The Restless Centuries

This circular arrangement of stones is the ruins of a flourishing pre-Columbian community that lived by hunting and agriculture. The circles within the ring of dwellings were underground places of religious worship. The canyon was abandoned shortly after the coming of Europeans. (Courtesy of Museum of the American Indian, Heye Foundation.)

The Restless Centuries

A History of the American People

Second Edition

Peter N. Carroll
San Francisco State University
San Francisco, California

David W. Noble
University of Minnesota
Minneapolis, Minnesota

Burgess Publishing Company
Minneapolis, Minnesota

For our teachers, colleagues, and students
who have seen another history

Editorial: Jeff Holtmeier, Marta Reynolds
Copy Editing: Marcia Bottoms, Elisabeth Sövik,
James Montgomery
Art: Joan Gordon, Lynn Guilfoyle Dwyer
Production: Morris Lundin, Pat Barnes

Cover photo: Courtesy of Grey Advertising Inc., for
The Department of Defense. Artist: Jim Butcher

0 9 8 7 6 5 4 3 2

Preface to
the First Edition

In writing this introductory history of the American people, we have worked with certain assumptions about the nature of history, the role of pedagogy, and the students to whom this book is directed.

First, we have assumed that the traditional textbooks — usually filled with the minutiae of American history — are needlessly detailed. Instead of presenting an overview of the historical process, they often overwhelm the student with a mass of information, much of which is either memorized by rote or soon forgotten. Some instructors, frustrated by these massive compendiums, have abandoned textbooks entirely and now prefer to work with selected "interpretive" pieces. Such essays or monographs, by illuminating specific aspects of American history, often engage the students' interest and provide an important basis for further learning. These works, however, usually lack a large structure in which to place the more specialized insights. Complaining that they do not know the "facts" of history, students often devote their energy to underlining and memorizing the data in these books and consequently ignore the more interpretive aspects of the works. For people who believe that students do not have to be burdened with comprehensive textbooks, but who also feel that they need some structure in which to place historical interpretation, *The Restless Centuries* provides a brief but orderly approach to the subject.

Second, we have assumed that American history involves considerably more than the study of national politics. In writing this history of the American *people*, we have tried to integrate social, economic, cultural, and political history. Moreover, we have avoided the elitist bias which usually emerges from traditional political history. Instead we have empha-

v

sized the role of minority groups, of women, of poorer people and we have endeavored to explain how these out-groups related to the male WASP majority.

Third, we have assumed that students appreciate the subtleties of history rather than the tidy, but overly simplistic, approaches characteristic of traditional texts. Such problems as ideological commitments or ethnic diversity or political dissent need not be avoided in presenting the data of American history to contemporary students. We have tried, therefore, to incorporate the most recent historical scholarship, even in areas where professional historians are reexamining long-standing beliefs about the American past.

Finally, we have assumed that *The Restless Centuries* is merely an introduction to American history. Hopefully, students will be stimulated to pursue specific areas of interest either from the supplementary readings listed at the end of each chapter or from collateral assignments. Wherever possible, we have attempted to liberate, rather than close, further discussion.

Preface to the Second Edition

We have undertaken a major revision of *The Restless Centuries*. We have held fast to our original strategy of providing a brief, core text which captures the main flow of American history in a way that allows maximum teaching flexibility. The text is presented in two forms: a combined version which covers American history from colonial times to the present, and a two-volume text that breaks at the time of Reconstruction. Our own teaching has convinced us that the richness of the literature available for students to read in American history should not go unexplored. Each instructor has his or her own way of making American history exciting to students, and the available literature provides an opportunity for this valuable exploration. The size of our text encourages investigation of outside sources, which we feel is one of its principal strengths.

When we wrote the book at the beginning of the 1970s, we were aware of a movement among historians to make society and culture, rather than politics, the foundation of the historical narrative. We attempted to build our book around that shift. But, at the end of 1970s, scholarship has become much more sophisticated in describing the clash of European, African, and American Indian cultures during the colonial period. And the interrelationships among the dominant Anglo-American culture and those of the new immigrants at the end of the nineteenth century have been brought into sharper focus; so have the problems of adolescence and the concept of the generation gap. Scholarship has been most productive during the 1970s in the area of the history of women.

We have tried to take these new materials and insights into account. Because of the richness of the materials on social and cultural history and their integration into the main patterns of American development, we were able to change the organization of the second volume from separate chapters on politics, economics, and society to that of chapters that combine themes from these areas in chronological sequences. We are delighted that our decision in the early 1970s to write a different kind of textbook that deemphasizes political history seems to have found support in the great outpouring of scholarly studies on so many aspects of American social history. We have tried now, in 1978, as we did in 1973, to keep *The Restless Centuries* on the cutting edge of historical scholarship.

Acknowledgments

In preparing the second edition, we have received invaluable help from many people. Lois Noble, in addition to typing the manuscript, provided constructive editorial criticism. David Ammerman, The Florida State University; Michael Batinski, Southern Illinois University; Randolph Campbell, North Texas State University; Valerie Conner, The Florida State University; Joseph Dowling, Lehigh University; Edward Pluth, St. Cloud State University; Leo Ribuffo, The George Washington University; and Harry Ward, University of Richmond, read the manuscript and improved it greatly with their suggestions for revisions. The late Alex Fraser and Gary Brahms encouraged us to go forward with the new edition. Jeff Holtmeier, who served as the editor of the revision, contributed the rare qualities of a perceptive critic and a warm friend. We appreciate the enthusiasm and skill with which Marta Reynolds carried out the indispensable task of coordinating the many details of the project. We also want to thank Marcia Bottoms and Ann Seivert for their careful reading and editing of the manuscript.

Contents

Chapter 1

The Two Americas

For nearly five centuries, the voyage of Christopher Columbus has been considered a major turning point in world history. By opening the Western Hemisphere to European colonization, Columbus's "discovery" paved the way for the global expansion of European civilization. But long before Columbus's ships touched land in the Bahamas on October 12, 1492, the first American settlers already had built flourishing societies that extended from the Arctic Circle to the tip of South America.

The Cultures of the American Indians

The first Americans — Asiatic hunters who had pursued large animals across a land bridge over what is now the Bering Sea near Alaska — began arriving in the Western Hemisphere about 30,000 B.C. This migration continued at irregular intervals for about 20,000 years until approximately 10,000 B.C., when the last Ice Age began to end and melting glaciers raised the level of the sea, thus submerging the land bridge.

The first American colonists came originally from different parts of the Asian continent and had different cultures. These differences were reinforced in the Western Hemisphere as the pursuit of mammals led these migrants in various geographical directions. Over the centuries, the groups divided and subdivided so that separate communities existed throughout the vast area of the American continents. After about 8000 B.C., however, massive climatic changes began to reduce the size of the animal population upon which the first Americans depended for food. Many human communities disappeared, but many others learned to broaden their food supply by mixing hunting with gathering, and still others began to adopt agricultural techniques that assured their survival.

The shift to agriculture had a profound impact on the life-styles of the American peoples. In hunting societies, such as the desert tribes of western North America, mobility was a fundamental aspect of life. But agriculture required a settled population, even though hunting was never entirely abandoned. In southwestern North America, groups such as the Zunis and the Hopis resided in the same areas for centuries before the arrival of Europeans. Agriculture also stabilized the food supply, thus leading to a significant rise in the human population.

In adapting to the natural environment, each social group created a unique culture that not only assured group survival but also stabilized social interaction within the group. The first Americans recognized that their survival depended upon maintaining an ecological balance. As a result, many of their religious and social customs served to protect the valuable animal species from extinction. For example, fishing often was prohibited during spawning seasons. The importance of group harmony for survival also affected social organization. Social patterns such as the division of labor, the distribution of food, and the rules of family relations were designed to maximize the chances of the group's survival. For example, in societies that lived on the edge of starvation, hunters might have enjoyed special prestige, but they were required to share their kill with the other members of the group; in areas of more abundance, hunters might have had lower status than the people who were responsible for a fair division of resources.

Although it is impossible to determine a precise relationship between natural environment and social organization, it is evident that the first Americans created a wide variety of cultures partly because of geographical circumstances. In the northern woodlands of North America, for example, Algonquian villages consisted of rectangular wooden houses built with curved roofs that deflected snow; in the western intermountain desert, where the land was arid and wood was not available, Shoshonean people erected temporary brush shelters that could be dismantled easily and taken to another site; where bison wandered in great herds, the Sioux covered their teepees with bison skins. These different housing arrangements suggest the great diversity of life-styles that existed among the American populations. There were also extensive variations in clothing, nutrition, and language. Scholars estimate that there were as many as 2,000 different languages spoken in the Western Hemisphere at the time of Columbus's historic voyage.

The diversity of cultures also can be seen in the wide variety of political organizations, which ranged from simple clan relationships in the smaller groups to such powerful empires as those of the Aztec of Mexico, the Maya of Central America, and the Inca of Peru. In the Ohio River valley, a flourishing "Mound Builder" culture existed about 2,000 years ago and was succeeded by a "Mississippian" culture that influenced most of the Atlantic seaboard and the part of the North American continent now called the Midwest of the United States. These ancestors of the Creek, Cherokee, and Natchez tribes left behind huge earthworks, which testify to extensive trade networks and a large population. In northeastern North America, later Iroquois peoples formed a loose political confederation known as the League of Five Nations (a sixth was added later), which united the tribes against common enemies. In what is now called the Pacific Northwest, such peoples as the Yurok, the Chinook, and the Nootka established complicated social groups in which distinctions of status and wealth were paramount.

The availability of abundant food not only encouraged social differentiation, it enabled some American societies to support dense populations, particularly in Central and South America, the areas first affected by European colonizers. Recent estimates suggest that there were between 50 and 100 million people living in the Western Hemisphere in 1492. Of these, approximately 10 million lived in what is now the United States. Portions of the Western Hemisphere were more densely populated than comparable areas of Europe at the same time. These statistics demonstrate that the American continents certainly were not a vacant wilderness waiting for the arrival of European colonists.

The first European contact with the first Americans probably occurred in the early eleventh century when Leif Ericson led a group of Norsemen from Greenland to an area in North America called Vinland. It is possible that other Europeans explored the American coasts in succeeding centuries. Yet, these early exploratory efforts had little impact either on European society or on the customs of the native population. Nor was the knowledge gained by the first pioneering seamen utilized by later explorers.

In the early hours of October 12, 1492, a member of Columbus's crew sighted an island the explorers named San Salvador. Upon landing, Columbus encountered members of the Arawak tribe, but he called them Indians. This nomenclature revealed that Columbus mistakenly believed that he had reached the East Indies (the main object of his voyage).

The term *Indian* soon was used throughout western Europe. Despite the complexity of American Indian culture and despite the diversity of the Indians' societies and their relatively large populations, European explorers generally treated the first Americans as one race. Such attitudes reflected the ethnocentrism (or self-centeredness) of the Europeans and the fact that most European explorers interacted with only one local American Indian culture. Moreover, when the Europeans failed to find a

Drawings of American Indians made by John White, an artist and colonial promoter, who accompanied the first English settlers to Roanoke Island. These pictures emphasized the visible differences between American Indians and Europeans. (Courtesy of Library of Congress.)

culture like their own in America, they promptly concluded that the American people had *no* culture and so were inferior to Europeans. For this reason, the European colonists and their descendents remained largely indifferent to the fate of the native peoples. As the mortality rate among American Indians soared into the millions because of the introduction of European diseases, the Europeans simply asserted that their Christian god had eliminated the heathen to provide room for their own settlements. Even people sympathetic to the Indians usually shared these ethnocentric attitudes.

The Background of European Expansion

The expansion of Europe depended upon important economic, political, and intellectual developments. Between the eleventh and the fourteenth centuries, Christian crusaders periodically invaded the Islam Empire in Asia Minor in an attempt to recover the holy city of Jerusalem from its Muslim rulers. Although the crusaders failed in their primary mission, they returned to Europe with luxurious items such as silks, jewels, and spices. Europeans particularly valued spices as food preservatives, important items in a world without refrigeration. In response to a growing demand for such products, trade with the Middle East increased. The trading was controlled by Italian merchants, who had acquired a monopoly over this commerce. The precariousness of trade with the Middle East, as well as the rich profits earned by the Italians, led other Europeans to seek alternative shipping routes.

The expansion of trade in luxury items represented but one aspect of a larger commercial revolution taking place in western Europe. The merchants and bankers who profited from trade acquired surplus capital that then could be reinvested in other mercantile adventures. The investors also developed a more sophisticated system of credit. The availability of surplus capital and the existence of adequate credit procedures were necessary antecedents for expansion in overseas mercantile activity.

Besides economic developments, important political changes occurred in western Europe between the thirteenth and the sixteenth centuries. As powerful kings emerged in such countries as Portugal, Spain, France, and England, the monarchs allied themselves with wealthy merchants and attempted to consolidate national power and national wealth by limiting the privileges and power of the medieval nobility. These centralizing tendencies associated with the rise of national states later enabled the monarchs to acquire sufficient resources to invest in the exploration and colonization of the New World.

The political and economic changes facilitated European expansion in the Western Hemisphere. Without such changes — as the Norse failure to capitalize on their discoveries seems to attest — Europeans could not have taken advantage so rapidly of the opportunities opened by Columbus. Yet, in themselves, the changes in economic and political practices do not explain the widespread European interest in America.

By about the fifteenth century, innovative European scholars had begun to question the traditional explanations of the natural world. Not since classical antiquity had scholars shown a more profound interest in learning about history, geography, and the physical sciences. As part of a wider cultural movement known as the Renaissance, this growing curiosity led Europeans in quest of new inventions, new discoveries, and new worlds.

During the late Middle Ages, shipbuilders and seamen — particularly the Portuguese — made several technological improvements that facilitated transoceanic voyages. New ship design led to the construction of caravels, small but speedy sailing ships that could traverse the ocean waves more effectively than older ships. Portuguese sailors also began employing an instrument, known as the astrolabe, for determining latitude.

The navigational advances enabled European seamen to sail into unknown waters, which in turn led to an increase in geographical information. Travelers' accounts from people like the Venetian merchant Marco Polo (who ventured to China during the thirteenth century) and from Christian missionaries in Asia whetted the European appetite for knowledge of exotic places. The information gleaned from mariners' reports and travelers' stories served to advance the level of cartography, the science of mapmaking, and it became possible to produce more accurate charts. But, while most educated people of the fifteenth century believed that the world was round, they disagreed considerably on the distance between Asia and Europe. Moreover, many seamen and mapmakers believed that there were definite limits beyond which it was not safe to sail.

The Portuguese

Systematic exploration and discovery began under the patronage of the Portuguese prince Henry the Navigator (1394-1460). Motivated primarily by a desire to enrich his nation through trade, Henry encouraged Portuguese seamen to sail on voyages of discovery along the West African coast. He also established a school of navigation in which sailors could acquire new skills and mapmakers could coordinate the newly obtained geographical information. After many voyages along the West African coast by Portuguese captains, Bartholomeu Diaz sailed around the Cape of Good Hope at the southern tip of Africa in 1488. Ten years later, Vasco de Gama sailed to India. In 1500, Pedro Cabral, blown off course while on a voyage to India, landed in Brazil. As a result of this mishap, the Portuguese claimed much of South America.

These early Portuguese voyages led to the creation of the first major European overseas empire. Based almost entirely on trade and "factory" (trading post) settlements, the Portuguese Empire reached as far as China. Early mercantile successes brought great profits and demonstrated that lucrative rewards could come from exploratory ventures. In addition, the Portuguese opened black Africa to European commerce. Less than 100 years after Prince Henry's death, Spanish, English, and Dutch mariners found new wealth in the slave trade. Portugal's small population prevented a consolidation of its empire, and so other European nations, larger and more prosperous, eventually supplanted the Portuguese in Asia.

The Spanish

The voyage of Christopher Columbus in 1492 should be considered in this context of European expansion. Columbus believed that he could discover a shorter route to Asia (and its wealth of spices) by sailing westward. Columbus's initial scheme failed to win wide support, not because people doubted that the world was round, but rather because the Italian navigator estimated the circumference of the globe to be far less than most people believed it to be. This miscalculation moved Columbus to undertake the voyage in the first place; the same error in reasoning convinced him in 1492 that he had landed in the East Indies rather than in a new world. But the Spanish monarchs, King Ferdinand and Queen Isabella, decided to finance Columbus's first westward voyage (as well as his three later ones) as a somewhat desperate challenge to Portugal's commercial empire.

Upon Columbus's return to Europe with news of his landing in the "Indies," Portugal protested Spain's intrusion into her trading empire. Pope Alexander VI mediated the dispute by drawing a demarcation line (1493) dividing the heathen country between Spain and Portugal. In 1494, this line was renegotiated in the Treaty of Tordesillas, which, in effect, gave Brazil to Portugal and the rest of America to Spain. Of course, the nations that had not agreed to the treaty simply ignored it.

Following Columbus's "discovery" of America, the Spanish monarchs supported several other exploratory ventures to the western lands. The primary object of these voyages remained the opening of Asia to Spanish trade. Columbus himself sailed in 1493, 1498, and 1502 in search of a water route to Asian wealth. He did not recognize that the lands he had found possessed other, less obvious, riches. It remained for a Florentine seaman, Amerigo Vespucci, who sailed under the Spanish captain Ojeda, to recognize that the newly found lands constituted a new continent; in this sense, Vespucci can be viewed as the "discoverer" of America! Other Spanish voyages of exploration included that of Balboa, who crossed the Isthmus of Panama (1513), and the remarkable circumnavigation of the globe (1519-1522) by the crew of Ferdinand Magellan. These voyages provided the background for the creation of a Spanish empire in America.

Although the Spanish explorers failed to discover the spice treasures of Asia, they did find gold. Thus, mining replaced trade as the economic basis of the Spanish Empire. In his second voyage (1493), Columbus brought 1,500 Spaniards to Hispaniola (Haiti); by 1515, the Spanish had settled Puerto Rico, Jamaica, and Cuba. The colonists proceeded to enslave the natives and force them to work in the gold mines. The death rate among the native peoples was enormous — reaching into the millions — primarily because they lacked immunity to European diseases such as smallpox. When the Indians succumbed to epidemics and maltreatment, the Spanish replaced them with black slaves imported from Africa. Despite huge death rates among these slaves, too, the Spanish shipped large amounts of gold back to Europe, thus claiming considerable profit for their efforts.

On the American mainland, the Spanish continued to kill and enslave the native populations. Led by minor nobles known as *conquistadores*, the subjugation of the Indians helped to bring immense wealth to Spain. Hernando Cortes (1519-1521) conquered the Aztec Empire, and Francisco Pizarro (1531-1535) conquered the Inca Empire. These relatively easy victories were made possible by the Europeans' superior weapons, the apparent lack of unity among the native peoples, and the diseases that ravaged the Indians. Although a large proportion of the native population was already subjugated by an Aztec ruling class, the disruption of the Indian empires brought profound confusion and death.

As the *conquistadores* subdued the native societies, the Spanish established a system of large colonial estates known as *encomiendas*. Under the almost absolute control of a nobleman or *encomiendo*, these estates incorporated the subjugated lands as well as the Indians who lived on them. Although the natives remained legally free, they were obligated to work as virtual slaves for the *encomiendo*. To some extent, the presence of Catholic missionaries mitigated the worst evils of this labor system. Moreover, the government in Spain attempted to ease the Indians' plight by ordering the colonial nobles to treat the natives with humanity and to attempt to convert them to Christianity. These edicts, which were issued repeatedly throughout the sixteenth century, reflected official Spanish colonial policy. But declarations made in Spain had little relation to the reality of the Indians' situation in America. Despite royal decrees, the *encomiendos* made no noticeable distinctions between free people and slaves in the native population.

During the sixteenth century, the Spanish crown attempted to increase its control in the colonies by strengthening the powers of colonial viceroys. Unlike the *encomiendos*, the viceroys were directly responsible to the king and served only at the king's pleasure. The viceroys received advisory and judicial assistance from councils known as *audiencias*. But Spanish law continued to be ignored by the colonists in America despite this attempt to strengthen royal institutions. In many ways, this problem also appeared in the British colonies of North America [see below, pp. 83-84].

The search for gold led several *conquistadores* to explore regions in North America. Ponce de Leon sailed along the Florida coast (1513); Panfilo de Narvaez explored the northern parts of Florida (1528); Hernando de Soto journeyed through the southeastern region of what is now the United States (1539-1543); Francisco Coronado penetrated as far as what is today Kansas in search of the legendary cities of gold. The failure of these explorers to find gold or silver deterred the Spanish from colonizing North America for decades. Not until 1565, when French adventurers occupied Florida, did the Spanish establish a town at St. Augustine. Toward the end

BaffinBay

GREENLAND

Iceland

Baffin, 1616

Baffin Island

Vikings, c. 1000

Baffin 1616

Frobisher, 1576-78

Gilbert 1583

Hudson Bay

Hudson, 1610

Cartier 1535

Cabot 1497

NORTH   AMERICA

Saint Lawrence R.

Cartier 1534

Cabot 1497

Newfoundland

Hudson 1609

Missouri R.

Mississippi R.

Great   Lakes

Nova Scotia

Hudson R.

Verrazano 1524

Long Island

Gilbert 1583

Coronado, 1540-1542

Ohio   R.

ATLANTIC

Onate, 1596-1598

Colorado R.

Arkansas R.

Jamestown

Verrazano 1524

Vespucci 1497-1498

ate, 1604-1605

De Soto, 1539-1542

Red R.

OCEAN

Narvaez, 1528

Ponce de Leon 1513

Columbus 1492

Cabenza, 1535-1536

Rio Grande

Columbus 1492

Vespucci, 1497-1498

Columbus 1493

Gulf of Mexico

Ponce de Leon 1513

MEXICO

Cortez, 1519-1521

Cuba

Amadas & Barlow 1584

Mexico City

Yucatan

Jamaica

Columbus 1493

Drake, 1577-1580

CENTRAL AMERICA

Hispaniola

Columbus 1502

Caribbean   Sea

Vespucci 1497-1498

Balboa, 1510-1513

Columbus 1498

PACIFIC OCEAN

Santo Domingo

Equator

Galapagos Islands

Pizzaro, 1530-1533

Amazon R.

Cajamarca

SOUTH   AMERICA

PERU

VOYAGES OF DISCOVERY

- - - - - - - - - - — Dutch
———————— English
— - — - — - — French
— · — · — · — Spanish
———————— Viking

of the sixteenth century, the Spanish also moved into what is now New Mexico and Arizona, where they built missions designed to expand Spanish control and to convert the Indians to Christianity. Not all Indians accepted the Spanish presence. In 1680, the Pueblos, angered by the behavior of the Spanish, rebelled and drove the Spanish from their lands. In 1692, the Spanish reconquered the territory, but nevertheless, the Pueblos retained a significant amount of autonomy.

Spain's early successes in the New World convinced other European nations that great wealth could be obtained through colonization, and so the French, the Dutch, and the English founded colonies of their own.

The French

French activity in the New World began with the voyage of Giovanni da Verazzano (1524), who searched along the Atlantic coast for a water route through the continent (the fabled northwest passage), which could open the Asian trade to France. A decade later, Jacques Cartier explored the coast of Newfoundland and in 1535 sailed up the St. Lawrence River in search of a channel to China.

During the sixteenth century, civil and religious wars prevented the French monarchs from pursuing the further colonization of North America. In the latter part of the century, however, fur traders returned from the St. Lawrence valley with a wealth of beaver skins; such commodities renewed French interest in the area. Samuel de Champlain made eleven exploratory voyages to North America and founded Quebec in 1608. Later in the seventeenth century, French traders and explorers followed the Mississippi River to its mouth in the Gulf of Mexico. Recognizing the value of the fur trade, Champlain encouraged friendly relations with the Indians and envisioned a flourishing empire in Canada.

Despite this optimism, however, New France grew slowly. In the early years, the French crown attempted to regulate colonial affairs by granting royal monopolies to French traders; in 1674, Louis XIV assumed direct control of the colony. Under both forms of government, French authorities attempted to institute a rigidly hierarchical social order in which every person had a specifically assigned place in society. This attempt to create a social structure similar to that of the mother country proved unworkable in the Canadian wilderness. A shortage of workers forced colonial officials to make basic concessions in order to attract a voluntary labor force. Moreover, since the fur trade promised easy wealth, many colonists ignored royal instructions and abandoned their agricultural pursuits. Thus, the colonists undermined royal efforts to establish a static social system. After 1685, the crown prohibited French Protestants (Huguenots) from settling in America. For these reasons, the population of New France remained small and badly divided.

The Dutch

Like those of the other Europeans, Dutch fortunes in the New World depended on the strength of the home country in Europe. In the late six-teenth century, the Netherlands successfully revolted against the Spanish Empire and emerged as a major commercial power. Although Spain did not acknowledge Dutch independence until 1648, Dutch merchants began attacking the Portuguese trading empire in Asia much earlier. The found-ing of the Dutch East India Company (1602) enabled the Dutch to consoli-date their interests and supplant the Portuguese. This company financed the voyage of Henry Hudson (1609) in his search for the northwest pas-sage in America. Twelve years later, the Dutch created a West India Com-pany, which successfully attacked Spanish trade in the Caribbean.

Dutch colonization in North America began when the West India Company planted a colony on Manhattan Island (1626) to serve as a base for its fur-trading operations, which had been established earlier. The com-pany attempted to attract settlers by instituting a system of patroons; the company would grant large estates to wealthy men who promised in return to transport tenant farmers to New Netherland. Because of the abun-dance of free land, however, this system proved unattractive (only one patroonship was settled), and the company thereafter concentrated its efforts on exploiting the fur trade. Dutch aggression provoked several wars with the Indian population, which weakened the colony. Under the last Dutch governor, Peter Stuyvesant, New Netherland annexed a small Swedish settlement at the mouth of the Delaware River in an attempt to remove its rivals in the fur trade. The home government proved more interested in its Asian empire, however, and paid little attention to New Netherland. In 1664, the English seized the colony and renamed it New York [see below, p. 44].

Supplementary Reading

For descriptions of the American Indians see A. M. Josephy, Jr., *The Indian Heritage of America* (1968), and P. Farb, *Man's Rise to Civilization* (1968). The best overview of the expansion of Europe is J. H. Parry, *The Age of Reconnaissance* (1963). It may be supple-mented by J. H. Elliott, *The Old World and the New: 1492-1650* (1972). Other studies of Euro-pean exploration are J. Brebner, *The Explorers of North America* (1933), and two recent volumes by S. E. Morison, *The European Discovery of America* (1971, 1974). For an environ-mental history of the period, see A. Crosby, Jr., *The Columbian Exchange: Biological and Cultural Consequences of 1492* (1972). A brilliant but difficult interpretation of the discovery of America is E. O'Gorman, *The Invention of America* (1961). The best study of Columbus remains S. E. Morison, *Admiral of the Ocean Sea* (1942). A thorough discussion of coloniza-tion before 1612 is in D. Quinn, *North America from Earliest Discovery to First Settlements* (1977). For a survey of the Spanish Empire, see C. Gibson, *Spain in America* (1966); for one of New Netherland, see T. Condon, *New York Commercial Beginnings* (1968); for one of New France, see W. J. Eccles, *France in America* (1972); and for one of Portuguese Brazil, see C. Prado, *The Colonial Background of Modern Brazil* (1969). For a comparative treatment, see the essays in H. Peckham and C. Gibson, *Attitudes of Colonial Powers toward the American Indian* (1969).

Chapter 2

The English Background of Colonization

Although England's claim to North America dated from the exploratory voyage of John Cabot (1497), internal political problems delayed English colonization in the Western Hemisphere. By the end of the sixteenth century, however, the Tudor monarchs had transformed England into a major European power that was prepared to exploit the opportunities in the New World. The changes that occurred in this period influenced the structure of the English Empire in fundamental ways. For this reason, English America differed enormously from the Spanish colonies founded 100 years earlier.

Tudor Centralization

Throughout the fifteenth century, England suffered from a series of dynastic crises known as the Wars of the Roses. However, the first Tudor monarchs — Henry VII (1485-1509) and Henry VIII (1509-1547) — succeeded in limiting the influence of the nobles by expanding royal power. Using the institutions of local government that had existed for centuries, the Tudors bypassed the higher nobility and sought to unite the counties directly to the crown. English county officials — the sheriff, the justices of the peace, the lord lieutenant — became more responsive to royal authority, thus bringing greater institutional unity to the nation. Appointed directly by the king, each of these officials exercised wide administrative, judicial, and military powers, which were increased during the sixteenth century. These institutions were exported to the colonies in the following century and played a prominent role in American political life.

By the middle of his reign, Henry VIII had destroyed his dynastic rivals, and the Tudor monarchy seemed secure on the throne. Only the ecclesiastical representatives of the pope at Rome acknowledged an authority higher than the king. But this supranational power posed the greatest threat to Henry's dynasty.

When Henry's first wife, Catherine of Aragon, failed to bear a male heir, the king appealed to the pope to annul the marriage. When the pope refused, Henry defied him and summoned Parliament to sever England's ties to the Roman Catholic church. In a series of statutes passed between 1532 and 1534, Parliament created a national church with the king as the supreme head. These laws also enabled Henry to confiscate church revenues and monastic lands. Although Henry himself probably remained unsympathetic to the Protestant Reformation then occurring on the continent (as a young man he had denounced Martin Luther as a heretic), his attack on papal authority opened the way for ecclesiastical reform. The introduction of an English Bible and the destruction of the monasteries lent unwitting support to English Protestants.

Economic Changes

The Henrician "reformation" was in part an outgrowth of political and economic centralization. Both Henrys had attempted to increase the crown's revenues by supporting foreign trade. Instead of exporting raw wool, English merchants were encouraged to manufacture and sell finished woolen products. Moreover, the Tudors supported the growth of an English merchant fleet, which lessened England's dependence on foreign ships.

These economic policies, besides enriching the crown, produced profound social and economic changes in sixteenth-century England. The increased demand for woolen products led to the "enclosure" movement, whereby lands that previously had been available to everyone's flocks were fenced by the landlord for his own use. The confiscation and sale of monastic lands after 1539 accelerated the enclosures. Landowners who purchased the monastic lands from the king enclosed their holdings in order to increase their profits. The steady rise in prices (which occurred throughout western Europe because of the importation of gold and silver from America) encouraged wool production. Stated simply, raising sheep proved more profitable than traditional farming, and many landowners took advantage of the new opportunity.

Not only did enclosed lands bring larger profits for the landlords, the increased export of woolen products brought large rewards to English merchants. Such profits led to an accumulation of surplus capital. In seeking to invest this capital, the merchants turned to foreign trade. Since major commercial undertakings were both costly and risky, English merchants began to form chartered corporations, known as joint-stock companies, in order to pool their resources and thus share the risks and profits. The most important of these companies were the Muscovy Company (1555) (which attempted to open trade routes to Russia), the Levant Company (1581), and the East India Company (1599). During the latter part of the sixteenth century, these joint-stock companies flourished and undertook various overseas projects. In the seventeenth century, the chartered companies served as the typical English instrument for colonization in North America. Private ownership meant that the joint-stock companies had more limited goals than the royally financed projects of England's Continental rivals.

Although the enclosure movement benefited the already prosperous landlords and merchants, it produced serious problems for the people who were forced off their lands. Unable to survive with their traditional occupations, many people migrated to towns and cities; the population of London probably tripled between 1560 and 1625, despite serious plagues. Other people became itinerant laborers who wandered through the countryside in search of livings. The Elizabethan Poor Laws did not alleviate their plight. Poor people seemed to abound, and many concerned English people came to believe that their island was overpopulated.

Some writers declared that the establishment of colonies would provide answers for England's troubles. Idle people, instead of draining the national wealth by requiring charitable assistance, could be transported to colonies, where they could produce raw materials for the benefit of England. Moreover, the colonies could supply England with precious metals, just as New Spain had enriched the Spanish. Finally, colonies could serve as markets for the finished products made at home. These arguments, reflecting mercantilist ideas, implied that the colonies would remain subservient to the mother country.

English-Spanish Rivalry

The foremost proponent of English colonization was Richard Hakluyt, who attempted to win support for his colonizing schemes by publishing numerous travel accounts written by explorers of America. Arguing that colonies would make England self-sufficient, Hakluyt also pointed to the growing rivalry between England and Spain and stressed the political advantages of weakening the Spanish Empire. Under the reign of Elizabeth I (1558-1603), the tenuous alliance between England and Spain collapsed, partly because Henry's break with Rome had led England to support the Dutch Protestants against Catholic Spain. No doubt, England's jealousy of Spanish successes aggravated the religious dispute.

Although England and Spain remained technically at peace during the first thirty years of Elizabeth's reign, the queen secretly supported the raids of English "seadogs" on Spanish commerce. In the 1560s, John Hawkins made numerous raids on Caribbean ports and sold African slaves to the sugar planters in violation of Spanish regulations. Despite Hawkins's

Queen Elizabeth I (1533-1603), daughter of Henry VIII and half-sister of the Catholic Queen Mary and the Protestant Edward VI, led the Church of England to a moderate Protestant position between the traditional Catholics and the extreme Puritans. (The Granger Collection.)

activities, English participation in the slave trade did not flourish until the following century. But, while Elizabethan English people first encountered the African as merely a different *type* of person (rather than as a *slave*), nevertheless they regarded blackness as a sign of savagery, sin, and heathenism. In short, for Elizabethans, blackness symbolized the basic inferiority of the African peoples.

Hawkins's younger cousin, Francis Drake, also raided the Spanish West Indies during the 1570s. On one voyage (1577-1580), he captured Spanish gold ships in the Pacific Ocean, refitted his own vessels in present-day California, and circumnavigated the globe on his voyage home. Meanwhile, the Cathay Company financed three voyages by Martin Frobisher (1576-1578), which resulted in the English exploration of Canada's eastern coast. England's intervention in Spanish America precipitated open warfare between the rival nations that climaxed with the destruction of the Spanish fleet (1588). The defeat of the Spanish Armada hastened England's ascendance as mistress of the seas; it also thwarted Spanish plans to destroy England's first colony in America.

Colonization

More than anyone else, Sir Humphrey Gilbert was responsible for England's first attempt at colonization. In 1578, he persuaded Queen Elizabeth to grant him a charter to establish a colony in North America. Following an abortive voyage in that year, Gilbert, with 200 prospective settlers, landed at Newfoundland (1583). But after only two weeks, the settlers abandoned the settlement for unknown reasons and returned to England. Gilbert died in 1583, and his interests in the American projects passed to his half-brother, Sir Walter Raleigh, one of the queen's favorites.

Like Gilbert, Raleigh hoped to establish a permanent colony in order to challenge the Spanish Empire. Upon receiving a charter from the queen (1584), he immediately launched an exploratory voyage to the lands that he named Virginia in honor of Elizabeth, the Virgin Queen. In 1585, Raleigh dispatched a group of settlers to Roanoke Island, just off what is now the coast of North Carolina. The colonists included John White, who made some excellent drawings of the Indians, and Thomas Hariot, a scientist who later wrote a detailed description of the natural life of the region. Instead of building a permanent settlement, however, the colonists devoted themselves to a futile search for gold. Moreover, the settlers needlessly antagonized the local Indians, thus jeopardizing their trade in food. When Francis Drake visited Roanoke in 1586, the settlers abandoned the colony and returned with him to England. The following year, Raleigh again attempted to found a settlement on Roanoke and sent 120 colonists to the island. These settlers also quarreled with the local tribes. After the encounter with the Spanish Armada prevented the sailing of a supply fleet from

Sir Francis Drake (1543-1596), one of the great Elizabethan sea dogs, attacked Spanish shipping in the Old World and the New. After a series of dramatic raids in New Spain brought Drake to the California coast, he commanded his ships across the Pacific in the second circumnavigation of the globe. (The Granger Collection.)

England, the settlers either starved to death or were killed by hostile Indians. English ships that arrived in 1590 found no survivors.

The failure of these colonizing endeavors taught Elizabethan adventurers several important lessons. First, successful colonies needed sufficient resources to free them from dependence on the Indians; second, the colonists had to maintain direct links with the mother country; third, the resources of one individual, or even of a group of individuals, could not adequately support colonial development. In the future, joint-stock companies, with larger capital resources, would finance many English colonizing activities. Permanent settlement would await the first decade of the next century.

English Society

On the eve of colonization, England was in the midst of a major social crisis. The economic changes of the sixteenth century were transforming the nation from an insular manorial country into an expanding capitalistic society. Yet, the English people, to a great extent, continued to live much as they always had. More important, they were not always conscious of the changes occurring around them, and they continued to cherish social ideals that reflected an earlier time.

Despite the major social dislocations of the period, Elizabethan English people continued to believe in the essential harmony and order of the universe. As Shakespeare wrote, "The heavens themselves, the planets, and this centre/Observe degree, priority, and place." Elizabethans believed that the orderliness of the universe should be duplicated in social arrangements. They stressed the organic nature of society, the idea that society was an organism like the human body in which each part of the body politic depended for its health on the other parts. Using the metaphor of the commonwealth, sixteenth-century English people argued that it was impossible for one part of society to benefit at the expense of another. Any illness in one segment of society would soon poison the entire organism.

These ideas represented the social values of Elizabethan English people; this was the way society was supposed to function. The ideal of social harmony provided the standard against which the English measured the realities of their world. For example, no one doubted that the government had the right to supervise economic activities in order to protect society as a whole from the selfish activities of a few individuals. Thus, the crown retained the right to charter (and regulate) joint-stock companies. Such economic supervision remained vital in local government as well. Towns and counties continued to regulate the affairs of the marketplace in order to prevent inequities in food prices or in wages due to laborers. To be sure, it was not always possible to enforce the principles of the organic society, and, throughout the period, people found ways to violate and ignore their professed ideals; indeed, many people continued to assert these values even as they practiced forms of behavior that contradicted their values. These social values, nevertheless, remained largely unchanged despite behavioral deviations. Such contradictory patterns were transported to the New World in the minds of the first colonists. Thus, throughout the colonial period, people continued to profess the importance of a regulated economy, often at the same time they ignored its principles in practice.

The ideals of the organic society were more clearly demonstrated in the social structure itself. Maintaining that certain people were better than others, Elizabethans paid deference to their superiors and expected similar respect from their inferiors. Society was characterized by clearly defined distinctions of status, which everyone recognized and most people accepted. There were various gradations in society ranging from the poorest tenant farmer to the richest aristocrat, and each status group retained certain privileges to itself; one's choices in dress, education, and marriage were limited and defined by one's place in society. Although social mobility was not rare, families generally moved only slightly upward or downward during one generation. It was not a caste society, but neither was it the more open society associated with the modern world.

At the top of society, the aristocracy and the rural gentry (who comprised only 5 to 7 percent of the total population) possessed the most wealth and ruled the country. According to organic social values, power belonged in the hands of the wealthy and prestigious families. The elite had the responsibility to rule that went along with the privileges of birth. As county officials, members of Parliament, and the crown's advisors, individuals from the highest-status group ran the country. And people of lesser status *expected* them to rule. These political ideas, which were also transmitted to the English colonies, were hardly democratic.

The hierarchical social arrangements appeared in miniature in the familial structure of sixteenth- and seventeenth-century England. As the poor were expected to obey their betters, so were children expected to obey their fathers and mothers. The average English family was nuclear in structure (that is, it usually contained only parents and their children). Families, moreover, were not simply biological units; they worked as economic units as well. Family businesses and family farms typified the economic situation of most people in Tudor England.

Because of a high death rate and the real possibility of malnutrition, life remained extremely precarious. The proximity of famine and pestilence explains why the English took seriously the need to regulate the prices of food and fuel. Moreover, because English families could not be sure of feeding many children, they may have practiced some forms of birth control. Thus, the number of children remained relatively low, ranging on the average from five to seven, and about half the children did not live to their twenty-first birthdays. The precariousness of life also meant that offspring could not afford to marry until they could support a family of their own. As a result, marriages usually were delayed until the middle or late twenties. Late marriages also discouraged large families, since they reduced the number of years of marital fertility. When a son did marry, he was expected to support his family in an independent household; thus, marriage became for Elizabethans the primary way of achieving full membership in society. The age at marriage and the birthrate varied among the status groups. Wealthier families did not worry about starvation and could afford to raise more children and see them married younger.

The fragility of life and the resulting tenuousness of social relations (a plague, for example, could destroy an entire village; the death of one man could abruptly terminate a business concern) led Tudor English people to cherish those institutions that seemed to be most permanent. The church, the aristocracy, customs from time immemorial were exalted because they alone seemed to provide continuity in a world of insecurity and sudden death.

Religious Upheaval

But, during the sixteenth century, even some of these durable institutions seemed to be decaying. Henry VIII's decision to separate from the Roman Catholic church destroyed the traditional religious order of England. The situation was aggravated by frequent religious changes made by Henry's children. Under Edward VI (1547-1553), England experimented with Protestantism; Henry's daughter Mary (1553-1558) tried to return England to the Church of Rome; Elizabeth attempted to steer a middle course between those who advocated a Protestant church and those who wished to retain Catholic practices within the national church.

Puritanism

During the reign of Mary, many Protestants fled to the European continent to avoid persecution. Having acquired extreme Protestant ideas, they returned to England when Elizabeth ascended to the throne. Dissatisfied with the queen's religious compromises, particularly the retention of certain Catholic ceremonies and offices, the Protestants demanded a reformation or a purification (therefore, the name Puritans) of the Church of England.

Although the Puritan movement began as the protest of a few dissatisfied ministers, it won support from people in all status groups. For one thing, the quality of the clergy in the established church was notoriously poor. Many ministers of the Church of England simply ignored their pastoral responsibilities; Puritan clergymen, by contrast, brought exceptional zeal to their work. Puritanism especially appealed to those English people who suffered most from the social dislocations of the sixteenth century, because it provided psychological security for them. In a world of rapid social change, Puritanism emphasized the importance of orderliness in religious and social affairs. Like other religious movements, it criticized worldliness and materialism, the search for worldly wealth rather than spiritual godliness. To people who suffered from the exploitation of enclosing landlords and the inflation of rents, the criticism of worldliness was particularly reassuring. Moreover, by emphasizing the spiritual transformation that would come to believers in the next world, Puritanism offered its adherents the possibility of religious security, despite the confusion of human affairs. In a sense, then, people became Puritans because that religion not only *explained* what they were experiencing but also provided them with religious *solutions* to difficult social questions. The Puritans, as founders of New England, left an important imprint on American society [see below, pp. 31-37].

The same social dislocations that impelled some people to embrace Puritanism led others to consider emigration to the New World. Aristocrats and members of the gentry whose real incomes were declining because of inflation, yeoman farmers who were losing their lands, and Protestants who were dismayed at the failure of religious reform all considered uprooting themselves in search of a more prosperous and stable society. Thus, the English colonies were settled both because of the attractiveness of America and because England seemed inhospitable to many of its inhabitants.

Supplementary Reading

For a lively survey of this period of English history, see L. B. Smith, *This Realm of England* (1966). English expansion and the rivalry with Spain are discussed in D. Quinn, *Raleigh and the British Empire* (1949), and G. Mattingly, *The Spanish Armada* (1962). For a discussion of the Elizabethan world view, see E. M. Tillyard, *The Elizabethan World Picture* (1943). Early English attitudes toward black people are analyzed in W. Jordan, *White Over Black* (1968). The best social history of the period is P. Laslett, *The World We Have Lost* (1965); also helpful are W. Notestein, *The English People on the Eve of Colonization* (1954), and C. Bridenbaugh, *Vexed and Troubled Englishmen* (1968). For an excellent analysis of social life in a slightly later period, see A. Macfarlane, *The Family Life of Ralph Josselin* (1970).

A complete discussion of the English Reformation may be found in A. G. Dickens, *The English Reformation* (1964). The origins of the Puritan movement are discussed in P. Collinson, *The Elizabethan Puritan Movement* (1967); W. Haller, *The Rise of Puritanism* (1938); and M. Walzer, *The Revolution of the Saints* (1965). For a discussion of the debate between Puritans and Anglicans, see C. and K. George, *The Protestant Mind of the English Reformation* (1961), and J. New, *Anglican and Puritan* (1964).

Chapter

3

The Beginning
of Colonization

With the death of Elizabeth I (1603), the English crown passed to James I (1603-1625), the first of the Stuart monarchs in England. Concerned that the war with Spain was needlessly draining the nation's resources, James negotiated a treaty of peace (1604), which brought an end to English raids on Spanish shipping. English people who hoped to acquire easy wealth in America adjusted their plans and began to think anew of planting a colony in North America.

Motivated primarily by a desire for commercial profits, two groups of merchants — one called the Virginia Company of London, the other the Virginia Company of Plymouth — petitioned the king for permission to establish a joint-stock company to finance a colonial enterprise. In response, James granted a charter to the Virginia Company (1606), authorizing the London group to settle the southern part of North America (34°-38°) and reserving the northern regions (41°-45°) for the Plymouth merchants. Later grants enlarged the territorial provisions of the charter, ultimately granting the companies territorial claims as far west as the Pacific Ocean. The charter provided that the government of each colony would be shared by a royal council appointed by the king in England and by a local council in the colony appointed by the royal council. A second charter (1609) transferred authority from the crown to the company. The revised charter also asserted that each planter in the colony had an equal economic interest with the investor (or adventurer) who remained at home. The Plymouth group attempted unsuccessfully to plant a colony on the Maine coast (1607) and then became dormant; it had no connection with the later Pilgrim colony at Plymouth [see below, pp. 31-32].

The Founding of Virginia

In May 1607, three vessels carrying slightly more than a hundred colonists dropped anchor in the James River. Lacking adequate experience, the settlers chose a swampy, malarial site to build a village, which they named Jamestown. During the early years of the settlement, the colonists succumbed to disease and starvation at an alarming rate. Meanwhile, the London Company in England obtained a new charter that allowed it to sell stocks to the public. The extensive revenue obtained from these sales enabled the company to support the faltering colony. By sending supplies at critical times, the investors prevented the abandonment of the settlement. Ironically, however, the influx of new immigrants, who often lacked adequate provisions, sorely tested the colony's resources.

The immense death rate — of 6,000 migrants, fewer than 2,000 remained in Virginia in 1622 — resulted primarily from poor organization, faulty planning, and personal rivalry. Since the London Company knew little about Virginia, it failed to offer sensible leadership for the settlers. By retaining ownership of all the land in Virginia, the company discouraged initiative on the part of the individual colonists, who worked as hired laborers. Experiments in communal agriculture also proved unsatisfactory. The company's interest in quick profits led the colonists to expend their energies in searching for gold or the fabled water routes through the continent. Moreover, English work habits, which traditionally provided for considerable slack time, discouraged intense activity. For these reasons, the colonists neglected agriculture and other necessary improvements in the settlement.

These problems were aggravated by internal squabbling among the members of the local council. Only the appearance of strong leaders such as John Smith, an early member of the Virginia council, prevented the complete collapse of authority. To make matters worse, the colonists, after receiving valuable assistance from the Indians during the "starving times," treated the natives with ruthless hostility. Besides trading unfairly with the Indians, the settlers committed numerous atrocities against them, thus destroying an essential source of assistance.

The English colonists' provocation of the Virginia tribes reflected the racial prejudices of English culture. During the Elizabethan period, English writers expressed two images of the Indians. The first suggested that the native Americans were more like animals than humans; the Indians were savage, cannibalistic, wild, and uncivilized. But the belief that the Indians

INDIAN TRIBES IN COLONIAL AMERICA
1600 - 1700

would be useful allies in trade led to the statement of an alternative image — the friendly Indian interested in cooperating with the English. Even this positive image, however, assumed that the native peoples were religiously and culturally inferior to the English. Moreover, once the English became determined to colonize North America (as opposed to trading on the coasts), the positive image of the Indians faded. In order to justify their claims to the lands, the English defined the natives as something less than human. These negative attitudes were aggravated by the fears and difficulties associated with colonization. The English tended to suspect the worst of the natives, even when Indian charity was the only reason for the colonists' survival. As the two cultures continued to clash during the seventeenth century, especially as land ownership became a major source of conflict, the English increasingly depicted the Indians as a savage race. Such racial images justified a policy of killing the Indians or pushing them beyond the frontiers of European settlement.

Native American attitudes toward the English, on the other hand, were predicated on an assumption that *they* were culturally superior to the newcomers. At the time of Virginia's settlement by whites, the Indian leader Powhatan could influence, if not control, about thirty Algonquian-speaking tribes. But Powhatan still wished to consolidate his power, and, initially, he saw the English as potential allies. Powhatan also recognized the benefits of trade with Europeans. Despite these advantages, there is little evidence to suggest that the local Indians wished to adapt to English ways. Only when the English settlements continued to encroach on their traditional territories did the native peoples realize that the colonists represented a serious threat to their survival. Thereafter, they became less willing to share their supplies with the struggling colony and eventually attempted to drive the English from their lands.

Despite the floundering condition of Virginia, the settlers continued to search for a staple commodity that might enrich the colony. John Rolfe's experiments in tobacco culture (1612) proved remarkably successful, and by 1617 Virginians were shipping substantial amounts of tobacco to England. As exports rose, the English began again investing in the company. With prospects brightening, the officers of the company attempted to protect their investments by making Virginia more attractive to potential settlers and adventurers.

Led by Sir Edwin Sandys, a member of the Virginia Company, the merchants instituted a number of changes designed to stabilize the colony. In the early years, a shortage of labor severely limited the amount of tobacco that could be cultivated. Most labor was performed by indentured servants, who sold their services for a period of time (usually from five to seven years) in exchange for transportation to Virginia and a promise of land at the end of that time. To encourage the importation of these workers, the company offered fifty acres (known as a headright) to anyone who paid the passage of a settler to the colony. Besides offering the possibility of land ownership to a colonist of modest means, this system encouraged the amassing of large landholdings by wealthy merchants who could afford to sponsor many servants. The Virginia Company itself transported many servants, often without adequate supplies, to work on company estates. In Virginia, these servants became prey for the wealthy colonial merchants (including the officials of the company) who had monopolized the available supplies. In exchange for basic necessities, these merchants cruelly exploited the labor of the servants; some Virginians treated their workers more as commodities than as people, and sold their labor to others. Such patterns served as grim forerunners of the treatment that blacks received later in the century.

In an effort to unify the struggling settlement, the company instructed its officials in Virginia to summon the first legislative assembly in American history (1619). The House of Burgesses, composed of two delegates from each district, was supposed to advise and consult with the governor and the council. Although any adult male, even an indentured servant, could vote for the first representatives, decisions made by the Burgesses could not bind the company, and later suffrage laws reduced the size of the electorate. While this representative system seems unusually democratic for its time, the changes were more illusory than real. Throughout the immediate future, the governor and the council, which consisted of the wealthiest men in Virginia, continued to control political power.

Despite these attempted reforms, Virginia brought no profits to the English investors, and only a few local merchants seem to have found modest wealth. In 1622, an Indian attack provoked by English encroachments on Indian territory, almost destroyed the colony, leaving over 300 colonists dead. Meanwhile, in England, members of the company continued to disagree about policy. James I, hoping to increase customs revenues by dismantling the company, accused the officers of mismanagement and had the company's charter revoked (1624). Thereafter, Virginia became a royal colony subject to the direct control of the crown.

As a royal colony, Virginia was ruled by a governor and a council selected by the king and an assembly elected by the male property owners in the colony. The survival of the House of Burgesses was fortunate for the colonists, for, in later years, the assembly assumed a greater role in enacting legislation. Although the king could veto laws passed by the assembly, Virginians enjoyed considerable self-rule, especially after 1624, when the Burgesses won the right to levy taxes. These political institutions became typical in other royal colonies as well. [See chapter 6.]

Virginia Society

The political history of Virginia in the middle decades of the seventeenth century was marked by minor disputes between the governor and the colonists. During the English civil wars (1641-1660), which pitted king against Parliament and Anglican against Puritan, Virginia was able to develop in isolation. The economic and social changes that occurred during these years appear more dramatic than the political events and had more lasting effects on the colony's history.

Despite the efforts of Virginia's officials to build a diversified economy, the settlers persisted in expanding tobacco production. After recovering from the massacre of 1622, the population of the colony increased slowly, largely because of an extremely high death rate. In 1635, only 5,000 people

inhabited the colony, despite continued emigration from England. The
shortage of women in the colony also helps to explain the low birthrate. By
mid-century, however, the death rate began to decline, possibly because
of better dietary conditions, and the population reached 30,000 by 1660.
The growth of the population encouraged geographical dispersal within
the colony. Although most Virginians owned relatively small holdings
worked by indentured servants and occasionally by slaves (the slave population in 1650 was barely 500), tobacco planting encouraged dispersal since
it rapidly depleted the fertility of the soil. The arrival of new settlers and the
ease of acquiring lands under the headright system also stimulated geographic expansion.

As settlement spread along the rivers, it became necessary to decen-
tralize the government by dividing the colony into counties (1634). The
regulation of county government duplicated the patterns of local administration in England [see above, pp. 13-14]. In each county, the governor
and the council appointed justices of the peace, sheriffs, clerks, and coro-
ners. As in England, these local officials administered justice, executed the
laws of the assembly, and maintained the peace. In compensation for their
public service, they received fees and the respect that colonial Americans
generally paid to their local leaders.

Besides resulting in these institutional adjustments, the expansion of
Virginia created serious strains in the colony's social structure. Sharing
the social ideals of the organic society [see above, pp. 19-20], most Virginians expected the traditional aristocracy to control political power; and,
under the rule of the Virginia Company, power, wealth, and social status
went hand in hand. Within one generation, however, most of the original
colonial leaders had died or returned to England. They had left behind a
vacuum at the top of the political structure, which soon was filled by the
wealthiest survivors in the colony. These new leaders were aristocrats of
mere wealth, rather than of birth, and lacked the status that people traditionally associated with political power. Thus, Virginians sensed a gap
between their social ideals (which said that only men of high status should
exercise political power) and the realities of the colony's politics. Rapid
economic mobility thereby undermined the colonists' attempt to create a
traditional social order in Virginia.

To make matters more complicated (for the colonists as well as for
the historian), the extreme fluidity of this early society soon undermined
the power of even the new elite. During the English civil wars, many ambitious English people of wealth fled to Virginia to escape the confusions of
the mother country. In Virginia, their inherited wealth enabled them to
acquire large landed estates. These newer immigrants (who immigrated to
Virginia between 1640 and 1660) rapidly consolidated their power and
emerged as the leaders in the colony. Not all the people from this group
acquired the same social and political standing. Consequently, jealousies
and tensions appeared periodically, eventually climaxing in Bacon's Rebel-

lion (1675) [see below, pp. 53-55]. But, by 1660, the "first families" of Virginia, who provided political leadership through the eighteenth century, had staked out their claims to status and power.

Maryland

Many of these same social problems emerged, though to a lesser extent, in the neighboring colony of Maryland. Unlike Virginia, Maryland was founded by a single proprietor, George Calvert, the first Lord Baltimore, rather than by a commercial company. Calvert, a prominent Roman Catholic, hoped to establish a haven for persecuted adherents of his faith. In 1632, the second Stuart monarch, Charles I (1625-1649), granted him a tract of land north of the Potomac River on which to found a colony. As proprietor, Calvert owned all the land, retained exclusive rights to colonial trade, and exercised wide legislative powers subject to the approval of the settlers.

First settled at St. Mary's in 1634, the colony soon produced prosperous harvests of tobacco, wheat, and corn. The proprietor attempted to create a feudal domain by granting large manors to wealthy settlers, who imported indentured servants to the colony. The shortage of labor, however, soon forced the proprietors to offer headrights to potential settlers, thereby undermining the manorial system. The Calvert family made similar concessions in political affairs. From the beginning of settlement, in Maryland they permitted an elected assembly to regulate local affairs, and by 1650 this body had developed into a legislature similar to the House of Burgesses.

Although Calvert conceived of Maryland as a refuge for English Catholics, the majority of colonists worshipped as Protestants. To protect the Catholic minority from religious persecution, the proprietors encouraged the passage of the Toleration Act (1649), which granted religious liberty to all Christians. This legislation failed to diminish religious rivalry in the colony. The proprietary leadership remained Catholic, and resentment of the proprietors usually was mixed with anti-Catholicism. Despite the proprietors' concessions in political affairs, patterns of landholding, and religious worship, numerous rebellions against proprietary rule disrupted the peace of the colony throughout the seventeenth century.

By 1660, the Chesapeake colonies of Virginia and Maryland had developed in parallel ways. Both possessed a staple agricultural economy based on tobacco production. Both had developed political institutions for self-government. Land policies in both colonies offered acreage to indentured servants upon completion of their service. This feature aggravated the labor shortage in both regions and would lead Virginians and Marylanders to institute black slavery as a cheap way of establishing a permanent labor force [see below, pp. 55-57].

Puritanism

Unlike the settlers who immigrated to the Chesapeake colonies because of the attractiveness of the New World, the people who colonized New England departed from their native land because of the social and religious troubles at home. In creating the Church of England, Henry VIII and his daughter Elizabeth had been motivated more by dynastic considerations than by religious beliefs [see above, pp. 15-16]. The Anglican church represented a compromise between those who wished to retain aspects of the Catholic church and those who wished to erect an orthodox Protestant church. The Protestant dissenters objected to the "popish" practices in the established church and hoped to further the Reformation by eliminating such "impurities." In particular, they wished to simplify the religious service by curtailing certain ceremonies, and they advocated the removal of higher church officers such as bishops and archbishops. Some reformers, such as the Presbyterians, proposed an alternative national church. But the founders of New England, who were primarily Congregationalists, instead conceived of a church in which each congregation controlled its own affairs. In many other respects, these Protestant dissenters shared beliefs and principles with their Anglican opponents. The New England colonists took their religions seriously, however, and refused to overlook even minor areas of disagreement.

The Congregationalist dissenters were divided into two groups: the Separatists and the Puritans (or Non-Separatists). Although both groups agreed on most of the essentials of religion, they differed in their willingness — or unwillingness — to remain within the established church. The Puritans, more moderate and more numerous than the Separatists, believed that the Church of England was a true church even though it desperately needed reformation. According to the Puritans, it was necessary for true Christians to remain within the Anglican church in order to maximize their reforming influence. The Separatists, on the other hand, insisted that the established church was beyond salvation and felt that a believer who worshipped in that church would be contaminated by its sins.

These ecclesiastical differences should not obscure the basic agreement among Puritans and Separatists. Influenced by the teachings of the sixteenth-century theologian John Calvin, these English dissenters believed that God selected a few saints as His chosen people and condemned the remainder of humanity to eternal damnation. Whether one was saved or damned depended not on human action or the quality of one's life but rather on the inscrutable will of God. The Lord, according to the adherents of Puritanism, imputed His grace into the souls of otherwise corrupt people, thereby confirming their eternal salvation. This act of conversion became the central aspect of Puritanism, the single event that separated the saint from the sinner for eternity. Although, in theory, a belief in these principles of predestination freed the saints from specific moral obligations in this world, Puritans expected believers to live godly lives on earth as a way of preparing for the comforts of heaven.

For many Puritans, the conversion experience was a physical experience in which the saint was struck down by a sense of sinfulness and total dependence on God's grace. This experience reveals the deep emotionalism of Puritanism and explains perhaps why the movement appealed to the victims of social dislocation [see above, pp. 21-22]. Confused by the chaos of the times, many people turned to Puritanism, because it offered salvation and a sense of security in the next world, if not in this one. The emotionalism also explains the self-assurance of the Puritans, the sense of confidence that enabled the Puritans to immigrate to the New World in the 1620s and 1630s and to wage civil war against Charles I during the following decade in England.

Besides this emotionalism, Puritanism had a rational side as well. Without denying the omnipotence of God, the Puritans attempted to make the ways of the Lord seem more intelligible by arguing that God used logical means to effect His ends. Puritan ministers suggested that God willingly bound Himself by a covenant, or contract, in dealing with His saints. As a result, the actions of God seemed less arbitrary and more predictable. The ideas of covenant theology enabled the Puritans to defend themselves against accusations that only God Himself could know His will.

Plymouth Colony

The Pilgrim Separatists established the first permanent settlement in New England (1620). Originally a Separatist sect in Scrooby, England, the Pilgrims had moved to Holland in 1607 to escape persecution for their radical religious views. Although they found religious freedom in the Netherlands, the Pilgrims suffered from economic deprivation and worried that their children were abandoning the faith. To solve these problems, the Pilgrims decided to immigrate to the New World, where, they hoped, economic prosperity would reinforce their solidarity.

First the Pilgrims obtained a grant of land from the London Company, which was attempting to populate its extensive domains. Then, to finance the voyage to America, they formed a joint-stock company with a group of London merchants. The settlers were to obtain one share of stock each (backed by their labor in the colony); the merchants purchased shares of stock in hopes of acquiring a large return. As in Virginia, commercial capitalism was closely linked to the founding of the colony.

Having chartered the *Mayflower,* the Pilgrims sailed for America in 1620. Blown off course by severe storms, the *Mayflower* dropped anchor off the Massachusetts coast just as winter was approaching. Exhausted by the voyage, the Pilgrims decided to remain in New England and in December began building a settlement at Plymouth. Possessing scant provisions, the Pilgrims barely survived the first winter. Timely assistance from the local Indians kept them from starving to death, but the mortality rate was high nevertheless.

Of the colonists aboard the *Mayflower*, only about one-third were Separatists; the remainder were ordinary Londoners ("strangers"). Recognizing that they had landed beyond the reaches of any government and that apparently they lacked title to the lands, the Pilgrim leaders persuaded all the immigrants to sign the Mayflower Compact, in which the colonists agreed to create "civil Body Politick" and promised to obey laws of their making. While the Mayflower Compact stands as a landmark of self-government in American history, the agreement also served as an instrument of social control to keep the "strangers" from undermining the religious principles of the Pilgrim leadership. In 1621, the colonists obtained a patent to the lands from the Council of New England, which had replaced the Virginia Company as owner of the region.

Because of its poverty and the unpopular views of the Separatists who led it, Plymouth colony grew slowly. To encourage agricultural production, the settlers abandoned their communal farming in 1623. Four years later, they dissolved their partnership with the London merchants who had helped to finance the enterprise. Despite attempts to develop a fur trade, few settlers became rich in the colony, and the London merchants realized little return from their investments. During the seventeenth century, the Pilgrim colony fell under the influence of its larger neighbor at Massachusetts Bay, finally being absorbed by the Bay colony in 1691 after failing to obtain a royal charter of its own.

Massachusetts Bay

The founding of Massachusetts Bay (1630) climaxed a decade of corporate development. In 1620, control of New England passed from the old Plymouth Company to the Council of New England, a revived joint-stock company interested in developing the region. In 1623, the council authorized a group of merchants, known as the Dorchester Company, to fish and trade in New England. In 1626, this company erected a small fishing station at Salem. When the Dorchester Company proved unsuccessful, several Puritan investors organized the New England Company (1628) to consider colonization in New England.

These complicated business transactions threatened the validity of various claims to the region. To avoid confusion, the Puritan investors obtained a new charter for the Massachusetts Bay Company (1629), which gave them power to govern the colony. It was this organization, led by Governor John Winthrop (1588-1649), that directed the colonization of Massachusetts Bay. In August 1629, the leaders of the company adopted the Cambridge Agreement, in which they promised to immigrate to New England, provided that the company charter and the governing body also were transferred to the colony. Since a government in America would be free from direct royal interference, this provision constituted the basis for a self-governing enterprise.

In 1630, Winthrop led the first contingent of about 1,000 settlers to what is now Boston, Massachusetts. Within a decade, the population of New England approached 20,000. The motives behind this mass movement obviously varied considerably. But, to a great extent, the religious and social turmoil of Stuart England explains the origins of the Great Migration.

Like other English people who shared the ideals of the organic society [see above, pp. 19-20], the Puritans believed that God was closely involved in all human concerns. Nothing could occur in the world that did not reflect, in some way, the will of God. These ideas led the English to attach religious significance to all human activities. During the 1620s, many Puritans interpreted the social troubles in England to mean that God was punishing England for its failure to "purify" the Anglican church. A depression in the wool industry, poor harvests, epidemics, and the dislocations associated with the enclosure movement all seemed to indicate that God was unhappy with England. By 1630, the future looked desperate. The silencing of Puritan ministers by Archbishop William Laud and the refusal of Charles I to cooperate with Parliament led the Puritans to believe that God would soon unleash His wrath. For these people, New England appeared as a place of safety for the Lord's chosen people, a refuge in which they could escape the coming devastation.

The immediate causes of the Great Migration appear to have been the economic and social turmoil of the times. But the Puritans believed that such troubles were *symptoms* of the pervasiveness of sin within the established church. They hoped by immigrating to New England not merely to escape from this sinfulness but also to stimulate a reformation at home. Like later utopians in American history, the Puritan colonists believed that they had a special mission, inspired by God, to create an ideal community — a wilderness Zion — in the New World. Such a community would serve as a social blueprint for all the world to imitate. John Winthrop assured his fellow voyagers that they would be a "city upon a hill," a beacon of hope amidst a world of sin. Presumably, the success of a Bible commonwealth would convince other communities to restructure their societies according to the divinely inspired blueprint. The magnitude of this mission required the leaders of the colony to exercise careful guidance lest sin creep in and undermine the godly experiment.

The charter that Winthrop transferred to Massachusetts in 1630 placed the government of the colony in the hands of a governor and his assistants, who were chosen by the stockholders. This meant that most of the colonists had no political voice. In 1631, in response to the protests of some outsiders, Winthrop and his associates redefined the meaning of the term *freeman* (which in England had meant *stockholder*) to mean *citizen* and still allowed all freemen to vote. This decision broadened the base of participation in voting. At the same time, however, an equally important decision restricted freemanship to members of Puritan churches. In this way, the Massachusetts authorities hoped to link the fortunes of the state with those of the church. In 1634, after hearing protests against granting all legislative power to the governor and his assistants, the colony legislature (called the General Court) authorized each town to send representatives to the General Court. These delegates, or deputies, met with the assistants to levy taxes and draft legislation. In 1644, the deputies and assistants divided into separate legislative branches.

Although church and state were legally separate in New England, they remained closely intertwined. The Puritans implemented their belief in a congregational church system and permitted each church to regulate its own affairs. After about 1634, a person had to demonstrate to his brethren that he had undergone a conversion experience before he could attain full membership in the church; women, who were considered weaker, were allowed to testify to their conversion in private. This rigorous standard of admission was especially significant, because only full church members could vote in colony elections (those who were not freemen, however, could participate in local elections). Those people who could not meet the requirements for admission to the church were compelled to attend the meeting house regularly, where they could hear the words of the Lord

The New England meeting house served as the center of town life. In the early days of settlement, colonists were required to live near the church to reinforce a sense of community and to prevent moral decline. (The Granger Collection.)

preached by such ministers as John Cotton, Thomas Hooker, and Thomas Shepard. To assure the church's close supervision of the settlers, the General Court prohibited the construction of houses more than a half-mile from the church and required all unmarried residents to live with a godly family. Such oversight, they believed, would preserve the Bible commonwealth from internal subversion.

Puritan Families

The Puritans' commitment to their religious mission led the colonists to exercise caution in raising their children. Like the English family, the average family in New England was nuclear in structure. A lower death rate in the healthier atmosphere of America seems to have permitted slightly larger families, and the abundance of available land made possible a lower average age of marriage. Education continued to be a function of the family. But, in 1647, perhaps because families were neglecting their responsibilities, the General Court ordered the Massachusetts towns to support godly schoolmasters.

Concern for the religious welfare of future generations also led to the founding of Harvard College (1636) to assure a supply of educated ministers. Despite these obvious religious motives, the Harvard curriculum imitated the traditional liberal arts education of the English universities. Prior to admission, a freshman had to possess a reading knowledge of Latin. College studies entailed work in Latin, Greek, Hebrew, mathematics, science, and philosophy, as well as in religion. More than half of the Harvard graduates of the seventeenth century became ministers.

The architecture of New England housing reinforced family interdependence. Most dwellings had one main room, called the hall, which was dominated by a large fireplace. There were usually only a few windows, since glass was expensive, and the ceilings were low in order to conserve heat. During the long New England winters, most social activity was moved indoors, and the close living arrangements accentuated family solidarity.

The importance of good family relations affected business affairs as well. Because of the high risk of commerce and the slowness of communications, merchants had to rely on trusted agents to transact their business. Puritan merchants preferred to deal with other Puritans, usually with family members and personal acquaintances who lived in other parts of the Atlantic world. Similarly, Quaker and Jewish merchants in Rhode Island and New York preferred to do business with their own trusted kin and coreligionists. This mixing of family and business in the colonial period reflected the personal nature of economic activity even over great distances.

Because of their desire to erect a godly commonwealth, Puritan leaders consciously attempted to avoid the dispersal that characterized the

A   In *Adam's* Fall
     We Sinned all.

B   Thy Life to Mend
     This *Book* Attend.

C   The Cat doth play
     And after flay.

D   A *Dog* will bite
     A Thief at night.

E   An *Eagles* flight
     Is out of sight.

F   The Idle *Fool*
     Is whipt at School.

The New England Primer, widely used in the late seventeenth and eighteenth centuries, simultaneously provided lessons in spelling and religious morality. As the sixth rhyme indicated, parents and teachers relied upon corporal punishment to correct misbehavior. But by the mid-eighteenth century, some pedagogues were calling for greater moderation. (The Granger Collection.)

settlement of Virginia. The influx of thousands of immigrants prevented the creation of a single community. Thus, colony officials relied on the town system as an instrument of social control. In distributing the lands, the General Court granted the land directly to towns, which then divided the acreage among the residents. From the beginning of settlement, no one was permitted to live beyond the confines of some town. When over-crowding compelled inland expansion, the General Court insisted that new settlements be made by several families and that they arrange to support an orthodox minister among them.

In the early decades of settlement, town life reflected the cohesive purposes of the Puritan experiment. Town dwellers lived together, worked together, and prayed together. Town meetings were open forums in which nonfreemen could participate. Besides overseeing land distribution, the towns hired the schoolmaster, laid out the roads, and protected the unfortunate. The town also served as the unit of political representation in the colonial legislature. More subtly, the closeness of town life enabled the godly to oversee the behavior of their neighbors. As a conservative force, the town system retarded the disintegration of Puritan social ideals.

Political and social theory in New England derived from the principles of the organic society. While the Puritans thought that all the saints were equal in the eyes of God, they did not assume that all people were equal on earth. Aside from the racial prejudices they shared with other English people, the Puritans believed that leadership belonged in the hands of the better sort of people. Despite a relatively large suffrage, political power remained in the hands of the elite. Democracy had no place in the Puritan scheme of things.

In emphasizing the importance of social status, the Puritans, like the settlers of the Chesapeake colonies, failed to consider the changes that would occur in colonial society. It was one thing to assume that society should be hierarchical; it was quite another to preserve such a system in practice. The original leaders of the Great Migration, men such as John Winthrop and Deputy-Governor Thomas Dudley, were members of the English gentry and retained high-status positions in New England. However, as the colonial economy prospered, several merchants acquired sizable fortunes. Desirous of attaining a social status equivalent to their wealth, these merchants often resented the restraints of the traditional order. On the town level, too, the harmony and order that had characterized the formative period of settlement often deteriorated as people bickered about land allotments or seating in the meeting house (the placement of seats reflected the social status of the saints). To be sure, New England remained remarkably homogeneous throughout the century. But, by 1660, Puritan ministers complained of a decline in religiosity and lamented a betrayal of the original mission.

Religious Deviation

With hindsight, it is not difficult to locate the sources of disintegration. What is more striking is the tenacity with which the Puritans attempted to defend their way of life. The need to maintain religious orthodoxy had been one of the primary goals of the Puritan colonists. Thus, the Puritans attempted to stifle all religious deviation. In the 1630s, they banished Roger Williams and Anne Hutchinson; twenty years later, they executed several Quakers who persisted in returning to the Bay colony after they had been banished.

Roger Williams, pastor of the church at Salem, was the first serious challenge to the Massachusetts orthodoxy. Taking a Separatist position, Williams argued that the Lord's saints should remain aloof from the affairs of the world, and he proposed a complete separation of church and state. By meddling with political affairs, he declared, God's chosen people would be contaminated by the sins of ordinary mortals. Although this was hardly a democratic position, the logic of the argument eventually led Williams to support religious toleration; after all, no one could know with certainty the state of another person's soul. Even though these positions were logical outgrowths of orthodox Puritan doctrine, the Massachusetts authorities viewed Williams as a potential subversive because he questioned the ecclesiastical system that they had created. For this heresy, Williams was banished from Massachusetts in 1635. In the dead of winter, he traveled southward and eventually founded a settlement, named Providence, on land purchased from the Indians near Narragansett Bay. Other deviants soon followed Williams to Rhode Island.

Although the Puritan ministers claimed that a person's moral behavior did not necessarily reflect the state of his or her soul, they nevertheless insisted that a saint would not engage in immoral conduct. These ideas influenced the leaders of New England, who felt responsible for preserving the moral order of their holy community. However, one Puritan dissenter, Anne Hutchinson, a member of the church at Boston, protested the emphasis on good works in Puritan sermons. Like Roger Williams, she carried Puritanism to its logical conclusion and argued that salvation was unrelated to a person's behavior in this world. Besides challenging established religious values, Hutchinson also violated the tradition of women's silence in public affairs. Instead of accepting the "correction" of the leadership, she ably defended herself in court. But her refusal to submit emphasized her threat to the social order, and, in 1638, like Roger Williams, she was banished from Massachusetts. She too fled southward, finally settling at Portsmouth. Other religious dissenters founded Newport (1639) and Warwick (1643) in Rhode Island. In 1644, Roger Williams obtained a parliamentary charter for the settlements of Rhode Island. Marked by provisions that authorized complete religious freedom, this charter was confirmed by Charles II in 1663.

Connecticut and New Haven

Unlike the deviant settlements of Rhode Island that were the results of fundamental theological differences, the founding of Connecticut (1635) and New Haven (1638) reflected the problem of overcrowding and the weakening of community attachments in Massachusetts Bay. Many of the settlers around Massachusetts Bay, complaining of a lack of arable land and attracted by the fertility of the Connecticut River valley, sold their holdings to new colonists from England and traveled overland to establish towns at Hartford, Wethersfield, and Windsor. Led by the Cambridge minister Thomas Hooker, some of these migrants may have resented a tightening of the standards of church admission. But, for the most part, the founders of Connecticut shared the political and social aspirations of their coreligionists at Massachusetts. The Fundamental Orders of Connecticut (1639) articulated the essential political principles of the colony, which remained firmly Puritan.

Shortly after the settlement of Connecticut, the local Pequot Indians, resenting the invasion, began to harass the Puritan communities. In the ensuing Pequot War (1637), the Puritans destroyed the Pequot villages, slaughtering the inhabitants and enslaving the survivors. Other Indian tribes, who had supported the Puritans in the conflict, found that they were not immune to the settlers' encroachment on their land. During the war, the Puritans had found fertile lands west of the Connecticut River. Reports of this discovery reached Boston just as a group of emigrants from London was searching for a suitable location to establish a colony. Encouraged by optimistic reports, these Londoners, led by John Davenport and Theophilus Eaton, founded a colony at New Haven. Composed of several towns spread along the northern coast of the Long Island Sound, New Haven colony was characterized by its rigid Puritan orthodoxy. In 1662, a royal charter attached New Haven to the colony of Connecticut.

In 1643, the major colonies of New England — Massachusetts Bay, Connecticut, Plymouth, and New Haven — established a loose confederation to challenge Dutch claims to Connecticut and to formulate a common policy toward the Indians. With civil war raging in the mother country, New Englanders realized that England would provide no assistance in time of crisis. On the other hand, the troubles at home enabled the Puritan colonies, like those on the Chesapeake, to develop independent of English interference. With the Restoration of the Stuart monarchy in the person of Charles II (1660-1685), however, England could afford once again to concern itself with its American possessions.

Supplementary Reading

A thorough discussion of British colonization during the seventeenth century may be found in C. Andrews, *The Colonial Period of American History,* four volumes (1934-1938). A more recent overview is J. Pomfret and F. Shumway, *Founding the American Colonies, 1583-1660* (1970). The best study of Virginia in this period is E. Morgan, *American Slavery, American Freedom: The Ordeal of Colonial Virginia* (1975); also helpful is A. Vaughan, *American Genesis: Captain John Smith and the Founding of Virginia* (1975). A more detailed study of the Chesapeake colonies is W. Craven, *The Southern Colonies in the Seventeenth Century* (1949).

The literature on the New England colonies is vast. The best survey of the Plymouth settlement is G. Langdon, Jr., *Pilgrim Colony: A History of New Plymouth* (1966). The founding of Massachusetts Bay is described in E. Morgan, *The Puritan Dilemma: The Story of John Winthrop* (1958). Also helpful are S. E. Morison, *Builders of the Bay Colony* (1930), and R. Wall, *Massachusetts Bay: The Crucial Decade, 1640-1650* (1972).

Numerous historians have examined the ideas related to Puritanism. For a convenient overview, see F. Bremer, *The Puritan Experiment* (1976). Perry Miller's outstanding works have stressed the intellectual aspects of Puritan life; see *Orthodoxy in Massachusetts* (1933), *The New England Mind: The Seventeenth Century* (1939), and the essays in *Errand into the Wilderness* (1956). Puritan emotionalism is explained in A. Simpson, *Puritanism in Old and New England* (1955). E. Morgan, *Visible Saints* (1963), analyzes the church structure, and D. Hall, *The Faithful Shepherd: A History of the New England Ministry in the Seventeenth Century* (1972), traces the changing role of the clergy. For a study of changing Puritan attitudes over three generations, see R. Middlekauff, *The Mathers* (1971).

Puritan attitudes toward education are explained in S. E. Morison's works; see *The Founding of Harvard College* (1935), *Harvard in the Seventeenth Century* (1956), and *The Intellectual Life of Colonial New England* (1956). A seminal essay on the relationship between education and the family is B. Bailyn, *Education in the Forming of American Society* (1960). Also suggested is K. Lockridge, *Literacy in Colonial New England* (1974). The family structure in New England is analyzed in E. Morgan, *The Puritan Family* (revised edition, 1966); J. Demos, *A Little Commonwealth: Family Life in Plymouth Colony* (1970); and P. Greven, *Four Generations: Population, Land, and Family in Colonial Andover, Massachusetts* (1970). For new research on Puritan child-rearing practices, see J. Illick's essay in L. deMause, *The History of Childhood* (1974). Puritan attitudes toward death and dying are analyzed in D. Stannard, *The Puritan Way of Death* (1977). Besides the work of Demos and Greven, there are several valuable studies of Puritan communities; see S. Powell, *Puritan Village* (1963); K. Lockridge, *A New England Town: The First Hundred Years* (1970); and D. Rutman, *Winthrop's Boston* (1965). Another aspect of social and economic history is presented in B. Bailyn, *The New England Merchants in the Seventeenth Century* (1955). Puritan attitudes toward the environment are treated in P. Carroll, *Puritanism and the Wilderness* (1969). For a critical assessment of Puritan relations with the Indians, see F. Jennings, *The Invasion of America* (1975). For a geographical study, see D. McManis, *Colonial New England: A Historical Geography* (1975).

Religious deviation is examined in a sociological framework in K. Erikson, *Wayward Puritans* (1966). For a discussion of the career of Roger Williams, see O. Winslow, *Master Roger Williams* (1957); Williams's ideas are analyzed in E. Morgan, *Roger Williams: The Church and the State* (1967). For an analysis of the controversy surrounding Anne Hutchinson, see E. Battis, *Saints and Sectaries* (1962). For a study of Puritan legal arrangements, see D. Flaherty, *Privacy in Colonial New England* (1972).

The Connecticut settlements are described in M. Jones, *Congregational Commonwealth* (1968). Also helpful is the biography of a leading settler by R. Black III, *The Younger John Winthrop* (1967). For a discussion of colonial New Haven, see I. Calder, *The New Haven Colony* (1934). A brief social history of Rhode Island is C. Bridenbaugh, *Fat Mutton and Liberty of Conscience* (1974).

Chapter
4

The Expansion of Empire
1660-1700

The English civil wars and the period of Oliver Cromwell's Protectorate (1653-1658) distracted the English people from their colonial empire. But the Restoration of Charles II (1660) stabilized the political situation at home and enabled enterprising people to think again of colonial ventures. In the latter half of the century, proprietary colonies were established in the Carolinas, New York, New Jersey, and Pennsylvania. Attracted by promotional pamphlets and promises of religious toleration, thousands immigrated to America. By 1700, the population of English North America totaled 250,000.

With the exception of Maryland (which had drawn upon the resources of nearby Virginia), the success of colonization in the early seventeenth century had depended on the extensive investments of joint-stock companies. The colonies settled during the Restoration period, however, were organized and settled by proprietors. Charles II owed large political debts to his loyal supporters; he often repaid them with proprietary grants in the New World. Besides being good politics, the bestowal of such gifts did not drain the royal coffers, since the lands in America were worthless without people to develop them. Also proprietary enterprises were not as risky during the Restoration period as they had been earlier in the century. The existence of nearby English settlements assured assistance and protection, however minimal, to the newer colonies. Moreover, transatlantic trade had become more common, and people were experienced in the problems of colonization.

The Carolinas

Charles II made the first of the proprietary grants to a group of eight powerful lords for the region south of Virginia (1663). Hoping to create baronial estates in the warm climate of the Carolinas, the proprietors expected to produce such exotic commodities as silk and wine. One of the proprietors, the future earl of Shaftesbury, and his protege, the philosopher John Locke, drafted an elaborate quasi-feudal plan for the colony known as the Fundamental Constitutions (1669). Attempting to implement the ideals of the organic society, the proprietors envisioned a community in which wealth, high social status, and political power all belonged to the same people. Ruled by a hereditary nobility with enormous landed estates, men of lesser wealth were to assume proportional political rights. Only a small portion of this program was ever developed in the colony, largely because few people wanted to work as virtual peasants when land was so abundant. By 1693, the proprietors abandoned even the facade of the Fundamental Constitutions.

It is likely that Shaftesbury proposed this scheme to make the colony more attractive to potential English investors. Certain other provisions, moreover, revealed an attempt to appeal to specific settlers already in the New World. Rather than transporting colonists from England, the proprietors hoped to populate their lands with inhabitants from other colonies. Thus, while the Constitutions suggested that the Anglican church would become the official religion in the colony at some future date, the plan promised religious liberty to all — even Jews and heathens — to attract potential immigrants among Puritans and Quakers already in America.

More numerous than these settlers, however, were emigrants from the West Indies, particularly those from Barbados. To attract planters from this region, the Fundamental Constitutions promised to protect the ownership of black slaves, even if the slaves had converted to Christianity. The islands of the West Indies, including Barbados (first colonized by the English in 1627) and Jamaica (taken from Spain in 1655), had been settled to produce sugar as a cash crop. The emphasis on capitalistic agriculture led to the consolidation of large plantations and the importation of black slaves. Small landowners (who might even have been slaveholders) could not compete with the wealthier estates. Many of these lesser planters immigrated to the Carolinas, where their economic prospects seemed brighter. Some wealthy planters, concerned about establishing their children, also deserted the crowded islands for the Carolina mainland. Both groups brought their slaves with them.

The first English inhabitants of the Carolinas had migrated from Virginia and settled in the region around Albemarle Sound. The original settlements resisted the efforts of the proprietors to attach them to the legal government and eventually formed the separate colony of North Carolina (1712). Isolated by hazardous sandbars from the coastal trade, the settlements explanded slowly. Based primarily on small-scale subsistence agriculture, North Carolina lacked internal political unity until the 1740s.

The settlements to the south, however, were more diversified. Settled by English colonists from Barbados (1670), the area around Charles Town (later Charleston) developed a flourishing trade in deer skins with the nearby Indians. The sharp Carolina traders soon expanded this commerce to include large numbers of Indian slaves, who were exported to other colonies. As with African slavery, the trade in Indian slaves depended upon intertribal rivalry and the willingness of the coastal tribes to enslave and sell people from the interior. The Carolina settlers were especially adept at playing off one tribe against another, a strategy that hastened the destruction of such groups as the Westos, Savannahs, Tuscaroras (who fled to New York), and the Yamasees.

Besides the trade in deer skins and slaves, the expansion of rice culture during the 1690s, together with the arrival of non-English immigrants such as Huguenots and African slaves (who were experienced cultivators of rice), created a thriving economy in South Carolina. By the early eighteenth century, an entrenched oligarchy owned large rice plantations, which were worked by numerous slaves. This society contrasted with the small farms and the free labor found in North Carolina. In 1729, when the proprietors sold their interests to the crown, each region became a separate royal colony.

New York

Just as the Carolina proprietors based their plans on an already existing colonial population, so did the proprietor of New York. In 1664, Charles II granted his brother, the duke of York (later James II), proprietary rights to the territory between Connecticut and Maryland. With this patent, the duke sent four ships to conquer the Dutch settlement of New Netherland (1664).

As has been suggested [see above, p. 11], the colony of New Netherland grew slowly and suffered from sporadic wars with the local Indians. Direct competition from the nearby settlers of New England aggravated these problems. Dutch claims to the fur trade in Connecticut, for example, had hastened the creation of the New England Confederation (1643). Even more threatening to Dutch control was the steady migration of New Englanders to the eastern end of Long Island. Although the Dutch under Governor Peter Stuyvesant had challenged the legality of the English claims, the small colony could not thwart English expansion. In 1650, the Dutch and English negotiated the Treaty of Hartford, which established a boundary between Connecticut and New Netherland and divided the claims to Long Island.

International events further weakened the Dutch colony. During the 1650s, the first of three Anglo-Dutch wars underscored the growing commercial competition between the two nations. As the English became more concerned with consolidating their empire and removing foreign interlopers, they resented the presence of a Dutch government between the Chesapeake and New England colonies. With a second war with the Dutch looming on the horizon, Charles II authorized the conquest of New Netherland. After a brief delay, Stuyvesant capitulated to the superior English forces and New Netherland became New York. During the third Anglo-Dutch war (1672-1674), the Dutch reconquered the colony but returned it to England as part of the peace settlement.

The local representatives of the duke of York did not drastically change the internal structure of the colony. Interested in acquiring revenue for the proprietor, they encouraged the Dutch to continue the fur trade (although the pelts then would be sold in England rather than in the Netherlands). Soon after the conquest, Governor Richard Nicolls drafted a body of laws (the Duke's Laws, 1665) that extended English law to areas outside New York City. Nicolls was interested in bringing English institutions to the existing English population and thought that such a policy would make New York more attractive to colonists in other areas. For similar purposes and to facilitate the integration of Dutch culture, the Duke's Laws also offered religious toleration to all Protestants. Although each town retained the right to elect local officials, the duke showed little interest in creating a provincial legislature. Only after continued pressure from the colonists did he at last authorize the summoning of a representative assembly (1683). The delegates promptly enacted a Charter of Liberties, which asserted the need for regular assemblies to levy taxes. Upon his accession as James II, however, the duke eliminated the legislature and placed New York under the administration of the Dominion of New England [see below, p. 58].

The Jerseys

Shortly after seizing New Netherland, the duke of York granted the southern portions of his domain (later to become New Jersey) to two loyal supporters of the Stuart throne, Lord John Berkeley and Sir George Carteret. Although the proprietors technically owned only the land, they claimed political authority as well. A Concession and Agreement (1665) provided for a government that included an elected assembly. In 1665, the population of New Jersey consisted of scattered Swedes and Finns settled along the Delaware River, Dutch farmers on the Hudson, and a small but rapidly growing number of Puritans from New England.

COLONIAL SETTLEMENT, 1700

In 1674, Lord Berkeley sold his interest in the area to two Quakers, leading to the formal division of the colony into East Jersey (adjacent to New York) and West Jersey (adjacent to Pennsylvania). East Jersey appealed to New Englanders in search of fertile lands and an opportunity to establish new religious institutions. West Jersey generally attracted English Quakers, who were later instrumental in founding Pennsylvania. In 1702, the Jerseys became a single royal colony known as New Jersey.

Pennsylvania

In 1681, to settle an old family debt, Charles II granted a proprietary colony to William Penn, a wealthy English Quaker and a former investor in the Jerseys. The Society of Friends, or Quakers, was a radical offshoot of English Puritanism. The Quakers rejected all earthly distinctions between people and criticized the existence of all religious ceremonies. Believing that all people retained an "inner light" of divinity within them, the Quakers preached a religion of spiritual equality and brotherly love. To other religious groups, the Quakers' refusal to take oaths or to pay respect to proper authorities seemed socially anarchistic and religiously blasphemous. For these reasons, the Puritans had executed several Quakers rather than permit them to undermine authority in New England. Many Quakers settled in Rhode Island, where they enjoyed religious toleration. Nevertheless, the Quakers hoped to establish a colony based on their own principles; Pennsylvania would be the proving ground of their "holy experiment."

As proprietor of Pennsylvania, William Penn possessed wide powers. The colony charter (1681) required obedience to English law but otherwise allowed Penn to organize the colony as he wished. Not content with a royal grant to Pennsylvania and hoping to establish friendly relations with the local tribes, he purchased the Indian claims to the territory. To administer his proprietorship, Penn formulated a Frame of Government (1682), which provided for a representative assembly. This body, however, lacked the power to initiate legislation until 1696, when the proprietor finally capitulated to pressure from the colonists. In a later draft called The Charter of Privileges (1701), Penn reaffirmed his policy of religious liberty and created a single-house legislature with power effectively in the hands of an elected assembly.

Penn also proved himself to be a successful promoter of colonization. The policy of religious toleration and the liberal political structure made Pennsylvania attractive to potential colonists. Penn made it even more enticing by offering land for sale or rent on easy terms. To publicize these opportunities, Penn launched a vigorous promotional campaign. In a series of pamphlets that received wide distribution in England and, in translation, on the Continent, Penn described the natural abundance of the New World and the particular advantages that his colony offered prospective

True to his Quaker principles, William Penn (1644-1718) attempted to compensate the local tribes for the land taken by the settlers of Pennsylvania. But many of Penn's disciples proved to be less upright in later negotiations. (Courtesy of American Museum of Natural History.)

settlers. By 1700, settlers from Germany and Scotland swelled the colony's population to 12,000. Surplus production of such cereals as corn, wheat, and rye assured prosperity not only to the farmers but also to the Quaker merchants of Philadelphia, who traded those commodities in the West Indies.

Georgia

Though founded fifty years after Pennsylvania, the colony of Georgia shared similar experiences with the proprietary colonies of the Restoration period. In 1732, George II granted the region between the Savannah and the Altamaha rivers to a group of weathly Englishmen to establish a colony. Bound by the charter to receive no land and obtain no profits, the proprietors, led by James Oglethorpe, were to oversee the development of the colony for twenty-one years, at which time Georgia would revert to the crown. Meanwhile, control of colonial affairs remained in the hands of the trustees, who resided in England.

In proposing the establishment of Georgia, the proprietors had various motives. Ostensibly, they wanted to create a haven for the able-bodied debtors who crowded English jails. This humanitarian impulse coincided with popular economic theory, which suggested that national wealth depended on the full employment of healthy workers. Oglethorpe also declared that Georgia would provide a barrier between the Carolinas and the Spanish settlements in Florida. By transporting troops to Georgia, the English would possess military resources adequate to prevent Spanish expansion northward.

Georgia grew slowly because of its management by the trustees. The colony's planners restricted land holdings to 500 acres (which could be inherited only by male heirs), prohibited slavery, and forbade the consumption of rum and brandy. Since private monies (supplemented by royal funds) were expected to finance the colony, the trustees made no provision for a local legislature to levy taxes. Many of these restrictions antagonized the settlers, and continued agitation in the colony compelled the trustees to compromise their program. By 1752, when Georgia became a royal colony, its population was less than 10,000, and many of the settlers were not of an English background.

English Mercantilism

The planting of proprietary colonies during the Restoration period revealed that the English were again interested in developing the North American continent. Yet, despite the fact that private individuals directed and controlled the newer colonies, the crown attempted to supervise colonial activities. The age of haphazard settlement had ended. The later Stuarts and their Hanoverian successors endeavored to centralize the British Empire in order to strengthen the mother country.

Royal interest in supervising colonial affairs reflected the widespread belief in a series of economic ideas loosely called *mercantilism*. According to mercantilist ideas, a nation's wealth depended on the amount of gold and silver it hoarded. Believing that the amount of wealth in the world remained relatively constant, proponents of mercantilism urged each nation to acquire as much precious metal as possible in order to weaken its international competitors. By the mid-seventeenth century, mercantilists agreed that the wisest and safest source of such revenues was the creation of a self-sufficient economy capable of exporting more commodities than it imported. To achieve this goal, advocates of mercantilism stressed the value of colonial possessions. Colonies could serve as sources of raw materials that might otherwise have to be purchased from some rival nation. Colonies also could serve as markets for the consumption of products manufactured in the mother country. In both cases, colonies existed solely for the benefit of the mother country.

An attempt to enforce the principles of mercantilism led to the passage of a series of Navigation Acts in the seventeenth century. The central assumption behind such laws was that the interests of the whole country were more important than the interests of any particular group. Equally important, no one doubted that government had the right to regulate economic matters. The significance of the laws of trade passed after 1650 lies not only in the content of the laws but also in the attempt to create an organized *system* of trade regulations.

The expansion of Dutch commerce during the seventeenth century motivated the Puritan Parliament to pass the first of the Navigation Acts in 1651. The provisions of the law declared that (1) products of Asia, Africa, and America imported into England, Ireland, or the colonies had to be transported in English ships; (2) foreign products had to be brought to England directly from the place of production; and (3) European goods shipped to England had to be carried in English vessels or in vessels belonging to the country that produced the goods. Each of these provisions attempted to remove foreign merchants from England's trade by supporting English shippers. (The definition of English shippers included English colonies.)

Since all parliamentary legislation passed after the execution of Charles I (1649) became void at the Restoration of Charles II, the act of 1651 was reenacted by Parliament in 1660. At that time, however, the government strengthened the law by eliminating certain loopholes. The act of 1660 required that all exports from, and imports into, an English colony had to be carried by an English vessel, of which three-quarters of the crew had to be English, thereby preventing the colonists from importing directly from Europe. Again, the law did not distinguish English from English colonies. Equally important, the law "enumerated" certain valuable commodities — tobacco, sugar, cotton, indigo, dye woods, and ginger — that could be sold only in England. Subsequent legislation extended the "enumerated" list to include rice, furs, iron, lumber, and naval stores.

Because mercantilism held that all the people should benefit from economic legislation, the law of 1660 attempted to compensate the American colonies by prohibiting the cultivation of tobacco in England and by banning its importation from all other countries. Still, this monopoly of the English tobacco market failed to compensate the Chesapeake colonies for the loss of sales in Europe. And the rebates (or drawbacks) on the tobacco reexported from England to the Continent did not cover the costs of transshipping and storage. The enumeration of tobacco, as well as its overproduction, caused a depressed tobacco market in the late 1600s.

To enforce the law of 1660, the Navigation Act of 1663 provided that all European commodities bound for the colonies had to pass through English ports, and the Navigation Act of 1673 attempted to prevent violations by requiring merchants to post a bond (or plantation duty) as a guarantee that the commodities would not be transshipped to an illegal destination. In 1696, Parliament passed another law to assure enforcement of the Navigation Acts. It provided for the establishment of vice-admiralty courts (which lacked juries) in the colonies to punish smugglers, required colonial governors to take an oath to uphold the mercantile laws, and authorized the courts to issue writs of assistance to permit officials to search warehouses for contraband.

The Molasses Act (1733) placed prohibitive duties on all sugar, molasses, and rum imported into North America from foreign plantations. Passed through the parliamentary influence of West Indies sugar planters, the act would have severely injured the economy of New England because of the large volume of molasses it needed to manufacture rum (an export commodity). This act, however, was never strictly enforced.

In addition to these acts of trade and navigation, the commitment to mercantilist theory led England to regulate colonial manufacturing. The Woolens Act (1699), which was directed more against Ireland than the American colonies, prohibited the export of woolen cloth beyond a colony's borders. Its impact upon America was indirect in that it aborted colonial woolen manufacturing *before* such activity developed. The Hat Act (1732), on the other hand, directly attacked the hat industry in New York and New England for the benefit of English manufacturers. The Iron Act (1750) encouraged colonial manufacturers of pig and bar iron, while it protected English producers of other types of iron.

The economic effects of the British mercantile system varied from colony to colony and from industry to industry. Although on paper it appears as though the Navigation Acts forced Americans to trade with England, it is significant that much of this trade would have occurred anyway. In an age in which successful mercantile activity necessitated the existence of loyal agents abroad, the colonists, as English people and offspring of English people, probably would have slipped into England's trading network regardless of parliamentary legislation. In addition, England's relatively advanced stage of industrialization meant that the country's manufactured products were, in many cases, better made and cheaper than commodities from the Continent.

There is no doubt that the Navigation Acts stimulated the growth of New England's shipbuilding industry; by 1776, one-third of British commerce was shipped in American bottoms. England also subsidized other colonial commodities — particularly naval stores and indigo — by offering generous bounties for their production. Colonial products on the enumerated list enjoyed a monopoly on the English market. Finally, American commerce benefited from the protection of the Royal Navy.

These advantages did not always compensate colonials for the economic costs of other aspects of the navigation system. The tobacco and rice industries, for example, suffered directly from the law requiring the shipment of those commodities to England. Since England could not absorb the entire market, these goods had to be reexported to the Continent. Rebates paid to colonials for this second shipment did not cover the extra costs involved. The impact of the Navigation Acts upon the American economy seems to have been greatest at the end of the seventeenth century, when enforcement was strictest and when the young colonial economy was most vulnerable. This economic burden, when added to certain internal pressures, contributed to the proliferation of social and political conflict in America during the last quarter of the seventeenth century.

Colonial Administration

Although the English agreed that colonies should serve the interests of the mother country, in the early years of colonization, the crown administered the empire in a haphazard way. After the Restoration, however, Charles II created two groups to advise him on colonial matters. These bodies were superseded by a new agency of administration, the Lords of Trade (1675). In 1696, the desire to enforce the Navigation Acts resulted in the replacement of the Lords of Trade by a subcommittee of the Privy Council known as the Board of Trade and Plantations. The board performed legislative, judicial, and executive functions for the crown until the American War for Independence.

During the Restoration period, the Lords of Trade attempted to centralize and coordinate colonial policy. Believing in the importance of royal authority, this group opposed — unsuccessfully — the bestowal of proprietary grants to the king's friends. Their influence could be seen in the clauses of the Pennsylvania charter that required the proprietor to enforce the laws of trade. They also advocated, without success, the revocation of all existing proprietary grants. The failure of the Lords of Trade to change the structure of the empire revealed the chaotic nature of the English bureaucracy. But it did not mean that their policies were without effect in America. To the contrary, the reinvigoration of royal government influenced political and social developments in the colonies in profound ways. In the eighteenth century, the British government revoked several proprietary charters and replaced them with royal governments.

The Restoration in Virginia

With the exception of a single parliamentary commission that deposed Virginia's Royalist governor William Berkeley, the English civil wars left the colony's political institutions virtually untouched. However, during this period of crisis in England, many sons of well-to-do families immigrated to Virginia. With the Restoration of Charles II, Berkeley was reappointed governor of the colony and authorized, together with a royally appointed council, to oversee the economic activities of Virginia. Among other things, the governor and the council supervised tax collection, conferred grants of land, and collected the customs duties. Each of these powers was enormously important in a society based on commercial agriculture, particularly because the staple crop, tobacco, quickly depleted the fertility of the soil.

To assist him in his various responsibilities, Berkeley appointed men who had arrived in the colony in the two decades before 1660. Because of the potential power of their assignments and because of their obvious friendship with the governor, these colonists constituted the upper echelons of Virginia's elite. Their power centered around the colonial council.

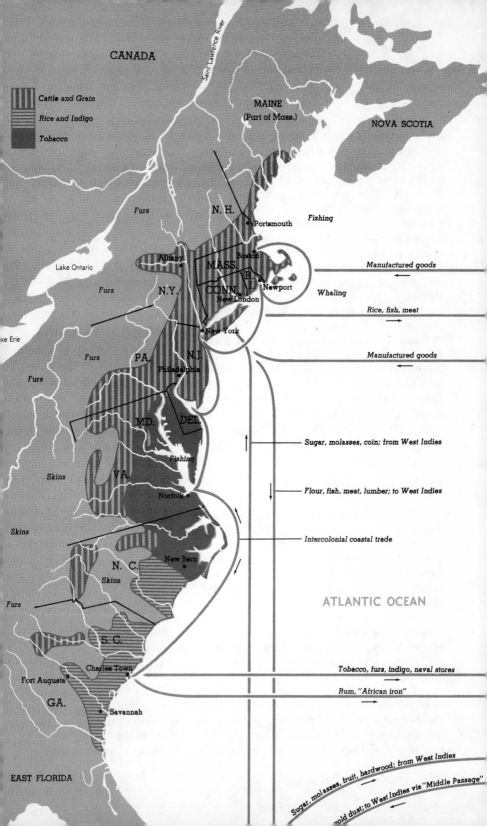

ICELAND

NORTH ATLANTIC OCEAN

NORWAY

SWEDEN

SCOTLAND

IRELAND

ENGLAND

Bristol London

GERMANY

EUROPE

FRANCE

Manufactured goods

Tobacco, furs, indigo, naval stores

Manufactured goods

Sugar, molasses, fruit, hardwood; from West Indies

Wine, fruit

SPAIN

ITALY

Lisbon

Rice, fish, meat

Cadiz

MADEIRA

CANARY ISLANDS

AFRICA

CAPE VERDE ISLANDS

Rum, "African iron"

GUINEA COAST

Slaves, gold dust; to West Indies via "Middle Passage"

SOUTH ATLANTIC OCEAN

COLONIAL ECONOMY AND TRADE ROUTES

*American colonies are shown here
on a much larger scale than Europe.*

The colonists of wealth who did *not* win Berkeley's favor sought to consolidate their power in the local levels of government in the numerous counties that had been created after 1634. As county officials, these local leaders supervised elections and relied upon their control of the House of Burgesses to offset the power of the governor and the council. The decision made about 1663 to separate the legislature into two distinct houses reflects the growing rift between members of the two political groups.

By 1670, the power structure of Virginia rested in the hands of these "new" men who had acquired their wealth most rapidly. They did *not* possess the traditional status that Virginians, like other seventeenth-century English people, expected of their leaders. Moreover, various men of equal wealth had been denied power by this entrenched elite. The out-group resented the selfish use of power by Berkeley's faction, and they also objected to a government ruled by men of "new" wealth. These frustrations provided the background for Bacon's Rebellion (1676).

The immediate cause of the uprising can be traced to land hunger and an abiding hostility toward the Doeg and Susquehannock tribes that inhabited the western frontier of the colony. In the latter part of the seventeenth century, the tobacco economy became depressed, partly because of the restrictions of the Navigation Acts and partly because of overproduction. New settlers in the colony, as well as indentured servants whose terms of service had expired, felt frustrated by this decline of opportunity. To improve their situation, they requested that Governor Berkeley open up the lands that had been reserved for the Indians. When Berkeley refused, the dissatisfied colonists took the law into their own hands.

Led by Nathaniel Bacon, a member of the council who had lived in Virginia for less than two years, an unauthorized army challenged Berkeley's authority in Jamestown, attacked the local Indian tribes, and convened an assembly that enacted various political "reforms." Bacon's sudden death ended the rebellion. Berkeley proved merciless in destroying his opponents. After he had executed twenty-three colonists for treason, Berkeley was recalled to England by the king.

Bacon's Rebellion revealed the deep conflicts in Virginia's social structure. The rebel's support had come from settlers who were new to the colony or who had recently completed their terms of indentured service. Bacon also had attracted many servants who shared the interests of these two groups. All wanted an opportunity to acquire western land, and all resented the selfish rule of Virginia's self-made leaders that made it impossible to remove the Indians from the colony's frontier. Other supporters of Bacon had come from members of the local elite who had been denied access to the governor and so felt isolated from colonial power. In protesting against Berkeley's rule, the rebels complained not only about the governor's favoritism toward his friends but also about the relatively low social status of the men who claimed leadership in the colony. In other words, Bacon's Rebellion was as much a protest against the political system as it was against Berkeley's Indian policy.

While Bacon's Rebellion represented a widespread dissatisfaction with the ruling groups, it is significant that the protestors were defeated. Instead of surrendering to the rebels, Virginia's leaders not only maintained their power, they increased it during the subsequent decades. As wealth and power were consolidated in the same families, the colony's leadership became more stable and more respectable. Eventually, the "new" leaders that Bacon had attacked became the established leaders of the colony. By the early eighteenth century, most Virginians acknowledged the authority of their local leaders.

The Institutionalization of Slavery

The shifts at the top of the social order were paralleled by changes occurring at the lower levels of society. In the early years of settlement, Virginia (and, after 1634, Maryland) relied upon the labor of indentured servants to harvest tobacco. Such servitude was limited by contractual arrangements, and, upon fulfillment of their contracts, the indentured servants attempted to acquire their own lands. It was this desire for independent farms that encouraged the dispersal of settlement in the Chesapeake colonies. Pressed for a stable labor force, Virginians and Marylanders turned increasingly to black slaves.

Economic considerations alone do not explain the expansion of black slavery in the southern colonies. Slavery, of course, was economically profitable — at least in the short run. But societies do not necessarily enslave whole populations for mere profits. The institution of black slavery rested firmly on widespread racial prejudice. From the "discovery" of black Africans in the fifteenth and sixteenth centuries, the English had treated blacks as an inferior race that lacked Christianity and civilization. The English — like other Europeans — justified slavery as a way of uplifting the blacks by converting them to Christianity. At the same time, however, the enslavement of blacks encouraged their further debasement. The notion that all slaves were black would be inverted to mean that all blacks were slaves. By the late seventeenth century, conversion to Christianity no longer liberated a slave. In English North America, slavery came to mean permanent hereditary servitude for blacks.

Although slavery existed in Africa before the arrival of Europeans, African slavery had not necessarily functioned as it did later in English America. Among African peoples, slavery was often a temporary status through which one society incorporated new members, such as prisoners taken in war. Children born of such slaves usually enjoyed full membership in the group. For Europeans, however, the enslavement of Africans became a convenient way of creating a permanent labor force. The Atlantic slave trade, however, did depend upon the participation of African slave traders. The use of African slaves in America expanded rapidly with the rise of large sugar plantations in the Caribbean at the end of the sixteenth century. It was from this area that North Americans imported most of their slaves.

The process of enslavement varied considerably from colony to colony, but, in each case, the institutional patterns of slavery were intimately related to other social developments. The first blacks arrived in Virginia without particular notice in 1619. It is impossible from surviving evidence to determine whether they were free or slaves or even how they were regarded by white society. But judging from the cruel treatment meted out to white indentured servants, it is certain that blacks also were exploited by tobacco planters. After about 1640, it appears that the legal authorities viewed some blacks — though not all — as slaves. Twenty years later, the legislatures of Virginia and Maryland enacted statutes dealing explicitly with slavery. After 1690, the expansion of tobacco production led to a mass importation of black slaves. Alarmed perhaps by the growing number of blacks and fearful of a slave revolt, Virginians codified the laws regulating slavery in 1705. By that time, blackness and slavery, for all practical purposes, meant one and the same thing.

The pattern of racial legislation in seventeenth-century Virginia reflected the changing nature of the colony's social structure. At mid-century, the status of blacks, like the status of elites, remained fluid and uncertain; by 1700, the status of blacks, like the status of elites, had become fixed and defined. Fearful of a loss of status and threatened by the possibility of black revolt, the white planters attempted, perhaps unconsciously, to create a semblance of certainty and order at the bottom layers of society. If blackness meant slavery and slavery meant blackness, then no matter how far a white person might fall in status, he or she would always have someone beneath him or her. The clarification of the blacks' status may have facilitated the adjustment to a local ruling class.

Although New Englanders shared the racial prejudices of their countrymen on the Chesapeake, slavery never became firmly entrenched in the Puritan colonies. Settlement in compact towns assured the availability of helping hands, and the absence of a staple crop like tobacco removed the need for mass labor. Relying upon Biblical precedents, the Puritans justified slavery either as a punishment for a crime or as a result of captivity in war. The Pequot War (1637) brought New Englanders Indian slaves, who were considered too dangerous for the safety of the colonies. By this time, Puritan merchants had already developed trade networks with the West Indies, and it was decided to replace the Indian slaves with blacks.

Although slavery came to New England in 1638, the blacks of New England received mild treatment compared to the slaves in the southern colonies. Unlike the blacks on the Chesapeake, New England slaves retained basic legal rights, could testify in courts against whites, and received equal punishment from the courts. (The Puritans afforded the same civil rights to the Indians.) Blacks in New England possessed certain property rights and received about the same treatment as white servants. Not until the 1680s did Puritan statutes deal specifically with blacks as a class. Then a series of laws attempted to regulate the social activities of blacks, who were forbidden to purchase alcoholic beverages and were restricted by a curfew. Limits were placed on the freeing of black slaves (1703), and interracial marriage and sexual intercourse were prohibited (1705). As was the case in Virginia and Maryland, this racial legislation betrayed an underlying anxiety among members of white society, a fear of the deterioration of all social relations. As in the southern colonies, the source of this malaise could be traced, in part, to Restoration politics.

The Restoration in New England

The Restoration of Charles II meant more to colonial New Englanders than a shift in political fortunes; it signified the failure of their mission to bring religious truth to the mother country. Even when English Puritans had rejected the New England model because its policy of religious intolerance was too strict for a multi-religious country, Puritans in America maintained their belief that one day England would accept their religious order. The accession of Charles II ended whatever hopes remained.

More critical for the Puritans was the apparent internal erosion of the wilderness community. Within fifteen years of colonization, Puritan ministers lamented a decline in religious zeal, particularly among the younger generation. If Puritanism flourished in an atmosphere of social dislocation (as in Elizabethan England), then the relative stability of New England may have retarded religious conversions. Since the high standards for church admission required new members to demonstrate their conversion experience, church membership began to decline. To broaden the base of *potential* saints without lowering the standards of admission, the ministers agreed to a Half-Way Covenant (1662), which permitted the children of baptized parents (who had not undergone a conversion experience) to be baptized. The Half-Way Covenant did not represent a decline in religiosity in New England. First, it reaffirmed the high standards for participating in the Lord's Supper set by the founding fathers. Second, the compromise was favored by the ministers (with a few exceptions) but opposed by the congregations. Finally, most people did not take advantage of the system and preferred to remain outside the church rather than risk the state of their souls by participating in half-way membership. Thus, the Half-Way Covenant did not solve the immediate problems of the New England churches, and Puritan sermons continued to deplore the low state of religion. Convinced that sin lurked within the wilderness communities, the ministers warned that God would soon punish New England with His wrath.

To many New Englanders, the failure of the Puritan revolution in England seemed to confirm these warnings. In 1662, Connecticut obtained a royal charter that called for the absorption of New Haven. Frustrated by the loss of their independence, many New Haven colonists migrated to

New Jersey [see above, p. 44]. In 1664, the king appointed a delegation to investigate the state of New England, to settle boundary disputes among the colonies, and to advise the crown on appropriate policy. Despite the efforts of moderates to negotiate with the royal commissioners, Massachusetts authorities refused to cooperate and adopted a policy of delay. In the short run, these stalling tactics proved successful, but, in 1676, the Lords of Trade commissioned Edward Randolph to investigate charges that Massachusetts was not enforcing the Acts of Navigation. Confirmation of these accusations led to the revocation of the colony's charter (1684). Two years later, Massachusetts was incorporated into a larger administrative unit known as the Dominion of New England.

Composed of the New England colonies, New York, and New Jersey, the Dominion represented an attempt by the Lords of Trade to centralize colonial administration. Government was placed in the hands of a royal governor, Sir Edmund Andros, and a royally appointed council. No provisions were made for a representative assembly. Andros also threatened the stability of New England by questioning the validity of land grants, by instituting taxes without consent, by enforcing the Navigation Acts, and by introducing the worship services of the Church of England in Boston. Upon learning of the Glorious Revolution in England (1689), which placed William and Mary on the throne, New Englanders revolted against the Dominion and attempted to restore the old charter government. In 1691, however, the new monarchs granted a revised charter that made Massachusetts a royal colony in which the governor was chosen by the king.

Besides these imperial problems, a bloody war with the Wampanoag tribe (King Phillip's War, 1675-1676) also had threatened the survival of the colonies. This prolonged period of political crisis seriously weakened the sense of social stability in New England. In the 1680s, rising merchants had supported the Andros regime until they discovered that the royal governor intended to enforce the laws of trade and ignored their aspirations for political power. People with landed wealth feared the loss of property when Andros investigated their land titles. The unwillingness of Andros to grant political power to his colonial allies explains why many of them later supported his overthrow.

Puritan believers interpreted these political problems as a divine punishment for abandoning the religious mission of the first generation. Worship within the Church of England in Massachusetts (and the forced acceptance of religious toleration) seemed the most obvious repudiation of Winthrop's "city upon a hill." These feelings of betrayal, together with the problems caused by the Dominion government, provided the background for the witch trials at Salem, Massachusetts (1692-1694). Confused by their social problems, people were prepared to believe that the devil was assaulting the Lord's saints. More subtly, this belief in the devil's presence reaffirmed the importance of New England in the divine scheme of things. While New England might be subject to the changes of English politics, it obviously remained sufficiently important for the devil to attempt its destruction. The witch trials, therefore, represent not the decline of Puritanism in New England but rather a *reassertion* of the religious position of the founding fathers.

Leisler's Rebellion

The rebellion against the Dominion of New England in Boston ignited a similar revolt in New York. As in Massachusetts, the colony of New York had undergone numerous political crises in the years after 1664. These frequent changes of government, particularly the formation of the Dominion (which eliminated the colony's assembly), undermined the colonists' sense of security. Fears of a Catholic conspiracy to overthrow the colony added to the tensions. When news of the arrest of Andros reached New York, the dissatisfied colonists rallied behind Jacob Leisler, a wealthy merchant, and joined the rebellion. Although lacking royal approval, Leisler ruled the colony until 1691, when he was arrested by royal officers and hanged as a traitor. Leisler's Rebellion did not radically alter the social structure of New York. Like Bacon's Rebellion in Virginia, however, it reflected the severe social and political strains that confronted people throughout the colonies. A new charter (1691) eased some of the political difficulties by establishing a representative assembly. But Leisler's Rebellion remained a politically divisive issue for decades.

The political rebellions of the late seventeenth century were symptoms, rather than causes, of rapid social change. In the years after 1689, the colonists adjusted to these developments and endeavored to create a stable social order. The reinvigoration of royal authority, however, had lasting effects on American society.

Supplementary Reading

A good overview of this period is C. Ver Steeg, *The Formative Years* (1964). A more detailed treatment is W. Craven, *The Colonies in Transition, 1660-1713* (1968). These books should be supplemented by G. Nash, *Red, White, and Black: The Peoples of Early America* (1974), which examines colonial history in the context of the African and Indian cultures. Also helpful in drawing together diverse material is D. Lovejoy, *The Glorious Revolution in America* (1972).

The history of the Carolinas is presented in V. Crane, *The Southern Frontier, 1670-1732* (1956), and E. Sirmans, *Colonial South Carolina* (1966). The influence of the West Indies on Carolina may be seen in R. Dunn, *Sugar and Slaves* (1972). The best survey of colonial New York is P. Bonomi, *A Factious People: Politics and Society in Colonial New York* (1971). J. Reich's *Leisler's Rebellion* (1953) is the standard work on that subject. It should be supplemented by L. Leder, *Robert Livingston, 1654-1728, and the Politics of Colonial New York* (1961), and D. R. Fox, *Caleb Heathcote: Gentleman Colonist* (1926). For a discussion of early New Jersey, see two works by J. Pomfret, *The Province of West New Jersey, 1609-1702* (1956) and *The Province of East New Jersey, 1601-1702* (1962). For discussions of the founding of Pennsylvania, see E. Bronner, *William Penn's "Holy Experiment"* (1962), and M. M. Dunn, *William Penn, Politics and Conscience* (1967).

British mercantile policies are discussed by C. Andrews, *The Colonial Period of American History,* Volume IV (1938); L. Harper, *The English Navigation Laws* (1939); and , most recently, M. Kammen, *Empire and Interest: The American Colonies and the Politics of Mercantilism* (1970).

The best social history of seventeenth-century Virginia is E. Morgan's *American Slavery, American Freedom* (1975). For an analysis of Bacon's Rebellion, see B. Bailyn, "Politics and Social Structure in Virginia," in J. Smith, ed., *17th-Century America* (1959), and W. Washburn, *The Governor and the Rebel* (1957). Restoration Virginia is described from the perspective of the colony's leaders in L. Wright, *The First Gentlemen of Virginia* (1940). W. Jordan, *White Over Black* (1968), provides sophisticated analysis of colonial slavery. Also provocative is D. Bertelson, *The Lazy South* (1967).

The impact of the Restoration in New England is discussed in M. Hall, *Edward Randolph and the American Colonies* (1960), and V. Barnes, *The Dominion of New England* (1923). The finest analysis of Puritanism in this period is P. Miller, *The New England Mind: From Colony to Province* (1953). R. Pope, *The Half-Way Covenant* (1969), examines the problem of church membership; T. Breen, *The Character of the Good Ruler* (1970), explores changes in Puritan political ideas; P. Gay, *A Loss of Mastery* (1966), sketches Puritan historical writings; R. Dunn, *Puritans and Yankees* (1962), studies the changes from the perspective of the Winthrop family; and D. Leach, *Flintlock and Tomahawk* (1958), describes King Phillip's War. For a discussion of the Salem witch trials, see C. Hansen, *Witchcraft at Salem* (1969). P. Boyer and S. Nissenbaum, in *Salem Possessed: The Social Origins of Witchcraft* (1974), view the trials in terms of the social and economic divisions within the town. For a comparative perspective, see A. Macfarlane, *Witchcraft in Tudor and Stuart England* (1970). Biographies of people of the period include W. Barrett, *Cotton Mather: The Puritan Priest* (1891); K. Murdock, *Increase Mather, the Foremost American Puritan* (1925); and O. Winslow, *Samuel Sewall of Boston* (1964).

Chapter 5

Provincial Societies
1689-1776

The original colonists had attempted to transplant the ideals and values of English society to America. Believing in the importance of social cohesion, they discouraged needless dispersal, endeavored to regulate the colonial economy, and attempted to perpetuate the status distinctions of the Old World. Such environmental forces as the difficulty of clearing wilderness lands and the presence of Indian inhabitants supported these cohesive tendencies. A perennial shortage of labor further retarded colonial expansion. By the late seventeenth century, however, certain internal pressures — particularly the sheer growth of the population — weakened the traditional social structure.

At the close of the seventeenth century, 250,000 people lived in English North America; by 1776, the population approached 2,500,000. This immense growth (about 75 percent of which was caused by natural increase, the remainder by foreign immigration) brought qualitative changes to colonial society. As the colonies became more densely populated, there was an appreciable decline of opportunity in the older areas of settlement. Soil exhaustion led some farmers to seek new lands on the frontier. Other colonists sought to improve their fortunes in nonagricultural employment in the burgeoning port cities of Charleston, Philadelphia, New York, and Boston. By the end of the colonial period, the population shifts suggested a more general tightening of the social structure in all the colonies.

The Southern Colonies

In the southern colonies, where commercial agriculture had gained a dominant foothold, land was a particularly important commodity, since wasteful agricultural methods had forced Virginia tobacco planters to amass large land holdings. By the late seventeenth century, wealthy Virginia planters had acquired large estates by investing in headrights (by paying the passage costs of immigrants) and by exercising politicial influence with the colonial council (which bestowed grants of land). The importance of exporting tobacco to England led the early Virginia planters to settle along inland rivers that could be navigated by English ships. Often, these planters became merchants for their less favorably located neighbors. Thus, the production of tobacco encouraged mercantile activity even as it made the establishment of an urban port unnecessary. Overproduction plagued the tobacco planters intermittently throughout the colonial period, but until about 1750, the colonists were careful to avoid becoming overly indebted to British merchants who extended credit. After 1750, the colonists began to purchase large quantities of British goods on credit; and, by the eve of the American Revolution, many Americans, especially in the southern colonies, were deeply indebted to British merchants.

Such economic uncertainty apparently did not weaken Virginia's social structure. Prior to the institutionalization of slavery [see above, pp. 55-57], Virginians had relied upon white indentured servants to work the plantations. Upon completing their tenure as servants, these settlers seem to have acquired small quantities of land. Meanwhile, the larger planters turned to slave labor to satisfy their labor needs. By the mid-eighteenth century, black slaves amounted to over one-third of Virginia's population. Throughout the colonial period, the Virginia elite, with heavy investments in land and slaves, dominated the social and political life of the colony. As political leaders with wealth and high status, members of this group seemed to fulfill the traditional ideal that suggested that power properly belonged to the "better" people. Rapid social mobility, so common in the early days of colonization, became increasingly rare during the eighteenth century.

Society in South Carolina was even more aristocratic than in Virginia. Carolina planters acquired rapid wealth from the production of indigo (thanks to generous bounties from the British government) and from the cultivation of rice (which benefited from the previous experience of West African slaves). To avoid the malarial swamps in which they cultivated their rice, the Carolinian elite lived in Charleston and relied upon overseers to run the plantations. Based on a flourishing trade, Charleston supported a sophisticated culture in which the local aristocrats ostentatiously displayed their newly acquired wealth. The elite controlled both the economic life and the political structure of the colony. The western counties remained underrepresented in the legislature and lacked an effective judicial system. During the 1760s, protests from the smaller planters produced minor concessions. But royal authorities prohibited the expansion of the size of the colony's assembly and thus prevented significant reform.

The success of the plantation aristocracy in South Carolina came from its ability to mobilize the labor of black slaves. Many planters had immigrated from Barbados on the condition that the Carolina proprietors recognized their ownership of slaves. There they instituted a rigorous system of slavery based on their experience in the West Indies. During the 1690s, South Carolina approved a slave code (derived from the Barbados pattern) that deprived the slaves of virtually all rights. In the early 1700s, blacks constituted about half of the colony's population; by the time of the Stamp Act crisis (1765), they outnumbered whites two to one.

Although black slavery was not limited to the southern colonies [see below, pp. 66-67], it was on the tobacco and rice plantations that the slave population expanded most dramatically. In 1700, the black population of English North America numbered about 28,000; by 1780, it approached 570,000. During that period, only about 250,000 blacks were imported from abroad; as with whites, then, the population increase resulted primarily from natural reproduction. Unlike slaves on the sugar islands of the West Indies who died at an appalling rate, North American slaves lived in a healthier environment, ate more nutritious food, and enjoyed a more balanced sex ratio. All these factors increased the slaves' fertility.

The dispersal of the black population in North America also influenced an emerging Afro-American culture. Because North American slaves had frequent contact with the white population, they were under great pressure to adopt the values and behavioral patterns of their masters. Slaves who understood English, for example, enjoyed preferential treatment. The slaves' tendency toward assimilation was reinforced by the lack of knowledge about their African past. After 1720, the majority of North American blacks were native born.

In adjusting to slavery, however, North American blacks did not easily surrender their African cultures. Newly imported blacks drew upon their traditional sense of community and organized group rebellions and mass escapes. More "seasoned," or assimilated, blacks, by contrast, relied upon individual strategies (such as slowing down their work or faking illness), to alleviate the drudgery of slavery. Besides open resistance to the slave system, blacks preserved portions of their African heritage by blending their traditional values with the culture of their masters. When whites encouraged slaves to convert to Christianity, for example, blacks emphasized those aspects of the Christian religion — such as the conversion experience — that were compatible with their own religious traditions. Similarly, in adopting the English language, blacks retained African styles of speech that communicated on different levels than standard English.

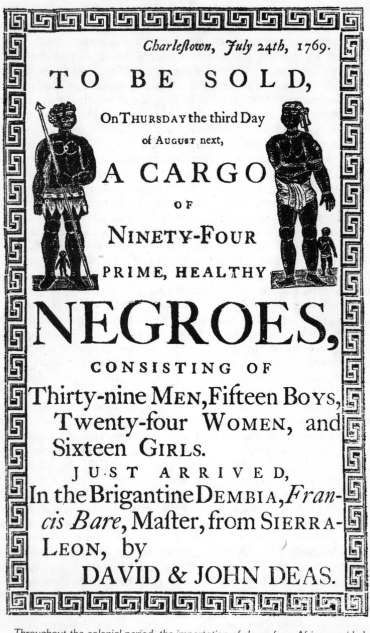

Charlestown, July 24th, 1769.

TO BE SOLD,

On Thursday the third Day
of August next,

A CARGO

OF

NINETY-FOUR

PRIME, HEALTHY

NEGROES,

CONSISTING OF

Thirty-nine MEN, Fifteen BOYS,
Twenty-four WOMEN, and
Sixteen GIRLS.

JUST ARRIVED,

In the Brigantine DEMBIA, *Francis Bare*, Master, from SIERRA-
LEON, by

DAVID & JOHN DEAS.

Throughout the colonial period, the importation of slaves from Africa provided American blacks with direct contact with their African traditions. But after 1720, more slaves were born in the colonies than were imported from Africa. (The Granger Collection.)

The presence of so many slaves in the colonies created anxiety among members of the master class. These fears proved justifiable in 1739, when an uprising of slaves at Stono, South Carolina, led to a pitched battle before the slaves were killed. While other smaller revolts occurred sporadically, nervousness among whites about the possibility of such uprisings was even more pervasive and betrayed the underlying fear created by slavery. White masters often expressed this fear of slave insurrections in sexual metaphors that suggested that the black slaves wished to rape white women; white men articulated such statements as a way of easing their consciences about their own sexual license with slave women. During the early eighteenth century, Carolinians attempted to restrict the freeing of slaves by requiring freed blacks to leave the colony.

Southern planters attempted to secure protection from Indian attacks by encouraging the settlement of the western regions. Yet, in creating a slave caste, they unwittingly discouraged the immigration of free white workers who could not compete economically with the labor of black slaves. Such colonists usually migrated to the middle colonies of Pennsylvania and New York. Many of these immigrants came as redemptioners — a form of indentured servitude in which the colonists did not bind themselves to a particular labor contract until they had arrived in America; upon arrival, the newcomers had a brief period of time in which to sell their labor to pay the cost of their transportation. This system represented a transition between the policy of indentured servitude and the self-supporting immigration characteristic of later times.

Non-English Immigration

Before 1690, most white settlers came from England and brought their English culture and institutions with them. After this time, immigrants from Germany, Scotland, and Ireland joined the colonial ranks. These non-English settlers often established ethnically homogeneous communities in which a single ethnic group predominated and avoided (or were excluded from) the problems of public affairs. Although some of these ethnic groups became anglicized in the eighteenth century, many retained their cultural vitality and made important contributions to the intellectual and religious life of the colonies.

William Penn's promotional campaign, together with his liberal offers of land and religious toleration, attracted many of the non-English settlers to Pennsylvania. German Pietists, led by Francis Daniel Pastorius, established Germantown, just north of Philadelphia, as early as 1683. In the decades after 1710, the trickle of German immigrants became a floodtide as members of numerous sects escaped religious oppression and the economic and social turmoil caused by the European wars. By 1776, about 250,000 Germans had immigrated to America, most of them settling in New York, Pennsylvania, and New Jersey.

The Scotch-Irish (or Ulster Scots) constituted another source of mass immigration to the middle colonies in the early part of the eighteenth century. Originally settled in Northern Ireland, these Presbyterian Scots suffered from religious discrimination and the economic consequences of the Woolens Act (1699), which prohibited some kinds of textile manufacturing. Like the Germans, some of these people immigrated to New York and New Jersey, but most settled in Pennsylvania. As lands in the eastern counties became crowded, many of the Scotch-Irish, like the Germans before them, moved westward and then to areas further south in the western parts of the Carolinas and Georgia. Living on small farms or in tiny villages, these frontier people enjoyed a life-style far different from the eastern elites who controlled political power in the southern colonies. Their desire for land often created conflicts with the native tribes.

Other non-English groups immigrated to America in smaller numbers. Following the revocation of the Edict of Nantes (1685), which had granted religious privileges to French Protestants, numerous Huguenots sought refuge in the English colonies. Possessing modest wealth and experience as merchants and lawyers, many Huguenots settled in urban areas, such as Charleston and New York, and rapidly attained high social status and wealth. A large group of Scottish Highlanders fled to North Carolina at mid-century after an abortive attempt to overthrow the Hanoverian dynasty. Clustering around Fayetteville, they developed a thriving trade in naval stores. Small groups of Jews from Portugal, Spain, and the West Indies also settled as merchants in the port cities of Philadelphia, New York, Charleston, and Newport.

The Middle Colonies

In the middle colonies, the newer immigrants, like the English before them, devoted themselves primarily to agriculture. The Germans were especially careful farmers and flourished on their Pennsylvania farms. Farmers in New York and Pennsylvania produced large surpluses of grain, pork, and beef, which were exported to the West Indies and other colonies. Such commercial agriculture brought prosperity not only to the people who cultivated the soil but also to the merchants of Philadelphia and New York City who exchanged the goods in other markets.

Not everyone, of course, shared equally in this prosperity. Philadelphia, whose population surged from 10,000 to 40,000 between 1720 and 1776, showed signs of social stratification by the mid-eighteenth century. By investing in overseas trade, speculating in lands swindled from the Indians, and tapping the fur trade, a group of merchants — many of them assiduous Quakers — acquired great wealth and emerged as an urban aristocracy. Like many Puritan merchants in New England, Quaker merchants often pursued material wealth at the expense of religious orthodoxy. Despite a belief in the equality of souls, for example, Quakers readily participated in the Atlantic slave trade. Meanwhile, the influx of indentured servants and redemptioners created a poor, urban working class at the lower levels of society, and beneath the white propertyless workers was a class of Indian and black slaves. Unlike Benjamin Franklin, whose rags-to-riches story has become fable, most of the lower-class people of this pre-revolutionary period found few opportunities to obtain much property or rise in status. Similar patterns of economic stratification appeared in other areas of Pennsylvania as well. This disparity of wealth led to the accumulation of political power in the hands of the Quaker elite.

The social structure of New York revealed a similar process of stratification. The English rulers of New York, like the Dutch before them, granted enormous estates to individual landowners. Instead of selling tracts of land to incoming settlers, these wealthy landlords rented farms, thus creating a class of tenant farmers who were economically (and often politically) dependent on the ruling elite. As in Philadelphia, the export of furs, naval stores, and food products created a merchant aristocracy in New York City. Intermarriages among the landed and mercantile elites also enabled the wealthier families to cement political alliances that assured them control of the colony's political institutions.

While New York's skilled artisans might have hoped to acquire modest wealth, the poor, semi-skilled and unskilled workers had a slim chance of moving anywhere. New York City, like Philadelphia, also had a sizable slave population, most of them artisans and house servants. In 1712 and again in 1740, New York authorities were horrified to discover the existence of slave conspiracies against the white masters, and the colonial government reacted with extremely cruel punishments. As in the south, the presence of blacks may have encouraged poor whites to quiet their own class antagonisms.

The Northern Colonies

The New England colonies, like those to the south, entered a period of economic expansion and increasing social stratification. The availability of labor in compact towns discouraged immigration from abroad. However, the healthfulness of the climate (as compared to England) and a slightly higher birthrate supported a steady growth of population. The increase of inhabitants strained the social order of New England considerably. In the older towns, the growing scarcity of land led to the development of a propertyless class of workers who depended on more affluent residents for employment. The stratification of the social structure was most evident in Boston. There wealthy merchants dominated the city's economy, skilled artisans prospered proportionally, poorer urban workers struggled to survive, and slaves made up 10 percent of the population.

Overcrowding in the older areas led third- and fourth-generation New Englanders to migrate to virgin tracts to build new communities. The

expansion of settlement offered opportunities for enterprising land speculators, and, in some infant towns, whole communities invested in real estate. As in the older towns, those who arrived first usually benefited from
the later inflation of land prices. Although most New England farmers
owned fairly small holdings, grazing and the production of beef and pork
provided commodities for export. These products, together with fish
caught off the Newfoundland coast and rum manufactured in the colonies,
brought great wealth to Yankee merchants who traded in the West Indies
and Europe.

Provincial Society

Despite the regional differences, a certain uniformity appeared in the
social structures of the British colonies. By the mid-eighteenth century,
local elites had emerged in all areas. Unlike the social leaders of the previous century, this elite generally commanded the respect of people of
lesser status (although, in some New England towns, the reverse might
have been true). Although the gap between the upper and lower levels of
society was less conspicuous in America than in England, most colonists
recognized the importance of rank and status. Yale and Harvard colleges
ranked students according to the standing of their families rather than on
the basis of intellectual achievement. In the port cities, aristocratic merchants ostentatiously imitated the fashions of the mother country and built
elaborate town houses to display their wealth.

Few Americans attained the prestige and property of the upper class.
But most white property owners probably aspired to a high social status
and so did not question the existence of social stratification. Most colonial
Americans belonged to middle-status groups and prospered accordingly.
In the southern colonies, many small-scale farmers and tobacco planters
worked their own lands and perhaps owned a few slaves; in New England
and the middle colonies, self-sufficient farms were quite common; artisans,
shopkeepers, and small-scale merchants populated all colonial cities.

At the lowest levels of the social structure, propertyless workers eked
out a livelihood. During the eighteenth century, rural and urban poverty
became more evident, and the rolls of those requiring charitable assistance rose proportionally. By the end of the colonial period, each port city
contained a sizable population of day-laborers, longshoremen, and sailors
who lacked not only property but also the privileges that traditionally
accompanied property, as well as a smaller proportion of unemployable
persons supported by charity. In all the colonies, however, the lowest-
status group consisted of black slaves and servants, victims of racial, as
well as economic, discrimination.

During the eighteenth century, the possibility of rapid social mobility
decreased significantly. As the colonial elites became entrenched, they
consolidated their claims to status and power. American society, of

course, did not become a caste society (as the rapid ascent of men such as George Washington and Benjamin Franklin attests), but people of lesser standing possessed fewer opportunities to obtain elite status. Mobility within the middle-status groups appeared more frequently, enabling people to rise slightly in status and thus easing the worst frustrations of social stratification. Yet, the poorer people often resented the social and political dominance of their rulers.

Such hostility occasionally led to open rebellion. In eighteenth-century Pennsylvania, times of economic depression often led to radical political activity when members of the lower class challenged the power of the mercantile elite. Such protests also revealed ethnic antagonism among Germans and Scotch-Irish against the Quaker and Anglican rulers. The unwillingness of the pacifist Quaker assembly to provide adequate protection against Indian attacks inflamed the western farmers in the colony. A partial withdrawal of Quakers from the colony's legislature (1756) temporarily solved the problem. But the western regions remained underrepresented in the assembly and, when the legislature again failed to supply military aid, a mob of Scotch-Irish, known as the Paxton Boys (1763), destroyed a peaceful village of Conestoga Indians and then marched on Philadelphia. Only the shrewd negotiations of Benjamin Franklin prevented a bloody insurrection. Yet, the representational imbalance persisted until 1776.

Hostility to certain aspects of the hierarchical social order appeared in other colonies as well. During the 1760s, tenant farmers in Dutchess and Westchester counties in New York appealed to their landlords to convert the rented property into independent holdings. When the landlords refused, the tenants withheld their rents. The landlords then issued notices of eviction. The result was a violent insurrection. The rebels, however, failed to win the support of the urban working class, and British troops were used to squash the uprising.

Similar disturbances erupted on the Carolina frontier. Backcountry farmers in North Carolina, plagued by extortionist tax collectors and corrupt judicial officials, formed a Regulator movement to pressure the government to bring about administrative reform. Resorting to arms, the Regulators finally were defeated by the colony militia at the Battle of Alamance (1771). The Regulators of South Carolina, unlike those of North Carolina, constituted more of a vigilante group and never seriously challenged the provincial status quo. Small-property owners on the make, these frontier people relied upon extralegal violence to eliminate criminals and outlaws.

Urban violence erupted spontaneously in all the major cities. These riots usually amounted to little more than drunken brawls or rivalry between lower-class ethnic groups. At times, however, such violence constituted a form of political protest against the social and economic order. Bread riots in Boston (1710, 1713, 1729), electoral violence in Philadelphia (1742), and opposition to impressment in cities such as Boston, Newport,

The Old Stone House in Georgetown, Washington, D. C. A restored eighteenth-century urban dwelling with exterior staircase typical of the South. (Courtesy Jack Boucher for the Historic American Buildings Survey.)

and Norfolk represented organized and purposive political behavior by deprived groups in colonial America. This tradition of political violence culminated in the Stamp Act riots (1765-1766) and the Boston Massacre (1770) [see below, p. 96]. The dissatisfaction expressed by these protests should not obscure the more general acceptance of the colonial social order. The possibility of social mobility — however slight — served to ease the worst tensions of class conflict.

Drinker's Court, 238 Delancy Street, Philadelphia. A pre-Revolutionary northern town-house, where smallness reinforced the intimacy of family life. (Courtesy of Cervin Robinson for the Historic American Buildings Survey.)

The Culture of Provincialism

Besides bringing wealth to urban merchants, commercial activity in the eighteenth century served to disseminate English culture and English ideas throughout the colonies. Despite the presence of numerous non-English cultures, most colonial intellectuals viewed England as the standard of cultural achievement and attempted to imitate the metropolitan accomplishments of London society. The importation of books, magazines, and newspapers published in the mother country informed the colonists of the latest English fashions and the most recent intellectual trends. This communication served to heighten a sense of provincialism in eighteenth-century America — a recognition of the superiority of English society and a realization of the inadequacy of American cultural activity. Intellectual leaders in all colonies shared this provincial perspective and, by attempting to duplicate English patterns, created a common but derivative intellectual community.

During the colonial period, higher education generally remained a privilege of wealthier families. Thus, the political and economic leaders often formed an intellectual elite as well. Their attempt to legitimize their high social status helps explain their conscious efforts to reproduce English culture in America. People of lesser status, no doubt, ignored the problem of intellectual refinement and read whatever books and pamphlets were available. A fairly high literacy rate, particularly in New England, enabled such people to follow the political debates that often appeared in print.

Education

Education in provincial America was primarily a family affair. Despite the passage of local school laws in the seventeenth century, primary education in New England remained rudimentary outside such urban centers as Boston. In the middle colonies, such schools as existed were conducted by private sectarian groups. Wealthy planters in the southern colonies exhibited little confidence in the few private schools there and employed private tutors or sent their children to England to be educated.

Institutions of higher education in colonial America usually maintained sectarian affiliations, but most colleges attempted to provide more than a ministerial education. The earliest colonial colleges — Harvard (1636), William and Mary (1693), and Yale (1701) — were designed to prevent the "barbarization" of colonial boys who were born in wilderness communities. In the wake of a religious revival known as the Great Awakening (1740-1742), various religious denominations established colleges in order to ensure that their children received an orthodox education [see below, pp. 74-75]. Evangelical Presbyterians established the College of New Jersey (Princeton) in 1747; Anglicans founded King's College (Columbia) in 1754 and the College of Philadelphia (1755); Baptists supported Brown (1764); the Dutch Reformed Church sponsored Queen's College (Rutgers) in 1766; and Eleazer Wheelock, a Congregational minister, turned a small Indian missionary school into Dartmouth (1770). Most of these schools offered a traditional liberal arts curriculum, but the Philadelphia Academy (stimulated by Franklin) and King's College (headed by Samuel Johnson) endeavored to bring the latest European writings to colonial boys. (As in Europe, these institutions were for men only.)

During the seventeenth century, a printing press at Cambridge, Massachusetts (founded in 1639), produced an enormous volume of religious literature. Until late in the colonial period, Americans preferred to read sermons (which, incidentally, indicate the state of popular culture) and doctrinal essays. The development of a provincial consciousness, however, influenced the reading habits of the American colonists, and readers turned increasingly to contemporary English writing. Hopeful American intellectuals, like the young Benjamin Franklin, imitated the style of such imaginative writers as Pope, Addison, and Steele, while more learned colonials imbibed the philosophical works of John Locke, Bishop Berkeley, and Sir Isaac Newton.

The development of more popular forms of publication brought many of these ideas to people of lesser status. After the founding of the *Boston Newsletter* (1704), the number of newspapers steadily increased; by the time of the War for Independence, thirty-seven newspapers appeared regularly. The press reported events in England and in other colonies, since the editors assumed that residents knew what occurred nearby. This policy, by emphasizing news from the English metropolis, supported provincial attitudes; it also encouraged an intercolonial culture, since people in all colonies shared provincial experiences. Newspapers in colonial America, although they were usually cautious about offending government officials, often endorsed controversial positions. Despite John Peter Zenger's acquittal in a celebrated trial (1735) involving censorship of the press, printers were still subject to libel suits for attacking public officials. Frequently, they relied on anonymous letters to the printer to convey their opinions. Thus, the colonial newspapers remained in the vanguard of protest throughout the crisis that led to the War for Independence.

In addition to newspapers, popular fare such as almanacs brought varieties of wisdom to the average colonist. In the seventeenth century, almanacs served to introduce new scientific ideas to residents of New England. Benjamin Franklin's *Poor Richard's Almanack* (first published in 1732), the most widely read almanac, offered business advice to hopeful entrepreneurs throughout the colonies. American publishers also reached colonists of lesser status by reprinting popular English political pamphlets. Besides demonstrating the provincialism of colonial political ideas, these publications provided a large number of literate Americans with an elaborate political ideology [see below, pp. 88-89]. Many colonials also produced pamphlets to publicize their views on such issues as paper money and public education.

Provincial Science

Of all the areas of intellectual achievement, colonial science appeared the most derivative and parochial. Surrounded by a variety of strange plants and animals, American naturalists, like the Quaker John Bartram, faithfully transmitted specimens and descriptions to naturalists in England and on the Continent, who interpreted the raw data. The inadequacy of scientific training and the difficulty of coordinating correspondence with other naturalists forced colonial scientists to play this secondary role. Only Benjamin Franklin made lasting theoretical contributions to eighteenth-century science (in the field of electricity). The dependence of American scientists on the European scientific community also retarded the development of intercolonial scientific societies. After several earlier failures, Franklin and Bartram founded the American Philosophical Society (1743) in Philadelphia. Publications of the society attempted to introduce new scientific agricultural techniques to colonial farmers. Jared Eliot of Connecticut also published several essays to encourage "field husbandry" in the 1740s. But most colonial Americans preferred the advice of their almanacs and continued to practice traditional agricultural methods.

Much of this scientific work, particularly the emphasis on utilitarian achievements, reflected the influence of the European Enlightenment of the eighteenth century. Captivated by the brilliance of Newton's explanation of the laws of gravitation, European intellectuals emphasized the importance of natural laws in all human activities. They suggested that such laws could be discovered by human reason rather than by divine revelation. An understanding of these laws would lead to inventions and social reforms that would improve the human condition and assure universal progress. Such theological concepts — known as deism — appealed to such young American intellectuals as Thomas Jefferson and James Madison. But most educated men stopped short of deism and attempted instead to blend enlightened rationalism with traditional Christianity.

Provincial Religion

Favorable reception of the ideas of Enlightenment was confined to a small segment of the intellectual elite in colonial America. By the early decades of the eighteenth century, however, rationalism had subtly invaded the older evangelical faiths. More seriously, the behavior of the expanding provincial communities no longer seemed compatible with the professed beliefs of social harmony and Christian love. Instead, the pursuit of wealth seemed to be undermining the older sense of community. This disparity between ideals and practices created anxiety among certain colonials, who felt guilty for departing from the social ideals of previous generations. These anxieties were intensified by the prospect of war against the French, by renewed fear of slave revolts, and by unsettled economic conditions.

The arrival of George Whitefield, an evangelical preacher, into this troubled atmosphere ignited a mass religious revival known as the Great Awakening (1740-1742). Earlier local revivals had laid the groundwork for Whitefield's evangelical successes. During the 1720s, the preaching of Theodore Frelinghuysen and William Tennant had inspired people in the middle colonies; in the following decade, Jonathan Edwards had brought religious fervor to his congregation in Northampton, Massachusetts. The evangelicals emphasized the utter dependence of people on God's grace and called for the return of a Christian spirit. Moving from one pulpit to another, Whitefield and his disciples won numerous converts for the Lord, and in some areas the revival spirit persisted until the 1750s.

The most visible effect of the awakening was a renewed sense of religiosity among some people and a marked rise in church membership. The revival also split the Presbyterian and Congregational churches into rival groups; "New Sides" and "New Lights" supported the revival, while "Old Sides" and "Old Lights" remained staunchly opposed. A side effect of this competition for souls was the founding of denominational colleges in many colonies. The proliferation of religious groups also encouraged the acceptance of religious toleration, since people were forced to live with neighbors of different beliefs. In most colonies, however, official churches retained their privileged positions and continued to enjoy the financial support of local governments. Not all religious Americans sympathized with the awakening, and many (particularly the Anglicans) became outspoken opponents of emotional theology.

Since the awakening cut across colony lines, it reinforced a growing sense of cultural unity in provincial America. The expansion of the coastal trade and the reorganization of the postal service by Franklin (1753) accelerated these intercolonial trends. Despite its obvious pluralism and diversity, provincial society appeared increasingly similar in all regions. Such common patterns, to be sure, did not then indicate the existence of a national culture (a failing that American nationalists would lament after 1776). But provincialism and a cultural dependence on England served as a common denominator. In a paradoxical way, Americans became more unified as they became more anglicized.

Supplementary Reading

A good synthesis of American social history is R. Berthoff, *An Unsettled People: Social Order and Disorder in American History* (1971), of which part I deals with the colonial period. J. Henretta, *The Evolution of American Society, 1700-1815* (1973), traces long-term demographic trends from an interdisciplinary perspective. For a cross-section of American society, see R. Hofstadter, *America at 1750: A Social Portrait* (1971). G. Nash, *Red, White, and Black* (1974), also has many provocative insights. Somewhat dated but still helpful is J. T. Adams, *Provincial Society: 1690-1763* (1927).

For an overview of American immigration, see M. Hansen, *The Atlantic Migration: 1607-1860* (1940). G. Mullin, *Flight and Rebellion: Slave Resistance in Eighteenth-Century Virginia* (1972), explores the question of African assimilation and acculturation. A comprehensive treatment of labor in this period is R. Morris, *Government and Labor in Early America* (1946); it should be supplemented with A. E. Smith, *Colonists in Bondage* (1947), and C. Bridenbaugh, *The Colonial Craftsman* (1950).

For studies of society in the southern colonies, see C. Bridenbaugh, *Myths and Realities: Societies of the Colonial South* (1952); H. Merrens, *Colonial North Carolina in the Eighteenth Century: A Study in Historical Geography* (1964); R. M. Brown, *The South Carolina Regulators* (1963); and J. Spruill, *Women's Life and Work in the Southern Colonies* (1938). An anthology of recent essays is T. Breen, *Shaping Southern Society: The Colonial Experience* (1976).

There are several excellent studies of life in the middle colonies. Among these are G. Nash, *Quakers and Politics* (1968), and F. Tolles, *Meetinghouse and Countinghouse* (1948). C. Bridenbaugh, *Rebels and Gentlemen* (1942), examines Philadelphia, while two other works by him deal with several colonial cities: *Cities in the Wilderness* (1938) and *Cities in Revolt* (1955).

Historians have closely scrutinized society in New England. C. Grant's *Democracy in the Connecticut Frontier Town of Kent* (1961) is a pioneering effort in local history. It has influenced such studies as M. Zuckerman, *Peaceable Kingdoms: New England Towns in the Eighteenth Century* (1970), and P. Greven, *Four Generations* (1970). R. Bushman, *From Puritan to Yankee* (1967), attempts to demonstrate the social basis of cultural change in eighteenth-century Connecticut. The role of elites can be seen in two family studies: J. B. Hedges, *The Browns of Providence Plantations* (1952), and J. Waters, *The Otis Family in Provincial and Revolutionary Massachusetts* (1968).

Several historians have written syntheses of colonial culture. The most encyclopedic of these is M. Savelle, *Seeds of Liberty* (1948). Also useful are L. B. Wright, *The Cultural Life of the American Colonies* (1957); M. Kraus, *The Atlantic Civilization: Eighteenth-Century Origins* (1949); and C. Cowing, *The Great Awakening and the American Revolution: Colonial Thought in the 18th Century* (1971).

For information on secondary education in America, see R. Middlekauff, *Ancients and Axioms* (1963), and J. Axtell, *The School upon a Hill; Education and Society in Colonial New England* (1974). For studies of college life at Yale and King's colleges, see R. Warch, *School of the Prophets: Yale College, 1701-1740* (1973), and D. Humphrey, *From King's College to Columbia, 1746-1800* (1976). Also valuable are two biographies of Yale presidents: L. Tucker, *Puritan Protagonist: President Thomas Clap of Yale College* (1962), and E. Morgan, *The Gentle Puritan: A Life of Ezra Stiles* (1962). American science has been studied in B. Hindle, *The Pursuit of Science in Revolutionary America: 1735-1789* (1956), and R. Stearns, *Science in the British Colonies of America* (1970). The role of Benjamin Franklin in provincial culture is discussed in C. Van Doren's biography, *Benjamin Franklin* (1941); Franklin's social ideas are analyzed in P. Connor, *Poor Richard's Politicks* (1965). Provincial art is discussed in J. Flexner, *American Painting* (1947).

A comprehensive treatment of eighteenth-century religion that emphasizes the evangelical contribution to the Revolution is A. Heimert, *Religion and the American Mind from the Great Awakening to the Revolution* (1966). P. Greven's *The Protestant Temperament* (1977) analyzes the relationship between child-rearing patterns and adult religious experience in colonial America. The Great Awakening is described in E. Gaustad, *The Great Awakening in New England* (1957), and· W. Gewehr, *The Great Awakening in Virginia* (1930). The revival in the South is analyzed in G. Pilcher, *Samuel Davies* (1971). There are numerous studies of the major proponent of the awakening, Jonathan Edwards; see P. Miller, *Jonathan Edwards* (1948), and O. Winslow, *Jonathan Edwards* (1940). For a biography of an opponent of the revival, Jonathan Mayhew, see C. Akers, *Called Unto Liberty* (1964). For an excellent study of an Anglican leader, see J. Ellis, *The New England Mind in Transition: Samuel Johnson of Connecticut* (1973). C. Bridenbaugh, *Mitre and Sceptre* (1962), examines the expansion of the Anglican church. A thorough treatment of colonial Presbyterianism is L. Trinterud, *The Forming of an American Tradition* (1949). For a discussion of the origin of the Baptist church, see W. McLoughlin, *Isaac Backus and the American Pietistic Tradition* (1967).

Chapter 6

Provinical Politics
1689-1763

Government in colonial America operated in three interdependent spheres: in the counties and townships, in the colony-wide institutions, and on the level of imperial politics. The interaction of power in these areas produced a unique pattern of political arrangements, which enabled the colonists to obtain a large measure of self-government in practice, if not in principle. Despite variations in the political institutions of the different provinces, to a large degree, the colonies reacted to royal authority in parallel ways. The similarities reflected the derivative nature of American politics. As in other areas of culture, the colonists borrowed (both consciously and unconsciously) the political ideals and institutions of the mother country. In a limited way, they introduced English legal protections (such as the right to counsel, the defense against self-incrimination, and the use of grand juries). Many of these safeguards, however, were modified by colonial circumstances. Yet, Americans continued to measure their political order against standards taken from England. This dialogue between English ideals and colonial practices culminated in the formulation of a sophisticated political ideology.

Local Government

For most colonials, local government was the most immediate and most important base of power. Borrowed from England by the first settlers, the institutions of local government flourished in America. Local officials — such as the justices of the peace — remained powerful political figures with wide-ranging administrative and judicial duties. Among other things, they assessed taxes, probated wills, maintained roads, and licensed taverns. Most people looked to their local government — the town in New England and the counties elsewhere — to provide them with basic political services and ignored the larger structure of provincial power. County officials were chosen by the colony's governor from a list of nominees submitted by the entrenched local leaders. In theory, a governor could reject this slate, but, in practice, he was bound to honor the will of the county court. Only members of the local elite were nominated to serve in local government. Thus, local power remained in the hands of a self-perpetuating oligarchy consisting of the social leaders of the community. Such a system fulfilled the ideals of the organic society and provided colonials with political stability and continuity. Although major shifts occurred in colony-wide politics, local administration generally operated with little change.

The units of local government served as the base of representation in the provincial legislatures. Colony elections generally were supervised by the county sheriffs, who were members of the local oligarchy. In all colonies, property requirements limited the number of eligible voters. Yet, because of the abundance of land and the relative prosperity of people of middle status, these qualifications were easily met by adult males. It is estimated that, in the northern colonies, 75 percent of the adult males were qualified to vote; in the southern colonies, the figure was slightly lower (about 50 percent). Women, slaves, servants, and children usually were excluded from voting, because it was believed that they were dependent upon other men's will — the male heads of the household — and because they did not have a sufficient "stake in society" since they owned no property. In most colonies, Jews and Catholics also were denied the vote because of their religious persuasions. The ease with which adult white males achieved the minimal property requirements, however, did not mean that most of them exercised their rights. And it should not be assumed that wide suffrage signified the operation of a democratic political system, for the right to vote is not equivalent to the exercise of power.

Despite the fairly widespread suffrage, the colonists (like other eighteenth-century English people) expected their "betters" to wield power and thus deferred to them at the polls. The fact that political candidates generally were members of the elite — either because of the higher property qualifications that existed for holding office or because they were nominated by the self-perpetuating local oligarchs — further discouraged political democracy. Many qualified voters ignored the electoral process because all the candidates represented similar interests. The use of oral

Boundary by Proclamation of 1763

QUEBEC

MAINE
(Part of Mass.)

NOVA SCOTIA

Saint Lawrence River

N. H.

• Falmouth

• Portsmouth

Lake Ontario

Albany •

Fort Stanwyx

MASS.

• Boston   Cape Cod

• Plymouth

PLYMOUTH

N. Y.

Hartford •

• Providence

R. I.

CONN.

Lake Erie

PA.

Long Island

• New York

• Perth Amboy

N. J.

Harrisburg •

• Burlington

Philadelphia •

Ohio R.

MD.   DEL.

ATLANTIC OCEAN

Charlottesville •

VA.

• Williamsburg

Cape Hatteras

Hillsboro •

Salem •

N. C.

• New Bern

• Wilmington

Camden •

Savannah R.

S. C.

Fort Augusta •

• Charles Town

GA.

• Savannah

COLONIAL SETTLEMENT, 1760

FLORIDA

balloting procedures further assured the reelection of upper-class candidates, for people of lower status could hardly afford to offend the local oligarchs.

Provincial Politics

In contrast to the stability of local politics, colony-wide politics often were characterized by factional strife as various members of the colonial elite competed for political power. Such rivalry revealed the structural problems of the imperial system, as well as the social and political aspirations of the provincial elite. Although issues varied from colony to colony, this competition appeared in all regions and reflected the tensions of provincial status.

The colonial governor represented the keystone of the provincial political structure. In most colonies, the governor was appointed by the crown and received explicit instructions from the Privy Council. Such men usually were selected to satisfy the political debts of English politicians. Consequently, few Americans achieved the distinction of such an appointment, and many of the governors were politically inept and unable to cope effectively with the difficulties of colonial politics. Regardless of their personal competence, royal governors faced an array of duties that would have overwhelmed the best politicians.

The governor possessed executive powers that obligated him to enforce parliamentary and colonial legislation, to bestow grants of land (with the approval of the provincial council), to serve as commander-in-chief of the colony's militia, and to supervise the operation of the Navigation Acts. His legislative functions included summoning and dissolving the colony's assembly, controlling appropriations and expenditures, and approving (or vetoing) provincial legislation. The governor, together with the council, constituted the highest court of appeal in the colony, and he could dismiss judicial officials almost at will. Many of these powers — the right to veto legislation, for example — made the governor's executive authority seem greater than the royal power in England. During the eighteenth century, however, the provincial assemblies challenged the governors' powers and assumed greater control of colonial affairs. This process did not evolve peacefully, and disputes between the governor and assembly appeared in all colonies.

The colonial council, usually composed of twelve men, constituted the second most important branch of provincial government. Councillors were appointed by the crown in most royal colonies upon the recommendation of the royal governors. In addition to advising the governor on matters of policy, the council, together with the governor, represented the highest judicial court in the colony. Assuming a function somewhat parallel to that of the British House of Lords, the council also served as the upper house of the provincial assembly. Although the council theoretically was

William Shirley (1694-1771), appointed royal governor of Massachusetts in 1741, demonstrated considerable skill in managing rival colonial politicians. Like other governors, however, Shirley could not always accommodate colonial demands and still preserve the power of the crown. (Courtesy of Frick Art Reference Library.)

independent of the governor in legislative matters, the governor often presided over council sessions in practice. Members of the council received no payment for their services but usually held other royally controlled positions to augment their incomes. This reliance upon royal favor further reduced the council's independence from the governor.

Councillors represented the in-group of the colonial elite. As the wealthiest and most powerful provincials, the councillors generally supported the royal governor. However, this alliance had not always existed. During the late seventeenth century, the colonial councils had wrested important concessions from the governors in certain executive spheres. Thus, for example, the council had the right to approve land grants and judicial appointments. Such powers enabled the provincial elite to protect some of its vested interests from the interference of royal authority.

Provincial Assemblies

By the early eighteenth century, the colonial assembly, rather than the council, emerged to challenge the royal prerogative. Although the members of the assembly, like other public officials, belonged to the provincial elite, they usually lacked the special favor of the royal governor and consequently were willing to weaken his power. Moreover, they represented specific geographic constituencies with interests that were often at variance with royal policy. The existence of relatively widespread suffrage and the frequency of provincial elections made these delegates especially responsive to the people who supported them. To be sure, provincial Americans believed that representatives should be independent of the changing whims of the people. Yet, their responsibility to their constituents made these politicians less pliable in the hands of the royal governor.

If the council represented the in-group of the colonial elite, the assembly attracted members of the political out-group whose base of power remained in the area of local government. As people with wealth and high standing in their _local_ communities, these representatives endeavored to strengthen their claims to elite status by acquiring political power at the expense of royal government. This persistent quest for status and power — the result of the absence of a hereditary aristocracy — created intense rivalry among members of the elite. The search for political security led these out-group leaders to challenge the provincial power structure, an action that ironically, undermined the stability of the political order.

In nearly every colony, members of the assemblies quarreled with each other and with the royal governors on such issues as taxes, land distribution, representation in the legislature, emission of money, payment of salaries, control of appointments, Indian trade, and colonial defense. Two things are significant about this pervasive strife. First, factional rivalry appeared in each colony as members of the provincial elite attempted to manipulate the issues to acquire additional power. These factions —

unlike the political parties of later eras — represented a series of shifting alliances in which the personal and familial affiliations of the politicians were more important than any institutional or party loyalties. Although representatives could not afford to alienate their constituencies on especially controversial issues, the general apathy of the voters usually enabled the politicians to take independent positions.

Second, the prevalence of factional rivalry undermined the attempts of royal governors to create stable political alliances. The quest for power among competing factions led to the so-called rise of the assembly whereby the lower houses of the provincial legislatures acquired political powers at the expense of the royal prerogative. By paralleling the rise of Parliament in the seventeenth and eighteenth centuries, the provincial assemblies won many basic concessions from the royal governors. For example, by controlling the expenditure of public monies, the legislatures not only supervised the provincial budget but also reduced the governor's patronage by deciding where and how funds should be spent. In similar fashion, the assemblies weakened the governors' power of appointment by regulating the disbursement of salaries. In stripping the governor of his patronage privileges, the assembly seriously undermined the power of the executive to reward his political allies or punish his enemies. The result was that the governors in America, unlike the king or the Privy Council in England, could not wield political power effectively.

Imperial Administration

The aggressiveness of the colonial assemblies should be viewed not simply in the context of the executive power in America but also within the perspective of imperial government. Throughout the colonial period, Americans also confronted the power of the political bureaucracy of the mother country. In England, the Board of Trade and Plantations (created in 1696) supervised colonial affairs, issued instructions to the royal governors, proposed legislation to Parliament, and reviewed laws passed by the provincial assemblies. Government at a distance encouraged inefficiency and administrative inflexibility. To make matters worse, other sections of the bureaucracy exercised authority in a variety of colonial affairs. The secretary of state for the Southern Department issued instructions to the colonial governors; a bureau of the Treasury Board collected customs duties, the admiralty courts retained jurisdiction in matters relating to the laws of trade, and the Privy Council approved legislation and made appointments in the name of the king. Finally, Parliament, increasingly conscious of its power, insisted on the right to legislate on certain imperial matters, such as the Navigation Acts.

The complexity of this bureaucracy and the overlapping of jurisdictions compelled the colonies to appoint agents in England to protect each colony's interests. Boundary disputes between colonies became a perennial problem for English administrators. In America, the selection of the agent remained a source of contention until the mid-eighteenth century when the assemblies won the power of appointment. The colonial agents proved most effective in obtaining the repeal of the Stamp Act (1766), but, for the most part, English politicians and bureaucrats viewed American interests as subservient to the wider concerns of Great Britain.

Nor was the imperial bureaucracy content to let matters slide. English politicians frequently intervened in colonial affairs, thereby undermining the colonists' search for political stability. The problem of imperial interference reflected not the maliciousness of the English administrators but the confusions created by an external source of power. Thus, while the Privy Council did not often veto colonial legislation, all bills did require the approval of the royal government in England *before* they became law; delays and vetoes were not unknown. These denials added to the uncertainty of political power in the colonies. In addition, English politicians viewed the colonial governments as a gold mine of patronage positions for rewarding politicial allies. Royal governors and lesser officials remained in office only for as long as their patrons in England possessed power. The vagaries of English politics created an unstable political atmosphere in America, because governors frequently were recalled with short notice. For provincial politicians searching for political and social security, such shifts of power brought renewed insecurity.

English interference in colonial society applied not only to political matters but to economic affairs as well. Aside from the Navigation Acts and the restrictions on colonial manufacturing [see above, pp. 48-50], royal authorities nullified colonial policies that appeared to threaten the king's prerogative. Thus, when Virginia attempted to prevent the overproduction of tobacco by prohibiting the slave trade, the Privy Council vetoed the statute, arguing that only Parliament could legislate on matters of trade. Similar decisions prevented the colonies from issuing paper currencies to alleviate the shortage of a circulating medium. In 1741, an act of Parliament prohibited the formation of land banks (which used land to back currency emissions); ten years later, the Currency Act restrained the colonies of New England from printing paper money (this law was extended to all colonies in 1764). Such decisions often seemed capricious to colonials and aggravated their sense of powerlessness. From the colonial perspective, only the acquisition of power would have produced a stable political order.

The Wars for Empire

Although provincial Americans resented the arbitrary interference of English politicians in colonial matters, they, nevertheless, conceded that the mother country should implement foreign policy and negotiate international relations. Between 1689 and 1763, a series of wars between England

and France involved the colonists in military operations. The presence of hostile Indians and the militant French probably increased the sense of insecurity in English America. Yet, as long as these enemies remained nearby, provincial Americans depended on English military strength for survival.

The rivalry between England and France originated in the power politics of European diplomacy and the desire of each nation to establish international supremacy. The battles were waged not only in Europe but also in areas where French and English colonists collided. In North America, the contest focused in the West Indies and on the frontiers of New York, New England, and New France. As the French settlements in Canada approached the expanding northern provinces of America, both nations competed for the Indian trade, and friction developed as a result of boundary disputes.

To attain a military advantage, England and France attempted to forge alliances with the neighboring Indian tribes. But, while the Indians recognized the advantages of such treaties, they were unwilling to become mere pawns of European diplomacy. Instead, the Indians exploited their strategic importance to further their own economic and political interests. By playing off the English and the French, for example, the Iroquois around New York were able to preserve their political sovereignty and win valuable trading concessions. In the southeast, the Creeks and Cherokees managed to balance the power of the English, French, and Spanish while preserving their trade connections. Such strategies, while beneficial in the short run, increased the Indians' dependence on European trade. More serious, by pitting tribe against tribe, these military alliances with Europeans prevented a united Indian policy. Finally, the Indians could effectively manipulate the balance of power only while no one nation predominated. Once the English had eliminated the French and Spanish power in America, the Indians lost their strategic advantage.

The first of these contests, the War of the League of Augsburg (known in America as King William's War, 1689-1697), commenced when William of Orange ascended to the English throne following the Glorious Revolution (1688-1689). As a prince in the Netherlands, William had opposed the expansion of French power under Louis XIV. After 1689, he brought English pressure to bear on his old enemy. The decisive battles of the war were fought in Europe; in America, the results proved inconclusive. The French, under Count Frontenac, initiated several raids in upper New York and New England, the most important being a massacre at Schenectady (1690). The New England colonists, determined to show their loyalty to the new monarchs, captured Port Royal in Acadia (Nova Scotia) but failed to conquer Quebec. The Peace of Ryswick (1697) resulted in the restoration of all occupied territory.

A second confrontation between England and France erupted when Louis XIV attempted to place his grandson on the Spanish throne. England, fearing a threat to the European balance of power, intervened, along with Austria and Holland, to block Louis's ambitions. The resulting War of the Spanish Succession (known in America as Queen Anne's War, 1701-1713) embroiled the English in the southern and New England colonies. The colonists in South Carolina thwarted two Spanish invasions from Florida but were unsuccessful in an attack on St. Augustine. In New England, the French instigated Indian attacks along the Massachusetts frontier, including the Deerfield Massacre (1704) and resulting in bloody Puritan reprisals. An expedition from New England again occupied Port Royal but failed to take Quebec. The Treaty of Utrecht (1713), which ended the war, recognized England's victories in Europe and required France to surrender Newfoundland, the region around Hudson's Bay, and Acadia (Nova Scotia).

Minor colonial disputes between England and Spain over trading rights in the West Indies and territorial claims between Spanish Florida and Georgia led to the outbreak of the War of Jenkins' Ear (1739). This minor conflagration was soon absorbed by the larger European War of the Austrian Succession (known in America as King George's War, 1744-1748). Before the war had ended, a contingent of New England troops had conquered the French fortress of Louisbourg at the Gulf of the St. Lawrence River. This victory was greeted with jubilation throughout the colonies, but the Treaty of Aix-la-Chapelle (1748), which ended the war, required the return of all conquered territories to their original claimants.

The prolonged contest for European leadership between France and England climaxed in the Seven Years' War (known in America as the French and Indian War, 1754-1763). Although part of the wider global rivalry between the European powers, the early confrontations began in the Ohio River valley during the years after 1748. By mid-century, the French had established a network of inland settlements between Quebec in the north and Louisiana in the south. Following the peace of Aix-la-Chapelle, however, a group of Virginians, possessing a royal charter for the Ohio Company of Virginia, began planning a trading settlement in the interior. Colonists from Pennsylvania, led by the Indian trader George Croghan, also penetrated the region. The French responded by attacking the English outposts and began constructing a chain of forts along the Pennsylvania frontier. Minor confrontations in this region exploded into the Great War for Empire. At stake were the western lands of North America.

The French held decided military advantages at the outbreak of war. With a unity of command and well-trained troops, the French army seemed superior to the colonial militia. By contrast, the English colonies lacked essential unity and relied upon the assistance of British troops. On the eve of war, the British government had urged the summoning of a colonial conference to discuss matters of mutual defense. At the Albany Congress (1754), delegates from New England, New York, Pennsylvania, and Maryland examined various alternatives and finally recommended the Plan of Union submitted by Benjamin Franklin. The scheme proposed the

A nineteenth-century portrayal of the nighttime massacre of the St. Francis Indians (1755) by British soldiers on the northern frontier during the French and Indian war.

formation of a Grand Council composed of delegates elected by the provincial assemblies every three years to administer the western lands and to regulate the Indian trade, thus eliminating individual colonies from those functions. The council would also levy colonial taxes. The plan suggested that the crown appoint a governor general to exercise such executive authority as negotiating Indian treaties and declaring war. The governor, moreover, would retain veto powers over council legislation. Despite the approval of the congress, the provincial assemblies, which were more concerned with local politics, rejected this proposal. The failure of the plan to win wider support revealed the basic disunity that would plague the British through the war.

Between 1754 and 1757, British troops suffered humiliating defeats before the French army. The defeat of General Edward Braddock in Pennsylvania was followed by losses at Niagara, Crown Point, Oswego, Fort William Henry, Ticonderoga, and Louisbourg. In 1757, however, William Pitt assumed leadership of the British government and reinvigorated British military efforts. Recognizing that success depended on the American theater of war, Pitt began sending supplies, troops, and capable officers to the colonies. Moreover, he formulated strategic plans for the conquest of Canada. Under the leadership of General John Forbes and Lord Amherst, the British captured many of the French forts. These victories climaxed in the Battle of Quebec (1759) on the Plains of Abraham, which saw British troops under General James Wolfe defeat the French forces under the Marquis de Montcalm. Montreal, the last French stronghold, capitulated in 1760. The war officially ended with the Peace of Paris (1763) in which France surrendered all her possessions in North America except for two islands in the West Indies.

The Seven Years' War, aside from altering the military balance in North America, aggravated certain imperial problems that culminated in the War for Independence [see below, pp. 91-93]. For the Indians, the war doomed their balance-of-power strategy and made them more vulnerable to English expansion. Taken as a whole, moreover, the wars against the French affected colonial society in important ways. First, the colonists provided large amounts of manpower and military supplies, particularly in the campaigns against Canada. Second, the colonists suffered from the close proximity of enemy troops not only during wartime but also at times of impending crisis. The effect of such anxiety is difficult to measure, but it may relate to the fear of slave conspiracies (as in New York City in 1741) or the timing of evangelical revivals (as in the Great Awakening). Finally, throughout the period after 1689, domestic tranquility in America depended on England's position in world affairs. To be sure, Americans considered themselves English and accepted their role as active members of the empire. The imperial wars, however, revealed how English political decisions could undermine the security and stability of the American provinces.

Political Ideology

The sense of dependence upon English power, of which the imperial wars were a constant reminder, provided the background for the development and articulation of a sophisticated political ideology (that is, a body of political ideas) in eighteenth-century America. The system of political power did not *cause* provincial Americans to accept a specific type of ideology, but the colonists seem to have embraced certain modes of thought because those ideas made sense to them, given the nature of imperial power relations.

As provincials, the colonists borrowed their political ideas and ideals from the mother country. Influenced by English publications and proud of their heritage as English people, provincial Americans accepted the political wisdom of England and measured their politics accordingly. Like their compatriots in England, the colonists praised the rise of Parliament in the seventeenth century and welcomed the decline of royal power. They attempted to model their provincial legislatures in the image of the House of Commons by claiming the rights that Parliament had won a century earlier. Thereby, the colonial quest for power could be given deeper historical roots. In adopting English political attitudes, eighteenth-century

Americans emphasized certain aspects of English theory more than others. This selective process, although not always conscious, reveals the colonists' attempt to understand their own political situation. Numerous political pamphlets and essays appeared in colonial newspapers, and, by 1763, articulate Americans possessed a mature political ideology.

Central to their political ideology was a fear of power. Believing that power tended to accumulate and extend itself beyond its proper limits, the more popular writers warned their readers to be vigilant in protecting their rights and liberties. Most Anglo-Americans praised the unwritten English constitution — the unique mixture of power represented by the king, the House of Lords, and the House of Commons — because it seemed to limit the accumulation of power. They believed, nevertheless, that this balance of power remained vulnerable to the encroachments of corrupt politicians. Such people, it was believed, would try to destroy the fragile constitution and erect a tyranny on its ruins.

In England, the most articulate spokesmen of this ideology were men who had been denied access to power and who consequently resented the informal political dealings that kept them out of power. Their publications, particularly *The Independent Whig* and *Cato's Letters* (written by John Trenchard and Thomas Gordon), achieved widespread popularity in America. The critiques of "tyrannical" leaders who sought to subvert the English constitution confirmed the colonists' suspicions of royal governors in America and the Privy Council in England. Realizing that the interference of English politicians had undermined their political stability, eighteenth-century Americans saw in this ideology a likely explanation of the encroachments of imperial power upon local initiative. Victimized by the workings of patronage politics, provincial Americans emphasized the corruptions of the system and questioned the morality of English officials.

By the mid-eighteenth century, these attitudes led provincial Americans to believe in the existence of a conspiracy among English leaders to destroy American rights. The widespread acceptance of this viewpoint can be explained by the colonists' perceptions of British power. The veto of a colonial law or the recall of a royal governor often seemed arbitrary and inexplicable to provincial Americans. The ideology of distrust, however, provided a framework that seemed to clarify these otherwise confusing procedures. From this perspective, articulate Americans responded to the imperial laws passed by Parliament after 1763 [see below, pp. 93-94].

The prevalence of these ideas does not mean that they were shared universally. Many Americans, both in and out of power, accepted the workings of government as legal and natural; such people viewed spokesmen of the ideology of distrust with dismay. Moreover, it is improbable that people of lower status even cared about such political discourse. People who worked from sunup to sundown, six days a week, probably looked at their American employers as greater threats to their liberty than royal officials. Although inarticulate, many of these workers supported the revolutionary protests of the 1760s and 1770s, but, of course, many did not. To examine the position of these people, we must rely on their visible behavior rather than on the spoken word. More often than not, they permitted members of the elite to speak for them.

Supplementary Reading

A brief overview of political values and institutions in the colonies is G. Dargo, *Roots of the Republic: A New Perspective on Early American Constitutionalism* (1974). A more detailed study is L. Labaree, *Royal Government in America* (1930). Voting patterns are discussed in R. Brown, *Middle-Class Democracy and the Revolution in Massachusetts* (1955), and R. and K. Brown, *Virginia, 1705-1786: Democracy or Aristocracy?* (1964), both of which emphasize the widespread franchise. An important criticism of the Browns' book, which also explains the relationship between county government and provincial power, is C. Sydnor, *Gentlemen Freeholders* (1952). The best synthesis of colonial politics is B. Bailyn, *The Origins of American Politics* (1967). Studies of the "rise of the assemblies" include J. Greene, *The Quest for Power* (1963), which deals with the southern colonies; and M. Kammen, *Deputyes and Libertyes: The Origins of Representative Government in Colonial America* (1969).

For studies of colonial power from the perspective of the governors, see J. Schutz, *William Shirley: King's Governor of Massachusetts* (1961); S. Katz, *Newcastle's New York* (1968); and W. Abbott, *The Royal Governors of Georgia* (1959). The colonial councils are described in J. T. Main, *The Upper House in Revolutionary America* (1967). For a case study of political leadership in Massachusetts, see R. Zemsky, *Merchants, Farmers, and River Gods: An Essay on Eighteenth-Century American Politics* (1971). Also helpful are several specific studies; see, for example, J. Hutson, *Pennsylvania Politics, 1746-1770: The Movement for Royal Government and Its Consequences* (1972); W. Hanna, *Benjamin Franklin and the Politics of Pennsylvania* (1965); or D. Dillon, *The New York Triumvirate* (1949). The best study of the colonial agents, which emphasizes the revolutionary era, is M. Kammen, *A Rope of Sand* (1966).

The relationship between English politics and colonial politics is described in J. Henretta, *"Salutary Neglect": Colonial Administration under the Duke of Newcastle* (1972), and J. Ernst, *Money and Politics in America, 1755-1775: A study in the Currency Act of 1764* (1973). The imperial wars in America are discussed in H. Peckham, *The Colonial Wars, 1689-1763* (1964). Also helpful is M. Savelle, *The Origins of American Diplomacy* (1967). Indian relations are illuminated by D. Leach, *The Northern Colonial Frontier* (1966); J. T. Flexner, *Mohawk Baronet: Sir William Johnson of New York* (1959); and W. Jacobs, *Diplomacy and Indian Gifts* (1950).

The best analysis of political ideology in the colonies is B. Bailyn, *The Ideological Origins of the American Revolution* (1967). L. Leder, *Liberty and Authority: Early American Political Ideology* (1968), summarizes a large body of colonial thought. Also helpful are the later chapters of T. Breen, *The Character of the Good Ruler* (1971). For a comparative perspective, see C. Robbins, *The Eighteenth-Century Commonwealthmen* (1959).

Chapter 7

The Imperial Crisis 1763-1776

Most of the English and the Americans expected the signing of the Treaty of Paris (1763), which concluded the Great War for Empire, to bring tranquility to the British imperial system. The British triumph, however, raised more problems than it solved on both sides of the Atlantic. To Americans, the victory meant release from the threat of French power on the frontier, opening the West to provincial expansion. To the English, the war dramatized the problems of administering an overseas empire. Different vantage points on numerous issues made an accommodation between the colonies and the mother country increasingly difficult.

The failure of the colonies to give England active support during the Seven Years' War demonstrated the existence of serious imperial problems. Despite the gravity of the situation, colonial merchants had traded with the French and Spanish islands in the West Indies. This illegal trade passed through neutral ports in the West Indies, usually with the connivance of the colonial governors. In addition, the colonists permitted the exportation to Canada of foodstuffs that were used to feed the French armies. Trading with the enemy was bad enough. But the colonists aggravated the situation by providing only limited support to the mother country. England attempted to meet its wartime needs by relying on requisitions from the colonial governments. Such a policy avoided the need to tax the colonists directly, but only New York, Connecticut, and Massachusetts provided sufficient money and manpower. Moreover, some colonial governments revealed their parochial orientation by refusing to assist their neighbors during the crisis.

The lack of colonial cooperation appeared not only in relations with the mother country but also in dealings with the Indians. During the war, the British government became concerned that indiscriminate appropriation of Indian lands would undermine the prospect of a lasting peace on the frontier. These fears were reinforced by the inability of the colonial governments to agree on a uniform Indian policy and by the continued use of fraud to acquire western lands. The wartime crisis also led the royal government to adopt a conciliatory policy toward its Indian allies by promising to limit land purchases in the West. These decisions resulted in the Proclamation of 1763, which (1) prohibited settlement west of a proclamation line drawn along the Appalachian Mountains, (2) stationed British soldiers in the West to oversee the fur trade and to enforce the restriction of white settlement, and (3) opened the newly acquired territories of Florida and Quebec to settlement.

The formulation of a land policy in London, however, did not mean that colonists in America would be willing or able to implement those decisions. Meanwhile, the Indians took matters into their own hands. Inspired by the prophet Neolin, the Ottawa chief Pontiac determined to reassert Indian independence by driving the English into the sea. In May 1763, Pontiac attacked British forts in the West and succeeded in capturing several trading posts and killing numerous settlers. But, by September 1764, British military power prevailed and the West appear pacified. The failure of the British army to prevent these attacks, however, troubled the colonial population.

Colonial displeasure with Britain's western policy emerged not only from the failure of the troops to protect exposed settlements from the Indians but also from the desire of colonial land speculators to acquire lands beyond the proclamation line. Pressure from these land speculators led the royal government to modify the proclamation line by renegotiating treaties with the Indians. For example, the Treaty of Fort Stanwix (1768) opened new territory for settlements. Such adjustments of the boundary lines encouraged colonial land speculation by groups like the Grand Ohio Company, which attempted to establish a new colony in the interior. By 1776, the English colonists had penetrated into western Pennsylvania, Kentucky, and Tennessee.

Reorganization of Empire

The failure of the colonists to comply with British policies during the Seven Years' War and the acquisition of new territory as a result of the peace settlement led the British government to consider reorganizing the empire in the years after 1763. English politicians, however, remained a diverse group and disagreed about the wisdom and nature of such reforms. Some, like William Pitt (who became Lord Chatham in 1766) and the "Old Whigs" (who included Edmund Burke), sought to expand parliamentary power at the expense of the crown by opposing executive plans to tax the colonists. Some, like the "King's Friends" (who included Lord North and the earl of Bute), wished to reassert royal authority throughout the empire. Other British officials moved in and out of a variety of political factions. Regardless of their viewpoints, however, the English politicians placed the interests of Great Britain above those of the American colonists. Few English people understood, or cared to understand, the political and social structure of the provinces.

In America, the elimination of the French colonial forces freed the colonists from their dependence upon England's military power. Yet, the conclusion of hostilities also brought a postwar depression that threatened the economic interests of people in all status groups. A reduction of trade hurt not only urban merchants but also the workers whom they employed. In Virginia, the tobacco planters, heavily indebted to English merchants, teetered on the edge of bankruptcy. No less serious, the reorganization of the empire threatened to limit political opportunities within the imperial system at a time when the provincial elite needed more political positions to satisfy its growing numbers. The insecurity created by these economic and political conditions may explain why many colonists were willing to listen to exponents of the ideology of distrust, who accused English politicians of attempting to subvert American liberty [see above, pp. 88-89].

From the perspective of many articulate provincials, the British attempt to streamline the empire seemed arbitrary and unnecessary. Convinced by pamphleteers that a conspiracy existed, the colonists responded not to what was actually happening in London but to what they thought lay behind imperial decisions. The sense of provincialism reinforced this distrust of British policy. Believing that the provinces, for all their cultural immaturity, remained "purer" than the mother country, provincials viewed England as a den of iniquity, a land of sin and corruption. It was entirely plausible to believe that English political leaders were equally corrupt and deceitful. These feelings were reinforced by English haughtiness toward American provincials.

Signs of dissent appeared during the Seven Years' War. In 1761, James Otis, acting as a spokesman for several Boston merchants, challenged the authority of Parliament to issue writs of assistance (general search warrants), which were used to stop smuggling. Although the Massachusetts courts upheld the use of the writs, Otis's position represented a fundamental assault on Parliament's right to legislate for the colonies.

The refusal of the Privy Council to approve a Virginia law that would have lowered the salaries of colonial clergymen led to a prolonged legal dispute known as the Parson's Cause. In 1763, Patrick Henry was catapulted to fame by his challenging of the right of the Privy Council to disallow

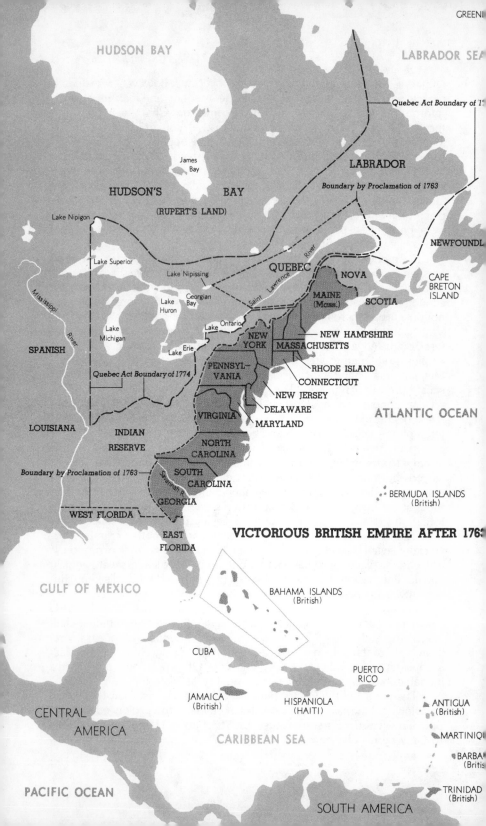

HUDSON BAY

GREENL

LABRADOR SEA

Quebec Act Boundary of 1

LABRADOR

HUDSON'S   BAY

(RUPERT'S LAND)

James
Bay

Boundary by Proclamation of 1763

Lake Nipigon

NEWFOUNDL

Lake Superior

Lake Nipissing

QUEBEC

NOVA

CAPE
BRETON
ISLAND

Saint Lawrence River

MAINE
(Mass.)

SCOTIA

Lake
Huron

Georgian
Bay

Lake
Michigan

Lake   Ontario

Lake   Erie

NEW
YORK

MASSACHUSETTS

NEW HAMPSHIRE

SPANISH

Mississippi River

Quebec Act Boundary of 1774

PENNSYL-
VANIA

RHODE ISLAND

CONNECTICUT

NEW JERSEY

DELAWARE

MARYLAND

ATLANTIC OCEAN

LOUISIANA

INDIAN
RESERVE

VIRGINIA

NORTH
CAROLINA

Boundary by Proclamation of 1763

Savannah R.

SOUTH
CAROLINA

GEORGIA

BERMUDA ISLANDS
(British)

WEST FLORIDA

EAST
FLORIDA

VICTORIOUS BRITISH EMPIRE AFTER 176

GULF OF MEXICO

BAHAMA ISLANDS
(British)

CUBA

PUERTO
RICO

JAMAICA
(British)

HISPANIOLA
(HAITI)

ANTIGUA
(British)

CENTRAL

MARTINIQ

AMERICA

CARIBBEAN SEA

BARBA
(Britis

PACIFIC OCEAN

TRINIDAD
(British)

SOUTH AMERICA

colonial legislation and his accusing the king of treason. The jury responded by awarding the clergymen only one penny in damages; Henry's prominence led to his election to the House of Burgesses.

The protests of Henry and Otis were *not* representative of American feeling during the early 1760s. But both men revealed their underlying distrust of the imperial system and their deep hostility toward English interference in American affairs. The attempt to reform the empire after 1763 brought these feelings forward. Not all Americans, of course, reacted to British policy in the same way. Many colonists from all social groups accepted its wisdom and stressed the importance of colonial obedience. More subtly, however, the political and social tensions *within* the colonies often influenced the factional alignments on questions of imperial policy. Thus, tenant farmers in New York often supported British decisions because their landlords opposed them. Similarly, in Pennsylvania, opposition to the Penn family led some Quakers to side with the royal government, while the Germans and Scotch-Irish backed the proprietors. Such divisions confused the political issues in most provinces.

A Source of Revenue

At the end of the Seven Years' War, the British government searched for a source of revenue to support the expanded empire. Since English taxpayers already were paying higher taxes because of the cost of the war, the government turned to the colonies to finance the stationing of troops in America.

In 1764, the Grenville ministry obtained the passage of the Sugar Act, which (1) provided for a lower duty on French and Spanish molasses, (2) levied new taxes on sugar, and (3) forbade the importation of rum. While the new duties meant a reduction in some of the existing tax rates, the British government hoped to increase revenues by a vigorous enforcement of the laws. More significantly, the Sugar Act (officially called the Revenue Act) was the first major parliamentary legislation aimed at raising money in the colonies. (Earlier laws had been intended to regulate trade rather than to acquire revenue.) Parliament further aggravated the situation by passing the Currency Act (1764), which restricted the emission of paper money in the colonies. This law reduced the amount of available currency just as the Sugar Act demanded increased payments to Britain.

The passage of these laws opened a constitutional debate that lasted over a decade and ended only with the Declaration of Independence. At issue was the question of whether sovereign power — supreme power — could be divided. During the middle decades of the eighteenth century, English legislators had argued that political sovereignty could not be shared, and they had attempted to expand parliamentary powers at the expense of the crown. Such assumptions also justified laws that taxed the colonists. Americans, on the other hand, had traditionally raised funds through the provincial legislatures on which the people had a direct influence through their representatives. The new revenue laws seemed to threaten these basic rights. In protesting against these policies, Americans emphasized the constitutional issues at stake, as well as the economic hardships that the new laws would bring. Besides petitioning Parliament for redress, merchants in such cities as New York and Boston swore not to purchase certain English products until the laws were repealed, thereby inaugurating a form of protest that became increasingly common in later years. Such economic coercion, by attacking English pocketbooks, aimed at forcing English merchants to pressure Parliament to reconsider the measure.

But the Grenville ministry remained untouched. In 1765, Parliament passed the Stamp Act, which required revenue stamps to be attached to certain legal documents, newspapers, and other printed matter. Like the Sugar Act, this law was designed primarily to raise money without having to rely on the laws of the colonial legislatures. At this time, Parliament also enacted the Quartering Act, which required the colonies to suppy British troops with adequate housing and supplies.

Colonial Dissent

Americans insisted that their basic right of taxation by consent was being challenged, and they responded with strong protest. Those who believed in the ideology of distrust claimed they saw a sordid conspiracy to destroy colonial liberties through the expansion of executive and military powers. Partly because the Stamp Act affected the more vocal elements of the population, such as lawyers, merchants, and printers, colonial dissent was especially articulate. In one tract, Maryland's Daniel Dulany challenged the British concept of representative government. Defenders of the Stamp Act had suggested that the colonists were "virtually" represented in Parliament, since the members of Parliament represented all the estates of the realm. Dulany denied this idea of "virtual" representation and argued that the interests of Parliament and the colonies were no longer identical. He maintained that Americans could be represented in Parliament only by sending "actual" delegates to England, an expensive procedure that few colonists endorsed.

Nor were the colonists content to stop with words. In the cities, secret organizations known as the Sons of Liberty emerged, and they harassed royal officials and prevented the distribution of the stamps. Composed largely of mechanics, laborers, and sailors, these mobs revealed that political protest did not belong solely to the elites who managed the provincial power structure; in later years, people of all classes attended mass meetings and participated freely in extralegal bodies. In October 1765, delegates from nine colonies attended a Stamp Act Congress in New York City and endorsed a Declaration of Rights and Grievances, which denied

The passage of the Stamp Act provoked opposition throughout the colonies. In urban areas, poorer workers joined skilled laborers and merchants in protesting the legislation. (Courtesy of Library of Congress.)

the right of Parliament to tax the colonists without their consent. In the aftermath of the congress, merchants throughout the colonies established nonimportation and nonconsumption agreements in which they vowed not to use English goods until Parliament repealed the Stamp Act. Merchants who preferred to acknowledge the supremacy of Parliament usually capitulated to the pressure of more militant protestors.

Such economic coercion, together with the political maneuvering of the colonial agents in England, persuaded Parliament to repeal the Stamp Act (1766). But, at the same time, Parliament announced in the Declaratory Act that it retained the right to legislate for the colonies. Parliament would concede the issue, but not the principle, of being the sole sovereign power in the empire.

Throughout the colonies, the repeal of the Stamp Act was greeted with jubilation. Many Americans believed that proper vigilance had enabled them to thwart a sordid conspiracy against their rights. In a perverse way, they believed that the repeal of the Stamp Act even confirmed the existence of a plot against liberty, because, if the law were basically sound, England would not have buckled to colonial pressure. Such was the logic of conspiracy theories.

The Townshend Acts

The success of colonial protest in 1766 did not remove England's desire to raise money in America to finance the empire. Nor were English politicians content to permit the colonists to go their own way. In 1767, Parliament passed several laws known as the Townshend Acts, which (1) provided for a series of new customs duties on such products as glass, paper, and tea; (2) created a new Board of Customs Commissioners based in America to enforce the Navigation Acts (the commissioners could bring suspects to trial in vice-admiralty courts that did not use juries); (3) permitted the use of funds from the duties to pay the salaries of royal officials, thus freeing them from their dependence on the colonial legislatures; and (4) suspended the New York Assembly for refusing to comply with the Quartering Act. This last act was particularly offensive to colonists who thought that they were again witnessing an attack on their right of representation.

The colonists responded with the forms of protest they had used periodically. John Dickinson published *Letters from a Farmer in Pennsylvania* (1767), which denied that revenue measures on trade (external taxes) were preferable to internal tax laws (like the Stamp Act). Both, he argued, were a violation of Americans' rights to tax themselves. In addition to these constitutional arguments, colonial merchants again formed nonimportation agreements, hoping to attack English pocketbooks. The Massachusetts legislature, influenced by the popular Sam Adams and James Otis, endorsed a circular letter urging all Americans to support these mercantile agreements.

Many prominent merchants engaged in smuggling, and the new customs administrators often employed dishonest methods in enforcing the Navigation Acts. Such activities, while technically legal, outraged colonial opinion. In June 1768, the royal customs commissioners seized John Hancock's sloop *Liberty* for failing to pay a duty on wine. In reprisal, a Boston mob attacked the commissioners. Upon learning of this violence, the British government transported four regiments of troops to Boston. The presence of British redcoats in the city convinced many provincials that their fears of a conspiracy against American liberty were justified. Worse still, the British troops antagonized many Boston workers by moonlighting at odd jobs. A series of minor brawls between citizens and redcoats climaxed in the Boston Massacre (March 1770), in which British soldiers fired on civilians and killed five men. Although the soldiers were acquitted in a jury trial, colonial propagandists exploited the atrocity to rally support for the cause.

Prior to learning of this outburst, British officials had decided to repeal the Townshend Acts in April 1770. However, they retained the tax on tea to uphold the principle of Parliament's right to tax the colonists. Most Americans, rejoicing in yet another defense of colonial rights, ignored the implications of this policy and allowed the nonimportation agreements to lapse.

In the months after the repeal of the Townshend Acts, calm seemed to return to British imperial relations. Provincial trade expanded, bringing prosperity to colonial merchants and the people they employed. Such peace might have persisted had politicians been able to deal with specific problems as pragmatic political questions rather than as disagreements of principle. The widespread belief in a conspiracy, however, prevented such accommodation and made colonists reluctant to ignore minor issues.

Continued enforcement of the Navigation Acts and the presence of British redcoats served as constant reminders of the powerlessness of provincial politics. In 1772, a British patrol ship, the *Gaspee*, ran aground off Rhode Island while pursuing suspected smugglers. A local mob burned the vessel to the waterline, horrifying British officials by the wanton destruction of property. Meanwhile, colonial juries refused to cooperate with royal officials in ending illegal trade. When Massachusetts governor Thomas Hutchinson announced in 1772 that certain judges would be paid from the royal treasury (thus freeing them from financial dependence on the colonial legislature), Boston's Sam Adams responded by establishing a committee of correspondence to coordinate news and grievances with similar groups in other New England towns.

The Tea Act

It was amidst this tenuous peace that the British government, led by Lord North, introduced the Tea Act (1773) to bolster the financial condition of the East India Company. The law granted the company a monopoly on the tea trade to America and reduced the export tax on tea, thereby enabling the company to reap large profits while cutting the retail price of tea. Such a law promised to curtail the smuggling of tea by underselling illegal imports. Although at first attracted by the lower price, many Americans soon realized that acceptance of such a law conceded Parliament's right to tax the colonies. Many merchants also feared that the creation of a monopoly by Parliament might set a precedent for other monopolies that would injure American business interests. Radicals again announced the existence of a secret plot against colonial rights. In every port, mobs attempted to prevent the consignment of tea, and, in Boston, a group of colonists disguised as Indians unloaded the tea chests into the sea.

Word of this destruction of property and defiance of authority horrified conservative Americans and infuriated English politicians. Parliament responded by passing the Coercive Acts (known in America as the Intolerable Acts, 1774), which (1) closed the port of Boston until the colony paid for the tea; (2) drastically revised the charter of Massachusetts by making the council appointive rather than elective, by restricting town meetings, and by strengthening the power of the royal governor; (3) permitted the transfer of legal cases outside the colony to enable fair trials; and (4) reenacted the Quartering Act to provide for the stationing of troops in America. At this time, Parliament also enacted the Quebec Act, which expanded the size of Quebec at the expense of other colonial claims, reaffirmed the unrepresentative government established by the French, and granted religious toleration to the Roman Catholics of Canada.

The colonists examined these laws from the perspective of their political ideology. The indiscriminate punishment of Bostonians, the arbitrary alteration of the Massachusetts charter, and the extension of the Quartering Act frightened many Americans. They feared that similar laws would apply to their own colonies. The conspiracy theory seemed more plausible, and colonists everywhere sent aid to the besieged New Englanders.

A Continental Congress

In 1774, a Continental Congress, composed of delegates from all the colonies but Georgia, convened in Philadelphia to discuss the imperial crisis. The congress revealed its political views by adopting the Suffolk Resolves, which declared the Coercive Acts to be null and void. Then, it adopted a Declaration of Rights and Grievances, which pledged allegiance to the king while denying Parliament's right to tax the colonists. Many moderate delegates supported a plan submitted by Joseph Galloway to restructure colonial administration. The proposal recommended the creation of a colonial union in which a president-general appointed by the king and a grand council elected by the provincial legislatures supervised colonial affairs and maintained a veto power over Parliamentary acts relating to the colonies. After narrowly defeating this plan, the congress proceeded to adopt more radical measures.

After a long debate, the congress endorsed the Continental Association, an elaborate plan of nonimportation, nonexportation, and nonconsumption of trade goods between England and the colonies. The importation of English goods was prohibited after December 1774. But, to enable southern planters to sell their crops, the embargo on exports was delayed until September 1775. To enforce the association, the congress advised the establishment of committees of safety in the local levels of government that would seize contraband and boycott uncooperative merchants. A provincial committee would coordinate local activities. The congress then adjourned, to meet again in May 1775 if the grievances remained unredressed.

The local committees, controlled by the radicals, effectively enforced the commercial boycott, bringing the importation of English products to a virtual standstill. The radicals often offended provincial conservatives by resorting to violence to assure compliance. At this time, most Americans probably expected economic coercion to bring peaceful administrative reform and feared that violent activity would prevent a political compromise. Few desired or anticipated a separation from the British Empire.

In response to the Continental Congress, British authorities resolved to bring the colonies to submission. While some English politicians, such as Pitt and Burke, appealed for conciliation, most members of Parliament preferred decisive action. They voted to transport more troops to Boston, declared that a rebellion existed in Massachusetts, and limited New England's trade to Great Britain and the British West Indies. This latter provision later included all the colonies but New York (an abortive attempt to divide and conquer). A simultaneous resolution in which Parliament promised to end taxation in any colony that would finance its own defense and civil government was rejected in America.

Meanwhile, Massachusetts radicals established an extralegal provincial government, commenced training soldiers, and began collecting supplies. In April 1775, General Thomas Gage (who had been appointed military governor of Massachusetts) ordered a detachment to seize some powder and weapons that were stockpiled at Concord. Warned by Paul Revere and William Dawes, the Massachusetts "minutemen" briefly confronted the troops at Lexington Green, allowed the redcoats to proceed to Concord, and then fired at the soldiers on their march back to Boston, causing 273 British casualties. News of the fighting spread throughout the colonies, exciting passions everywhere. In Virginia, the royal governor seized the public powder, and New England volunteers led by Ethan Allen captured Ticonderoga and Crown Point.

The Second Continental Congress

In this tense atmosphere, the Second Continental Congress convened in Philadelphia on May 10, 1775. Although more radical in composition than the first congress, the delegates still opposed independence and adopted instead an Olive Branch Petition drafted by Pennsylvania's John Dickinson. However, most of the representatives recognized the immediate importance of providing assistance to the people of Massachusetts. Assuming control of the provincial troops, congress appointed George Washington commander-in-chief of the Continental army and dispatched him to Boston to protect the besieged city.

Prior to Washington's arrival, British and American soldiers had clashed at Bunker Hill and Breed's Hill. In territorial terms, the British attained their ends, but they suffered enormous casualties. General William Howe replaced Gage at Boston and, after allowing Washington to fortify the surrounding heights, withdrew his troops to Nova Scotia (March 1776). Meanwhile, one American force conquered Montreal, and another failed to capture Quebec. In the South, Carolinians repulsed the British invasion of Charleston (June 1776).

These military engagements obviously reduced the possibility of a compromise between England and the colonies. Still, many Americans, including the delegates at the congress, remained reluctant to break with the empire and feared the consequences of independence. Moreover, conservatives viewed with alarm the increasing reliance on mob violence. The political takeover of Pennsylvania by common people confused elitist provincials everywhere. Yet, several events that occurred during the winter of 1775-1776 made independence seem increasingly logical.

In December, Parliament declared all colonial ports closed to trade until the colonists recognized British sovereignty. Continued political dependence on England, therefore, meant economic suicide for many Americans. In January, the colonists learned that the king had hired Hessian mercenaries to wage war in the colonies. Exploited by American publicists, this decision aroused the fears of many provincials. Even more important in crystalizing colonial opinion for independence was the publication of Thomas Paine's *Common Sense* (January 1776). In the enormously popular tract (about 150,000 copies were sold between January and July 1776), Paine attacked not simply the imperial system and the king but also the notion of monarchy itself. Urging Americans to create a republican form of government, he pressed for immediate independence. The Continental Congress responded in the spring by opening American ports to foreign shipping and in May 1776 recommended that the provincial governments draft new state constitutions.

The Declaration of Independence

On June 7, 1776, Richard Henry Lee of Virginia offered a resolution calling for American independence from England. Congress, in an attempt to win a wider consensus, appointed a committee headed by Thomas

Thomas Paine (1737-1809), author of Common Sense, migrated to America in 1774, carrying with him a radical ideology which justified American independence and the creation of a republican government. Paine later supported the French Revolution and drafted The Rights of Man. But his atheistic ideas made him unpopular in America and he died in obscurity in New York in 1809. (By John Wesley Jarvis, courtesy of National Gallery of Art, Washington, D. C., gift of Marian B. Maurice.)

Jefferson to prepare a rationale for such a move. Congress approved Lee's motion on July 2 and then endorsed the Declaration of Independence two days later. Jefferson's statement contained two sections. In the preamble, he justified the rebellion on the basis on the natural and inalienable rights of humans to revolt and establish a new form of government based on the consent of the governed. The longer portion of the document indicted the king for violating the specific rights of the colonists and protested the persistent interference of royal power in colonial government.

In condemning George III (rather than Parliament), Jefferson enabled colonials to focus their dissent on a specific enemy of American liberty, thereby fulfilling the logic of the conspiracy theory. Moreover, by 1776, most colonials had repudiated all parliamentary control and insisted that only the king united the empire. In attacking King George, Jefferson severed this last imperial connection. Nevertheless, the emphasis on the problems of royal administration reflected over a century of provincial frustration and a sense of powerlessness that could only be alleviated by the acquisition of home rule. American revolutionaries expected the transfer of political power to America to bring social stability and economic security. But it was one thing to declare independence and quite another to enjoy its expected advantages.

Supplementary Reading

The most complete discussion of the prerevolutionary era is L. H. Gipson, *The British Empire before the American Revolution*, 13 volumes (1936-1967). A shorter version is Gipson's *The Coming of the Revolution, 1763-1775* (1954). Other synthetic studies include J. C. Miller, *The Origins of the American Revolution* (1943), and E. Morgan, *The Birth of the Republic* (1956). For the English side, see L. B. Namier, *England in the Age of the American Revolution* (1930). The influence of Indian affairs on English policy making is described in J. Sosin, *Whitehall and the Wilderness* (1961); it should be supplemented with T. Abernethy, *Western Lands and the American Revolution* (1937).

More specialized studies include B. Bailyn, *The Ideological Origins of the American Revolution* (1967), which explains the prevalence of conspiracy theories; E. S. and H. Morgan, *The Stamp Act Crisis* (1953); B. Knollenberg, *Origin of the American Revolution* (1960), which treats the early crises; A. M. Schlesinger, *The Colonial Merchants and the American Revolution* (1917); B. Labaree, *The Boston Tea Party* (1964); and J. Shy, *Toward Lexington: The Role of the British Army in the Coming of the Revolution* (1965). For a collection of original essays dealing with the socioeconomic aspects of the Revolution, see A. Young, editor, *The American Revolution: Explorations in the History of American Radicalism* (1976).

For a discussion of the relationship between the provincial political structure and the reorganization of the British Empire after 1763, see J. Martin, *Men in Rebellion: Higher Governmental Leaders and the Coming of the American Revolution* (1973). The role of the colonial mobs is described in P. Maier, *From Resistance to Revolution: Colonial Radicals and the Development of American Opposition to Britain* (1972). Several local studies are also useful; see especially C. Becker, *The History of Political Parties in the Province of New York, 1760-1776* (1909); D. Lovejoy, *Rhode Island Politics and the American Revolution* (1958); O. Zeichner, *Connecticut's Years of Controversy* (1950); and J. Hutson, *Pennsylvania Politics, 1746-1770* (1972). The relationship between ideology and social structure in Pennsylvania is examined in E. Foner, *Tom Paine and Revolutionary America* (1976).

For biographical studies of two provincial leaders, one a supporter of independence and the other an opponent, see R. Beeman, *Patrick Henry: A Biography* (1974), and B. Bailyn, *The Ordeal of Thomas Hutchinson* (1974).

Chapter 8

The War for Independence

1776-1783

The War for Independence pitted thirteen diverse and disunited colonies against the forces of the most powerful empire in the world. Yet, the men who signed the Declaration of Independence, no doubt, held some expectations of success. A decade of colonial protests and English retreats had taught American revolutionaries that the British Empire, for all its might, suffered from administrative inefficiency and a lack of unified purpose, as well as a multitude of international enemies. Early military victories against British soliders at Lexington and Concord, Bunker Hill, and Charleston bolstered American optimism.

At the outbreak of war, Great Britain appeared to have a decided military advantage. Possessing a trained army (reinforced by Hessian mercenaries), the largest navy in the world, and superior economic resources, the British expected a quick victory and a harsh peace. These advantages, however, were offset by certain strategic and logistic problems. British soldiers and munitions had to be transported 3,000 miles from the base of supplies, while colonial soldiers could live off the land and conveniently disappear into the friendly countryside. The dispersed nature of colonial settlement further complicated the British position, for a victory in one region did not assure a final triumph. Moreover, the British authorities disagreed about military policy. Many shrank from waging all-out war against His Majesty's former subjects; others questioned the wisdom of depleting the

European army while France and Spain remained hostile enemies. British confusion can be seen in the dual roles of General William Howe and Admiral Richard Howe, who were simultaneously military commanders and peace commissioners. The British unrealistically hoped to frighten Americans into acknowledging the authority of the king and the Parliament.

The colonial cause suffered from weaknesses and division of another sort. Militarily, the Continental army revealed the problems of a citizen-soldiery. Composed primarily of short-term recruits prone to desertion, the army never exceeded 20,000 men at one time. More serious, colonial soldiers (and many of their officers) lacked fighting experience, and, in the early battles in New York, the colonial militia scattered before the oncoming redcoats. Preservation of the army became Washington's major concern. Equally serious was the chronic shortage of military and medical supplies, a particularly acute problem during the early stages of the war.

The Loyalists

Besides these military problems, the revolutionaries also confronted complex political questions. Numerous Americans, for a variety of reasons, refused to support the revolutionary cause and remained loyal to England. The presence of these loyalists (or Tories) confused British plans. English administrators underestimated the strength of the revolutionaries and expected the loyalists to rally behind the king's armies, thus shortening the rebellion. The fact that many New England loyalists had accompanied Howe's troops to Nova Scotia enhanced this British misconception. British planners mistakenly assumed that the Continental Congress was a group of plotters rather than a gathering of the delegates of the people. Throughout the war, the British waited for a rising of loyal subjects against the congressional rebels.

The failure of the support to materialize should not obscure the depth of the loyalist sentiment in 1776. Like the revolutionaries (or patriots, as they called themselves), the loyalists had searched for a clear political position in the years after 1763. Most of them had opposed such laws as the Stamp Act, just as they had condemned the violence of the Sons of Liberty. But they believed that colonial liberties depended upon the protection of the British government and that a separation from the empire was politically unwise, if not treasonous. As supporters of the status quo, the loyalists lacked a program to rally public support. They remained apathetic and disorganized and allowed the patriots to take the initiative. Not until the conclusion of the first Continental Congress (1774) did they begin to publish specific critiques of the revolutionary position.

The number of loyalists is difficult to determine, since many, if not most, Americans remained indifferent to the shifting political crisis. It is estimated that only 6 percent of Connecticut's population became loyalists, whereas in areas of New York perhaps half the people supported the king. In terms of the entire colonial population, recent studies suggest that Tory strength numbered about 20 percent of the people. Although loyalism appeared in all status groups and in all regions, it appealed to certain types of people. Colonists who depended on the British government for power and status often became Tories. Thus, royal appointees and certain favored merchants often entered the loyalist camp. Loyalism also attracted members of ethnic minorities who hoped to find protection from the cultural encroachments of the provincial majority. In New England, parishioners of the Church of England, who had been harassed by the Congregational majority, frequently supported the king rather than their American opponents. Minority groups that already had been anglicized (like the English-speaking members of the Dutch Reformed Church) tended to support the Revolution, whereas culturally isolated minorities often defended the king. In some areas, loyalism revealed the tensions of the provincial social structure. In New York, many tenant farmers became Tories because their landlords were patriots. For similar reasons, blacks often assisted the British armies and served as volunteers. After 1776, American revolutionaries attempted to create a consensus by ostracizing the loyalists, many of whom sought protection behind British lines. Although statistics remain inaccurate, perhaps 30,000 loyalists fought with the British and between 80,000 to 100,000 left the country at the end of the war.

Besides these political divisions, Americans also faced the problem of supplying their soldiers and financing the war. The issue of centralized taxation had created the imperial crisis originally, and Americans were reluctant to delegate the power of taxation to the Continental Congress. Hence, the congress relied upon requisitions of money and supplies from the states. In addition, the congress borrowed about $15 million by selling bonds at home and abroad. Both the states and the congress issued paper currency that rapidly depreciated in value. The resulting inflation adversely affected many people, who thereby paid for the war indirectly. Americans also received financial assistance from England's traditional European enemies, France and Spain. However, to a large extent, the colonists supplied themselves either by developing home manufactures or by trading their agricultural surplus in the West Indies. Only with a sophisticated economy could the new nation have challenged the British Empire effectively.

To offset these relative disadvantages, both the British and the patriots hoped to benefit through alliances with the Indian tribes. In previous wars in the colonies, the interior tribes, particularly the Iroquois in the North and the Creek and Cherokee in the South, had used their military power to obtain trading privileges and to preserve their independence. Since the departure of the French in 1763, these Indians had been severely pressed by white frontier people who wanted their lands. Therefore, the Indians understood that the War for Independence involved more than bargaining for economic advantage; what was at stake was control of their lands and, consequently, their own political independence. Even before

A revolutionary broadside printed and engraved on handmade rag paper. "The Thirteen States united in one Ring/Join heart to hand & Independence sing." (Courtesy of Minnesota Historical Society.)

the Declaration of Independence, the Continental Congress had sent delegates to the Indians to urge them to remain neutral. The British, on the other hand, worked to turn the Indians into active allies against the colonists.

In the North, the Iroquois Six Nations at the start of the war had a policy of neutrality. But, when Americans invaded their territory to capture British agents, the Senecas agreed to enter the war on the British side. They participated in battles around New York and attacked frontier settlements in Pennsylvania and New York. By 1777, the Continental Congress also had abandoned a policy of Indian neutrality and had managed to persuade other Iroquois to support the patriots' side. Eventually, Iroquois fought against Iroquois, undermining the unity of the Six Nations and leaving all the Iroquois more vulnerable to white encroachments. In the South, the Creeks initially chose neutrality, but the Cherokees, angered by colonial invasions of their lands, joined the British side. When Cherokees attacked along the southern frontier in 1776, Americans retaliated quickly, destroyed Cherokee opposition, and forced them to surrender a large portion of their lands. The fate of the Cherokees discouraged the Creeks from joining the British. But, when colonials continued to raid their lands, the Creeks agreed to fight with the British along the Georgia frontier.

The Early Battles

The strengths and weaknesses of the two forces emerged soon after the Congress declared independence. On July 2, 1776, General Howe (who had first removed his besieged troops from Boston to Nova Scotia) landed in force on Staten Island. Washington, anticipating an attack had moved south from New England. In the ensuing Battle of Long Island (August 1776), the British roundly defeated the Continental forces. A resourceful British general (which Howe was not) could have followed up this victory by entrapping a substantial part of the American army. Instead, Howe permitted Washington to escape to Manhattan. Then, in a series of skirmishes, he pursued the American army from New York City to Harlem Heights to White Plains. Despite defeats at each place, Washington managed to keep his army intact and, in the autumn of 1776, led a retreat through New Jersey. When Howe's soldiers went into winter quarters, Washington surprised a Hessian post at Trenton (Christmas 1776) by crossing the Delaware River at night. After another minor victory at Princeton, Washington also retired for the winter.

Besides demonstrating the weakness of the Continental army and the ineptness of the British command, this first campaign revealed the secret of America's ultimate success. The British fought for *territory*, seizing such crucial areas as New York City. Washington fought for *armies*. As in modern guerrilla wars, the American revolutionaries sacrificed territory to preserve the army, and, as long as the army existed, the British could not claim a victory. Thus, Washington's persistence gave the colonists additional time to strengthen their cause. The victories in New Jersey, moreover, boosted the morale of the new nation.

In the spring of 1777, the British commenced an elaborate campaign designed to end the colonial uprising. General John Burgoyne was to lead a contingent of troops south from Canada toward Albany while a smaller force, under the command of Barry St. Leger, marched from Lake Ontario to the Albany region. Meanwhile, Howe was to bring his soldiers from New York City up the Hudson River. When this strategy was consummated, the British expected to destroy the rebel forces in New York, rally the local loyalists, and thereby isolate New England from the other colonies. The failure of these plans revealed the essential problems of waging warfare in a hostile country while surrounded by a dense wilderness and an uncooperative population.

Instead of coordinating the attack, Howe transferred his army southward, defeated Washington at Brandywine (September 1777), and occupied Philadelphia, the headquarters of the Continental Congress. He left behind a small force in New York under the command of General Henry Clinton. Meanwhile, Burgoyne had moved southward from Canada and captured Fort Ticonderoga. Thereafter, things became more difficult for the British. The loyalist support failed to materialize, and local patriots hindered Burgoyne's passage by felling trees and harassing his soldiers. As Burgoyne's progress stalled, a small American force, commanded by Nicholas Herkimer, encountered St. Leger's army at Oriskany and forced the British to withdraw to Fort Oswego on Lake Ontario. Burgoyne, bogged down in the forests of New York and surrounded by patriot militia, attempted to destroy colonial resistance by attacking American defenses near Saratoga. Beaten back twice by patriot forces and anticipating no assistance from Clinton (who, after a shortened march from New York City, returned to his base), Burgoyne surrendered his army (October 1777).

The French Alliance

The victory at Saratoga demonstrated to the world the tenacity of colonial resistance. Louis XVI responded by granting French recognition to the United States. French sympathy for the American cause had emerged shortly after the outbreak of hostilities. Frustrated by the loss of France's American empire and desirous of revenge, the French foreign minister, Comte de Vergennes, persuaded Louis XVI to convey supplies secretly to America through a fictitious firm (to avoid antagonizing England prematurely). The king also permitted the colonists to outfit privateers in French ports. Thus, French assistance, based on a self-interested desire to weaken Great Britain, contributed to the revolutionary struggle.

The European powers, recognizing the significance of the Battle of Saratoga, endeavored to protect their national interests. Lord North, concerned that France would intervene on the American side, proposed a ser-

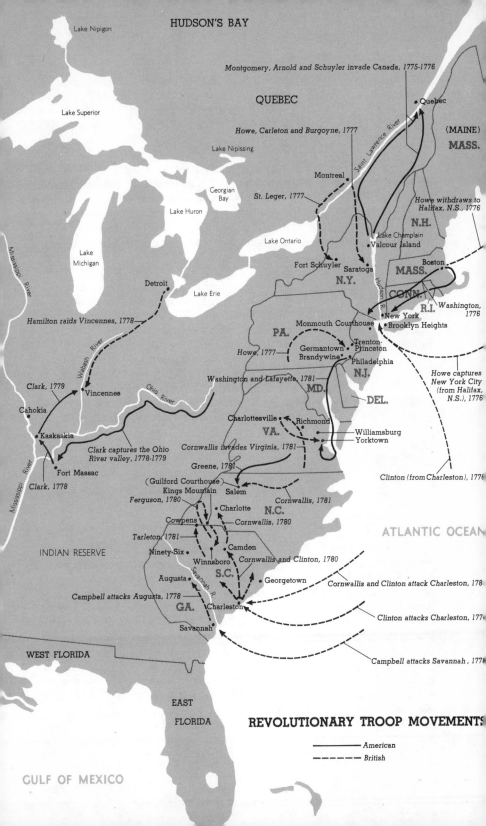

HUDSON'S BAY

Lake Nipigon

Lake Superior

QUEBEC

Montgomery, Arnold and Schuyler invade Canada, 1775-1776

• Quebec

(MAINE)

MASS.

Howe, Carleton and Burgoyne, 1777

Lake Nipissing

Montreal •

St. Leger, 1777

Howe withdraws to Halifax, N.S., 1776

N.H.

Georgian Bay

Lake Huron

Lake Ontario

Lake Champlain
Valcour Island

Lake Michigan

Fort Schuyler • Saratoga

N.Y.

MASS. Boston

CONN.

Detroit •

Lake Erie

Hamilton raids Vincennes, 1778

Hudson R.

R.I. *Washington, 1776*

• New York
• Brooklyn Heights

Monmouth Courthouse •

PA.

Howe, 1777

Germantown • Trenton-Princeton
Brandywine •

Mississippi River

Wabash River

Clark, 1779

Vincennes •

Ohio River

Washington and Lafayette, 1781

• Philadelphia

N.J.

Howe captures New York City (from Halifax, N.S.), 1776

Cahokia •

MD.

DEL.

Kaskaskia •

Clark captures the Ohio River valley, 1778-1779

Charlottesville • • Richmond

VA.

Fort Massac •

Clark, 1778

Cornwallis invades Virginia, 1781

• Williamsburg
Yorktown

Greene, 1781

(Guilford Courthouse)
Kings Mountain •

Clinton (from Charleston), 1776

Salem •

Ferguson, 1780

• Charlotte

Cornwallis, 1781

N.C.

Cornwallis, 1780

Cowpens •

Tarleton, 1781

ATLANTIC OCEAN

INDIAN RESERVE

Ninety-Six •

Savannah R.

• Camden

Cornwallis and Clinton, 1780

Winnsboro •

S.C.

Augusta •

Campbell attacks Augusta, 1778

GA. • Charleston

Cornwallis and Clinton attack Charleston, 178-

• Georgetown

Clinton attacks Charleston, 177-

Savannah •

Campbell attacks Savannah, 177-

WEST FLORIDA

EAST

FLORIDA

REVOLUTIONARY TROOP MOVEMENTS

———— *American*
- - - - *British*

GULF OF MEXICO

ies of measures that would have conceded all colonial demands short of independence. Despite the urgency of the situation, Parliament responded slowly and British peace commissioners did not arrive at Philadelphia until June 1778. By that time, the United States and France had concluded a commercial treaty, which afforded certain privileges to American merchants, and a formal treaty of alliance, which bound both nations to continue the war until England recognized American independence and agreed to a treaty of peace. Aside from weakening the British Empire, France hoped to acquire territory in the West Indies.

Announcement of the alliance led England to declare war against France. This policy forced the British to maintain a large home army. More important, the French began openly to transport money, munitions, manpower, and naval assistance to America. The absence of an American navy made this last item particularly valuable. France's ally, Spain, remained reluctant to enter the war, fearing that the revolutionary zeal might spread to the Spanish Empire in Latin America. However, Vergennes offered to support the Spanish until they won Gibraltar from England. An alliance between France and Spain (June 1779) presented Great Britain with yet another European enemy.

Other Continental alliances eventually isolated England from Europe. British interference with Baltic shipping led Denmark, Sweden, the Netherlands, Portugal, and Russia to form a League of Armed Neutrality (1780) to protect the rights of neutrals. The English became especially antagonistic toward the Dutch, who had capitalized on Britain's preoccupation with the war by acquiring England's carrying trade. England responded by declaring war on Holland (December 1780). The Dutch contributed to the Revolution by selling supplies on credit and by purchasing American bonds.

The Late Battles

The formation of international alliances, however, did not assure an American victory. Following the debacle at Saratoga, Howe spent the winter at Philadelphia, while Washington attempted to preserve his depleted army at Valley Forge. In the spring, Henry Clinton, the equally indecisive general who replaced Howe as commander of the British forces, moved his army from Philadelphia toward New York. Pursuing the redcoats, Washington attacked at Monmouth, New Jersey (June 1778), nearly defeating the British army. Benedict Arnold's attempted treason at West Point (1780) and an abortive British assault at Newport, Rhode Island, represented the last military activity in the northern states. In the West, a small American force led by George Rogers Clarke captured several British posts in Indiana and Illinois (1778-1779).

After 1778, the British, relying upon their superior sea power and hoping to find pockets of loyalist supporters, directed their energies to the southern states. Following a successful invasion of Savannah (1778), the

British captured 5,000 American soldiers at Charleston, South Carolina (1780), a serious loss of manpower. General Cornwallis subsequently defeated an American force under Horatio Gates at the Battle of Camden (1780), but a small patriot contingent vanquished a Tory band at the Battle of King's Mountain. General Nathanael Greene replaced Gates in command and directed several minor raids on Cornwallis's numerically superior troops. An American triumph at Cowpens, South Carolina (January 1781), cost the British heavy casualties that were made more severe by a costly victory at the Battle of Guilford Court House (March 1781). Nursing his wounds, Cornwallis retreated to Wilmington, North Carolina.

In the spring of 1781, Cornwallis moved northward to Virginia and established a base at Yorktown on a peninsula jutting out into Chesapeake Bay, where he expected the support of the British navy. However, a French fleet commanded by Admiral De Grasse fought off a small British flotilla and blocked a British escape by sea. Meanwhile, Washington feigned an attack on Clinton in New York and raced his army to Virginia. Confronting over 16,000 American troops, Cornwallis, with 7,000 redcoats, capitulated on October 19, 1781. Thus ended the military side of the war.

The Treaty of Paris

Plagued by enormous war debts, vanquished by the Continentals at Yorktown, and pressed by the armies of Spain and France throughout the world, Great Britain looked for peace. In March 1782, following the fall of the North ministry, the English agreed to negotiate with an American peace delegation. In April, the British agent, Richard Oswald, traveled to Paris and opened discussions with Benjamin Franklin, the United States emissary in France.

A series of wartime alliances complicated the peace negotiations. The Franco-American pact bound each nation to reject a separate treaty, while France remained obligated to fight until Spain captured Gibraltar. Moreover, neither European ally wished to see a strong United States in the Western Hemisphere, and Spain still hoped to establish an empire west of the Appalachian Mountains in the Mississippi Valley. Vergennes, for all his professed loyalty to the American cause, wanted to protect French interests at all costs. Attempting to outmaneuver the American peace commissioners (Benjamin Franklin, John Jay, and John Adams) by offering Spain territory in the West, Vergennes overplayed his hand. Jay, who had served as an American representative in Spain, recognized Vergennes's duplicity and persuaded his colleagues to deviate from their instructions and begin separate negotiations with Oswald. The British, believing that they had divided their enemies and preferring a weak republic to a Spanish Empire in North America, accepted the offer. By November 1782, the negotiators agreed to a preliminary treaty, which was formally signed September 3, 1783.

In the Treaty of Paris, George III recognized the independence of the United States, thus conceding the major issue of the war. Other provisions (1) established boundaries for the new nation, extending north to the Great Lakes, west to the Mississippi River, and south to 31° (a secret clause also provided that, if England rather than Spain eventually acquired Florida, the southern boundary would be drawn at 32°28'); (2) granted Americans fishing rights in Canadian waters; (3) assured both nations rights of navigation on the Mississippi River; (4) promised that no legal impediments would prevent the collection of prewar debts; and (5) provided that the Continental Congress would recommend that the states restore the property confiscated from the loyalists and that further seizures would cease. England's willingness to consent to this treaty reflected British war weariness and the desire to maintain the European balance of power by preventing further French or Spanish expansion in North America. In agreeing to American sovereignty east of the Mississippi, the British broke their wartime promises to their Indian allies in the West. Lacking British support, these Indians soon became victims of American expansion.

The "Inner" Revolution

The War for Independence represented more than a war for national liberation. Prior to 1781, Americans remained preoccupied with military affairs and recognized the importance of eliminating the British army. Yet, the Declaration of Independence, by ending traditional political ties, enabled Americans to effect an "inner" revolution that altered the structure of power. These political changes, however, did not necessarily lead to shifts in the social structure. Many of the social changes that have been associated with the Revolution emerged less as consequences of independence than as a result of longer-term trends.

In May 1776, the Continental Congress recommended that the individual states replace their provincial governments with new governments based on republican principles. Each state, except Rhode Island and Connecticut, adopted a new constitution that was drafted by either a provincial congress or an extralegal body claiming to represent the people. These constitutions reflected the political ideology that had led to the War for Independence. In some cases, the draft constitutions were submitted to the citizens for ratification.

The political assumptions that influenced the state constitutions represented a logical outcome of the prerevolutionary ideology of distrust [see above, pp. 88-89]. Americans still viewed power as a threat to popular liberty and endeavored to protect the people from the encroachments of executive authority. Consequently, in most states, the constitutions stripped the governors of their legislative and judicial powers, reduced their power of patronage and, in Pennsylvania (where radicals controlled state politics), replaced the office of governor with an elective council. The

Lake Nipigon

e of the Woods

BRITISH CANADA

Indefinite boundary

efinite
ndary

Lake Superior

Quebec

St. Lawrence River

St. John R.

MAINE
(Part of Mass.)

St. Croix R.

Green
Bay

Georgian
Bay

Lake Nipissing

Lake Huron

Lake Michigan

Lake Ontario

Fort Niagara

NEW
HAMPSHIRE

River

NEW YORK

MASS.

Boston

Detroit

Lake Erie

CONN.

R.I.

Cape Cod

NORTHWEST   TERRITORY

PENNSYLVANIA

New York

Illinois R.

Wabash R.

Ohio R.

Philadelphia

Baltimore

MD.

Ohio R.

Kentucky admitted 1792

VIRGINIA

ANISH

UISIANA

TERRITORY SOUTH OF

THE OHIO RIVER

Tennessee admitted 1796

NORTH CAROLINA

Cape Hatteras

Mississippi River

Yazoo R.

Tombigbee R.

Alabama R.

GEORGIA

SOUTH CAROLINA

MISSISSIPPI TERRITORY
Claimed by Spain until 1795

Savannah

ATLANTIC OCEAN

SPANISH

FLORIDA

St. Augustine

PEACE OF 1783

GULF OF MEXICO

states endeavored to separate powers but, nevertheless, allowed the legislatures to control judicial and executive affairs. Other powers granted to the legislative branch included the right to regulate foreign relations, issue money, and supervise appointments.

While eliminating the monarchy from government, the constitutions continued to accept the idea of balancing power within the states. With the exception of Pennsylvania, which created a unicameral legislature, the states established a bicameral system in which the lower houses theoretically represented the people while the state senators constituted an aristocracy. In practice, however, men from similar classes — usually the more affluent — were elected to both houses. During this period, the upper houses of the legislatures became less aristocratic as men of lesser status sat in their proceedings. To protect the people from the expansion of legislative power, the state constitutions included bills of rights that defined the civil liberties of the citizens.

In strengthening the power of the legislatures, the state constitutions assumed that the legislative branch represented specific constituencies and thus reflected the will of the people. But the men who drafted these fundamental laws still feared the anarchic power of the mob to dictate to the legislature. To protect government from the masses, the states maintained some property requirements for voting (which were usually slightly lower than the older colonial standards) and established higher property qualifications for holding office. Thus, the politics of deference — the idea that voters should defer to their "betters" — survived the revolutionary crisis and withstood the radical demands for wider democracy.

In writing their constitutions, several states attempted to reapportion legislative representation to account for shifts in population. Some states also removed such feudal limitations on land tenure as primogeniture and entail, which had restricted the sale of real estate. Since most colonists had ignored these ideas in practice, the social consequences remained insignificant; usually, the wealthier landholders with large estates supported the elimination of these feudal vestiges because the sale of land was profitable. In some states, government-supported religions lost their privileged status, but many areas maintained some religious establishment. Massachusetts and Connecticut did not formally separate church and state until the first quarter of the nineteenth century.

Liberty and Slavery

Despite the widespread commitment to civil liberty, provincial Americans generally believed in the inferiority of blacks and accepted the institution of slavery. The Quakers, with few exceptions, were the only articulate advocates of abolitionism during the colonial era (even though they maintained segregated burial grounds). However, in expressing the idea that "all men are created equal," Thomas Jefferson fostered a lengthy debate among whites about the alleged inferiority of black people. This discussion, which focused more on the question of racial prejudice than on the institution of slavery, revealed the revolutionary *potential* of the War for Independence and weakened the bondage of some American slaves.

During the War for Independence, many Americans opposed the use of black troops, arguing that the blacks were either unreliable or subversive. Yet, the need for manpower finally forced the states (with the exception of South Carolina and Georgia) to accept black enlistees. Thus, free and slave blacks, many of them enticed by promises of freedom, fought with the patriots. Even when blacks earned their personal freedom, however, the persistence of racial prejudice limited the application of the principles of the Declaration of Independence. The British offered similar terms to black slaves, and the royal governor of Virginia, Lord Dunmore; recruited many fugitives. But, while the redcoats confiscated the slave property of southern planters, relatively few blacks obtained the promised freedom; most were sold as slaves in the West Indies.

Indirectly, the effect of the Revolution on slavery appeared more significant. Antislavery societies emerged in such states as New York and Pennsylvania, and states throughout the North instituted programs of gradual emancipation whereby blacks born after a certain date were freed upon attaining maturity. The conservative nature of this legislation can be seen by the existence of thousands of slaves in northern states well into the nineteenth century. Such programs also did not consider the more subtle problem of racial discrimination. All states eventually prohibited international slave trade and, with some exceptions, facilitated the process of voluntary emancipation. Moved by the revolutionary rhetoric of natural rights, such planters as Henry Laurens (one of the American peace delegates at Paris) liberated their slaves. While thousands of slaves obtained their liberty in this era, the more typical pattern involved bestowing freedom on slaves as part of one's last will and testament. Many southern states outlawed this procedure during the nineteenth century.

A Limited Revolution

The conservative approach to the problem of slavery revealed the conservative tone of the American Revolution. Many of the *implications* of the revolutionary position — the articulation of the natural rights of humans, for example — appear radical even in modern times. But, most often, control of the Revolution remained in the hands of moderates who could accommodate the pressures of conservatives and radicals. This middle group moved cautiously, seeking to reform the worst problems of colonial society without threatening the traditional social order. In New York, for example, the secret ballot was extended only in gubernatorial elections.

Respect for the rights of property, of which slaves were considered one type, retarded the democratic tendencies of the revolutionary spirit. State governments often confiscated the property of Tories to raise revenue to finance the war. Seldom did they attempt to redistribute this wealth throughout society. Such lands were sold, not given away, and most often wealthy land speculators benefited from the procedure. Of course, much of this acreage eventually trickled down to smaller farmers, but it did so by processes separate from the War for Independence. In terms of class, the American Revolution enabled more men of lesser status to obtain public office. Radicals in Pennsylvania also managed to open suffrage and office holding to white males without regard to the ownership of property, and even the conservative Massachusetts constitution required popular approval.

But American democracy was still limited by custom and law. Although articulate women such as Abigail Adams protested the denial of political rights to women, the revolutionary leadership never seriously considered expanding full political citizenship to such "dependent" groups. The electorate still was limited to adult white males who (with the exception of Pennsylvanians) owned some property and were willing to allow their "betters" to rule. Thus, despite the ideological importance of government by consent and the widespread belief that power properly derived from the people — ideas that were truly revolutionary — political leadership generally remained in the hands of a social elite.

The economic impact of the War for Independence also reinforced long-range patterns of stratification. The disruption of commerce during the war brought economic distress to revolutionary merchants and especially to the people who depended upon the merchants for jobs. Serious wartime inflation, caused by the overissuance of paper money by the revolutionary governments, increased the problems of the urban poor by raising the cost of food. American cities, as a result, saw a significant decline in population. Among the people who departed from the cities at that time were wealthy loyalist merchants who fled to Canada and England. Their places in the social structure were filled by patriot leaders who already possessed ample wealth. Thus, the war did not alter the basis structure of American society or undermine distinctions of status; if anything, it accentuated the distance between the very rich and the very poor.

The Articles of Confederation

Until the middle of the nineteenth century, most Americans considered their state governments more important than the national government. The state constitutions, based upon republican principles, provided the first line of protection for American liberty. A fear of unguarded power also led most of the revolutionaries to oppose a strong national government. Recognizing the need for central coordination, the congress before the Articles of Confederation appointed a committee, headed by John Dickinson, to draft a plan of union (1776). Quarrels about representation and disputes over western lands delayed congressional adoption of this draft until November 1777. Congress then sent the Articles of Confederation to the states for ratification.

Although far from enthusiastic, all the states but Maryland approved the articles by 1779. Maryland refused to ratify the document until those states that claimed lands west of the Appalachians ceded that territory to the national government. In part, Maryland wished to prevent an imbalance in state power, since some states claimed territory as far west as the Pacific Ocean. Maryland politicians also wished to protect the investments of certain land speculators. Competing claims by Maryland and Virginia speculators created a political deadlock. But, after considerable delay, the growing menace of Cornwallis's army forced the states to end their quarreling. In 1781, Virginia ceded its title to the western lands to the congress. Maryland then ratified the articles, which went into effect on March 1, 1781.

For over 150 years, provincial Americans had rejected all suggestions for creating a continental union. The presence of a common enemy had compelled the colonies to cooperate during the War for Independence. Yet, Americans viewed the war less as a struggle for *national* liberation than as a bid for home rule in the thirteen separate states. Moreover, the drive for independence had been complicated by local issues and local rivalries within each colony. For this reason, revolutionary Americans emphasized the importance of drafting state constitutions and concerned themselves primarily with state politics. These attitudes found support in the widely held view that republics could only flourish in small geographic areas where the people and their representatives shared political interests. Thus, the search for political stability and home rule logically culminated in a confederation of autonomous states.

Supplementary Reading

Two good general surveys of the American Revolution are J. Alden, *A History of the American Revolution* (1969), and M. Jensen, *The Founding of a Nation* (1968). The best military history is D. Higginbotham, *The War of American Independence: Military Attitudes, Policies and Practice, 1763-1789* (1971). The problems of the British are described in I. Gruber, *The Howe Brothers and the American Revolution* (1972). Also insightful is J. Flexner, *Washington: The Indispensable Man* (1974), a condensed version of the four-volume biography of Washington.

There are numerous studies of the loyalists; see W. Nelson, *The American Tory* (1961); W. Brown, *The King's Friends* (1966); M. Norton, *The British-Americans: The Loyalist Exiles in England* (1972); and R. Calhoon, *The Loyalists in Revolutionary America, 1760-1781* (1973). Two biographies of loyalists are B. Bailyn, *The Ordeal of Thomas Hutchinson* (1974), and C. Berkin, *Jonathan Sewall: Odyssey of an American Loyalist* (1974).

For discussions of diplomacy during the war, see R. Van Alstyne, *Empire and Independence* (1965), and S. Bemis, *The Diplomacy of the American Revolution* (1935); for a treatment of the treaty negotiations, see R. Morris, *The Peacemakers* (1965). Wartime finance is discussed in E. Ferguson, *The Power of the Purse* (1961), which covers the period through 1790.

A detailed study of state government and society during the war is J. T. Main, *The Sovereign States, 1775-1783* (1973). The most sophisticated study of the relationship between political ideas and government is G. Wood, *The Creation of the American Republic* (1969). Also provocative is S. Lynd, *Intellectual Origins of American Radicalism* (1968). The "inner" revolution in politics is also examined in E. Douglass, *Rebels and Democrats* (1955), and J. T. Main, *The Upper House in Revolutionary America* (1967).

Many historians have studied the Revolution in the context of social and economic trends. The pioneering work is J. F. Jameson, *The American Revolution Considered as a Social Movement* (1926), which stresses the democratizing impact of the war. For studies that suggest the conservative nature of the changes, see J. T. Main, *The Social Structure of Revolutionary America* (1965), and R. Morris, *The American Revolution Reconsidered* (1967). For a different perspective, see the relevant chapters of J. Henretta, *The Evolution of American Society* (1973). The best treatment of the relationship between the war and slavery is W. Jordan, *White Over Black* (1968); also helpful are A. Zilversmit, *The First Emancipation* (1967), and B. Quarles, *The Negro in the American Revolution* (1961). For discussions of the Indians' role, see B. Graymont, *The Iroquois in the American Revolution* (1972), and J. O'Donnell, *Southern Indians in the American Revolution* (1973).

Chapter 9

Confederation and Constitution

1781-1789

The Articles of Confederation established a loose administrative union in which each state retained its sovereignty and independence. Fearful of government at a distance, the states delegated few powers to the national legislature and jealously guarded their local interests. According to the articles, Congress could (1) declare war and peace; (2) negotiate treaties and alliances; (3) regulate Indian affairs; (4) establish a system of coinage, weights, and measures; and (5) operate a postal service. The states retained the power to tax, which forced Congress to rely upon requisitions and the sale of bonds to finance the government. The states also continued to regulate commerce, thus impeding the creation of a uniform policy. Congress, moreover, could not coerce individual citizens or the states.

Lacking an executive or a judicial branch, power rested entirely in Congress, in which each state wielded one vote. Nine states had to approve any legislation, and amendments required a unanimous vote. To handle the business of government, Congress created several administrative departments and appointed Robert Morris to head the office of finance. Morris's ability to float foreign loans and his creative policies (which included the creation of a congressionally chartered bank) prevented the utter collapse of American credit.

The national government, like the state governments, reflected the political thinking of American revolutionaries. Believing that power and liberty rested at opposite poles, they preferred a decentralized government with a weak executive branch. Because the revolutionary leaders had matured during the colonial period, they lacked experience with national power and assumed that the state governments could provide all the services necessary for public happiness. The formation of a weak central government thus reflected a century of provincial experience and a generation of political protest.

The Western Lands

Maryland's insistence that Virginia give its western lands to the national government created a precedent whereby other states with claims to the West also surrendered their titles (Georgia, the last, did so in 1802). These grants placed the problem of the administration of western lands before Congress. Already settlers in the West clamored for a legal government. In western North Carolina, frontier people organized the state of Franklin (1784) and claimed sovereignty in the area. Despite the presence of numerous Indian tribes, political leaders assumed that the Indians should be forced to sell their lands and move further west or be killed.

To establish a uniform policy of land sales and to assure the orderly development of the West, Congress adopted the Land Ordinance of 1785, which required the western territories to be surveyed into townships six miles square. Alternate townships would be subdivided into 640-acre (one square mile) sections, and each section would be sold at public auction at a minimum price of one dollar an acre. This system, by requiring surveys before settlement, eliminated conflicting land claims. The introduction of geometrically uniform land divisions was intended primarily to facilitate land transfers. Since few farmers could afford 640-acre units, they had to buy smaller units from speculators who subdivided the land. In this way, speculation in real estate was responsible for the rectangular geography of the American West.

Besides providing for the distribution of western lands, Congress also created a system of political organization for the West. From the beginning, Congress endorsed the principle that the western territory eventually should be formed into sovereign states on an equal footing with the original thirteen. A committee, headed by Thomas Jefferson, drafted the Northwest Ordinance of 1784. The ordinance reaffirmed the equality of new states and formulated a procedure for their admission into the union. Although approved in principle, this scheme was never implemented in practice. Meanwhile, a group of land speculators formed the Ohio Company (1786) and delegated Rev. Manasseh Cutler to obtain congressional consent for a massive land purchase. Congress appeared uninterested until Cutler agreed to accept the Scioto Company, composed of congressmen and other public officials, into partnership. Together, they agreed to purchase 5 million acres of land in Ohio. Cutler, however, refused to complete the purchase until Congress provided for a legal government.

Congress responded by passing the Northwest Ordinance of 1787. This law created a precedent for the establishment of governments in the western states throughout the nineteenth century. The ordinance declared that the area north of the Ohio River should be divided into not less than three and no more than five territories. Each area would pass through three stages of political development. In the early phase, each would be administered by a governor and three judges appointed by Congress; when the adult male population reached 5,000, the citizens would elect a legislature and send a nonvoting delegate to Congress; finally, when 60,000 people inhabited a territory, it could enter the union as a state. A bill of rights protected the liberty of the settlers and prohibited slavery in the region. In adopting this system, Congress avoided the worst features of the British Empire, which had endeavored to keep colonies permanently subservient to the mother country. To be sure, territorial governors possessed the power to veto legislation and territorial delegates lacked voting rights in Congress. But, in allowing for the equality of new states, the Northwest Ordinance reflected the republican theory that power belonged in the hands of elected representatives who understood and shared the interests of their constituents. The prohibition of slavery also revealed that American political leaders, while willing to accept slavery where it existed, wanted to limit its future expansion and expected it to die out naturally.

International Relations

The formulation of a settlement policy solved only some of the problems facing the United States in the West, for, despite the provisions of the Treaty of Paris, Great Britain refused to relinquish the posts it held at Oswego, Niagara, Detroit, and other points south of Canada. By retaining these posts, Britain maintained control of the lucrative fur trade, and British intrigue with the Indians threatened the safety of American settlers. The northwestern tribes opposed further American expansion, and Britain justified its occupation of the Northwest by citing the refusal of the states to restore property confiscated from the loyalists or to reimburse English creditors for debts owed by the colonists. John Adams, the United States ambassador to Great Britain, failed to negotiate a solution to this dispute. In part, the problem derived from the inability of Congress to coerce the states and force a compliance with the Treaty of Paris [see above, p. 114]. However, it is unlikely that Congress supported reimbursement, and it is doubtful that the British would have abandoned the posts anyway. The real problem facing the United States was not the disunity of the states but the absence of military power to force the withdrawal of the British.

Similar problems with Spain confused the situation on the southern frontier as well. In Florida, both the United States and Spain claimed the area between 31° and 32°28′ according to the provisions of the treaties of 1783. More serious, the Spanish, who controlled the mouth of the Mississippi, closed the river to American commerce, thereby threatening the farmers of the Ohio Valley, who needed an inland water route to ship their products abroad. The desire of American mechants to open trade with the Spanish West Indies complicated relations between the nations.

After prolonged negotiations, Spain proposed a commercial treaty in exchange for closing the Mississippi for twenty-five years. The offer produced a heated debate between northern and southern delegates in Congress, and the proposal was rejected (1786). The failure of Congress to win trade concessions discouraged northern merchants. But the willingness of the northern states to accept the Spanish offer and thereby jeopardize expansion in the southwest infuriated frontier people (whose economic interests were threatened) and alarmed southern expansionists who realized that western development was essential to southern prosperity. Some of the westerners, influenced by Spanish bribes, began to talk about separating the Kentucky area from the United States. The movement was never very popular, however, and it collapsed in 1788 when Spain reopened the Mississippi, even though Americans still paid high duties for their goods. But southern fears about losing the West were more lasting. It was partly to protect the possibility of western development that southern expansionists such as James Madison then began talking about creating a stronger national government.

Foreign Trade

Besides the problems of diplomacy, the War for Independence affected American foreign relations by freeing the United States from the restrictions of British mercantilism. In the short run, the war seriously impaired American commerce. During the 1780s, American merchants started profitable trade arrangements with France (including the French West Indies), Holland, and East Asia. However, the loss of British bounties severely hurt producers of naval stores and indigo. British merchants also curtailed their orders for American-built ships, thereby injuring the shipbuilders of New England. Finally, independence meant the end of British naval protection on the high seas, and Mediterranean pirates began preying on American cargoes.

To a large extent, Americans preferred British products and attempted to restore the mercantile arrangements that had lapsed during the war. Although Britain rejected a commercial treaty in 1783, subsequent decisions granted Americans favorable privileges in English ports. However, British officials, still smarting from the loss of the colonies, tried to prohibit certain lines of trade while supporting the export of British goods to American markets. In 1783, the British Privy Council prohibited importation of

American meat and fish products into the West Indies and permitted other products to enter the islands only in British ships. By barring the fish and meat, the British hoped to stimulate production in Canada and Newfoundland. But these areas could not furnish adequate supplies, and Americans continued to ship products to the Caribbean in defiance of the law. Thus, a combination of West Indian necessity and American smuggling overcame the worst effects of British policy. Nevertheless, many New England merchants suffered by being excluded from the West Indian ports. Commercial treaties with Sweden (1783) and Prussia (1785) did not entirely compensate for such losses.

The War for Independence, by closing American trade with Britain, also acted as a natural tariff to stimulate American manufacturing. During the postwar period, Americans built new factories, expanded banking facilities, and founded societies to promote manufacturing. Yet, native production could not satisfy the demands of the marketplace. Americans, deprived of British commodities by the war, welcomed the influx of British manufactures after the peace. British merchants, anxious to unload surplus commodities that had accumulated after 1775, dumped large quantities of inexpensive goods on American markets, thereby satisfying American consumers but threatening domestic manufacturers. As Americans imported more than they exported (a symptom of the continued dependence of the economy), specie (hard money) was drained out of the country, and the postwar depression was aggravated.

The depression of 1784-1786 primarily affected commercial areas, although crop failures added to economic woes. Merchants and artisans suffered most from the competition of cheaper British goods. Congress dispatched John Adams to Great Britain, hoping that a commercial agreement would alleviate the problem. But Britain, riding a crest of prosperity, ignored Adams's appeals. The separate states responded by erecting protective tariffs, but, since they lacked uniformity, commerce moved to low-tariff states such as Rhode Island. Nor could Congress coerce the states to accept a standard policy. In 1781, Congress had requested authority to levy a 5 percent revenue tariff, but Rhode Island had refused its consent. A second proposal had been thwarted by New York. Yet, the depression did not touch everyone equally, and, by 1786, the economy appeared to be recovering.

Finance

An impost tariff might have provided Congress with an independent means of financial support (which explains why such nationalists as Robert Morris supported the proposal). Without this income, the government relied on land sales (which offered small returns), loans from European bankers, and requisitions from the states. During the depression, the states refused to divert money to Congress. Since most Americans expected their local governments to provide basic services, this policy seemed appropriate; few people regretted the failure of Congress to pay its bills. Many states responded to the shortage of money (caused by the depression and the imbalance of imports to exports) by issuing paper currency. In some states, this proved to be sound fiscal policy. In others, such as Rhode Island, the emission of paper money caused runaway inflation. Merchants in Rhode Island closed their shops rather than accept the paper money, and the state supreme court backed them by declaring a force act that required the acceptance of paper money to be unconstitutional.

Some states endeavored to protect debtors by enacting stay laws that prevented the foreclosure of mortgages for indefinite periods. Many creditors feared a permanent loss of their loans and complained about the effects of uncontrolled republicanism. In western Massachusetts, high taxes and a contracted currency led to frequent foreclosures. Respectable but debt-ridden farmers, led by Daniel Shays, prevented the courts from sitting (1786). The appearance of the state militia, however, quickly ended the rebellion. Although the uprising did not threaten the social order, many conservatives throughout the nation viewed the affair as a symbol of rampant democracy and yearned for a more stable government. They regretted not the impotence of *Congress* but the inability or unwillingness of the *states* to protect private property.

A National Culture

Americans had deliberately formed a loose confederation, because they feared the accumulation of power in strange hands. Since local republics were expected to protect liberty, only avowed nationalists regretted the inability of Congress to influence the state governments. In creating these republican governments, most Americans believed that they had undertaken a grand political experiment. The commitment to republicanism influenced American attitudes toward politics and power under the Articles of Confederation and provided a standard against which citizens measured the success of their government. Traditional political thought had warned against the anarchistic tendencies of democratic republics. Nevertheless, revolutionary Americans remained optimistic about their political institutions. They believed that the American people possessed special virtue and that a virtuous people could be trusted with self-government. This notion of American virtue derived from the provincial attitudes of the eighteenth century, which suggested that the provinces were "purer" than the corrupt English metropolis [see above, p. 89]. The sense of special "purity" explains not only the political ideology of the period of confederation but also the rise of American nationalism.

On the eve of the Revolution, colonial Americans remained culturally and politically divided. Few possessed the vision of Benjamin Franklin. Yet, since eighteenth-century colonials viewed themselves as Anglo-Americans, a sense of provincialism cut across colony lines and brought Americans everywhere a common standard of culture. The War for Independence, by stimulating intercolonial cooperation, strengthened these cultural bonds. In creating republican governments, citizens in all states expressed pride in the nation's political achievements. Thus, a sense of nationalism *followed* independence and reflected a self-conscious desire to transcend the historical divisions of American society.

After 1776, a variety of intellectual leaders called for the creation of a national culture to articulate the special genius of the American people. Noah Webster (later famous for his *American Dictionary of the English Language*, 1828) published a *Spelling Book* (1783) and an *American Reader* (1785) to emphasize the superiority of the American language and its unique grammatical usages. Through these immensely popular books, he attempted to instill a sense of patriotism in the American people. A group of Connecticut writers (known as the Connecticut Wits), who included John Trumbull, Timothy Dwight, and Joel Barlow, produced numerous poems that extolled American virtue and glorified the spirit of young America. Jedidiah Morse's *The American Geography* (1789) praised the uniqueness of American progress. In painting, Charles Willson Peale advocated the advancement of American art, while John Trumbull produced historical canvases depicting the great moments of the Revolution.

The self-consciousness with which Americans called for a national culture betrayed the absence of national cultural traditions. Colonial scientists had paid deference to their patrons in England and remained dependent upon European correspondents. In many cases, the War for Independence destroyed these intellectual connections, thereby retarding scientific advances within the United States. The era of the Articles of Confederation witnessed the publication of two national histories of the American Revolution by David Ramsay and William Gordon. Yet, local and state histories remained more popular. For all the emphasis on national character, revolutionary Americans continued to identify with their states and regions. The national motto, *E pluribus unum* (from many one), reflected more the wishful thinking of the nationalists than the realities of American life in 1787.

Republican Politics

While the fulfillment of American *nationalism* awaited a later age, the sense of political uniqueness remained undisputed. Believing in the virtue of the American people, republicans accepted the notion that all power derived from the people. During the war, crowds that claimed to represent the people attempted to regulate the economy by preventing wartime profiteering. Shays' Rebellion in western Massachusetts [see above, p. 126] constituted a logical outgrowth of the idea that the people should protect themselves from unrepresentative legislatures. Residence requirements forced the delegates to share some of the interests of their constituencies, while popular conventions informed the representatives of the will of the

"George Washington" by Charles Willson Peale. Such portraits transformed the nation's first president into the "father" of his country, a political symbol that fulfilled the traditional expectation that political leaders should be patriarchal figures. (Courtesy of New York Historical Society, New York City.)

people. Nevertheless, during the 1780s, some republicans began to fear that the state legislatures no longer represented the people on such issues as the enactment of stay laws or the levying of taxes. Meanwhile, conservatives protested the dependence of the legislatures on popular opinion and worried that the representatives would attack the rights of property. This widespread suspicion of the state legislatures permeated American society by the mid-1780s.

Because of their local orientation, Americans evaluated their society from the perspective of the *state* governments. In declaring independence, the revolutionary generation hoped to create a more stable political system. Thus, people in those states that had achieved a semblance of order remained satisfied under the Articles of Confederation. In many areas, however, state governments failed to provide the political security that people desired. In Georgia, for example, farmers distrusted the Indians on the southern frontier and recognized the military expediency of a stronger union. Bostonians, suffering from a decline in business and shaken by the Shays affair, similarly appreciated the possible advantages of more centralized government. The social and economic problems in the states aggravated a sense of frustration at the political failures of republicanism. People in all groups lost faith in the state legislatures and increasingly viewed the reform of the national government as the best way to preserve the republican experiment.

These frustrated republicans, motivated primarily by a desire for political stability in the states, joined a group of self-conscious nationalists to propose a restructuring of the Articles of Confederation. As early as 1781, such ardent nationalists as Robert Morris and Alexander Hamilton had advocated the strengthening of the national government to assure the independence of the United States. However, the failure of the proposed tariff and the signing of the treaty of peace weakened their position. For a time, a few committed nationalists considered using a coalition of public creditors and the power of the army to force Congress to accept a political reorganization. But George Washington exerted his prestige with the army to squash the effort. During the period of Confederation, the nationalists won increasing support throughout the states. Their success revealed the growing disillusionment with the structure of state power.

The Philadelphia Convention

Since Congress lacked the power to regulate interstate commerce, disputes among the states were resolved by negotiation. In 1785, delegates from Virginia and Maryland met at Alexandria to consider improving navigation on the Potomac River. They recommended a conference of all the states to examine the broader problem of commerce in the United States. The resulting Annapolis Conference (1786) proved disappointing. Only five states sent delegates, too few to propose specific revisions of the articles. Nevertheless, the conference endorsed a proposal by Alexander

Hamilton to summon another delegation to Philadelphia to discuss amending the national government. In February 1787, Congress sanctioned the meeting, and, in May, delegates from all the states but Rhode Island converged on Philadelphia.

The delegates were relatively young (their average age was forty-two), and they were sympathetic to the strengthening of the national government. Leading state politicians such as Patrick Henry were satisfied with the Confederation and refused to serve as delegates. Generally men of wealth, the representatives reflected the persistent belief that politics belonged in the hands of the "better" sort. They chose George Washington, the first national hero, to preside over the sessions.

In principle, the delegates agreed on the importance of preserving the republican experiment by protecting the people from arbitrary government while at the same time protecting government from the caprice of the people. Thus, they accepted the idea of balancing power to prevent one segment of society from acquiring unrestricted control of government. Power would be divided between the states and the central government. No single branch of government could become all-powerful. Early in the convention, the delegates abandoned the idea of revising the Articles of Confederation and chose instead to create a centralized government. They disagreed, however, about the structure of government and the division of political power.

The delegates from Virginia, led by James Madison, presented a plan that granted wide powers to the national government. The Virginia Plan proposed (1) the creation of a bicameral legislature with membership based on population (which appealed to the larger states); (2) the election of the upper house by the lower house; (3) voting in the legislature by individuals, not by states; and (4) the establishment of an executive and a judicial system whose officials would be chosen by the legislature. But the smaller states supported the New Jersey (or Paterson) Plan, which recommended a single legislative unit in which each state possessed one vote and separately chosen executive and judicial branches. The resulting debate ultimately produced the Great Compromise, which provided that (1) membership in the House of Representatives should be proportional to population, (2) each state would have two delegates in the upper house (or Senate), who would vote as individuals, and (3) revenue bills would originate in the lower house.

The resolution of this controversy opened a new debate between the northern and southern states over the apportionment of the slave population. In the Three-fifths Compromise, the delegates agreed that five slaves would be counted as three freemen for the purpose of taxation and representation. Fearful of destroying the Convention, the delegates avoided discussing slavery itself.

The convention avoided the problem of the slave trade by denying Congress the power to interfere with the trade before 1808. To alleviate the fears of commercial farmers (particularly southerners), the delegates prohibited the enactment of export taxes. By September 1787, the convention had completed its work and the United States Constitution had been written.

The Constitution provided for a bicameral legislature, a strong executive branch, and an independent judiciary. The Constitution authorized Congress to levy taxes, to regulate foreign and interstate commerce, to coin or borrow money, to maintain an army and a navy, to declare war, to create a post office, and to pass any laws necessary to exercise these delegated powers. The structure of Congress reflected the political frustrations of the era of Confederation. Based on the idea that power derived from the people, the Constitution authorized the states to establish voting qualifications for the election of delegates to the House of Representatives. Yet, to protect the representatives from the whims of popular politics, senators were to be chosen by the state legislatures and would serve six-year terms of office. The Constitution required the Senate's approval of all executive appointments and foreign treaties. In theory, the Senate was to represent not only the states but also the most stable (aristocratic) segments of society.

The idea of balancing the power of the democracy (as represented in the lower house) and the power of the aristocracy (in the Senate) led the founding fathers to create a strong, independent executive. The president was to be elected indirectly by an electoral college, thus freeing the executive from dependence on either Congress or the people. The framers of the Constitution hoped that such a system would enable the president to rise above the influence of interest groups and avoid the entanglements of faction. The Constitution granted the president powers to execute the laws of the land, to make foreign treaties, to serve as commander-in-chief of the army, to appoint judges and other public officials, and to veto congressional legislation (vetoes could be overridden only with a two-thirds vote of each house). In departing from the revolutionary tradition of weak executives, the Constitution reflected an underlying distrust of the representatives of the people. Moreover, since the framers of the Constitution expected the prestigious Washington to serve as chief executive, they were more willing to expand presidential powers.

The Constitution also provided for a judicial system consisting of a Supreme Court and such lower courts as Congress might wish to create. Judges were appointed for life (as long as they remained on their good behavior), thus freeing them from executive and legislative interference. The federal courts were granted jurisdiction in matters related to the Constitution, national laws, and treaties, and they heard cases involving the states or citizens of more than one state. The Constitution did not explicitly establish the right of judicial review (whereby the courts could nullify a law for being unconstitutional), but, in subsequent years, federal judges assumed that power.

Finally, the Constitution provided for amendment procedures that could be initiated either by Congress or by popular conventions of two-thirds of the states. To be ratified, amendments required the consent of three-quarters of the states acting through either the legislatures or special conventions. This procedure endeavored to protect the people from representatives who ignored their will.

Aside from balancing power, the Constitution delegated certain powers to the national government and reserved all other powers for the states. Thus, in the lives of average citizens, the state governments continued to be more important than the central authority. Yet, the national government derived not simply from the sovereign states but also from the people at large. A system of dual citizenship emerged and enabled the national government to exercise power directly on the people by levying taxes and by compelling the enforcement of congressional legislation. In time, this power became more actual than potential and facilitated the development of a strong national government.

The Ratification of the Constitution

The delegates at Philadelphia believed that the people constituted the ultimate source of authority and provided for the ratification of the Constitution by special state conventions. Ignoring the clause that insisted that all states had to approve amendments to the Articles of Confederation, the convention declared that the Constitution would become effective upon ratification by nine states. The transmission of the document to the states opened an intense debate between the supporters of the Constitution (known as Federalists) and its opponents (known as Anti-Federalists).

The debate over the ratification of the Constitution reflected both the political tensions of the era and the ideological considerations of republicanism. State politics usually determined the composition of the rival political movements. Politicians who had disagreed about taxes and finance in the state legislatures then disagreed again about the Constitution. Often, there was a direct continuity between the legislative voting blocs of the period of Confederation and the political alignments during the debate over ratification. In general, the Federalists articulated an ideology that stressed the importance of protecting the rights of property from the onslaughts of the popularly controlled legislatures. During the 1780s, these politicians had opposed stay laws, supported high salaries for government officials, and urged the restoration of the political rights of loyalists. Criticizing the democratic tendencies of revolutionary politics, the Federalists called for the restoration of an aristocracy of talent to control political power. The Anti-Federalists, on the other hand, wished to preserve the status quo and claimed to represent the people against the expansion of aristocratic power. Earlier, they had favored paper money, low land prices, and a reduction of government costs, as well as the confiscation of loyalists' property.

The Anti-Federalists were state-centered men whose primary loyalty remained with state governments. Their opposition to the Constitution reflected a fear of central authority and strong government. Anti-Federalists also protested the absence of protection for civil liberties. Such criticism later led to the adoption of the first ten amendments to the Constitution [see below, p. 153]. The Anti-Federalists often were men who had had acquired power in the states as a result of the Revolution. As members of the local in-group, the Anti-Federalists would suffer the most by a transfer of power to the national government. The Anti-Federalists appealed primarily to people *without* interstate interests, men who owned small farms and engaged in subsistence agriculture. They were often regionally isolated and cared little for the affairs of other areas.

The Federalists, by contrast, won the support of commercial farmers, merchants, urban workers, and public creditors. Men from these groups shared *national* concerns and suffered most from the lack of a strong central authority. Many of the Federalists constituted an out-group in state politics that resented the power of entrenched politicians. While representing a conservative elite concerned with protecting private property, the Federalists nevertheless found a large following among urban workers. Such support reflected either common economic interests, shared ideological perspectives, or the subtle forms of influence wielded by local political leaders.

Throughout the debate, the Federalists and the Anti-Federalists shared certain assumptions about politics and power. Both feared the accumulation of power, and both recognized the importance of balancing power to protect the interests of all people. Neither group claimed to be truly democratic, and both expected the masses to pay deference to their political superiors.

In accepting republicanism, however, they disagreed about the best means of balancing liberty and authority. The Anti-Federalists believed that legislative institutions should be miniature reproductions of society at large. Such a system, they argued, could be created only in *small* geographical regions, where the number of delegates permitted the representation of all interest groups. Jealous of power, they wished to keep sovereignty close to home, where all citizens could watch its workings. This commitment to state republicanism coincided with the Anti-Federalists' retention of local power. They articulated this ideology, because it seemed to explain and justify what they had been doing in state politics in the decade after independence.

The Federalists responded to this position by arguing that republicanism could flourish best in *large* heterogeneous (or pluralistic) states. In the *Federalist Papers,* a series of essays written by Alexander Hamilton, John Jay, and James Madison, the authors suggested that the existence of a large pluralistic society would prevent any *single* group from acquiring absolute power because of the difficulty of forging a numerical majority. The pluralism of the American people, they maintained, would protect republicanism from the encroachments of power. This ideological position also reinforced the social and political experiences of the Federalists, many of whom had acted in national affairs during the Revolution.

In 1787, Delaware became the first state to ratify the Constitution. Other states followed soon after. The major battle over ratification occurred in New York, where the Federalists — led by Hamilton — confronted the numerically superior Anti-Federalists at the ratifying convention. After considerable political maneuvering, the convention approved the Constitution by a narrow vote (thirty to twenty-seven), thus paving the way for the creation of a new national government. Rhode Island became the last state to ratify the Constitution in May 1790.

Although a majority of citizens probably had been satisfied with the government under the Articles of Confederation, the nationalists possessed certain advantages that enabled them to overcome Anti-Federalist resistance. First, the Federalists offered a specific program for reorganizing the national government, thereby seizing the initiative and leaving the Anti-Federalists to defend the existing system. Many supporters of state sovereignty had recognized the problems of the Articles of Confederation but, after the defeat of the New Jersey Plan at Philadelphia, had no concrete proposal to bring to the voters. Second, the Federalists proliferated near urban centers that were close to lines of interstate communication. Therefore, it was relatively easy for the Federalists to create an interstate organization, while the Anti-Federalists, as locally oriented politicians, lacked adequate connections with like-minded people in other states. Third, the Anti-Federalists represented people who were generally satisfied with the Confederation and thus relatively indifferent to political debates. Only a small percentage of eligible voters participated in the selection of delegates to many of the ratifying conventions.

More significant than the defeat of the Anti-Federalists was the rapidity with which Americans came to accept the validity of the new government. Like the framers of the Constitution, most Americans remained suspicious of the "excesses" of liberty and accepted the idea of rule by the elite. Thus, if the Constitution appeared undemocratic, so too was American society in 1789. Moreover, Americans evidently recognized that the Constitution, for all its *implications* concerning national power, changed very little. Powers not expressly granted to Congress remained with the states, and people continued to emphasize the power of state and local governments. Voting participation remained higher in state elections than in national contests, most taxes were paid to state governments, and citizens went about their business as usual. In the long run, the Constitution enabled the national government to acquire vast power. But most people, living in the short run, simply hoped that the Constitution would at last bring political stability to the nation.

Supplementary Reading

The nineteenth-century view of the 1780s, which emphasized the problems of decentralization, is elucidated in J. Fiske, *The Critical Period of American History* (1880). M. Jensen, *The New Nation* (1950), stresses the viability of government under the Articles of Confederation. For a cogent analysis of congressional issues, see H. J. Henderson's essay in S. Kurtz and J. Hutson, editors, *Essays on the American Revolution* (1973), or his fuller study, *Party*

Politics in the Continental Congress (1974). Also insightful is D. Robinson, *Slavery in the Structure of American Politics: 1765-1820* (1971).

The best study of state politics is J. T. Main, *Political Parties before the Constitution* (1973). Also helpful is F. McDonald, *E Pluribus Unum* (1965). The ideological questions are analyzed in G. Wood, *The Creation of the American Republic* (1969). For a study of finance, see E. Ferguson, *The Power of the Purse* (1961).

A lively account of the Philadelphia convention is C. Rossiter, *1787: The Grand Convention* (1966). Much can be learned of the politics of the period from I. Brant's *James Madison: Father of the Constitution* (1950). More controversial is C. Beard, *An Economic Interpretation of the Constitution* (1913), which has been answered by R. Brown, *Charles Beard and the Constitution* (1956), and F. McDonald, *We the People* (1958). For the debate over ratification, see J. T. Main, *The Antifederalists* (1961). An outstanding state study that spans this era is A. Young, *The Democratic Republicans of New York: The Origins, 1763-1799* (1967).

Chapter 10

An Expanding Society

1789-1819

The history of the United States government begins in 1789. In that year, the American people elected their first congressional representatives, and George Washington took the oath of office as the nation's first president. Yet, 1789 is only a *political* date; it marks a shift in national power arrangements and denotes the beginning of new political institutions. Most Americans remained indifferent to national politics and continued to pursue their accustomed ways of life. During the early years of the nation's history, national power seldom impinged directly on the lives of ordinary citizens. People reacted first to social pressures and then to politics. Thus, the political history of the period needs to be seen in the context of the American social order.

The decades after 1790 witnessed the steady expansion of the American economy. These economic changes profoundly affected social arrangements throughout the country. Many people welcomed the changes as a sign of progress and a confirmation of American virtue. Others regretted the loss of a traditional social structure and complained of moral deterioration. This dialogue, a product of social and economic developments, influenced the political activity of the American people in the states and in the nation.

A Mobile People

In 1790, the American population numbered 4 million; by 1815, it had reached nearly 9 million. During this period, wars in Europe reduced immigration to a total of about 250,000 people. Thus, the remarkable growth of population resulted largely from natural increase. The United States remained a nation of farmers, and the perennial shortage of agricultural labor encouraged large families. By 1800, it was not uncommon for a family to have seven or eight children. The rapid growth of population placed great strains on the traditional social institutions. Overcrowding in older areas meant that parents could no longer provide for all their children, and young people began moving to new regions in search of economic opportunities.

Population pressure combined with soil exhaustion to stimulate migration into the western territories. New England farmers, facing a depletion of natural resources, moved westward into Vermont and western New York. People from the middle-Atlantic states pressed into the eastern portions of the Ohio Valley. Southern planters, having exhausted the fertility of the soil with repeated crops of tobacco, flocked to the fertile acres of Kentucky and Tennessee. The availability of land on easy credit and at moderate prices (even when purchased from land speculators) served to lure people from their native states. Experienced as farmers in the East, the settlers remained farmers in the West, often settling on soil that was similar to their old lands and trying to cultivate crops that they had grown in the East.

In moving into the western territories, American farmers brought with them a world view that saw the land as a commodity to be purchased, improved, and later resold. This attitude toward the land differed greatly from the views of the Indian peoples who inhabited the West. While white Americans emphasized the economic value of the land, Indians saw the land as a sacred home in which humans and other forms of natural life interacted harmoniously. The Indian's spiritual ideas convinced white Americans that the Indians were a childish race that had to be "uplifted" by the superior American society. In seeking to "civilize" the Indians and convert them to Christianity, the American government worked with private missionaries to subvert the traditional Indian cultures. Traders introduced the products of American technology, which increased the natives' economic dependence on white society. Indiscriminate sale of alcohol further disrupted the Indians' traditional cultures. And many died from the epidemic diseases introduced by the whites.

When these subtle forms of aggression failed to destroy the Indian tribes, Americans turned to armed warfare to remove the native inhabitants from the lands they coveted in the West. In the Northwest Territory, American encroachment on Indian lands had alarmed the natives. In defense of their traditional lands and their way of life, the Indians attacked advancing settlers and defeated two military expeditions sent to remove them (1790, 1791). But an American army under the command of "Mad"

Anthony Wayne decisively routed the Indian warriors at the Battle of Fallen Timbers (1794). With the Treaty of Fort Greenville (1795), Wayne compelled the Indians to surrender large areas of southern Ohio and Indiana to the United States. After 1800, equally coercive land treaties negotiated by William Henry Harrison, governor of the Indiana Territory, infuriated the Indians. Led by the Shawnee chief Tecumseh and his brother the Prophet, the tribes of the Northwest formed a confederation pledged to keep their lands. Violation of this compact by certain tribes and Harrison's insistent campaign to remove the Indians provoked open warfare. The Battle of Tippecanoe (November 1811) proved indecisive, but later confrontations (which were related to the War of 1812) continued until the Battle of the Thames (October 1813) resulted in the death of Tecumseh and his confederation. The Indians who survived these battles became victims of the white traders who continued to undermine the Indians' traditional life-styles. The northwestern tribes also were forced to surrender their lands and moved to other reserved areas. But even these agreements could not protect them from later waves of settlers.

In the Southwest, the Creek Indians also defended their homelands from American settlers and, in 1813, commenced open warfare. Andrew Jackson led an expedition against the Indians and, after a number of extremely bloody battles, defeated them at the Battle of Horse Shoe Bend (1814). With the Treaty of Fort Jackson, the American general forced the Creeks to relinquish their best lands to the United States. But even these concessions did not satisfy southern farmers who wanted the removal of all Indians to areas west of the Mississippi River [see below, pp. 194-195].

In political terms, the geographical expansion of the period led to the admission of new states into the union: Kentucky (1792), Tennessee (1796), Ohio (1803), Louisiana (1812), Indiana (1816), Mississippi (1817), Illinois (1818), and Alabama (1819). The order of admission reveals the thrust of migration. By 1820, over 2 million Americans inhabited the Mississippi Valley. In social terms, the availability of western lands offered wide opportunities for the first settlers. Many frontier people bought choice lands and watched their investments grow in value as later settlers moved westward. Within a relatively short time, the social structure of the western states became as differentiated and as stratified as that of the eastern regions. Later and poorer settlers often resented the entrenched western elites, and their hostility spilled over into state politics. Equally important, the reduced sense of opportunity led many people to pull up stakes again and head further west.

Not all easterners moved westward in search of economic opportunity. Instead, a small proportion headed for cities such as Philadelphia and New York, hoping for success as artisans and merchants. Between 1790 and 1820, Philadelphia's population grew from 40,000 to 110,000 and New York's quadrupled from 30,000 to 120,000. To be sure, in 1820, less than 10 percent of the population lived in urban centers. Yet, the pronounced trend of urbanization reflected the growing opportunities of an increasingly diversified economy. Skilled and semiskilled artisans found moderate

Tecumseh (1768-1813), a Shawnee chief, led American Indian opposition to the American invasion of the Old Northwest Territory. In 1811, Tecumseh organized a tribal confederation to stop white aggression, but the outbreak of the War of 1812 blocked his efforts. He was killed in the Battle of the Thames. (Courtesy of Library of Congress.)

wealth in the cities at this time and formed a middle class beneath the wealthy merchants. The expansion of commerce also created a large class of dependent wage earners who owned little property. Even in times of relative prosperity, the almshouses of New York remained crowded with unemployed laborers.

Commerce and Transportation

The expansion of the American population into the western states and the eastern cities represented part of a larger expansion of the American economy that began in the decades after the War for Independence. Although the wars in Europe often interfered with American foreign trade [see below, pp. 171-172], many merchants accumulated large profits. Moreover, domestic commerce thrived as eastern merchants transacted more business with western farmers. The profits acquired from such mercantile activity provided the capital for other types of economic investments.

Because of the poor condition of American roads, most commerce followed available water routes. In the West, the Mississippi River system provided a convenient, but expensive, channel for the exportation of western products to the east coast. Aside from the high costs of transportation (which, in part, explain an economic depression in the West on the eve of the War of 1812), the process was extremely slow and unreliable. And eastern commodities could not be shipped upstream conveniently. To facilitate transportation, private investors formed joint-stock companies and began constructing roads and bridges capable of handling the traffic of heavy wagons. By the War of 1812, an extensive network of turnpikes (toll roads) connected the major towns and cities of the Northeast. The national government also sponsored interstate roadways, the most extensive of which was the National or Cumberland Road, which connected Cumberland, Maryland, with Wheeling, West Virginia, on the Ohio River (1811-1818). Technological improvements in bridge design also enabled the construction of spans to replace cumbersome and erratic ferry service.

These improvements in land travel facilitated the transportation of bulky commodities to the newly settled areas of the West. Overland travel, nevertheless, remained fairly expensive, and improved water transportation was highly desirable. During the 1780s, John Fitch of Pennsylvania experimented with a steamboat and established a regular ferry service (1790). Lacking financial support, however, he could not sustain his operations profitably. After several technological improvements in steam boilers, Robert Fulton launched the *Clermont* (1807) and acquired monopoly rights on New York waters. Other inventors soon repeated his success, and, by 1820, steamboats sailed on every major river east of the Mississippi. Although steamboat transportation did not reach its peak until later in the century, its impact on American commerce was apparent by 1820.

Besides increasing the volume of trade between the East and the West, the steamboat brought a dramatic drop in prices in the interior. Reduced costs stimulated increased sales in the West, supporting eastern manufacturers. Another facet of improved water transportation — the artificial canal — remained in its infancy during this period, although people were already planning such waterways as the Erie Canal [see below, p. 196].

Manufacturing

The growth of the population and the improvements in transportation encouraged the growth of American manufacturing by opening new markets, but most manufacturing remained in the hands of self-employed artisans and their apprentices who produced goods for a local market. Because of the shortage of labor and the difficulty of gathering industrial workers, manufacturers often let out raw materials to home craftsmen who performed piecework. The manufacturers then collected the finished products for distribution to consumers. To reduce costs, manufacturers placed greater emphasis on the quantity than the quality of production, and work tasks were divided to increase specialization.

The attempt to streamline production appeared most clearly in the growth of factories. During the eighteenth century, the mechanization of textile manufacturing in England had demonstrated the advantages of machine production. American manufacturers wanted to establish similar factories. But England attempted to maintain a monopoly on textile machinery by prohibiting its export. Efforts to duplicate English factories in America proved unsuccessful until 1789, when Samuel Slater, an English mechanic, memorized the plans of the complicated machines and fled to Rhode Island. Financed by the merchant Moses Brown, Slater reconstructed the necessary machinery and began the first profitable factory in the United States (1790). Factory-made cotton proved remarkably successful, and, by 1815, over 200 mills were operating in the United States. Although profits from manufacturing swiftly exceeded the returns from commercial investments, it is significant that the early factories were financed initially by capital accumulated in commerce. Since factory production coexisted with traditional hand labor, few skilled craftsmen became factory workers. Factory owners preferred to employ the cheaper labor of women and children to operate the machinery. Although child labor was not unknown at this time, the employment of whole families in textile factories suggests the growing impoverishment of northern industrial workers.

The Southern Reaction

The rise of textile factories created an increased demand for raw cotton. American cotton producers, however, lacked an efficient means of removing the oily seeds from the type of cotton grown in the United States. Thus, textile manufacturers in England and the Northeast imported most of their cotton from Egypt and India. Then, in 1793, Eli Whitney perfected the cotton gin, which facilitated the extraction of the seeds from the cotton fibers, and thereby transformed the southern economy. Cotton production soared from 10,000 bales in 1793 to nearly 100,000 in 1800 and exceeded 250,000 bales by 1816. As cotton became king, southern planters assiduously cultivated the crop, moving into the fertile "black belt" of Alabama and Mississippi. Land values rose and even inefficient growers made large profits.

The proliferation of cotton production in the South bolstered the economy of the nation as a whole. While most of the cotton was exported to Europe from such southern ports as New Orleans and Charleston, northern merchants controlled a large portion of the trade. Aside from accruing large profits from the carrying trade, northern merchants also imported European manufactured goods for sale throughout the nation. The development of a plantation economy also made the South dependent on the North for manufactured goods. Thus, southern profits often were absorbed by northern merchants and manufacturers.

The expansion of cotton production also served to reinvigorate black slavery in the South. Although it is doubtful that slavery was dying out in the late eighteenth century, the cotton boom did raise the value of slave labor. As the price of black slaves increased in the decade after Whitney's invention, planters began importing them from abroad, first in violation of state laws and after 1804 with the legal approval of the South Carolina legislature. Between 1790 and 1808 (when Congress voted to prohibit the foreign slave trade as it was allowed to do under the Constitution), over 100,000 slaves entered the United States, more than in any previous twenty-year period. Since planters heading West usually took their slaves with them, the center of the black population also shifted from the seaboard states toward the southwestern frontier.

The renewed economic interest in slavery coincided with a decline of liberal sentiment regarding the emancipation of slaves. In the years after the Declaration of Independence, the number of voluntary manumissions increased throughout the South. In 1810, over 100,000 free blacks resided in the southern states. Although restricted by discriminatory legislation, the free black population managed to create and support independent cultural institutions, such as churches and schools. Racism among white workers limited black employment opportunities, but the general shortage of labor in the nation enabled some blacks to initiate successful businesses. Free blacks recognized important differences in status within the black community and emphasized their distinction from slaves. Yet, free blacks actively supported fugitive slaves, worked to eliminate the institution (which was "peculiar" to the South), and served as important symbols of freedom for less-favored blacks.

The presence of large numbers of free blacks, particularly in southern cities, alarmed many whites who had never abandoned their racial prejudices. News of the atrocities that followed a successful slave revolt in Santo Domingo (1793) horrified Americans everywhere. Many southern states, fearing internal subversion, attempted to quarantine their own slaves from recently imported West Indian slaves and free West Indian blacks. Meanwhile, white refugees from Santo Domingo were received by sympathetic Americans throughout the country. Fears of a domestic insurrection found support in the discovery of a slave conspiracy near Richmond, Virginia, led by Gabriel Prosser (1800). Virginians quickly eliminated the threat by executing thirty or forty suspected plotters.

Fear of a slave revolt, frustration with a small but vocal antislavery movement composed largely of Quakers and free blacks, and the shifts in southern agriculture created a rigid reaction to slavery in the South. After 1800, slave codes were tightened to restrict the social and economic activities of black slaves and establish stringent requirements for private manumissions. Moreover, in response to the growing number of free blacks, the southern states enacted discriminatory legislation restricting the liberty of the free black population. Similar laws often appeared in northern states — an indication that racial prejudice was more than a sectional problem. More subtle but no less obvious than the legal restraints was the economic discrimination that placed black people at the bottom of the social structure throughout the nation.

Government and Business

The expansion of the American economy, particularly in the area of transportation, found active support from all levels of government. As in the colonial period, few Americans believed in laissez-faire and instead expected government to assist private business in bringing the benefits of technology to all people. The absence of large accumulations of investment capital made such assistance especially important during this period. Moreover, by participating in the economy, the state and local governments could regulate business activity in the interest of the community. Thus, the states chartered joint-stock companies to build particular roads or bridges and permitted the investors to collect tolls to pay for their investments. Such corporate charters established minimum standards for each project and provided for a specific scale of tolls. Since these undertakings often required more capital investment than private enterprise could provide, the companies depended on the sale of stock to the local and state governments that benefited from the public utilities.

The creation of chartered corporations by the state governments also supported the accumulation of capital by facilitating the sale of stock. Each corporate charter required a specific act of the legislature so the governments were able to regulate corporate development. Frequent application for such charters by business groups led some states (New York and Massachusetts, for example) to enact general laws of incorporation, which permitted the creation of some corporations without specific legislation. Most states, however, remained cautious about incorporation and were reluctant to free individual investors from liability in case of corporate failures. Not until the 1830s did the American people accept incorporation as a right for all business people.

State regulation of economic activity also appeared in the field of banking. During the early national period, the American banking system consisted of a national bank chartered by Congress (the charter expired in 1811)[see below, pp. 153-154] and private banks chartered by the state legislatures. In theory, the banks sold stocks to investors and loaned the capital at interest to individual businesses. Yet, banking became even more profitable when bankers loaned *more* than the fixed investment capital through the issuance of bank notes (a form of paper money), which circulated safely as long as people maintained confidence in the issuing bank. Thus, the banks controlled the amount of available capital by issuing or recalling their notes. After the War of 1812, numerous state banks were chartered, thus increasing the amount of investment resources and stimulating the expanding economy. An abrupt contraction of credit, however, created the Panic of 1819, a severe economic depression.

The small scale of American factories minimized the importance of government assistance to manufacturing, and capitalization came entirely from private investments. Nevertheless, the states granted land, water rights, and in some cases, tax exemptions to manufacturing companies. In labor disputes, the judicial system favored business interests over those of workers. Although numerous craft unions existed, strikes were considered illegal conspiracies in restraint of trade. Wage cuts and extended hours were common occurrences in times of economic stagnation.

The national government limited its interference in business to the establishment of protective tariffs, the creation of the Bank of the United States, and the regulation of interstate steamboat traffic. In several important decisions, the Supreme Court, under the influence of Chief Justice John Marshall, attempted to protect private business from the interference of state legislatures by interpreting strictly the rights of contracts. Thus, in *Dartmouth College* v. *Woodward* (1819), Marshall ruled that corporation charters were contracts that could not be rescinded or impaired by the states. By protecting the rights of corporate investors, this decision encouraged capital investment at a time of capital scarcity, thus supporting economic expansion. The relative absence of national government regulation of the economy reflects not so much a belief in laissez-faire as a recognition that the state and local governments adequately supervised economic activity. These economic attitudes thereby reinforced the essential localism of American society at the time.

Ideological Responses

Although the economic changes of the early national period constituted but an early stage of a larger transformation of the nation's economy, contemporary Americans did recognize some of the social implications of these trends. The response to these alterations varied considerably from region to region and class to class. People interpreted the changes from different ideological perspectives and attempted to blend their viewpoints with their interests. These clashing ideological responses affected the political alignments in the states and ultimately shaped the positions of the first political parties.

Eighteenth-century Americans (like most of their contemporaries in others parts of the world) believed in the natural harmony of the universe. Whether these ideas derived from natural laws or a belief in God's goodness, most Americans assumed that orderliness and organic unity were natural states and that disorder stemmed from individual perversity. But, while agreeing in the abstract that an orderly society was desirable, people disagreed about the structure of that order in the concrete world of human affairs. The economic and social changes of the late eighteenth century brought these dilemmas to the forefront and compelled the generation of the founding fathers to reassess their society.

Traditionally, the American social order was based on a balance of status groups, in which the social and economic elites dominated the political institutions. The wealthiest men in the community were deemed the natural leaders of society and received proper deference from their inferiors. Such a vision of society was static and unchanging; it left little room for individualism, equality, or rapid social mobility.

In the face of economic and social change, many conservatives retained a belief in an organic community controlled by natural elites. They criticized the westward migrations as socially disruptive and questioned the leveling tendencies of social mobility. To explain the chaos that seemed to beset them, conservatives blamed the anarchistic democracy that had been unleashed by the War for Independence. Believing that masses of people lacked the virtue necessary to wield political power, these conservatives opposed the idea of majority rule and preferred that government be in the hands of an aristocracy. They acknowledged that a republican form of government was necessary to preserve liberty but nevertheless insisted that government had to be stable enough to protect the rights of property as well.

The complexity of state and local politics in this period makes it difficult to generalize about the political ramifications of this conservative ideology. It appears, however, that in many areas these ideas appealed to people who had benefited *least* from the social and economic changes of the period. Unable or unwilling to participate in the changing order, the conservatives looked back to a more peaceful age when social relations seemed more harmonious and orderly. The conservative ideas also attracted some people who felt socially or politically displaced by a new ruling elite. But commitment to a conservative ideology was not confined to a frustrated aristocracy. Many people of lesser status shared the elitist ideals of the conservatives and maintained their allegiance to their older leaders. Moreover, it was often in their own interest that lower-class people supported the political preferences of their employers. Thus, the conservative ideas appealed to people from all areas and in all status groups, although not always for the same reasons.

Many Americans, unlike the conservatives, viewed the social and economic changes as progressive improvements in the social order. Critical of rigid class distinctions, these proponents of social change believed that economic mobility reinforced the political principles of republicanism by offering liberty and property to all. Yet, these advocates of change did not repudiate the importance of social order; they simply denied that economic change was weakening the social fabric. Instead, they claimed that traditional class distinctions represented an artifical, manmade order. They wished to replace this artificial order with a society based on natural or cosmic order. As individuals freed themselves from traditional social restraints, they moved closer to the harmony and order of the universe. Thus, individual mobility and political democracy were made compatible with order and stability. The ideology of change, like the ideas articulated by conservative Americans, seems to have appealed to people in a variety of circumstances. In the North, people on the move — geographically and socially — seemed to have embraced the tenets of individual achievement. In other areas, people endorsed these ideas because they seemed to reinforce earlier commitments to republican liberty and political equality.

State Politics

During the 1790s, ideological differences combined with conflicts of interest to shape the political alliances in the states. Despite the creation of a central government in 1789, people still responded primarily to state and local issues. As in the colonial period, factionalism appeared in all regions, and political out-groups attempted to supplant their opponents in power. To achieve their political goals, state politicians gradually transformed the loosely knit political factions into vigorous political organizations capable of appealing to a popular electorate. In many cases, national political questions, particularly those dealing with international relations, served as catalysts that hastened the development of efficient political parties. For example, in New York, the Clintonian faction (which centered around Governor George Clinton) swiftly became the Republican party in response to President Washington's pro-British foreign policy [see below, pp. 157-158].

The importance of national questions, however, should not obscure the state orientation of American politics. Because of a variety of ideological, social, and political pressures (often related to the changing nature of American society), people were predisposed to support certain political positions. These pressures remained overwhelmingly regional and local. In New York City, for example, a well-publicized legal dispute involving two Irish laborers apparently led thousands of workers to desert the Federalist party because of its professed elitism. During the 1790s, it was the exist-

Governor George Clinton (1739-1812) was the shrewd political leader of New York during the revolutionary era (1777-1795). Typical of his age, Clinton developed a strong personal following that enabled him to dominate state politics. (Courtesy of Library of Congress.)

ence of these well-developed political groups that enabled such politicians as Alexander Hamilton and Thomas Jefferson to build the first national party system in the United States. Such national structures were superimposed on the bedrock of political, social, and economic rivalry in the separate states.

Supplementary Reading

The best synthesis of American social expansion is R. Berthoff, *An Unsettled People* (1971). For a survey of westward expansion, see F. Philbrick, *The Rise of the West, 1754-1830*

(1965), and M. Rohrbough, *The Land Office Business* (1968). For a discussion of the American provocation of and conflict with, the Indians, see the relevant chapter of W. Washburn, *The Indian in America* (1975); see also B. Sheehan, *Seeds of Extinction: Jeffersonian Philanthropy and the American Indian* (1973), and M. Rogin, *Fathers and Children: Andrew Jackson and the Subjugation of the American Indian* (1975).

Economic development is examined in D. North, *The Economic Growth of the United States* (1961), and T. Cochran and W. Miller, *The Age of Enterprise* (1942). For a discussion of improvements in transportation, see P. Jordan, *The National Road* (1948); and G. Dangerfield, *Robert R. Livingston of New York* (1960), which discusses the steamboat. For a lucid illustrated study of early technology, see E. Sloane, *Diary of an Early American Boy: Noah Blake, 1805* (1965). The relationship between business and state government is analyzed in O. and M. Handlin, *Commonwealth: A Study of the Role of Government in the American Economy* (1947), and L. Hartz, *Economic Policy and Democratic Thought* (1948), which treat Massachusetts and Pennsylvania, respectively. For a discussion of the Marshall Court, see E. Corwin, *John Marshall and the Constitution* (1919). Also helpful is B. Hammon, *Banks and Politics from the Revolution to the Civil War* (1957).

Information on the social consequences of economic expansion in this period is harder to find. R. Mohl, *Poverty in New York, 1783-1825* (1971), deals with the problem of relief for the poor. Particularly useful are the studies of state politics; see especially P. Goodman, *The Democratic-Republicans in Massachusetts* (1964); J. Banner, *To the Hartford Convention* (1970), which deals with the Massachusetts Federalists; and A. Young, *The Democratic Republicans of New York* (1967). The impact of the cotton boom on slavery is discussed in W. Jordan, *White Over Black* (1968), and R. Fogel and S. Engerman, *Time on the Cross: The Economics of American Negro Slavery* (1974). For studies of black society, see G. Mullin, *Flight and Rebellion: Slave Resistance in Eighteenth-Century Virginia* (1972), and I. Berlin, *Slaves without Masters: The Free Negro in the Antebellum South* (1974).

Several studies treat the ideological context of early politics. For a discussion of the Jeffersonians, see A. Koch, *The Philosophy of Thomas Jefferson* (1943); D. Boorstin, *The Lost World of Thomas Jefferson* (1948); and F. Brodie's exceptionally good biography, *Thomas Jefferson: An Intimate History* (1974). For a discussion of the Federalists, see L. Kerber, *Federalists in Dissent* (1970); J. Howe, *The Changing Political Thought of John Adams* (1966); and P. Shaw, *The Character of John Adams* (1976).

The Politics
of Nationhood
1789-1800

The Federalist supporters of the Constitution, as the most nationally minded people in the country, easily assumed leadership of the new government. Virginia's George Washington, chairman of the Philadelphia Constitutional Convention, was unanimously chosen the first president; Massachusetts's John Adams, a former ambassador to France and Great Britain and a staunch nationalist, assumed the vice-presidency; both houses of Congress had large Federalist majorities. This original leadership attempted to stabilize national power by resolving the older problems of finance and diplomacy. In less than a decade, however, disagreements about policy divided politically aware Americans into warring camps — some known as Federalists and some as Republicans — and paved the way for the formation of rival political parties.

The founding fathers continued to share a commitment to republicanism and viewed the new nation as a grand experiment in politics [see above, p. 127]. By balancing liberty and authority, the United States would demonstrate to the world the viability of republican forms of government. Yet, in formulating specific programs, the national leaders disagreed about which side of the balance needed to be strengthened. Some, like Washington's secretary of the treasury, Alexander Hamilton, advocated placing the government in the hands of an economic elite in order to protect the new nation from popular anarchy. Others, like Speaker of the

House of Representatives James Madison, stressed the need to erect safeguards to protect the liberty of the people from the power of government. Such differing perspectives often led to heated clashes over specific political questions.

Despite these quarrels, the founding fathers agreed that republics were fragile governments that were easily subverted by conspiratorial politicians. They disagreed, however, about the nature of these threats. Some, like Hamilton, warned that popular demagogues would unleash the power of the masses against the institutions of authority and order. Others, like Madison, believed that an entrenched minority, if it were not checked, would destroy the liberty of the majority. Both groups feared that power-hungry politicians would manipulate the machinery of government in order to seize power and destroy the republic. For this reason, the nation's leaders condemned political factions and made no provisions for political parties. Such groups, they believed, sought the interest of a few people rather than the welfare of all. This fear of factions led American politicians to distrust political dissenters. Suspicious of their critics, the founding fathers could not comprehend the notion of a loyal opposition. Instead, they viewed dissent as subversive and resorted to conspiracy theories to explain the behavior of political opponents.

The New Government

In undertaking the presidency, George Washington attempted to avoid the factional quarreling that had characterized revolutionary politics. In selecting a cabinet (a body not specifically authorized by the Constitution), Washington ignored factional considerations and chose men of ability. Thomas Jefferson served as secretary of state, Hamilton as secretary of the treasury, Henry Knox as secretary of war, and Edmund Randolph as attorney general. In dealing with Congress, Washington strictly interpreted the separation of powers and remained aloof from congressional affairs. Early in his administration, the president appeared in the Senate to discuss an Indian treaty, following the constitutional provision that treaties required the "advice and consent" of that body. The resulting discussion proved unsatisfactory, and thereafter the president negotiated treaties independently and then submitted the documents for ratification.

The first Congress established the administrative Departments of State, Treasury, and War. Cautious of executive power, Congress required the secretary of the treasury to report to the legislature as well as to the president. The Judiciary Act (1789) created a Supreme Court with six justices, three circuit courts, and thirteen district courts. To prevent the national judiciary from swallowing the state courts, the act limited the jurisdiction of the national courts and defined appellate procedures. To raise revenue, Congress approved a tariff on foreign imports and enacted a duty on tonnage that taxed foreign shipping heavily, an attempt to support the American carrying trade. A proposal by Madison to establish discriminatory duties against English shipping antagonized northern commercial interests and was rejected by the Senate.

Finally, in 1791, Congress adopted twelve amendments to the Constitution (ten of which were ratified) designed to protect civil liberty from governmental encroachment. These amendments, known as the Bill of Rights, represented a fulfillment of Federalist promises made during the debate on ratification of the Constitution and eased Anti-Federalist fears about the dangers of a strong central government. The amendments included guarantees of freedom of speech, the press, and religion; assured the right of trial by jury; and protected citizens from unreasonable search and seizure and from self-incriminating testimony. Above all, the Bill of Rights attempted to preserve the balance of liberty and power in the United States.

Hamilton's Financial Program

The new government had inherited an unstable financial structure from the government under the Confederation. Bonds dating back to the War for Independence exceeded $50 million, and the nation's credit was insecure. In a *Report on the Public Credit* (1790), Alexander Hamilton proposed a series of laws designed to restore American credit at home and abroad and, at the same time, to win the allegiance of the business elite to the national government. By stabilizing the economy, Hamilton hoped to protect the young republic from domestic turbulence and foreign domination. He suggested that the national debt (of which $12 million was in foreign hands) be funded at par (face value), even though most of the domestic bonds were owned by northern speculators who had purchased them at a small percentage of the par value. Hamilton's desire to reward the speculators represented an attempt to tie the interests of the business community to the United States, thereby strengthening the national government. Despite the opposition of the southern states (which would benefit least from the program), Congress agreed to fund the entire debt at par.

For similar reasons, Hamilton also recommended that the United States assume all state debts (about $20 million) on similar terms, thereby making state creditors more dependent on the national government. Again, the southern states, which had already funded most of their debts, opposed the proposal. To overcome this resistance, Hamilton entered into a bargain with Jefferson and Madison to transfer the seat of government of the United States to an area near the Potomac River in exchange for the passage of the assumption proposal. Hamilton also agreed to offer bounties to states that already had paid their debts. In accepting the compromise, Jefferson and Madison expected the southern states to benefit by the proximity of the national capital.

In 1791, Hamilton requested Congress to charter a national bank with a capital investment of $10 million, of which one-fifth would be subscribed

Alexander Hamilton (1755-1804) supported a strong national government during the debates over the Constitution and later as Washington's secretary of the treasury. His strong political passions antagonized his opponents and one of them, Aaron Burr, killed him in a duel. (The Granger Collection.)

by the government. Such a bank would serve as a depository for federal funds and would facilitate the collection and expenditure of public money. Moreover, the bank would issue paper money (bank notes) based on the securities it held, thus providing the country with a circulating medium. The direct beneficiaries of the proposed bank would be investors in the bank's stock and business people who took advantage of the bank's credit; Hamilton argued that other Americans would also benefit indirectly since the bank facilitated governmental administration. Although Congress passed the bank bill (1791), Washington questioned its constitutionality and solicited the opinions of the members of his cabinet. In defending the bank, Hamilton articulated a "loose" interpretation of the Constitution, arguing that Congress had "implied" powers that permitted it to legislate in areas not specifically prohibited by the Constitution. Jefferson, on the other hand, denied the constitutionality of the bank and insisted that Congress could only exercise powers specifically authorized by the Constitution. To some extent, the debate reflected countering versions of republican ideas; Hamilton wanted to extend the government's legal authority in order to stabilize the country, while Jefferson preferred to limit the power of the national government lest popular liberty be restrained. Washington, persuaded by Hamilton's logic, signed the bill into law. Within a brief period, the Bank of the United States proved successful. Its emission of bank notes increased the available capital and stimulated the expanding economy [see above, p. 145].

Hamilton followed his proposal for a bank with a *Report on Manufactures* (1791) in which he urged government support for American industry through tariffs and bounties. As a nationalist, Hamilton recognized the advantages of a self-sufficient economy, even though the immediate beneficiaries of the program once again would be northern business people. Congress refused to enact the recommendations, but a Tariff Act (1792) incorporated many of Hamilton's suggestions, including a bounty for American fisheries.

To finance the retirement of the national debt, Hamilton persuaded Congress to establish an excise tax on whiskey (1791). The tax fell largely upon western farmers who usually converted their grain into whiskey because of the high cost of transportation. The failure of the administration to alleviate the farmers' grievances led to the Whiskey Rebellion (1794) in western Pennsylvania, in which the dissidents prevented the collection of excise taxes. In response, Washington summoned the militia, and the rebellion rapidly disintegrated. In suppressing the rebellion, Washington not only demonstrated the strength of the national government, he also denied the right of revolution that had been expressed in Jefferson's Declaration of Independence. Washington's attack on popular politics (which he blamed for instigating the uprising) reflected a belief that governmental authority was of primary importance.

In economic terms, Hamilton's financial program proved remarkably successful. By bolstering American credit, it facilitated the influx of foreign capital into the United States. In addition, the Bank of the United States encouraged the chartering of state banks, which increased the amount of investment capital [see above, p. 145]. In political terms, the debates in Congress over aspects of the program led Hamilton to begin forging a coalition in the legislature. By exercising executive leadership in Congress, Hamilton inadvertently commenced the process of national party formation. Moreover, the founding of the *National Gazette* (1791) by Madison and Jefferson to popularize sentiment against Hamilton's measures also represented a rudimentary step in the development of political parties. Public invective between this newspaper and the pro-Hamilton *Gazette of the United States* revealed the growing rift in national politics. Significantly, however, the financial program had only a small impact upon state politics. Local interests, more than political affiliation, determined how people reacted to such measures as funding and assumption.

Foreign Problems

American political opinion divided more clearly on questions of foreign policy. In 1789, most Americans responded enthusiastically to the commencement of the French Revolution. The overthrow of the monarchy seemed to be a logical fulfillment of the American War for Independence and consequently reinforced the American mission of extending the blessings of liberty to all humankind. The execution of Louis XVI

(1793), however, horrified many people, and the outbreak of war between France and the other major European nations further complicated American attitudes toward the Revolution. Conservative Americans condemned the anarchy and atheism of the French radicals and viewed Britain as the defender of property rights and social order. More radical Americans took up the French revolutionary cry of "liberty, equality, fraternity."

Amidst this divided atmosphere, President Washington faced the question of whether the United States should honor the French alliance of 1778. Hamilton opposed assisting France since American commerce was closely tied to Britain; Jefferson, although sympathetic to France, acknowledged the dangers of a war with Britain. Washington accepted a compromise whereby he formally recognized the French Republic, while at the same time he issued a Proclamation of Neutrality (1793) designed to keep the United States out of war. Nevertheless, the arrival of a French ambassador (Edmond Genet) the following month aroused political passions in the new nation. As he traveled northward from Charleston, Genet was greeted by enthusiastic crowds. Misinterpreting American sentiment, Genet, in violation of Washington's proclamation, commissioned privateers to assault British commerce and issued military commands to American adventurers to attack Spanish and British possessions in North America. Washington, infuriated by Genet's activities, requested the ambassador's recall. Meanwhile, Hamilton organized mass meetings around the nation to discredit Genet and influence public opinion. Pro-French supporters, with less success, tried to coordinate similar public meetings. In the end, the Genet mission aggravated political divisions and served to popularize political debates.

Washington's Proclamation of Neutrality initially proved beneficial to American merchants who traded with both Britain and France (including the French West Indies). American ports prospered as the European wars increased the demands for American goods. Both belligerents, however, began to attack neutral shipping as part of their war efforts and by 1794 had confiscated hundreds of American ships. Because of Britain's larger navy, British interference proved more effective and consequently more irritating to Americans. The British government, moreover, announced that it would enforce a policy toward neutrals called the Rule of 1756, which declared that trade closed to a nation in time of peace could not be opened in time of war. Following this policy, Britain confiscated over 200 American ships engaged in trade between France and the French West Indies. These attacks, together with the continued presence of British troops in the Northwest, revived the patriotic sentiments of 1776. As hostility toward Great Britain increased, grassroots organizations (known as Democratic Societies) emerged throughout the nation and advocated American support for France.

In an attempt to avoid war, Washington sent John Jay to Britain to negotiate a settlement. But the British saw no reason to satisfy American demands, and the Jay Treaty (1794) contained few concessions to American rights. The British agreed to evacuate the northwestern posts by 1796 and consented to reimburse American shippers for goods confiscated by the Royal Navy. The treaty opened trade with the West Indies to ships under seventy tons but imposed so many conditions that the Senate refused to ratify this provision. The British refused to retract their definition of neutral rights, and Jay acceded to the Rule of 1756. Finally, Jay promised that the national government would seek to reimburse British merchants for prerevolutionary debts. Nothing was said about the British confiscation of slaves during the War for Independence. Announcement of the Jay Treaty infuriated opponents of Britain throughout the United States. After much debate, the Senate ratified the treaty by only one vote.

The agreement between Britain and the United States also enabled the new nation to settle its differences with Spain regarding the southwestern frontier. Spain desired a separate peace with France but feared that her ally (Britain) would retaliate. The Spanish interpreted the Jay Treaty as part of an Anglo-American design against Spanish possessions in North America. Meanwhile, Spanish policy in America had proven unsuccessful. A series of conspiracies to separate Tennessee and Kentucky from the United States won little support; few Americans accepted Spanish offers to migrate to Louisiana; and an alliance with the Indians had failed to thwart American expansion. Thus, to forestall an Anglo-American attack, Spain offered to negotiate a settlement with the United States. The resulting treaty, signed by Thomas Pinckney, granted Americans navigation rights on the Mississippi River, conceded their "right of deposit" of goods at New Orleans, and accepted American claims to the disputed boundary with Florida.

The Formation of Political Parties

Although the Jay Treaty solved some of the foreign problems facing the United States, it greatly aggravated domestic tensions. Proponents of the treaty, who were led by Alexander Hamilton, attempted to organize support in Congress and in the states, thereby coalescing as the Federalist party. Opponents of the pro-British foreign policy grouped around Madison and Jefferson and formed the Democratic-Republican (or Republican) party. During the debate on the treaty, the Republicans held the first congressional caucus. By 1796, party affiliation, more than sectional interests, influenced voting alignments in Congress on such questions as the appropriation of funds to implement the Jay Treaty. The debate on foreign policy not only reflected disagreements about American interests but also introduced an ideological dimension to political activity. Pro-French politicians spoke about preserving national honor (by fulfilling the obligations of the alliance of 1778) and invoked the spirit of '76. Their Federalist opponents discussed the need to protect the new nation from the atheistic madness of the French Revolution. These appeals to a broader ideology meshed with the grassroots sentiments in the states and accelerated the creation of national political organizations.

The debate over the Jay Treaty revealed more than conflicting interests. Americans reacted to the treaty from the common perspective of the ideology of republicanism. Yet, a belief in republicanism could lead well-meaning politicians to contradictory conclusions. Thus, the Federalists viewed an alliance with Great Britain as the only effective way of preserving the fragile American republic from the excesses of liberty. They believed that a commercial treaty with Britain would provide economic stability and thereby enable conservative leaders to maintain the social order. Democratic-Republicans, on the other hand, saw the Jay Treaty as a repudiation of the spirit of liberty and feared that the Federalists would overthrow the republic and erect a new monarchy. Such contradictory perceptions influenced the political behavior of the American people. The belief in a conspiracy, which was shared by members of both parties, explains the bitterness of political debate during the 1790s.

Although the Federalist and Republican parties clearly represented different positions on national issues, the pattern of voting support in the states remains difficult to detect. The prominence of individual politicians, which reflected the personal nature of American politics, influenced voting behavior in all states. It appears, nevertheless, that the Federalists appealed to entrenched elites and to merchants and farmers with national interests, while the Republicans attracted small-scale farmers, people on the make, and, increasingly, urban workers [see above, p. 147]. Such patterns, however, could be offset by regional and ethnic considerations. Yet, the fuzziness of social and economic categories did not diminish the intensity of party rivalry. Thus, when George Washington drafted his Farewell Address (1796), he warned the American people of the dangers of political factionalism and urged them to avoid foreign entanglements that would breed domestic discord. The president's hostility toward political parties revealed that the notion of a loyal opposition had not yet emerged in 1796.

The Adams Administration

Despite Washington's efforts to calm political passions, the election of 1796 further increased the cleavage between the Federalists and Republicans. Partisan reaction to the Jay Treaty influenced the congressional elections and dominated the selection of presidential electors. The Republicans nominated Thomas Jefferson for president and New York's Aaron Burr for vice-president. The Federalists bypassed the unpopular Hamilton and nominated John Adams and Thomas Pinckney. Hamilton, who disliked Adams, attempted to maintain his political influence by manipulating the presidential balloting in Pinckney's favor. Adams's supporters, upon learning of the scheme, dropped Pinckney. In the ensuing balloting, the Federalist Adams was elected president and the Republican Jefferson vice-president. Republicans attributed their defeat to the clumsy attempt of the French ambassador (Citizen Adet) to influence the election by threatening attacks on American shipping. Meanwhile, Hamilton's machinations served only to fragment the Federalist coalition.

Adams took office amidst a renewed series of French assaults on American shipping. Hoping to avert a war, Adams sent three emissaries (Charles C. Pinckney, John Marshall, and Elbridge Gerry) to Paris to negotiate a settlement. But the French foreign minister, Talleyrand, refused to negotiate with them until they paid a sizable bribe to three French agents (later referred to as X, Y, and Z). Insulted by this demand, the delegates refused to cooperate and returned to the United States. The subsequent publication of their correspondence describing the XYZ affair created a national furor. Americans everywhere demanded a war with France to satisfy the nation's honor. Congress responded to popular pressure by cancelling the French alliance and by authorizing war preparations. Creating a Navy Department, Congress approved the construction of warships and licensed privateers to prey on French shipping. Only the restraint of John Adams, who feared the consequences of a foreign war and who opposed Congress's appointment of Alexander Hamilton to lead the army, prevented a formal declaration of war. Nevertheless, an undeclared naval war between the United States and France lasted for more than two years (1798-1800).

Republican opposition to congressional war plans moved the Federalist majority to attempt the destruction of the Republican minority by enacting a series of laws known as the Alien and Sedition Acts (1798). The alien laws lengthened the period of residence required for naturalized citizenship from five to fourteen years and authorized the president to deport dangerous aliens. In enacting this legislation, the Federalists revealed their fear of French radicalism as they attempted to insulate American politics from French influence. Meanwhile, the sedition laws endeavored to suppress public criticism of the administration by prohibiting organized opposition to the legal measures of the government and by banning the publication of false or malicious statements that would bring the president or congress into disrepute. The Federalists believed that such laws would protect the United States from the anarchistic tendencies of democratic politics and thereby preserve the republican experiment in government. It seemed inconceivable to Federalists that dissent from the legal government could be construed as anything but subversive. The Adams administration enforced the sedition laws, and Federalist judges imprisoned several Republican editors for questioning Federalist policies.

The expansion of the power of government under the sedition laws alarmed many Republicans. Jefferson and Madison drafted protests that were passed by the state legislatures of Kentucky and Virginia (1798). These resolutions asserted that the states could refuse to obey laws passed by Congress that were unconstitutional. In articulating this doctrine of nullification, Jefferson was concerned primarily with protesting Federalist policies. Thus, the Virginia and Kentucky resolutions did not interfere with the enforcement of the laws but served to publicize an alternate political position.

Amidst this domestic turmoil, the French had a change of heart. Talleyrand, who had been surprised by the vehement reaction to the XYZ affair, informed Adams that a new American ambassador would be received with honor. Recognizing the importance of peace, the president responded favorably to the French proposal. However, several conservative members of the cabinet, influenced by Hamilton, believed that war with France would permit the destruction of American radicalism and opposed a rapprochement with the French government. Nevertheless, Adams displayed an uncommon example of executive independence and refused to capitulate. By the time the American delegates arrived in France, Napoleon controlled the government. Desirous of peace, he agreed to the Convention of 1800, which ended all treaties between the two nations and guaranteed the rights of neutrals during wartime. The pact did not mention the question of indemnities, but Adams had brought peace to the new nation.

The relatively easy resolution of the quarrel with France betrayed the artificiality of Federalist war hysteria and the recklessness of the Alien and Sedition Acts. Voters resented the high taxes that had been levied in preparation for war. The Federalist party, moreover, had divided into rival factions. Yet, many people respected Adams's independence and believed that the Federalist leadership could best preserve American republicanism. Thus, the presidential election of 1800 brought only a narrow victory (seventy-three to sixty-five) for the Republican party. But the Constitution had not provided for political parties and hence did not distinguish between votes cast for presidential and vice-presidential candidates. The Constitution had provided that the person receiving the most electoral votes would become the chief executive, while the runnerup would assume the vice-presidency. Jefferson and his running mate Aaron Burr had obtained the same number of electoral votes. The tie placed the election in the House of Representatives (which voted by states), where the Federalists maintained a considerable influence. After several deadlocks, Hamilton threw his support to Jefferson, thereby assuring a peaceful transition of power. To avoid a repetition of the crisis situation, Congress drafted the Twelfth Amendment (ratified in 1804), which provided for separate ballots for presidential and vice-presidential candidates in the electoral college.

Despite the closeness of the presidential contest, the election of 1800 gave the Republicans a substantial majority in Congress. Thus, the new administration faced few obstacles in the implementation of policy. Yet, the party of Jefferson and Madison proved remarkably conservative in the years after 1800. This caution facilitated the accommodation of the Federalists to the Jefferson administration and thereby assured the perpetuation of the American republic.

Supplementary Reading

The best survey of the 1790s is J. Miller, *The Federalist Era, 1789-1801* (1960). Much about the period can be learned from the biographies of the political leaders; see J. Miller, *Alexander Hamilton: Portrait in Paradox* (1959); D. Malone, *Jefferson and His Time* (1948-1974), of which Volume III deals with the 1790s; G. Chinard, *Honest John Adams* (1933); I. Brant, *James Madison: Father of the Constitution* (1950); and J. Flexner, *Washington: The Indispensable Man* (1974). For an administrative history of the decade, see L. White, *The Federalists* (1948).

There are many books dealing with the parties of the 1790s, most of them emphasizing the maneuverings in Congress. These include J. Charles, *The Origins of the American Party System* (1961); W. Chambers, *Political Parties in a New Nation* (1963); N. Cunningham, *The Jeffersonian Republicans, 1789-1801* (1958); and R. Bell, *Party and Faction in American Politics: The House of Representatives, 1789-1801* (1973). Also useful is H. Ammon, *The Genet Mission* (1973). For a discussion of the political climate, see R. Hofstadter, *The Idea of a Party System, 1780-1840* (1969), and R. Buel, *Securing the Revolution: Ideology in American Politics, 1789-1815* (1972). These titles should be supplemented by the studies of states by Goodman, Banner, and Young listed after Chapter 10, as well as by R. Beeman, *The Old Dominion and the New Nation, 1788-1801* (1972), a study of Virginia.

The diplomacy of the period is examined in S. Bemis, *Jay's Treaty* (1923); A. DeConde, *Entangling Alliance* (1958) and *The Quasi-War* (1966); and B. Perkins, *The First Rapprochement: England and the United States* (1955). Also helpful for understanding American foreign policy is F. Gilbert, *To the Farewell Address* (1961).

The Adams administration is best discussed in S. Kurtz, *The Presidency of John Adams* (1957). For information on the Alien and Sedition Acts, see J. M. Smith, *Freedom's Fetters* (1956), and L. Levy, *Legacy of Suppression* (1960). The early Supreme Court is examined in R. Morris, *John Jay, the Nation, and the Court* (1967).

Chapter 12

Jeffersonian Politics

1801-1815

On March 4, 1801, Thomas Jefferson became the first president to be inaugurated in the national capital at Washington, D.C. Ten years earlier, the founding fathers had commissioned Major Pierre L'Enfant to plan the city. To a remarkable degree, his design reflected, in geographical terms, the political principles of the Constitution. The capital was divided into separate regions, each centering around one branch of government. Roads ran directly from the public buildings to main highways leading to the states and underscored the republican idea that government should be responsive to the people. Moreover, Washington lacked independent economic resources and remained dependent on the citizens for support. Thus, a fear of uncontrolled power not only influenced the political behavior of the nation's leaders, it also structured the physical layout of the nation's capital.

If the blueprint of Washington implied a constituency-oriented leadership, the geographic realities of the capital reinforced those attitudes in practice. Built on virtually uninhabited land, the town offered politicians few cultural diversions. Surrounded by partially completed buildings and plagued by scorching summers, government officials hastened to their home districts at the first opportunity. During the early nineteenth century, the small scale of government operations encouraged prolonged

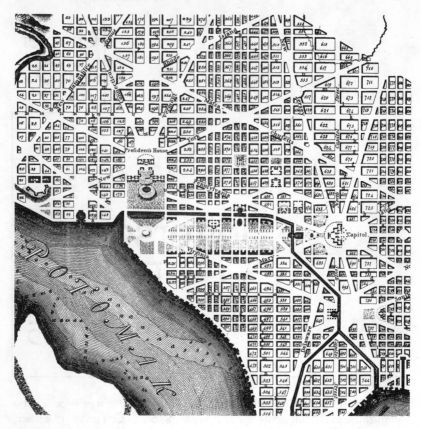

The blueprint of the national capital (1792), placing the executive, legislative, and judicial branches of government in separate parts of the city. (Courtesy of Library of Congress.)

departures from the capital, and for months at a stretch clerks and bureaucrats transacted governmental business. The relative unimportance of the national government created a rapid turnover among public officials, who resigned their posts in Washington and returned to the state capitals, where political affairs seemed more substantial.

The Young Federalists

Jefferson's victory in 1800 spelled the decline of the Federalists as a *national* party. The congressional vote in 1802 brought Republicans an even larger majority in both Houses, and in 1804 Jefferson easily defeated his Federalist opponent, Charles C. Pinckney, in the presidential contest. The preponderance of Republicans on the national level, however, did not mean that the Federalists had disappeared from American politics. Instead, during the years after 1800, the Federalist party, often led by a new breed of younger politicians, continued to wield power in New England and attempted to rebuild a national structure.

The younger Federalist leaders, like the founding fathers whom they idealized, never abandoned their elitist ideas about government and continued to criticize democratic politics. Yet, while insisting that government belonged in the hands of the "better sort," these Federalist politicians recognized the need to appeal to a mass electorate. Using such devices as nominating conventions (instead of private caucuses), party newspapers, public rallies, and political clubs, the Federalists attempted to build a popular following in the states. To be sure, these conservatives never accepted the democratization of the party structure and generally allowed a party elite to make crucial decisions. Yet, by strengthening the party apparatus, the Federalists achieved numerous victories in the states.

The Federalists appealed primarily to conservative citizens who opposed political democracy and lamented the passing of the old order. In the North (where the party was most successful), the Federalists offered a traditional social order to voters frustrated by the social and economic changes of the period [see above, p. 146]. To New Englanders, they stood for ethnic homogeneity against foreign immigration and appealed more to traditional Congregationalists than to Baptists, Methodists, and Unitarians. In other areas, the Federalists attracted voters who resented the rule of an entrenched Republican elite. Thus, areas of western Virginia remained Federalist strongholds, because small-scale farmers opposed the political domination of the slave-holding planter aristocracy. The insistence on elite leadership did not make the Federalists a class party, for many Americans of lower status retained deferential voting habits and expected their "betters" to rule.

The strengthening of the Federalist party structure brought a resurgence of party competition in the states after 1800. Traditionally, state and local issues proved more important than national politics, and citizens seemed more interested in gubernatorial elections than in the results of presidential contests. But, during Jefferson's second administration (1805-1809), national questions again intruded into state politics and affected voting patterns. As the rival parties competed for votes, the amount of voter participation increased. This activity, ironically, doomed the Federalist party, for masses of voters preferred the democratic ideology of the Republicans to the elitism of their opponents. Thus, the Federalists' attempts to broaden their appeal merely hastened the demise of their party.

The First Jefferson Administration

On the national level, President Jefferson further undermined the Federalists by demonstrating the effectiveness of negative government. In his inaugural address of 1801, Jefferson offered to heal the breaches of partisan conflict and attempted to ease the fears of the defeated party. Yet, in filling government offices, he was determined to replace arch-Federalists with dutiful Republicans until each party held about half the positions. Few Federalists were dismissed, but, as positions fell vacant, they were given to Republicans. Jefferson revealed his political skills in providing executive leadership in Congress. Making use of floor leaders and loyal followers, Jefferson drafted legislation and guided a moderate program through a sympathetic Congress.

Despite his desire to eliminate certain Federalist policies, Jefferson carefully avoided a direct attack on the party out of power. Thus, while repealing federal excise taxes (including the whiskey tax), the Republicans preserved the Hamiltonian financial structure. Rigid economies in government and an increase in revenues from customs duties (resulting from an expansion of American commerce) enabled the administration to reduce the national debt. Congress also reduced the residence requirement for naturalization to five years and allowed other aspects of the Alien and Sedition Acts to lapse [see above, p. 159]. Such moderation discredited many Federalist politicians who had accused the Jeffersonians of wanting rebellion and anarchy.

The Republican president, however, proved to be less temperate in dealing with the judiciary. Washington and Adams had filled the federal courts with Federalist judges, many of whom had interpreted the sedition laws for partisan purposes. On the eve of its retirement, a Federalist-controlled Congress had passed the Judiciary Act of 1801, which created sixteen new judgeships and a variety of minor judicial offices. Moreover, President Adams had attempted to protect the courts from the Jeffersonians by appointing conservative Federalists to the new positions. The new Republican Congress, infuriated by these midnight appointments, immediately repealed the law, and Jefferson refused to honor judicial commissions that had not yet been distributed. The president's intransigence led one of Adams's appointees, William Marbury, to ask the Supreme Court for a writ of *mandamus* ordering Secretary of State James Madison to deliver his commission. In rendering his decision in *Marbury v. Madison* (1803), Chief Justice John Marshall (an Adams appointee himself) ruled that, while Marbury deserved his commission, the Supreme Court did not have original jurisdiction in the case and hence could not order Madison to comply. Marshall thereby declared that a section of the Judiciary Act of 1789 (which had originally granted the Court such jurisdiction) had exceeded the limits established by the Constitution and consequently was void. This case established the precedent of judicial review, whereby the Supreme Court assumed the power of declaring on the constitutionality of legislation.

Jefferson next attempted to purge the courts of the more partisan Federalist judges. He succeeded in obtaining the impeachment and conviction of one district judge, who apparently was insane. The attempt to remove the Federalist Samuel Chase from the Supreme Court, however, did not succeed. Although Chase had demonstrated political prejudice in hearing cases under the sedition laws, the Senate refused to convict him (1805). The decision thereby protected the independence of the American judiciary.

The domestic successes of Jefferson's first administration were matched by minor and major triumphs in foreign affairs. For decades, a group of Arab potentates in North Africa had levied tolls on shipping in the southern Mediterranean. Under the Federalist presidents, the United States had joined the European nations in paying this tribute. But, when Tripoli raised the charges for American vessels, Jefferson refused to comply. Tripoli then declared war on the United States (1801); the war lasted for over three years. American naval forays brought indecisive results; yet, in 1805, Tripoli offered more favorable rates. The United States continued to pay tribute to the Barbary pirates until 1815.

The Louisiana Purchase

Jefferson's greatest triumph, the purchase of Louisiana (1803), was the culmination of a complex history of European diplomacy. Spain, which obtained Louisiana in 1763, viewed the territory as a barrier between Mexico and the expanding American frontier. But, following the resolution of differences with the United States (in the Pinckney Treaty of 1795) [see above, p. 157], Spain was prepared to sell the territory. Meanwhile, Napoleon became interested in reestablishing a French empire in the Western Hemisphere and pressed Spain to relinquish her claims to Louisiana. The secret Treaty of San Ildefonso (1800) completed the transfer. Napoleon expected Louisiana to supply foodstuffs for the sugar-producing islands in the West Indies. To fulfill these plans, however, France first had to crush a slave rebellion in Santo Domingo. But a French military expedition, ravaged by an epidemic of yellow fever, failed to quell the uprising.

The replacement of a weak Spanish neighbor with an aggressive French empire alarmed President Jefferson, and, when Spanish officials at New Orleans suspended the right of deposit (1802), his fears seemed confirmed. With western economic interests seriously imperiled, Jefferson dispatched James Monroe to France with instructions to negotiate the purchase of New Orleans. However, the failure of the expedition to Santo Domingo and the need for resources to finance a war with Britain had led Napoleon to abandon his imperial schemes. By the time Monroe joined American ambassador Robert R. Livingston in Paris, the French emperor had offered to sell the entire Louisiana territory, a geographical area nearly equal in size to the existing United States. After a brief delay, the American ambassadors exceeded their instructions and agreed to purchase Louisiana for $15 million.

Jefferson received the treaty with reservations, for the Constitution included no provisions for the acquisition of new territories. As a believer in the strict interpretation of the Constitution, the president considered

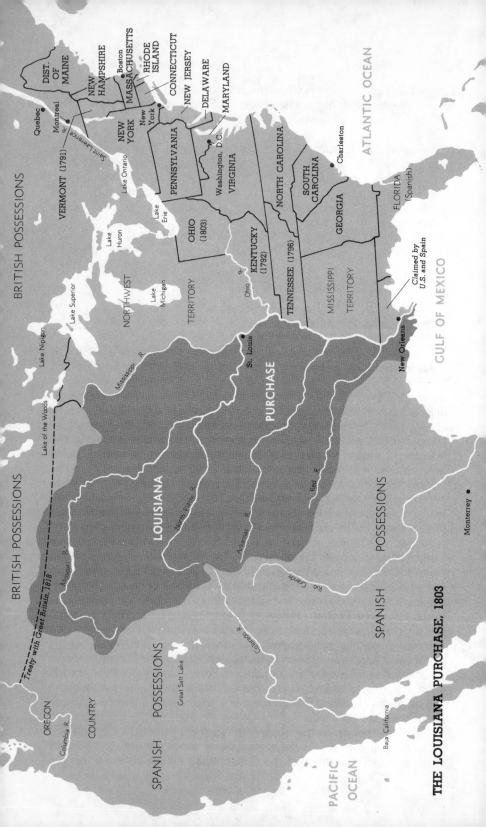

THE LOUISIANA PURCHASE, 1803

introducing a constitutional amendment to legitimize the purchase. But warnings that Napoleon might withdraw his offer compelled haste, and Jefferson consented to overlook his constitutional scruples. In reversing his interpretation of the implied powers of the Constitution, Jefferson revealed his deeper commitment to creating an agrarian republic in the West.

Believing that the ownership of landed property provided the surest defense of an individual's liberty, Jefferson envisioned the United States as a nation of self-sufficient farmers. By doubling the size of the union, the purchase of Louisiana provided room for geographic expansion. Such expansion would enable the American people to prosper without facing the social problems associated with industrialization and urbanization. Jefferson, in effect, hoped to protect Americans from the evils of artificial institutions by opening a virgin land to settlement. In the West, the Jeffersonian hero would escape from an artificial social order and enter a more natural cosmic order free from human corruption. Jefferson's ideological perspective thus could reconcile individual mobility with social order [see above, pp. 146-147].

Opposition to the Louisiana Purchase came largely from New England Federalists who reacted differently to American expansion. As conservatives committed to an organic social order, the Federalists feared the consequences of social disintegration and wanted a more stable society. Their criticism of westward expansion also reflected a sense of regional isolation. As the population moved westward, new states would enter the union (Ohio already had been admitted in 1803), thereby weakening the political influence of the older states. Already estranged from the Jeffersonian administration, New England Federalists lamented the consequences of territorial expansion. Yet, as proponents of a broad interpretation of the Constitution, they lacked a convincing political rationale for their opposition.

To explore the resources of the newly acquired territory, Jefferson commissioned several western expeditions. Between 1804 and 1806, a group led by Meriwether Lewis and William Clark ascended the Missouri River, crossed the Rocky Mountains, and descended the Columbia River to the Pacific Ocean. Besides obtaining geographical information, the explorers returned with a wealth of scientific data, including a variety of specimens found in the western wilderness. Jefferson also encouraged expeditions by Zebulon Pike, who explored the upper Mississippi Valley (1805) and the southern regions of the Rocky Mountains (1806).

Republicans in Opposition

The ratification of the Louisiana Purchase increased Jefferson's popularity even in New England, thereby alienating the Federalists even more. A small group of extreme conservatives, led by Timothy Pickering, became convinced of the impossibility of Federalist success in a democratic country and formed a secessionist plan to establish a Northern Confederacy (1804). The scheme called for the election of Aaron Burr as governor of New York; Burr then would lead that state into a union with New England. The plot collapsed when Burr lost the election. The former vice-president blamed his defeat on the opposition of Alexander Hamilton and challenged him to a duel. The two met at Weehawken, New Jersey, and Hamilton was killed (July 1804).

Burr's willingness to consider the Northern Confederacy reflected his personal alienation from the Jefferson administration. For unknown reasons, Burr earlier had approached the British ambassador with a scheme to separate the western states from the union. Although the British refused to cooperate, Burr proceeded westward, intending to form a republic either in the western portions of the United States or in Spanish-owned territory. In any case, he soon joined forces with James Wilkinson, the governor of Louisiana, and in 1806 launched a small expedition down the Ohio River. Whatever the goals of the mission, Wilkinson apparently realized its futility and betrayed the scheme to President Jefferson. Burr fled toward Spanish Florida but was captured and returned to Richmond, Virginia, to stand trial for treason. Jefferson, for personal reasons, attempted to secure Burr's conviction. But Chief Justice Marshall, who presided over the circuit court that tried Burr, proved equally prejudiced in favor of Burr. Marshall, perhaps interested in preventing a political murder, offered an extremely narrow definition of treason that resulted in Burr's acquittal.

During his first administration, Jefferson had relied heavily upon John Randolph of Roanoke, Virginia, as a liaison with Congress. Randolph, like Jefferson, feared the potential power of government and believed in a narrow interpretation of the Constitution. But Jefferson's flexibility in this respect offended Randolph, leading to a split within the Republican party. Randolph had first challenged the president in 1804 over the settlement of the Yazoo land frauds. In 1795, a bribed Georgia legislature had sold 35 million acres of western lands to four land companies at less than two cents an acre. The next legislature, upon learning of the corruption, rescinded the sale, but not before the companies had sold some of the land to third parties. These purchasers appealed to the national government for relief. Jefferson supported their petition for 5 million acres, but Randolph refused to countenance the original fraud and prevented the passage of a relief bill. The case finally reached the Supreme Court as *Fletcher v. Peck* (1810). Marshall ruled that the Georgia legislature could not legally rescind the original sale (despite the corruption) because of the constitutional prohibition against the impairment of the obligation of contracts. Together with the Dartmouth College decision [see above, p. 145], this ruling revealed Marshall's attempt to protect the rights of property from the capricious interference of government.

In subsequent years, Randolph, together with a group of like-minded congressmen known as Quids, became a strong opponent of governmental expansion. When Jefferson attempted to obtain funds to acquire western Florida from Spain, Randolph openly broke with the administration. Despite their frequent protests against the administration's policy, the Quids remained a small and ineffective group within the Republican party. As strict interpreters of the Constitution, they tried unsuccessfully to limit the power of the president and endeavored to impede his foreign policy. Yet, they proved no match for the resourceful Jefferson.

The Rights of Neutrals

The outbreak of a new war between Britain and France (1803) swiftly destroyed the relative tranquility of American politics. In the early stages of the conflict, American commerce benefited greatly by the increased demand for American goods in Europe. This commercial expansion had been facilitated by a decision of the British courts in the *Polly* case (1801), which ruled that American ships could participate in trade between France and the French West Indies, provided that they passed first through neutral ports. In the *Essex* case (1805), however, the British courts reversed themselves and prohibited the profitable trade between France and her colonies under the Rule of 1756 [see above, pp. 156-157]. This reversal reflected the altered nature of the European conflict.

The British navy had won mastery of the seas by destroying the French fleet in the Battle of Trafalgar (1805), and Napoleon had asserted his dominance of the land war in Europe in the Battle of Austerlitz (1805). Secure in their own realms, neither nation could attack the other directly. They resorted instead to economic warfare, hoping to starve the enemy into submission. Napoleon created a Continental system designed to end Britain's trade with the world. In the Berlin Decree (November 1806), he established a paper (unenforced) blockade around Great Britain and forbade British ships to enter Continental ports under his control. The British responded by issuing an Order in Council (1807), which placed a blockade around all ports occupied by France and prohibited neutral vessels from entering them unless they had first paid customs duties in Britain. Napoleon then issued the Milan Decree (December 1807), which ruled that any neutral ship that had acquiesced in the British orders had become British property and consequently was subject to seizure. Under these rulings, both Britain and France began to confiscate American vessels (over 700 ships by 1807). Yet, American commerce continued to thrive.

Foreign interference in American shipping proved more inflammatory on the question of the impressment of sailors in international waters. Locked in a mortal struggle with Napoleon, the Royal Navy asserted its right to impress British subjects from neutral vessels to man its warships. Problems arose, however, in identifying British seamen and distinguishing between naturalized American citizens born in Great Britain and ordinary British deserters. The willingness of American sea captains to wink at violations of the naturalization law complicated the problem. The issue of impressment climaxed in the *Chesapeake-Leopard* affair (June 1807). A British frigate, *Leopard*, ordered the American *Chesapeake* to allow a boarding party to search for four deserters. When the *Chesapeake* refused to comply, the British opened fire and forced the American vessel to surrender. Of the four suspected deserters who were seized, only one was English. Outraged public opinion in the United States demanded a war with Britain to revenge this insult to national honor. However, Jefferson, fearful of the consequences of war, chose to pacify American bellicosity.

Realizing that the European powers depended upon American shipping, Jefferson hoped to use economic coercion to force the belligerents to recognize the rights of neutrals. The president persuaded Congress to enact the Embargo Act (December 1807), which prohibited all American trade with foreign ports. In effect, this policy hurt Britain more than France, since the Royal Navy already had obstructed much of America's trade with France. From Jefferson's point of view, the embargo served the additional purpose of protecting American property from attacks on the high seas, thereby avoiding further insults to the nation's honor. More subtly, the policy also betrayed a Jeffersonian notion that Americans, because they were more virtuous and frugal than Old World Europeans, could better surmount the economic deprivations caused by the curtailment of the nation's commerce. Moreover, Jefferson felt that commerce, by its nature, embroiled the "pure" New World in the vices of the Old.

The optimistic Jefferson, however, had failed to consider the reaction of American merchants. The embargo accomplished peacefully what neither Britain nor France could do by force; it drastically reduced American trade. As ships rotted at the docks, unemployment increased and prices fell. Despite a considerable amount of smuggling, the economy ground to a halt. Jefferson's attempt to enforce the law (often in violation of individual civil liberties) further infuriated the American public. Although Jefferson's favored candidate, Secretary of State Madison, easily won the presidential contest, the congressional elections of 1808 brought victories to men pledged to repeal the obnoxious law.

In the waning days of the Jefferson administration, Congress finally lifted the embargo and substituted the Nonintercourse Act (March 1809), which reopened American commerce with all nations but Britain and France and provided for the resumption of trade with either belligerent upon the elimination of earlier trade restrictions. Responding to this measure, Britain authorized its ambassador, David Erskine, to negotiate a conditional settlement with the Madison administration. When the president balked at the terms, Erskine exceeded his instructions and modified the proposal. Upon Madison's acceptance of the new offer, 600 American vessels sailed for Britain. However, the British government immediately repudiated the Erskine Agreement, further inflaming American opinion.

The Nonintercourse Act proved ineffectual in halting American commerce with the belligerents. Thus, at the suggestion of the administration, Congress replaced the law with a measure known as Macon's Bill Number 2 (May 1810), which repealed all restrictions on American commerce. But, to avoid complete submission to European authority, the law provided that, if either Britain or France eliminated their commercial restrictions, the United States would reestablish nonintercourse with the other power. Since the Royal Navy controlled the seas, this measure primarily stimulated American commerce with Britain. Napoleon, fearful of the consequences of this shift, instructed Foreign Minister Cadore to inform Madison that the Berlin and Milan decrees would be rescinded by November 1810, provided that Britain agreed to suspend the Orders in Council. Although Madison probably knew that this letter did not constitute a change in French policy (Napoleon continued to seize American vessels), the president restored the nonintercourse policy against Britain (February 1811). A minor confrontation between British and American vessels near New York, known as the *Little Belt* affair (May 1811), rallied public support for Madison's anti-British policy. Motivated by a desire to appear independent, Madison ignored British revelations of Napoleon's hypocrisy and led a divided nation toward war. Meanwhile, the American restrictions on trade with Britain aggravated the economic crisis in that country. Pressured by English industrialists, the British government finally agreed to repeal the Orders in Council. But, by that time, a Republican Congress already had declared war on Britain (June 18, 1812).

The War of 1812

The decision to declare war culminated a decade of frustration with the European disregard of American rights. In his war message to Congress, President Madison stressed the role of maritime grievances — the violation of neutral rights, the commerical restrictions, and the impressment of American citizens. He also alluded to American suspicions that British officers had stirred Tecumseh to attack settlers in the Northwest Territory (November 1811) [see above, p. 139]. Western settlers, however, seemed more concerned with a depression in farm prices (caused largely by high transportation costs), which they blamed on British interference with American exports. Thus, in terms of grievances, Americans seemed to respond primarily to the British Orders in Council, which had disrupted the nation's commerce.

Yet, British violations had occurred long before 1812 without bringing war. Moreover, neither sectional nor economic patterns emerged in the congressional vote to declare war. Nor was Congress driven to declare war by a small band of "War Hawks." Instead, the vote followed party lines. Most Republicans opposed war but reluctantly agreed to support Madison's policy. The Federalists were staunchly opposed. But, by 1812, the United States had few choices. Diplomacy had failed, and the young nation faced the alternative of declaring war in defense of national honor or abjectly submitting to the power of Great Britain.

The decision to declare war was made easier for the Jeffersonians by their commitment to the republican experiment in government. Believing that the success of the United States would demonstrate the value of republicanism, they had to prove (perhaps to themselves as much as to outsiders) that a republican government could not only preserve liberty but also could protect the property of its citizens. The Republicans believed, moreover, that Federalist oppostion to the administration's foreign policy represented part of a monarchist plot to discredit the infant republic. Still unable to accept the idea of loyal dissent, the Republicans viewed their opponents as conspiring subversives. In rallying behind President Madison in 1812, therefore, these moderate Republicans affirmed the importance of maintaining national honor as the best way to preserve the republican experiment.

A war to defend national honor logically required the party in power to demonstrate a semblance of valor. Yet, the Madison administration provided poor leadership in Congress, made few war preparations, and failed to rally public support. Although Congress authorized the creation of a 35,000-man army, only 7,000 men enlisted. The shortage of army manpower forced the nation to rely upon state militiamen (many of whom refused to leave their home states). The military leadership proved equally unenthusiastic. The United States Navy, although well seasoned by the battles with France and the Barbary pirates, nevertheless appeared hopelessly puny in comparison to the Royal Navy.

The state of public finance seemed equally fragile. To finance the government, the United States had relied upon customs duties, but the outbreak of war reduced the income from that source. Secretary of the Treasury Albert Gallatin persuaded a reluctant Congress to establish excise taxes, but these too proved inadequate and the government was forced to borrow money. A Republican Congress had allowed the first Bank of the United States to expire (1811), and the banking systems of the states were inadequate for public borrowing. Thus, Gallatin depended on the sale of bonds, which brought in far less money than was anticipated largely because New Englanders contributed little support for the unpopular war.

American strategy called for the invasion of Canada as the easiest way to strike at Great Britain. (In planning the attack, annexationist dreams seemed less important than military strategy.) During 1812, the United States launched three attacks on Canada. One expedition, led by General William Hull, crossed the Detroit River but found that a small British force had cut the army's supply lines to Ohio. Fearful of being isolated, Hull retreated to Detroit, where he surrendered his army to an attacking force of Canadians and Indians (August 1812). A second army successfully crossed the Niagara River and captured Queenstown but was forced to withdraw when a detachment of New York militiamen refused to cross state lines to participate in the battle. The third force, under General Henry Dearborn, approached the Canadian border near Lake Champlain but also retreated when militiamen refused to fight in foreign territory.

In the early stages, the war at sea seemed more hopeful, as the badly outnumbered navy achieved several stunning victories. Triumphs of the

Constitution over the *Guerriere,* the *United States* over the *Macedonian,* and the *Wasp* over the *Frolic* demonstrated the skill of such naval officers as Stephen Decatur. By the spring of 1813, however, the superior British navy had bottled up the American ships in port and thereafter dominated the Atlantic waters. Only an extensive fleet of privateers remained to harass British shipping.

In the Northwest Territory, the British were supported by a confederation of Indian tribes that hoped to stop further American expansion in the area. Captain Oliver Hazard Perry destroyed a British fleet in the bloody Battle of Lake Erie (September 1813). William Henry Harrison then ferried his troops across the lake and pursued the British across the border to the Thames River, where the American army defeated a combined British and Indian force.

American successes prior to 1814 revealed less the prowess of American troops than Britain's preoccupation with the European theater of war. With the defeat of Napoleon, however, British strategists planned an elaborate assault on the United States. One army marched southward from Montreal along Lake Champlain, intending to isolate the northern states from the union. Despite overwhelming superiority, the British general halted at Plattsburg to await naval support on Lake Champlain. However, an American squadron defeated the British fleet at the Battle of Lake Champlain (September 1814). The British, fearful of flank attacks, retreated to Canada. A second British army landed on the Chesapeake Bay and rapidly marched toward Washington (1814). Overpowering a small defense force, the redcoats burned most of the public buildings, including the White House. An attempted assault on Baltimore, however, met stiff resistance from forces at Fort McHenry, and the British were forced to retreat.

The Hartford Convention

For the Federalists, the burning of the capital symbolized the degradation of the nation. The War of 1812 had never been popular in Federalist New England. During the electoral contests of 1812, Federalist politicians had campaigned vigorously against the war and had won numerous state elections. Yet, it had become increasingly apparent that the party no longer influenced national politics. The stagnation of American commerce, the conscription of state militias, and the continued domination of Republicans in national politics further alienated the Federalist minority. The humiliating military defeats and the unlikelihood of peace led several frustrated Federalists to summon a convention to protest the war and suggest reform of the national union.

Meeting at Hartford, Connecticut (December 1814), the Federalists avoided the question of secession and instead proposed a series of amendments to the Constitution. Reflecting a fear of a loss of power in the national government, the Federalist convention proposed that (1) appor-

THE WAR OF 1812

——————— Americans

- - - - - - - - - - British

tionment for purposes of taxation and representation be based on the white population, thus eliminating the Three-fifths Compromise, which had given the southern states additional representation; (2) admission of new states require a two-thirds vote of Congress, thereby delaying territorial expansion; (3) embargoes be limited to sixty days and require a two-thirds vote of Congress; (4) declarations of war require a two-thirds vote of

Congress; (5) naturalized citizens be barred from public office, thus protecting the ethnic homogeneity of the country; and (6) presidents be
limited to one term in office. Such proposals revealed two decades of frustration with the changing nature of American society. In offering these
reforms, the Federalists viewed themselves as defenders of the republican
tradition of the founding fathers. Convinced that the Jeffersonians had
perverted the American dream, the Federalists posed as restorers seeking
to recapture an original vision.

The despair of the Hartford Convention quickly dissipated following
news of a stunning military victory at New Orleans. While one British force
had descended from Canada and another had penetrated the Chesapeake, a third army of about 10,000 troops had landed near New Orleans
(December 1814). Andrew Jackson, assigned to defend the city, confronted a superior British force just south of the city and inflicted an overwhelming defeat (January 1815). Overnight, Jackson became a national
hero, and Americans everywhere celebrated the victory of the Kentucky
riflemen at New Orleans. Although the war had involved a series of military
failures, the Battle of New Orleans salvaged American pride and fed the
budding patriotism of the people. To many, the triumph became a symbol
of American virtue and proof of the superiority of republican institutions.

The Treaty of Ghent

Yet, neither the victory at New Orleans nor the protests of the Hartford Convention influenced the outcome of the war. Prior to both events,
American and British delegates had negotiated the Treaty of Ghent
(December 1814), which officially ended the war. The negotiations had
lasted for over four months. In the early stages, the British, confident that
their military offensive would succeed, offered no concessions regarding
the rights of neutrals and demanded that the United States surrender most
of the Northwest Territory to the Indians and portions of Maine to Canada. The American representatives refused to concede any territory and
instead requested that Britain recognize the United States's interpretation
of maritime law. As the peace talks dragged on, news of the American victory at Plattsburg weakened the British position. In addition, the duke of
Wellington advised the British negotiators that the United States could not
be defeated without long and expensive military operations.

As British territorial claims evaporated, so too did the other substantive issues. The defeat of Napoleon, ending the European wars, had eliminated such grievances as commercial restrictions and impressment.
Anxious to end the war, the peace commissioners agreed to a treaty that
provided for the restoration of all conquests. The pact ignored such questions as maritime rights but instead established several commissions to
deal with specific problems. On paper, the United States had won no concessions by going to war!

Yet, in the aftermath of the war, the United States and Great Britain
settled many of the disputes that had been omitted from the Treaty of

Ghent. The nations agreed to a commercial convention (July 1815), which expanded American trade with all parts of the British Empire (but continued to limit American shipping in the West Indies). The Rush-Bagot Agreement (1818) provided for the demilitarization of the Great Lakes, thereby establishing a precedent for an unfortified boundary between Canada and the United States. A fisheries convention (1818) settled a long-standing dispute by confirming American rights to fish off the coast of Newfoundland. Finally, a boundaries commission (1818) established the forty-ninth parallel as the northern boundary of the Louisiana Territory and provided for the joint occupation of Oregon for ten years. In 1827, this latter clause was extended indefinitely. Each of these agreements revealed the altered face of Anglo-American relations after 1815.

These diplomatic settlements, nevertheless, represented but one consequence of the War of 1812. Despite the obvious failure of American armies, the war had demonstrated the durability of the American republic. The sense of national autonomy, in turn, encouraged domestic security, and politicians ceased to worry about political subversion. During the next decades, this self-confidence accelerated the democratization of American politics.

Supplementary Reading

A solid overview of the Jeffersonian era is M. Smelser, *The Democratic Republic, 1801-1815* (1968). L. White, *The Jeffersonians* (1951), presents a standard account of government administration. It should be supplemented by the more imaginative J. Young, *The Washington Community* (1966). An account of the Republican party is N. Cunningham, *The Jeffersonians in Power* (1963); for an account of the Federalist party, see D. Fischer, *The Revolution in American Conservatism* (1965). For an examination of the schisms within the Republican party, see N. Risjord, *The Old Republicans* (1965), and T. Abernethy, *The Burr Conspiracy* (1954). R. Walters, *Albert Gallatin* (1957), describes the career of a leading Jeffersonian.

The best study of the origins of the War of 1812 is B. Perkins, *Prologue to War* (1961). Also helpful is I. Brant, *James Madison: The President* (1956), and R. Horsman, *The Causes of the War of 1812* (1962). R. H. Brown, *The Republic in Peril: 1812* (1963), places the war in the context of Jeffersonian ideology. For the role of France, see L. Kaplan, *Jefferson and France* (1967).

A brief survey of the war itself is H. Coles, *The War of 1812* (1965); also helpful is I. Brant, *James Madison: Commander in Chief* (1961). For discussions of Federalist opposition to the war, see J. Banner, *To the Hartford Convention* (1970), and S. E. Morison, *Harrison Gray Otis* (1969). The Treaty of Ghent is examined in F. Engelman, *The Peace of Christmas Eve* (1962). For examinations of postwar diplomacy, see G. Dangerfield, *The Era of Good Feelings* (1952); S. Bemis, *John Quincy Adams and the Foundations of American Foreign Policy* (1949); and B. Perkins, *Castlereagh and Adams* (1964).

Chapter

13

A Nation of Sections

1816-1828

At the time the United States was founded, many Americans lamented the absence of strong national traditions. Formed from culturally diverse colonies, the United States lacked a common history. Numerous Americans hoped to fill the void by fostering nationalistic sentiments, by glorifying the founding fathers, by reinterpreting the past. Such nationalistic statements, however, should not obscure the local and regional orientation of most Americans. On such questions as tariffs and western development, politicans rallied first to their states and then to the union.

During the first decades of independence, American nationalists focused on the superiority of the new nation to Great Britain. Thus, Noah Webster's proposal for a new American language represented a patriotic assertion of cultural independence. Similarly, Royall Tyler's play *The Contrast* (1787) lauded American virtue at the expense of British culture. Nor did many Americans doubt the natural superiority of American political institutions. The War of 1812 revived these anti-British feelings. After 1815, for example, Americans rebelled against British "immorality" by replacing popular English books on etiquette with American publications that extolled "republican manners."

Cultural Nationalism

The creation of a national culture, however, required not only condemnations of Britain but also positive assertions of American uniqueness. Gilbert Stuart painted numerous portraits of the founding fathers, producing idealized versions of such patriots as George Washington. As in the colonial period, Americans continued to believe in the educational value of great lives, and heroic biographies of national figures became popular fare. Washington, as the father of his country, seemed to be a perfect model for young boys to imitate. John Marshall's five-volume *Life of Washington* (1804-1807) emphasized the Federalist policies of the first president. But Mason Locke Weems's *Life of Washington* (1800) was far more popular and influential, going through nearly eighty printings during the nineteenth century. Interested in Washington as an ideal for American boys, Parson Weems transformed the national hero into a veritable monument. Austere and aloof, Washington appeared as the personification of American virtue, the citizen-soldier who selflessly served his nation in time of need.

The War of 1812 stimulated the glorification of other national heroes. Perry's victory on Lake Erie and Jackson's triumph at New Orleans catapulted both men to national fame. As "Old Hickory," Jackson seemed to symbolize the vitality of the young republic, a nation of farmers uncorrupted by the luxury and vice of the Old World. In the aftermath of the war, the study of American history grew more popular, and, in 1827, Massachusetts became the first of many states to require its teaching in public schools. The search for a national past led to the popularity of such mythmakers as William Wirt, whose biography of Patrick Henry (1817) attempted to teach republican ideals to the nation's youth.

The enthusiastic rhetoric of nationalism, nevertheless, did not easily destroy the traditional regionalism of American society. Washington Irving, for example, achieved wide popularity by developing regional themes in such works as *Diedrich Knickerbocker's History of New York* (1809). The *self-consciousness* of American nationalism, indeed, seems to betray a recognition of the lack of a national heritage. People who had been raised as Virginians or New Englanders could not abruptly establish a national identity. Yet, by the third decade of the nineteenth century, many of the founding fathers had died or retired from politics. They were replaced by a new generation of leaders who had matured after 1789. These new leaders had not created the republic; they had inherited it. Their ideas about republicanism had not been acquired late in life, but had been learned from earliest youth. Men of this generation believed in the ideals of political democracy that were expressed by patriotic orators on national holidays. And, as second-generation republicans became active politically, they attempted to put their ideals into practice — at least for white males.

THE LIFE

OF

GEORGE WASHINGTON;

WITH

CURIOUS ANECDOTES,

EQUALLY HONOURABLE TO HIMSELF,

AND

EXEMPLARY TO HIS YOUNG COUNTRYMEN.

A life how useful to his country led !
How loved ! while living !—how revered ! now dead !
Lisp ! lisp ! his name, ye children yet unborn !
And with like deeds your own great names adorn.

EMBELLISHED WITH SIX ENGRAVINGS.

BY M. L. WEEMS,

FORMERLY RECTOR OF MOUNT VERNON PARISH.

The Author has treated this great subject with admirable,
" success in a new way. He turns all the actions of Washington, to the encouragement of virtue, by a careful application of
numerous exemplifications drawn from the conduct of the
founder of our republic from his earliest life.'
H. Lee, *Major-General, Army U. S.*

PHILADELPHIA:

PUBLISHED BY JOSEPH ALLEN,

AND SOLD BY J. GRIGG,

No. 9, North Fourth Street.

1832.

---

*Title page of Parson Weems's famous biography, which invented such
historical legends as the chopping of the cherry tree.*

Political Reform

During the revolutionary crisis, the second Continental Congress had instructed the states to create republican governments. Concerned primarily with reducing the power of the executive branch, the states had drafted republican constitutions that gave the greatest power to the legislatures. These constitutions further reflected the spirit of the times by limiting political democracy. Accustomed to colonial voting habits, the revolutionary leaders perpetuated property requirements for suffrage and for holding office [see above, p. 116]. For second-generation republicans, the inconsistencies of these constitutions required reform. If republican politics was the essence of American uniqueness, it appeared necessary to eliminate the obstacles to political democracy.

These ideological impulses for political reform were reinforced by changes in the states. Population growth, geographical dispersal, and religious and ethnic complexity had produced an altered social order by 1820. People in newly settled regions, members of religious minorities, and propertyless wage earners demanded the protection of their republican rights. The western states that had entered the union after 1816 generally imitated the state constitutions of the East but had provided for universal suffrage for white males. Pressure for reform in the older states led to the summoning of constitutional conventions in many states in the years after the War of 1812. At each convention, specific local issues often complicated the proceedings. Moreover, conservative politicians did not collapse before the onslaughts of democratic reformers. Thus, in many states, conservative politics continued to be written into the new constitutions. In Massachusetts, the government continued to support the Congregational churches; in New York, the convention disfranchised the free blacks of the state (about 30,000 voters); in Virginia, the western counties remained underrepresented. Yet, such undemocratic provisions should not obscure the major contributions of the state constitutional conventions. By expanding the suffrage to include virtually all adult white males, the new constitutions radically altered the nature of American politics.

The emergence of a new generation of political leaders also affected political practices in the United States. As the sons of revolutionaries, these politicians had not experienced the trouble of the revolutionary era and were not plagued by fears of political subversion [see above, p. 152]. They viewed the War of 1812 as a confirmation of the stability of the republic. In creating a mass electorate through political reform, they demonstrated their confidence in republican institutions. As the Federalist party lost its popular appeal, fears of political dissent vanished, and Americans gradually accepted the notion of a loyal opposition. The idea of majority rule replaced the older notion of political consensus; it was no longer necessary for politicians to appeal to *all* the voters. The expansion of suffrage, nevertheless, required politicians to organize supporters even to obtain a mere majority. This need stimulated such modern electioneering tactics as mass meetings, rallies, and parades. Political parties, viewed by the founding fathers as subversive factions, became acceptable instruments for harnessing the electorate. Instead of shunning parties, the new leaders emphasized the importance of party loyalty and attempted to organize mass followings.

During the 1820s, the process of party formation remained unbalanced and a single party usually dominated each state. As a result, the constitutional reforms did not produce a surge in voter participation. A lack of significant choices combined with voter apathy to restrict the size of the electorate even in state elections (which remained more competitive than presidential contests). As rival politicians organized the voters, however, party competition stiffened. In later years, voters who faced real alternatives turned out in greater numbers [see below, pp. 203-204]. Thus, if democratic reform stimulated party formation, competition among the candidates, in turn, transformed potential voters into active participants in the political process.

The Marshall Court

Although republican nationalism accelerated the acceptance of political democracy, the first American nationalists had been Federalist conservatives. Of these, the most influential was John Marshall, chief justice of the Supreme Court (1801-1835). In a series of major rulings, Marshall upheld the expansion of national power while limiting the authority of the state governments. In the *United States* v. *Peters* (1809), the Supreme Court established its right to coerce a state legislature by ordering a Pennsylvania court to issue a verdict despite a legislative act prohibiting such a step. A later judgment (*Martin* v. *Hunter's Lessee*, 1816) confirmed the Court's right to overrule a state court. Two cases involving the right of contract (*Fletcher* v. *Peck*, 1810, and *Dartmouth College* v. *Woodward*, 1819) established the principle that state laws were invalid when in conflict with the United States Constitution [see above, p. 170]. Marshall's commitment to a strong national government often had vast economic implications. Thus, in *McCulloch* v. *Maryland* (1819), the Court upheld the constitutionality of a national bank (something that President Washington had assumed much earlier) and denied that the states could tax the institutions of the central government. In *Gibbons* v. *Ogden* (1824), Marshall invalidated a New York steamboat monopoly that operated on the Hudson River between New York and New Jersey by broadly defining *commerce* to include not only buying and selling but also other forms of intercourse (including navigation). This ruling gave the national government undisputed control of interstate commerce *within*, as well as between, the states. Such decisions reinforced national support of economic expansion and provided precedents for later regulation of American business.

The Foreign Policy of John Quincy Adams

The rulings of John Marshall, like the oratory of American patriots, reflected a self-conscious nationalism, a determined effort to strengthen the bonds of national union. John Quincy Adams, son of the second president, shared these nationalistic feelings. As James Monroe's secretary of state (1817-1825), Adams attempted to implement his sentiments by forging a foreign policy of independence.

Although Spain claimed legal ownership of Florida, the United States wanted to seize the territory. Florida long had been a haven for runaway slaves, who often formed communities with the Seminole Indians (sometimes as their slaves). Like the other southern tribes, the Seminoles resisted American invasion of their lands, and, in 1817, the Seminoles joined with blacks in open warfare against the United States. President Monroe ordered Andrew Jackson to lead a punitive expedition into Spanish territory (1818), allegedly in defense of American property. In pursuing the Seminoles, Jackson captured two Spanish garrisons and executed two British subjects who, Jackson claimed, had been instigating the Indians' attacks. The affair had important international repercussions. Despite fears in Washington that Jackson might have provoked a war with Spain and Britain, Adams eased diplomatic tensions by relinquishing the captured towns. Meanwhile, Spain realized its inability to restrain American expansion and feared a loss not only of Florida but also of northern Mexico. To protect its interests in Mexico, Spain was prepared to sacrifice Florida and instructed Ambassador Onis to negotiate a treaty. In a series of tough negotiating sessions, Adams persuaded Onis to transfer eastern Florida to the United States for $5 million, which would be used to reimburse American citizens for claims they held against Spain. Adams also agreed to a western division of the Louisiana Territory that preserved Spanish control in Texas. But he persuaded Onis to relinquish Spanish claims to a large tract of land west of the Rocky Mountains, thus providing the United States with a claim to the Pacific coast. Adams, long a proponent of nationalism, had provided a legal basis for continental expansion. The Adams-Onis Treaty, also known as the Transcontinental Treaty (1819), was not ratified until 1821, because Spain wished to delay American recognition of the Latin American states that had revolted against the Spanish Empire.

By 1821, nearly all the nations of Latin America had declared their independence from Spain. Such nationalists as Henry Clay, interested in expanding trade with Latin America, urged the administration to grant formal recognition to these states. Monroe, however, waited for Spanish approval of the Adams-Onis Treaty before taking that step (March 1822). Meanwhile, the conservative European monarchs, intent on preserving the legitimacy of existing regimes, devised a scheme to send a French army to reestablish Spanish authority in South America. This proposal alarmed not only Adams and Monroe but also Foreign Secretary George Canning, who wished to protect British economic interests in Latin America. Canning suggested that the United States and Britain issue a joint statement repudiating French interference in South America and disavowing any intention of annexing the area themselves.

President Monroe seemed agreeable to Canning's gesture, but Adams pointed out several disadvantages of such a procedure. First, he realized that the British navy would prevent French military operations in South America regardless of the position of the United States. Second, it was not in the best interest of the United States to preserve Britain's trade with Latin America. Third, a promise to renounce annexationist interests might prevent the later acquisition of such territories as Cuba and Mexico. Finally, the British proposal ignored the problem of Russian expansion along the Pacific coast. Hence, in his annual message to Congress (December 1823), Monroe independently announced an American foreign policy. The Monroe Doctrine articulated the principles of (1) noncolonization, which forbade further colonization of the Western Hemisphere by any European power, and (2) nonintervention, which renounced American interference in European affairs (a reference to the Greek and Spanish rebellions then in progress) and conversely opposed any attempts of European nations to intercede in the affairs of the Western Hemisphere. An additional implicit position was that of "no-transfer," whereby the United States opposed the transfer of any possession in the Western Hemisphere from one European nation to another. The Monroe Doctrine had little impact on European diplomacy, but, for reasons unrelated to the statement, the European powers abandoned their plans. The Russian czar, lacking serious interest in the Pacific coast, agreed to a treaty renouncing all claims south of 54°40′ (the southern border of Alaska). Although unimpressive at the time, the Monroe Doctrine provided later Americans with a precedent for restricting European activities in the Western Hemisphere. Equally important, by making United States policy independent of Britain, the Monroe Doctrine provided the basis for the expansion of an informal empire in Latin America.

National Politics

The self-conscious nationalism of men like Adams and Marshall did not eliminate the essential localism of American politics. Prior to the War of 1812, the Jefferson administration had relied upon customs revenues to fund governmental operations and to retire the national debt. Wartime expenses led Congress to double all tariffs (to about 25 percent). Meanwhile, Jefferson's embargo and the war itself had stimulated American industry. Following the Treaty of Ghent, American manufacturers demanded that Congress protect the infant industries from British competition. Such nationalists as John C. Calhoun of South Carolina and Henry Clay of Kentucky supported the Tariff of 1816 (which maintained the wartime levels) partly because they expected the measure to benefit their *home districts*. (Kentucky's hemp industry required protection, while

Calhoun held visions of flourishing textile mills in South Carolina.) The northern states were divided on the issue; manufacturers supported the tariff, while merchants, fearful of a loss of commerce, opposed it.

Clay and Calhoun also combined forces to win congressional support for a program of internal improvements (that is, the construction of roads and canals) funded by the national government (1816). Partly a reaction to the transportation difficulties encountered during the war, the proposal would facilitate interstate trade and reduce American economic dependence on Europe. Despite the opposition of congressmen from New England (who opposed westward expansion) and many southerners (who doubted the constitutionality of the proposal), the bill passed in Congress only to be vetoed by President Madison, who denied the constitutionality of the measure.

The absence of a national bank had seriously hampered the war effort. The Bank of the United States had expired in 1811 and failed at renewal. State banks had been unable to finance public loans, and wartime crises (particularly the burning of Washington) had disrupted banking credit, causing a suspension of specie payments outside New England. After the war, Congress voted to charter a second Bank of the United States (1816) capitalized at $35 million to restore financial stability. Chartered for twenty years, the bank was authorized to establish branches throughout the nation. Only the New England states, which already possessed adequate banking facilities, opposed the measure.

The bank had been intended to promote a stable economy. But poor management by the bank's officials instead produced an overexpansion of credit both by the state banks and by the branch banks. The resulting inflation was reinforced by a rise in agricultural prices caused by the reopening of markets in war-torn Europe. Many farmers borrowed money to buy western lands at this time. But, as European farmers recovered from the war, the demand for American goods dropped, causing a decrease in prices. Amidst this depression, the national bank began tightening credit by accumulating the notes of state banks that had overissued their credit and then presenting them for redemption. To meet these demands, the banks called in their loans, forcing debtors to liquidate their holdings. In the ensuing crisis, known as the Panic of 1819, banks failed, businesses closed, trade ceased, and farmers faced eviction from their lands. Congress assisted the farmers by lowering the price of land, permitting the purchase of smaller acreage, and allowing farmers to return portions of their land to the government. More frequently, state legislatures enacted stay laws to delay execution on debtors' property. Such relief measures assisted many hard-pressed farmers in the South and West.

Nevertheless, the Panic of 1819 aggravated sectional tensions. Western and southern farmers, hit hardest by the depression, blamed the Bank of the United States for their troubles and became strong opponents of a national bank. Northern manufacturers, suffering from a loss of markets, appealed to Congress for a higher protective tariff (1820). Southern representatives, realizing by this time that tariffs primarily favored northern

THE UNITED STATES, 1820

manufacturers, managed to defeat the proposal in the Senate. Four years later, the manufacturers again pressed for higher tariffs. Support came from the Northeast and from western farmers, who hoped to find domestic markets for their products. The South voted almost unanimously against the measure in the House of Representatives. Despite such opposition, the Tariff of 1824 raised duties on textiles, iron, hemp, and raw wool. Sectional alignments also emerged in discussions of federally financed internal improvements. Congressional voting on such matters revealed strong western support for internal development programs, while eastern regions, both northern and southern, often dissented.

Political divisions on such issues as banking, tariffs, and internal improvements illustrated two aspects of American politics in this period. First, congressional representatives defended the interests of their constituents on most questions, thereby preserving the republican attitude toward political leadership. Second, the rhetoric of nationalism, however prevalent, concealed a more fundamental commitment to regional and state interests.

The Missouri Compromise

The importance of sectional interests appeared even more obvious on the question of the expansion of slavery in the western territories. In the years after 1815, the territory of Missouri filled rapidly with southern settlers. By 1819 — with over 60,000 inhabitants — the territory petitioned for statehood. Expected to be a routine matter, the admission of Missouri provoked an intense debate when New York representative James Tallmadge presented an amendment (in February 1819) forbidding the importation of slaves into Missouri and freeing the children of all slaves already there at the age of twenty-five. Introducing this proposal, Tallmadge departed from tradition by ignoring the composition of the free population of the territory. (Such earlier limitations on slavery as the Northwest Ordinance of 1787 had restricted the institution *prior* to settlement.) In any case, the Tallmadge amendment passed the House of Representatives, which voted along sectional lines; the Senate, however, overwhelmingly defeated the proposal. The next Congress (1819-1820) confronted the issue anew.

The intense debate over the status of slavery in Missouri centered on the problem of power. The southern states realized that the more heavily populated North effectively controlled the House of Representatives. The Senate, however, representing eleven free states and eleven slave states remained a safeguard of southern interests. Moreover, Arkansas and Florida were the only proslave territories about to be admitted into the union, while three free territories soon would become states. In this situation, the status of Missouri seemed fundamental to southern power. The northern states, on the other hand, objected to Missouri as a slave state, because, under the Three-fifths Compromise, it would obtain additional representatives in Congress. During this crisis, few politicians spoke about the rights of blacks or the morality of slavery. The absence of moral imperatives facilitated a resolution of the controversy. Missouri would enter the union as a slave state, and Maine, which recently had been formed as a separate district, would be admitted as a free state, thus preserving the political balance in the Senate. Moreover, Congress agreed to prohibit slavery in all other parts of the Louisiana Territory north of 36°30′ (the southern boundary of Missouri).

The Missouri Compromise, however, did not immediately conclude the crisis. The Missouri Compromise prohibited the admission of free blacks into the state, a policy often practiced in older states. Northern congressmen argued that the provision violated the Constitution by denying the privileges of citizenship to free blacks. Henry Clay then introduced a second compromise in which Congress forbade Missouri from abridging the rights of citizenship (1821). In this manner, pragmatic politicians dodged the more inflammatory questions of slavery and racism. The prolonged debate on the Missouri question, nevertheless, emphasized the sectional nature of American politics. Concerned with protecting regional interests, politicians often ignored the problem of national interest.

The Adams Administration

The presidential election of 1824 reflected both the rudimentary level of political parties and the sectional interests of the American people. Although four candidates campaigned for office — William Crawford of Georgia, John Quincy Adams of Massachusetts, Henry Clay of Kentucky, and Andrew Jackson of Tennessee — voters in the states apparently noticed little competition locally and barely 25 percent of the eligible voters cast ballots. Moreover, with the exception of Jackson, the candidates triumphed only in their home regions. In the electoral college, Jackson obtained ninety-nine votes; Adams, eighty-four; Crawford, forty-one; and Clay, thirty-seven. Since no candidate controlled a majority, the election moved to the House of Representatives, where each state had one vote. As Speaker of the House, Clay possessed sufficient influence to control the election. Fearing Jackson as a rival from the West and sympathetic to Adams's nationalism, Clay supported Adams, thereby assuring his election. When Adams subsequently appointed Clay his secretary of state, the Jacksonians accused the president of having bargained with Clay for his support. The notion of a "corrupt bargain" haunted the remainder of Adams's administration.

Adams, the adept exponent of national interests under Monroe, proved less effective as a nationalist president. Unwilling to accept the rules of partisan politics, he tried to rise above party interests. Thus, he refused to use presidential patronage to win a personal following and failed to provide executive leadership in Congress. He recommended an ambitious program of internal improvements and government aid to agriculture and manufacturing and yet failed to rally support for his ideas. Consequently, Congress allotted insufficient funds for the program.

By refusing to appease sectional interests, Adams became a scapegoat of sectional antagonism. When Colombia and Mexico invited the United States to attend a conference at Panama intended to pressure Spain to acknowledge their independence, Adams's political enemies attacked the proposal, and southern representatives warned that the presence of black delegates from Haiti posed a threat to American slavery. After much debate, Congress appropriated funds to finance the mission (1826), but one delegate died en route and the other arrived in Panama after the sessions had ended.

Sectional antipathy reached a peak in a debate over the revision of the Tariff of 1824. Since producers of raw materials joined manufacturers in demanding protection from foreign competition, the tariff bill of 1828 included high duties on such commodities as hemp, raw wool, and flax. New England manufacturers protested the high rates on these raw materials and proposed a series of amendments to lower the duties. Southern representatives believed that northern congressmen would certainly defeat any bill that included high tariffs on raw materials. Therefore, they hoped to kill the entire tariff by voting against the northern amendments. New England, however, was too committed to a policy of protection and reluctantly approved the Tariff of 1828, even with its high duties on raw materials. The antitariff strategy of the South had backfired, forcing southerners to live with the Tariff of Abominations. South Carolina's John Calhoun, frustrated by the vote, drafted the Exposition and Protest (1828), which criticized the tariff and stated a theory of states' rights that justified the nullification of a congressional law by an act of a state legislature. Yet, Calhoun hoped that the next administration would lower the tariff and so made no effort to implement his ideas.

Conflicts over tariffs, the Panama conference, and internal improvements undermined the nationalist policies of President Adams. As sections became somewhat more specialized — the North as a manufacturing center, the South as a cotton producer, and the West as an agricultural region — it became increasingly difficult to effect political compromise. By 1828, a successful leader had to transcend the divisions of American society and appeal to people in all sections. As a national hero, Andrew Jackson seemed well suited to the task. In 1828, he easily defeated the presidential incumbent and assumed the leadership of the United States.

Supplementary Reading

For a survey of the period after the War of 1812, see G. Dangerfield, *The Awakening of American Nationalism, 1815-1828* (1965). The search for a national culture is described in R. Nye, *The Cultural Life of the New Nation, 1776-1830* (1960), and P. Nagel, *One Nation Indivisible* (1964). For a discussion of Jackson as a cultural hero, see J. W. Ward, *Andrew Jackson: Symbol for an Age* (1955).

Studies of the relationship between state politics and reform include C. S. Sydnor, *The Development of Southern Sectionalism, 1819-1848* (1948); R. Remini, *Martin Van Buren and the Making of the Democratic Party* (1959); R. Hofstadter, *The Idea of a Party System* (1969); and L. Benson, *The Concept of Jacksonian Democracy: New York as a Test Case* (1961). Also helpful is S. Livermore, *The Twilight of Federalism* (1962).

For a discussion of the Marshall Court, see E. Corwin, *John Marshall and the Constitution* (1919). For an examination of the career of J. Q. Adams, see S. Bemis's two-volume study, *John Quincy Adams* (1949-1956). The standard work on the fifth president is W. Cressor, *James Monroe* (1946). In addition to Bemis, several historians have examined the Monroe Doctrine; see D. Perkins, *The Monroe Doctrine* (1927); A. Whitaker, *The United States and the Independence of Latin America: 1800-1830* (1941); and J. Logan, *No Transfer* (1961).

The standard work on the Missouri Compromise is G. Moore, *the Missouri Controversy, 1819-1821* (1953), but see also D. Robinson, *Slavery in the Structure of American Politics: 1765-1820* (1971). Much of the politics of the period can be learned from the biographies of the leaders; see H. Ammon, *James Monroe: The Quest for National Identity* (1971); C. Wiltse, *John C. Calhoun: Nationalist, 1782-1828* (1944); G. Van Deusen, *The Life of Henry Clay* (1937); C. Eaton, *Henry Clay and the Art of American Politics* (1957); and J. Curtis, *Andrew Jackson and the Search for Vindication* (1976). A good study of national politics is R. Remini, *The Election of Andrew Jackson* (1964).

The Politics of Social Change
1828-1844

The Panic of 1819 and the ensuing depression (1819-1821) severely upset the American economy. The contraction of credit squeezed western land purchasers and eastern manufacturers alike, and antagonism toward the Bank of the United States, state banks, and paper money developed throughout the nation. But, by the mid-1820s, the return of prosperity again encouraged economic expansion. Sound fiscal policies, promoted by the director of the second Bank of the United States, Nicholas Biddle, stimulated capital investments from abroad and allowed the expansion of credit from domestic banks. Economic prosperity, however, did not spread equally, and many Americans resented the economic and social developments of the period. Varying attitudes toward economic and social issues influenced political behavior and shaped the political party alignments.

Immigration

Following the conclusion of the Napoleonic wars, waves of immigrants from England, Ireland, and Germany contributed to the expansion of American society. Before 1840, the immigrants were usually either artisans unable to compete with the mechanization of European industries or farmers who had become victims of overproduction. Concerned about declining incomes and a loss of status, more and more Europeans undertook the difficult journey to America. First, they traveled to such ports as Hamburg, Bremen, Le Havre, and Liverpool. There, they were packed aboard freighters, where they endured four to six weeks at sea, often plagued by disease and hunger. They entered the United States through port cities such as Boston, New York, Baltimore, and New Orleans. Many immigrants, lacking the funds to go further, remained in those ports. Others, who were more prosperous, traveled inland and settled in Cincinnati, St. Louis, and Buffalo. As experienced craftsmen, industrial workers, and miners, these immigrants brought needed skills to developing American industry. The relative prosperity of American agriculture, moreover, offered many immigrant farmers the opportunity to regain their status as successful farmers. This wave of immigration contrasted with the later arrival of poorer groups [see below, pp. 222-223].

Western Expansion

The influx of European immigrants, combined with the natural increase of the American population, encouraged westward expansion. Mostly young people in search of opportunity and eastern farmers unable to compete with the production of more fertile acreage in the West, the migrants swelled the population of the western territories. The abundant wheat harvests of the West often compelled eastern farmers to shift to wool production, to attempt more diversified farming that brought smaller profits, or simply to abandon their farms for urban employment. More adventurous people packed their furnishings and joined the westward movement.

Supported by government policy, the American settlers ignored the claims of the Indians and moved quickly into the virgin lands. The Black Hawk War (1832) ended Indian opposition in the Northwest, while the Seminole War (1837-1842) reduced the populations of the tribes in Florida. It was in Georgia, however, that the American people most blatantly disregarded the rights of the Indians and ignored the treaties of the national government. The state of Georgia, interested in land development, attempted to force the Creeks and Cherokees from their traditional homeland.

During the Adams administration, the national government settled a long-standing dispute with the Creeks with the Treaty of Washington (1827), in which the Indians ceded their lands to Georgia. During the treaty negotiations, Adams had offended many Georgians by seeking greater equity for the Creeks. The Cherokee tribe of northwestern Georgia attempted to forestall a controversy with the state by adopting a constitution (1827) and declaring themselves dependents of the United States not

MAJOR GENERAL SCOTT, of the United States Army, sends to the Cherokee people, remaining in North Carolina, Georgia, Tennessee, and Alabama, this

ADDRESS.

Cherokees! The President of the United States has sent me, with a powerful army, to cause you, in obedience to the Treaty of 1835, to join that part of your people who are already established in prosperity, on the other side of the Mississippi. Unhappily, the two years which were allowed for the purpose, you have suffered to pass away without following, and without making any preparation to follow, and now, or by the time that this solemn *address* shall reach your distant settlements, the emigration must be commenced in haste, but, I hope, without disorder. I have no power, by granting a farther delay, to correct the error that you have committed. The full moon of May is already on the wane, and before another shall have passed away, every Cherokee man, woman and child, in those States, must be in motion to join their brethren in the far West.

My Friends! This is no sudden determination on the part of the President, whom you and I must now obey. By the treaty, the emigration was to have been completed on, or before, the 23rd of this month; and the President has constantly kept you warned, during the two years allowed, through all his officers and agents in this country, that the Treaty would be enforced.

I am come to carry out that determination. My troops already occupy many positions in the country that you are to abandon, and thousands, and thousands are approaching, from every quarter, to render resistance and escape alike hopeless. All those troops, regular and militia, are your friends. Receive them and confide in them as such. Obey them when they tell you that you can remain no longer in this country. Soldiers are as kind hearted as brave, and the desire of every one of us is to execute our painful duty in mercy. We are commanded by the President to act towards you in that spirit, and such is also the wish of the whole people of America.

Chiefs, head-men and warriors! Will you, then, by resistance, compel us to resort to arms? God forbid! Or will you, by flight, seek to hide yourselves in mountains and forests, and thus oblige us to hunt you down? Remember that, in pursuit, it may be impossible to avoid conflicts. The blood of the white man, or the blood of the red man, may be spilt, and if spilt, however accidentally, it may be impossible for the discreet and humane among you, or among us to prevent a general war and carnage. Think of this, my Cherokee brethren! I am an old warrior, and have been present at many a scene of slaughter; but spare me, I beseech you, the horror of witnessing the destruction of the Cherokees.

Do not, I invite you, even wait for the close approach of the troops; but make such preparations for emigration as you can, and hasten to this place, to Ross' Landing, or to Gunter's Landing, where you all will be received in kindness by officers selected for the purpose. You will find food for all, and clothing for the destitute, at either of those places, and thence at your ease, and in comfort, be transported to your new homes according to the terms of the Treaty.

This is the address of a warrior to warriors. May his entreaties be kindly received, and may the God of both prosper the Americans and Cherokees, and preserve them long in peace and friendship with each other!

WINFIELD SCOTT.

Cherokee Agency, }
May 10, 1838. }

General Winfield Scott, following the president's instructions, orders the Cherokee nation to remove to the west of the Mississippi River. (Courtesy of Special Collections Department, University of Georgia Libraries.)

subject to the laws of Georgia. Although treaties with the national government confirmed the legitimacy of the Cherokee nation, Georgia ignored the law and opened the Cherokees' lands for settlement (1828). When the Cherokees protested, Congress proved equally unsympathetic and simply offered them lands farther west. The Cherokees brought their case to the Supreme Court, where Chief Justice John Marshall appeared more interested in justice. In *Worcester* v. *Georgia* (1832), he ruled that the Cherokees constituted a separate nation independent of Georgia's jurisdiction. But President Jackson criticized Marshall's judgment and refused to enforce the decision. Jackson claimed that the United States was doing the Cherokees a favor by transporting them to the West at no cost, and he suggested that many white Americans would have been happy to receive similar treatment. But the Cherokees, as well as the other southern tribes, suffered immensely during their forced march to Oklahoma, and their infamous ordeal became known as the Trail of Tears.

Even before the Cherokees were forced to leave their homes, white settlers, more interested in real estate than in legal and moral claims, filled the states of Alabama, Mississippi, and Arkansas. The fertile acres encourged cotton production, and plantation owners, large and small, found prosperity as the demand for cotton increased. Black slaves, transported involuntarily to the Southwest, constituted a major source of cheap labor. Slavery discouraged the settlement of European immigrants in the southern states. The persistence of slavery further solidified the political alliance between the Southwest and the Southeast.

American agriculture expanded with the migration into new lands and benefited greatly by such inventions as the reaper by Cyrus McCormick (1831), the thresher (1836), and the steel plow (1837). Yet, without adequate transportation, western products could not have found adequate markets. The geographic dispersal of the American people stimulated improvements in transportation, which, in turn, accelerated the development of the West.

During the first quarter of the nineteenth century, turnpikes had improved overland transportation [see above, p. 141]. Water travel, however, proved more convenient and cheaper. After the War of 1812, the state governments began to construct artificial canals to connect interior settlements with the eastern ports. The construction of the Erie Canal in New York (1817-1825) represented the most ambitious engineering feat of the period. Connecting the Hudson River with Lake Erie, the canal increased the trade of New York City and brought prosperity to such towns as Buffalo and Rochester. Within a few years, the Erie Canal had paid for itself, setting off a canal boom throughout the nation. Although New York City had surpassed Philadelphia in trade before the construction of the Erie Canal, other eastern states, hoping to recapture the western commerce, began constructing canals. A Pennsylvania Canal System (1825-1835) connected Philadelphia and Pittsburgh with a complicated network of canals, and Maryland chartered the Chesapeake and Ohio Canal Company (1828) to connect Baltimore with the Ohio River. Yet, neither of these projects challenged the supremacy of the New York system. Such western states as Ohio, Indiana, and Illinois built a series of canals to link the Great Lakes with the northern river system. In 1830, there were more than 1,000 miles of canals; in another twenty years, that figure nearly tripled.

The increased use of steamboats also reduced freight costs on inland waterways. Hundreds of steamers sailed the Mississippi River system, shortening the length of voyages (to five days between New Orleans and Louisville) and lowering prices. Foreign commerce also expanded as sailing ships conquered the Atlantic. Besides reducing the time of transportation, transatlantic service became more regular, enabling merchants to move their products on schedule. The completion of the Erie Canal confirmed New York City's commercial leadership by opening the West to European manufactured goods. Thus, western farmers as well as business people profited from improvements in transportation. Yet, by opening the East to western foodstuffs, the transportation system imperiled eastern farmers who cultivated less productive soil. Many of the easterners, facing declining profits, sought to protect their incomes by following the transportation routes to the West. Ironically, profits for some brought deprivation for others.

Industrial Expansion

Commercial expansion generated investment capital that was used to finance American manufacturing. Textile factories, which were centered in New England, continued to mushroom, bringing large profits to industrial investors. The availability of water power, investment capital, and labor explains why industrialization began in the Northeast. Similarly, the abundance of anthracite coal, used for smelting, made Pennsylvania the center of iron production. The mass production of timepieces in this period signified the increased emphasis on industrial efficiency and underscored the attempt to harness time as well as labor and capital.

European immigrants provided much of the skilled labor in early American factories. Unskilled workers, however, usually came from the rural areas that surrounded the first factory towns. New England farmers, unable to compete with western agriculture and unwilling to migrate to the West, moved to urban centers. Ironically, the growth of factories had helped to undermine their economic position in the first place. On marginal farms, many families had engaged in domestic manufacturing to augment declining incomes from agriculture. As factory competition eliminated these household industries, rural families abandoned their farms for the nearby mills. Some of the larger New England industrialists developed the Waltham System to recruit a labor force of unmarried farm women. Living in company dormitories that were strictly supervised, the mill girls worked seventy-five hour weeks and contributed their meager earnings to their struggling families or tried to accumulate a modest dowry.

The textile mills of Lowell, Massachusetts, symbolized the expansion of industrial technology in the early nineteenth century. Besides producing vast quantities of cloth, the founders of Lowell also hoped to create a healthy moral climate to protect the virtue of the predominantly female employees. (Courtesy of Library of Congress.)

Besides being an inexpensive source of labor (costing two to three dollars per week), the girls provided an elastic work force that could be sent back home during depressed times and recalled to meet increased demands. By the 1840s, however, these young women were being replaced by a cheaper source of labor — the immigrants from Ireland and Germany [see below, p. 222].

The economic expansion in the eastern cities created a rising demand for skilled craftsmen during the 1820s. Taking advantage of this situation, many artisans formed workers' unions to demand a variety of reforms. In Philadelphia, a city-wide organization led a ten-hour day strike (1827) and later established a political party. The Workingmen's party, which spread throughout the eastern states, consisted not only of artisans but also of radical reformers and merchants. They demanded a ten-hour work day, free public education, the abolition of imprisonment for debt, and mechanics' lien laws (to give laborers first claims against bankrupt employers). Many states responded by establishing lien laws and ending imprisonment for debt. The demands of labor included more than economic improvements and revealed the fact that skilled workers shared many of the middle-class ideals of their employers.

A depression that struck the United States after 1837, however, enabled employers to break the infant unions and abolish such victories as the limitation of the length of the workday. Since unions did not obtain judicial sanction until a Massachusetts court decision of 1842 (*Common-*

wealth v. *Hunt*), the workers had few defenses against their employers. An executive order issued by President Martin Van Buren (1840) instituted a ten-hour workday for federal employees. But little was done to ease the plight of a growing urban proletariat made up of unskilled and semiskilled workers.

Although American economic development remained dependent on foreign investments, American capital increasingly provided the resources for American business. A series of complex changes in international markets involving the importation of silver from Mexico, the influx of capital from Britain, and the rise in cotton prices led to the accumulation of large amounts of specie in the United States. The increase in hard money enabled American banks to extend credit safely for a variety of economic activities. This extension of credit stimulated prosperity during the early 1830s. Moreover, the rise in cotton prices led farmers throughout the nation to invest heavily in western lands. Such land investments, by removing capital from other areas of the economy, served a deflationary role.

By the mid-1830s, a crisis in international trade led English bankers to reduce their capital investments in the United States. This policy, which was related to a decline in cotton prices, forced bankers in the United States to suspend specie payments and created the Panic of 1837. However, the deflation was moderated by changes in other segments of the economy. President Jackson had issued the Specie Circular (1836) which required land purchases to be made in hard money rather than on credit. Although this policy did not raise the price of public land, it did reduce the optimism of land speculators and led to a reduction of land purchases. The end of the land boom freed American capital to work in other areas of the economy, thus buffering the depression caused by the financial panic.

The return of English investments in 1838 alleviated the deflation, and prosperity returned to the nation. But a series of crop failures in England, combined with a drop in cotton prices, again moved British investors to curtail capital exports to the United States in 1839. This policy caused a second depression that lasted for several years. State governments repudiated their debts, further deterring British investments. Yet, agricultural production did not decline and unemployment appeared to be sporadic. Above all, these economic trends seem to be unrelated to the fiscal policies of President Jackson [see below, p. 207].

Social Structure

During the mid-nineteenth century, most Americans were still farmers, and American society was overwhelmingly rural. But, during the third and fourth decades of the nineteenth century, the expansion of American society — the influx of European immigrants, the migration to new lands, urbanization, and industrialization — offered many people the possibility of upward social mobility. Foreign visitors, like the Frenchman

Alexis de Tocqueville, observed that the American people seemed to be interested primarily in acquiring wealth and material possessions. Yet, Americans did not share equally the benefits of the altered economy. Few people found easy wealth; most found their chances for success increasingly restricted.

In the eastern states, the growth of manufacturing brought great wealth to a fortunate few, most of whom already possessed some capital — usually inherited wealth — with which to make their initial investments. Although the rise of an industrial elite might have displaced an older commercial elite, the new rich usually had family connections with the old order and continued to respect traditional social distinctions. Only by retaining traditional social values could they legitimize their new status. Artisans and craftsmen who were not directly challenged by factory production also prospered, as the formation of trade unions seems to suggest. But workers in the domestic industries that faced mechanized competition struggled to survive and often entered the ranks of a swelling industrial labor force. Unskilled workers formed an urban labor force that was economically dependent on merchants and industrial capitalists. Although frequently on the move between jobs, the urban laborers had few opportunities to change occupations or to raise their incomes. Lowest on the social scale were free blacks, who were concentrated in urban centers. Although some blacks managed to start small businesses, most were unskilled laborers who worked in occupations that were subject to frequent unemployment. Racial discrimination in employment occurred frequently.

The pattern of social stratification emerged not only in eastern cities but also in the newly settled areas of the West. In the Gulf plains states, cotton and sugar production accelerated the rise of a planter elite that had heavy investments in land and slaves. Although comprised of "new" people with capitalistic attitudes toward agriculture, many members of the southwestern elite attempted to imitate the gentility of the eastern planter aristocracy. The industrial demands for American cotton also offered proportional wealth to farmers with smaller investments. Thus, small-scale farms, operated with few or no slaves, flourished throughout the South.

In the Northwest, a similar pattern of stratification existed. Many farmers speculated in western lands and acquired large profits when later settlers purchased their holdings. As in the colonial period, people from all classes participated in such speculation, particularly during the land boom of the 1830s. Although the northern social structure appeared more fluid than that of the South, a rural elite emerged throughout the Northwest. Farmers in this region generally sold their products to merchants in nearby towns for reshipment east. Thus, agricultural prosperity encouraged the development of such western cities as St. Louis, Cincinnati, Pittsburgh, and Louisville. Such towns offered wide opportunities to merchants, lawyers, artisans, and manufacturers. Within a relatively brief period, these urban centers also revealed patterns of social stratification. As the urban elite became entrenched, newcomers and people of lesser status found

Upper-class fashions in 1844 revealed the acceptance of "egalitarian" trousers and the popularity of hooped dresses. (From Godey's Lady's Book, *1844.)*

fewer opportunities for social mobility. Yet, the hardening of social distinctions in the West did not eliminate further mobility, for western settlers frustrated in one region frequently moved to another.

Ideological Responses

Economic expansion affected the American people in various ways. Some took advantage of available opportunities, acquired greater wealth, and rose in status. Others sadly watched their incomes decline and witnessed the erosion of their social standing. In between were people who welcomed the economic changes and aspired to higher status but who found their hopes blocked by entrenched groups. These variations of status influenced American attitudes toward the economic and social changes of the period. Stated generally, people with expectations of improvement supported the direction of change, while those who feared the consequences of economic expansion lamented the loss of social order.

Despite such differences, Americans generally shared a commitment to the principle that all people deserved equal economic opportunities. To be sure, such ideals were seldom practiced, for white Americans continued to discriminate against racial and ethnic minorities and women. Yet, within the native-born white male population, Americans claimed that individual initiative, if moral in intent, would bring economic rewards. People used moral language to explain their economic and social conditions and they assumed a close correlation between prosperity and virtue, poverty and vice. Thus, as nineteenth-century Americans evaluated their society, morality served to rationalize economic status. Such attitudes helped to shape the political divisions of the period as Americans attempted to protect their social and economic interests.

The revitalization of political parties that occurred during the 1820s encouraged candidates to appeal directly to American voters [see above, pp. 182-183]. The close alliance between various interests and the government in areas relating to economic development also forced politicians to discuss economic issues. Electoral competition revealed two rival approaches to social and economic questions. One group of politicians, who comprised the Democratic party, opposed the pattern of economic development. A second group, which later formed the core of the Whig party, emphasized the advantages of economic expansion.

Democratic orators generally criticized the changing nature of American society. Coalescing around Andrew Jackson, the Democrats viewed the expansion of American commerce and industry as a radical departure from the yeoman republic of the founding fathers. They believed that the *natural* harmony and order of the Jeffersonian farmer had been perverted by materialistic and *artificial* institutions [see above, pp. 146-147]. Above all, they condemned such artificial devices as chartered corporations, banks, and paper money. Such unnatural contrivances had enabled privileged groups to benefit at the expense of the people. Thus, the Jacksonians stood as restorers, hoping to return the United States to its original republican purity by destroying such unnatural monsters as the Bank of the United States.

By contrast, anti-Jacksonian politicians, who later established the Whig party, praised the economic transformation of the United States and exalted the material progress of the nineteenth century. Popularized by the American System of Kentucky's Henry Clay, the Whigs' program advocated government support for economic expansion through protective tariffs, the continuation of a national bank, federally financed internal improvements, and the rapid settlement of the West. As nationalists, they envisioned an integrated self-sufficient economy. Whig politicians like Clay and Massachusetts's Daniel Webster promised that economic nationalism would bring the fruits of progress to all Americans by increasing economic opportunities in all regions. Emphasizing the democratic nature of their program, the Whigs declared that banks and tariffs had brought prosperity to numerous Americans by encouraging individual initiative. Developing the theme of rags-to-riches success, Whig spokesmen insisted that the United States was a nation of self-made men. Thus, they accepted the economic changes of the age and simply promised to extend the economic bounties to more Americans.

Political Competition

The politicians who eventually formed the Whig and Democratic parties attempted to appeal to all Americans. Neither group attracted all the members of a particular class. In some states, intangible factors such as party loyalty and ethnic affiliation influenced voting behavior more clearly than class interest. Moreover, political leaders avoided contradicting the regional or economic interests of their constituents. Webster defended the manufacturers who supported his candidacies; Clay protected the hemp industry of Kentucky; Calhoun spoke for the antitariff interests of South Carolina. In short, politics did not merely reflect attitudes toward social and economic change.

Such qualifications aside, certain generalizations may be made about voting alignments. The Whigs attracted support from people who believed that they might *rise* in status as a result of the expansion of the American economy. Land speculators, western farmers and business people, and eastern manufacturers endorsed the Whigs' economic program. The Jacksonians, on the other hand, won support from people who believed that they might *decline* in status or lose opportunities as a result of privileged economic practices. Thus, state bankers who resented the privileged position of the national bank advocated its elimination. Urban workers who were paid in bank notes (which circulated at less than face value) condemned paper money as the source of evil. Eastern farmers forced off their land by western competition, artisans and craftsmen drawn into factories, and other victims of inflation blamed the expanding industrial economy for their problems. They all advocated an economy of small independent producers, and they all found solace in the party of Andrew Jackson.

Despite the potential mass base of the competing politicians, the presidential election of 1828 between Jackson and John Quincy Adams focused more on the candidates' personalities than on substantive political issues. Both men had national reputations, but their party organizations remained immature. Consequently, in some states, one party dominated the other. But, in states where the parties competed with equal vigor, voter participation increased. Aside from his popularity as the hero of New Orleans, Jackson benefited by a powerful political alliance forged by New York's Martin Van Buren and southern leaders opposed to Adams. John Calhoun, as Jackson's running mate, strengthened the ticket in the South. Winning the support of voters in all sections and from all classes, Jackson easily defeated his rival.

President Jackson

Jackson's ability to transcend the sectionalism of the 1820s bolstered his image as a president of the people. Believing himself to be the only government official elected by all citizens, Jackson endeavored to protect the people from the power of other branches of government. Thus, his support of Georgia over the Cherokees [see above, p. 196] reflected his desire to advance the interests of the white majority. At other times, he vetoed congressional legislation and challenged state legislatures when he felt their actions contravened the interests of their constituents.

The president's attitude toward the people emerged visibly on inaugural day, when he opened the White House to all celebrants, rich and poor. Unlike his predecessor, Jackson sought to consolidate his following by rewarding his loyal adherents with presidental patronage. The use of the spoils system, although practiced by earlier presidents such as the elder Adams, reflected the growing importance of party organizations, which obliged successful candidates to reward party workers. Jackson also justified his appointments by arguing that party appointees represented the people better than entrenched civil servants. Jackson relied heavily on an informal Kitchen Cabinet composed of such friends as Amos Kendall of Kentucky, William B. Lewis of Tennessee, and Francis P. Blair, editor of the *Washington Globe*. Supporters of John Calhoun, who hoped to succeed Jackson, ominously were frozen out of the administration, while Martin Van Buren was appointed secretary of state.

Sectional Rivalry

Jackson's personal distrust of the instruments of economic expansion led him to pursue a moderate policy during this first administration. Although as a westerner he approved federally funded internal improvements, he vetoed a bill to finance a turnpike between Maysville and Lexington, Kentucky (1830), arguing that the road was a local improvement that was not eligible constitutionally for federal support. The veto, besides revealing the president's desire to reduce government expenditures, also underscored the growing influence of Van Buren. As a representative of New York (which wanted no competition with the state-supported Erie Canal), the secretary of state persuaded Jackson to reduce government aid for internal improvements.

The question of a western land policy also brought sectional conflict into focus. Henry Clay had proposed that proceeds from the sale of public lands be distributed to the states to finance internal improvements. The suggestion met with opposition from westerners, who preferred to see land prices reduced, and from southerners, who feared that further expenditures would necessitate a higher tariff. Such sectional interests provided the backdrop for a major debate in the Senate. Samuel Foote of Connecticut, reflecting New England's dislike of westward expansion, introduced a resolution calling for the cessation of the sale of government lands (1829). Senator Robert Hayne of South Carolina denounced the resolution and used the floor of the Senate to propose a West-South alliance to support cheap land and a low tariff. Daniel Webster attempted to defend the interests of the Northeast by steering the discussion away from the land question to a consideration of the nature of the union. By virtually accusing Hayne of treason, Webster cleverly undermined the formation of a West-South alliance. Equally important in subverting the alliance, however, was the fear of eastern cotton planters that the rapid development of the West would threaten their own prosperity.

The Webster-Hayne debate (1830) also aggravated a growing rift between Jackson and Calhoun over two personal matters. The first involved a minor social dispute among the wives of cabinet members in which Mrs. Calhoun alienated the president. The second issue related to Jackson's discovery that Calhoun, as secretary of war during the Monroe administration, had recommended that Jackson be tried for his invasion of Florida in 1818 [see above, p. 184]. Such personal enmity, together with the dispute on the question of nullification, led Jackson to drop Calhoun and select Van Buren as his running mate in 1832.

Nullification

Southerners like Calhoun hoped that the Jackson administration would seek to reduce the extravagant rates of the Tariff of Abominations [see above, p. 190]. A protectionist Congress, however, adopted only minor revisions (1832). South Carolina Nullifers reacted by summoning a popularly elected convention, which declared the tariff laws to be null and void and forbade their enforcement in South Carolina (November 1832). The movement for nullification reflected more than just a protest over economic grievances. Like the New England Federalists of an earlier generation, the Nullifiers felt increasingly powerless in national affairs.

During the 1820s, northern abolitionists had begun a moderate campaign against slavery, but, in 1831, William Lloyd Garrison established *The Liberator,* which signified the beginning of a more militant abolitionist crusade [see below, pp. 225-226]. Meanwhile, the foundations of South Carolina slavery seemed threatened from within. The discovery of an imminent slave revolt led by Denmark Vesey in Charleston (1822) horrified the white population. News of Nat Turner's Insurrection (1831) in nearby Virginia further alarmed South Carolinians. Thus, fear of a slave revolt, hostility toward northern abolitionists, and a sense of political impotence on the question of tariff reform enabled the Nullifiers to rally public support.

Jackson responded to the Nullification Convention by issuing a proclamation to the citizens of South Carolina calling on them to demonstrate their loyalty to the union, and he requested Congress to reduce the tariff rates of 1832. Yet, he also asked Congress to pass a force act permitting him to enforce the revenue laws in South Carolina by any means necessary. Congress reacted by passing the force act and by adopting the Compromise Tariff (1833), which provided for a gradual reduction of rates until 1842. South Carolina radicals, seizing the opportunity to save face, accepted the compromise measure and withdrew the Nullification Ordinance (March 1833) but, as a final gesture of defiance, nullifed the force act. The initial success of the Nullifiers should not obscure the existence of a strong unionist minority that opposed nullification and threatened civil war if the state resisted the national government. Equally significant, every southern legislature repudiated the doctrine of nullification, thereby isolating the South Carolina radicals. Throughout the country, Americans applauded Jackson's defense of national authority.

The Bank War

In confronting the Nullifiers, Jackson had benefited by his overwhelming victory over Henry Clay in the presidential election of 1832. In that campaign, the two candidates had taken contrary stands on the most controversial question of the decade: Jackson's veto of a bill to recharter the second Bank of the United States. Although the bank's charter would not expire until 1836, anti-Jacksonian politicians persuaded Nicholas Biddle, the president of the bank, to seek a new charter prior to the 1832 election. In suggesting this procedure, the anti-Jacksonians expected that the bank charter would be renewed (thereby assuring the continuation of their economic program) or that a presidential veto would inflame public opinion against Andrew Jackson. In July 1832, Congress passed the recharter bill; Jackson promptly vetoed it.

In the veto message, Jackson reaffirmed his opposition to the rapid development of the American economy. He described the bank as an artificial institution that had served the interests of foreign investors and a privileged segment of the American population. Viewing himself as a defender of republican virtue, the president condemned the use of paper money to enrich a monied aristocracy at the expense of the people. Such rhetoric expressed the feelings of numerous Americans who opposed the direction of economic expansion.

Following his electoral victory in 1832, the "president of all the people" was determined to hasten the destruction of the national bank by withdrawing the government's deposits from its vaults. When two successive secretaries of the treasury refused to cooperate, Jackson appointed Roger

B. Taney, a loyal Jacksonian. By spreading government deposits to sympathetic state banks, called "pet banks" by the Whigs, the administration drastically reduced the capital of the national bank. When Biddle exaggerated the problem by further contracting credit, a minor economic crisis developed. The Whigs blamed the president for the crisis, but the people supported the administration.

Although Jackson's withdrawal of government deposits from the Bank of the United States alarmed many business people, this policy did not cause the inflation that occurred after 1833. Jackson's approval of a distribution bill (1836) that divided surplus treasury funds among the states also had only a minor impact on the economy. Rather, the inflation of the period was a product of changes in international finance. Similarly, the Specie Circular (1836) did not provoke the Panic of 1837 [see above, p. 199]. Such economic patterns, however, did not minimize the *political* significance of Jackson's economic policies.

Jackson's attack on the privileged position of the national bank was paralleled by a Supreme Court ruling in the *Charles River Bridge* case (1837). In 1785, the Massachusetts legislature granted proprietary rights to a group of businessmen to construct a toll bridge across the Charles River. By reducing transportation costs, the bridge proved beneficial to the community and highly profitable to the investors, who watched the value of their stock rise dramatically. By the 1820s, however, numerous groups began demanding a free bridge, and, after several legislative disputes, the Massachusetts legislature chartered the Warren Bridge Corporation to erect a toll-free span. The original company then sued to prevent the construction of the new bridge, arguing that it would impair the property rights conferred upon them by their charter, a legal contract with Massachusetts. After several appeals, the Supreme Court, with the Jacksonian Roger Taney presiding, ruled against the old proprietors. Taney's opinion maintained that the Charles River Bridge Company constituted a monopoly of special privilege and that the interests of the community superseded the original legislative grant. Besides attacking the privileged monopoly, Taney's decision also revealed the altered state of the American economy. In the late eighteenth century, it had been necessary to make generous legislative grants to stimulate capital investment. By the 1830s, such grants seemed unnecessarily restrictive. In economic terms, Taney's ruling freed the creative entrepreneur from traditional legislative restraints, thereby encouraging a more rapid development of economic resources.

Foreign Policy

As during the nullification crisis and the Bank War, President Jackson used the full power of the government to effect several diplomatic triumphs. Secretary of State Van Buren initiated negotiations with Britain that opened the trade of the British West Indies to American shipping (1830). More dramatically, the president insisted that France reimburse

THE DOWNFALL OF MOTHER BANK.

Jackson's removal of government deposits from the Bank of the United States promised to destroy the aristocratic "money power" symbolized by the palatial columns. The bank's president, Nicholas Biddle, appears as the devil in this 1833 cartoon. (Courtesy of New York Historical Society, New York City.)

American claimants for damages dating back to the Napoleonic wars. The Claims Convention (1831) awarded the United States the equivalent of $5 million, payable in installments. When the French Chamber of Deputies declined to appropriate the money, Jackson adopted a rigid stand and asked Congress to authorize the seizure of French property. When Congress delayed action, the president severed diplomatic relations with France. Despite talk of war, the French agreed to restore the payments if Jackson apologized for his attacks on France. Jackson resisted, arguing that he had never intended to insult France. The French accepted this as an apology and paid the claims. Stubborn diplomacy, however rash, had served the national interest. Jackson revealed more prudence in refusing to annex the recently formed Republic of Texas. Fearing a war with Mexico, he waited until his last day in office to recognize the government. The resolution of the Texas problem was left to a later administration [see below, pp. 240-241].

As president, Jackson left important political legacies to the nation. As a nationalist, he transcended sectional divisions and strengthened popular ties to the presidency. Exercising strong executive leadership, he bypassed Congress and appealed directly to the people. Thus, his free use of his veto power forced congressional representatives to be more responsive to their constituents. Indirectly, Jackson's popularity compelled his opponents to form an equally responsive political organization capable of appealing to a mass electorate. In 1836, Jackson's handpicked successor, Martin Van Buren, easily defeated a group of rival candidates.

The Van Buren Administration

Van Buren inherited not only the blessings of "Old Hickory" but also a severe economic depression. To make matters worse, the president proposed a reform policy that perpetuated the deflation. First, he obtained the repeal of the Distribution Act (1836), which had provided the states with additional revenue for schools and internal improvements. This policy, together with the general depression, forced many southern and western states to repudiate the debts that they had contracted. Foreign investors, hurt most by the default of the debts, became reluctant to reinvest in American projects, and a major source of capital thus was eliminated.

Van Buren also recommended the creation of an independent treasury system that would enable the government to remove public funds from the banking system. Instead, the government would deposit its revenue in vaults (or subtreasuries) throughout the country. Moreover, payments to the government would have to be made in specie. In effect, the president proposed to contract the resources of the banks, thereby restricting the credit available for economic development. Pressure from business people and opposition by Clay and Webster delayed passage of the plan until 1840.

The Panic of 1837 convinced the states to implement reform of banking procedures in order to prevent a recurrence of runaway inflation. New York inaugurated a twofold system, which was later imitated by other states. It established a safety fund by requiring all banks to deposit securities in an independent fund, which would be used to redeem the notes of a defaulting bank. New York also approved the Free Banking Law (1838), which permitted the formation of banks without specific legislative approval, provided that investors satisfied minimum guidelines. Such policies, by abolishing certain legislative restraints, accelerated the expansion of the American economy in later years.

Tippecanoe and Tyler Too

The failure of Van Buren to cope with the economic crisis does not explain the Democratic defeat in the presidential election 1840. Rather, the Whig victory depended upon the rituals of mass politics. To challenge Van Buren, the Whigs passed over Henry Clay and nominated General William Henry Harrison, the hero of Tippecanoe. For the vice-presidency, they selected Virginia's John Tyler in order to attract southern voters. During the presidential campaign, the Whigs ignored the political issues of the day and simply glorified the personal attributes of the candidate. Branding Van Buren as an aristocrat, the Whigs portrayed Harrison as a frontiersman born in a log cabin who was committed to the common people. Parades, brass bands, and hard cider replaced political discourse. Yet, the intense party competition brought out 78 percent of the eligible voters (over 2.4 million people, an increase of nearly a million from 1836). Harrison's victory (234 electoral votes to 60) seemed to provide the Whigs with an opportunity to reverse some of the policies of their Democratic predecessors. But, within a month of his inauguration, Harrison died of pneumonia and was succeeded by John Tyler, until recently a Democrat and still a believer in a strict intepretation of the Constitution.

Henry Clay, frustrated by his inability to attain the Whig nomination, nevertheless hoped to persuade Tyler to accept his American System of tariffs, internal improvements, and a central bank. Clay easily obtained approval of a bill to repeal the independent treasury system (1841). But Tyler, taking a states' rights position, vetoed an act to create a third Bank of the United States. Furious with the president, Clay pushed a second bill through Congress only to see Tyler veto that measure also. The entire cabinet, except for Secretary of State Webster, then read the president out of the Whig party and resigned from office. Although Tyler attempted to forge an independent coalition in Congress, Whig antipathy and sectional controversy precluded any success.

Similar problems impeded the remainder of Clay's program. The senator from Kentucky introduced legislation for a protective tariff and for the distribution of revenues from land sales to the states to finance internal improvements. Southern states opposed the distribution measure because it would deplete the treasury and encourage a higher tariff. Western states feared that the program would maintain higher land prices. To appease both groups, Clay modified his proposal. The Preemption Act (1841) legalized the rights of squatters to occupy up to 160 acres of public land and then to purchase the land at a dollar and twenty-five cents an acre. Clay also accepted a southern amendment that declared that the distribution program would cease if the tariff rates exceeded 20 percent (the prevailing rate in 1842). When the Whigs ignored this second provision and attempted to raise tariffs, Tyler intervened and vetoed the measure. In the end, Congress repealed the Distribution Act and established a tariff (1842) that restored levels to those of 1832. Continued quarrels among rival groups prevented further legislation.

Foreign Affairs

Despite the factional rivalry, Webster had remained in the administration in order to complete diplomatic negotiations with Great Britain. Several problems, ranging from a boundary dispute to the slave trade, had strained relations between the two nations. During a small rebellion in Canada (1837), American citizens had smuggled supplies to insurrectionists. In response, Canadian militiamen boarded a Canadian vessel, the *Caroline*, which was moored in American territory, killed an American citizen, and burned the ship. Van Buren demanded reparations, but the British government denied complicity. The issue climaxed in 1840, when a Canadian citizen, Alexander McLeod, boasted in a New York saloon that he had participated in the raid. New York authorities arrested McLeod, and tried him for murder. Although Britain threatened war, McLeod's acquittal calmed tempers in both nations.

Britain and the United States also clashed over the boundary between Maine and New Brunswick. Vague wording in the peace treaty of 1783 enabled both countries to claim about 12,000 square miles, and attempts to compromise the dispute proved unsuccessful. When Canadian lumbermen began operating in the disputed area, the American inhabitants of Maine protested, and feelings were inflamed in both countries. Minor confrontations between Canadian and American militiamen, known as the Aroostock War (1838), nearly produced open warfare. However, Van Buren's emissary, General Winfield Scott, managed to arrange a temporary truce.

The two nations also disagreed about British attempts to suppress the slave trade by searching neutral ships on the high seas. The question of British interference became related to southern fears of slave revolts when Great Britain abolished slavery in 1833. Slaves aboard American ships that were forced into West Indian ports often were granted sanctuary by British officials. The problem climaxed when slaves aboard the *Creole* en route to New Orleans from Virginia mutinied and sailed into Nassau. British authorities freed all but the leaders of the insurrection. Vehement protests, however, forced the British to agree to respect American property rights, including their rights over slaves.

The appointment of a new British ambassador, Lord Ashburton, to the United States paved the way for a peaceful settlement. Negotiations soon produced the Webster-Ashburton Treaty (1842), which resolved the problems. Secretary of State Webster agreed to sacrifice American claims along the Maine boundary but obtained other territorial concessions along the Canadian border. The treaty also provided for the mutal extradition of criminals between Canada and the United States. Finally, Webster and Ashburton agreed to maintain squadrons in African waters to cooperate in suppressing the slave trade. Such compromises assured friendly relations between the two nations and thereby protected the economic interests of American exporters and British investors.

The administrations of Jackson, Van Buren, Harrison, and Tyler had emphasized the political significance of economic and social change. Such questions as westward migration and business expansion had rallied voters in Congress and in the states. The territorial expansion of the United States during the 1840s, however, swiftly undermined the importance of economic matters in national politics and forced the American people to confront anew the problem of slavery. Yet, Americans had not reacted to social questions simply by going to the polls. In a variety of nonpolitical ways, they had attempted to cope with a diverse assortment of social problems. Thus, the shifting nature of American politics represented, in part, a logical outgrowth of broader social concerns.

Supplementary Reading

A good introduction to the Jacksonian era is L. Richards, *The Advent of American Democracy: 1815-1848* (1977). It may be supplemented by a provocative collection of essays, T. Hareven, editor, *Anonymous Americans* (1971). For information on immigration, see M. Hansen, *The Atlantic Migration, 1607-1860* (1940). The westward movement is analyzed in R. Billington, *America's Frontier Heritage* (1966). American-Indian relations are examined in F. Prucha, *American Indian Policy in the Formative Years* (1962); B. Sheehan, *Seeds of Extinction* (1973); and R. Satz, *American Indian Policy in the Jacksonian Era* (1975). For a psycho-historical study, see M. Rogin, *Fathers and Children: Andrew Jackson and the Subjugation of the American Indian* (1975). The expansion of the American economy is described in several synthetic works; see G. Taylor, *The Transportation Revolution* (1951), and D. North, *The Economic Growth of the United States, 1790-1860* (1961). More specialized studies are R. Albion, *The Rise of the Port of New York* (1939), and R. Shaw, *Erie Water West: A History of the Erie Canal* (1966). These economic trends are placed in the context of international finance in P. Temin, *The Jacksonian Economy* (1969).

The social consequences of the economic changes are examined in several specialized works. The best study of the elites is E. Pessen, *Riches, Class, and Power before the Civil War* (1973). For studies of less affluent urban dwellers, see S. Thernstrom, *Poverty and Progress: Social Mobility in a Nineteenth Century City* (1964), a study of Newburyport that extends to 1880; and P. Knights, *The Plain People of Boston, 1830-1860* (1971). Also helpful are R. Wade, *The Urban Frontier* (1959); F. Owsley, *Plain Folk of the Old South* (1949); W. Hugins, *Jacksonian Democracy and the Working Class* (1960); E. Pessen, *Most Uncommon Jacksonians* (1968); and L. Richards, *"Gentlemen of Property and Standing": Anti-Abolition Mobs in Jacksonian America* (1970). A concise statement of Jacksonian ideologies is M. Meyers, *The Jacksonian Persuasion* (1957). Popular political songs are described in V. Lawrence, *Music for Patriots, Politicians, and Presidents* (1975).

Several works attempt to survey the politics of the period; see A. Schlesinger, Jr., *The Age of Jackson* (1945); G. Van Deusen, *The Jacksonian Era* (1959); L. White, *The Jacksonians* (1954); and R. McCormick, *The Second American Party System* (1966). A statistical study is L. Benson, *The Concept of Jacksonian Democracy* (1961). The political biographies of the period are especially useful; see J. Curtis, *Andrew Jackson and the Search for Vindication* (1976); C. Eaton, *Henry Clay* (1957); R. Current, *Daniel Webster and the Rise of National Conservatism* (1955); C. Wiltse, *John C. Calhoun: Nullifier* (1949); and C. Sellers, *James K. Polk: Jacksonian* (1957).

For discussions of the Bank War, see R. Remini, *Andrew Jackson and the Bank War* (1967), and T. Govan, *Nicholas Biddle* (1959). For information on nullification, see W. Freehling, *Prelude to Civil War: The Nullification Crisis in South Carolina* (1966). For a discussion of the *Charles River Bridge* case, see S. Kutler, *Privilege and Creative Destruction* (1971). The best study of Van Buren's administration is J. Curtis, *The Fox at Bay* (1970). For a discussion of the Tyler presidency, see O. Chitwood, *John Tyler* (1939).

Chapter 15

Reform and Reaction

1800-1860

The sense of living in a new nation uncorrupted by archaic traditions encouraged nineteenth-century Americans to view social institutions as impermanent and changeable. The creation of political institutions, the rapidity of economic change, and the sheer growth of population had demonstrated the flexibility of American society. Yet, by weakening the social order, these expansive tendencies undermined the stability of people in all classes and aggravated the divisions within the society as a whole. To a limited extent, party competition absorbed some of the social tension; members of competing ethnic groups, for example, usually voted for rival candidates. More often, people participated in various social movements designed to alleviate particular grievances. During the first half of the nineteenth century, innumerable reform movements flourished throughout the country. With varying intensity and popularity, men and women agitated to reform nearly every aspect of American life. Some people endorsed such visionary ideals as world pacifism and abolitionism, while others dealt with such mundane questions as diet and dress. Some groups attempted to legitimize their status by forming professional organizations; others worked to preserve their status by eliminating potential rivals. Some movements advocated the destruction of traditional institutions; still others sought to manipulate the existing institutions and coerce their opponents. Within single movements, moreover, members often disagreed about means and ends.

Despite such diversity, liberals and conservatives alike recognized the importance of appealing to common ideals and assumptions in order to justify their positions. Regardless of their internal consistency or specific purpose, all social activists tried to show that their movements were consistent with political democracy. Nineteenth-century Americans extolled individual liberty and equality of opportunity. The need to release the individual from institutional bondage became, therefore, a prominent theme among social reformers. To allow the individual to flourish free from corrupting restraints, it was necessary to eliminate the chains of illiteracy, drunkenness, and slavery. In seeking to improve society, however, many reformers ignored the question of individual rights and sought to coerce their neighbors by enacting restrictive legislation. Thus, the passage of prohibition laws and attacks on religious minorities constituted attempts to "free" the individual — by force, when necessary. Social activists buttressed their appeals to democratic individualism by demonstrating that their causes coincided with American nationalism. Appealing to the natural superiority of the American people, the reformers promised to accelerate the creation of a virtuous republic free from the remnants of European institutions.

Protestant America

The supporters of new social movements also endeavored to show that their programs were compatible with the Protestant religious values of the nation. Religious heterogeneity in the eighteenth century had led to the separation of church and state. (Only Connecticut and Massachusetts maintained established churches in the early nineteenth century.) Americans had not become less religious, nor had they become more receptive to atheistic infidelity. Instead, they emphasized the importance of religious voluntarism, the right of each individual to worship as he or she chose. Protestant ministers stressed that competition among denominations would strengthen American religion and hasten the creation of a Christian society.

The churches of nineteenth-century America, although still overwhelmingly Protestant, had undergone important changes after the War for Independence. The "rational" wing of American Protestantism had evolved toward the Unitarian church. Unitarianism replaced the Calvinist God of vengeance with a more benevolent God of love. According to the Unitarians, God respected the essential dignity of humanity and rationally offered salvation to all people. Such a religion, although limited in its appeal before the Civil War, reflected the democratic egalitarianism of the United States. The more popular Universalist religion similarly professed that God would save all people. Avoiding esoteric theology, these religions reduced Protestantism to a system of common-sense love.

Far more influential in shaping religious attitudes was the revitalization of evangelical Protestantism. Partly a reaction to the growth of secularism during the revolutionary era, partly a response to changing social conditions, the evangelical movements stimulated a wave of revivals throughout the nation. Along the western frontier, circuit-riding Baptists and Methodists won numerous converts in a series of revivals, which culminated in the second Great Awakening (1800-1801). Presbyterians, Congregationalists, and Episcopalians, who were less responsive to religious emotionalism, lost parishioners to the more evangelical faiths throughout the Mississippi Valley. Later in the century, evangelicalism spread eastward into the cities and brought several national revivals (1830-1833, 1857-1858). The foremost evangelical preacher of the age, Charles Grandison Finney, repudiated the pessimism of traditional American Protestantism and instead assured his hearers that God provided salvation to all sincere Christians. Equating sin with selfishness, Finney declared that people could be saved simply by replacing sinfulness with benevolence. Upon conversion, moreover, the true Christian had to continue his or her struggle against sin by seeking to convert others.

Thus, evangelicals suggested that the moral perfection of the individual could provide the basis for the regeneration of American society. Social imperfections, like sin itself, could be eradicated by moral activity. These ideas served conservative purposes. For, if social problems such as poverty and unemployment reflected individual failings, then there was little need to change the structure of society. The evangelical preachers also placed these appeals within a nationalistic context. Affirming the moral superiority of the American people, they advocated missionary activity to redeem the world. Religious revivalism thus reinforced American patriotism and justified various political causes. This missionary nationalism culminated eventually in the doctrine of manifest destiny, which rationalized the territorial expansion of the United States [see below, pp. 240-241].

Evangelical Protestantism, political democracy, and American nationalism provided the intellectual framework from which people evaluated the social changes of the nineteenth century. The American people condemned social activity that seemed to contradict any of these cultural ideals. Conversely, to legitimize new social movements, reformers attempted to demonstrate how a particular cause reinforced these values. In this way, the demands for social reform acquired a moral dimension and forced Americans to confront specific protests. These moral imperatives enabled certain radical minorities, such as the abolitionists, to agitate even for reforms that offended the conservative majority.

The Professions

The widespread commitment to egalitarianism made Americans suspicious of social elites. The Jacksonian defense of rotation in office [see above, p. 204] had denied the importance of expertise. Yet, during the

An illustration of a Shaker meeting, illuminating the "Sacred Whirling Dance" in which the dancer fell into a prophetic trance. Like other evangelical groups, the Shakers flourished in the decades before the Civil War.

early decades of the nineteenth century, two middle-class groups — lawyers and scientists — emerged to claim professional status in American society. In the colonial period, all intellectuals, in one form or another, had been esteemed scientists (or natural philosophers). By the mid-nineteenth century, science had become an esoteric discipline, subdivided by specialties and dependent on popularizers to inform the public of recent discoveries. The legal profession had undergone an even more visible change. Viewed with suspicion until after the Revolution, the American legal profession gradually surmounted popular hostility and had become a prestigious profession by the mid-nineteenth century. Yet, in acquiring legitimacy, both the scientists and the lawyers first had to demonstrate the orthodoxy of their organizations.

In appealing for public recognition, both groups stressed the nationalistic function of their professions. Scientific advances would bring fame to the nation and demonstrate the intellectual superiority of the United States. Lawyers stressed the important role of the legal profession in leading the War for Independence and in drafting the Constitution. Similarly, nineteenth-century professionals insisted that their activities were compatible with American religious values. Scientists viewed themselves as collaborators with theologians in studying God's creation in nature. Recognizing the importance of winning the approval of clergymen, American scientists stressed the moral function of their work. More important, they interpreted their work in an extremely narrow way to avoid challenging the religious orthodoxy. Scientists became mere gatherers of data who allowed theologians to interpret the meaning of the scientific facts. The major scientific achievements of the period involved the *classification* of factual material; scientific *explanation* remained in theological hands. The marriage of science and religion later retarded the introduction of Darwinian thought in the United States [see chapter 22]. Similarly, American lawyers took great pains to show that the pulpit and the bar were engaged in a common enterprise to uplift the morality of the people. Finally, both professions denied an aristocratic impulse and insisted that the complexity of their disciplines required professional standing. In this manner, two occupational groups endeavored to preserve their status in an age of social change.

The Communities

The social changes of the early nineteenth century also led other Americans to seek social stability through group activity. By joining various social organizations, men and women could create a semblance of order despite the weakening of traditional institutions. The proliferation of new religious sects following the separation of church and state, the strengthening of political parties (and party loyalty), and the rise of voluntary organizations provided Americans with numerous options for developing a sense of community. Business people established trade associations, farmers created agricultural societies, social critics joined reform movements, city dwellers enrolled in fraternal lodges, and immigrants founded ethnic associations.

The search for community amidst a changing social order reached its most direct expressions in the formation of utopian communes. Often inspired by religious leaders, numerous groups attempted to create a perfect social order by withdrawing from ordinary society. The Shakers, founded in the 1770s by Mother Ann Lee, a prophet who claimed to be a reincarnation of Christ, established numerous perfectionist communes that thrived during the nineteenth century. Believing in the imminent return of the Messiah, the Shakers practiced celibacy (it was unnecessary to propagate the race), emphasized equality of labor, and sought to create a Christian community. One of Charles Finney's converts, John Humphrey Noyes, established a prosperous community in the 1840s at Oneida, New York, which replaced private property and traditional marriage with communal ownership and a system of complex marriages. Several Pietist groups from Germany founded perfectionist societies. George Rapp led a millennial community of 600 to western Pennsylvania (1807) and influenced two secessionist groups in Bethel, Missouri, and Aurora,

Oregon. Several Pietists also formed the Amana Society, or Community of True Inspiration, near Buffalo, New York (1843).

Secular reformers, influenced by the writings of European thinkers, erected several communes based on socialistic principles. Robert Owen, a wealthy English industrialist, experimented with a factory town at New Lanark in Scotland before attempting an ambitious industrial community at New Harmony, Indiana (1825). Hampered by internal dissension, the socialist experiment proved an expensive failure. Owen's Declaration of Mental Independence (July 4, 1826), which condemned private property, organized religion, and the institution of marriage, undermined the popularity of the movement. To be successful, reform activity could not threaten the dominant values of Protestant America. One of Owen's disciples, Frances Wright, attempted to create a quasi-socialist community at Nashoba, Tennessee, which was to allow black slaves to labor for freedom (and eventual colonization in Africa). Wright's notorious radicalism (which included a condemnation of traditional marriage), however, horrified most Americans and doomed her efforts.

The ideas of the French socialist Charles Fourier became popular in the United States following the publication of such sympathetic pamphlets as Albert Brisbane's *The Social Destiny of Man* (1840). Fourier's proposal for a cooperative society divided into "phalanxes" led to the establishment of about fifty communities. George Ripley's Brook Farm, which served as a retreat for many New England intellectuals, experimented briefly with Fourierism. Besides offering escape to the few participants in communal living, these perfectionist groups attempted to reform American society by example. Hoping to create an ideal society, the communitarians expected that such utopias would prove irresistible to the remainder of humanity.

The most enduring communitarian movement was the Church of Jesus Christ of the Latter Day Saints (Mormons). Founded by Joseph Smith, who claimed to see visions and to have found and translated the Book of Mormon, the Mormon church rapidly grew in strength in the Midwest. Such practices as baptizing the dead and plural marriages, however, offended conservative Americans, while the Mormon economic prosperity aroused envy. Harassed by their neighbors, the Mormons moved from Ohio to Missouri and then to Nauvoo, Illinois (1838), where they erected a flourishing town. But again hostile unbelievers, fearful of Mormon expansion, attacked the community and killed Joseph Smith while he was in jail. Under the leadership of Brigham Young, the Mormons created a more secure haven on the Utah frontier (1847). The prosperous community, nevertheless, continued to antagonize American Protestants. Before Congress approved the admission of Utah as a state (1896), the Mormons first had to eliminate polygamy. The persecution of the Mormons revealed the limitations of political democracy in the nineteenth century and underscored the importance of conforming to the dominant values of American society.

The Family and the Child

In rejecting older notions of predestination, evangelical Protestantism placed great emphasis on the moral improvement of the individual. This attitude encouraged a more tender view of children. Seen as the victim of adult corruption (rather than as being inherently evil), the American child became an object of considerable attention during the early decades of the nineteenth century. Concerned about the moral consequences of social disintegration, numerous publications advised parents to inculcate Christian values in the young and urged them to maintain the stability of family life. Such fears reflected a subtle, but continuous, erosion of the American family.

As industrialization and urbanization transformed the economy of the Northeast, the family became less important as an economic unit. The use of women and children in factories weakened the cohesion of the nuclear family. Geographical mobility, by uprooting families from their kin and by encouraging the departure of adult children, further undermined the family unit. Moreover, parents apparently tried to inculcate a sense of independence in their children. European observers frequently noticed the lack of parental discipline and the prevalence of youthful autonomy. With such patterns of child rearing, American parents evidently tried to prepare their offspring for the rigors of an expanding society. The nineteenth century also witnessed a steady shrinkage in the size of the family due to a decline in the birthrate. Servants, once considered an integral part of the family unit, became hired help, mere outsiders who lived in a household.

The apparent disintegration of the family worried conservative leaders, who began to stress the importance of domesticity for women. Writers such as Catherine Beecher advised American mothers to remain in the home, where they could instill moral values in their children. They also asserted that women were too tender to participate in the world of business and, therefore, that they must accept the superiority of men. As they urged women to act like dependent children, they denied that virtuous females could have sexual feelings. The medical profession reinforced these values by treating sexuality of women as a disease. In the southern states, the exploitation of slave women for sexual purposes (including the nursing of white children) may have contributed to the white female's desexualization and her ascent to a mythical level of purity and innocence.

Many middle-class women rejected these ideas and sought personal fulfillment in public life by participating in such reform movements as abolitionism, temperance, and humanitarianism. But even these activities did not free American women from male domination. When an antislavery convention in London (1840) refused to admit Lucretia Mott and Elizabeth Cady Stanton, several women began to agitate for women's rights. Meeting at Seneca Falls, New York (1848), the feminist reformers issued a declaration of independence in which they demanded the rights of citizenship

A NATURAL CONSEQUENCE

Miss Lucy (*blushing extensively*).—Miss President and Ladies. It is my painful duty to resign my office as Corresponding Secretary of the Women's Rights Association—for I am to be married to-morrow.

After the Seneca Falls Convention, Harper's Monthly *published the view that women's rights meetings were attended only by ugly women. (From* Harper's Monthly, *November 1852.)*

and condemned male supremacists for attempting to lessen women's self-respect. Continued agitation brought only modest gains. Several state legislatures, persuaded by the logic of economic individualism, gave women the right to own property independently of their husbands. Women also were permitted occasional entries into professions, and Oberlin College became the first coeducational institution in 1837. Such technical victories, of course, did not eliminate the informal but pervasive discrimination against women.

The apparent erosion of the traditional family led many reformers to advocate the creation of public schools to assure the proper instruction of American children. The demand for free public education won support from the trade-union movement of the 1820s and 1830s. Labor leaders,

PROPER PRUDENCE

MISS PRUDENCE *(emphatically).*—Miss President, I repeat it—No conscientious Woman will ever marry until she is in a condition to support her Husband and Children in a suitable manner.

(From Harper's Monthly, *November 1852.)*

unable to accept the idea of a permanent proletariat, viewed education as a social equalizer that would remove the special privileges of their employ-ers. Some business people, like southern slaveowners, feared that educa-tion would breed a lower-class rebellion. But educational reformers argued that public schools would instill traditional American values in an other-wise potentially subversive group. Horace Mann, first secretary of the Massachusetts Board of Education and the foremost proponent of public schools, repeatedly articulated the idea that public schools would protect the United States from the chaos of social disintegration.

Such logic inspired numerous educational reforms in the decades before the Civil War. Most of the states outside the South created public elementary schools, lengthened the school year, and adopted uniform textbooks. In the South, governments also increased appropriations for education. Yet, public secondary schools remained rare outside New England, and most parents of wealth relied on private academies to instruct their children. Nevertheless, Americans viewed compulsory education as an intrusion on the rights of individuals, and no state required classroom attendance. American textbooks reflected the conservative principles of the educational reformers. The Peter Parley series on history and geography inculcated a sense of patriotism, Jared Sparks's Library of American Biography extolled the nation's heroes, and William H. McGuffey's readers (which sold 120 million copies) preached traditional morality to American children.

The evangelical commitment to the principle of self-improvement also encouraged the growth of adult-education movements. During the middle decades of the nineteenth century, the number of private subscription libraries grew throughout the nation and numerous communities established tax-supported public libraries. Josiah Holbrook founded the first lyceum in Massachusetts (1826), a self-improvement society that sponsored lectures and public discussions on a variety of subjects. The idea spread rapidly and enabled such prominent personalities as Ralph Waldo Emerson, Daniel Webster, and the scientist Louis Agassiz to reach popular audiences. Combining education and entertainment, the lyceum movement absorbed some of the frustrated energy of the American working classes.

Social Control

The use of public education to instill traditional values reflected the close relationship between reformism and social control. As the westward migration weakened institutions such as the family, the influx of foreign immigrants also seemed to threaten the social order. After 1840, repeated crop failures in Germany, Scandinavia, and, especially, Ireland forced hordes of impoverished and starving people to migrate to the United States.

The vast increase in the number of Jewish and Catholic immigrants frightened many conservatives. Although Jews had prospered in colonial America, these new immigrants, most of whom spoke German, were poorer and less educated. Between 1840 and 1860, the American Jewish population increased from 15,000 to 150,000. During the same period, Irish immigration brought 1.5 million people to the United States, most of them settling in port cities such as Boston and New York. The Irish constituted the lowest (white) status group and suffered the most. In the South, they performed dangerous tasks on public works projects, because slaveowners wanted to protect the lives of their slaves; in New England, Irish workers replaced Yankee farm girls in the textile factories.

Discontented by economic exploitation and victimized by ethnic and religious discrimination [see below, p. 236], the immigrant working class seemed for a time to have been completely unassimilated into Ameri-

can society. Poverty and ethnic antagonism led to crime and urban violence, further threatening the social order. Irish workers, whose traditional
culture approved the everyday use of alcohol, frequently expressed their
discontent by coming to work drunk or by not coming at all. To Protestant
Americans, however, the plight of the Irish reflected not so much economic conditions as their unwillingness to improve themselves. The main
argument of the public school reformers was that education would instill
the proper habits of industry in the working classes.

The emergence of popular journalism provided another instrument
for defusing lower-class antagonism. More efficient printing techniques
reduced the price of newspapers to one penny (*New York Sun,* 1833).
James Gordon Bennett founded the *New York Herald* (1835) to capitalize
on the growing readership by publishing sensational stories dealing with
crime and violence. Such stories (like contemporary mass-media violence)
may have provided vicarious relief for frustrated workers. More subtly,
nineteenth-century journalists frequently dramatized obituaries of wealthy
citizens who had emerged from poverty by hard work and frugal habits.
Popularizing the myth of the self-made man, such news articles helped to
implant middle-class values in the minds of exploited workers.

Efforts at social control appeared more obvious in the crusade to
reduce the consumption of alcoholic beverages. Since colonial times,
Americans had consumed vast quantities of liquor and medical leaders
such as Benjamin Rush had warned of the evils of alcoholism. The temperance movement grew rapidly in strength in the early nineteenth century
when it became apparent that poor workers were squandering their
meager earnings on liquor. Temperance crusaders pointed to the close
correlation between poverty, crime, and drunkenness and formed the
American Temperance Union (1826). Emphasizing voluntary self-
improvement, the temperance crusade began as a movement to moderate
the consumption of alcohol.

After 1840, however, the prevalence of drunkenness among immigrant workers led to a shift in tactics — a demand for total abstinence. The
Washington Temperance Societies (1840), composed of reformed drunk-
ards, attempted (with little success) to persuade alcoholics to abandon
liquor. The failure of voluntary abstinence moved reformers to demand
legislation to force the prohibition of alcohol. Several states responded by
enacting strict licensing laws and levying taxes on liquor. Under the leadership of Neal Dow, a wealthy businessman concerned about the intemper-
ance of his workers, the prohibition crusaders persuaded the state
legislature of Maine to prohibit alcoholic beverages (1846). Twelve other
states adopted similar laws during the 1850s.

Humanitarian Reform

As temperance reformers argued that prohibition freed the individual
from the clutches of demon rum, conservative Protestants, who founded
the American Bible Society (1816), the American Sunday School Union

(1824), and the American Tract Society (1825), believed that they could disseminate the good word and thereby liberate Americans from the slavery of sin and infidelity. Humanitarian reformers also struggled to release individuals from other types of bondage. Thomas Hopkins Gallaudet developed educational techniques for the deaf, and Samuel Gridley Howe experimented with raised letters for the the blind. Dorothea Dix exposed the maltreatment of the mentally ill and pressured numerous states to transfer the insane from jails to asylums. Brutal prison conditions led other humanitarians to advocate penal reform. They introduced the Philadelphia system, which kept criminals in solitary confinement to encourage them to repent and be cured. New York reformers introduced an alternative system (the Auburn system), which permitted prisoners to work together in silence during the day but separated them at night.

Antidemocratic "Reforms"

The desire to protect the nation from corrupting institutions also inspired several repressive movements. Despite their commitment to voluntarism, most Americans viewed secret organizations as potential threats to political democracy. Members of secret organizations, it was feared, might be more loyal to their private groups than to the republican government. Such attitudes led to a repressive campaign against the Order of the Masons, a secret fraternal organization. Following the murder (1826) of a former Mason (who was about to reveal the secrets of the society), politicians in New York and Vermont launched a political attack on the organization and formed the Anti-Mason party. Part of a popular crusade against aristocratic privileges, the party won several state elections but eventually was absorbed by the Whig party.

Seeking to liberate individuals from sin, Protestant reformers branded the Roman Catholic church as a corrupting institution dominated by a European hierarchy and demanded its destruction. In the early nineteenth century, the rapid growth of the Catholic church alarmed conservative Americans. Between 1830 and 1860, the Catholic population in the United States rose from 3 percent (318,000) to 10 percent (3,100,000) largely because of increased immigration. Since most of these immigrants filled the urban working class, fear of the urban poor reinforced traditional anti-Catholic bias. New England Federalists, concerned with preserving ethnic homogeniety, had supported immigration restrictions earlier in the century. After 1830, nativist publications denounced the Catholic immigrants for stealing the jobs of American workers, thereby provoking mob violence and the burning of Catholic schools and churches in northern cities.

The tendency of Irish and German immigrants to vote for Democratic candidates led nativists to accuse the immigrants of a conspiracy to destroy political democracy. Such allegations fostered the creation of nativist political parties. During the 1840s, when Roman Catholics protested the use of Protestant Bibles in public schools, nativist candidates found a lively issue and won several elections in New York and Philadelphia. Secret fraternal organizations, the Order of the Star Spangled Banner (1849) for example, emerged to oppose further immigration. The anti-Catholic, anti-immigration movement culminated in the formation of the American or Know-Nothing party, which won numerous elections in the 1850s. But, as the problem of slavery increasingly intruded into American politics, nativist stength waned in importance. At a later date, economic expansion and foreign immigration again combined to create a strong nativist movement [see chapter 21].

Abolitionism

The movement to free the individual from institutional servitude attained its clearest expression in the abolitionist crusade against slavery. During the late eighteenth century, a few Quakers and other liberals, inspired by humanitarianism and the rhetoric of egalitarianism, had begun to agitate against slavery. Such activity attracted only a small following until a group of Protestant conservatives founded the American Colonization Society (1817) which was designed to transport emancipated blacks back to Africa. The colonization movement attracted support from evangelical clergymen and Federalists (particularly from the upper South and border states), who viewed slavery as a potentially disruptive institution. They accepted racial prejudice as a permanent feature of American society and, therefore, proposed to solve the race question by removing the offensive minority. Their proposal to colonize Africa appealed to the missionary sentiments of evangelical Protestants but made no allowance for the blacks' feelings about the matter. The colonizationists also wished to preserve the American social order by compensating slaveowners for their property losses and by restoring the racial homogeneity of the nation. The society founded the Republic of Liberia and transported the first colonists there in 1822. But the colonization movement lost its appeal among whites after 1830 and only about 12,000 blacks ever settled in Africa.

The colonization movement failed largely because American blacks refused to surrender their birthrights as Americans. Equally significant in influencing white opinion was the emergence of a new type of radical abolitionist. Influenced by the evangelical commitment to individual perfectionism, radical abolitionists such as William Lloyd Garrison confronted the moral question of slavery and demanded its immediate elimination. Unlike the colonizationists, the abolitionists insisted that Americans *could* surmount their racial prejudice and create a Christian society. Besides founding an abolitionist newspaper, *The Liberator* (1831), Garrison also organized the American Antislavery Society (1833). A perfectionist, Garrison refused to dilute his appeal in order to win a wider following. Instead, he campaigned not only for abolition but also for such controversial issues as racial equality, temperance, and women's rights. When his ideas met stiff resistance, Garrison proposed that the North secede from the union to avoid the contamination of slavery.

Garrison's extremism offended many abolitionists who recognized the importance of appealing to the more conservative majority. Less extreme but equally dedicated abolitionists such as James G. Birney (who ran for president in 1840 and 1844 as the Liberty party's candidate), Wendell Phillips, Sarah and Angelina Grimke, Theodore Dwight Weld, and Arthur and Lewis Tappan recruited a mass following for abolitionism. Frederick Douglass, a fugitive slave, became an effective proponent of antislavery, as did numerous free blacks in northern cities, who constituted a majority of the subscribers to *The Liberator*. The abolition movement suffered from internal divisions. For example, white male abolitionists did not always accept the participation of women or blacks. But, by petitioning Congress to abolish slavery (despite the adoption of a gag rule in 1836, which required that such petitions be tabled without discussion), by agitating in northern communities, and by publicizing the brutality of slavery, the abolitionists brought the slavery issue directly into national politics and converted numerous northern liberals to the cause.

Despite its apparent strength, the crusade for abolition offended the majority of the white population. Outraged Bostonians attacked Garrison in the streets, and midwesterners murdered the abolitionist Elijah Lovejoy in Alton, Illinois (1837). White workers in the North, viewing free blacks as an economic and social threat, rioted against the black population on many occasions. Northwestern farmers, interested in excluding black competition in the West, prohibited the admission of all blacks to Indiana (1851) and Illinois (1853) and strongly supported the free-soil movements of the 1840s and 1850s [see below, p. 247]. In the North, blacks suffered racial discrimination, economic exploitation, and often political disfranchisement.

It was in the South, however, that the abolitionist movement produced the strongest reaction. During the 1820s, slaveowners in states such as South Carolina had bitterly opposed government assistance to colonization schemes. In the following decade, the emergence of radical abolitionism, together with Nat Turner's Insurrection, led slaveowners to develop a sophisticated rationale for slavery. Earlier defenders of slavery, like Thomas Jefferson, had adopted an environmentalist explanation for the inferiority of blacks and viewed slavery as a necessary evil to uplift the blacks to the level of whites. By the 1830s, however, slaveowners articulated a racial theory to justify slavery as a positive good. Southern apologists argued that the blacks were *inherently* and irreparably inferior. Such racial ideas obtained scientific sanction in the two decades before the Civil War. American ethnologists, including the prestigious Louis Agassiz, proposed a theory of polygenesis (plural origins of humankind) that implicitly suggested the permanence of racial characteristics. With scientific support, the defenders of slavery proclaimed the natural inferiority of blacks. Such ideas also appealed to northerners, who then could justify the discrimination against blacks on scientific grounds. North and south, egalitarianism meant political democracy for whites only.

Intellectuals and the Social Order

The reform movements of the nineteenth century attempted to solve fundamental social problems and eliminate obvious social evils. Many of these problems had resulted from the rapid expansion of American society in the early part of the century. Yet, Americans remained divided about the importance of preserving or changing the existing social order. The attack on the Catholic church, for example, was an attempt to preserve the traditional Protestant social order. The attack on slavery, on the other hand, suggested that individuals must be liberated from traditional institutions. But even these reformers insisted that the destruction of social institutions was not incompatible with a higher kind of order, a natural or cosmic order, in which the individual attained a harmony with the cosmos.

The tension between natural order and artifical (or social) order represented a major theme in the intellectual output of nineteenth-century America. Many writers welcomed the freeing of individuals from traditional restraints, while others feared that disintegration, once begun, would lead inevitably to chaos and destruction. The dialogue between proponents of natural order and advocates of social order was not confined to an intellectual elite; it appeared in popular writings as well. Popular works also reflected the cultural context of the period. Nationalism and regionalism, mobility and order appeared as dominant themes in a variety of publications.

The importance of achieving cosmic unity pervaded the writings of a group of New England intellectuals known as transcendentalists. Ralph Waldo Emerson, the leading spokesman of this loosely knit group, expressed his ideas in such essays as "Nature" (1836), "The American Scholar" (1837), and the "Harvard Divinity School Address" (1838). Emerson suggested that individuals could approach perfection by transcending human society and joining a mystical "oversoul." Social institutions became snares to be overcome.

Henry David Thoreau, a close friend of Emerson, carried these ideas into action by withdrawing to an isolated cabin at Walden Pond (1845). Thoreau's journal of his experiences, *Walden* (1854), described the attempt of one man to participate in the cosmic harmony by rejecting all forms of materialism. While at Walden, Thoreau protested the Mexican War (which he believed would support the expansion of slavery) by refusing to pay his poll tax. For this resistance, he was arrested. To explain his position, Thoreau drafted the "Essay on Civil Disobedience" (1848) in which he elaborated a theory of passive resistance. Arguing that governmental institutions corrupted the natural unity of humanity, Thoreau justified the violation of human laws.

"Mountain Ford" (1836). Emphasizing the sublime in American nature, Thomas Cole revealed the romantic interests of the Hudson River school. This celebration of natural wildness contrasted with the popular idea that the rugged American landscape ought to be tamed. (The Metropolitan Museum of Art, Bequest of Maria DeWitt Jesup, 1915.)

The poetry of Walt Whitman also emphasized the importance of liberating the individual from artificial restraints. Introducing a free-form verse style, Whitman published *Leaves of Grass* (1855), in which he endeavored to embrace the cosmos. Using ordinary language and metaphors, he captured the spirit of the people and extolled the expansion of the nation. In painting, these themes found expression in the works of a group of New York artists known as the Hudson River school. Producing magnificent paintings of wild nature, such painters as Thomas Cole glorified the majesty of the untrammeled earth. In a series of canvases called *The Course of Empire,* he suggested that the pursuit of materialism would destroy the virtuous American republic.

Many intellectuals feared the anarchistic tendencies of individual fulfillment and worried about the direction of American society. James Fenimore Cooper, a New York novelist and supporter of Andrew Jackson, decried the materialistic spirit of the nineteenth century (*The American Democrat* and *Home as Found*, both 1838) and questioned the virtue of frontier individualism in a series of Leatherstocking Tales, which included *The Last of the Mohicans* (1826) and *The Deerslayer* (1841). Nathaniel Hawthorne, drawing upon his New England heritage, reaffirmed the importance of social traditions and institutions in such works as *Twice-told Tales* (1837), *The Scarlet Letter* (1850), and *The House of the Seven Gables* (1851). The novelist Herman Melville similarly rejected the optimism of the transcendentalists. His magnificent novel of the sea, *Moby Dick* (1851), pointed to the destructiveness of individualistic achievement. Edgar Allen Poe, a southern writer of short stories, also lamented the social disintegration of his age.

Several American novelists dealt with the theme of materialism and social change in the context of regional rivalry. Anxious about the pace of economic change, these writers contrasted the acquisitiveness of northern society (symbolized by the aggressive Yankee) with an idealized image of a plantation-dominated South (symbolized by the aristocratic cavalier). The glorification of the southern aristocrat, however, represented a condemnation of materialism by popular writers throughout the nation. These themes emerged in the works of such southern novelists as John Pendleton Kennedy (*Swallow Barn*, 1832) and William Gilmore Simms (who published over 100 novels and stories). Such northern authors as James Paulding and Harriet Beecher Stowe employed the same genre. Even Stowe's *Uncle Tom's Cabin* (1852), a popular indictment of slavery, adopted the cavalier imagery and portrayed Simon Legree as a transplanted Yankee from Vermont. The plantation novels also depicted the slaves as essentially happy, loyal, and childlike. Abolitionist writers swiftly adopted those stereotypes and condemned the slaveowners for mistreating such innocent human beings. The images of the materialistic North and the cavalier South influenced the sectional dialogue on political questions in the decade before the Civil War.

At mid-century, a group of New England writers explored regional and historical themes and achieved wide popularity. Their works included Henry Wadsworth Longfellow's historical tales, John Greenleaf Whittier's abolitionist poems, and James Russell Lowell's *Bigelow Papers* (1848). This period also witnessed the publication of several major historical works by New Englanders. George Bancroft began a ten-volume *History of the United States* (1834-1874); William Prescott completed his studies of Spanish expansion in Latin America; and Francis Parkman began his multi-volume history of the Anglo-French wars for empire.

Most of these literary works, like the oratory of the politicians, extolled the virtue of the American people. Even the critics of the social order often asserted the natural superiority of American institutions. As a citadel of liberty (the United States had provided sanctuary for European radicals after the failure of the revolutions of 1848) and as the bastion of evangelical Protestantism, the American republic symbolized the progress of Western civilization. Beneath the facade of national greatness, however, lay the dilemma of black slavery.

Supplementary Reading

Two detailed and thorough analyses of nineteenth-century American culture are R. Nye, *Society and Culture in America: 1830-1860* (1974), and R. Welter, *The Mind of America: 1820-1860* (1975). For a briefer introduction, see I. Bartlett, *The American Mind of the Mid-Nineteenth Century* (1967). A brilliant but incomplete overview is P. Miller, *The Life of the Mind in America from the Revolution to the Civil War* (1965).

American religion is discussed in T. Smith, *Revivalism and Social Reform* (1957); C. Wright, *The Beginnings of Unitarianism* (1955); and W. Cross, *The Burned-Over District* (1950). Miller's *Life of the Mind* discusses the lawyers, while G. Daniels's *American Science in the Age of Jackson* (1968) is the best discussion of the scientific community. For a more general survey of science, see G. Daniels, *Science in American Society: A Social History* (1971). Also helpful is D. Calhoun, *Professional Lives in America* (1965).

A detailed synthesis of reformism is A. Tyler, *Freedom's Ferment* (1944); a briefer survey is C. Griffin, *The Ferment of Reform, 1830-1860* (1967). Very provocative is C. Griffin, *Their Brothers' Keepers: Moral Stewardship in the United States* (1960). For a discussion of the utopian communities, see A. Bestor, *The Backwoods Utopias* (1950). The Mormons are described from the perspective of Joseph Smith in F. Brodie, *No Man Knows My History* (1945).

American attitudes toward children are illuminated in B. Wishy, *The Child and the Republic: The Dawn of Modern American Child Nurture* (1968). For essays on the American family throughout American history, see M. Gordon, editor, *The American Family in Social-Historical Perspective* (1973). Educational values are conveyed in G. Mosier, *Making the American Mind: McGuffey Readers* (1947); and education reform is analyzed in M. Katz, *The Irony of Early School Reform* (1968). The conservative nature of the newspapers is suggested in S. Thernstrom, *Poverty and Progress* (1964). For a discussion of prohibition, see F. Byrne, *Prophet of Prohibition: Neal Dow and His Crusade* (1961). American attitudes toward deviance are described in D. Rothman, *The Discovery of the Asylum* (1971). The standard account of nativism during this period is R. Billington, *The Protestant Crusade, 1800-1860* (1938). New studies of the women's movement include E. DuBois, *Feminism and Suffrage* (1978), B. Berg, *The Remembered Gate: Origins of American Feminism* (1978), N. Cott, *The Bonds of Womanhood* (1977), and K. Melder, *Beginnings of Sisterhood* (1977).

Chapter 16

Expansion and Crisis

1844-1860

Nineteenth-century reformism, concerned with forging a new cosmic order, had stressed the importance of freeing the individual from artificial social restraints [see above, p. 214]. Similar attitudes toward economic activity encouraged the continued expansion of the American economy, ironically aggravating many of the social problems that had called for reform in the first place. Moreover, these economic developments reinforced the pattern of regional specialization — the Northeast as industrial center, the South as cotton producer, the West as food grower. Such differences heightened sectional tensions on such political matters as western expansion and the status of slavery in the territories. Instead of integrating American society, the creation of a national economy had worked to divide the nation.

Population Expansion

The persistent expansion of American society depended on the continued growth of population. In 1830, nearly 13 million people inhabited the United States; despite declining birthrates, by 1850, that figure increased to over 23 million and by 1860 exceeded 31 million. Such growth reflected the rising importance of immigration from abroad. During the 1840s and

1850s, a series of disastrous crop failures in Germany and Ireland moved over 4 million people to immigrate to the United States. Thousands of Germans and Scandinavians with modest means purchased farmland in the Midwest. But many immigrants lacked the necessary capital to move westward and remained in the port cities where they had entered. The population of New York City swelled from 200,000 in 1830 to over a million in 1860, and other urban centers experienced similar growth.

The pressure of population, the search for opportunity, and the opening of new territories for settlement greatly stimulated the western migration. Following the transportation networks westward, farmers filled most of the region east of the Mississippi River by the 1850s. Numerous adventurers, enticed by the newly discovered California gold, headed toward the Pacific; many, disillusioned by the difficulties of travel, stopped midway and settled in the Mississippi Valley. By 1850, half the population of the United States lived west of the Appalachian Mountains.

The rapid settlement of the West, together with improvements in transportation and agricultural machinery, encouraged the expansion of western agriculture. Britain repealed tariffs on grain (1846), while the outbreak of the Crimean War (1853) brought especially great demands for American foodstuffs. Thus, agricultural prices generally rose during the 1840s and 1850s. Western farmers then found it worthwhile to abandon self-sufficient farming practices and began to specialize their crops. During the 1850s, corn, wheat, and pork production nearly doubled throughout the West. Such advances in commercial agriculture made farmers more dependent on international markets; this led them to favor tariff reductions in 1846 (the Walker Tariff) and again in 1857.

The Railroads

The surge in farm production and the movement to specialized agriculture was stimulated by improvements in transportation. The canal system continued to carry ever-larger volumes of western goods to eastern cities. This commerce gradually tied the economic interests of the Northwest to the Northeast, and New York City replaced New Orleans as the major exporter of western produce. This process became more obvious with the construction of the first railroads. Rail transportation had developed slowly in the 1830s, hampered by the diversion of capital into canals and retarded by the deflation of the late 1830s. Moreover, inexpensive solutions to engineering problems awaited the invention of such devices as crossties and improved locomotives. The use of different rail gauges — designed to prevent competition from other railroads — further deterred railroad development. In 1848, most of the 6,000 miles of track in the United States lay east of the Appalachians.

During the 1850s, however, railroad construction increased dramatically, and, by 1860, over 30,000 miles of track had been laid. Four major trunk lines connected the eastern cities of New York, Philadelphia, and

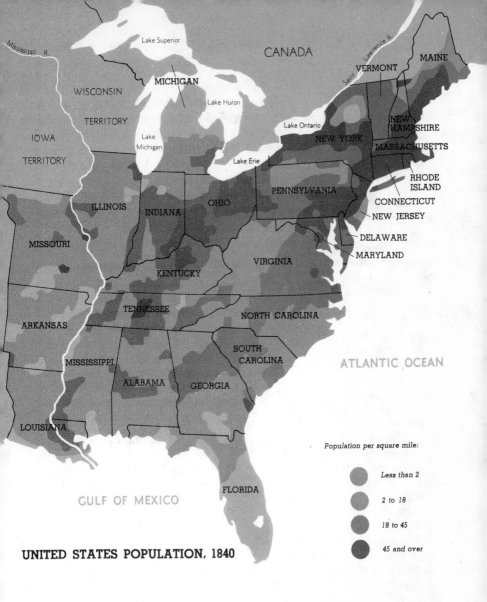

Population per square mile:

- Less than 2
- 2 to 18
- 18 to 45
- 45 and over

UNITED STATES POPULATION, 1840

Baltimore with interior areas in the Mississippi Valley. New railroads also expanded throughout the western states. As rail lines connected the western railroads with the eastern trunk lines, a national transportation system emerged, facilitating the flow of goods throughout the North. The implementation of the telegraph, invented by Samuel Morse, further reduced the sense of distance in the United States. In the southern states, however, railroad construction remained unsystematic. Relying on the river systems, southern capitalists ignored railroads and continued to invest primarily in land and slaves. By failing to create economic ties to the Northwest, southern merchants encouraged the development of a northern sectional alliance.

Railroad construction required large capital outlays, most of which came from private investors. Farmers and merchants living along the proposed right-of-way frequently mortgaged their property to invest in railroads. Besides bringing lucrative returns, such investments protected their business interests by assuring them connections with national markets. The merchants of Chicago, for example, aggressively supported railroad building, thereby enabling their city to emerge as a commercial and transportation center. Such nearby cities as St. Louis, lacking the competitive spirit of Chicago's boosters, enjoyed much slower growth. Foreign investors, particularly from England, also realized large profits from investment in American railroads.

In the densely populated eastern states, private capital proved sufficient for railroad construction. In the West, however, the sparsity of population and the greatness of distance forced the railroads to seek public assistance. State and local governments supported railroads by loans, subsidies, tax exemptions, and the purchase of stocks. Despite this public assistance, the companies retained the right to establish freight charges, thereby protecting the investors from government interference. Originally designed to encourage investment, this policy of laissez-faire seriously disadvantaged the smaller shippers in later decades. [See chapter 20.] Federal support of railroads began in 1850, when Senator Stephen Douglas of Illinois persuaded Congress to offer generous land grants to the Illinois Central Railroad so that it could build a line connecting Lake Michigan with the Gulf of Mexico. By 1860, American railroads had obtained nearly 30 million acres of public lands, establishing a precedent for the generous land grants of the post-Civil War era.

By facilitating domestic commerce, the railroads encouraged economic specialization in all regions. Western farmers found new markets for their products and, in turn, provided eastern manufacturers with new outlets for industrial goods. Capitalistic agriculture thus made American farmers dependent on other capitalists, a situation that contradicted their self-image as independent producers. This conflict nourished a variety of agrarian protests in the latter half of the century. Yet, the increase of farm production, by providing adequate food supplies, further stimulated industrial expansion and foreign commerce.

Industrial Growth

The desire to liberate American business from artificial restraints had led most states to enact general laws of incorporation by the 1850s. The corporate device, by facilitating the sale of stocks and bonds, encouraged the accumulation of capital from domestic and foreign investment. This expansion of capital, which was augmented by the discovery of gold in California, financed the increase of industrial production. Most American manufacturers remained small enterprises. Flour and meal milling, cotton textile production, lumbering, and meatpacking constituted the major industries. Yet, the volume of industrial production increased dramatically, and capital investment nearly doubled in the decade before the Civil War.

The introduction of steam power and such processes and inventions as the vulcanization of rubber (by Charles Goodyear) and the sewing machine (by Elias Howe) accelerated industrial development. The process of industrialization soon became self-generating. Developments in one industry swiftly stimulated technological advances in others, which encouraged still more. Thus, the proliferation of railroads encouraged the locomotive and tool industries, which depended on increased iron production, which stimulated smelting and mining.

The expansion of agriculture also supported foreign commerce. Southern cotton and western wheat found wide markets in Europe, while Americans imported large quantities of textiles and iron products from England. Since the volume of imports exceeded exports, the United States shipped large amounts of the gold discovered in California to Europe to balance accounts. In addition to the lucrative transatlantic trade, American merchants began to open commercial ties to China and Japan. Responding to the demands of northern merchants, President Tyler inaugurated negotiations with China that opened several Chinese ports to American shipping (Treaty of Wanghsia, 1844). Following the lead of European imperialists, the United States forced China to concede favorable commercial terms to American merchants throughout the century. American business also pressed the government to negotiate a commercial settlement with Japan. President Millard Fillmore responded by sending a fleet of warships, commanded by Commodore Matthew Perry, to open negotiations with the Japanese. Threatening war, Perry overcame stiff Japanese resistance and secured the Treaty of Kanagawa (1854), which relaxed trade restrictions.

The construction of railroads, by easing the transportation of agricultural goods, supported this commercial expansion. Foreign trade was stimulated by improvements in shipbuilding, which produced clipper ships (sleek many-sailed vessels) that reduced the time and cost of transatlantic commerce. Such ships also captured the valuable trade between the eastern ports and California, reducing the length of the voyage from five to three months. For a brief time, American shipping challenged British maritime supremacy. But the construction of a railroad across Panama and the development of steamships by the British undermined American competition, despite government subsidies to the shippers. Nevertheless, by reducing the cost of shipment, American merchants contributed to the expanding economy.

The Industrial Society

Commerce continued to bring large profits to northern merchants who distributed southern cotton and western foodstuffs abroad. Such commodities often were exchanged for manufactured goods and industrial machinery. These industrial imports occupied less space than the raw materials, leaving room for lighter cargo. More often than not, ship captains filled their holds with human ballast, providing immigrants with cheap shipboard accommodations. The flood of poor immigrants during the middle decades of the nineteenth century provided American manufacturers with an abundant source of cheap labor.

The process of industrialization reinforced the statification of northern society and accented the differences between the very rich and the very poor. The influx of immigrants created a surplus of labor in the eastern cities, forcing wages down and aggravating unemployment. Living in crowded neighborhoods that became identified as slums, whole families labored for subsistence wages. Despite the prevalence of the myth of the self-made man, few unskilled laborers had the opportunity for upward social mobility. Workers instead drifted from one town to another, searching for a meager livelihood. For semiskilled laborers, *slight* upward mobility remained possible. But the idea of rags-to-riches success served less as a description of reality than as a means of reinforcing traditional social values [see above, pp. 222-223].

The poverty of the industrial working classes contrasted starkly with the relative prosperity of the middle and upper classes. People with capital to invest acquired modest fortunes amidst the general economic expansion. Benefiting from the prosperity of the 1850s, skilled craftsmen again formed trade unions and won a ten-hour workday and certain restrictions on child labor. Skilled workers usually held middle-class aspirations and viewed industrial laborers as potential threats to their status. Equally significant, patterns of residential segregation along ethnic and economic lines emerged in the larger cities. Although rich and poor before that time had lived in close proximity, wealthier inhabitants began to move to more fashionable neighborhoods or to the outskirts of town to avoid social contact with people of lesser status. An urban elite patronized the arts, dined in fine restaurants, and attended the theater; at the same time, charity rolls grew, crime proliferated, and poor people starved.

The Southern Economy

Although northern reformers frequently criticized certain aspects of the industrial society, the most thorough condemnations of industrial capitalism came from southern planters. Because southern capitalists preferred to invest in plantation agriculture, southern manufacturing lagged behind northern production. A few industrial enterprises appeared in the South, but, in 1860, southern manufacturing represented only a small fraction of the total production of the United States. Although numerous economic reformers (such as William Gregg of South Carolina) urged southerners to support a more diversified economy by establishing textile mills, the South remained dependent on northern manufacturers for finished cotton products. In addition, the failure of the southern states to build railroad connections with the food-supplying Northwest retarded the development of urban centers that might have supported local manufacturing.

The apparent absence of industrialization, however, did not mean that southern agriculture was not capitalistic. Recent studies have suggested that investment in slaves was more profitable than comparable investments in manufacturing. In the older areas of the South, the depletion of the soil by continued tobacco cultivation stimulated a shift to such crops as corn and wheat. Agrarian reformers such as Edmund Ruffin also persuaded some planters to use artificial fertilizers to replenish the soil. Many southern farmers, moreover, worked small holdings and produced diversified crops to feed their families. Larger planters continued to produce valuable harvests of tobacco, rice, and sugar. For the most part, however, cotton remained king and dominated southern agriculture. Following the frontier westward through Alabama, Mississippi, Arkansas, and eastern Texas, cotton production (over 5 million bales during the 1850s) doubled. Tobacco production also doubled during that decade.

Slavery

The expansion of southern agriculture reinforced the institution of slavery. As planters moved westward, they brought their slaves with them; only a small percentage of slaves were sold in the interstate slave trade. The general rise of cotton prices steadily increased the value of slaves during the nineteenth century. The increasing price of slaves meant that fewer whites could afford to invest in blacks. By 1860, nearly 75 percent of the population of the white South owned no slaves. The concentration of wealth in the South also meant that a few slaveowners controlled a large proportion of the slave population (which approached 4 million people in 1860). As the center of cotton production moved westward, the concentration of slaveholdings in the upper South declined. Yet, slavery did not appear to be dying out in those regions. In 1859, only 3,000 slaves were emancipated throughout the entire South; Virginia freed only 277; Kentucky manumitted but 176.

As an institution, slavery varied immensely, depending upon the personalities of the masters and the slaves, the nature of the work, and the size of the plantation. On smaller holdings, the slaves and their masters often worked side by side. Such a pattern was fairly personal, but whether the system was gentle or harsh depended on the caprice of the master. Most slaves, however, worked on larger plantations (with more than twenty slaves), where the institution was more impersonal. Directed by white overseers or black slave drivers (selected members of the slave population who served as informal intermediaries who eased some of the brutality of slavery), the plantation slaves worked from sunup to sundown in exchange for scanty clothing and food. Their diet usually lacked sufficient protein (due more to ignorance than to cruelty). Household slaves fared somewhat better, since their close contact with the slaveowners often secured them better treatment. Some slaves were trained as craftsmen and were leased to neighboring plantations. In urban areas, slaves had greater mobility and could mingle with the free black population. Nevertheless, slaves had virtually no rights and remained at the mercy of their owners.

Since slaves were considered a form of property, they lacked traditional legal protections. They could not testify in courts against whites, they were subject to severe corporal punishment, and their marriages lacked legal sanction. Slave codes restricted their mobility and, in some states, prevented their attendance in churches and schools. Such limitations, however, often were ignored by white owners. No sane slaveowners interested in protecting their property would jeopardize the health of their slaves; recalcitrant slaves often were spared the brutality of the law and were simply sold to another plantation. Legally, the slaveowner could divide a slave family and sell individual slaves to different owners. Yet, in practice, slave families seem to have held together, despite the unhappy departures of individual members. Moreover, most slaves seem to have inhabited single-family housing units in slave quarters.

As a class, slaves managed to obtain many customary rights. They usually chose their own marriage partners. Their workweek was usually six days, like that of factory workers, and Sunday work was performed for an extra payment. Slaves came to expect a traditional Christmas holiday, which meant gifts of food, alcohol, and clothing, as well as a break in the regular work schedule. Blacks also created a unique Afro-American religion, which blended evangelical Christianity with traditional African religious beliefs. They directed their own funerals, for example, and often buried their dead at night, an African custom that also fit the practical needs of plantation society.

The impact of slavery on individual slaves varied considerably. White Americans, in justifying slavery, often portrayed blacks as happy, innocent, and childlike. This Sambo stereotype suggested that blacks were natural slaves, since they seemed to flourish in that condition. The metaphor, perhaps, eased guilty consciences about the enslavement of human beings. Yet, the widespread assertion that slaves appeared to be happy may reveal one defense mechanism employed by blacks to reduce the evils of the slave system. By pretending to be happy, by faking ignorance, and by acting childishly, some slaves may have attempted to anticipate the desires of their owners in order to avoid their masters' displeasure. Such behavior need not have been conscious.

More typical than Sambos, however, were the slaves who resisted the system deliberately. Such rebelliousness often involved subtle forms of subversion — the destruction of crops, the breakage of tools, the maltreatment of farm animals, fires in plantation buildings, faked illnesses, self-inflicted injuries, and plain laziness. Blacks also tried to escape the

harshness of slavery by hiding in the woods or the swamps that surrounded plantations or by escaping for freedom. Such activity indicates
that most black people did not respond to slavery with a grin or a shrug but
actively fought against the system. Advertisements for runaway slaves
betrayed the inherent brutality of enslavement. Slaveowners identified
their missing property by describing their brands and wounds and frequently mentioned the fact that the slaves stuttered. Such physical and
psychological scars suggest that slaves were not content with their status,
southern claims notwithstanding.

Besides individual subversion, black slaves occasionally planned
larger upheavals. The Gabriel plot in Virginia (1800) and the Vesey Conspiracy in South Carolina (1822) were betrayed by black informers. In
1831, however, Nat Turner staged a major rebellion in Virginia, killing fifty-
seven whites before being captured and executed. Southern whites
reacted to such rebellions with swift retribution. Suspected blacks were
brutally beaten and often killed as examples to others, even when they
posed no threat to whites. The savagery of such reprisals betrayed white
anxiety about slavery. Fearful of imminent slave revolts, southern whites
attempted to silence all opposition to slavery lest it inflame the black popu-
lace. Prohibiting education for blacks, restricting church attendance, and
censoring the mails became prime defenses of the peculiar institution.

Ideological Divisions

Anxiety about the rebelliousness of the slave population made southern whites extremely sensitive to abolitionist attacks. The articulation of
the plantation mythology that suggested that the slaves were happy
represented a defense against outside criticism [see above, p. 238].
Yankee peddlers were accused of causing slave uprisings and occasionally
became victims of mob violence. In southern minds, abolitionist criticism
seemed extremely dangerous, and southern politicians protested against a
northern conspiracy to destroy the southern way of life. Abolitionists
responded to such allegations by accusing a conspiratorial "slave power"
of subverting the republican mission of the founding fathers. Such charges
and countercharges reflected the social insecurities of both groups. Southerners feared that the destruction of slavery would undermine all social
institutions. Abolitionists worried that the spiritual regeneration of the
American people would be wrecked by the peculiar institution.

These ideological cleavages emphasized the growing differences between northern and southern society. Sectional rivalry entered the political arena in the 1840s over the question of the extension of slavery into the
western territories. To a limited extent, the debate involved the distribution of political power. Additional slave states would enable the southern
minority to retain some checks on the nonslave majority. But even John
Calhoun realized the futility of these hopes and proposed an alternate sys-

These advertisements — typical of the southern press before the Civil War — reveal a common method of slave resistance — running away. The "ingenious" Cumby, the owner warned, would attempt to pass as a freeman and would rely on his skills as a boatman to evade capture. Meanwhile, his facial scars and his slow speech betrayed the brutality of the "peculiar institution." (From Richmond Enquirer, November 5, 1824.)

TWENTY DOLLARS REWARD.

WILL be given for apprehending and delivering to me my negro man CUMBY, about twenty four years of age, of light complexion, about 5 feet 6 inches high, well set, has somewhat of a roman nose—has one or more small scars about the face, not particularly recollected—talks slow, has a pleasing countenance when spoken to, is plausible and ingenious in his manner of excusing himself, when any charge is made upon him. Cumby went off about the 1st of April last, since which I have not heard of him. I have no doubt he will attempt to pass as a free man, and probably has obtained false papers for that purpose. He was a waterman at the time I purchased him of James Cooke of this county, and the head man of a boat; it is probable that he is now at work on the river, and most likely above Lynchburg, or he may have gone out of the State. He carried off clothes of different sorts.

JOHN GILLIAM.
Powhatan, July 30.   25—wtf

TWENTY DOLLARS REWARD.

RUNAWAY from the subscriber on Thursday the 16th of September, a negro woman named SALLY, aged about twenty-two years, her complexion is a mulatto, but not very bright—she has spots in her face something like a ringworm—her height is between four and five feet—spare made, with a good countenance when spoken to—her dress when she ranaway was blue plains, and also carried with her a dress of coppers checked homespun—it is possible that she may have changed her dress. I purchased her from Richard Strawn, a negro buyer, and he purchased her from Benjamin Grimes in the county of King George—it s possible that she may have gone back to the same county, or is aiming to get back, as Mr Grimes owns her husband. I forwarn all masters of vessels from taking a negro of that description on board—It is possible that she may have obtained free papers—if any person or persons will apprehend the said woman and deliver her to me, or secure her in any jail in this state, and give information so that I get her again, they shall receive the above reward with all reasonable charges, and if the said woman should be apprehended out of the State of Virginia and brought home to me in said State, or delivered in any jail in the State of Virginia, and give information so that I get her again, the person or persons shall receive the reward of forty dollars, with all lawful charges

ROBERT ACREE.
Hanover co. Va. near Cold Harbour, Oct. 26. 51—w3t*
☞ The Fredericksburg Herald will publish the above weekly for 4 times and charge this office.

tem of "concurrent majority." The minority rights of the South would be protected by the election of two presidents, one to represent the South, the other the North; each would retain the right to veto congressional legislation. Calhoun's suggestion was never seriously considered outside the South.

A prime reason for southern support for the expansion of slavery into the West was the continued search for agricultural prosperity. While cotton prices remained high, planters sought to cultivate more acreage and expected the United States to expand into Mexico, Cuba, and South America, where plantation slavery would continue to flourish.

Since the North already dominated the political institutions of the United States, its opposition to the expansion of slavery also reflected economic considerations. As commercial agriculture expanded through the

Northwest, farmers brought new lands under the plow and eagerly invested in more. Agricultural workers commanded high wages, and western farmers feared that black labor, free or slave, would prove too competitive. For this reason, several free states prohibited the entrance of free blacks in the 1850s.

The desire to exclude blacks from the West also revealed a series of popularly held ideas known as Manifest Destiny. Advocates of American expansion argued that the United States had a divine destiny to extend republican institutions and Protestant churches throughout the American continent. These ideas, however, usually were placed in the evangelical context that suggested that individuals should be liberated from corrupting social institutions. As the "garden" of the world, the American West symbolized the absence of traditional social arrangements and represented a place where individual citizens could enjoy regeneration. To nineteenth-century Americans, it seemed self-defeating to corrupt the purity of the West by introducing the inferior black race. The search for social uniformity in the 1850s also led to a revitalization of the colonizationist movement. Even President Lincoln hoped to transplant the black population to Central America, but the scheme proved impractical for financial reasons and because the majority of blacks opposed it. In the aftermath of the Civil War, many Americans expected a voluntary migration of blacks to their natural climate in South America, thereby leaving the United States as a nation of white Anglo-Saxons.

Territorial Expansion

The western expansion of the American people had not been confined to the territorial limits of the United States. During the 1820s, numerous Americans, led by Stephen Austin, began to settle in Texas, a northern province of Mexico. These settlers, many of whom were slaveowners, soon established a prosperous colony based on cotton production. As native-born Americans, these Texans held little allegiance to the Mexican government and resented the absence of political representation. By 1830, Mexico had become alarmed at the presence of these alien citizens. To reduce the threat of subversion, the government prohibited further immigration from the United States and abolished domestic slavery. This policy merely aggravated the dispute and led to open rebellion. Amidst such military clashes as the Battle of the Alamo, Texas formally declared independence and elected Sam Houston first president of the Republic of Texas (1836).

Although the inhabitants of Texas appealed to the United States to annex the territory, Presidents Jackson and Van Buren, fearing a war with Mexico, ignored their pleas. As an independent nation, Texas formed closer ties with Great Britain, which was interested in an alternate supply of cotton. British policy in Texas alarmed many southerners, who feared that British abolitionists would undermine slavery in that region and threaten the continued westward expansion of the plantation economy. Meanwhile, President Tyler, searching for a policy to increase his political support, instructed his secretary of state, Abel Upshur, to open negotiations with the Texans. Before obtaining a formal treaty, however, Upshur was accidentally killed. In his place, Tyler appointed John Calhoun, who not only submitted a treaty for the annexation of Texas (1844) but also defended it as a bulwark of slavery. Northern abolitionists charged that the annexation of Texas represented part of a slave-power conspiracy. Fear of a war with Mexico led the Senate to reject the treaty. Texas became a prominent issue in the presidential election of 1844.

During this period, Americans also became interested in the Oregon Territory. American fur traders and merchants who traded with China had recognized the commercial value of the region since the beginning of the century. Both the United States and Great Britain claimed the territory, but both countries had accepted the principle of joint occupation (1818). In the early 1840s, however, Americans became fired with "Oregon fever" and commenced a mass exodus along the Oregon Trail from Independence, Missouri, to the Pacific coast. Searching for rich lands, many Americans settled in the Willamette Valley, a region claimed by the British Hudson's Bay Company. Meanwhile, other Americans, attracted by favorable reports, began moving into California, a province of Mexico. American merchants were particularly interested in the ports at San Diego, San Francisco, and Puget Sound and viewed these harbors as crucial for the growth of trade with China and Japan [see above, p. 235].

Expansion through the Great Plains undermined the government's previous policy toward the Indian tribes. The removal of the Indians beyond the Mississippi during the 1830s had been intended to create a geographical barrier that would benefit both whites (by freeing them from conflict with the Indians) and Indians (by enabling them sufficient time to assimilate into white society). But, as Americans crossed through Indian territory, they came into greater contact — and conflict — with the plains Indians who resented the invasion. Already, traditional tribal life had been altered by the introduction of horses and guns, and Indian societies had been disrupted by alcohol, disease, and dependence on white trade. The mounted tribes had become warlike. But not until whites invaded the area and threatened the food supply by destroying the buffalo did the intertribal wars become wars of extermination. The white invasion also provoked Indian attacks on American settlers. To pacify the area, the United States government decided in the late 1840s to create separate Indian reservations on the Great Plains. Besides reducing armed conflict, such reservations, it was believed, would protect the Indians until they had become sufficiently "civilized" to enter white society. Since the Indians did not accept the idea that white society was superior, they continued to oppose both the reservations and the white migration.

The Politics of Expansion

The question of territorial expansion played an important role in the presidential election of 1844. Martin Van Buren expected to receive the Democratic party nomination, but when he refused to support the annexation of Texas, he was passed over in favor of James K. Polk. The Whigs nominated Henry Clay. But when Clay took an ambiguous position on the Texas question, many northern Whigs deserted the party and voted for James G. Birney, the abolitionist candidate. Consequently, Polk won a narrow victory, carrying New York (with thirty-six electoral votes) by a mere 5,000 ballots. Nevertheless, President Tyler, who was determined to obtain Texas, treated Polk's victory as a mandate for expansion and asked Congress to annex the territory by a joint resolution (which required only a majority vote, rather than the two-thirds necessary to ratify a formal treaty). Despite heated opposition from some northern congressmen, the measure passed, and Texas became a state (December 1845).

During the presidential campaign, the Democrats had advocated the acquisition of Oregon as far north as the Alaska boundary (54°40'). Polk, however, wished to avoid a war with Britain (particularly as Mexican-American relations deteriorated) and offered to accept a compromise boundary at 49°. But, when the British ambassador rejected the offer, Polk asked Congress to authorize the termination of the joint occupation of Oregon. Meanwhile, American settlers flocked to an area along the Columbia River, and the Hudson's Bay Company prudently moved its headquarters to Vancouver Island. This transfer enabled the British government to offer to compromise the boundary dispute at 49°. After slight hesitation, Polk accepted this compromise (1846), and the United States obtained the valuable harbor at Puget Sound.

The Mexican War

While Polk negotiated with Great Britain, American expansion in the Southwest led to a war with Mexico. Following the annexation of Texas, Mexico severed diplomatic relations with the United States. Moreover, the two countries disagreed about the southern boundary of Texas; the United States demanded the Rio Grande, whereas Mexico insisted on the more northern Nueces River. To protect American claims, President Polk ordered General Zachary Taylor to occupy the disputed region. As Taylor's army moved southward, Polk sent a special ambassador, John Slidell, to Mexico City to negotiate a peaceful settlement. Besides transmitting an offer to resolve the boundary dispute, Polk instructed Slidell to propose (1) the assumption by the United States of all American claims against Mexico (about $2 million), (2) the purchase of New Mexico for

$5 million, and (3) the purchase of California for as much as $25 million. Mexican nationalists, upon learning of the proposed dismemberment of their country, overthrew the government and refused to receive the American ambassador. Infuriated by this obstinacy, Polk prepared for war. A minor dispute between Mexican soldiers and Taylor's army north of the Rio Grande (May 1846) provided a convenient excuse. At Polk's request, Congress declared war and appropriated funds to raise an army.

Despite widespread congressional approval, the Mexican War was far from popular in the United States. Abolitionists and antislavery Whigs (known as Conscience Whigs) opposed the war and accused the president of provoking the crisis. Transcendentalist Henry David Thoreau refused to pay his taxes in protest of the war, and Illinois congressman Abraham Lincoln created a minor stir when he introduced a "spot resolution" demanding that Polk reveal on which spot American blood had been spilled. Condemnations of a slave-power conspiracy behind the war indicated the depth of sectional distrust.

Such divisions never threatened an American military victory. Polk himself planned a three-part campaign against Mexico, New Mexico, and California. General Taylor's army moved southward from Texas, captured Monterrey, Mexico (September 1846), and defeated a numerically superior army under General Santa Anna at Buena Vista (February 1847). These victories brought national fame to Zachary Taylor, and Polk, fearful of the general's presidential aspirations, ordered him to remain at Buena Vista until the northern provinces were subdued.

Meanwhile, Colonel Stephen Kearney directed the capture of Santa Fe in New Mexico. Then, he proceeded to California to join other American forces. Led by the explorer John C. Frémont, American settlers in California had already declared their independence and established the Bear Flag Republic. Frémont, together with an American naval force, captured Monterey, California (July 1846), and drove the Mexican defenders from the province. By January 1847, the United States controlled California and New Mexico. In planning the final campaign, the conquest of Mexico City, Polk passed over General Taylor and appointed General Winfield Scott to lead the expedition. Landing at Vera Cruz, Scott fought his way to Mexico City and laid siege to the city. After several bloody battles, General Santa Anna conceded defeat (September 1847), and the American army entered the city.

To facilitate a peace settlement, Polk had ordered the chief clerk of the State Department, Nicholas P. Trist, to accompany Scott's army to Mexico. Trist's instructions essentially duplicated those of John Slidell. But, when postwar confusions delayed the opening of negotiations, Polk ordered Trist to return to Washington. Trist, however, was on the verge of concluding a treaty and ignored the president's instructions. Instead, he signed the Treaty of Guadalupe Hidalgo (February 1848), which transferred California, New Mexico, and the Rio Grande region to the United States in exchange for $15 million and the assumption of American claims against Mexico. Although Polk repudiated Trist's actions, he submitted the treaty to the Senate for ratification. At this time, several expansionists advocated the annexation of all of Mexico. In opposing this policy, anti-annexationists warned that the absorption of the "colored" population of Mexico would threaten national unity and weaken republican institutions. American racism thus served to counter expansionist impulses.

Slavery in the Territories

The acquisition of New Mexico and California reopened the controversy regarding the status of slavery in the territories. Shortly after the outbreak of the Mexican War, David Wilmot, a congressman from Pennsylvania, introduced an amendment to an appropriation bill that sought to prohibit slavery from all territory taken from Mexico. Although the proposal passed the House of Representatives twice, it was defeated in the Senate. Nevertheless, the Wilmot Proviso began a four-year debate on the question of territorial expansion.

Most northern Whigs and Democrats backed the proviso and most southern Whigs and Democrats opposed it. If a compromise was not found on the issue of slavery in the territories, the national party system was in danger of breaking down into sectional parties. When this occurred in 1860, secession and civil war resulted. But this division was avoided until after 1850, because the tensions of 1846 were temporarily resolved in the Compromise of 1850.

During the prolonged controversy, American politicans argued about the constitutional authority for congressional control over the territories. Three constitutional positions emerged from that debate. Antislavery northerners insisted that Congress had the right to legislate on the status of slavery; President Polk, by proposing to extend the Missouri Compromise line to the Pacific Ocean, implicitly supported that view. John Calhoun, however, introduced a series of resolutions that challenged the antislavery interpretation. Arguing that the Constitution provided for the protection of private property in the territories, Calhoun denied that Congress could prohibit slavery anywhere and even claimed that the Missouri Compromise was unconstitutional. A compromise view, introduced by Lewis Cass of Michigan and supported by Stephen Douglas of Illinois, articulated the idea of popular sovereignty, which suggested that the actual settlers in each territory should determine the status of slavery in their localities. This position, although eminently pragmatic, avoided the moral imperatives of the northern and southern interpretations. After six months of bitter debate, Congress prohibited slavery in Oregon, a region where even southern extremists acknowledged the futility of transplanting the peculiar institution.

Amidst the congressional deadlock, the presidential election of 1848 was held. The Democratic party, recognizing the need to attract southern voters, nominated Lewis Cass, an opponent of the Wilmot Proviso. The Whigs selected the military hero Zachary Taylor and chose not to adopt a

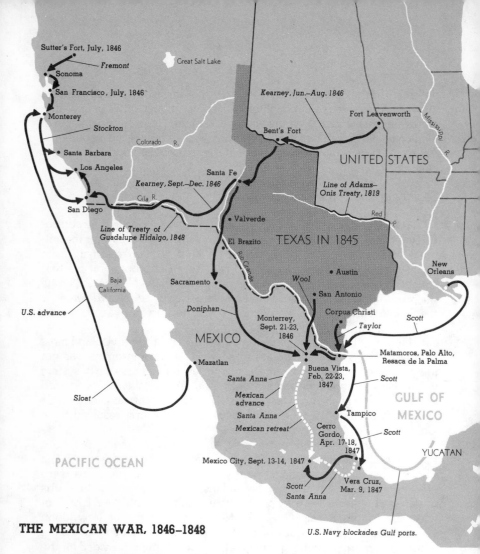

THE MEXICAN WAR, 1846–1848

U.S. Navy blockades Gulf ports.

Map labels:

- Sutter's Fort, July, 1846
- Fremont
- Sonoma
- San Francisco, July, 1846
- Monterey
- Stockton
- Santa Barbara
- Los Angeles
- San Diego
- Line of Treaty of Guadalupe Hidalgo, 1848
- Baja California
- U.S. advance
- Sloat
- PACIFIC OCEAN
- Great Salt Lake
- Colorado R.
- Gila R.
- Kearney, Sept.–Dec. 1846
- Santa Fe
- Sacramento
- Doniphan
- MEXICO
- Mazatlan
- Santa Anna
- Mexican advance
- Santa Anna
- Mexican retreat
- Kearney, Jun.–Aug. 1846
- Bent's Fort
- Fort Leavenworth
- Mississippi R.
- UNITED STATES
- Line of Adams–Onis Treaty, 1819
- Valverde
- El Brazito
- TEXAS IN 1845
- Rio Grande
- Wool
- Austin
- San Antonio
- Corpus Christi
- Taylor
- Red R.
- New Orleans
- Monterrey, Sept. 21-23, 1846
- Buena Vista, Feb. 22-23, 1847
- Matamoros, Palo Alto, Resaca de la Palma
- Scott
- Scott
- Tampico
- Cerro Gordo, Apr. 17-18, 1847
- Scott
- GULF OF MEXICO
- YUCATAN
- Mexico City, Sept. 13-14, 1847
- Scott
- Santa Anna
- Vera Cruz, Mar. 9, 1847

---

party platform. Northern antislavery supporters, unable to support either candidate, formed the Free-Soil party composed of abolitionists, Conscience Whigs, and Democratic supporters of Martin Van Buren. The party endorsed the Wilmot Proviso and nominated Van Buren for the presidency. Although the Free-Soil party won no electoral votes, it drew nearly 300,000 voters in an otherwise dull contest and won thirteen congressional seats. Personal popularity enabled Taylor to defeat the more experienced Cass.

By the time Congress reconvened, the problem of territorial government had become more pressing. Gold had been discovered near Sutter's Fort in California (1848), and thousands of "forty-niners" had rushed to find their fortunes in the California gold fields. By the end of 1849, the nearly 100,000 Americans inhabiting the territory required a civil government. President Tyler, hoping to avoid the sectional controversy, advised the settlers of California and New Mexico to draft constitutions and apply for admission to statehood. Both territories adopted antislavery constitutions. Southerners, led by Calhoun, immediately denounced the president's scheme and began to speak of secession.

Congressional moderates, led by Henry Clay and Stephen Douglas, managed to defuse the crisis by proposing a series of compromise resolutions. The Compromise of 1850 provided for (1) the admission of California as a free state; (2) the organization of the remainder of the Southwest without restrictions on slavery (slaveowners could legally bring slaves to New Mexico, but for geographical reasons few would actually do so); (3) the annexation of the disputed boundary lands of Texas to New Mexico, in compensation for which the United States would assume the $10 million debt of the Texas Republic; (4) the abolition of the slave trade (but not slavery) in Washington, D.C.; and (5) the enactment of a stringent fugitive slave law.

The introduction of these resolutions provided the background for a dramatic debate in the Senate. Calhoun and a newcomer, Jefferson Davis of Mississippi, opposed the compromise, arguing that the measures reduced the South to a minority status and threatened the southern way of life. William H. Seward, a New York Whig, adopted the opposite position and denounced the compromise for failing to confront the moral question of slavery. Ultimately, however, such moderates as Clay, Douglas, and Webster prevailed. The sudden death of Zachary Taylor (July 1850) removed presidential objections to the measures. Then, in a series of tense votes, the separate bills passed through Congress. In the voting, party alignments collapsed completely. A northern bloc supported antislavery measures; a southern bloc supported proslavery measures; and a compromise bloc provided the crucial majority for each bill. But no section actually compromised its position.

Despite regional dissatisfaction with certain features of the compromise, Americans welcomed the end of the four-year crisis. By avoiding moral questions and by dealing with political problems from a pragmatic perspective, the politicians had managed to create a political truce. But a continuation of the peace depended on the willingness of the American people to support the compromise in practice, to act in good faith. The presence of radical politicians in both sections — people like Jefferson Davis and William Seward — confirmed the fact that neither region would remain silent if its interests appeared to be threatened. Moreover, as soon as the new western territories *did* act on the question of slavery (either pro or con), the old constitutional questions about the right of a legislature to legislate against slavery would emerge again.

For the time being, however, a coalition in Congress, which included most southern Whigs and Democrats and most northern Democrats, managed to avoid both the extreme northern stand that wanted Congress to bar slavery from the territories and the extreme southern stand that wanted Congress to protect slavery in the territories. But most northern Whigs, with the exception of several major leaders such as Daniel Webster, opposed giving up what they saw as the national tradition of excluding slavery from the territories. In 1852, the northern and southern wings of the Democratic party managed to achieve unity in their national convention by agreeing on popular sovereignty. But, in that year, the Whig party, one of the great national institutions that held the sections together, began to disintegrate, because northern and southern Whigs could not agree on accepting the popular sovereignty aspect of the Compromise of 1850.

Supplementary Reading

For a survey of the United States in the decades before the Civil War, see R. Nichols, *The Stakes of Power, 1845-1877* (1961). Immigration is discussed in M. Hansen, *The Atlantic Migration* (1940); R. Berthoff, *British Immigrants in Industrial America* (1953); C. Wittke, *The Irish in America* (1956); and O. Handlin, *The Uprooted* (1951). For a discussion of westward expansion, see R. Billington, *The Far Western Frontier, 1830-1860* (1956). Railroad development is described in R. Fogel, *Railroads and American Economic Growth* (1964), and C. Goodrich, *Government Promotion of American Canals and Railroads* (1960). An insightful study is T. Cochran, *Railroad Leaders* (1953).

The impact of industrialization on northern society is examined in N. Ware, *The Industrial Worker, 1840-1860* (1924), as well as the studies by Thernstrom, Knights, and Pessen listed at the end of chapter 14. Southern society is viewed from a Marxian position in E. Genovese, *The Political Economy of Slavery* (1965) and *The World the Slaveholders Made* (1969). The best study of American slavery is E. Genovese's *Roll Jordan Roll: The World the Slaves Made* (1974); equally important is the statistical study of R. Fogel and S. Engerman, *Time on the Cross: The Economics of American Negro Slavery* (1974). Also valuable are J. Blassingame, *The Slave Community: Plantation Life in the Antebellum South* (1972); G. Rawick, *From Sundown to Sunup: The Making of the Black Community* (1972); R. Starobin, *Industrial Slavery in the Old South* (1970); and R. Wade, *Slavery in the Cities* (1964). For a provocative study of the Sambo personality, see S. Elkins, *Slavery* (1959). A good study of a major slave rebellion is S. Oates, *The Fires of Jubilee: Nat Turner's Fierce Rebellion* (1975). Southern defensiveness is analyzed in W. Taylor, *Cavalier and Yankee* (1961); G. Fredrickson, *The Black Image in the White Mind* (1971); and A. Craven, *The Growth of Southern Nationalism* (1953). Also provocative is D. Davis, *The Slave Power Conspiracy and the Paranoid Style* (1969).

The concept of Manifest Destiny is discussed in A. Weinberg, *Manifest Destiny* (1935); F. Merk, *Manifest Destiny and Mission in American History* (1963); and H. Smith, *Virgin Land* (1950). The impact of expansion on American Indian policy is discussed in R. Trennert, *Alternative to Extinction* (1975). The problems of racism in the West are described in R. Lapp, *Blacks in Gold Rush California* (1977). For an examination of black attitudes toward American destiny, see L. Sweet, *Black Images of America: 1784-1870* (1976). An economic explanation of expansion is offered in N. Graebner, *Empire on the Pacific* (1955). The politics of expansion are discussed in C. Sellers, *James K. Polk: Continentalist* (1966), and J. Paul, *Rift in the Democracy* (1961). For a discussion of Texas, see W. Binkley, *The Texas Revolution* (1952); for a discussion of Oregon, F. Merk, *The Oregon Question* (1967). A brief history of the Mexican War is O. Singletary, *The Mexican War* (1960). For an excellent analysis of the issues raised by the war and the peace settlement, see D. Potter, *The Impending Crisis: 1848-1861* (1976). For the debate over the Wilmot Proviso, see C. Morrison, *Democratic Politics and Sectionalism* (1967). The Compromise of 1850 is described in H. Hamilton, *Prologue to Conflict* (1964).

Chapter 17

The Politics of National Disunity

1852-1861

From 1840 until 1852, the nation had a strong and vital two-party system. Voters in the South during these twelve years divided their votes almost equally between the Whigs and the Democrats. When Whig President Harrison died, he was succeeded by the Democrat John Tyler, who opposed Henry Clay's desire for a third Bank of the United States and a higher tariff. Most of the southern Whigs in Congress turned against President Tyler and backed Clay. It was the unity of northern and southern Whigs behind Clay that enabled him to read Tyler out of the party by 1844 and to win the Whigs' presidential nomination for himself. Cotton planters from Georgia to eastern Texas, who continued to expand their investment in land and slaves, liked the Whig policy of a national bank and of the government's financial support for the building of roads, canals, and railroads that were necessary to get their crops to the seaports, where they would be sent to Europe or to the North. This was also true of the tobacco planters of Tennessee and Kentucky.

Alexander Stephens of Georgia was an example of a young southern Whig who supported Clay's economic program in 1844. Stephens was a lawyer who had become a political spokesman for the economic interests of the wealthy planters of the black belt in central Georgia. Many southern lawyers, bankers, and merchants were tied to the plantation economy and participated in politics as spokesmen for the planters.

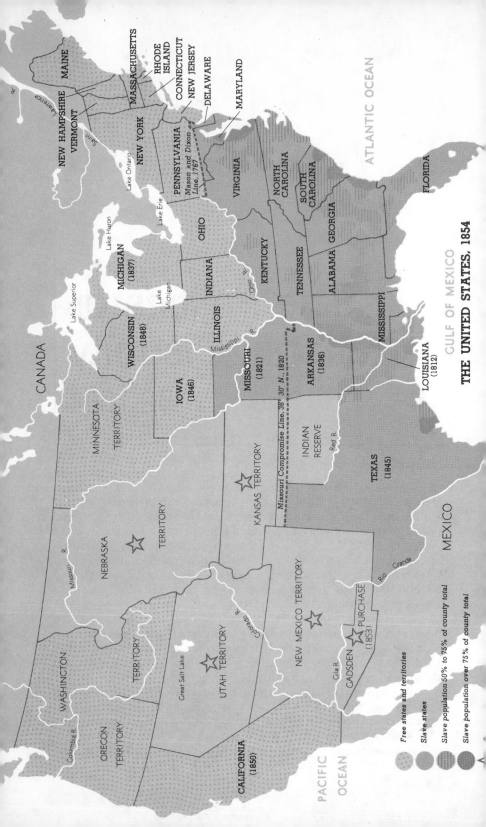

THE UNITED STATES, 1854

CANADA

ATLANTIC OCEAN

GULF OF MEXICO

PACIFIC OCEAN

MEXICO

MAINE
NEW HAMPSHIRE
VERMONT
MASSACHUSETTS
RHODE ISLAND
CONNECTICUT
NEW JERSEY
DELAWARE
MARYLAND
NEW YORK
PENNSYLVANIA
Mason and Dixon Line, 1767
VIRGINIA
NORTH CAROLINA
SOUTH CAROLINA
GEORGIA
ALABAMA
FLORIDA
OHIO
INDIANA
ILLINOIS
MICHIGAN (1837)
WISCONSIN (1848)
KENTUCKY
TENNESSEE
MISSISSIPPI
LOUISIANA (1812)
ARKANSAS (1836)
MISSOURI (1821)
IOWA (1846)
MINNESOTA TERRITORY
NEBRASKA TERRITORY
KANSAS TERRITORY
INDIAN RESERVE
TEXAS (1845)
NEW MEXICO TERRITORY
UTAH TERRITORY
WASHINGTON TERRITORY
OREGON TERRITORY
CALIFORNIA (1850)
GADSDEN PURCHASE (1853)

Missouri Compromise Line, 36° 30' N., 1820

Lake Superior
Lake Huron
Lake Michigan
Lake Erie
Lake Ontario
St. Lawrence R.
Ohio R.
Mississippi R.
Missouri R.
Red R.
Rio Grande
Gila R.
Colorado R.
Columbia R.
Great Salt Lake

Free states and territories
Slave states
Slave population 50% to 75% of county total
Slave population over 75% of county total

With most of their capital invested in land and slaves, the planters were very dependent upon the government for acquiring the capital necessary both to establish banks and to build transportation facilities. In Stephens's experience in Georgia in the 1830s and 1840s, the state government played an active role in establishing banks and various kinds of transportation. From the 1840s to 1860, the state government of Georgia financed and controlled the building of an extensive railroad system. In 1844, Stephens was eager for the national government to play a more active role in subsidizing railroad expansion. In return, the southern planters that Stephens represented were even willing to accept the tariffs that northern Whigs wanted.

When the Whig party disintegrated between 1846 and 1852, therefore, the divisive issues driving southern and northern Whigs apart were not those of a national bank, tariff, or government subsidization of transportation. The divisive issue was slavery in the territories.

The Democratic party disintegrated between 1856 and 1860. As in the case of southern and northern Whigs, there was substantial agreement among southern and northern Democrats on the economic issues. Most agreed on a low tariff and no national bank, and many were hesitant or doubtful about the government's responsibility to finance the building of railroads. From 1850 to 1856, northern and southern Democrats had agreed on popular sovereignty as the national policy toward the territories. In 1857, however, the Supreme Court ruled in the Dred Scott decision that both the old policy of excluding slavery from the territories and the new policy of popular sovereignty were unconstitutional. The Court's argument was that Congress, since it had the responsibility of governing the territories, had the responsibility of protecting the property that citizens brought into the territories. The definition of property necessarily included slaves. When Congress said that the people in the territories should decide for themselves whether they wanted slavery or not, it was, therefore, giving up its responsibility to govern the territory and to protect property there. The implication was that Congress must protect slavery in the territories.

Most southerners between 1846 and 1857 had not supported the extreme position of Calhoun and Jefferson Davis that Congress should protect slavery in the territories, and so most southerners accepted the Compromise of 1850 and popular sovereignty. After 1857, however, southerners believed that they had no choice but to accept the implications of the Supreme Court decision and to shift to the support of congressional protection of slavery in the territories. When southern Democrats made this shift in 1857, the collapse of the Democratic party in 1860 seemed assured, because most northern Democrats would not give up their position of popular sovereignty. In 1860, then, the country for the first time had political parties divided along sectional lines, and, without the unity provided by national parties, the nation divided and civil war resulted.

The Issue of Slavery

It has been difficult for historians to explain the importance of the issue of slavery in the territories as a cause of the Civil War, because, until recently, they have not worked with the assumption of cultural identity as an important part of a nation's history. When one brings the perspective of a cultural anthropologist to the study of American history, however, the symbolic importance of the territories in bringing about the Civil War becomes easier to explain.

An important part of the cultural identity of the nation in 1789 was the belief of the founding fathers that blacks were biologically incapable of becoming mature, rational, and responsible citizens. These leaders, including Jefferson, believed that the blacks must eventually be sent back to Africa.

Another important part of the cultural identity of the new nation was the role the western territories were to play in preserving the virtue of the new republic. Again, Jefferson, like the other founding fathers, believed that the rationality of responsible white citizens could only flourish where there was widespread ownership of agricultural property. For Jefferson, where rich and poor were crowded together (as in the European cities), politics were irrational and destructive. As the American population increased, the territories would be a safety valve through which the population could spread and acquire agricultural property, rather than being crowded together in cities as in Europe. For the founding fathers, therefore, the territories were associated with the preservation of national political virtue, and blacks were seen as a threat to that political virtue.

Jefferson's generation defined slavery as a necessary evil that kept the potentially corrupting blacks segregated from the virtuous whites. But the logic of the situation, for Jefferson, was that neither the unhealthy institution of slavery nor the inferior black should go to the territories. A significant consensus existed among northern and southern leaders in the 1780s about trying to restrict slavery to the areas where it already existed. Until the 1830s, most southern leaders continued to define slavery as a necessary evil, to hope that blacks could be sent to Africa, and to agree that Congress had the power and the responsibility to restrict the movement of slavery to the West.

The violent reaction of southern Whigs and Democrats to the Wilmot Proviso in 1846 revealed that southerners had changed dramatically since 1820 and no longer accepted the exclusion of slavery from the territories. This meant that most white southerners then defined slavery as a positive good.

The crucial role of the institution of black slavery in making possible the profitable spread of the cotton plantation across South Carolina beginning in the 1790s and its continuing profitable development from Georgia to eastern Texas down to the Civil War is one major factor in helping to explain this shift in southern attitude. When the center of slavery was localized in the upper South and the tobacco plantations there were relatively unprofitable, it was easier to think about ending slavery and sending the blacks to Africa than it was when the center of black population had spread southwest into Georgia, Alabama, Mississippi, and Louisiana and when the institution was profitable.

Another major factor in the shift, however, is the change in American culture from 1789 to the 1830s. The expansion of suffrage increased political participation among the lower-middle classes. Many of these people were converts to evangelical Protestantism, which was critical of the philosophic and religious values of the founding fathers. Suspicious of the outlook of eighteenth-century Enlightenment, with its emphasis on intelligence and science and reason, the evangelicals argued that truth could be found in a literal reading of the Bible, especially the Old Testament.

The numerous converts to the Methodist and Baptist churches were taught that they were escaping the moral corruption and compromises of the sinful world that had characterized upper-class life at the end of the eighteenth century. The converts were taught that they were becoming perfect saints. For southerners who were converting to the Methodist and Baptist churches (the largest such conversions took place in the South), it was difficult to continue to define slavery as a necessary evil. That was a compromise with corruption. But, if they defined slavery as a positive good, then they would not be compromising with evil.

For a South where probably 80 percent or more of the churchgoers after 1840 were Methodists and Baptists, the major defense of slavery was based on the existence of slavery in the Old Testament. Slavery was ordained by God. A God-given institution was a perfect institution. Historians in the past exaggerated the importance of the neo-medieval defense of slavery as a variety of the feudalism developed by a few literary figures in Virginia and South Carolina, such as George Fitzhugh.

As the majority of southerners came to hold a view of slavery as a positive good in the 1830s, they were also becoming very sensitive to the meaning of national citizenship. The founding fathers had tried to safeguard the presidency from identification with a majority by having the president chosen by the electoral college. But, when Jackson was elected in 1828, the electoral college had been made almost obsolete by the development of the national political parties that could mobilize a national majority for the election of a president. The election of Jackson was seen as a symbolic victory for the common man in achieving effective citizenship. Equality of citizenship — equal dignity for every adult white male — became an important part of the emotional background for the political and religious events of the 1830s.

For the average southern adult white male in the 1830s, therefore, evangelical Protestantism and political democracy were extremely important. If the issue of slavery in the territories had been raised and northerners had tried to continue a national policy of excluding slavery from any new territories, this policy would have made the southerner of the 1830s feel that his value of the positive good of slavery was under attack and that his right as a citizen to take his good institution into the territories was under attack. No one had a legitimate reason to deny this southerner his equal rights as an American Protestant and a democratic citizen.

The emphasis on political democracy that developed during the 1830s, however, made possible the compromise of popular sovereignty in 1850. Sharing the same democratic political culture, northerners and southerners could accept the idea that the people in the territories should decide their own policies. But southerners were so committed to slavery as a positive good that, when the Supreme Court ruled in the Dred Scott decision (1857) that Congress should protect slavery in the territories, they had no reason to reject the Court's position [see below, pp. 259-261].

Ironically, then, it was the growth of a common national culture around the ideals of political democracy and evangelical Protestantism that began to lead the nation toward civil war between 1830 and 1860. As many whites made the transition from lower-class to middle-class status in the early nineteenth century, they became more hostile toward blacks than the more aristocratic founding fathers had been. The white lower class of the eighteenth century had not participated in the white racist caste system that had denied the black male any equality with the white male. In the caste system, the black adult male was forced to act as a child or Sambo who could not be the equal of any adult white male and who could not sexually approach a white female. But in lower-class life in the eighteenth-century North, white and black men often worked together, and occasionally there could be open sexual relations between a black man and a white woman.

When many lower-class whites became members of the lower-middle class, however, they rejected this racial familiarity and defined democracy in caste terms. The white common man as a democratic citizen and an evangelical Protestant felt that he should not work as an equal with a black man and that the white women of the Protestant male citizens should not be available to black men. Steadily, from 1789 until 1860, the areas of citizenship allowed the free black by the northern states and the national government were restricted. And, in 1857, few important white leaders in the North protested the part of the Dred Scott decision that declared that a free black should not be considered a citizen of the United States and therefore had no right to sue to the federal court system.

Coming to despise the black more and more, the white northern political democrat and evangelical Protestant sympathized with its southern counterpart and was willing to tolerate the existence of slavery in the southern states as a necessary evil, as a necessary form of segregation that kept whites from corruption by blacks.

The northern political democrat and evangelical Protestant still thought of slavery as a necessary evil, as he shared in the Jacksonian political and religious reform movement to restore the virtuous simplicity of the old republic by purging the nation of all artificial institutions. Even more vehemently than Jefferson's generation, however, this Jacksonian genera-tion in the North wanted to keep both slavery and free blacks out of the West. As midwestern states from Indiana to Iowa joined the nation, they not only explicitly denied political citizenship to blacks but passed laws to stop their migration. These states then became the centers of the greatest hostility toward the possible spread of slavery into the territories taken from Mexico and then, in the 1850s, toward the possible spread of slavery into the Kansas and Nebraska territories.

Sympathetic to the reasons southern Methodists and Baptists had to compromise their perfect sainthood to keep blacks in their place in the South, northern Methodists and Baptists, however, did not want that com-promise to have a corrupting influence on the entire nation. By 1844, these churches had split into northern and southern branches, because north-erners did not want slaveholders to exercise national leadership, while southerners seceded from the national churches because they were not recognized as the moral equals of their northern counterparts. The motive of the southern Methodists and Baptists was expressed in politics in 1846, when southern Whigs and Democrats threatened to secede from the na-tion if they were defined as morally inferior citizens by having their institu-tion officially excluded by Congress from the territories to be taken from Mexico.

The Civil War, then, was not the result of the effort by southerners to create a new political state because they had a culture that differed strongly from that in the North. The major political tensions from 1846 to 1861 revolved around the efforts of most southerners to try to preserve their identity as first-class citizens of the United States who were in no way inferior to citizens in the North because they lived in a region that had the peculiar institution of slavery. They threatened secession in 1846, because they saw the Wilmot Proviso, if it were passed by the northern majority in Congress, officially defining them as Americans who were burdened by an immoral institution that had to be excluded from the national territories. The next major threat of secession did not come until 1860, when south-erners warned that the election of Lincoln would force them to consider secession.

The symbolic political crisis of Lincoln's election is related to the meaning of the presidency after Jackson became president in 1828. With Jackson's election, the president became the symbolic representative of a national majority and a national will. The president came to symbolize national identity. Lincoln and the Republican party of 1860 stood for the exclusion of slavery from the territories because it was not, as an institu-tion, a positive good but only a necessary evil where it existed in the south-ern states. Almost no southerner could identify with Lincoln in 1860; almost no southerner would vote Republican in 1860. The Lincoln who was elected in 1860, in the eyes of southerners, represented only the North. The southerner, therefore, was no longer a part of the nation, and the logic of the situation dictated that the southern states should secede and recreate the United States of America — South.

The Two Revolutions Compared

A comparison between the events leading to the American Revolution in 1776 and the secession of the southern states in 1860-1861 reveals the great differences between the two revolutions. In comparison to the clear-cut divisions between life in England and the colonies and the clear-cut conflict of political power between the British Parliament in which the colonists were not represented and the colonial governments whose autonomy Parliament refused to recognize, the main patterns of southern historical development — expansive capitalism, political democracy, and evangelical Protestantism — paralleled those of the North. Participation in the mainstream of national development made it possible for southerners to dominate the presidency, the Supreme Court, and congressional leadership until 1852. Their state governments had not been oppressed by a national government controlled by northerners. Southerners had no experience of being colonials under a foreign government.

When Parliament had passed the Stamp Act in 1765, the colonial legislatures had responded by creating an extralegal congress to force Parliament to withdraw this concrete legislation that directly affected the colonial economy. When the northern Whigs and Democrats threatened to pass the Wilmot Proviso, southern Whigs and Democrats responded by asking the southern states to send delegates to a convention at Nashville, Tennessee, to consider the crisis. When the crisis was resolved by the Compromise of 1850 and the establishment of the policy of popular sovereignty for the New Mexico Territory, the delegates returned to their states without taking any specific action.

Since Congress did not act to bar slavery from the territories between 1850 and 1860, there were no further regional conventions in the South. Again, the situation was unlike the American Revolution. Parliament had continued to pass concrete legislative acts that shaped colonial economic and political life. And the colonies again had responded by creating the Continental Congress to force Parliament to withdraw this legislation. By 1776, when Parliament refused to bow to colonial pressure, this extralegal congress had declared the independence of the colonies from Britain. Specific British actions had caused the creation of a revolutionary political organization, which linked the separate colonies before independence and which then provided the focus for a common revolutionary effort against Britain. And, in its Declaration of Independence, this revolutionary body had constructed a revolutionary ideology to justify the break from Britain. A clear distinction was made between an old and a new political identity, between monarchy and republicanism.

The Psychology of Sectional Conspiracy

In 1848, the Whigs had nominated a southerner, General Zachary Taylor, to be their presidential candidate. But many southern Whigs had been disillusioned by Taylor as president because he had shown no sympathy toward the issue of slavery in the territories. Instead, the southern Whigs saw a conspiracy on the part of northern Whigs to use Taylor to overcome southern resistance to the Wilmot Proviso. In 1852, the majority of northern Whigs again refused to approve the popular sovereignty aspect of the Compromise of 1850. Instead, they offered the southern Whigs another southern general, Winfield Scott (who had been a hero of the Mexican War), as the party's presidential candidate. Then, however, many southern Whigs refused to accept Scott, because it was clear that he, like Taylor, had no sympathy with the concern of so many southerners for popular sovereignty as the national policy for the territories. When Scott was nominated at the Whig convention without a commitment to the Compromise of 1850, many southern Whigs refused to support him, and the party ceased to be a strong national organization.

In 1852, the Democrats nominated a northerner, Franklin Pierce, as their candidate and stood firmly on popular sovereignty and the Compromise of 1850. United north and south, the Democrats won a smashing victory. Immediately, however, the party began to move toward disunity because of the issue of popular sovereignty for the Kansas and Nebraska territories. Stephen A. Douglas, a Democratic senator from Illinois who had played a major role in putting together the Compromise of 1850, was one of many northerners who wanted a railroad to be built from the Midwest to the Pacific coast. It was in the economic interest of midwesterners to have the first transcontinental railroad follow a northern route rather than go from Texas to the Pacific. To get government protection for settlers and railroad builders in the unorganized territories west of Missouri, however, territorial government would have to be established. This area, part of the Louisiana Purchase, had been barred to slavery by the Missouri Compromise of 1820. Douglas believed that the only way to get enough southern votes in Congress to organize the Kansas and Nebraska territories was to end the exclusion of slavery and establish the policy of popular sovereignty.

Douglas was not sensitive to the strong hostility toward the expansion of slavery in the North, which had been expressed in the Liberty party of 1844, the Free-Soil party of 1848, and the refusal of northern Whigs to accept popular sovereignty in 1852. Nor was he aware that many northern Democrats had accepted popular sovereignty in 1850 only because the alternative seemed to be civil war. When in 1854 Congress passed the Kansas-Nebraska Act repealing the Missouri Compromise and establishing popular sovereignty, Douglas was not prepared for the critical uproar in the North. In the Senate, antislavery politicians led by Salmon Chase and Charles Sumner (both future members of the Lincoln cabinet) published "An Appeal of the Independent Democrats," which condemned the repeal of the Missouri Compromise as a repudiation of an earlier congressional pledge. Many other northern Democrats renounced their party. Believing that they had made a mistake between 1848 and 1852 when they had given up the national tradition of barring slavery from the territories, they were able to make a new political alliance with a segment of the northern Whigs. The result was the birth in 1854 of the new Republican political party.

The Republican party, like the Liberty party of 1844 and the Free-Soil party of 1848, made the restriction of slavery its most important principle. Unlike the earlier parties, it could become a major party because of the collapse of the Whig party. The Republicans did not threaten to capture the government in 1856, because the Democrats remained united and because another party, the Native American, was able to attract a segment of the northern Whigs as well as most of the southern Whigs. The Native American, or Know-Nothing party, tried to overcome the growing sectional tension between North and South by uniting the northern and southern white Protestants in a crusade against the rapid buildup of Catholic population, which was due to Irish and German immigration.

By 1856, however, northern and southern Protestants were too far committed to seeing each other's section as the major source of conspiracy to join a crusade against a Catholic conspiracy. Starting in the 1830s, northern abolitionists had warned that the planter aristocracy was an un-American class with medieval values that wanted to destroy the freedom of white Americans by spreading slavery throughout the entire nation. The abolitionists had been able to persuade few northerners in the 1830s and 1840s to see the South in these terms, and many abolitionists were harassed by northern mobs; a few were even killed.

But, by 1856, abolitionists could point to a succession of events that they claimed proved the existence of the conspiracy to spread slavery — the annexation of Texas as a slave state, the end of the national policy of excluding slavery from the territories in 1850, and the repeal of the Missouri Compromise by the Kansas-Nebraska Act in 1854. They could also point to the foreign policy of the Pierce administration, in which the influence of Jefferson Davis was expressed, that attempted to get Cuba from Spain and add that slave territory to the United States. In 1856, the Republicans accepted the abolitionist theory of a slave-power conspiracy to spread slavery throughout the nation as a central part of their political appeals. According to the Republicans, slavery had to be excluded from the territories because the slaveholding conspiracy had to be stopped there; otherwise, the slaveholders would demand the next step of spreading slavery into the free states.

However, to southerners, especially Democrats, the emergence of the Republican party (which represented only northerners) seemed to be part of a northern aggressive conspiracy to destroy the simplicity and virtue of the Republic of 1789. Jefferson had warned that Hamilton had wanted to use the power of the national government to destroy the principles of 1789 and that the states must take responsibility for guarding their power so that they could resist any attempt to subvert the Constitution. Then, in 1856, southerners could argue that they were standing in Jefferson's tradition of states' rights. In 1856, northern Republicans saw southern Democrats as representing an un-American conspiracy that planned to destroy American liberty. And, in 1856, southern Democrats were committed to seeing northern Republicans in exactly the same way.

These mutual suspicions were reinforced by the conflict of free-soil and proslavery forces in the Kansas Territory. The New England Emigrant Aid Company was organized to send free-soil settlers into Kansas, and proslavery men from Missouri rode across the border to stuff ballot boxes and intimidate free-soil voters. John Brown, a militant abolitionist and an outspoken free-soiler, killed several proslavery settlers at Pottawotomie Creek; soon after, in a larger battle at Osawatomie, one of Brown's sons was killed and Brown was driven from the territory. The tension and conflict in Kansas spread to the United States Senate when Charles Sumner presented a violent antisouthern speech called "The Crime Against Kansas." Preston S. Brooks, a member of the House of Representatives, was angered by Sumner's personal insult of his relative, Senator Andrew P. Butler, and came to the Senate and gave Sumner a beating with his cane that left him an invalid for three years.

In political terms, the controversy in Kansas (known as Bleeding Kansas) resulted in two rival groups — one proslavery, one antislavery — claiming to represent the entire population in the drafting of a state constitution. When President Buchanan, hoping to end the long quarrel, accepted the proslavery Lecompton Constitution (despite the fact that the vote for ratification had been rigged), Senator Douglas attacked the administration for corrupting the idea of popular sovereignty. Douglas's stand further undermined his support among southern Democrats.

During the Democratic national convention of 1856, however, the northern and southern wings of the party managed to mend their disagreements long enough to agree on a candidate and a platform. The party could not nominate Pierce because of the unpopularity of the Kansas-Nebraska Act. Nor could northern delegates afford to nominate Douglas because of the hostility toward him in the North. Although some southern delegates were still friendly to Douglas, they preferred to compromise on James Buchanan, who had been out of the country in 1854. Despite severe sectional tensions, the Democrats managed to unite on the continuation of popular sovereignty as a national policy for the territories.

The Republicans nominated a national hero of the western expansion, John C. Frémont, and emphasized a platform of restoring the policy of congressional exclusion of slavery from the territories. Buchanan won 174 electoral votes; Fremont, 114; and Millard Fillmore, the Know-Nothing candidate, 8. But the Republicans won control of most of the northern state legislatures. Buchanan won the support of only five northern states, and his margin was very close in four of them. If anything undermined the unity of the Democratic party before the election of 1860, there was a strong possibility that, for the first time in American history, a sectional party might control the national government.

The Supreme Court's Dred Scott decision in 1857 accomplished the destruction of the Democratic party. The five southern justices and one of the northern justices ruled that blacks were not citizens of the United

UNITED STATES POPULATION, 1860

ATLANTIC OCEAN

GULF OF MEXICO

PACIFIC OCEAN

POSSESSIONS

BRITISH

MEXICO

MAINE
NEW HAMPSHIRE
VERMONT
MASSACHUSETTS
RHODE ISLAND
CONNECTICUT
NEW JERSEY
DELAWARE
MARYLAND
NEW YORK
PENNSYLVANIA
New York
Philadelphia
Pittsburgh
Washington, D.C.
Albany
Buffalo
Boston

VIRGINIA
NORTH CAROLINA
SOUTH CAROLINA
GEORGIA
FLORIDA
ALABAMA
MISSISSIPPI
LOUISIANA
TENNESSEE
KENTUCKY
ARKANSAS
MISSOURI
OHIO
INDIANA
ILLINOIS
IOWA
WISCONSIN
MICHIGAN
MINNESOTA
Charleston
New Orleans
Cincinnati
Louisville
Saint Louis
Chicago

UNORG. TERR.
TERRITORY
NEBRASKA
KANSAS TERRITORY
UNORGANIZED TERRITORY
TEXAS
NEW MEXICO TERRITORY
UTAH TERRITORY
WASHINGTON
OREGON
CALIFORNIA
San Francisco

Lake Superior
Lake Michigan
Lake Huron
Lake Erie
Lake Ontario

Total population, per square mile:
Less than 2
2 to 18
19 to 45
46 to 90

Slave population 50% to 75% of county total
Slave population over 75% of county total

States and that Congress had no right to exclude slavery from the territories, either directly through legislation or indirectly by giving territorial governments the power to decide for or against slavery.

When Abraham Lincoln campaigned in 1858 for Stephen Douglas's Senate seat, he focused attention on the way in which the Court had undermined the doctrine of popular sovereignty, which Douglas had helped to make a part of national politics in 1850 and 1854. Lincoln asked Douglas whether he accepted the Court's decision. Douglas said yes but that the existence of slavery in the territories was still dependent upon the will of the people who settled there. This Freeport Doctrine of Douglas insisted that popular sovereignty would determine the future of the territories in spite of the Court's decision.

Southern Democrats who had been in favor of popular sovereignty in 1856 and who supported Douglas as a presidential candidate then turned against him with great bitterness and damned him for being as bad as a Black Republican. Most of the leaders of the Democratic parties in the southern states then told northern Democrats that they would have to give up popular sovereignty when the party met at its national convention in 1860. Northern Democrats would have to accept the implication of the Supreme Court that Congress must protect slavery in the territories. Otherwise, the southern Democrats warned, they would split the party and allow the Republicans to win the presidency. If that happened, they would secede from the union.

As the Democrats approached their crucial convention in 1860, the psychology of sectional conspiracy was still escalating. Many northerners found the Fugitive Slave Act of 1850 to be evidence of the southern conspiracy. Some northern states were passing "personal liberty laws," which made it a crime to help federal officials enforce the Fugitive Slave Act. Some northern legislatures also were declaring the act unconstitutional. Southerners, however, had more dramatic evidence that fit their theory of an aggressive northern conspiracy when John Brown captured the federal arsenal at Harpers Ferry, Virginia (October 1859) in the hope of beginning a slave rebellion. Although most northern newspapers denounced Brown, southerners chose to believe that the New England poets Emerson and Thoreau were representative of northern opinion. Emerson and Thoreau declared Brown to be a martyr and a saint when he was hanged in December 1859 for conspiracy and treason against Virginia.

When the Democrats met at Charleston (April 1860), northern Democrats would not abandon popular sovereignty and accept the demand of southern Democrats for a plank in the party platform favoring congressional protection of slavery in the territories. When many southern delegates left the convention, the northern delegates moved to Baltimore, where they nominated Stephen Douglas. Douglas, who had been too prosouthern for northern delegates in 1856, was acceptable to the North after the South had turned against him. The southern Democrats nominated Vice-President John C. Breckinridge of Kentucky as the candidate of their Democratic party, with a platform of congressional protection of slavery in the territories.

The Republican convention in 1860 stood on the original party position of 1854 that slavery must be excluded from the territories. The Republicans also promised to accept slavery where it existed in the southern states and denounced John Brown and the extreme abolitionists. Absorbing most of the northern Whigs, the Republicans in 1860 accepted the Whig philosophy of economic growth. Their platform called for a high tariff and government financial support of railroads. The platform also promised free homesteads to settlers going into the western territories. The Republicans nominated Abraham Lincoln from Illinois as their presidential candidate. Lincoln was not a major political figure. He had served as a Whig congressman in Washington but had not made a national reputation, and, in 1858, he had been defeated in his effort to win Douglas's Senate seat. But the Republicans did not want a well-known figure, like William Seward, who had made enemies, and they wanted someone from the Midwest who would be popular in the doubtful states of Indiana and Illinois.

A fourth party, the Constitutional Union, nominated a presidential candidate. Southern Whigs had been homeless since they had left the national Whig party in 1852. They were reluctant to join the national Democratic party, because they did not share that party's hostility toward tariffs, a national bank, and national support for railroad building. They had drifted into the Native American party in 1856, and then they formed most of the strength of the Constitutional Unionists in 1860. Little separated them in 1860 from the Republican party but the issue of slavery in the territories. They agreed with most of the economic planks in the Republican platform. Nominating Senator John Bell of Tennessee for president, the Constitutional Unionists appealed to Americans to overcome sectional differences and to vote for national unity. This party, therefore, refused to take a specific stand on the issue of slavery in the territories.

When the votes were in, Douglas had won only in the slave state of Missouri. Bell had won the slave states of Virginia, Kentucky, and Tennessee. Breckinridge had won all the other slave states, even Delaware and Maryland. Lincoln won every free state. Since the northern population had grown faster than the southern because immigration had been concentrated in the North, northern states dominated the electoral college. Lincoln won the presidency with a minority of the popular vote, since Douglas ran very close behind him in most of the northern states. Lincoln had 1,866,452 votes; Douglas, 1,376,957; Breckinridge, 849,781; and Bell, 588,879.

Secession

The legislature of South Carolina immediately called for the election of a convention to consider secession. When the convention met, it unanimously declared on December 20, 1860, that South Carolina had seceded from the union. The convention insisted that it was not engaging in rebellion but was carrying out its right as a sovereign state, a right that

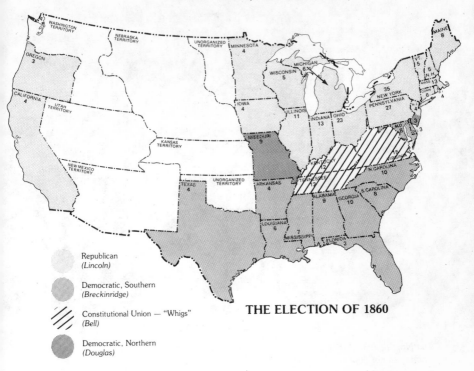

Republican
(Lincoln)

Democratic, Southern
(Breckinridge)

Constitutional Union — "Whigs"
(Bell)

Democratic, Northern
(Douglas)

THE ELECTION OF 1860

was established by the Declaration of Independence and the Articles of Confederation, which declared that each state retained "its sovereignty, freedom, and independence." The Constitution of 1789 was formed by a compact of the states who retained "reserved powers." In 1860 South Carolina had exercised part of this reserved power by withdrawing from the Compact of 1789. This was done because the union had fallen into the hands of a sectional party that was hostile to the institution of slavery. When Lincoln took the office of the presidency in March 1861, South Carolina's interests would no longer be represented in the national government. Rather than wait for this to happen, South Carolina seceded at once.

A secessionist movement headed by Robert Barnwell Rhett had existed in South Carolina since the 1820s [see above, pp. 205-206]. During the 1850s, Rhett joined Edmund Ruffin of Virginia and William L. Yancey of Alabama to try to create organizations in the southern states that paralleled the Committees of Correspondence in the early 1770s. Ruffin and Yancey shared Rhett's belief that the South had a unique culture and should, therefore, form a separate political nation. But they were unable to win converts during the 1850s, and they were rejected by the secessionist leaders of their own states. These leaders, like James Orr of South Carolina, thought the South was preserving the national values of 1789 rather than expressing a new southern culture. Fire-eaters like Rhett, Ruffin, and

The North claimed that it represented a national rather than a sectional position through traditional national symbols. (Courtesy of Library of Congress.)

Yancey were denied leadership in the Confederate States of America at Montgomery, Alabama, in February 1861, when delegates gathered from South Carolina, Georgia, Alabama, Florida, Mississippi, Louisiana, and Texas, the seven states that had seceded by that date.

The governors, as the heads of the Democratic parties of their states, were the decisive leaders in taking their states out of the union. The governors had committed themselves to Breckinridge in the election of 1860, and they had warned northern Democrats and Republicans that they would react to the election of Lincoln by calling state conventions to consider secession.

Breckinridge received 124,000 fewer votes in the southern states than the combined number of votes cast for Douglas and Bell. Democratic party leaders in the states from South Carolina to Texas did not represent, therefore, an overwhelming consensus for secession. Indeed, the conventions that called for secession were controlled by Breckinridge Democrats, because the Douglas Democrats and Constitutional Unionists divided the votes of those southerners who were opposed to immediate secession.

Since the secessionist governors were not ideological fanatics, they were able to recognize that the only consensus that existed in their states was a commitment to the right of states to secede from the union. Most Douglas Democrats and Constitutional Unionists shared this belief with the Breckinridge Democrats. The governors were not committed, then, to sending to Montgomery delegates who represented the fire-eaters' belief in a unique southern culture. Instead, they chose delegates who believed that the South was acting in the pattern of Jefferson in 1800 and Jackson in 1828 in preserving the virtues of the Old Republic of 1789. This is dramatized by the action of the secessionist governor of Georgia, Joseph E. Brown, who sent Alexander Stephens to Montgomery as a representative of Georgia. Stephens, who had been a Whig in the 1840s, had backed Douglas in 1860 because he was violently opposed to Georgia's secession from the union. Then, he had worked to keep the state convention from declaring secession.

Because so many of the delegates at Montgomery wanted to placate the large number of southerners, who like Stephens, had not wanted secession, they chose Stephens to be vice-president of the Confederacy. Jefferson Davis, who was chosen to be president, had not gone to Montgomery. Like Stephens, he had not played a positive role in taking his state (Mississippi) out of the union. Davis was born in a log cabin in Kentucky within a year of Lincoln's birth in a similar cabin in the same state. His older brother Joseph had gone to the Mississippi frontier and become a wealthy lawyer and planter. He decided to raise his younger brother as an aristocrat and sent him to West Point before he presented him with his own plantation to run.

Davis had been a United States senator from Mississippi when he opposed the Compromise of 1850 because he was committed to congressional protection of slavery in the territories. He was defeated in Mississippi in 1851 by a politician who favored acceptance of the compromise. He then became secretary of war in the Pierce administration and favored the annexation of Cuba. At the end of the 1850s, he became a United States senator again, and, in 1860, he disagreed with the Breckinridge Democrats in his state about the need to secede if Lincoln were elected. He remained in Washington trying to work out a compromise until he learned that Mississippi was seceding from the union. Then, he returned to his plantation, where he was notified that he had been chosen as president of the Confederate States of America.

The constitution worked out at Montgomery represented, therefore, an overwhelming desire to preserve the Constitution of 1789. To the extent that there were differences, these expressed a belief in strengthening states' rights and not in fulfilling southern nationalism. According to the Constitution, each state, in joining the Confederacy, was acting in "its sovereign and independent character," and federal officers could be impeached by the legislatures of the states where they were located. But the Confederate Constitution kept the provisions of the Constitution of 1789 dealing with money and diplomacy that made the federal government supreme over the states. And the federal Constitution, laws, and treaties were also to be the "supreme law of the land."

The Constitution prohibited the Confederate government from ending slavery and provided that slavery must be protected in any territories that the federal government acquired. Again, however, the fact that the secessionist leaders did not share the aggressive proslavery attitudes of men like Robert Barnwell Rhett is revealed by their refusal to legalize the foreign slave trade.

In March 1861, when Lincoln officially became president of the United States, only the deep southern states of South Carolina, Georgia, Alabama, Mississippi, Louisiana, Florida, and Texas had seceded from the union and had created a separate national government. These states represented the area where the expansion of the cotton plantation had made slavery profitable. They also represented the area of the South where the presence of blacks in large numbers made white southerners feel that slavery was a necessary social institution that kept blacks under control.

The tendency in the pattern of votes for and against secession in these states was for smaller planters to provide the leadership of the Breckinridge Democrats while larger planters tended to vote for the Constitutional Unionists. The nonslaveholding whites in counties where geographic factors like mountains or poor soil kept slavery from being an economic or social factor tended to vote for Douglas Democrats.

In the border states of the South, the Constitutional Unionists and Douglas Democrats were strong enough to block the drive of the Breckinridge Democrats for secession. In Virginia, for instance, the mountainous western part of the state was solidly Douglas Democratic and opposed to secession. The plantation areas in the eastern part of the state were split between Constitutional Unionists and Breckinridge Democrats. A convention was elected in Virginia, as in the cotton states, to consider the crisis of Lincoln's election, but a majority of Constitutional Unionists and Douglas Democrat delegates blocked the proposal of the Breckinridge Democrats for secession. This coalition lasted until Lincoln (April 1861) declared that he would use military force to suppress rebellion in South Carolina. Then the Constitutional Unionist delegates from the plantation areas joined the Breckinridge Democrats to vote Virginia out of the union. At this point, the Douglas Democrats from the mountainous area began to withdraw their counties to form the new state of West Virginia and remain within the union.

The Constitutional Unionists of Virginia agreed with the Constitutional Unionists of the cotton states that Lincoln's election should not be the cause for southern states to secede, but they also agreed that a state had the constitutional right to secede and that Lincoln had no constitutional right to coerce a state that had left the union. This was the reasoning that brought North Carolina, Virginia, Tennessee, and Arkansas to secede in April and May. However, the northernmost group of slave states — Maryland, Delaware, Kentucky, and Missouri — remained in the union. A map of states' rights and secessionist sentiments would show them strongest in the cotton South where slavery was most important in economic and social terms. But in nonslaveholding counties in those states, as well as in the border slave states, opinions favoring states' rights and the right of secession were not as strongly held.

Attempts at Compromise

During the months between December 1860 and February 1861, President Buchanan was unable to decide how to act toward the seceding cotton states. Nor would he vigorously support the attempts at compromise being made in Congress. Senator John J. Crittenden of Kentucky proposed that the division of the Louisiana Purchase territories worked out in the Missouri Compromise, which excluded slavery north of 36°30′ (the southern boundary of Missouri) and permitted it south of that line, be extended to the Pacific. It was also proposed that Congress should guarantee the security of slavery forever where it existed in the southern states and in the District of Columbia and that slaveowners should be compensated by the national government for runaway slaves.

Lincoln agreed to the last two principles. And, in February, the Republicans in the House of Representatives approved a thirteenth amendment to the Constitution, which would have guaranteed the security of slavery forever where it existed, and sent it to the states for ratification. But Lincoln would not compromise on the issue of excluding slavery from the territories.

In his inaugural address on March 4, 1861, Lincoln assured the South that slavery was secure where it existed and that he would enforce the Fugitive Slave Act. He also stated that secession was unconstitutional and that he would enforce the laws of the United States within all the states.

When Lincoln took office, the national forts along the southern coast already had surrendered to Confederate forces without armed conflict, except for Fort Pickens in Florida and Fort Sumter in the harbor of Charleston, South Carolina. Lincoln, like Buchanan, hesitated to send reinforcements and supplies to these forts because such an action might begin civil war. Lincoln knew that much unionist sentiment existed within the seceded states. If conflict was avoided, the Constitutional Unionists and Douglas Democrats might win political control in a number of the cotton states and bring them back into the union. And, as long as conflict was avoided, the border South remained within the union.

However, if Fort Sumter was not supplied and was taken over by South Carolina, the power of the secessionists to defy the authority of the United States of America would be established. Lincoln decided to send supplies but not military reinforcements to Sumter on April 6 and to make the expedition public. The problem was then in the hands of Jefferson Davis. He would have to make the decision to fire the first shot. He ordered Confederate officers to fire on the supply ships when they arrived. The officers began firing on Fort Sumter on April 12 and the fort surrendered on April 14.

On April 15, Lincoln called for 75,000 volunteers to suppress the rebellion in South Carolina. The Virginia Convention voted on April 17 in favor of secession. Arkansas, Tennessee, and North Carolina followed Virginia out of the union, and the Civil War began.

Supplementary Reading

The religious and philosophic commitment of Americans to the western territories was discussed in detail for the first time in H. N. Smith's *Virgin Land* (1950). Since then historians have become interested in the way in which Americans came to believe that a timeless perfection had been achieved by the 1830s. See, for example, E. L. Tuveson, *Redeemer Nation* (1968), and M. L. Wilson, "Time and the Political Dialogue in the United States, 1828-48," *American Quarterly*, XIX (1967), 619-44. The strength of white racism in pre-Civil War America has been described by L. Litwack in *North of Slavery* (1961), and G. M. Fredrickson, *The Black Image in the White Mind* (1971). The relationship of evangelical Protestantism to white racism is the subject of D. G. Mathew's *Slavery and Methodism* (1965), and H. S. Smith's *In His Image, But: Racism in Southern Religion, 1780-1910* (1972). The white racism of the Midwest, which tried to keep blacks out of the territories, is described in E. H. Berwanger, *The Frontier against Slavery* (1967), and V. J. Voegeli, *Free But Not Equal* (1967).

The most complete discussion of the political issues during the pre-Civil War decades is D. Potter, *The Impending Crisis: 1848-1861* (1976). Also valuable is W. Barney, *The Road to Secession* (1972). The values of the Republican party are analyzed in E. Foner, *Free Soil, Free Labor, Free Men* (1970). The political problems of the Democrats are described in R. Nichols, *The Disruption of American Democracy* (1948). For a good discussion of the decision for secession, see S. Channing, *Crisis of Fear: Secession in South Carolina* (1970). Several biographical studies are also helpful; see D. Donald, *Charles Sumner and the Coming of the Civil War* (1960); D. Fehrenbacher, *Prelude to Greatness: Lincoln in the 1850's* (1962); R. Johannsen, *Stephen A. Douglas* (1973); and S. Oates, *To Purge the Land with Blood: A Biography of John Brown* (1970). Several recent essays are collected in G. Fredrickson, editor, *A Nation Divided* (1975).

Chapter

18

The Civil War

When Lincoln became president in March of 1861, he recognized that the weak Republican party was the political institution that he had to use to hold the nation together. The result of the elections of November 1860 brought 29 Republicans to the Senate. They faced an opposition of 37 senators belonging to other parties. In the House, there were 108 Republicans opposed by 129 Democrats and Constitutional Unionists. The secession of the southern states and the withdrawal of their representatives and senators by the spring of 1861, however, left the Republicans with a working majority. But Lincoln was faced with the same members of the Supreme Court who had ruled in the Dred Scott decision of 1857 that the Republican policy toward slavery in the territories was unconstitutional.

To Preserve the Union

Lincoln had an almost fanatical devotion to the idea of the American nation as a divine experiment in establishing a democracy that could serve as a model for the whole world. Under no circumstances was he willing, therefore, to have the American nation divided. He was willing to use almost any means to preserve the unity of the nation.

The commercial and and banking interests of the eastern cities, which had transferred from the Whig to the Republican party, had put pressure on Lincoln to accept a compromise with the South during the winter of 1860-1861. But, by March of 1861, most of this group had reluctantly accepted the failure of the attempts at compromise and backed Lincoln in a policy of firmness in not recognizing the Confederacy. Some northern abolitionists had been calling for the separation of the northern states from the slave states so that the free states would no longer be corrupted by the evil institution of slavery, and their immediate response was to celebrate southern secession. But, by March 1861, they could see the alternative of purging slavery from the South and were willing to back Lincoln's policy of holding the nation together by force, if necessary. Many northern Democrats, as represented by Stephen Douglas, had worked desperately for compromise between November 1860 and March 1861. But, like the big business interests, they had reached the reluctant decision by March 1861 that Lincoln must use force as the last resort to preserve the nation. When fighting began in April, Douglas pledged his support to Lincoln.

Lincoln, as a former Whig, was opposed to the views of Andrew Jackson and the Democrats that the president had more power than the Congress or the Supreme Court because only the president directly expressed the will of the people. Throughout his presidency, Lincoln tried to involve Congress in the making of important decisions. But the emergency caused by the secession of the southern states, coupled with Lincoln's dedication to the preservation of the union, forced him — with great reluctance — to take decisive actions even when that meant ignoring constitutional limitations on presidential power.

Hoping for a brief war, Lincoln had called for volunteers to serve for three months to suppress rebellion in the South (April 1861). The war he began was technically not a violation of Congress's constitutional responsibility to declare war. Lincoln did not recognize the right of a state to secede, and he argued that the Civil War was not a conflict between two nations but the suppression of rebellion within the borders of the United States. According to this view, every southern soldier was a traitor and was subject to the death penalty if captured. In practice, however, Lincoln recognized southern soldiers as members of an army of a foreign nation, and those captured were treated as prisoners of war and not as traitors.

In the months of April, May, and June, Lincoln did violate explicitly the Constitution by increasing the regular army, taking money from the treasury to finance the military forces, and suspending the right to habeas corpus. According to the Constitution, these actions were the responsibility of Congress. When Congress met in July, it ratified Lincoln's actions by passing the necessary supporting legislation.

The North in 1861 had a much larger population and much greater industrial strength than the South. The northern population was 20,700,000, compared to 9,105,000 in the South. Blacks composed 3,654,000 of the southern population. There were 110,000 industrial plants in the North, employing 1,300,000 workers. The South had 18,000 industrial plants with 110,000 workers. The North had 22,000 miles of railroads; the South had 9,000 miles.

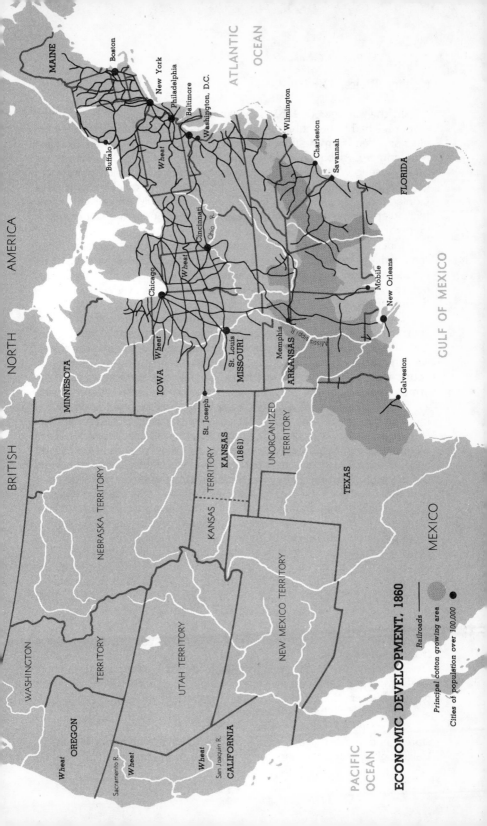

ECONOMIC DEVELOPMENT, 1860

Principal cotton growing area

Cities of population over 100,000

Railroads

PACIFIC OCEAN

WASHINGTON TERRITORY

OREGON

Wheat

CALIFORNIA

Wheat

San Joaquin R.

Sacramento R.

Wheat

UTAH TERRITORY

NEBRASKA TERRITORY

NEW MEXICO TERRITORY

KANSAS TERRITORY

KANSAS TERRITORY (1861)

UNORGANIZED TERRITORY

MEXICO

TEXAS

Galveston

GULF OF MEXICO

New Orleans

Mobile

ARKANSAS

Memphis

Mississippi R.

St. Louis

MISSOURI

St. Joseph

IOWA

Wheat

MINNESOTA

BRITISH NORTH AMERICA

Chicago

Wheat

Wheat

Cincinnati

Ohio R.

Buffalo

Wheat

MAINE

Boston

New York

Philadelphia

Baltimore

Washington, D.C.

Wilmington

Charleston

Savannah

FLORIDA

ATLANTIC OCEAN

Military Affairs, 1861

In the summer of 1861, Lincoln did not believe that the northern resources had to be mobilized to crush rebellion in the South. When Virginia seceded from the union, the Confederate capital was moved from Montgomery, Alabama, to Richmond, Virginia. With the Confederal capital so close to Washington, D.C., Lincoln sent the first Union army under General Irwin McDowell to capture Richmond and quickly destroy the Confederacy. But, at the first Battle of Bull Run in July, McDowell's volunteers were smashed by the Confederate army under the leadership of General Joseph E. Johnston.

Lincoln, who wanted to direct the strategy of the war personally, removed McDowell and replaced him with General George B. McClellan. McClellan spent the next year creating a disciplined, professional army before he was ready to try again in the summer of 1862 to capture Richmond.

Lincoln had better military success, however, in 1861 in holding Missouri, Kentucky, and Maryland in the union. The governors of Missouri and Kentucky favored the Confederacy, but the Unionists in these states, with the help of the federal army, kept control. The army set up military courts in these states to prosecute those citizens who worked against the armed forces by persuading young men not to enlist or to resist the draft.

As the North gradually built an army of 2 million men, it depended more on creating an emergency national army by using volunteers and the state militias than by expanding the regular army. By 1862, however, there were not enough volunteers to meet the manpower needs of the North, and Congress passed a conscription act that year that gave the governors the power to draft men between the ages of eighteen and forty-five into their state militias. However, this act worked so badly that Congress in 1863 passed another draft act that put federal officers in every state to conscript men. No right to be a conscientious objector was recognized in these draft acts. But, in 1864, Congress ruled that alternative duty, such as serving in a hospital, was acceptable in place of military service.

There was much resistance to these conscription acts throughout the entire North. The attitudes of the urban poor were most critical, because the well-to-do could buy a substitute for $300. In New York City, the Irish poor rioted for several days in July 1863. They used blacks as scapegoats for their frustrations and lynched several dozen black men. Dozens of people were killed before regular army troops brought from the Virginia front restored order.

Discontent with the war in the North caused a great upsurge of votes for Democratic candidates in the fall elections of 1862. The Republican party lost strength in every state, and the Democrats won control in Indiana and Illinois and almost won in Ohio.

Secret peace societies were especially strong in these midwestern states, and the army arrested a leading Ohio Democrat, Clement L. Vallandigham, for criticizing the war. The Republicans were able to keep

An Appeal to Patriots!

Minnesotians! Citizens of Dakota County!! Are you Cowards? Can you set a price upon your liberties! your honor? If not AROUSE! YOUR COUNTRY CALLS!! TO ARMS!!

The President, the head of the Nation, by proclamation, has called for 75,000 MEN! to defend the Constitution—to execute the laws—to protect the NATIONAL FLAG from INSULT and DISHONOR.

Minnesota is called upon by proclamation issued by the Governor of this State to furnish One Regiment to respond to the call of the President. Shall Old Dakota County be behind her sister counties in responding to this Our Country's Call? Dakota County must and shall be represented.

We are told that we cannot and must not "coerce" a Sovereign State. My God! Fellow-Citizens, are we guilty of listening to this senseless twaddle, and remain passive while the Sovereign Nation is "coerced" by these same twaddlers? No, never! in the name of the Eternal, NEVER !!

Holding as I do, the Commission of Adj't of the 13th Regiment, which comprises Dakota County, I hold it to be my right and duty to make this strong appeal to the citizen soldiery of this County to respond and furnish one noble, gallant and fearless company, who dare go where I will lead.

Volunteers will be received at this place forthwith, to proceed to the Capital of the State—thence to the Capital of the Nation; or wherever duty calls. Then, hurrah!! Who will Volunteer under

Capt. O. T. HAYES,

Hastings, Min, April 19th, 1861.

Recruiting posters appealing to sectional honor, of which this one is typical, were used in both the North and the South at the beginning of the Civil War to raise volunteer armies. (Minnesota Historical Society.)

control of Congress in 1862 only because the army suppressed the Democratic party in Maryland, Kentucky, and Missouri by arresting Democratic candidates and keeping them from campaigning.

Emancipation

The border states of Maryland, Kentucky, and Missouri were angry because Lincoln had announced in September 1862 that the slaves held by those active in rebellion against the union would be declared freemen as of January 1863. The people in the border states believed strongly, as Lincoln had in 1861, that slavery was a domestic institution (like marriage) and that it was the responsibility of the states to make the legislation appropriate to such domestic institutions. According to this view, the national government had no power over domestic institutions.

In 1861, Lincoln hoped that the slave states that had remained loyal to the union would agree to free the slaves within their boundaries. He also hoped that Congress would agree to pay the slaveholders in these states for the loss of their slave property. He hoped that this compensated emancipation would take place over several generations and that the freed slaves would be colonized either in Africa or Central America.

Lincoln had removed General John C. Frémont from military control of Missouri in 1861, when Frémont had declared the slaves of Missouri rebels to be freemen. In 1862, Lincoln had countermanded the order of General David Hunter that slaves in areas of South Carolina, Georgia, and Florida conquered by Union armies were to be considered freemen. Lincoln also refused to have blacks taken into the Union army as fighting men.

But, when he called a conference of leaders from the loyal slave states of Delaware, Maryland, West Virginia, Kentucky, and Missouri to consider the proposals for compensated, gradual emancipation, he was bitterly disappointed by their refusal to accept his ideas. By September of 1862, he felt that he was forced to accept the proposal of the abolitionists and the Radical Republicans that the slaves of the rebels be freed instantly and without compensation. The Emancipation Proclamation, which took effect in January 1863, however, did not free the slaves in the loyal slave states; nor did it free the slaves in those large areas of states, like Virginia and Louisiana, that had been occupied by Union armies. It declared that only slaves behind rebel lines were to be free. In a sense, the proclamation did not free any slave at the moment it went into effect. Slaves would become free only as Union armies penetrated the existing rebel lines.

Accepting the Radical Republican proposal for immediate, uncompensated emancipation without a plan for colonization, Lincoln also bowed to Radical pressure to use black men as soldiers. Beginning in 1863, 200,000 blacks became members of the northern army. They served in segregated units under white officers, and their pay was less than that of white soldiers.

Lincoln reluctantly bowed to the pressure of Radical Republicans to use blacks as combat troops against the Confederacy. He was reluctant because the national caste system prohibited black men from using violence against white men. And the participation of blacks in a citizen army pointed to their acceptance politically as citizens, an acceptance to which Lincoln was opposed. (Signal Corps photo.)

The Confederacy threatened to kill all black soldiers taken prisoner, and Lincoln, in return, threatened to kill a Confederate prisoner for every black killed by the Confederates. However, when several hundred black soldiers were massacred by a southern army at Fort Pillow, Tennessee, Lincoln did not order retaliation against Confederate prisoners.

Lincoln justified his Emancipation Proclamation as a necessary violation of the Constitution because of the war emergency. He asked Congress to make his action constitutional by accepting a constitutional amendment ending slavery in the rebel states and sending it to the states for ratification. The Republican party, which had promised the South in March 1861 a thirteenth amendment to the Constitution guaranteeing the security of slavery forever where it existed, then began action on another version of a thirteenth amendment, one that would abolish slavery. This amendment became a part of the Constitution in December 1865, after Lincoln's death. It abolished slavery, however, in every state in the union, not only the Confederate states. The loyal slaveholders of Maryland, Kentucky, Delaware, and Missouri who had refused compensated emancipation in 1861 then had their slave property confiscated as did the disloyal slaveholders of the cotton states.

One reason that Lincoln was pushed from the position on slavery held by the center of the Republican party toward that held by the Radical Republicans was the threat of the Radical Republicans to form a third party if Lincoln did not abolish slavery. With the Democrats gaining political strength and reaching almost equal strength with the Republicans in 1862, Lincoln could not afford to split his party. Given his total commitment to preserving the union, he was afraid that, if the Democrats won political control, they would stop the war without crushing the Confederacy.

Foreign Influences

The other major reason Lincoln changed his mind about emancipation was the pressure he felt in the area of foreign policy. He needed desperately to keep Britain and France from helping the Confederacy. Napoleon III, the emperor of France, was strongly tempted to help the Confederacy, because he had ambitions about establishing French power in Mexico. During the Civil War, a French army seized control of Mexico and made the Austrian archduke Maximilian the emperor of that country. If France was to violate the Monroe Doctrine and attempt to become a permanent power in the Western Hemisphere, it was in the French interest to have the power of the United States divided into two separate countries. But Napoleon III did not dare establish an openly pro-Confederate policy unless Britain also did so, because the British fleet commanded the Atlantic Ocean. British leaders were restrained from cooperating with France against the North because they did not want France to challenge the dominant British position in foreign trade throughout the Western Hemisphere. British leaders also recognized that it was in their economic interest to keep open the supply of northern wheat, which provided cheap bread for British industrial workers. A further economic concern was the fact that the North was Britain's best market for manufactured goods and surplus capital.

The small British aristocracy tended to sympathize with what it saw as a southern aristocracy. And British diplomats felt that British power would be enhanced by the division of American power. But a strong antislavery movement had developed in England in the early nineteenth century, which had resulted in the abolition of slavery in the British West Indies during the 1830s. The English antislavery movement continued to have very close ties with the American antislavery movement between 1830 and 1860. This movement, then, was very critical of the Confederacy and put pressure on the British government not to help the South. Some spokespeople for the British workers were also critical of a government based on slave labor.

The British government in 1861 and 1862, under the leadership of Lord Palmerston, took a cautious course in its relations with the United States and the Confederacy. It angered the United States by recognizing the belligerent status of the Confederacy, but it disappointed the South by not giving it formal recognition as an independent nation. It further disappointed the Confederacy by not denouncing the naval blockade of the southern coast proclaimed by Lincoln. The British government agreed with the Confederacy that the blockade was a violation of international law, but, since British naval strategy included such blockades by the British fleet, Palmerston was unwilling to take a strong stand against the United States.

An American warship had stopped a British ship, the *Trent*, in the fall of 1861 and had removed two Confederate diplomats traveling to Europe. This incident caused great anger on the part of the British government. The anger was eased when the United States political leaders made it clear that the American naval officer, Captain Charles Wilkes, had acted on his own and was not following orders from the government. The southern diplomats, James M. Mason and John Slidell, were allowed to proceed to Europe.

American anger at Britain developed when several ships, built in English ports, became Confederate raiders destroying northern shipping. In 1862, the *Alabama* and the *Florida* began operations, and, in 1863, two ironclad rams would be ready to go to sea. British law forbade the building of warships for belligerent nations, but the *Alabama* and *Florida* left England before they were fitted with their guns. By 1863, however, the British government declared that it would no longer accept this technicality and, emphasizing the intent of the shipbuilders to deliver the boats to the Confederacy, seized the new ships before they could be delivered.

In 1862, before the Emancipation Proclamation and the defeat of Lee's invasion of the North at the Battle of Antietam, the British government was giving serious consideration to recognizing the Confederacy. But, in 1863, after Confederate defeats at Vicksburg and Gettysburg, Britain was quite certain that the South would lose the war and stopped showing any signs of friendship toward the southern government.

Military Affairs, 1862-1863

Lincoln had become impatient with McClellan's emphasis on building a professional army before he attacked Richmond and ordered him to attack in the spring of 1862. McClellan chose to try to reach Richmond by coming up the James River from the ocean rather than by trying the direct overland route taken by McDowell in 1861. Upset by McClellan's slow maneuvering, Lincoln removed him and ordered his new general, John Pope, to make an attack along the old invasion route. Lee, who planned an invasion of Maryland, smashed Pope's army in August, and Lincoln was forced to depend once more on McClellan to stop Lee. McClellan did defeat Lee at Antietam in September. But Lincoln had lost faith in McClellan and removed him from all further command. General Ambrose Burnside then was chosen to capture Richmond, but his army was routed by Lee at Fredricksburg in December of 1862. Lincoln's desperate search for a winning general continued, and he replaced Burnside with General Joseph Hooker, who led the Union army to another bloody defeat at Chancellorsville in May 1863.

Once more Lee felt confident enough to invade the North, and he marched into Pennsylvania, where General George C. Meade defeated him at Gettysburg at the beginning of July 1863. The summer of 1863 was the turning point in the military history of the war. After Gettysburg, Lee would never again feel that he had the military strength to counterattack after he had repulsed northern invasions. For almost two more years, he could keep Union armies out of Richmond, but he did not consider another invasion of the North. More important, Union armies cracked the Confederate defenses in Tennessee and along the Mississippi River in the summer of 1863. This meant that the North would control the entire length of the Mississippi River, thus splitting the Confederacy. It also meant that General William T. Sherman could move out of Tennessee into Georgia in 1864 and begin a march that would take his army to the Georgia coast, where he turned north. By the spring of 1865, Sherman's army, coming north, had marched through South Carolina and North Carolina and had reached Virginia.

General Ulysses S. Grant commanded the Union army that captured Vicksburg, Mississippi, in July 1863. Grant then was put in charge of the Union armies under Confederate attack in eastern Tennessee. There, at Chattanooga, in November 1863, Grant with his best generals (George H. Thomas, William T. Sherman, and Philip H. Sheridan) shattered the Confederate army commanded by General Braxton Bragg.

In the spring of 1864, Lincoln rewarded Grant for these victories in the West by making him supreme commander of all the northern armies and by asking Grant to take personal responsibility for the military advance on

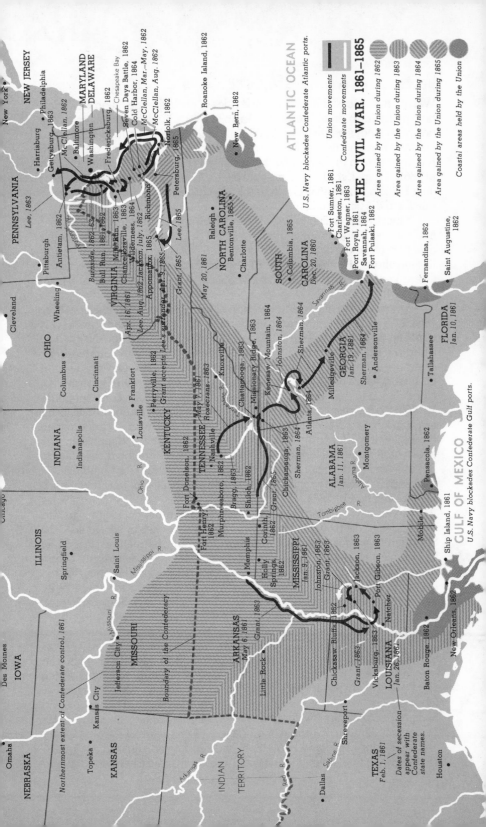

THE CIVIL WAR, 1861–1865

ATLANTIC OCEAN

GULF OF MEXICO

U.S. Navy blockades Confederate Atlantic ports.

U.S. Navy blockades Confederate Gulf ports.

Union movements

Confederate movements

Area gained by the Union during 1862

Area gained by the Union during 1863

Area gained by the Union during 1864

Area gained by the Union during 1865

Coastal areas held by the Union

Northernmost extent of Confederate control, 1861

Boundary of the Confederacy

Dates of secession appear with Confederate state names.

NEBRASKA

IOWA
Des Moines

KANSAS
Topeka

Omaha

Kansas City

ILLINOIS
Springfield

Chicago

Saint Louis

MISSOURI
Jefferson City

Missouri R.

Mississippi R.

INDIANA
Indianapolis

OHIO
Columbus
Cincinnati
Cleveland

Wheeling

Louisville

Frankfort

KENTUCKY

Ohio R.

PENNSYLVANIA
Pittsburgh
Harrisburg

NEW JERSEY
New York
Philadelphia

Lee, 1863

Antietam, 1862

MARYLAND
DELAWARE
Baltimore
McClellan, 1862
Washington
Gettysburg, 1863

Chesapeake Bay
Seven Days Battle, 1862
Cold Harbor, 1864
McClellan, Mar.–May, 1862
McClellan, Aug. 1862
Fredericksburg, 1862
Norfolk, 1862
Petersburg, 1865

VIRGINIA
Burnside, 1862–63
Bull Run, 1861, 1862
Manassas, 1863
Chancellorsville, 1863
Wilderness, 1864
Jackson, July, 1862
Appomattox, 1865
Grant, 1865
Lee, 1865
Richmond

Apr. 16, 1861
Jackson, Aug. 1862
Lee, Aug. 1862
Grant accepts Lee's surrender, Apr. 9, 1865

INDIAN TERRITORY

Arkansas R.

ARKANSAS
May 6, 1861
Little Rock
Grant, 1863

TEXAS
Feb. 1, 1861
Dallas
Houston

Red R.

Sabine R.

Shreveport

LOUISIANA
Jan. 26, 1861
Grant, 1863
Natchez
Baton Rouge, 1862
New Orleans, 1862

MISSISSIPPI
Jan. 9, 1861
Chickasaw Bluffs, 1862
Vicksburg, 1863
Port Gibson, 1863
Jackson, 1863
Johnston, 1863
Grant, 1863
Holly Springs, 1862
Memphis
Corinth, 1862

TENNESSEE
May 7, 1861
Fort Henry, 1862
Fort Donelson, 1862
Shiloh, 1862
Murphreesboro, 1862
Nashville
Perryville, 1862
Rosecrans, 1863
Bragg, 1863
Chattanooga, 1863
Knoxville
Missionary Ridge, 1863
Chickamauga, 1863
Grant, 1865

Tombigbee R.

ALABAMA
Jan. 11, 1861
Montgomery
Mobile
Ship Island, 1861

Alabama R.

GEORGIA
Jan. 19, 1861
Kenesaw Mountain, 1864
Atlanta, 1864
Johnston, 1864
Sherman, 1864
Milledgeville
Andersonville
Savannah R.

FLORIDA
Jan. 10, 1861
Tallahassee
Pensacola, 1862
Fernandina, 1862
Saint Augustine, 1862

SOUTH CAROLINA
Dec. 20, 1860
Columbia, 1865
Fort Sumter, 1861
Charleston, 1861
Fort Royal, 1861
Port Wagner, 1863
Savannah, 1864
Fort Pulaski, 1862

NORTH CAROLINA
May 20, 1861
Raleigh
Charlotte
Bentonville, 1865
New Bern, 1862
Roanoke Island, 1862
Sherman, 1864

Richmond. In May, Grant tried the direct invasion route between Washington and Richmond. In the Battles of the Wilderness and Cold Harbor, he failed to break Lee's lines in spite of the huge losses taken by the northern troops as they engaged in suicidal charges. By June, Grant had given up hope of success in this area, and he moved his troops to approach Richmond from the sea along the James River, following McClellan's plan of 1862. There Lee stopped his approach at the town of Petersburg. From July 1864 to April 1865, Grant and Lee engaged in trench warfare on the outskirts of Richmond.

Lincoln was willing to be patient with Grant as it became obvious that Lee's forces were slowly withering away. The Confederacy was no longer able to replace the dead and wounded, and it was becoming more difficult to feed those still able to fight. By putting Lee under constant pressure, Grant kept his army tied down while Sherman was able to approach from the south.

Sherman had started his invasion of Georgia from Tennessee in May 1864 at the same time Grant was attacking Lee. Sherman's army was opposed by that of General Joseph E. Johnston. Johnston planned to withdraw slowly and make Sherman's army vulnerable to counterattack when his supply lines became overextended. President Davis, however, disagreed with Johnston's strategy and replaced him with General J. B. Hood. Hood fought and lost two battles with Sherman, and on September 1, 1864, Sherman's army occupied Atlanta, Georgia. The ability of a northern army to penetrate into the very heart of the Confederacy undermined the political platform of the Democratic party that the Republican war effort had been a failure. Sherman's victories also blunted the Radical Republican criticism of Lincoln's handling of military strategy and made it impossible for them to replace Lincoln with another candidate for the presidential election of 1864.

Hood, having failed to defeat Sherman in battle, decided to go into Tennessee to destroy Sherman's supply lines. This, he hoped, would force Sherman to withdraw back into Tennessee. But Sherman responded by abandoning his supply lines and marching to the sea, where the Union navy would provide him with new supplies. Living off the country, the northern army destroyed and burned everything along the route of its march to Savannah, which he reached in December 1864. Sherman rested his army for a month in this seaport, and then he began an even more ruthless march through South Carolina, the state where secession had begun.

Every major South Carolina town close to the line of march was burned, including the state capital Columbia. By March 1865, Sherman was in North Carolina, close to Virginia. When Grant began his spring offensive against Lee at Petersburg, Lee's army no longer had the strength to resist, and it began to disintegrate. Lee then led those of his troops who had not been captured westward, but Grant pursued him, and, on April 9, Lee surrendered to Grant at the village of Appomattox.

President Davis and his cabinet had fled from Richmond on April 2. He asked General Johnston, whose army confronted Sherman's, to continue the war, but Johnston refused and surrendered to Sherman on April 26. The last Confederate forces in the Southwest surrendered on May 26. Meanwhile, Davis and his cabinet had been captured. And most of the people of the South accepted General Lee's advice that they not continue guerrilla warfare, that they give up all commitment to the Confederate States of America, and that they reclaim their citizenship within the United States of America.

Southern Loyalties

Robert E. Lee had been made commander-in-chief of all Confederate armies in February 1865. It is indicative of the problem of loyalty to the idea of a separate southern nation that Lee, the most important Confederate general, had little emotional loyalty to the Confederacy. As the descendent of a family that had been important in eighteenth-century Virginia, he had not lost the feeling of the founding fathers that slavery was an evil institution, and he had no sympathy for the idea of slavery as a positive good that became so strong in the South between 1830 and 1860. In November 1860, Lee's two loyalties were to the United States and to Virginia. He was a professional soldier who had served in the Mexican War and on the Indian frontier. Since he was not an apologist for slavery, he did not react negatively to Lincoln's election. In the spring of 1861, General Winfield Scott offered him command of the Union army. Lee refused, because he was so committed to his state of Virginia that, if it left the union, he felt that he would have to go with it. Asked by his state to defend it against the invasion of northern armies, he would do so. But, when Virginia was forced back into the union in April 1865, Lee was not reluctant to return to the United States of America.

His willingness to surrender totally any hope for a separate southern nation evidently was more representative of southern opinion than Jefferson Davis's that the ideal of the Confederacy would not die. Lee became a heroic figure for southerners in 1865 and was honored during the 1870s and 1880s. Davis, however, held no such heroic place among southerners between 1865 and 1890.

The southern states had been able to resist the northern armies so well in 1861 and 1862 because there was such great unanimity among southerners that a state had a constitutional right to secede from the union and that Lincoln had no constitutional right to attack a seceding state. In Georgia, for instance, Governor Joseph E. Brown could count on support from Douglas Democrats and Constitutional Unionists for resistance to Lincoln's war. He could call for volunteers for the state militia that could be sent to Virginia to turn back the Yankee invasion. He could count on the state legislature to support him in seizing the Union forts on the Georgia coast and to support him in constructing factories to turn out guns and uniforms for the state troops. The legislature could also try to control prices and ration goods for the people of the state. But Brown, who led Georgia out of the union, had no more loyalty to the Confederate States of America than had Lee.

When the Confederate Congess passed its first draft act in April 1862, Brown called it unconstitutional. He argued that Georgia had seceded from the union because northerners had seized control of the national government and were destroying the meaning of the Constitution of 1789 by suppressing states' rights. President Davis, too, was suppressing states' rights. Brown told Georgians to ignore or resist the draft act. Vice-President Alexander Stephens also declared that the draft act was unconstitutional and left Richmond to return to Georgia, where he joined Brown in advising resistance to President Davis's policy that took power from the states in order to build up national power in Richmond.

In 1864, when Sherman was invading Georgia, Governor Brown refused to cooperate with the generals President Davis sent into the state to defend it. Together with Stephens, he began talks with the state legislature about the possibility of seceding from the Confederacy and entering into negotiations with Lincoln about returning to the union.

Brown had been elected in 1857 and then reelected in 1859 and 1861 and was once more reelected governor in 1863. In the 1863 election, he was opposed by one candidate who said that the war was a failure and that Georgia should immediately stop fighting. He was opposed by another candidate who said that Georgia must cooperate fully with President Davis in winning the war. Brown ran on the platform of continuing the war as a state effort and received overwhelming support from the voters.

Like Lee, Brown and Stephens were admired by the people of Georgia after defeat in 1865, and both retained positions of political leadership. Stephens was elected governor in the 1870s and Brown was elected to the United States Senate in 1880.

The tension between President Davis and Governor Brown demonstrates the strange political position Davis had as the leader of a new nation in which there was no national political group dedicated to the success of the Confederacy. Since it was the state governors who led secession and then sent delegates to Montgomery, the Montgomery Convention did not have the lines of ideological connection linking local politicians in a larger unity as had the Continental Congress in 1776.

The Montgomery Convention called for a regular election of a president in November 1861. The state political leaders insisted that, for the duration of the war, there should not be partisan politics. And so Davis and Stephens were elected without opposition. But the American presidency as it had developed from Andrew Jackson in 1828 to Lincoln in 1860 made presidential leadership dependent upon the strength of the president's political party.

A president as the head of a Democrat or Whig or Republican party could hope for the support of state governors who were members of his party; a national party, starting at the caucus level, then built through county and state conventions to a national convention, where the presidential candidate who commanded the loyalty of this institutional hierarchy was chosen. Davis, therefore, was an American president who was not the head of a party. He commanded no institutional hierarchy reaching down to the local level in each state. This weakness, of course, was even more crucial when a president was trying to establish a new nation.

During the war, however, something like party divisions began to develop in the Confederacy. The states of North Carolina, South Carolina, Georgia, Alabama, and Mississippi did not experience much military pressure from the North between 1861 and 1865, and their state governments and delegates to the Confederate Congress tended to favor states' rights and obstruct the operations of the Confederate government.

The commitment to states' rights rather than southern nationalism as the more important motive for secession and resistance to Lincoln's military attacks in the South was expressed in the voting patterns within these states. The tendency was to vote the Breckinridge Democrats, who led the secessionist movement, out of office. Identifying the Breckinridge Democrats with the nationalism of the Jefferson Davis administration, voters in these southern states turned increasingly for political leadership to Douglas Democrats and Constitutional Unionists, who had opposed secession.

In the border states of the South, where military activity was constant, the Confederate army became the most important political factor. And, as Lincoln used the Union army to give political support for a national war effort, so the Confederate army gave political support for a national war effort. State governments under the army's control supported Davis's policy of national power and sent delegates who supported that policy to the Confederate Congress.

Davis's Strategy

Davis, like Lincoln, took an active interest in military affairs. His strategy was to repel northern invasions until the northern will to fight was broken. The Confederacy was able to import all the arms it needed through the Union blockade until the time when government-built arsenals, foundries, and powder mills, organized under the leadership of Josiah Gorgas, were in full production. Davis and his advisers knew of the growing Democratic strength in the North, the secret peace societies, the resistance to the draft, and the desertions from the Union armies, which came to total about 200,000 men. Unfortunately for Davis, however, the strong will to fight for the right of a state to secede held by southerners in 1861 had not been translated into a will to fight for the Confederacy in 1863.

By the summer of 1863, the northern will to fight did seem close to the breaking point. But the southern armies that were defeated at Gettysburg and Vicksburg and then at Chattanooga that summer and fall were weakened by the loss of about 100,000 deserters and by thousands of state troops the governors refused to commit to Confederate control. Governors such as Brown of Georgia and Zebulon B. Vance of North Carolina encouraged desertion. And secret peace societies were much more extensive throughout the South than they were in the North.

The hopes Davis held for help from Britain had been also dashed by 1863. He and his advisers believed that cotton was so crucial to the British economy that Britain had no choice but to recognize the independence of the Confederacy. But there was a surplus of cotton stored in Britain when the war came. And the British economy depended upon northern food to feed a huge urban population as much as British industry depended upon southern cotton. With offsetting economic pressures, British leaders finally made their decision not to recognize the Confederacy on other grounds.

The War Economy

Neither the northern nor the southern governments tried to pay for the war through taxes. In the North, a small income tax was used for the first time, and an excise tax was placed on almost everything bought and sold. But taxes provided only $667 million, compared to the $2.5 billion borrowed by the northern government. Taxes were an even smaller part of financing the cost of the war in the Confederacy, which resorted to printing $1.5 billion of paper money. This made inflation a much more serious issue in the South than in the North. The prices of many goods were 100 times higher in the Confederacy in 1865 than they had been in 1861. While the southern economy collapsed during the war, the northern economy grew and prospered.

Agricultural as well as industrial production increased in the North, but the Confederacy suffered more and more from a shortage of food. The specialized cotton plantations had depended upon the border South and the Midwest for food, and those sources were cut off during the war. The railroad system of the South also was designed to get cotton to seaports and not to distribute food and industrial goods within the South. Civilians in Richmond and Lee's soldiers were starving at the end of 1864 in a region that had the ability to grow food but did not have the ability to get the food to the cities and the armies.

The South's increasingly desperate need to mobilize all its resources can be found in the sequence of conscription acts passed by the Confederate Congress. The first, in April 1862, had drafted men between the ages of eighteen and thirty-five; the second, in September 1862, increased the age limit to forty-five; the third, in February 1864, made the ages seventeen to fifty. The later acts tried to reduce the number of exemptions established by the first act. The one that was most criticized benefited large planters by exempting one white man for every twenty slaves on a plantation. For example, a planter with a hundred slaves could keep five sons out of the army.

Wartime mobilization, of course, was forcing the South away from the kind of society that southern leaders had wanted to preserve in 1861.

Beyond the political and military centralization that leaders such as Brown and Stephens criticized as forcing the South away from states' rights, an attempt was made to increase industrialization to support the war effort. Industrialization threatened the distinction between the agricultural South and the North with its factories and commerce. Southern leaders also insisted that part of the South's uniqueness was the respect of men for southern women, ladies of fine manners who were separated spiritually from the materialistic world of men. But, with so many white men in the armed forces, women ran plantations, farms, and businesses.

The final irony in the way in which wartime pressure forced the South away from the values it wanted to defend in 1861 was the decision by the Confederate Congress in February 1865 to use slaves as soldiers. To make a black into a fighting man was a dramatic violation of the caste system imposed on the blacks by whites in both the North and the South. This caste system insisted that a black man was never to engage in physical competition with a white man. Both Lincoln and Davis had opposed making blacks into soldiers, but both eventually bowed to pressure from their generals. The Civil War was a modern war that was a preview of the total mobilization of national manpower in World Wars I and II. Telegraphs and railroads made it possible for generals to control the movement of masses of men in ways that had not been possible earlier. The generals of both the North and the South, however, continued to use tactics from earlier wars, trying to break through enemy lines with columns of troops. They did not take into account the dramatic increase in firepower made possible by new technologies in steel and gunpowder production that made artillery more effective. As a consequence, the 360,000 Union dead and the 250,000 Confederate dead were comparable to the huge numbers of casualties suffered by the European nations during World War I. Respect for artillery fire finally led Union and Confederate forces around Richmond, in 1865, to dig trench systems much like those used in Europe during World War I.

Reconstruction Plans

At the same time the Confederacy was collapsing, Lincoln was assassinated on the night of April 14 at Ford's Theater in Washington, D.C., by the actor John Wilkes Booth. Booth was from Maryland and was joined by several others who shared his view that Lincoln was a tyrant who had subverted traditional American liberties. This group also planned to assassinate Vice-President Johnson as well as several cabinet members. Booth was pursued and killed as he resisted arrest. The others were summarily hanged.

Vice-President Andrew Johnson, a Tennessee Democrat who had remained loyal to the union, then had the responsibility of trying to carry out Lincoln's plan for Reconstruction against the opposition of the Radical Republicans. The Radicals had opposed Lincoln from the beginning of the war, because they wanted abolition of slavery to be a major aim of the war and they demanded emancipation without the compensation of slave-holders. They had become angry at Lincoln's removal of General Frémont from his command in Missouri when he had declared the slaves of Missouri's rebels to be free. They had created a congressional committee, the Committee on the Conduct of the War, to put pressure on Lincoln and the generals he had chosen to lead the Union armies. Lincoln had brought Democrats and border-state men into his cabinet to unify the nation behind the war, and he appointed many Democrats to be generals for the same reason.

After Lincoln had proclaimed emancipation in 1863, the Radicals had found a new major issue that brought them into opposition to the president. In December 1863, Lincoln outlined his plan for the Reconstruction of the southern states as they returned to the union. He would pardon all Confederates who took an oath to uphold the Constitution of the United States. Whenever 10 percent of those who had voted in 1860 took this oath and abolished slavery, they could establish a state government that Lincoln would recognize as having returned to a normal relationship with the other states. These states could then send representatives to Congress.

Radical Republican leaders in Congress, such as Henry W. Davis, Benjamin F. Wade, Thaddeus Stevens, Charles Sumner, G. W. Julian, and Zachariah Chandler, violently opposed this plan. On July 2, 1864, they put their own plan into legislative form. The Wade-Davis bill demanded that a majority of white male citizens take an oath before they could create a convention to form a new state government. And the Radicals would not follow Lincoln in pardoning Confederates. In their plan, all Confederate government officials, all who had served in rebel state governments, and all who had volunteered for rebel military service would be barred from the state convention and from voting or office holding in the new state governments. Lincoln vetoed the Wade-Davis bill.

By 1864, Lincoln had recognized reconstructed state governments in Virginia, Tennessee, Arkansas, and Louisiana. But the Radicals in Congress refused to allow representatives from these states to be seated in the House or the Senate.

Believing that Lincoln would not punish the southern leaders who had begun the rebellion, many Radicals hoped to block his renomination in 1864. Some of the Radicals participated in a convention at Cleveland in April 1864, where they set up a new party and nominated General Fremont for the presidency on the platform of the Radical plan for Reconstruction. When the regular Republican convention met at Baltimore, Lincoln, a skill-ful politician, was in control and was easily renominated. Stressing national unity, Lincoln said that the Republican party should be known as the Union party and, therefore, should have a southern Democrat (Andrew Johnson) as its vice-presidential candidate.

By changing the name of the Republican party, Lincoln was making it easier for War Democrats, those who supported his war effort, to back him in 1864. But Peace Democrats, those who declared that the military attempt to crush rebellion in the South was a failure, were numerous enough to hold a vigorous convention, which nominated General McClellan as its presidential candidate. The platform of these Democrats was that the reunion of the northern and southern states should be accomplished by diplomatic negotiations rather than by armed force and that fighting should be stopped while negotiations went forward.

This platform was undercut by President Davis, who had made it clear that he would never consider a voluntary end of the Confederacy, and by Sherman's conquest of Atlanta early in September. Frémont dropped out of the election, and Lincoln won a smashing victory in the electoral college, losing only Kentucky, Delaware, and New Jersey. But McClellan's popular vote was only 400,000 less than Lincoln's, out of 4 million votes cast. The Democrats had substantial minorities in New York, Pennsylvania, Ohio, Indiana, and Illinois, while New England was most solidly behind Lincoln.

Religious and class differences also seem to have been a part of the political divisions. There was a tendency for Protestant farmers to vote Republican and Catholic farmers to vote Democratic. There was a tendency for skilled urban workers and the professional classes, both largely Protestant, to vote Republican. And the lower-income groups in the cities, heavily Catholic, tended to vote Democratic.

Lincoln's assassination then dramatically changed the political context in which Reconstruction would take place. The Radicals would have a much easier time in their attempt to dominate the policies of the Republican party when Lincoln, who had the strength of a skillful political leader and the strength of having successfully held the nation together, was no longer the head of the party.

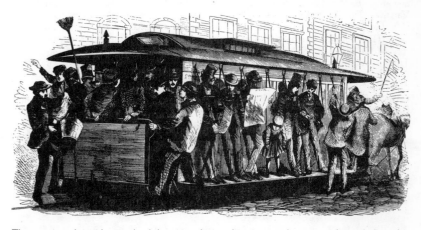

The continued rapid growth of the cities during the nineteenth century depended on the development of inexpensive forms of mass transit. This illustration reveals something of the fascination and the shock that the revolutionary beginnings of public transportation caused. (From Harper's Weekly, *November 16, 1867.)*

Johnson, as a Democrat, shared none of Lincoln's many friends and supporters within the Republican party. Nor did he have Lincoln's experience or knowledge of how to work within the framework of the Republican party. And, of course, as a southerner, he could not inherit Lincoln's prestige as the great national hero who had repressed rebellion in the South. Lincoln could be lenient toward the South in April 1865 because no one could question his motives. When Johnson tried to carry on these policies, his motives as a southerner could be questioned.

By April 1865, the issues that had caused the Civil War seemed settled. Slavery had been abolished, and the right of a state to secede from the union was no longer credible. The North could control western expansion and the growth of industrialism without effective competition from the South. The North could define the future meaning of American nationalism and exclude the South from its previous role of providing most of the nation's presidents and congressional leaders. But, in the spring of 1865, the Radical Republicans did not believe that military victory had brought these results. They believed that only the political, social, and economic Reconstruction of the South would ensure the dominance of northern values in the decades ahead.

Supplementary Reading

J. G. Randall and D. Donald, *The Civil War and Reconstruction* (1961), is the standard work on the period. Economic and social aspects of slavery are discussed in S. Bruchey, *Cotton and the Growth of the American Economy* (1965), and R. C. Wade, *Slavery in the Cities* (1964). D. T. Gilchrist and W. D. Lewis, editors, *Economic Change in the Civil War Era* (1965), give perspective on economic developments. T. J. Pressly, *Americans Interpret Their Civil War* (1954), analyzes changing interpretations of the Civil War. Views of the Confederacy are to be found in C. Eaton, *A History of the Southern Confederacy* (1954), and F. E. Vandiver, *Their Tattered Flags* (1970). Interpretive essays on the North and South are in *Why the North Won the Civil War* (1960), edited by D. Donald. A. Nevins, *Ordeal of the Union* (1947-1960), is the most detailed discussion of the political, economic, and military history of the years to 1863. T. H. Williams's *Lincoln and the Radicals* (1941) and H. L. Trefousse's *The Radical Republicans* (1969) discuss the differences between Lincoln and the Radical Republicans. Abolitionists and the role of blacks in the Civil War are discussed in J. M. McPherson, *The Struggle for Equality* (1964) and *The Negro's Civil War* (1965); D. T. Cornish, *The Sable Arm* (1956); Benjamin Quarles, *The Negro in the Civil War* (1969); and B. I. Wiley, *Southern Negroes* (1938). W. Barney, *Flawed Victory* (1975), provides an excellent recent interpretation of the Civil War.

Chapter 19

Reconstruction

Most northerners in 1865 shared Abraham Lincoln's belief that the Civil War had been a successful conservative struggle to preserve the national unity of 1860. They believed with Lincoln that some southerners had attempted to destroy the union because of their erroneous beliefs in the right of a state to secede and in the positive goodness of slavery. The war had cut these cancers out of the body politic. Thus, for Lincoln and the northern majority in 1865, there was no problem in reconstructing the union. The problem had been that of restoring national unity, and the goal had been achieved. This attitude was strengthened by Lincoln's strong feeling that only a minority of southerners had engaged in fomenting the secessionist rebellions in various southern states. His constitutional theory was that the southern states could not leave the union. And so, in 1863, he had announced that when 10 percent of the voters of 1860 in any southern state swore allegiance to the United States and accepted the Emancipation Proclamation, he would recognize that such a state was restored to a normal relationship with the national government.

The President Versus the Congress

The Radical Republicans in Congress opposed Lincoln's Reconstruction plan for governmental and ideological reasons. They argued that the

Charleston, South Carolina: the ruins of war. (Courtesy of U. S. War Dept. in the National Archives.)

Congress, not the president, had constitutional responsibility for bringing the southern states back into a normal relationship with the national government. This was especially true for the many Radical Republicans who argued that the southern states were conquered territory and that Congress had explicit power under the Constitution to govern territories before they became states.

Ideologically, the Radical Republicans differed with Lincoln on the specific issues of the plantation aristocracy and the future of the freedmen as citizens. Like Lincoln, the Radical Republicans believed that there was a strong plantation aristocracy in the South that had medieval, un-American values. Unlike Lincoln, however, the Radical Republicans believed this aristocracy had the strength in 1865 to try to force its unfree labor system on the rest of the country. To the Radical Republicans, this aristocracy had conspired to spread these foreign values throughout the country, and, when the conspiracy was checked by the Republican victory of 1860, these feudal aristocrats had attempted to destroy the nation by providing the treasonous leadership for the secession of the southern states. The Radical Republicans in 1865, unlike Lincoln, were sure that the conspiracy was still alive. Rather than allow the southern aristocracy to take the initiative, the Radical Republicans were ready to force free-enterprise capitalism, with its free labor system, on the South. Their radicalism was not socialism but a desire to force the South into accepting the patterns of northern commercial, financial, and industrial capitalism.

The Radical Republicans had expressed their fear of the southern aristocracy in their congressional plan for Reconstruction, the Wade-Davis bill of 1864, which barred Confederal political and military leaders from voting and office holding when their states returned to the union. Lincoln had vetoed the Wade-Davis bill, and, after his assassination in April 1865, the new president, Andrew Johnson, attempted to fulfill Lincoln's plan to restore the southern states to the union as quickly and easily as possible. Johnson shared Lincoln's view that the president had the constitutional authority to control Reconstruction, and he planned to have all the southern states back in a normal relationship with the nation by the time the congressional session began in December 1865. All he asked of a southern state was that the qualified voters of 1860 elect delegates to a convention that would reestablish a government that invalidated the state's ordinance of secession, ratified the Thirteenth Amendment, and repudiated Confederate war debts.

Johnson's political ideology was that of Jacksonian democracy. He believed that the yeomen of the South had been misled by the planter aristocracy, and he agreed that Confederate leaders and the wealthy planters, those with taxable property worth more than $20,000, should be formally excluded from southern politics. But he was very generous in giving pardons to those southern leaders who came to him and pledged their loyalty. As a poor white, Johnson was flattered when southern aristocrats were put in the humble position of asking him for favors.

When Congress began its session in December 1865, it was clear that Johnson had decided that the banking aristocracy of the Northeast was a greater threat to the yeoman democracy of the West and the South than was the planter aristocracy of the South.

A major reason for Johnson's shift in attitude was the issue of black citizenship. Johnson, like Lincoln, did not believe that blacks had the mental or moral capacity to be responsible citizens. But Johnson, unlike Lincoln, hated and feared black people. When the Radical Republicans agreed with him that the planter aristocracy must be destroyed, they told him that the only way to accomplish this was to liberate the planters' captive labor supply by making the blacks citizens. Before the Civil War, all of the southern states and many of the northern states had refused to define free blacks as citizens. If the free blacks were not citizens, their geographic mobility could be restricted by law. In 1865, the southern states used this legal precedent to pass Black Codes.

The restored southern state governments, which Johnson was willing to accept back into the union, defined the implications of the Thirteenth Amendment to mean that black marriages were to have legal recognition, that blacks could own some forms of property, and that they could sue and testify in the courts but that they were not to be considered equal to whites in the courts; that they could be denied the right to own some forms of property; and that they could not bear arms.

The legalization of marriage was very important to blacks, because their families had been important to them under slavery. Blacks had used their families to develop an Afro-American culture that kept its African roots through oral traditions passed from the old to the young. Families also provided an area of social independence, an alternative life to the daily work dominated by white masters. Many of the newly freed blacks traveled great distances to try to find family members who had been sold away from their plantations in the upper South to the developing cotton areas in the lower South.

But, in the South, white judges were given the right to set the wages that blacks were to be paid. Blacks could be ordered to stay on the plantations where they previously had been slaves. If they left, they would be arrested for vagrancy and forced to work for white men. Young blacks were subject to compulsory apprenticeships to white men. Blacks who had learned to be skilled mechanics in slavery were forbidden to use those skills. Economically, then, the majority of free blacks in the South were to be held on the plantations under the control of their former masters. And, since none of the southern states allowed blacks — even those who were literate and owned property — to vote or hold political office, there was no way in which they — although free from slavery — could alter the laws that restricted their economic and social freedom.

In 1865, there were only a few Radical Republicans, such as Senator Charles Sumner and Congressman Thaddeus Stevens, who believed that blacks were equal in moral and mental capacity to whites and, therefore,

President Andrew Johnson (above) wanted to destroy the planter aristocracy in the South, but he did not want blacks to become citizens of the United States. Radical Republicans, however, like Thaddeus Stevens (below) insisted that only national citizenship for blacks established through the passage of the Fourteenth Amendment could give the freedmen the right of geographic mobility necessary to break the power of the planters over their former slaves.

deserved to be fully integrated into the political life of the nation. A larger number of Radical Republicans reluctantly had committed themselves to the idea of black citizenship, because they felt it was necessary to destroy the plantation aristocracy. Only when the blacks were defined as citizens could they escape the Black Codes and have geographic mobility.

This majority of Radical Republicans, who did not believe in the equality of blacks, were joined in this belief by most of the moderate and conservative Republicans. Immediately after the Civil War, the northern states of Connecticut, New Jersey, Pennsylvania, Ohio, Wisconsin, Michigan, Minnesota, and Nebraska refused to give blacks the right to vote. Northern Democrats were even more hostile toward blacks than were the Republicans. In December 1865, therefore, it did not seem possible for the Radical Republicans to achieve their goal of making blacks citizens of the United States.

But the actions of southern political leaders and the attitude of President Johnson during 1866 forced the moderate and conservative Republicans to accept the Radical idea of black citizenship. The behavior of southern Democrats also weakened the popularity of northern Democrats and made it possible for the Republicans to win smashing victories in the congressional elections of 1866. Republican control of Congress became so complete that, for the first time in American history, Congress overcame a presidential veto of important legislation when President Johnson vetoed the Civil Rights Act and the Freedmen's Bureau Act.

When Congress met in December 1865, most of the moderate Republicans believed that Congress, rather than the president, had the responsibility for Reconstruction. They joined the Radical Republicans, therefore, in refusing to seat the representatives from the southern states. Together, the Radical and moderate Republicans created the Joint Committee on Reconstruction to investigate the political situation in the southern states. Only after such an investigation would the moderate Republicans consider the readmission of the southern states.

This congressional committee discovered that the southern states were refusing to exclude Confederates from political leadership. Seventy-four former Confederate leaders, generals, cabinet members, and the former vice-president, Alexander H. Stephens, had been elected to sit in the national Congress. South Carolina and Mississippi had refused to repudiate their Confederate debts. And, of course, every southern state had passed the Black Codes to preserve the plantation system.

Furthermore, southern Democrats were stating that they would try to control national policy when, in alliance with northern Democrats, the Democrats might become the majority party in the country. Southern Democrats were open in their criticism of the national banking system and the tariff passed by the Republicans during the Civil War. Some talked of repudiating the national war debt. Others talked of having the national government pay the Confederate debt.

All of this talk by southern Democrats frightened the business community in the North. Most business people, backing moderate Republicans, had been opposed to the idea of black citizenship. But, faced with the aggressiveness of Confederate leadership and the threat of a reversal of Republican economic policies by a strong Democratic party, much of the business community shifted to the Radical idea of citizenship for blacks.

Under the leadership of Republican moderates such as Senator Lyman Trumbull of Illinois, Senator John Sherman of Ohio, and Senator William P. Fessenden of Maine, Congress voted to expand the Freedmen's Bureau and passed a Civil Rights Act that denied the right of a state to restrict the rights of blacks in the courts and the right of a state to deny the right of a black to hold property.

In 1865, Congress had created a Bureau of Freedmen and Refugees to provide food and shelter for southern blacks and whites who had been uprooted by the war. In 1866, faced with the extreme prejudice of the southern state courts against blacks, Congress voted to establish federal military courts within the framework of the Freedmen's Bureau until the southern states were properly reconstructed. The purpose of these courts was to protect the lives and liberty of southern blacks.

President Johnson vetoed this Freedmen's Bureau Act and the Civil Rights Act. Johnson also advised the southern states to refuse to ratify the Fourteenth Amendment, which the Republican-dominated Congress had sent to the states. This amendment fulfilled the Radical Republican desire to create national citizenship by stating that "all persons born or naturalized in the United States, . . . are citizens of the United States and of the State wherein they reside." To stop the prejudice of southern courts, it further stated that "no State shall make or enforce any law which shall abridge the privileges or immunities of citizens . . . nor shall any state deprive any person of life, liberty, or property, without due process of law."

The amendment also barred Confederate leaders from holding political office. They could not be pardoned by the president but only by a congressional vote. Other clauses relieved the fears of the Republican business community by guaranteeing the national debt and outlawing the Confederate debt.

Johnson tried to rally northern public opinion against the two acts he had vetoed and against ratification of the Fourteenth Amendment. Many northerners interpreted his speeches as a defense of the South against the North. Republicans argued that support for Johnson was the same as support of the Confederacy, and some northern Democrats even voted for Republican congressmen in the fall elections of 1866. When Congress reconvened in December 1866, the Republicans had gained more than a two-thirds majority in both the House and the Senate, and they were able to pass the expanded Freedmen's Bureau Act and the Civil Rights Act over Johnson's veto.

The First Reconstruction Act

On March 2, 1867, the Republican majority passed its first Reconstruction Act. This act destroyed the state governments of all the former Confederate states except Tennessee and divided the ten states into five military districts, each under the control of an army general. It was the responsibility of the generals to see that white and black voters were registered, that Confederate leaders were disfranchised, and that constitutional conventions were called to write new state constitutions. The generals were to see that the conventions ratified the Fourteenth Amendment as a necessary prerequisite for their readmission as states to the union. The first of the states, Arkansas, returned to the union in June 1868, and the last, Georgia, in July 1870. Tennessee was not reconstructed because, under the leadership of native Republicans, it had quickly ratified the Fourteenth Amendment.

Because President Johnson had lost all control of the Republican party, national political leadership in 1867 and 1868 came from Congress. For the moment, therefore, the nation had something like parliamentary government. Congress moved to break down the traditional constitutional division of power among the executive, judicial, and legislative branches by asserting its dominance over both the president and the Supreme Court.

Congress reduced the size of the Supreme Court and intimidated the remaining justices who then refused to question the constitutionality of congressional Reconstruction legislation. Congress also declared that it, not the president, should control the army and passed a Tenure of Office act that denied the right of the president to dismiss any official who was appointed with the consent of the Senate. When President Johnson defied this act by dismissing Secretary of War Edwin M. Stanton, the House of Representatives immediately voted to impeach him. The Senate, which sat in judgment of the impeachment, came within one vote of finding Johnson guilty and dismissing him from the presidency.

A Positive or Negative Revolution?

While the Republican-dominated Congress of 1867 acted in a revolutionary manner in establishing military government in the southern states, in overriding the power of the president and the Supreme Court, and in creating national citizenship that included blacks, the extent of this revolution was severely limited by the continued commitment of most Republicans to the national tradition that declared that a virtuous revolution must be a negative one.

Americans in 1776 had defined their revolution as a defense of the status quo. The reform movements of Jefferson and Jackson had been seen as defenses of the status quo. Lincoln said the Civil War was another defense of the status quo. From 1776 until 1865, revolution and reform were considered good if they had a negative rather than a positive identity. This was because in the eighteenth century most Americans assumed that they had achieved liberty for the individual and that this liberty must be preserved. The great threat to that liberty was political power that conspired to impose institutional control over the free individual.

In 1867, most Republicans who backed Radical Reconstruction viewed their activities in these negative terms. The conspiracy of the southern aristocracy that had threatened to spread the institution of slavery throughout the country in 1860 was seen as still in existence in 1866. In order to guarantee the preservation of the liberty of white men from this conspiracy, it was necessary to give blacks the political liberties held by white men. When the black man, as citizen, had the right to leave the plantation, then the freedom of all white men to participate freely in the economic marketplace would be guaranteed.

Only a few Radical Republicans, like Sumner and Stevens and a group of black leaders, hoped to define Radical Reconstruction in positive terms. These men wanted the positive use of governmental power to change the whole structure of American society. They recognized that the proclamation of black citizenship would not end the patterns of economic and social segregation that existed in 1866.

Of the 4,441,000 blacks listed in the 1860 census, 4,097,000 were in the South, and 3,838,000 of these southern blacks were slaves. Even if these people were to be defined as citizens in 1867 by the passage of the Fourteenth Amendment, they were coming to citizenship without property and without literacy. They had been denied the experience of political participation. They had been denied the experience of economic responsibility in the competitive marketplace. They had been denied the experience of legal responsibility for their families. They had been denied the experience of much of their own social leadership. And they were becoming freemen in a society dominated by whites who traditionally had denied that free blacks were equal human beings and who had segregated free blacks in a caste system designed to keep white people from being made dirty by association with blacks.

Black men like the runaway slave Frederick Douglass (who had become an abolitionist leader) and James McCune Smith, William C. Neel, J. W. C. Pennington, and Martin R. Delany (all of whom had been educated in Europe and northern universities) believed that the national government must take a positive role in providing land and education for the freedmen. They believed that the national government must protect blacks from the hostility of southern whites for at least a generation until the blacks had gained enough economic strength and political skill to overcome the traditional social prejudice of the caste system.

Such a positive revolution would have required a dramatic change in the relationship of the American government to private property. The national government would have had to engage in economic planning on a large scale. Land would have had to have been taken from wealthy whites in the South and redistributed to the poor blacks. This kind of governmental control and planning, however, was a direct contradiction to the logic of the Republican attack upon the southern aristocracy. Slavery before 1860 and the Black Codes after 1865 kept the blacks from being free participants in the economic marketplace, and the Republicans, including most of the Radicals, argued that political citizenship would free the blacks to participate as fully and freely in the marketplace as did white laborers. This strong Republican commitment to the ideal of the free marketplace precluded, therefore, a contradictory commitment to government economic planning.

During the war, northern generals had turned over confiscated plantation land to blacks in the Sea Islands of South Carolina and along the river in Mississippi. The blacks who cultivated this land were very successful economically and had established stable social relationships. The Freedmen's Bureau Act also had empowered government officials to allot forty acres of abandoned land to black families. After three years of farming, the families would be given the opportunity to purchase the land.

Over the objections of a few white Radical Republicans, like Thaddeus Stevens, and the black leaders, most of the Radical Republicans joined with the moderate Republicans in destroying the Sea Island experiments and returned the land to white ownership. This Republican majority also chose not to carry out the allotment of forty acres to black families.

The Republican majority also refused to make permanent the national experiment in public education that was begun by the Freedmen's Bureau. The bureau established more than 4,000 schools, which enrolled 250,000 students, before its funds were cut off in 1870. As the slaves became free, they showed a tremendous desire for education. Many of the teachers were northern women, like Mary Peake and Charlotte Forten, who had been participants in the abolitionist movement.

Northern black leaders, who saw the continuation of economic and social discrimination against blacks in the North, called for a permanent national school system. Even though the conventions that were writing new constitutions for the southern states were establishing public school systems there for the first time, the black leaders recognized that control of these public schools by local whites would mean inferior education for blacks. Only the national government could guarantee equal expenditures and equal quality. But the decision of the Republican majority was to allow the control of public education to remain in the hands of the state governments and local authorities.

In spite of the sharp limitations on the revolutionary aspects of congressional Reconstruction, it was clear that the mood of northern voters had shifted dramatically between the congressional election of 1866 and the presidential election of 1868. There seems to have been a consensus in 1866 on the need to destroy the southern aristocracy. But, by 1868, northern whites were beginning to fear that blacks had gained too much, and

(Opposite page) The Radical Republicans created a political revolution in the South and in the nation in 1867 by bringing southern blacks into the political process. At first leaders of northern public opinion, like Harper's Weekly, *approved the revolution. Within several years, however, they became critical of Radical Reconstruction in the South. (From* Harper's Weekly, *November 16, 1867.)*

HARPER'S WEEKLY.

A JOURNAL OF CIVILIZATION.

Vol. XI.—No. 568.]   NEW YORK, SATURDAY, NOVEMBER 16, 1867.   [SINGLE COPIES TEN CENTS.
[$4.00 PER YEAR IN ADVANCE.

Entered according to Act of Congress, in the Year 1867, by Harper & Brothers, in the Clerk's Office of the District Court for the Southern District of New York.

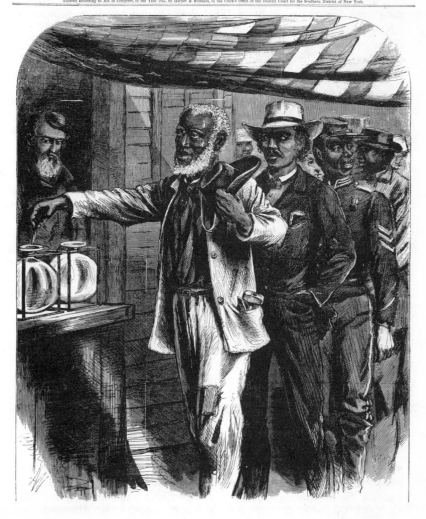

sympathy for southern whites was growing. The only Confederate officer who was executed for war crimes was Major Henry Wirz, who had commanded the prisoner of war camp at Andersonville, Georgia, where thousands of northerners had died of disease and malnutrition. Jefferson Davis was the only Confederate political leader who was kept in prison, and he was released in 1867. By 1868, northern public opinion was ready to pardon all former Confederate leaders and restore them to political participation. The feeling of northern whites that they were part of the same superior white racial caste as southern whites became stronger than their hostility toward Confederate leaders.

Therefore, although the Republicans nominated General Grant as their presidential candidate in 1868, they were not able to repeat their smashing victory of 1866. Grant defeated the Democratic candidate Horatio Seymour, a former governor of New York. But his popular vote was only 3 million, with 2.7 million for Seymour. More than 500,000 southern blacks voted for Grant. And so Republicans were faced with the fact that the majority of whites had voted for the Democratic party.

Their reaction was to try to make the black vote permanent in the southern states through a Fifteenth Amendment to the Constitution that stated that a person could not be kept from voting because of "race, color, or previous condition of servitude." Many black leaders feared that this amendment did not go far enough in protecting the right of blacks to vote, because it was still legally possible for the states to deny individuals the right to vote for failing to meet other qualifications, such as literacy and ownership of property. These fears were borne out in the years between 1890 and 1910, when the southern states established literacy and property qualifications for voting. It was obvious that, since the mass of blacks came out of slavery without property and without education, these qualifications would disfranchise many more blacks than whites. But blacks supported the amendment as better than nothing. It was the New England states and the southern states under Republican control that provided the greatest strength for the ratification of this amendment in 1870.

The Republican Party in the South

Republican parties dominated all of the southern states in 1869, with the exception of Virginia. The most solid bloc of Republican voters in each state was the blacks. They were joined by white northerners, who have come to be known as carpetbaggers, and white southerners, who are known as scalawags.

Until the 1960s, most history books described the carpetbaggers and scalawags as cynical and selfish men who wanted to exercise political power to gain personal fortunes by robbing the state treasuries under their control. Since the 1960s, however, historians have made a distinction between those cynical northerners like Henry Clay Warmoth, who became governor of Louisiana, and the idealistic northerners like Adelbert

Ames, who became governor of Mississippi. Many white northerners came south hoping to make themselves a permanent and responsible part of the local community.

Similarly, many white southerners joined the Republican parties in their states in 1868, because they believed that Republican leadership could improve their states. While there were some cynical scalawags like Governor Franklin J. Moses of South Carolina, there were many more responsible men like Governor James L. Alcorn of Mississippi.

Alcorn represents the many former southern Whigs who shared the same economic philosophy as the northern Whigs. Since the northern Whigs had become Republicans and had made the economic philosophy of that party reflect their traditional commitment to mercantilistic capitalism, the southern Whigs saw no good reason why they should not become Republicans. The issue of slavery in the territories that had divided northern and southern Whigs was gone. And, as northern and southern Democrats had reunited in 1868 after their split on the same issue in 1860, northern and southern Whigs could reunite in the Republican party in 1868.

A number of poor whites who, like many wealthy Whigs, had opposed secession in 1860 turned to the Republican party because they identified the Democratic party with secession. Other poor whites, like S. G. W. Dill in South Carolina, became political leaders in the Republican party because it promised to carry through such major reforms as the establishment of public education. Also, under Republican leadership, the overrepresentation of plantation counties was ended by giving more political representation to poor white counties.

Strong and lasting areas of white support for the Republican party did not develop in the southern states, however, except in the mountainous areas of western North Carolina and eastern Tennessee. The major reasons for the failure of the Republicans to become a permanent and strong second party in the South were the issues of carpetbag influence and black leadership.

In the generation before the Civil War, white southerners had struggled to retain their identity as first-class citizens within the United States of America. They had seen the issue of slavery in the territories as a threat to that status. And the major reason for secession in 1861 was that white southerners saw Lincoln's election as a destruction of their equal citizenship with white northerners. The North had elected Lincoln, who did not represent a national party that included both northerners and southerners. With the abolition of slavery in 1865, most white southerners felt they could return to the union as citizens of equal worth with northerners. The peculiar institution of slavery, which had set them apart from the rest of the country, was gone, and in 1865, there no longer seemed to be any way in which northerners could define southerners as inferior citizens.

But congressional Reconstruction once more had placed white southerners outside the national consensus. Once more white southerners were being defined as inferior or second-class citizens. The Fourteenth

Amendment had excluded Confederate leaders from political participation. This meant that most of the established white political leaders of the
South were taken out of political life, at least temporarily. This vacuum in
leadership was to be filled by northern white carpetbaggers and by southern blacks. Most white southerners believed these actions were creating
an unprecedented and unjustified situation for them; it was a situation that
put the southern states in a peculiar and, in their view, an inferior relationship to the northern states. No class of northern whites was barred from
political leadership. And no significant group of outsiders was coming into
northern states to exercise political leadership.

It was the Republican party that in 1860 had stood for the exclusion of
slavery from the territories. It was the Republican party that had declared
that white southerners were responsible for a morally evil institution of
slavery. Then it was the Republican party that declared that a group of
white southerners were morally evil because of their participation in the
Confederacy. If southerners were to regain full and equal citizenship
within the nation, they would have to escape this abnormal situation in
which a northern political party, the Republicans, was using the institutional power of the national government to dictate the patterns of white
political leadership in the southern states.

Even more important in the eyes of white southerners was the way in
which the Republican party had used congressional Reconstruction to
create the abnormal situation in the southern states in which there was the
possibility of black political leadership. White southerners knew that
blacks had been defined as unclean inferiors by the caste system operating
in the North before the Civil War. They knew that the passage of the Fourteenth Amendment had not ended that caste system in the North. Not
only had many northern states voted to exclude blacks from political life in
1866 and 1867 but the Republican party had assured northern whites in
1868 that black participation in political life in the South would not have a
parallel in the North. Many Republicans in 1868 had appealed to white
racism in the North by arguing that making blacks political participants in
the South would ensure that blacks would be happy in the South and,
therefore, would not move into the North.

Certainly, southern whites in 1868 were aware that the revolutionary
implications of the Fourteenth Amendment, which made blacks citizens,
were interpreted by white northerners as making blacks, at best, second-
class citizens. The distinction between first- and second-class citizenship
was that leadership was a monopoly of white men, the first-class citizens,
and that black men, as second-class citizens, must be content to be followers. No black was elected to the House of Representatives in the North
until Oscar DePriest won election from the black ghetto in Chicago in
1928. No black was elected to the United States Senate in the North until
Edward Brooke won election in Massachusetts in 1966.

But the Republican parties in the southern states, created by the
northern Republican party through its control of Congress and the army in
1868, did provide vehicles for the emergence of vigorous black leadership

in the South during Reconstruction. The concept of second-class citizenship did not radically challenge the national caste system, which denied blacks the right to compete as equals with white men. And white southerners did not react hysterically to the passage of the Fourteenth and Fifteenth Amendments because they could tolerate the concept of second-class citizenship. Black leadership, however, as first-class citizenship was a dramatic denial of the caste system. White southerners would refuse to allow northern Republicans to threaten the caste system in the southern states while it was still operational in the northern states. Indeed, most northern Republicans were so committed to the caste system that they never encouraged a full attack upon it in the southern states. The white carpetbaggers and scalawags kept most of the political power in their own hands.

Black Leadership in the South

No black became governor of a southern state. And blacks never controlled the judicial or legislative bodies of a southern state, even though the population of South Carolina was more than 60 percent black and the populations of Mississippi and Louisiana were more than 50 percent black. Only in South Carolina did the lower house have a black majority, but the Senate had a white majority. Two blacks, Hiram R. Revels and Blanche K. Bruce, both from Mississippi, served in the United States Senate. During the entire period of Reconstruction, twenty blacks were elected from the southern states to serve in the House of Representatives. The largest number, however, serving in any single congressional session was seven. Many blacks were elected to local offices in the southern states. This was especially true in South Carolina, where blacks frequently served in the lower courts.

In addition to skilled political leaders like the two senators from Mississippi and congressmen Richard H. Cain of South Carolina, James T. Rapier of Alabama, and John R. Lynch of Mississippi, skillful black social leaders also emerged. In South Carolina, these included Francis L. Cardozo, Prince Rivers, and Professor Richard T. Greener. Greener helped establish the public school system in that state. Paul Trevigne provided vigorous leadership as editor of the *New Orleans Tribune*.

Black political and social leadership was recruited in part from the North and from Canada, where there was a colony of runaway slaves. Many leaders came from among the free blacks who were numerous in the upper South and New Orleans in 1860. But a significant number of leaders came from among the ex-slaves, as in the case of Senator Bruce and Congressman Lynch from Mississippi.

There was a tendency for social divisions to develop among these black leaders. One of these divisions was between the former slaves and those blacks who had been free before 1860. Another social division tended to form between those leaders of lighter and darker color. In addition to the small number of blacks who became lawyers, doctors, school teachers, ministers, and business people, there was a somewhat larger group of skilled urban workers who had received under slavery their training as carpenters and bricklayers and in other crafts. But the great majority of blacks continued to work on the land. A major division developed on the issue of priorities between black leaders who tended to emphasize political and civil rights and the black masses who tended to emphasize economic issues. The black masses had never forgotten the possibility of family ownership of forty acres that had been included in the Freedmen's Bureau Act. And they were dismayed by the pattern of sharecropping in which most of them had become trapped.

Freedom from the forced gang-work patterns of slavery on the plantation had not meant the ownership of their own family farms. And the shortage of cash to meet payrolls had meant that the black families worked as tenant farmers on the white planters' land. Local storekeepers, who borrowed money from the North to purchase the supplies necessary to start the new pattern of farming, became an important part of southern agriculture. The white landowners and the black tenant farmers all went into debt to the storekeepers to get their supplies for the coming year. And the next year's crop was pledged to pay off the debts. The sharecropper usually kept a third of the crop, the landowner received a third, and the storekeeper claimed the other third.

This system caused most of southern agriculture to become even more tightly tied to cash crops. These cash crops lost value on the world market as the price of cotton dropped from 16.5 cents a pound in 1869 to 9.7 cents in 1876 and tobacco dropped from 11.6 cents a pound in 1866 to 7.3 cents in 1876. These economic conditions made it almost impossible for black sharecroppers to get out of debt for the food, clothing, fertilizer, and agricultural equipment they used each year. Few blacks were in a position to accumulate capital to buy their own land.

White Leadership and the Democratic Party

The white carpetbaggers and scalawags who controlled the Republican parties in the southern states were separated socially and economically from the mass of blacks whose votes kept them in power. Because of the caste system, the white carpetbaggers and scalawags felt social solidarity with their political enemies, the disfranchised Confederate leaders, rather than with their black political allies. The white carpetbaggers and scalawags also wanted to be part of the economic establishment of the southern states in which they held political power. Again, it was their political enemies, the Confederate leaders, rather than their political allies, the blacks, who controlled the economic establishment.

As the pressure grew within the white populations of the southern states to restore the states to a normal position within the nation by ending what the southern whites saw as their peculiar and discriminated-against situation of not being able to choose freely white leaders and of having to accept black leaders, the scalawags were asked to abandon the Republican party. Since the Republican party was seen as the agency in every southern state that forced an inferior, regional status on southern whites, the Democratic party increasingly was seen as the agency that could restore equal national status to southern whites by replacing carpetbag leaders with local leaders and by ending black aspirations for first-class citizenship.

A case study of these pressures can be seen in Mississippi, where Governor Alcorn was persuaded to abandon the Republicans and join the Democrats. Tension existed between the scalawags like Alcorn and the carpetbaggers like Adelbert Ames who became governor when the scalawags shifted to the Democratic party. Much of this tension was the result of the increasingly important role blacks were playing within the Mississippi Republican party. As the blacks developed more and more skill in political and social leadership between 1867 and 1872, they believed that, because they constituted more than 50 percent of the state's population, they should not be relegated to positions of secondary leadership.

When Alcorn and other former Whigs joined the Democratic party, the white minority made a successful effort to drive the carpetbaggers out of political power and to force the blacks into a passive acceptance of second-class citizenship. In Mississippi and South Carolina, the black majorities had been armed as units in the state militia, and white Democrats used organized violence in Mississippi in 1875 and in South Carolina in 1876 to destroy the black political majority.

The leaders of the triumph of the Democratic parties in these states, L. Q. C. Lamar in Mississippi and Wade Hampton in South Carolina, interpreted their victories as the restoration of their states to equal status with northern states. They were not struggling to preserve a unique regional way of life against the attempt of the North to push them into national patterns. Rather, they were struggling to have their states escape from the unique regional identity forced upon them by the Republican party in 1868. No longer would Mississippi and South Carolina be different from northern states because they had carpetbag leaders. No longer would they be different from northern states because they had black leaders.

Because most white southerners were struggling to preserve their status as first-class citizens within the United States from 1840 to 1860, few major leaders developed who spoke for the whole southern region. Each southern state had leaders trying to keep that state within the union as long as northerners did not deny the right of slavery to expand in the territories. After the war, the struggle of white southerners to restore their status as first-class citizens within the United States also worked through leaders in each particular state. The effort was to bring Virginia or Mississippi or any other former Confederate state back into the union without the stigma placed on whites by the Radical Republicans. No powerful political leaders who spoke for the entire southern region, therefore, developed between 1867 and 1877.

This second struggle, like the first, emphasized states' rights. The struggle was for the restoration of Virginia or North Carolina or Georgia to a status equal to that of Massachusetts or Pennsylvania or Ohio. The white populations of Virginia and Tennessee were free of the regional discrimination of carpetbag and black leadership by 1869. Those in North Carolina and Georgia were free by 1871. The Democratic political leaders of these states did not try to organize a regional southern political bloc to help the whites in Mississippi or South Carolina or Louisiana. It was a local problem for the white population in each southern state to regain the privilege held by the white population in each northern state not to experience external political control or black leadership.

Lamar in Mississippi in 1875 and Hampton in South Carolina in 1876, therefore, did not intend to defy the Fourteenth and Fifteenth Amendments. They only wanted those amendments to mean the same thing in their states as they meant in northern states — that blacks were passive, second-class citizens. To define second-class citizenship in a southern state with a large black population was, of course, different and more difficult than in a northern state with a small black population. In a state like South Carolina, the black majority had to be made into a political minority by a variety of means. But Hampton allowed a reduced number of blacks to vote and hold office. He even allowed a minority of the state militia to remain black. It was not until the 1890s that the attempt would be made in Mississippi, South Carolina, and the rest of the South to destroy second-class citizenship for blacks.

It was ironic that the effort of the former southern Whigs to restore their states to a normal political relationship with the nation should have forced them into the Democratic party. The emancipation of the slaves had ended the plantation as the major form of capitalistic expansion in the South. Most southern leaders recognized in 1865 that the future of capitalism in their region would have to resemble northern forms of industrial, commercial, and financial capitalism. In Virginia in 1865, for example, the ex-Confederate leaders immediately began an economic program for their state very similar to that which Alexander Hamilton had proposed in 1789 to stimulate industrial growth for the nation. A study of the careers of several hundred Confederate political and military leaders has revealed that the majority became executives in transportation, commercial, financial, and insurance companies that depended upon money invested from the North.

The overwhelming majority of southern political leaders between 1865 and 1877, whether they had been Whigs or Democrats, hoped to share in the national economic expansion that they identified with the Republican party. They realized that economic growth depended upon the rebuilding and expansion of their railroad system. And it was the national Republican party, rather than the national Democratic party, that was committed to providing government subsidies for building railroads.

During the years between 1900 and 1950, when historians were bitterly critical of the Republican administrations imposed on the southern states by congressional Reconstruction, they stressed the financial irresponsibility of these administrations by pointing to the rapid growth of state debts. Since 1950, however, historians have demonstrated that most of this increase in state indebtedness was caused by the state governments' financial aid to railroads. And, when Democrats replaced Republicans in office in states such as Georgia and Alabama, they were equally eager to subsidize railroad building.

The other major reason for the rise of state indebtedness during Reconstruction was the socially constructive role taken by the southern state governments under the new constitutions written by Republican carpetbaggers, scalawags, and blacks. In addition to repairing the damage caused by the war, the state governments established public school systems for the first time, as well as other social services such as hospitals and orphanages.

Southern leaders, whether Republican or Democratic, also were eager to industrialize their region as quickly as possible by attracting northern and European capital through promises of exemption from taxes and an adequate supply of cheap, docile labor. There was an 80 percent increase in the number of manufacturing establishments in the South during Reconstruction. Most of these were in tobacco factories and cotton mills and in the development of iron manufacturing in Birmingham, Alabama. The rate of industrial expansion in the South, however, was far below that of the North, which had achieved the base for its industrial boom in the generation before the Civil War.

By 1876, northern Republicans recognized their mistake in believing that the plantation aristocracy was anticapitalistic and that the Republican party had to be imposed in the South, with leaders from the North who would mobilize southern blacks as a voting base. They recognized that the strong Whig political groups in the southern states shared the same economic philosophy as the Republican party. A powerful Republican party in the southern states in the long run would have to depend on these white leaders of the economic and social establishment, rather than on the economically and socially weak black population.

The problem for northern Republicans in 1876 was to persuade the former Whigs to leave the Democratic party and join the Republican party with which they had obvious economic alliances. Northern Republicans in 1876 were ready to abandon their former strategy of protecting the blacks in the South. This they had done in 1870-1871 by passing congressional legislation to give federal protection to black voters who were being intimidated by secret societies in the South, such as the Ku Klux Klan. The last such attempt by northern Republicans came in 1875, when they passed a Civil Rights Act that outlawed discrimination in transportation, theaters, restaurants, and hotels. In 1883, the Supreme Court ruled this act unconstitutional, because it said that the Fourteenth Amendment did not protect citizens from discrimination by private individuals.

Because of the many scandals of the Grant administration and the collapse of the national economy in 1873, the Democrats were able to win control of the House of Representatives in 1874, and it was clear that the Republicans would have great difficulty in retaining the presidency in 1876. The Republicans nominated Governor Rutherford B. Hayes of Ohio to get a candidate who was not associated with the problems of the party in Congress or with the Grant administration.

The Democrats nominated Governor Samuel J. Tilden of New York. Their campaign stressed the corruption of the Republican party. Tilden had helped to destroy the corrupt Tweed Ring in New York City. Tilden won all the southern states except South Carolina, Louisiana, and Florida, which still had Republican state governments. He also won a number of northern states and had more popular votes than Hayes. The decision in the electoral college depended upon the votes of the three Republican-controlled southern states. Congress had to create an electoral commission to decide whether Hayes or Tilden had carried these states. The commission had eight Republicans and seven Democrats and voted eight to seven that Hayes should receive the electoral votes of these states and become the president. The Democrats, who controlled the House of Representatives, had the power to refuse to accept this decision and to leave the country without a president.

A compromise was worked out during February 1877. Congress accepted the commission's decision on March 2, and Hayes became president. The compromise was made possible by the willingness of a number of southern Democrats to accept a Republican as president. The nature of the compromise was revealed when Hayes recalled the last federal troops stationed in the South from South Carolina and Louisiana. Northern Republicans would no longer try to impose political patterns on the South. Hayes then named a Democratic political leader from Tennessee, David M. Key (a former Confederate general) to his cabinet as postmaster general. His hope was that Key could persuade a number of important southern Democrats to switch their allegiance to the Republican party.

Hayes could hope for this, knowing that a number of southern Democrats in Congress had voted for his election because they knew that a Democratic president would never subsidize the building of a railroad from Texas to California, while a Republican might. He recognized how many former Whigs had become leaders of the Democratic parties in the southern states. But, in 1877, it was too late for the northern Republicans to win the former southern Whigs into open participation in the national Republican party.

Industrial development in the South between 1865 and 1877 had not been rapid enough to offer alternate employment opportunities to those in agriculture. The rapid increase in both the white and the black populations made jobs difficult to find in the rural South, where the decrease in the price of tobacco and cotton was causing greater and greater poverty. The overwhelming majority of southern white farmers had come to blame their economic plight on the national Republican party.

Officially Democrats, the former southern Whigs did not openly ally with the national Republican party. If they had declared themselves

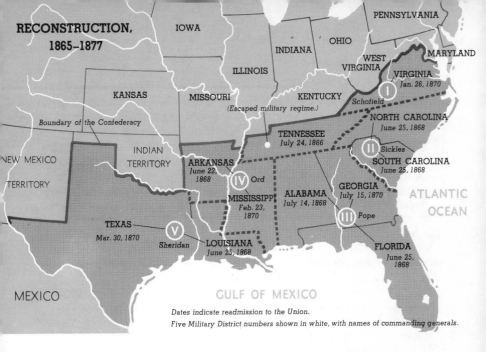

RECONSTRUCTION, 1865–1877

Boundary of the Confederacy

VIRGINIA
Jan. 26, 1870

Schofield
(Escaped military regime.)

NORTH CAROLINA
June 25, 1868

TENNESSEE
July 24, 1866

Sickles

SOUTH CAROLINA
June 25, 1868

ARKANSAS
June 22, 1868

Ord

MISSISSIPPI
Feb. 23, 1870

ALABAMA
July 14, 1868

GEORGIA
July 15, 1870

Pope

TEXAS
Mar. 30, 1870

Sheridan

LOUISIANA
June 25, 1868

FLORIDA
June 25, 1868

ATLANTIC OCEAN

GULF OF MEXICO

MEXICO

Dates indicate readmission to the Union.
Five Military District numbers shown in white, with names of commanding generals.

Republicans in 1877, they would have given up their positions of political power in their states' majority parties. They would have had to gamble that they could persuade a majority of their states' white population to join the Republican party. Given the economic hostility of southern white farmers toward the Republican party in 1877, there was no rational reason to believe such a gamble could have succeeded. The sensible compromise seemed to have beeen one of continuing to exercise power within the state Democratic party but of urging the state's Democratic congressmen in Washington to cooperate with northern Republicans.

The majority of the white leaders in the southern states in 1877, then, were committed to building a New South characterized by industrial expansion and urban growth. They wanted to integrate the South into national economic patterns. They also were willing to accept the new national social and political patterns established by the Fourteenth and Fifteenth Amendments, which had made blacks citizens but which defined that citizenship within the framework of the nation's caste system. White racism insisted that blacks must be passive followers rather than active leaders.

Reconstructed Racial Patterns

Nevertheless, for southern blacks in 1877, citizenship within the caste system was greatly more liberating than slavery within the caste system had been in 1860. Their role as passive followers was dramatically different from what it had been under slavery.

Under slavery, whites had worked to create the psychological and social conditions that would condition the black personality to be dependent rather than independent. To program the adult black male to have a childish personality and look to his white master as an authoritarian father figure, white southerners had tried to keep the black male's area of responsibility to a minimum. The male slave, of course, had no political responsibility; nor did he have the responsibility of being a participant in the court system of the community. The male slave was denied the right to own property and had no economic responsibility. Slaves were denied the right to legal marriage and had no social responsibility. Laws in the southern states ordered masters not to educate their slaves or to allow them to hold all-black religious services. Leadership qualities and a sense of responsibility might have developed if slaves had been educated or had become religious leaders.

Under the Fourteenth and Fifteenth Amendments, the freedman did gain political responsibility, even if it was that of being a political follower. The courts were opened to the freedman as a citizen. The freedman had the right to own property, and even the sharecropper worked under his own initiative rather than under the whip of the slaveowner. The freedman had the right of legal marriage and the responsibility for his own family. Education became legally possible for the freedman, and he had the right to hold his own all-black religious services.

The Fourteenth and Fifteenth Amendments pushed through by the Radical Republicans did, therefore, permanently reconstruct racial patterns in the South and in the entire nation. The amendments changed the North as well as the South by making male blacks citizens and voters for the first time in a large number of northern states. Patterns of public and private education for blacks established in the South have persisted down to the present. And, in the long run, the education of blacks undermined the white racist myth that blacks were inherently childish and incapable of educational achievement.

By current standards, the segregated public schools for blacks established by the Republican state governments in the South were of poor quality. But they were revolutionary in contrast to legal denial of education under slavery. Most of these public schools offered only the fundamentals of education for a few grades. Northern white church groups, however, came into the South during Reconstruction to subsidize the establishment of private high schools and colleges that could help blacks reach higher levels of education and develop leadership skills. Northern Congregationalists, working through the American Missionary Association, established seven colleges between 1866 and 1869. And other groups had established thirty-two more by the end of the 1870s. Black churches also established several colleges, and the state governments of Mississippi and South Carolina began public colleges for blacks.

The greatest opportunity, however, for blacks to escape the psychological conditioning of slavery and develop independent personalities and leadership skills came from the establishment of 10,000 black churches.

Black ministers and black congregations together could develop both a sense of independence and the skill of running a social institution.

Blacks who had been forced to be members of the white Methodist, Baptist, and Presbyterian churches of the South under slavery deserted those churches as they became free. Two hundred and fifty thousand southern blacks affiliated with the northern Methodist church, which sent aggressive white missionaries into the South to preach a gospel of racial equality. But more southern blacks were not content to form all-black congregations within a white-dominated church, and 400,000 joined the African Methodist Episcopal church, while 200,000 more established the African Methodist Episcopal Zion church. The largest number of blacks, however, formed all-black Baptist congregations that had no relationship to southern white Baptist congregations. The citizenship of the Fourteenth Amendment gave blacks the opportunity to segregate themselves voluntarily in their own churches, where they could develop a sense of black dignity and black pride.

The dream of a larger revolution during Reconstruction, held by Thaddeus Stevens and a few other white Radical Republicans and by many black leaders, in which the national government would work to undermine the national caste system by providing freedmen with property, a good public education system, and the right of first-class citizenship, had been defeated by 1877. Historians, tending to focus on this defeat, have neglected to describe how the Radical Republicans and the black population were able to achieve a constructive, positive revolution between 1867 and 1877 in the creation of conditions in which blacks could begin to challenge the caste system and white racism.

Supplementary Reading

The hostile interpretation of Reconstruction held by historians from 1900 to the 1960s was best expressed by W. A. Dunning in his *Reconstruction, Political and Economic* (1907). The first major challenge to this view came from the black historian W. E. B. DuBois in his *Black Reconstruction* (1935). It was not until the 1960s, however, that white historians such as K. Stampp in his *The Era of Reconstruction* (1965) came to support the perspective of DuBois. W. L. Rose, *Rehearsal for Reconstruction* (1964), and J. Williamson, *After Slavery: The Negro in South Carolina during Reconstruction* (1965), describe the constructive roles of southern blacks at the end of the Civil War. *Reunion and Reaction* (1951) by C. Vann Woodward was a pioneering effort to demonstrate the commitment of southern leaders during Reconstruction to northern forms of capitalism, and Woodward pointed to the economic issues in the Compromise of 1877.

The racism of Andrew Johnson's administration is the subject of E. L. McKitrick, *Andrew Johnson and Reconstruction* (1960), and L. and J. H. Cox, *Politics, Principle, and Prejudice: 1865-1866* (1963), as well as F. G. Wood, *Black Scare: The Racist Response to Emancipation and Reconstruction* (1968). W. R. Brock, *An American Crisis: Congress and Reconstruction* (1963), F. Brodie, *Thaddeus Stevens* (1959), and D. Donald, *Charles Sumner and the Rights of Man* (1970), provide perspective on the Radical Republicans. W. S. McFeeley, *General O. O. Howard and the Freedmen* (1968), points to the constructive role of the Freedmen's Bureau.

R. Johannsen's *Reconstruction* (1970) is a good analysis of the period.

Chapter 20

Triumph and Crisis for the New Middle Class

1876-1892

Between 1876 and 1892, corporations became the keys to American economic growth. Most had their headquarters in the Northeast, although some were located in the Midwest. The large corporations, however, operated throughout a national marketplace, and their power and influence created regional resentments in the South and the West, as well as class resentments among lower-income groups.

The extreme speed with which industrial production surpassed agricultural production during these years caused great cultural confusion throughout the country. Not only were farmers and industrial workers bewildered by the revolutionary economic changes that centralized so much wealth and power, the leaders of the revolution were themselves bewildered. Men like John D. Rockefeller and Andrew Carnegie saw themselves as upholding the American tradition of the self-made man, but the huge corporate empires that they built in oil and steel were run by managers who had to think of themselves in relationship to the thousands of people who were parts of the company teams.

Industrial Organization and the New Middle Class

This confusion between the traditional values of individualism and the new values of organizational teamwork also influenced the new middle

313

class of doctors, lawyers, and college professors, who thought of themselves as more national and professional in their outlook than the previous generation of doctors, lawyers, and professors. The members of the old middle class had gained their skills by apprenticeships to individuals, and the communities that they had served were localized. But the new professional middle class was learning its skills in impersonal professional schools, whose standards and interests were national, not local. Throughout the years between the 1870s and the 1920s, there was considerable conflict between the rising new middle class in the major cities and large universities and the declining old middle class in the small towns and small colleges. But the conflict was not clear cut, since individuals in one group often held some values typical of individuals in the other group.

The aggressive business people who had directed the industrialization of America and who had gained control of Congress after the secession of the southern states, had used the Republican party to further their economic interests through the legislation of tariffs, national banks, and the Homestead Act. Government buying to supply the massive mobilization of men and materials during the Civil War resulted in the increase of the number of factories in the North from 140,000 to 250,000.

The industrial capitalists had steadily been gaining strength in their competition with the old commercial capitalists who had dominated the northern economy before 1860. These individuals from the new middle class had destroyed the power of the old planter capitalists of the South during the Civil War and the Reconstruction. Northern industrialists had been more willing to fight the Civil War than had the northern commercial capitalists; they had been the leaders of the Radical Reconstruction, while the commercial capitalists had been the leaders of the moderate Republicans in 1865.

The newer business leaders in 1860 were working to replace local and regional economies with a single, standardized national economy. Their goal was to be accomplished by the creation of a national railroad network and a national banking system. It was to be facilitated by technological advances and by the development of more efficient forms of large-scale human organization.

During the Civil War, the huge officer corps of the northern army, most of whom had been civilians in 1860 (like Ulysses S. Grant, who rose to the position of commander-in-chief), developed skills and outlooks that were helpful to the growth of large-scale industrial capitalism. They had mobilized a million and a half men and had moved the men and the vast supplies they needed by an expanding rail system that followed the northern armies as they penetrated into the South. They were eager for new technology in weapons as well as in transportation and were quick to accept breech-loading rifles, Gatling guns, and rifled cannons, as well as ironclad ships and submarines. They tied this vast organization together with the construction of telegraph lines, sending six million telegrams during the war.

The Peacetime Railroad Empire

There were 35,000 miles of railroad tracks in 1865, an amount doubled by 1875. This rapid expansion had reached 166,700 miles by 1890. Army officers returned to civilian life and often became the officers of railroad companies. As the Union army had been massively larger in manpower and budget than the civilian government, so the new railroad companies were massively larger than the United States government. In 1890, the income of the railroad companies was more than a billion dollars, while the income of the national government was only $403 million. Railroad debt in 1890 was $5 billion, the national debt was only $1 billion. With hundreds of thousands of employees, many more than the number who worked for the national and state governments, the railroad companies organized themselves like armies. Under the company director as commander-in-chief and his advisers, there were separate divisions with their own commanders. Within these divisions, there was a hierarchy of officers stretching down to the unskilled workers at the bottom. The telegraph and, eventually, the telephone allowed orders to flow down through the chain of command with speed and efficiency. The railroad leaders moved to standardize time in four time zones that stretched from the Atlantic to the Pacific. This standardization of time, as well as the standardization of the width of railroad tracks, was accomplished during the 1880s.

The Railroads and the American Indians

Industrial capitalists had seen the Civil War as an opportunity to destroy the planter aristocracy. They believed that slavery made the operation of a national marketplace impossible. During Reconstruction, they continued to use the army to force the southern regionalists into standardized national economic, social, and political patterns. (Some white southerners, however, wanted to create a New South that accepted northern patterns.) This willingness to use the army to expand the national marketplace also had characterized the government's policy toward the Indians of the Great Plains and Rocky Mountains. In 1860, most of the territory from the Mississippi to the Pacific was under the control of Indian tribes. By 1890, however, all of these tribes had been militarily defeated; many of their lands had been taken over by the national government; and the surviving Indians had been restricted to reservations, where they subsisted on government doles.

Union troops had marched east out of California and into Arizona and New Mexico in order to keep the territories out of the control of the Confederacy. They easily defeated the Navaho and Pueblo tribes, who were farmers. The more nomadic Apache, however, continued to resist under powerful chiefs such as Geronimo until 1886. The pressure of white settlers also brought war in 1862 in Minnesota, where the Sioux fought to save their land. The Santee Sioux were defeated, and thirty-eight of their

leaders were hanged by the government in the largest mass execution in the history of the United States. Other Sioux tribes under Red Cloud, however, defeated the government's forces when they tried to move west into Dakota Territory in 1868. In 1876, Sioux and Cheyenne warriors destroyed the regiment led by George Custer, who was attempting to reach the sacred Black Hills of the western Dakotas.

By 1877, however, the army's policy, developed by such generals as Philip Sheridan, of deliberately destroying the vast buffalo herds was making the Indians' resistance impossible. The military tactics of the tribes were those used in modern-day guerrilla warfare. They ambushed invading groups of soldiers and then moved their camps to avoid confrontation with the larger units of white soldiers sent to crush them. Such movements depended on the Indians' ability to live off the land, to be able to hunt the buffalo for the food, clothing, and shelter these animals provided.

The army's plan to destroy the buffalo was facilitated by the construction of the Union Pacific Railroad, which avoided the Apache in the south and the Sioux in the north by pushing west through Nebraska. Large numbers of Irish laborers were imported during the 1860s to build this railroad under the protection of the army. Meanwhile, Chinese were imported to construct the Central Pacific from California into Utah, where it was to meet the Union Pacific. Many of the tribes from the central plains were sent, after their military defeat, into exile in the Oklahoma Indian Territory, which had been given to the Civilized Tribes (the Cherokees, Creeks, Choctaws, Chickasaws, and Seminoles) when they had been displaced from Florida, Georgia, Alabama, and Mississippi during the 1830s. Hunters, brought into the center of the plains by the railroad, soon reduced the buffalo herd from 9 million to a few hundred, and the buffalo hides were carried back to profitable eastern markets. In 1877, the army pursued the Sioux chiefs Crazy Horse and Sitting Bull and forced them to surrender their bands or find temporary refuge in Canada. And the army continued its domination into the northern Rockies, where Chief Joseph and his Nez Perce band were hunted until exhaustion forced them accept imprisonment on a reservation.

Government leaders, however, intended that the Indians eventually would leave the reservations and give up their heritage of communal ownership of land and their philosophy of nature that rejected continual economic growth. To this end, boarding schools were established so that children could be sent away from the reservations and separated from the values of their parents. More important was the passage by Congress of the Dawes Severalty Act (1887), which was intended to encourage the Indians to accept the Anglo-American tradition of private property. Much of the communal property of the reservations was to be broken into 160-acre farms to go to the heads of each family.

Farms of 160 acres on the dry plains and the southwestern deserts could not support families. Furthermore, many Indians did not understand the concept of private property and their land was easily taken from them by whites. Although some Indians refused to accept their allotments and

INDIAN TRIBES, 1865-1890

kept the communal lands of the reservations intact, 86 million acres of reservation land had passed into white hands by 1935, when Congress reversed itself and decided to encourage the preservation of tribal lands. The most sustained tragedy for the American Indians came in Oklahoma when government leaders in Washington decided to break the treaties promising to preserve an Indian territory forever. During the 1890s, the governmental and educational systems established by the Five Civilized Tribes were destroyed, and much of their land, as well as that of the other tribes resettled there during the 1870s and 1880s, was thrown open to waves of white settlers.

Historians usually date the massacre of a Sioux band by the United States Cavalry at Wounded Knee, South Dakota, in 1890 as the end of the Indians' military resistance to the whites. But Wounded Knee was not a battle; it was a massacre of an Indian religious group. By 1880, when it had become apparent that the Indians could not stem the whites' invasion, many tribes began to develop religious visions to sustain their hope for freedom from the whites some time in the future. The most important religious prophet was Wovoka, a Paiute from Nevada. Wovoka believed that he was a red Christ, and he taught that God had turned His face away from white people because they had rejected Christ's message of love and peace. God was to destroy the whites by burying them under a layer of soil that would cover the earth. Wovoka taught the tribes a ghost dance that was to elevate them as the earth was covered. Then, the Indians could return to a new earth covered with grass and buffalo, where they could live in peace and prosperity.

Members of tribes from all over the country made pilgrimages to Wovoka. Some of them were members of the Sioux from South Dakota tribes who brought the dance back to their people. White officials could not believe that this was a new religion of gentleness, and they moved to arrest the tribal leaders. When Sitting Bull was killed as he was arrested, one of the Sioux bands, fearful that they too would be killed, fled the reservation. Tracked down by the cavalry, they surrendered. But, for reasons that remain obscure, the cavalry fired into the band, killing many men, women, and children. Even after the massacre, American Indians continued to use religion, traditional as well as that from new visions, to preserve a separate cultural identity. But the new visions, such as those that created the Native American Church, no longer promised the destruction of all white people. Instead, they offered the hope that Indian values could survive in a world dominated by whites.

The Railroads and the Cattle Frontier

As industrial production increased, workers were concentrated in urban factories and became dependent on food transported by the railroads. A huge herd of longhorn cattle, brought from Spain to Mexico, had developed on the plains of Texas. When the Missouri Pacific Railroad was built from St. Louis to the Kansas-Missouri border, a long drive of cattle to Sedalia, Missouri, took place; from there, the cattle were shipped to eastern city markets. As the railroad moved farther west, the cattle were driven north along the Chisholm Trail to Abilene, Wichita, and Dodge City, Kansas. White Anglo-Saxon Protestants controlled the ranches in Texas and hired cowboys to work the long drives. The majority of these cowboys were of black or Mexican ancestry.

By 1880, with the military defeat of the Sioux and the destruction of the buffalo, it was possible to develop herds of millions of cattle on the plains of Colorado, Wyoming, Montana, and the Dakotas. This northern herd ended the need for the long drive. So too did the development of the Southern Pacific Railroad, which shipped cattle directly out of Texas. By 1885, overproduction of cattle caused a drop in price from $30 to $10 a steer, and many small ranchers went out of business when their herds were almost destroyed in blizzards during the winter of 1886-1887. Large corporations then consolidated cattle ranching. Financed in part by invest-

THE AMERICAN FRONTIER, 1860–1890

ments from Britain, the ranges were fenced in with newly invented barbed wire, and the longhorns were replaced by English beef cattle, the short-horned Herefords.

The Railroads and the Meatpacking Industry

Until the Civil War, meatpacking was a local industry. Then, packers (such as Philip Armour) in Milwaukee and Chicago obtained large government contracts to supply salted and pickled beef to the Union army. After the Civil War, these large packers managed to keep control of a national market by buying the beef from the long drives. Gustavus Swift soon challenged Armour by using refrigerated railroad cars. The meatpackers organized their national companies along the patterns developed by the railroad corporations, breaking them into divisions that specialized in marketing, slaughtering, and packing. One reason that the giant meatpackers of Chicago gained more profit than their small competitors was because they were in a better position to use the slaughterhouse waste products for fertilizer, glue, and soap. The ability to buy and sell on a large scale made it possible for the big packers, as well as other major corporations, to cut costs and still make profits while charging less than many of their smaller competitors could.

The Railroads and the Mining Frontier

The discovery of gold had attracted many Americans to California during the 1840s and 1850s, and farmers had established themselves in the rich valleys of Oregon and Washington. Further discoveries of gold and silver in the Rockies brought whites eastward from their settlements along the Pacific coast. The Indians native to California had been almost completely annihilated during the 1850s, and their numbers had been severely reduced in Oregon and Washington. Custer and his command were heading for the Black Hills in 1876, because gold had been discovered there. During the 1860s and 1870s, there was the same kind of anarchy and violence in the mining towns of Nevada, Montana, Colorado, and South Dakota that there was in the cattle towns of Kansas. But, by the 1880s, the large corporations were taking over from the individual prospectors, bringing the order of large-scale industrial production to the mines. Miners, like most of the cowboys, then worked for weekly wages. The prospector Henry Comstock sold his claim at Virginia City, Nevada, for $10,000 to a mining corporation, which took $306 million of gold and silver from the Comstock lode.

The gold rush around Deadwood, South Dakota (which produced such personalities as Calamity Jane, Wild Bill Hickok, and Deadwood Dick, who were romanticized in popular dime novels and later in the movies), found all the mines eventually owned by a single company, Homestake Mining. As in other sectors of the economy, the mining industry depended upon the railroads, which were used to ship ore to the East. The increase in mineral wealth helped the North pay for the Civil War and was used to increase the money supply for the expanding economy during the 1870s and 1880s.

The Railroads and the Agricultural Frontier

In 1890, approximately 100,000 white settlers lined up on the border of the Oklahoma Indian Territory. They waited astride horses and in wagons for the signal that would allow them to rush into the territory and claim a homestead on the last good agricultural land left to be settled in the West. In the single generation that it took to dispossess the American Indians, their lands had been settled and the agricultural frontier had ended. In Minnesota, for example, as the Sioux were driven west into the Dakota Territory between 1860 and 1870, the white population increased from 172,000 to 780,000 and the number of farms from 18,000 to 92,000. By 1890, the number of farms in the nation had almost tripled, from 2 to 6 million, and

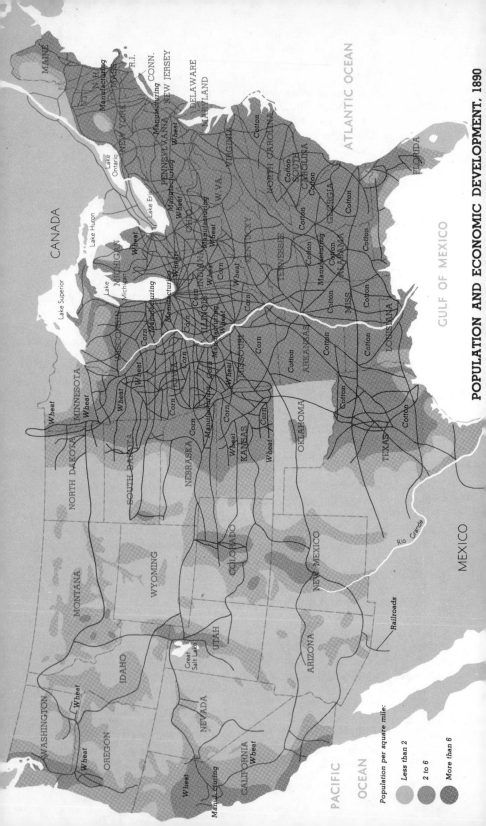

POPULATION AND ECONOMIC DEVELOPMENT, 1890

Population per square mile:

Less than 2

2 to 6

More than 6

Railroads

the number of cultivated acres had risen from 163 to 415 million. By the end of the nineteenth century, 60 percent of the wheat, 50 percent of the cattle, 60 percent of the sheep, and 25 percent of the hogs produced in the United States were produced on land west of the Mississippi.

The Homestead Act of 1862 provided land for some of the settlers. But the railroads provided even more and were primarily responsible for the speed of settlement. The government had given the railroads 155 million acres of western land to encourage them to build the transcontinental lines. So, on both sides of their right-of-way, the Northern Pacific; the Union Pacific; the Central Pacific; the Atchison, Topeka, and Santa Fe; and the Southern Pacific controlled vast tracts of land. The government even forbade homesteading near the railroad property to give further support to railroads' land sales. The railroads sent agents into the older midwestern states of Illinois, Indiana, and Ohio, to the east coast, and to Europe to attract people to their land. Farmers from the eastern areas, under stress because they had large families with more children than their farms could support and because they were faced with soil exhaustion from poor farming practices, moved into the central plains. The railroad agents also attracted hundreds of thousands of settlers from Scandinavia, Germany, and the British Isles to Wisconsin, northern Iowa, Minnesota, and the Dakotas.

The Railroads, the Farmers, and the American Dream

The dominant American value system, which had developed with the emergence of Jacksonian democracy in the 1830s and the simultaneous conversion of many people to the evangelical Protestantism of the Baptists and Methodists, visualized a permanent society of small, independent, capitalistic producers basically equal to one another in the competition of the economic marketplace. The majority of these producers were expected to be farmers, and, in 1870, 70 percent of Americans worked in agriculture. These small agricultural capitalists were joined by small business people and small industrialists who also could be considered producers because no sharp line divided the owners of small shops from the people who worked for them.

Then, just as the expansion of the agricultural frontier seemed to strengthen the economic base for this dream of a nation of small and independent producers, farmers became aware of their dependence on the railroads. To sell their products in the national marketplace, farmers had to ship them by rail. They had no choice but to pay what the single railroads that passed through their towns charged them. Farmers learned that to send butter from western New York to New York City might cost 50 percent more than to send it from Wisconsin or that similar shipments of wheat might be more costly to send from Ohio than from Illinois. Beyond the unfair rate differences, the railroads raised and lowered their freight charges at will and often in a matter of weeks, so farmers could not anticipate shipping costs.

The Regulation of the Railroads and the Political Parties

In 1865, the Democratic party adopted a laissez faire position that suggested that government should allow the economic marketplace to regulate itself. The Republicans shared this belief in self-regulation, but they also wanted the government to encourage the growth of the marketplace through tariffs and subsidies. During the 1870s, therefore, just as many farmers began to feel that the ideal marketplace of competition between equal producers was threatened by the monopolistic power of railroads, they found that neither of the two major parties was in favor of government action to ensure economic justice. Some farmers then believed that the railroad corporations had to be regulated by the state and national governments in order to preserve fair competition. But neither the Democrats nor the Republicans held a philosophy of government regulation, even for this negative purpose of saving the free marketplace.

The first major movement for government regulation of the railroads came, therefore, from a social rather than a political organization. Oliver H. Kelley had founded the National Grange of the Patrons of Husbandry in 1867 in order to provide farmers with an organization that could help them overcome the sense of loneliness and isolation that came from living on the new and widely spaced farms. As they gathered together, farmers found that they had common worries. They also found that, with group organization, they were able to put pressure on both political parties in the midwestern states and force them to consider the regulation of the railroads.

The 800,000 Grangers won their first victory when the legislature of Illinois established maximum rates and denied discrimination through a state regulatory commission. The United States Supreme Court upheld the constitutionality of this Granger legislation in *Munn* v. *Illinois* (1877). But, in 1886, the Supreme Court ruled in the *Wabash* case that these state regulatory commissions could not control railroad discrimination, which applied to interstate commerce. The pressure from the nation's farmers then became one factor in causing the United States Congress to establish the Interstate Commerce Commission (1887). It was intended that the commission should prevent rate discrimination and stabilize rates by demanding that railroads publish their rates and give public notice when rate changes were planned.

By the end of the 1880s, many railroad executives were ready to accept such regulation, because they hoped it would end the cutthroat competition among the major railroad companies. Like the leaders of other large corporations, railroad executives were becoming afraid of the price competition that threatened the stability of corporations, which had fixed expenses for payrolls, machinery, and buildings. The financial condition of many railroad companies was so bad that they went bankrupt during the 1893 depression. Large bankers then consolidated several railroad lines to reduce the amount of competition.

The Sherman Anti-Trust Act

Farmers wanted state and national commissions to regulate the large railroad corporations in order to preserve a marketplace of small and equal producers. This also was the motivation for farmers in the South and West who wanted their states to pass antitrust legislation. The national marketplace established by the railroads created the conditions that had made it possible for other massive national corporations to develop. John D. Rockefeller in oil and Andrew Carnegie in steel, like Armour and Swift in meatpacking, built huge companies by destroying or absorbing small businesses.

In 1865, when Rockefeller entered the oil industry, there were many small producers and refineries. Rockefeller opposed the confusion and chaos of the competition among these small firms, and he attempted to impose order by gaining a monopoly in the refining and distribution of oil. In return for his business, he persuaded railroads to ship his oil at a lower rate than they did his competitors' and to give him a rebate on each barrel of oil shipped by other companies. Grocery stores that sold only Rockefeller's kerosene were supplied by his corporation with other products, such as sugar, below their usual costs. Groceries that sold rival kerosene brands and bought their supplies at usual prices were driven out of business or agreed to sell only Rockefeller's brand. By 1879, Rockefeller controlled 90 percent of the oil business in the nation. The companies that were absorbed by Rockefeller became part of the Standard Oil Trust. The stocks of the different companies were put in the hands of trustees, and the stockholders were paid dividends on the trust certificates they received in return for their stocks. Chaos in the production and the price levels of oil was ended by Rockefeller's monopoly, which gave him a fortune of $800 million by 1892.

Andrew Carnegie was building a similar empire in steel. Like Rockefeller, he was not a specialist in his product but had the skills to eliminate his competitors and to hire loyal specialists who pushed through new technical processes as rapidly as possible. Carnegie and other steel producers had their profits protected by tariffs that made imports of cheaper English steel unprofitable.

State antitrust legislation, like the state railroad regulatory commissions, could not deal with corporations that did business on a national level. Pressure from farmers and small business people encouraged Congress to pass the Sherman Anti-Trust Act (1890). This legislation declared business combinations that restrained trade to be illegal. The United States Supreme Court, however, which had made it difficult for the Interstate Commerce Commission to regulate the railroads, then severely limited the effectiveness of the Sherman Anti-Trust Act. The ICC did not have the power to fix rates but had to take the railroads to court to prove that they were charging rates that were unreasonably high. In almost every case brought before them, judges refused to find that the railroads' prices were unreasonable. The Court decided in *United States v. E. C. Knight Company* (1895) that the sugar trust that controlled 98 percent of sugar refining was not restraining trade. The Court's position was that, even if the sugar trust controlled 100 percent of the refining in the country, the control of refining was not the same as the control of trade.

Farmers, Prices, and Economic Protest

The use of energy from coal to produce steam to run machines in factories, as well as to run railroad engines, was paralleled by the channeling of human energy to invent or improve machines to speed the process of manufacturing. The 2 million horsepower of energy used by industry in 1870 had jumped to 10 million by 1890, and the number of inventions patented jumped from 12,000 in 1870 to 25,000 in 1890. Much of the new machinery was developed for agriculture. Improved plows and cultivators and steam-driven threshers and reapers made it possible for one farmer in 1890 to do work that had required several in 1870. This mechanization of American agriculture, however, was accompanied by the increase of commercial agriculture in many parts of the world. Farm production, therefore, increased more rapidly than expanding American and European populations.

As American cotton production went from 5 to 8 million bales and wheat production from 173 to 449 million bushels, prices dropped from fifteen cents to six cents a pound for cotton and from a dollar to sixty cents a bushel for wheat on the world market. Farmers found themselves in a position of having to double their production to pay for mortgages that they had taken out ten years earlier. It was in their interest to try to get a national policy of currency inflation. The amount of money in circulation was related to the amount of gold and silver held in the United States Treasury. This amount had not increased as rapidly as the expanding economy had, and the shortage of money kept interest rates high. Farmers urged the government to buy more silver to overcome the shortage of gold. Many business and banking groups, on the other hand, wanted to restrict the use of silver and depend only on gold. They had momentarily achieved this end with the Coinage Act of 1873, but pressure from farmers and silver miners had brought back the purchase of silver with the Bland-Allison Act of 1878 and the Sherman Silver Purchase Act of 1890. This legislation, however, did not increase the amount of silver held by the treasury enough to halt the deflationary trend of the 1870s and 1880s.

Farmers and Political Protest

Farmers' Alliances had spread from Texas into the cotton South and among the wheat growers of the Great Plains. Thousands of speakers and

In the 1880s the major labor organization, the Knights of Labor, protested the growing economic and social divisions brought by industrialism. By 1900, however, the Knights had been replaced by the American Federation of Labor (AFL) as the major labor organization, and the AFL refused to engage in social criticism. But from 1910 until it was destroyed by World War I, a small, vital, radical labor group, the Industrial Workers of the World (IWW), tried to revive the criticism of the hierarchical nature of American society. This poster expresses their social criticism. (Courtesy of Wilson Library, University of Minnesota.)

hundreds of newspapers had educated people in these regions to the need for a decentralized, democratic society controlled by the people at the local level. A key issue in avoiding an undemocratic, centralized society was breaking the control of the money supply held by a few large bankers in the East. The leaders of the Farmers' Alliances, therefore, stressed the need for financial cooperatives to keep credit in the hands of the people. Between 1888 and 1892, however, these rebels decided that they needed help from the national government to break the centralized power of the New York bankers. They came together at a national convention in Omaha, Nebraska, in July 1892 to establish the People's party, better known as the Populists. A major concern of the Populist party's platform was the feared destruction of a society of small and equal producers.

Some of the Populists hoped to restore the old-type marketplace of small farmers and business people, but other Populists felt that the only way to end the power of large corporations was to develop a socialist society. Both the right and the left wings of the Populist movement agreed in the 1892 platform on a graduated income tax that would check the development of an upper class. They also agreed that there should be national ownership of the railroads and the telegraph and telephone companies. They argued that these natural monopolies must be controlled by the people, not by the privileged few. As a first step to destroying the eastern bankers' control of the national money supply, government warehouses in which farmers could store their crops were to be constructed. Holding crops off the market at harvest time would allow farmers to sell them later at higher rates. This Sub-Treasury Plan, according to the Populists, would help farmers escape the high interest rates on the credit that they received from storekeepers and bankers. And the national government, by providing low-interest loans, would also be increasing the amount of money in circulation, thus encouraging inflation. To further encourage inflation and raise farm prices, the platform also called for the unlimited coinage of silver.

Believing that political power had fallen into the hands of a new plutocracy, located in the Northeast, which controlled the major political parties, the Populists recommended that the people be able to express their will directly through the initiative and the referendum. As another step in their program for a decentralized, democratic society, the Populists wanted a constitutional amendment that would have United States senators elected by popular vote, rather than by the state legislatures as provided by the Constitution of 1789. The Populists believed that the new millionaires were bribing the state legislatures to get them to send them to Washington and that the Senate was becoming a rich man's club.

Farmers and the Crisis of Industrialism

The Populists hoped that urban labor would join with the farmers in 1892. To attract the workers, the Populist platform supported the eight-hour workday, called for an end to the use of private police (such as the Pinkerton detectives) in labor conflicts, and advocated the restriction of the immigration that kept wages down. The fact, however, that most Populist farmers were white Anglo-Saxon Protestants (WASPs) while Catholic immigrants from southern and eastern Europe were becoming the largest part of the industrial work force made such an alliance difficult. And the Populist desire for higher food prices obviously was contrary to the interests of urban workers, who needed inexpensive food. However, a more important factor that kept farmers and industrial workers apart was the issue of small-scale capitalism. Most farmers continued to own their own means of production in 1890, but most industrial workers by that time had become wage earners with little, if any, control of what went on in the factories owned by wealthy industrialists.

In 1865, most industrial wage earners had worked in small shops. They had thought of the owners and themselves as producers in an essentially classless society. The few larger factories in New England in the generation before the Civil War employed women and Irish immigrants. It was not until the end of the 1860s, then, that the male, white Anglo-Saxon Protestants, who were the majority of the work force at that time, began to experience the worst of the impersonality that came with the specialization of work in the large railroad companies and the other large corporations producing meat, oil, and steel for the national marketplace.

National craft unions had grown rapidly during the Civil War and, with a combined membership of 300,000, formed the National Labor Union (1866) under the leadership of William Sylvis of the Iron Molder's Union. Already aware that the Jacksonian ideal of a marketplace of small and equal producers could not be preserved in a large-scale urban-industrial context, Sylvis and other labor leaders advocated that the workers preserve their ideal of a classless productive society by forming producers' and consumers' cooperatives. The workers would own the factories collectively and operate them under their own leadership.

Efforts to establish such cooperatives were defeated by people, like Rockefeller and Carnegie, who were willing to use any economic means to defeat their competitors and were able to persuade or bribe political leaders to give them competitive advantages. This warlike environment worsened during a sharp economic depression in 1873. Many workers lost their jobs, union memberships declined, and efforts to establish cooperatives collapsed.

By 1877, many workers, especially those in the railroads, had become desperate as they saw themselves become a propertyless proletariat totally dependent economically and politically on a small group of new industrial corporations. Bitter strikes among railroad workers broke out from the east coast to the west coast; and, in many cities, scores of men, women, and children were shot down in the streets by federal and state troops.

Despite the failures of 1877, the labor movement survived in another national organization, the Knights of Labor. Headed by Terence V.

Powderly, the Knights also were opposed to the creation of a propertyless wage-earning class. They, too, wanted worker-owned and worker-operated factories. Asking for the support of all producers — white and black, male and female, skilled and unskilled — the Knights were trying to build a national political movement, the equivalent of the labor parties that were growing among the industrial workers of England and Germany.

Although the number of nonagricultural workers more than doubled, from 6 million in 1870 to 13 million in 1890, agricultural workers remained a much more important part of the economy than they did in England and Germany, and the number of agricultural workers increased from 7 million to 10 million. The tradition of the independence of the family farm, so strong among rural people, often led to a suspicion of the cities. Largely evangelical Protestants (Baptists and Methodists), they felt at odds with Episcopalians, Presbyterians, Congregationalists, and Unitarians, whom they identified as upper-class urban leaders. Traditionally hostile toward Roman Catholics and Jews, they also identified the city by the time of the Civil War with the immigration of large numbers of Irish and German Catholics and German Jews to the urban Northeast.

Urban labor itself was divided in ways that did not exist in Germany and England. Racism tended to separate white from black workers. Protestant workers often opposed Catholic workers, and this separation also applied to Jewish immigrants, whose numbers were increasing rapidly. German, Slavic, and Italian immigrants, of course, did not speak English when they arrived, and it was easy for employers to turn various groups of Catholics against one another. Usually, when employers brought in outside workers to replace their striking workers, they used blacks as strikebreakers against whites, or Irish against WASPs, or Italian Catholics against Slavic Catholics. Much of the expanding industrial work force between 1870 and 1890 was recruited from among the immigrants, and the cultural diversity of the immigrants created a work force in which it was much easier for employers to divide and conquer their workers than in industrial Europe.

Haymarket Square and the Collapse of the Knights of Labor

With its vision of industrial unionism, the Knights expanded from 40,000 members in 1882 to 700,000 in 1886. Throughout the country, the number of strikes in 1886 doubled those of any previous year. Members of the Knights engaged in these strikes even though the top leadership was opposed to such activity and hoped that the workers would concentrate on building cooperatives. In Chicago, a crowd of workers meeting in Haymarket Square to protest the shooting of strikers in 1886 erupted in violence. A bomb was thrown at the attacking police, and seven of them were killed. Known anarchists were arrested, and although there was no evidence to connect them with the bombing, four were executed. Business people and cultural leaders throughout the country associated the Knights with anarchism, and they defined anarchism as a form of European, un-American radicalism. Although most labor leaders were WASPs, an attempt was made to link union activity with recent immigrants, thus emphasizing its alien characteristics. Industrialists increased their efforts to break strikes. As they succeeded, the morale of the Knights disintegrated. By 1892, almost nothing was left of the mass movement of the 1880s. The success of the industrialists in stopping the development of a strong labor movement, especially one concerned with producers' and consumers' cooperatives, was completed in 1892, when management destroyed the strong Amalgamated Association of Iron and Steel Workers Union at Andrew Carnegie's Homestead Steel Plant in Pittsburgh. At first, the union fought off the army of Pinkerton detectives who were bringing in new workers. But, as always, the force and violence available to the establishment was greater than that of the unions, and a nonunion work force soon displaced the organized workers. The challenge to the new industrial middle class by the dissident farmers of the Populist party seemed less dangerous with the collapse of the Knights of Labor in 1892. Industrialists did not have to fear a strong labor element in the upcoming presidential election.

The New Middle Class and the Cities

The new business and professional middle class had not achieved self-discipline by 1892. Chaotic competition still characterized much of the business world and was one cause of a major economic depression in 1893. Significant differences in values and distrust still separated much of the old commercial middle class from the new industrial middle class.

The small-town bankers, business people, lawyers, doctors, ministers, and college teachers, who were the dominant middle-class elites of 1870, feared the mushrooming cities associated with industrialism. No longer could they believe that cities were something that existed only along the east coast. Chicago doubled in size from 500,000 to 1 million between 1880 and 1890; Minneapolis, Milwaukee, St. Paul, Kansas City, and Denver tripled in size from cities of about 50,000 to ones of about 150,000. To the old middle class, cities meant dirt, disease, epidemics, and crime (the nation's crime rate quadrupled between 1880 and 1890). Cities also housed Catholics and Jews, who threatened the Protestantism of small-town America. In short, cities meant political corruption and moral decay, as well as a threat to physical health.

The new middle-class business people and engineers, who had developed the new technology that was the basis for the explosive growth of cities after the Civil War, then began to use that technology to solve the problems of dirt and disease in the cities. The introduction of first horse-drawn carriages on tracks and then electric trolley cars made it possible for cities to extend their boundaries beyond the reasonable distance that a person could be expected to walk to work. Whereas the boundaries of the old "walking" city could not extend more than two miles from the city's center, the boundaries of the new "streetcar" city could extend up to four times that distance. Outbreaks of epidemic disease such as cholera were decreased by the introduction of water purification systems, which provided clean drinking water, and sewage facilities, which removed the rapidly increasing volume of waste produced by the new factories and the denser populations. City leaders also began taking steps to impose minimum standards on housing in order to force landlords to supply water and toilet facilities, as well as ventilation, in their tenements. However, the living conditions in some parts of New York City and Chicago remained even more overcrowded than those of the worst Asian cities.

The Cities and the Preservation of Ethnicity

By the 1880s, several hundred thousand Jews had entered the United States from Germany. Jews in Germany were more fully integrated into economic and cultural life than in any other European country, even England. They brought to America, therefore, urban and industrial skills, since Germany also was modernizing very rapidly during the nineteenth century. The German Jews also gave their greatest commitment to political life and to participation as universal citizens, rather than to an emphasis on the religious traditions that set them apart from other citizens. Most of the Jewish immigrants had rejected the tradition of Zionism, which prophesied that someday God would restore Israel to the Jews. Many of the Jews had given up traditional religious practices and committed themselves to an ethical philosophy that they could share with non-Jews. Others became Unitarians and Congregationalists.

Joining the religions of the upper-middle-class WASPs seemed plausible because German Jews had achieved levels of wealth and education comparable to the older American elite. Both the old and the new middle classes, however, rejected integration with the German Jews. Jewish students were systematically kept out of private schools, and quotas were used to limit their membership in elite colleges. Well-to-do WASPs often withdrew into suburbs, from which Jews were excluded, and Jews were denied membership not only to suburban country clubs but also to the city clubs of the WASP business people.

The new industrial middle class, therefore, was contradicting its ideal of a uniform national community. It was reinforcing cultural divisions that would make it more difficult to impose standardization.

The Cities and the Catholics

In the case of the Jews, as with blacks during Reconstruction, WASP elites had denied their own philosophy of universal citizenship and had imposed segregation on groups who seemed to want to be integrated into the national community. Catholics, however, seemed more like the American Indians in their desire to preserve their separate identity. Irish and German immigration from the 1830s to the 1880s had created a large Catholic community of several million. The Catholics were concentrated in the industrial cities of the Northeast to St. Louis, Missouri, and St. Paul, Minnesota. The church leaders had decided by the 1880s to create a coherent Catholic community by building a Catholic school system. The leaders were sure that the public schools were dominated by Protestants and that the Catholic children could easily lose their faith within such an environment.

Most Catholic leaders were enthusiastic about the American political and economic system. Nevertheless, they wanted to teach a greater emphasis on the family and the need to place economic interest below loyalty to the family. In this sense, church doctrine was critical of the Protestant ideal of the totally self-made man. Thus, Catholics began to create alternative institutions to those of the Protestant majority, including not only schools from kindergartens to colleges and graduate schools but also a system of hospitals. Catholics developed their own fraternal organizations, such as the Knights of Columbus, in opposition to the anti-Catholic Masons. The emphasis on ethnic homogeneity was made easier to maintain as the growing cities broke down into ethnic neighborhoods, with concentrations of Irish, Germans, Italians, Jews, and WASPs living in specific areas. Baptized in a Catholic church and educated in Catholic schools, an individual usually married a Catholic and belonged to Catholic voluntary organizations and finally was buried in a Catholic cemetery.

The Cities and Politics

As the major cities doubled their populations every ten years, political chaos characterized the urban scene. Huge fortunes were made in the building of water and sewer facilities for the cities, the paving of streets, and the constructing of trolley systems. Business people were as willing to bribe city officials to win the contracts for these jobs as they had been willing to bribe state and national officials to get rights-of-way for the railroads and supply contracts during the Civil War. Urban populations were unstable because of their rapid growth and because of the overall geographic mobility of people at the time. Several hundred thousand people moved into cities such as Boston and then moved out again within less than a decade. The poorer people of the United States seemed to be in constant motion, as they moved from place to place in search of jobs.

Powerful city bosses, such as Boss William Tweed of New York, emerged to control this chaos. Using vast amounts of graft, they won support from slum dwellers by providing the only available welfare through their personal expenditures. Food baskets, buckets of coal, and construction jobs were given away by the political machine in an economy where there was no unemployment insurance and no social security legislation.

The majority of the immigrants from the 1880s to World War I were from Southern and Eastern Europe. Poor when they left Europe, most of these "new" immigrants, Catholics and Jews, were crowded into densely populated urban ghettos. This is a picture of one of the Jewish neighborhoods in New York City in 1898. (Photograph by Byron, The Byron Collection, Museum of the City of New York.)

By the 1880s, WASP bosses were being replaced by Irish bosses in Boston, New York, and Philadelphia. The Irish were the first of the nineteenth-century immigrant groups to achieve local political power because they could speak English.

The WASP Middle Class

The dominant tradition among the WASP political and cultural leaders originally had defined America as a frontier that was waiting to have people and economic growth put into its open spaces, whereas Europe was seen as a world of closed opportunities. Until the 1870s, most of the population growth and most of the economic opportunities for those leaving Europe and coming to America were on the agricultural frontier. In 1893, the young historian Frederick Jackson Turner of the University of Wisconsin pointed out that the census of 1890 indicated the end of frontiers unsettled by white Anglo-Saxon Protestants. Even before the Civil War, however, the WASP middle class had begun to limit its birthrate. Throughout the colonial period and into the early nineteenth century, the WASPs had an extremely high birthrate, doubling their population every generation. By the 1870s, however, the birthrate among middle- and upper-level-income Americans had slowed dramatically, partly as a result of declining opportunity for the middle class and partly because of the loss of many young men in the Civil War. Much of the population explosion from 40 million in 1870 to 70 million in 1890, therefore, came from Catholic and Jewish immigrants. For at least a generation, these newcomers continued to have the very large families that had characterized the disorganized social situation of the lower-income people of southern and eastern Europe. That social disorganization had caused the overpopulation of those parts of the Old World and had driven millions of immigrants to America.

The Anglo-Americans who were the nation's cultural, economic, and political leaders began to worry that their America would be lost to the new immigrants and their many children. Theodore Roosevelt, a young man during the 1880s, warned of racial suicide for the WASPs if they did not once again increase their birthrate.

It was difficult for the WASP middle class, however, to consider immigration restrictions. Their capitalistic philosophy was one of the endless expansion of the marketplace. Their experience from 1865 until 1890 was one of successfully channeling creativity into the invention of new technology, and this technology had expanded the frontiers of industrial production. The expansion was so great that there was a shortage of labor to work the machines. The immigration of Catholic and Jewish aliens from southern and eastern Europe seemed essential to America's economic growth. WASP leadership had been willing to stop immigration of the Chinese in 1882 because they represented a different race and an alien civilization. But it resisted the demands of large numbers of farmers and workers throughout the 1880s to place limits on immigration from Europe.

The End of the Geographic Frontier and the Crisis of the Middle-Class Family

American cultural leaders were worried about the rising divorce rate among middle-class families during the 1880s, as well as about the declining birthrate for Anglo-Americans. The divorce rate had doubled between 1870 and 1890, and a government report in 1889 announced that the nation had a divorce problem. Although political, educational, and religious leaders held a series of meetings between 1890 and World War I to find ways to check the rising divorce rate, they failed completely in their conservative efforts.

In their discussions of the divorce problem, male Anglo-American leaders seldom considered the possibility that family instability might be caused by the new industrial economy. Instead, they seemed to see the social problems of divorce and the declining birthrate as problems that had to do with women, whereas they seemed to see economic problems as the concerns of men. This sharp sexual separation of social and economic experience may have been the result of the tremendous wall placed by the nineteenth-century middle class between the home and the marketplace and between women and men.

Throughout the nineteenth century, the Cult of True Womanhood defined the home as the world of women and the economy as the world of men. Men were to be tough and competitive in the marketplace. Women were to be gentle and cooperative in the home. This Cult of True Womanhood seems to have been the climax of a trend that began during the transition between medieval and modern Europe. In medieval society, both men and women worked at home. As this home economy was replaced by the marketplace economy of capitalism, the only major function of the home seemed to be that of raising children.

During the 1880s and 1890s, as middle-class women had fewer children, they seemed to grow restless with the segregated role they were given under the Cult of True Womanhood. This restlessness also seemed to challenge the definition of a middle-class woman as an innocent who was incapable of sexual pleasure. The possibility that women did have sexual feelings also threatened the middle-class ideal of innocent children. Children were not supposed to have sexual interests; this ideal was expressed in Mark Twain's stories about young people and in L. Frank Baum's Oz stories.

By 1890, therefore, the Anglo-American middle class was deeply troubled by a growing challenge to family stability and to the traditional identities given to women and children.

The Despair of the Novelists

The great novelists of Anglo-American culture from the 1870s to the 1890s, such as Mark Twain, Henry James, and William Dean Howells, expressed concern about the stability of the family and the identities of women and children. Much more than political leaders such as Theodore Roosevelt, however, they linked family instability to the end of the agricultural frontier and the coming of industrialism. They were much more pessimistic, therefore, about the future than were the political leaders. Of the three, Twain had the least hope for the future. American history, for him, had been the story of liberty. In Europe, people were dependent on one

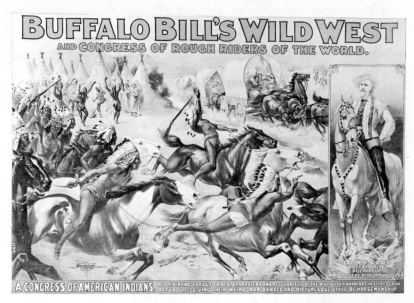

As Americans became aware in the 1880s and 1890s that the western frontier was vanishing, they tried to preserve the national identity of a people always moving west by making books about cowboys bestsellers and by going in their cities to Buffalo Bill's Wild West Show. More than any other American, Buffalo Bill was used in the years from 1890 to World War I to demonstrate that urban-industrial America was still the land of the independent pioneer. (Courtesy of Library of Congress.)

another, they were part of a complex web of relationships. Leaving Europe, a person could become independent on the American frontier. In his book *The Prince and the Pauper* (1882), Twain described the way in which two boys had defeated their corrupt fathers, marking the victory of modern youth over medieval elders. But, in *The Adventures of Huckleberry Finn* (1884), Twain presented an America where young people could no longer escape from or defeat the older generation. And, in *A Connecticut Yankee in King Arthur's Court* (1889), an enterprising young American transported back in time to medieval England is able to liberate the people from the superstitions and tyrannies of the Dark Ages only through the use of modern weapons that destroy the population. Like Twain, William Dean Howells and Henry James described the closing of the geographic frontier that had made America different from Europe. They agreed with Twain that American life would become more like that of Europe since the western expansion had ended.

It is interesting to note that L. Frank Baum began to write his Oz stories during the 1890s. Baum wanted to write American fairy tales that offered more happiness to children than European fairy tales did. But Baum began his stories in Kansas, where a young girl (Dorothy) faced the end of the agricultural frontier. The land in Kansas, as Baum described it, was brown and parched, and Uncle Henry and Aunt Em's farm was about to be foreclosed upon. For Baum, America no longer was a land where dreams came true. Dreams of the good life had to be fulfilled in the fantasy world of Oz.

But other cultural spokespeople of the 1880s believed that new frontiers could take the place of the West. Perhaps the city could be made as pure as rural America and offer new homes for the expanding population. Perhaps new overseas frontiers could make it possible for the young to continue to leave their elders behind.

One of the most popular books of the period was *Our Country* (1885), written by the Congregational minister Josiah Strong. Strong warned that the real Americans, Anglo-Saxon Protestants and capitalists, were on the verge of losing their country to the alien forces of socialism and Catholicism. The only way for Anglo-Americans to restore their vigor, Strong warned, was to return to being frontier people. They must restore their vitality by spreading Americanism — Protestantism and capitalism — to Latin America, Asia, and Africa. Such expansionism would give them the confidence to impose order in American cities and to regain discipline in their families.

A strange pattern of events during the 1890s was to make it possible for the new middle class to move toward the goals outlined by Strong.

Supplementary Reading

The political patterns of the 1870s and 1880s are discussed in H. Morgan, editor, *The Gilded Age: A Reappraisal* (1963), and J. Garraty, *The New Commonwealth* (1968). R. Higgs, *The Transformation of the American Economy* (1971), and D. North, *Growth and Welfare in the American Past* (1974), analyze the growth of industrialism. The development of the new middle class is the subject of R. Wiebe, *The Search for Order* (1967), and A. Chandler, Jr., *The Visible Hand: The Managerial Revolution in American Business* (1977). The caste and class attitudes of the WASP establishment in 1890 are described in E. Baltzell, *The Protestant Establishment* (1964). Western expansion by whites is discussed in R. Bartlett, *The New Country: A Social History of the American Frontier* (1974). J. Frantz and J. Chaote, *The American Cowboy* (1955), look at the Anglo-American cowboy; P. Durham and E. Jones, *The Adventures of the Negro Cowboy* (1966), mark the rediscovery of the fact that there were a large number of blacks on the cattle frontier.

R. Bruce, *1877: Year of Violence* (1959), and H. David, *The History of the Haymarket Affair* (1936), analyze the difficulties faced by workers in the new industrial frontier. G. Grob, *Workers and Utopia* (1961), looks at the anticapitalist ideology of the workers during the 1870s and 1880s.

The history of the American Indians during these years is the subject of W. Washburn, *The Indian in America* (1975); D. Brown, *Bury My Heart at Wounded Knee* (1971); and R. Andrist, *The Long Death* (1964). H. Fritz, *The Movement for Indian Assimilation* (1963), points to an attitude held by whites toward Indians and to a different attitude toward blacks. G. Fredrickson, *The Black Image in the White Mind* (1971), is an excellent analysis of white racism throughout the nineteenth century.

The crisis in WASP culture during the 1880s is the subject of R. Hofstadter, *The Age of Reform* (1955); F. Jaher, *Doubters and Dissenters* (1964); P. Carter, *The Spiritual Crisis of* the *Gilded Age* (1973); and W. LaFeber, *The New Empire* (1967). W. O'Neill, *Divorce in the Progressive Era* (1967), P. Filene, *HimHerself* (1974), and G. Barker-Benfield, *The Horrors of the Half-known Life* (1976), provide good descriptions of the crisis in the middle-class family.

The New Middle Class, the New Politics, and the New Diplomacy

1892-1904

The confusions of American society between 1876 and 1892 were expressed in the political patterns of those years. A Republican, James Garfield, was elected president in 1880; a Democrat, Grover Cleveland, was elected in 1884. Benjamin Harrison, a Republican, defeated Cleveland in 1888, but Cleveland won a clear-cut victory in 1892. During this period, neither party was able to control the presidency and both houses of Congress at the same time. The defection of many discontented Democrats to the Populist party in 1892 left the conservative Democrats in firm control of the party. President Cleveland, representing the conservative wing of the party, was prepared to hold to the gold standard and veto any efforts to inflate the currency. Totally committed to the laissez-faire tradition, he also rejected the efforts of farmers to bring the government into the economy to try to save a marketplace of small producers.

Political Loyalties in 1892

In the Northeast, many large bankers were Democrats because they opposed the Republican policy on tariffs. The bankers wanted a free flow of international trade to help transfer billions of dollars from European capitalists for investment in America. Merchants who shipped wheat and cotton to Europe also opposed tariffs. Moreover, many small business people in the Northeast and Midwest allied themselves with the Democratic party because they saw the Republicans as friends of large corporations.

Political representatives of the upper-class and middle-class groups were able to dominate the national Democratic party because the average voter, as worker, farmer, or lower-middle-class clerk, was interested primarily in local issues. Irish and German Catholics had turned to the Democratic party in large numbers because it had a tradition of localism and decentralization that contrasted with the Republican emphasis on nationalism and centralization. Catholics looked to the Democrats to help them preserve their unique ethnic culture. This attitude also influenced many German and Scandinavian Lutherans who wanted to preserve their Old World heritage.

The Republican party, on the other hand, held the loyalty of many lower-middle-class and lower-class Protestants in New England and the Midwest. These people had become emotionally committed to the Republicans as the party that ended slavery and preserved the union. They also clung to the Republican party as the symbol of Protestant control of the nation's culture in the face of the seeming threats from Catholics, Jews, and Lutherans.

Politics and the Depression of 1893

In 1893, a much more terrible depression than that of 1873 struck the country. Fifteen to twenty percent of the industrial work force was unemployed until 1896. True to his laissez-faire principles, President Cleveland never considered government intervention to control the business cycle or to provide relief for the unemployed and the poor. A small "army" of unemployed workers marched on Washington, D.C., under the leadership of an Ohio businessman, Jacob Coxey, to ask the president to create jobs through federally financed public works and to stimulate the economy by financing roadbuilding administered by local governments. (Some of the New Deal measures taken to meet the depression of 1933 were similar to Coxey's suggestions.) Coxey was arrested when he arrived in Washington, and his followers were driven away from the White House by the police. Cleveland also sent federal troops to repress a strike of railroad workers in support of the workers who manufactured Pullman sleeping cars for the railroads (1894). More than twenty strikers were killed and many were wounded in Chicago, and the strike leader, Eugene Debs, was sent to jail.

The depression was responsible for the crushing defeat of the Democratic party in the congressional elections of 1894. A Democratic majority of 61 percent in 1892 became a minority of 29 percent in the House of Representatives. Populist candidates in the South and West won 50 percent more votes than they had in 1892. It was the Republicans, however, especially in the Northeast, who benefited most from the Democrats' losses. Republicans won control of every major city in the Northeast, a control that they largely held until 1928. Many Catholic and Lutheran workers who had been loyal Democrats reacted to the depression by voting against their party.

As the Democrats approached their presidential convention in 1896, the conservative Cleveland Democrats from the Northeast and Midwest lost control of the party and the more radical southern and western Democrats were in a position to take over. They nominated William Jennings Bryan, a thirty-six-year-old political leader from Nebraska, as their presidential candidate. The specific issue emphasized by Bryan in the campaign was the increased coinage of silver to encourage inflation. This economic issue was beneficial to the cotton farmers of the South and the wheat farmers of the Great Plains. Bryan added an important emotional issue by suggesting that the farmers were the "real America," the America where the small producer still preserved the equal competition of the marketplace. Bryan warned that this virtuous area of the economy was being threatened by the modern corporations, which were creating a European class system composed of a very rich plutocracy and a poverty-stricken proletariat.

Many urban workers found Bryan's rural orientation no more attractive than Cleveland's conservative financial policies. Higher prices for food would not help the problems of unemployment and low wages in the cities. The saving of the family farm and small-town businesses would not solve the problems of industrial factory workers. More dramatically, as Catholics and Lutherans, urban voters were faced with a Democratic party that seemed to be imposing evangelical Protestant culture on their ethnic groups. Ninety percent of the southern whites were Baptists and Methodists, and Great Plains farmers also were predominantly evangelical Protestant. When they talked about the evils of the city, they seemed to be talking about the evils of Catholics and Jews. They also talked about the need to impose prohibition to end national corruption. Beer and wine drinking was a strong part of the ethnic culture of many Catholics, Jews, and Lutherans. Although Bryan campaigned hard in the cities, the Democratic party under Bryan suddenly seemed to be taking over the Republican role of imposing a Protestant national culture and denying the right to local and decentralized cultural autonomy.

The Democrats and the Populists

Many Populist leaders, however, were impressed by the capture of the Democratic party by its southern and western wings and decided that they should support Bryan. Unable to win the presidency themselves, the Populists hoped to share the victory of the Democrats. But bitter divisions developed within the Populist convention. The Populists finally nominated Bryan for the presidency but endorsed Tom Watson from Georgia as a separate vice-presidential candidate.

Deeply opposed to fusion of the Populists with the Democrats, Watson had become a rebel against the business leaders who ran the Democratic party in his native state of Georgia during the 1880s. Angered that these leaders were neglecting the problems of farmers who were the majority of the population, Watson had joined in the creation of a Populist party in Georgia and then helped to create a national Populist party. Watson, like white agrarian rebels in a number of southern states, was prepared to join with black farmers to break the political control of southern Democrats. During the 1880s, a coalition of lower-income white and black farmers captured control of the state government of Virginia, and, in 1894, a similar coalition won control in North Carolina.

Democratic leaders who wanted to bring industrialism to the South attempted to break the reform parties in their states by using the issue of racism to divide the white farmers from the black. In Virginia, at the end of the 1880s, they invented a false history of Reconstruction to help them in this effort. According to these Democratic leaders, all white men — rich and poor, merchants and farmers — had joined together in the Democratic party at the end of the 1860s to preserve white supremacy from the Republican party's threat to let blacks and whites intermarry. Such events, of course, had not occurred, but the Democratic leaders used their newspapers to persuade voters anyway. The logic of their argument was clear. If white farmers joined with black farmers to create a second political party, they threatened white supremacy. Black voters in a two-party situation could be the balance of power. With such power, they could control the state, and, by controlling the state, they could claim white women and destroy the purity of Anglo-Saxon blood. The novelist Thomas Dixon manufactured the most elaborate mythical history of Reconstruction in his novels *The Leopard's Spots* (1902) and *The Clansmen* (1905). They were written to justify the concept of racist democracy. Ben Tillman, the governor of South Carolina, however, was the most powerful spokesman of the theory of racist democracy. Anglo-Saxon people, he argued, had a single will that needed to be expressed by a single party and a single leader.

Disfranchising Blacks and Jim Crow Segregation

Mississippi, in 1890, was the first state in which a constitutional convention was called for the purpose of disfranchising blacks. By 1905, every southern state had adopted similar restrictions. To get around the Fifteenth Amendment, which stated that people could not be kept from voting because of their race, these conventions established literacy tests, property qualifications, and poll taxes that applied to all voters. But, since most blacks owned little property and could not read, the laws applied more to them than to whites. Although white southern leaders publicly admitted that the legislation was intended to remove blacks from politics, the Supreme Court ruled that the laws were not a violation of the Fifteenth Amendment because they applied to whites as well as to blacks. The

The conservatives of the 1890s symbolized farmers' demands for government aid as representing an un-American philosophy. This illustration of the "foreignness" of these demands also reflects the growing anti-Semitism of that decade. (From Judge, *January 17, 1891.)*

Court, however, did rule that Grandfather Clauses were unconstitutional. These clauses in the rewritten southern state constitutions exempted men from the literacy and property qualifications for voting if their grandfathers had voted before 1876. Only white men, of course, had voted before that date.

The elimination of blacks from southern politics was accelerated after the collapse of the Populist parties in 1896. As Tom Watson had feared, the fusion of populism with the Democratic party enabled the New South's Democratic leaders to regain their power. Most of the southern states operated with a single party from 1896 until 1948. In this situation, the Populists' demand for political primaries worked against blacks. Between 1900 and 1910, southern states adopted primaries with the hope that political leadership would be chosen by the average voter, rather than by professional politicians in conventions. In a one-party state, however, a candidate chosen in the primary necessarily won the general election. Blacks were explicitly barred from participation in the primaries of the state Democratic parties. Until 1944, the Supreme Court found this discrimination acceptable because the Court defined political parties as private organizations. In 1944, however, the Court ruled that the parties were part of the political process and that the constitutional guarantees of equal citizenship without racial discrimination applied to them.

Some Jim Crow legislation had been passed before 1890, but it was not until the 1890s that all southern states systematically established the Jim Crow principle of the physical separation of whites from blacks in public life. Many new laws divided the races in public transportation facilities. In some localities, it even became illegal for whites and blacks to play checkers together. The Supreme Court announced that racial segregation did not violate the provision for equal citizenship in the Fourteenth Amendment. In *Plessy v. Ferguson* (1896), the Court ruled that separate-but-equal facilities were constitutional. This decision was not reversed until 1954. Most members of the Supreme Court were sympathetic to the crusade against the blacks. In 1890, the southern states spent about $2 for a white child's education, but only $1 for a black child's; between 1890 and 1914, the difference grew to be almost $10 to $1. The Court, however, ignored this evidence of discrimination until the end of the 1930s.

The Supreme Court justices, congressional leaders, and the presidents of the 1890s, although overwhelmingly from the North, tolerated the crusade against blacks in the South because they, too, had become defensive about their Anglo-Saxon culture in the face of increasing Catholic and Jewish immigration. They were willing to tolerate the attempt of many southern whites to destroy the second-class citizenship held by the blacks during the 1870s and 1880s. An important example of this attitude was the unwillingness of President Harrison and other Republican leaders to fight hard for the passage of a federal elections bill, sponsored by Congressman Henry Cabot Lodge in 1890-1891. This bill would have authorized federal supervision of federal elections in the states. The presence of such federal election officials could have checked the disfranchising of blacks. (Somewhat similar legislation was passed during the 1960s.) Harrison also refused to give leadership to federal antilynching laws that would have controlled the rapid increase in the number of lynchings of blacks throughout the South.

Booker T. Washington and the Black Response to Jim Crow

Many aspects of the crusade against blacks during the 1890s were comparable to the crusade against Jews in Nazi Germany during the 1930s, when Jews were barred from political life and physically segregated. German Jews during the 1930s, like blacks during the 1890s, had no protection from physical violence. The number of lynchings of blacks rose sharply in the 1880s, and the lynchings continued throughout the 1890s. Often, lynching was a ritual in which a black was burned alive in the presence of the entire white community. Local sheriffs often led the lynchings; governors, like Ben Tillman, encouraged the practice; and northern political leaders refused to send federal troops into the South to protect the blacks.

In this desperate situation, there was a sharp change in black leadership. Through the 1880s, Frederick Douglass, the ex-slave and abolitionist leader, had criticized the failure of blacks to achieve first-class citizenship. He was not satisfied with the pattern of second-class citizenship in which blacks had to be followers rather than leaders. But, by 1894, Booker T.

Washington and other southern black leaders were forced to try to save those parts of second-class citizenship that had not been lost already. Washington feared that blacks might be barred from education as they had been under slavery. Also, if they lost all aspects of citizenship, they would lose the right to geographic mobility. The caste system and the prejudice of white racists kept most blacks working in unskilled and poorly paid jobs. But they were not legally prohibited from being teachers, lawyers, doctors, and business people, as they might have been if they were stripped of their citizenship.

Speaking to a white audience in Atlanta (1895), Washington said that blacks were willing to forego social equality and political participation. But he argued that black workers were necessary for the agricultural and industrial prosperity of the white South and that industrial workers needed the training and discipline that black schools could provide for them. By speaking in a humble and subservient way, Washington persuaded southern whites that the education of blacks posed no threat to the caste system. Washington believed that an inferior public school system and inferior colleges were better than no schools for blacks and that the possibility of a few blacks achieving professional status was better than nothing.

Faced with a totalitarian, one-party system in the South and an unsympathetic system dominated by whites in the North, Washington and most other southern black leaders felt that they must appear to be unaggressive in public. Washington, for instance, supplied money anonymously to lawyers to wage legal battles against Jim Crow laws. Meanwhile, the continued mobility of blacks brought more of them into southern cities, where the new Jim Crow patterns cut them off from white leadership and permitted black leaders some self-reliance within the ghettos. A distinct black culture, rooted in African traditions and the slave experience, lived vigorously at the beginning of the twentieth century.

Progressivism and the "Responsible" Voter

The Populist fusion with the Democrats did not result in a victory for Bryan in 1896 as a leader of farmers, workers, and small business people against big business. Instead, William McKinley won the presidency for the Republicans and solidified the Republican majority that had emerged in 1894. Holding the states of the Northeast and Midwest, the Republicans remained the majority party until 1932. Many industrial workers voted for McKinley in 1896 because the Republicans promised to end the depression that had begun in 1893. Other workers were attracted to McKinley because he seemed to promise that, under his leadership, the Republicans would be more tolerant of ethnic culture, in contrast to the image of Bryan as a defender of Protestant fundamentalism. It was difficult, however, to find an emphasis on political reform in McKinley's campaign. Reform politics on the national level within the Republican party did not appear until Theodore Roosevelt became president in 1901. But his reform politics

THE AMERICAN SOUTH, 1920

Population per square mile:
- Less than 5
- 5 to 45
- 46 to 90
- More than 90

were built on movements led by Republicans at the city and state level throughout the 1890s.

During the 1890s, middle-class voters had begun to accept the importance of political reform. Calling themselves progressives, middle-class reformers stressed the importance of virtue and efficiency in all areas of the government, the economy, and the society. An early sign of this mood had been the Pendleton Act, passed by Congress in 1883. This act had placed a number of government workers under civil service, so their appointments depended upon skills demonstrated in tests, rather than upon their political influence.

Like the farmers of the 1870s, the new urban middle class of the 1890s was angry at the ability of corporations to corrupt politics, to charge outrageous prices for their products, to sell shoddy and unsafe goods (especially food), and to avoid taxes by shifting them to average taxpayers. But the urban middle class, unlike the farmers and workers, still welcomed the corporations that provided increasing numbers of white-collar jobs. This class was small compared to the workers and farmers, but it had grown eight times faster than the total population between 1870 and 1900. This middle class wanted responsible corporations. Part of the blame for corporate corruption, according to many middle-class leaders, was the ease with which corporations could buy the votes of lower-class immigrants. Electoral reforms establishing a secret ballot, making registration much more difficult, and taking the printing of ballots out of the hands of the political parties were passed. In this manner, voter participation was significantly reduced in northern cities after 1896, although not as drastically as the fall-off of poor white voting in the South and, of course, not as overwhelmingly as the almost total elimination of black voting in the South.

Another reform pushed by the urban middle class was the at-large election of city councilmen and school board members by all the city voters, rather than those from particular wards. Election by wards was bound to give ethnic voters who formed majorities in some neighborhoods a voice on city councils and school boards. Election at large gave the Anglo-American middle class a chance for complete control, because its members were more apt to vote than were the immigrants and the poor. To run a city-wide election campaign cost more money than to run one at the neighborhood level. This gave another advantage to the WASP middle class and also allowed them to use in the election campaigns the city-wide social and economic networks developed by the elites. Other reforms advocated by the new urban middle class were having city commissions and city managers take over much of the power of mayors and city coun-

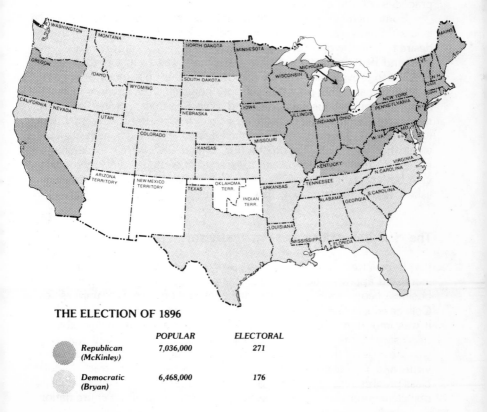

THE ELECTION OF 1896

		POPULAR	ELECTORAL
Republican (McKinley)		7,036,000	271
Democratic (Bryan)		6,468,000	176

cils. Commissioners and city managers — nonelected officials who were to represent professionalism and scientific objectivity — were preferred by the WASP middle class, which was coming to trust highly educated specialists and to distrust politicians elected by uninformed average voters.

From Urban to State Progressivism

The development of progressivism in the cities soon had parallels at the state level of government. Robert LaFollette gained control of the Republican party in Wisconsin in 1900 by uniting farmers, workers, and members of the urban middle class. He campaigned against the control of the state by irresponsible railroad and public-utility groups. His reform legislation passed new laws taxing the railroads, ending rebates, and lowering the shipping rates. Small business people and farmers liked this legislation. The urban middle class also wanted fair and regular standards. Depending on gas and electricity to make the city livable, they wanted the regulation of the public utilities and the lowering of rates. They also approved a corrupt practices act and a state income tax.

Some members of the urban middle class were developing a paternalistic attitude toward the poor and the workers. A deep idealism and a desire to help the oppressed was felt by many WASP reformers between 1890 and 1918. In most cases, however, there was a sense of the need of WASPs to provide all the highest levels of leadership in the reform movements against crime, poverty, and poor housing. If the city was to be livable, minimum housing codes and police and fire protection were necessary. Crime would be reduced if children went to school rather than work. And, if lower-class women had adequate working conditions, they would not be driven into prostitution. Under LaFollette's leadership, a state industrial commission was created to encourage employers to provide better working conditions, restrictions on child labor were established, and a minimum-wage law for women was passed.

The New Universities and Progressivism

LaFollette and many other progressive governors dramatically increased appropriations for their state universities. At the same time, business people were increasing their contributions to private universities. College education was of great importance for the new urban middle class. It was important because it provided the specialized training and skills necessary for the complex industrial economy. More important, however, was the belief of the middle class that college education made possible the virtue and objectivity essential to the new progressive democracy. Middle-class progressives argued that democracy depended on disinterested and objective voters who were able to see the concerns of the entire nation.

The logical implication of this theory was that workers and farmers, even though they were the majority of the population, could not establish a democracy for all the people, because they represented only the special interests of labor and agriculture. But educated business people and professionals, although a small minority of the population, could establish a democracy for all the other people, because their education made it possible for them to see the concerns of all kinds of people.

As the new urban middle class emerged between 1870 and 1900, therefore, a revolutionary change took place in higher education. Until the 1870s, colleges had represented various Protestant denominations and largely drew students from their immediate regions. Doctors, lawyers, teachers, and ministers were trained in local colleges or by apprenticeships with senior members of their professions. But, from 1870 until 1900, there was pressure to transform some of these older colleges, such as Harvard, Yale, and Princeton, into universities drawing faculty and students from throughout the nation. New private universities such as Johns Hopkins, the University of Chicago, and Stanford, as well as midwestern state universities such as Michigan, Wisconsin, and Minnesota, also served as "national" universities. The purpose of the national universities was to train professionals with standardized qualifications that could be applied everywhere in the country. National professional associations in law and medicine (such as the American Medical Association [AMA]) were developed, and apprenticeships in the professions were prohibited.

A national profession of college teachers was needed to staff the national universities. This was accomplished by importing from Germany the doctor of philosophy (Ph.D.) degree. As part of the most rapidly industrializing and urbanizing nation in Europe by 1870, German universities were world leaders in science, medicine, and the social sciences. Central to the German universities was the seminar, where college teachers were trained. The essence of the seminar, according to the leaders of German middle-class culture, was its ability to teach methods of complete impersonality and objectivity and methods of achieving scholarly progress. During the 1870s and 1880s, many Americans studied in German universities, earned Ph.D.s, and returned to establish Ph.D. programs in the new American universities. In this, too, national organizations developed quickly, including the American Historical Association, the American Political Science Association, and the American Economic Association.

By 1900, therefore, a great gap existed between the national universities and the many colleges that continued to have religious and regional roots. It was assumed by WASP cultural leaders that Catholics and Jews could not be objective, and social pressure kept them, for the most part, from teaching in the national universities. Catholic scholars and professionals had their own university system, which included Holy Cross in Massachusetts, Fordham in New York, Catholic University in Washington, D.C., Notre Dame in Indiana, and St. Louis University. The professionals trained there were mostly Irish and German Catholics.

Italian and Polish Catholics who, along with Russian Jews, were the largest immigrant groups between 1900 and 1914 experienced less social and economic mobility than Irish and German Catholics until after World War II. The newer immigrants often stayed in the industrial and mining jobs that were available to them in 1900. They had strong family ties, and their children were encouraged to work and help the family buy houses in ethnic neighborhoods, rather than to pursue individual careers that would take them away from their families. The Italians and Poles were suspicious and fearful not only of the WASP establishment but also of the American Catholic establishment dominated by Irish and Germans.

A vast influx of Russian Jews, almost 2 million between 1890 and 1914, settled mostly in New York City. Much poorer than the earlier German Jewish immigrants, they were just as dedicated to education and soon were sending their children to colleges in large numbers. Wherever there was a large Jewish urban population, Jewish social organizations, hospitals, and cemeteries were established. In New York City, there was a flourishing cultural life, with newspapers, magazines, books, and plays written in Yiddish. Yeshiva University was established in New York, but most Jews went to publicly supported universities, such as the City College of New York. As they became doctors, lawyers, and business people, much of their practice and business was carried on in the Jewish community. Jews were excluded from leadership in the national banks and corporations, and Jewish lawyers were not recruited by the national corporations.

One of the tests of objectivity used by the national universities was the acceptance of the concept of evolution. Evolution was linked with progress by the new academic leaders. Southern Baptist and Methodist colleges, because of their fundamentalist and antievolutionary theology, were defined as outside the enlightened national community. This was also true for the Lutheran colleges of the Midwest. These colleges could train local leaders but not national leaders.

Upper-middle-class Episcopalians, Presbyterians, Congregationalists, and Unitarians and those middle-class northern Methodists and Baptists who accepted evolution — a small minority of the national population — defined themselves as the only acceptable national leaders who could lead the progressive crusade to purify the cities, regulate the corporations and restore democracy to the country.

Education and Discipline

The center of the national middle class was in the northeastern cities where many of the national corporations and banks were headquartered. But business leaders in midwestern and southern cities could consider themselves part of this national class. The business leaders of most midwestern and western cities were WASPs from the East. The major businesses and banks in cities such as Minneapolis were dominated by former New Englanders, who were mostly Episcopalians, Presbyterians, Congre-

Industrial production created vast wealth for a few Americans at the end of the nineteenth century. Many of the new rich began to move out of the cities into the suburbs by the 1880s. Some, however, built palatial residences within the city, as along New York's Fifth Avenue. This illustration demonstrates the ability of the rich to keep open space for themselves with the densely populated urban areas. (Courtesy of Library of Congress.)

gationalists, and Unitarians. They sent their children to private schools in the cities or to boarding schools in the East. The children then attended eastern Ivy League universities. When they returned to Minneapolis, St. Louis, or Denver, they had strengthened the web of personal relationships binding the national middle class together through the friendships formed in prep school and college.

A lower level of leadership with a local focus was trained in states such as Minnesota in Lutheran and Catholic colleges that served the state population. Minnesota was 40-percent Lutheran and 30-percent Catholic. The state university also trained local leaders; however, its professional and graduate schools were part of the national network.

The progressive urban middle class was able to provide leadership for the majority of Americans who were kept by social pressure from participation in national leadership because of their race, religion, region, or occupation, because the urban middle class was able to control what was taught in the public schools. During the 1890s, many states began to make school attendance compulsory to the age of sixteen. Public school teaching was defined as a profession. Teachers' colleges looked to the national universities to provide them with instruction. It became necessary that the public schools be efficient and businesslike and that they be run by professional administrators. These school administrators studied at the major universities, belonged to national professional organizations, and went to national conventions.

History and civics, taught in the grade schools and high schools, came from textbooks written or influenced by the professional historians of the American Historical Association. American history was taught as the political history of male WASPs. American literature was taught with the novels and poetry written by male Anglo-Americans. American heroes, presented in history and literature from John Winthrop to Abraham Lincoln, were male WASPs. Anglo-American women, as well as all other American women, therefore, were conditioned to accept their absence from the American story. Blacks and American Indians; Catholics and Jews; southern white, evangelical Protestants; midwestern Lutherans; and the poor, too, were invisible and unheard. Children were taught that America was a democracy run by the people. But the only people in the textbooks were middle-class and upper-middle-class male WASPs. Middle-class WASPs could, therefore, believe that their progressivism was a democratic movement of the people.

The Cult of Masculinity

Although urban progressives talked about objectivity, efficiency, rational control, and impersonal standards, they were also concerned with energy, power, and will. Many new magazines appealed to the interests of middle-class readers, and almost every one of them carried a story about Napoleon. The new middle class seemed to be waiting for the appearance of an American Napoleon who would create military order in the nation and expand the nation's influence through military power.

Already the upper-middle class during the 1880s seemed to be preparing its young people in the hope of producing a Napoleon. Private schools often established military discipline. Incoming freshmen received a hazing from upperclassmen. They had to show that they were manly enough to withstand pressure before they would be accepted as brave and soldierly sophomores. This system of hazing then spread upward to the national universities, as did the emphasis on uniformed and body-contact sports.

Baseball was the nonviolent sport of lower-middle-class, agricultural America. It expressed the individualism of Jacksonian America, since each member of each team took a turn at bat and made an individual contribution. Football rapidly became the sport of the upper-middle class. As in corporate structures, most offensive play in football depended on team blocking. There was also great violence in trying to march through the enemy's territory. Unlike the relaxed attitude toward time in baseball, football was played with a clock that was running down. Ivy League universities, especially Yale, were the stronghold of football during the 1890s. The state universities of the Midwest soon began to build formidable football teams. (When Notre Dame tried to prove that a Catholic university was as good as the national universities dominated by Protestants, it mobilized a football team that could compete successfully with any team during the 1920s.)

The Ivy League and Foreign Policy

After the election of 1896, the Republicans became the majority party in the nation, a position they held until 1932. This gave the new national middle class a more powerful political position. But, in making domestic policies, the new Republican middle class still had to win support from workers and farmers who voted Republican and from small business people who were opposed to large corporations. Furthermore, national policies needed to flow through state governments, whose politicians had to face local issues in order to gain election. Political power, in other words, did not assure the passage of specific legislation.

Foreign policy, however, was a different situation. In this, the Constitution gave the president tremendous power. In foreign policy, therefore, the president was much more like a football quarterback who called the plays without consultation and expected instant obedience and cohesive teamwork in running the play.

Already in 1896, when William McKinley was elected president, representatives of the new middle class were well on their way to making the foreign policy of the United States one of systematic and continual overseas expansion, of moving the American team into the other team's territory. Between 1888 and 1896, presidents, secretaries of state, and other diplomatic advisers had begun to think of America as a major world power. American leaders had been interested in expansion during the 1870s and 1880s, but they had not developed a systematic policy that would be carried on from one administration to the next. Rather, American leaders reacted to specific issues that might involve American interests in various parts of the world.

In the Harrison, Cleveland, and McKinley administrations, a consistent policy toward Latin America began to develop. Throughout the nineteenth century, the Monroe Doctrine had been enforced through the power of the British navy. The Monroe Doctrine had warned European powers not to interfere with the new Latin American republics. Britain approved of this policy because it allowed trade to flow freely between South America and Britain.

By 1890, American leaders knew that the American population and American industrial production were surpassing those of Britain. They urged the expansion of the American navy to assume responsibility for enforcing the Monroe Doctrine. They also planned to increase trade between the United States and Latin America. Both positions were designed to drive British naval and economic power out of the Western Hemisphere.

Production of Iron in Millions of Tons

	1880	1890	1900
England	7	8	9
Germany	2	4	7
United States	3	9	14

Production of Steel in Millions of Tons

	1880	1890	1900
England	2	4	5
Germany	1	3	7
United States	1	5	11

The Depression of 1893 and American Expansion

The collapse of the economy in 1893 convinced many business leaders that overseas markets were needed to absorb America's surplus industrial production. There was then substantial economic and political support for an overseas frontier to replace the dying agricultural frontier. They found encouragement from Captain Alfred T. Mahan, a teacher at the newly founded Naval War College. Mahan argued that naval bases were needed throughout the world if the navy was to be able to protect the expansion of American overseas trade and allow America to compete successfully with other world powers.

The Hawaiian Islands were seen as one such naval base necessary to the growth of American trade in Asia. American missionary activity in Asia doubled during the 1880s and 1890s. A strong interlocking group of WASP religious, economic, and naval leaders — concerned with expanding American religious, economic, and naval influence in Asia — existed by 1896. There was not as much consensus, however, about the emerging Asian policy as there was about the Latin American policy. American business people and missionaries in Hawaii had engineered a revolution with the help of American diplomats that overthrew the Hawaiian queen, Liliuokalani. President Cleveland, however, refused to annex the islands. But President William McKinley, who took office in March 1897, was committed to American expansion in Asia. In 1898, the United States annexed Hawaii.

Cuba and the Spanish-American War

Cuba and Puerto Rico, during the 1890s, were the last Spanish possessions in the New World, and revolutionaries were trying to establish Cuba's independence. The revolution provided an opportunity for WASP leaders to demonstrate their ability to enforce the Monroe Doctrine. The Cleveland and McKinley administrations pressured Spain to recognize the independence of Cuba and withdraw from the Western Hemisphere. This policy had support from many major newspapers and Protestant and academic leaders. To drive Catholic Spain from the New World would help WASPs overcome the fears of the 1890s, the fears that the end of the geographic frontier meant the end of their vitality. These fears had been strengthened by the extensive Catholic immigration. During the 1890s, WASPs were setting themselves apart from the new immigrants as they established many exclusive organizations, such as the Daughters of the American Revolution and the Sons of the American Revolution. Many business leaders, including those who had large sugar interests in Cuba, also wanted an aggressive policy that might expand their markets and make crucial raw materials more available.

Many big-city newspapers operated as a yellow press at the beginning of 1898, printing sensational but unverified stories about Spanish atrocities in Cuba in order to increase circulation. This was especially true of the *New York World,* published by Joseph Pulitzer, and the *New York Journal,* published by William Randolph Hearst. When the American warship *Maine* was blown up in the harbor at Havana, Cuba, these newspapers ran headlines calling for war, even though there was conflicting evidence about who was responsible for the explosion. They also demanded war when the *New York Journal* printed a copy of a personal letter sent by the Spanish minister Depuy De Lôme, that made insulting references to President McKinley. But McKinley and his advisers were in control of the timetable for the war. The President sent a war message to Congress in April 1898. Since his inauguration in March 1897, McKinley and his advisers had been trying to force Spain to accept American control of the peacemaking process in Cuba. Under an American ultimatum, Spain agreed to many of McKinley's demands. But, when the Spanish government was reluctant to give the United States complete control over Cuba, the president asked for war. All of the psychological factors (proving American vitality), the economic factors (expanding overseas trade), and the strategic factors (developing overseas bases) played a part in the president's decision and the enthusiastic backing he received from Congress.

The navy proved that it had attained the status of a great power by destroying the Spanish fleet in Cuba and in the Philippine Islands. Already in 1895, naval officers had worked out plans for an attack on Spanish possessions in Asia, which were seen as part of a chain of strategic bases that would reach from Hawaii to the China market. During three months of war, the United States captured Cuba, Puerto Rico, Guam, and the Philippines. The McKinley administration planned to keep Puerto Rico and the Philippines as colonies. Since the war had been fought for the official reason of helping the Cubans become an independent republic, Congress had written the Teller Amendment in its declaration of war to guarantee that it would respect Cuban independence and not make it into an official American colony. After four years of government by the American military, Cuba was permitted to establish its own government in 1902. But the treaty with the United States forced Cuba to place the Platt Amendment in its constitution. This amendment granted the United States the right to build naval bases in Cuba and also granted the United States the right of military intervention to preserve political and economic stability. Meanwhile, the United States Army suppressed a lengthy rebellion in the Philippines, where the people wanted to create their own independent republic.

China and the Open Door Policy

By 1900, the United States had developed a consistent Asian policy to go with its Latin American policy. Secretary of State John Hay sent notes to the major European powers interested in trade with China to announce that America wanted an Open Door policy toward China. The intent of this policy was similar to that of the Monroe Doctrine. Throughout the nineteenth century, American diplomats had tried to keep European powers from ending the independence of the Latin American republics. It was American policy to keep those republics open to trade with all nations. At the beginning of the twentieth century, the United States wanted China to remain an independent nation open to trade with all nations; it did not want China broken into colonies that were parts of European empires as Africa had been during the nineteenth century.

The Open Door Empire

WASP political, economic, and naval leaders did not plan to develop an empire comparable to that of the major European powers. Knowing that the American economy was the most dynamic and powerful in the world, they believed that American business could defeat any other businesses in competition for markets in South America and China. Someday, they hoped, European empires would break down, and an open-door policy would spread throughout the entire world.

Recent historians have called this American policy that of the Open Door empire because it intended to make the American economy dominate the whole world. The United States would become the center of world finance and trade, drawing profits from Asia, Africa, South America, and Europe. The seizure of Hawaii, Puerto Rico, and the Philippines did not mean, therefore, the beginning of a European-type empire. These were strategic bases from which the United States Navy could protect the open door aspects of the Monroe Doctrine in Latin America and the Open Door policy in China.

In this concept of Open Door empire, independent nations had no right to refuse to trade with the United States. But the Boxer Rebellion in China (1900) was led by people who wanted to drive all foreigners out of their country and return it to the self-sufficiency that had existed before 1850. United States troops joined forces from Britain, France, Germany, Russia, and Japan to smash the rebellion and keep China open to trade.

The Roosevelt Corollary to the Monroe Doctrine

During the 1880s, Theodore Roosevelt had feared that WASPs were losing their will to be vital and expand. By 1890, he believed that only war could restore virtue and discipline to the nation. He was delighted when war came in 1898, and he raised a volunteer cavalry unit, the Rough Riders, made up in part of cowboys. The newspapers and magazines, which had been calling for a Napoleonic hero, made Colonel Roosevelt a national figure by exaggerating his military exploits. When McKinley was reelected in 1900, Roosevelt became vice-president. Six months after McKinley's inauguration, he was assassinated, and Roosevelt, at age forty-two, became the youngest man to hold the presidency.

In his first three years in office, Roosevelt was able to act in a Napoleonic fashion in the area of foreign policy. He wanted swift action to build a canal connecting the Atlantic and Pacific across the narrow part of Central America. He and his naval advisers believed such a canal was a strategic necessity that would enable the navy to move quickly to support either the Latin American policy or the Asian policy.

The Hay-Pauncefote Treaty (1901) marked the official withdrawal of British power from Latin America. For fifty years, Britain and the United States had had an agreement to share in the control of any canal that was built. In 1901, Britain granted the United State sole control. Unable to match the growth of the German navy without bringing some of its forces back from around the world, British leaders welcomed the United States as a potential ally against Germany.

With the British obstacle gone, Roosevelt became impatient with the financial demands made by Colombia for the right to build a canal across the Colombian province of Panama. When a revolutionary group declared the independence of Panama from Colombia, Roosevelt used the United States Navy to keep Colombia's armed forces from suppressing the revolution. He then gave almost instant recognition to the revolutionary government. In later years, he boasted that he had personally taken Panama because he had moved swiftly to approve a treaty with the revolutionaries that granted the United States a ten-mile-wide canal zone for perpetuity in return for $10 million and an annual rent of $250,000.

On May 1, 1898, a week after Congress declared war on Spain for the stated purpose of liberating Cuba from Spanish imperialism, American warships destroyed the Spanish fleet in the Philippines. As early as 1895, naval officers had planned such an attack. It was their thinking, guided by the theories of Captain Alfred T. Mahan, that the United States needed naval bases stretching across the Pacific in order to exploit the vast China market. Unlike Cuba, the Philippines were taken from Spain and made a part of an American empire. For the next three years, American troops were used to suppress attempts by the people of the Philippines to achieve independence from American rule. (Courtesy of Library of Congress.)

With this increase of American strategic commitments in Central America, Roosevelt declared a corollary to the Monroe Doctrine (1904). The United States, he announced, had the right to intervene in any Caribbean or Central American country to keep or to restore political and economic stability. The intention of this policy, he argued, was to avoid giving European powers an excuse for intervening in these countries.

The White Man's Burden and Progressivism

For many political leaders, especially Senator Albert Beveridge of Indiana, the overseas expansion related to the Spanish-American War was a rebirth of the Manifest Destiny that had swept Anglo-Saxon Protestants across the North American continent. Just as WASPs had brought the liberty of English representative institutions, capitalism, and Protestantism to the New World, it was then their destiny to spread Anglo-Saxon civilization to the entire world. Just as the progressives saw no conflict with democracy when they allowed the end of black voting in the South and reduced the political participation of new immigrants in the northern cities, they believed they were expanding democracy when they brought Hawaii, Puerto Rico, and the Philippines under colonial control. It seemed to them that they were preserving democracy when troops were sent to intervene in Cuba, Nicaragua, Santo Domingo, and Haiti. They believed that many people, because of their race or religion, were incapable of self-government and that WASPs had the responsibility of providing government for those who were incapable of self-government. Under this theory of paternalism, even the female half of the WASP population was barred from political participation. The male WASPs, who claimed that blacks and Latins and Slavs were too emotional, too unpredictable, too lacking in intelligence to be able to govern themselves, also claimed that biology made all women too emotional, too unpredictable, and too lacking in intelligence to be capable of self-government.

The Women's Suffrage Movement of the 1890s

The first middle-class women who opposed being limited to life in the home had become active in the abolitionist movement during the mid-nineteenth century. Gaining the right to vote would have been a major sign of being accepted in public life. They were bitterly disappointed when black men were given the right to vote with the Fifteenth Amendment in 1870 while women were still denied the vote.

From 1870 until 1890, women suffragists were divided into two major groups. The National Woman's Suffrage Association (NWSA), headed by Elizabeth Cady Stanton and Susan B. Anthony, saw the vote as only one part of changing the status of women in society. The other group, the American Woman's Suffrage Association (AWSA), headed by Lucy Stone and Julia Ward Howe, wanted to focus only on the vote. Women, they argued, could bring their unique virtues of the home, their gentleness and purity, into politics. The merger of two organizations in 1890 as the National American Women's Suffrage Association (NAWSA) was a victory for Lucy Stone's group. Elizabeth Cady Stanton had decided that there was no immediate chance to change radically the place of women in society and that victory on the vote should be won before women fought for other issues.

NAWSA concentrated on persuading legislatures to give women the right to vote in state elections. Women hoped that, when enough states had made such a change, they would find it easier to win a constitutional amendment and establish a national pattern. Victories were won in Colorado (1893) and in Utah and Idaho (1896). Wyoming had granted women the right to vote in 1869, when it was still a territory. One of the arguments made in these western states whose populations were basically WASP was that the vote of the wives of the established first generation of settlers would help overcome the votes of the next wave of settlers, who were challenging the establishment.

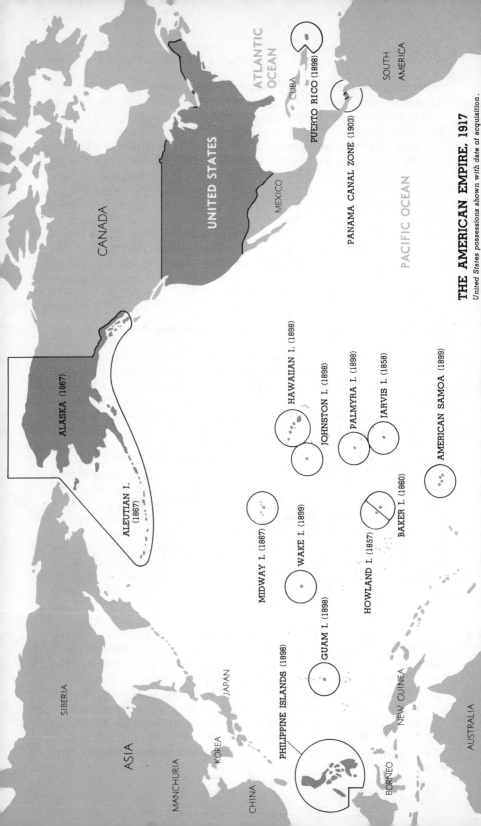

ATLANTIC OCEAN

SOUTH AMERICA

PUERTO RICO (1898)

CUBA

CANADA

UNITED STATES

MEXICO

PANAMA CANAL ZONE (1903)

PACIFIC OCEAN

THE AMERICAN EMPIRE, 1917

United States possessions shown with date of acquisition.

ALASKA (1867)

ALEUTIAN I. (1867)

HAWAIIAN I. (1898)

JOHNSTON I. (1898)

PALMYRA I. (1898)

JARVIS I. (1858)

AMERICAN SAMOA (1899)

MIDWAY I. (1867)

WAKE I. (1899)

HOWLAND I. (1857)

BAKER I. (1860)

GUAM I. (1898)

PHILIPPINE ISLANDS (1898)

SIBERIA

JAPAN

KOREA

MANCHURIA

CHINA

ASIA

NEW GUINEA

BORNEO

AUSTRALIA

In the eastern states, a number of women leaders in the 1890s abandoned their earlier argument that women were being kept from universal
rights that applied to all people. They began to argue that blacks and Slavic
and Latin Europeans who were coming into the cities in large numbers
should be kept from voting because they were biologically inferior. To
counter the argument of WASP men that all women were biologically inferior and, therefore, should not vote, many Anglo-American women began
to claim that they shared the biological superiority of the Anglo-Saxon
race. They argued that, if Anglo-Saxons were divided as males and
females, they could be conquered by inferior races but, if they were united,
they could continue to lead the United States.

Women Radicals during the 1890s

Not all women leaders joined the WASP reaction of the 1890s. One of
the most powerful radicals was Charlotte Perkins Gilman. In *Women and
Economics* (1898), she argued that the vote for women would be meaningless as long as they were economically dependent on men. Only by leaving
the home and entering the work force could women become independent.
To free women from the home necessitated the socialization of child rearing. Children should be reared, she argued, in collective nurseries. Equally
radical in a different way was Kate Chopin's novel *The Awakening* (1899),
which attacked the double standard in sexual relationships. The heroine of
the novel, Edna Pontellier, was a respectable middle-class mother who had
become frustrated because her sexual needs were not satisfied by her husband. Finally, she left him and her children for a lover. Chopin realistically
saw that there could be no social acceptance of a liberated woman in 1899
and had her heroine commit suicide by walking into the sea after meeting
overwhelming hostility after her act of independence. Kate Chopin herself
found nothing but social and literary rejection for having written such a
daring book. Less scandalous but just as frightening to males was the sentiment expressed by the popular writer Mary Freeman. Her story "A New
England Nun" (1891) suggested that middle-class Protestant women could
find fulfillment by rejecting marriage and choosing a celibate life.

These stories expressed the reality of choices made by many college-
educated WASP women. The new colleges for women, such as Vassar
(1865), Smith (1875), Wellesley (1875), and Bryn Mawr (1885), expected
their students to become cultured housewives. But a significant minority
of the women chose instead to become lawyers, doctors, professors, ministers, and writers. Others in the 1880s and 1890s pioneered the development of social work in settlement houses. Most of these women did not
marry. A small number did establish themselves in the professions and
served other women as lawyers and doctors and as teachers in the colleges for women. But, between 1900 and 1970, there was no significant
increase in the number of women in the professions. And fewer college
women chose an unmarried life after 1900.

But male Anglo-Americans by 1900 had failed to keep their women in the position they had held in 1870, when marriage and motherhood without the possibility of divorce or any significant social, economic, or political life outside the home seemed to be the only role for respectable females. And the signs in 1900 pointed to even more dramatic changes in the lifestyles of women in the future.

Supplementary Reading

Ethnic and regional influences in politics are discussed in R. Jensen, *The Winning of the Midwest* (1971), and P. Kleppner, *The Cross of Culture* (1970). Populism is analyzed in N. Pollack, *The Populist Response to Industrial America* (1962); J. Youngdale, *Populism: A Psychohistorical Perspective* (1975); and L. Goodwyn, *Democratic Promise: The Populist Movement in America* (1976). The union of populism with the Democratic party is described by R. Durden, *The Climax of Populism: The Election of 1896* (1965).

C. Woodward, *The Strange Career of Jim Crow* (1954), was the first book on the role of racism in the crisis of the 1890s. J. Kousser, *The Shaping of Southern Politics: Suffrage Restriction and the Establishment of the One Party South, 1880-1920* (1974), demonstrates the role of wealthy whites in creating the crusade against blacks.

A. Weinberg, *Manifest Destiny* (1935), H. and M. Sprout, *The Rise of American Naval Power* (1939), and D. Healy, *U.S. Expansionism: The Imperialist Urge in the 1890s* (1970), describe the new foreign policy of the 1890s; R. Beisner, *Twelve against Empire: the Anti-Imperialists* (1968), discusses the critics of that policy.

The confusion of the different cultures in the city is the subject of H. Chudacoff, *The Evolution of American Urban Society* (1975); S. Thernstrom, *The Other Bostonians* (1973); M. Rischin, *The Promised City: New York's Jews, 1870-1914* (1970); and P. Messbarger, *Fiction with a Parochial Purpose: Social Use of American Catholic Literature, 1884-1900* (1970).

J. Kett, *Rites of Passage* (1977), analyzes the new adolescence. B. Bledstein, *The Culture of Professionalism* (1976), and T. Haskell, *The Emergence of Professional Social Science* (1977), outline the new universities. A. Kraditor, *The Ideas of the Woman Suffrage Movement: 1890-1920* (1965), demonstrates the tendency toward racism among middle-class women during the 1890s.

The growth of a middle-class reform movement is the subject of R. Bremner, *From the Depths: The Discovery of Poverty in the United States* (1965), and A. Davis, *Spearheads for Reform: The Social Settlements and the Progressive Movement* (1967). Useful collections of essays on urban reform are B. Brownell and W. Stickle, editors, *Bosses and Reformers: Urban Politics in America, 1880-1920* (1973), and B. Stave, editor, *Urban Bosses, Machines, and Progressive Reforms* (1972). D. Thelen describes the development of progressivism in Wisconsin in *The New Citizenship: Origins of Progressivism in Wisconsin, 1885-1900* (1972) and *Robert LaFollette* (1976).

The Attempt to Create a National Progressivism
1901-1916

Progressivism began in the cities of the 1890s with strong mayors. It had spread to the states with strong governors. Then, in 1901, Theodore Roosevelt had the opportunity to create a national progressive movement around a strong presidency.

The professionals of the new urban middle class distrusted city councils, state legislatures, and the national Congress because they believed elected representatives were concerned only with local and special interests. They distrusted courts because most judges seemed committed to the older, small-scale capitalism and did not seem to understand the legal needs of large-scale national corporations. Only the mayor and trained experts in the civil service could represent a whole city. Only the governor and his appointed experts could represent a whole state. But only a president and his experts could represent the whole nation.

Theodore Roosevelt and the Strong Presidency

The new urban middle class tended to distrust the idea of constitutional checks and balances. Planning and efficiency could be disrupted by a disorganized legislature that was unable to reach a consensus and pass

By 1913 Henry Ford had established an effective assembly line that greatly speeded the production of cars and lowered their cost. Ford was able to recruit workers who endured the pressure and monotony of this repetitive work by paying wages somewhat higher than average. But recruitment was aided by the need for jobs on the part of people being driven off the farm by the mechanization of agriculture. (Courtesy of the Ford Archives, Dearborn, Michigan.)

needed legislation. Courts, by ruling legislation unconstitutional, also could disrupt the establishment of an effective policy. Efficient government was to be like the management of the new large corporations. Stockholders voted to accept or reject corporate policy that was made by company managers. Within the corporation, the policies of these executives were not frustrated by a slow-moving and disorganized legislature. Nor was there a court to veto policy. As president, therefore, Theodore Roosevelt wanted to be in the position of defining the national interest with the help of nonelected experts.

Roosevelt and the Large Corporations

Roosevelt, unlike LaFollette, accepted the national corporations as the necessary foundation of the national economy. LaFollette and many other state leaders of progressivism wanted an economy of regional and small-scale corporations and businesses that could be regulated by state commissions. The state progressives were frightened by the explosive growth of the large national corporations. Between 1896 and 1904, the 300 largest corporations gained control of 40 percent of all manufacturing in the United States. Unhappy with the economic disorganization and cut-throat competition that marked the depression years of 1893-1897, the powerful New York banker J. P. Morgan and other bankers controlled by the huge Rockefeller fortune decided to merge steel companies, railroads, and other important businesses into huge corporations. In 1901, Morgan bought Andrew Carnegie's steel company and merged it with others to form United States Steel, the first billion-dollar corporation. The new corporation had 213 manufacturing plants, its own railroads, ore boats, and coal and iron mines. It employed an army of 170,000 people. Executives from the Morgan and Rockefeller banks became directors of 112 of the largest corporations in the country, making it possible for an interlocked group of a few men to control financial interests valued at $22 billion and play a vital role in the nation's economic development. The creation of United States Steel was part of a major movement toward the merger of several smaller companies into a single large conglomerate. The number of mergers had jumped from 26 in 1896, to 69 in 1897, to 303 in 1898, and to 1,208 in 1899. After that time, the trend slowed, dropping back to 340 in 1900 and 423 in 1901.

Roosevelt believed that even the leaders of the largest corporations were limited in their understanding of national problems by the special interests of their own companies. They had to learn to depend on the president and the government experts to oversee the entire national economy. In 1902, Roosevelt initiated a successful antitrust suit against the Northern Securities Company. Morgan and Rockefeller had combined the major railroads of the Northwest without consulting Roosevelt or considering the impact of their actions on public opinion. The preservation of corporate capitalism depended, for Roosevelt, on persuading average voters that the corporations did not threaten their independence through their ability to dominate and manipulate the marketplace. Roosevelt took this opportunity to enforce the Sherman Anti-Trust Act for the first time to show the public that the national government was more powerful than the corporations. Such vigorous action against the most powerful corporate leaders would teach, Roosevelt hoped, other corporations to act in a "responsible" manner, to consider the public interest, and to respect the power of the national government. Through his antitrust policy, therefore, Roosevelt was not trying to destroy or even limit the size of large corporations. He was teaching them to be sensitive to the public interest, as well as to public opinion, and to rely on guidance from the president.

Many young men of the Anglo-American upper and upper-middle class who came of age in the 1880s and 1890s felt that their fathers had not faced the problems of the cities, factories, and immigration. They developed a philosophy of vigorous leadership focused on strengthening the power of the president to solve these problems. President Theodore Roosevelt (1858-1919) was immensely popular because of the energetic style he gave to the presidency. (Courtesy of Library of Congress.)

Roosevelt and the Power of the Presidency

Roosevelt was a very popular president. He had a magnetic, charismatic personality. He knew how to use the newspapers to present his image to the public. His image was not that of an upper-middle-class easterner, a Harvard graduate, and a writer of books. Instead, Roosevelt continued to emphasize the image he acquired during the Spanish-American War. He was a westerner, a cowboy, an athlete, and a man of action. He defended the violence of football. He demonstrated that the solitary and self-reliant frontiersman could survive in the corporate, urban-industrial world. Farmers and state progressives could vote for him because they saw his trust-busting as an attempt to restore the nineteenth-century marketplace of the small producer.

Adolescence and the Masculinity Crisis

Roosevelt was honest in his commitment to the Wild West. He believed that the future expansion of urban and corporate America depended on the preservation of the fighting spirit that had conquered the western frontier. He approved of his eastern friend Owen Wister, who wrote the first major cowboy novel, *The Virginian* (1902). Wister's hero was an eastern civilian who was also a warrior in the West.

In England and Germany, as well as in the United States, the upper-middle classes were creating the concept of adolescence. Instead of young men entering into adult sexual relationships and adult jobs at an early age, as they had for centuries, it was argued that childhood extended to age eighteen or later. Between the ages of about twelve and eighteen, boys, it was argued, were naturally violent and warlike. What was necessary then was for society to discipline and channel their primitive instincts.

One of these disciplines — the Boy Scouts — was developed in England. Similar organizations were developed in Germany, and the Boy Scouts were borrowed directly by the United States. Boys in uniforms learned to follow orders and give their allegiance to the nation. In England, Edgar Rice Burroughs created another hero, Tarzan, to teach militant manliness to boys and the solution of problems through simple acts of violence.

Public education through adolescence was made compulsory in the United States as in western Europe. Academic achievement was not as important as teaching young people to be able to stay in one place for an entire day as they would as adults in their office and factory jobs. School administrators consciously borrowed from efficiency experts such as Frederick J. Taylor, who pioneered time and motion studies in factories to find ways of getting workers to produce more during each hour of work. One of the new techniques of professional school administrators was having a class march under almost military discipline at the end of an hour's study to the next classroom. Great emphasis was placed on a class leaving one room in an orderly and silent fashion and getting seated in another room with a minimum of noise and confusion. The importance of getting to school on time was stressed as preparation for later work. The students were taught the importance of grades. The work world of the corporation had many levels from the top to the bottom. The school taught this sense of hierarchy by teaching students to see themselves as divided into those who were most successful in winning high grades and those who failed and stayed at the bottom. Schools consistently placed about 40 percent of the students at the bottom. This was a figure close to the half of the national population that was living in poverty in 1900. Spreading from the private to the public schools was also a great emphasis on organized and uniformed sports. Young males were taught that the greatest school heroes were the best athletes.

The world of work was presented to young men as a world of war, where they must fight for survival. They were taught that they must not masturbate because they needed to save their energy for becoming economic successes. Dr. J. H. Kellogg, founder of the Kellogg breakfast cereal company, for instance, wrote a book, *Natural History and Hygiene* (1900), that told worried parents how to identify the thirty-nine telltale signs that indicated whether or not their sons were masturbating. One of the reasons that women were defined as free from sexual desire was that passionless wives would not drain their husbands of their energy. Many of the male WASPs, like Theodore Roosevelt, were very upset by the rising divorce rate and the increasing number of middle-class women seeking careers outside the home. Women were defined as gentle and passive. Men were defined as violent and aggressive in public life. If women left home and became stronger, men would become weaker.

These fears were expressed by two important novelists, Frank Norris and Theodore Dreiser. In his novels *Vandover and the Brute* (1895) and *McTeague* (1899), Norris described men who were destroyed by the aggressive sexuality of women. Theodore Dreiser had great difficulty in finding a publisher for his novel *Sister Carrie* (1900), because it challenged the stereotype of the weak woman. In his autobiographical novel *The Genius* (1912), Dreiser directly expressed his fear of the sexual power women had over men.

The Purity Crusade

By defining adolescence as a period of late childhood rather than early adulthood and by using compulsory education to force a dependent status upon children, middle-class reformers created a new type of crime, juvenile delinquency. To avoid compulsory education, to become a worker, and to engage in adult sex had become criminal. Most of the middle-class women who were leaving the home to go into public life saw themselves as bringing the purity and the sexlessness of the home into the corrupt world of men, where there was far too much sex. They were eager, therefore, to help control juvenile delinquency and to help the young people in reform schools. The many WASP women who were interested in social reform were using the ideal of the home, however, to challenge the WASP masculine ideal of extreme competition in the marketplace. Much of the motivation of these middle-class women, therefore, was not to prolong adolescence in order to create manlier men but to soften the market-place ideology of the survival of the fittest. It was the hope of many of these women reformers that young people would not be put in jails, where they would be corrupted by hardened criminals.

Women reformers tried to end prostitution, which they saw as an institution that made the double standard for middle-class men and women possible. Women also were active in making abortion illegal. Until state laws were instituted during the late nineteenth century, most states had accepted abortion during the first part of pregnancy. The major part of the women's purity crusade was against alcohol through the Women's Christian Temperance Union (WCTU), headed by Frances Willard. Also, there was rising pressure to stop the across-the-counter sales of opium and cocaine. By World War I, laws had been passed that banned the sale of such drugs except by a doctor's prescription. And the Mann Act (1910) made it illegal to transport a woman across state lines for the purpose of prostitution.

Middle-Class and Lower-Class Women

By 1900, northern Protestantism had been influenced by a social gospel movement that came in part from Germany and England. The movement argued that life in the city and in the factory was making it impossible for poor people to achieve decent lives. Overcrowded and dirty tenements encouraged sexual immorality. Poverty destroyed a sense of responsibility. Working children and women undermined the stability of the family. Unsafe working conditions crippled fathers and forced families into poverty. The churches, according to theologians such as the Baptist Walter Rauschenbusch, must work to end these evil conditions. But, while the theologians of the social gospel were males, most of the social welfare activities of the churches were carried out by women. Some of the middle-class women who were choosing to remain unmarried and who wanted to lead a life of social service began settlement houses in the major cities. In the most famous of them, Hull House in Chicago, Jane Addams and other WASP women worked to provide some order for new immigrants in the slums. Well-to-do women of German-Jewish background, such as Lillian Wald, also began settlement houses. An example was the Henry Street Settlement House, which served poor Russian Jews in New York City.

Jane Addams (1860-1935), often called "Saint Jane," was one of the strongest leaders of the group of young Anglo-American women who rejected their traditional roles as housewives and became active in urban reform during the Progressive Era. They established settlement houses in the slums of the new immigrants and tried to strengthen the families of the poor by teaching homemaking skills and alternative social activities to those of the saloon and the street. (The Granger Collection.)

The settlement house reformers worked for health and housing laws in the cities and for the passage of state laws limiting child and woman labor. They also pushed for minimum-wage laws for women and workmen's compensation. By 1914, more than thirty states had passed such legislation. Other middle-class women, such as Florence Kelley, also worked through the Consumer's League and the National Women's Trade Union League to encourage the economic and political activism of lower-class women.

Most immigrant women worked in factories or as maids until they married. After marriage, they often did piecework for wages in their homes. In the South, most black women, before and after marriage, worked in the fields or as domestic help. Many lower-income white women were employed in the cotton mills of the South. Of all these women, Jewish workers were most successful in unionizing. Jews, much more than Italians and Poles, had had industrial experience in Europe. Well-acquainted with unionism and socialist criticism of capitalism, Jewish leaders and workers kept in touch through newspapers published in Yiddish. New York's Jewish *Daily Forward,* edited by Abraham Cahan, helped create the community solidarity that made possible the unionization of the many Jewish women in the garment industry. The International Ladies' Garment Worker's Union (ILGWU) was one of the few successful unionizations of women until the 1940s.

The National Civic Federation and the American Federation of Labor

At the end of the 1880s when the Knights of Labor collapsed, unions of skilled workers began to form the American Federation of Labor (AFL). Leaders such as Samuel Gompers of the Cigar Maker's Union and leaders of other trade unions had decided that there was no hope of stopping the growth of the large corporations. They believed that it was inevitable that there would be a class of workers who labored in factories owned by capitalists. The only thing these workers could hope for was to use the pressure of their unions and the threat of strikes to win higher wages, shorter hours, and better working conditions. They also believed that only skilled workers had the economic power and the unity necessary for this kind of collective bargaining. The AFL did not try to unionize unskilled workers.

In 1896, about 200,000 workers were members of AFL unions. By 1904, there were 2 million. But there would be no further growth until 1917. The restoration of prosperity and the rise of employment helped the growth of the unions after 1896. AFL unions also benefited from the support of some of the corporate leaders. Mark Hanna, a millionaire from Ohio who was President McKinley's chief adviser, believed that a safe labor movement was better than a radical one. Hanna disagreed with those industrialists, like the members of the National Association of Manufacturers (NAM) who wanted to destroy all unions. Hanna argued that such a hostile policy would encourage the development of a socialist movement. Therefore, he helped form the National Civic Federation, which was to express the cooperation of capitalists and unions, and he invited Samuel Gompers to become an officer of the federation.

Theodore Roosevelt strongly agreed with Hanna about the need for a conservative labor movement. He decided to use the power of the presidency to persuade business leaders that there was such a need when there was a major coal strike in 1902. Roosevelt was angry at the mine owners who refused to recognize the union, and he warned them that he would seize the mines if they continued to refuse to negotiate with the workers. Roosevelt's pressure helped to place a representative of the United Mine Worker's Union on the board of conciliation established to keep peace in the coal industry. Once more, Roosevelt was trying to teach corporate leaders that labor must be brought within the establishment. Successful in this case, Roosevelt failed, however, to increase the number of business people who would accept the AFL unions after 1904. State courts and the Supreme Court, especially, used their powers against union activities. They strongly enforced the Sherman Anti-Trust Act against union boycotts.

The Socialist Party

After the chaos of the depression of 1893 and the collapse of the Knights of Labor, many workers did not accept the conservative approach of the AFL. Eugene Debs, who had gone to prison after the Pullman strike (1894), was converted to socialism there. But he agreed with Samuel Gompers that there was no hope in the efforts of the Knights of Labor to create cooperatives as alternatives to the corporations. Socialist theory said that it was inevitable that capitalism would move from a large number of small capitalists to a concentration of ownership and control by large corporations. Debs became the leader of the Socialist party, which grew rapidly between 1900 and 1914. The Socialists believed that they could become the majority party. When they took legal control of the nation's government without violent revolution, they could take over an economy that already had been collectivized by the large corporations.

The Socialists gained supporters from all regions, from all ethnic groups, and from all classes. There was strong Socialist support among the Jewish workers and intellectuals in New York, as there was among German writers and intellectuals in Milwaukee. WASP farmers in former Populist areas of the South and West became Socialists in great numbers. The largest Socialist newspaper was published in Kansas, and, in Oklahoma, Socialists made up a greater proportion of the voters than in any other state. Some Protestant ministers who converted to the social gospel became Socialists, and Socialist groups were formed at many colleges. By the time of the presidential election of 1912, when Debs won almost a million votes, there were Socialist mayors in a number of towns and cities.

The IWW

The Socialist party, like the AFL, made little effort to help the unskilled workers who provided most of the labor for the major industries. New immigrants from Europe made up at least half of the work force in the coal, copper, and iron mines, in meat and leather processing, in rubber and steel production, and in textiles and breweries and three-fourths of the work force in the clothing industries. The AFL believed that these workers could not be organized because of their many ethnic divisions. Many Socialist leaders agreed but promised help in the future, when they won electoral control of the government.

Eugene Debs (1855-1926) was the major leader of socialism in America from 1900 to 1920. A native of Indiana, he kept his home in Terre Haute although much of his time was spent traveling across the country giving speeches as he tried to convert Americans to socialism. Debs hated the capitalist system for teaching people to fight each other. He was dismayed that most churches accepted the capitalist system of self-interest, and he saw socialism as offering an alternative spiritual as well as an economic philosophy of brotherhood. (UPI.)

Groups of radical miners, lumberjacks, and agricultural workers from the West challenged these AFL and Socialist policies. The Western Federation of Miners, under the leadership of Big Bill Haywood, sought the support of other western workers in forming the Industrial Workers of the World (IWW). Unlike the AFL, the IWW tried to organize unskilled workers. Unlike the Socialist party, it hoped for an immediate overthrow of corporate capitalism through a series of massive strikes that would mobilize the majority of working Americans.

In Lawrence, Massachusetts, in 1912, the IWW proved that unskilled workers divided into many ethnic groups could be organized. Of the city's 84,000 people, 74,000 were foreign born. The majority of the Italians, Jews, Greeks, French-Canadians, Poles, and Lithuanians worked in the woolen mills. There was a small AFL union of skilled WASP, German, and Irish workers. Enduring a sixty-hour week for low wages, many unskilled workers spontaneously walked off the job when the machines were speeded up and their wages were lowered. IWW leaders came to the city and organized the rebels into an effective strike, which withstood violence from the police and the state militia. When the strikers won their wage and hour demands from the mill owners, however, they had won only a short-term victory. They did not have the support of a national union organization like the AFL, and the IWW had no strategy for long-term industrial unionization. Quickly the union fell apart. Unskilled workers from ethnic minorities would have to wait for the appearance of the CIO (1935 and 1936) to make their unionization permanent.

Roosevelt and the Progressive Party of 1912

In 1912, Theodore Roosevelt left the Republican party to become the leader of the newly formed Progressive party. Roosevelt believed that he had failed to educate the nation's leaders during his presidency from 1901 to 1908. Roosevelt believed that under his succcessor, William Howard Taft, the Republican party had gone back to letting business people act in a completely selfish manner. Republicans had not acted in the supportive manner toward labor that Roosevelt had wanted, and, therefore, socialism was growing. During his presidency, Roosevelt had begun to worry about the health of rural America and so had established a commission to study country life. A few years later, discontented farmers in the Midwest were strengthening the Democratic party, which defeated many Republican congressmen in the elections of 1910. Roosevelt felt that it would be disastrous for the Democrats to regain control of the nation. He believed that they would either move toward socialism or would try to return to the small-scale capitalism of the nineteenth century.

Roosevelt wanted a responsible corporate capitalism with leadership from government experts. He had worked for the Elkins Act (1903) and the Hepburn Act (1906), which gave the ICC more power to regulate the railroads. Most railroad leaders approved of this legislation, which limited cutthroat competition. Roosevelt also persuaded Congress to establish a Bureau of Corporations to oversee the policies of the major corporations. He backed the passage of a Pure Food and Drug Act (1906) and a Meat Inspection Act (1906). The growing consumer movement praised Roosevelt's leadership in these areas, but so did the large drug and meat corporations because the legislation made it more difficult for small companies to meet government standards. As a result of the legislation, the large companies gained greater control over the production and distribution of drugs and meats. The new legislation also helped the large corporations expand their overseas markets because government standards made it possible for the companies to meet the production standards demanded by many foreign countries. Large companies also approved of Roosevelt's conservation policies, while small companies objected. Roosevelt increased national forest reserves from 50 million to 200 million acres and created a Forest Service, which was headed by Gifford Pinchot. Pinchot, like Roosevelt and Owen Wister, was an upper-middle-class easterner who wanted the nation's resources used in a rational and efficient way. The interests of Pinchot's civil service coincided with the need of large corporations for long-range planning. The policy of sustained yield was opposed by small lumbermen and ranchers, who were concerned with immediate profits.

Taft as President

Although Roosevelt had chosen Taft as his successor, the new president had not believed in Roosevelt's effort to create a responsible corporate capitalism. Taft's antitrust policy harassed large corporations without Roosevelt's attempt to educate them. He also supported a higher tariff, which angered progressive Republicans who supported the consumers' movement. Inflation had become serious after 1900, and the new tariff made it worse. It also angered farmers in the Midwest, who then turned toward the Democrats. Taft also backed Secretary of the Interior Richard Ballinger in a conflict with Gifford Pinchot. Ballinger wanted natural resources exploited quickly, without concern for the future, and like Taft, wanted the control of natural resources decentralized. Many Roosevelt progressives, like Pinchot, thought that such a policy was not designed to achieve decentralization but rather would lead to ruthless exploitation.

Roosevelt and the New Nationalism

In 1909, Roosevelt had gone to challenge the jungles of South America and Africa in order to preserve his vitality in case the nation needed him again. In 1912, he decided to challenge Taft. Roosevelt won the Republican primaries, but the politicians who controlled the convention renominated Taft. Outraged, Roosevelt was easily persuaded to lead the new Progressive party (nicknamed the Bull Moose party), which expressed his political position. Roosevelt favored two new amendments to the Constitution that would make an income tax possible and would have United States senators elected by popular vote, rather than by state legislatures. He also wanted an inheritance tax. All these laws would help make corporations more responsible, as would a national commission to regulate corporate activities. He favored the vote for women and the initiative, referendum, and recall. He favored the eight-hour workday for labor, the end of child labor, and minimum wages for women. He wanted limitations on the courts that would make it difficult for them to declare laws unconstitutional. All of this New Nationalism, which would overcome constitutional checks and balances, was to be guided by a strong president and an efficient civil service.

Roosevelt's major contributors and advisers were corporate executives such as George Perkins of United States Steel. Roosevelt also won strong support from the professionals of the new middle class, from consumers' groups, and from women leaders such as Jane Addams. Taking many progressives out of the Republican party, Roosevelt won 4.2 million votes to Taft's 3.5 million. Debs, the Socialist, won 900,000. But, with the Republican majority split, it was the Democratic candidate Woodrow Wilson who gained the presidency with 6.3 million votes. Taking advantage of the disintegration of the Republican party, the Democrats also captured the majority in the Senate and the House of Representatives.

Woodrow Wilson and the New Freedom

Until 1912, the Democratic party had not been very attractive to the new middle-class professionals except in the South. It was the party of rural radicalism, corrupt city bosses, and eastern millionaires who wanted to preserve nineteenth-century competitive capitalism. But Woodrow Wilson was able to win many progressives over to the Democrats.

Wilson called his program the New Freedom, in contrast to Roosevelt's New Nationalism. Wilson's speeches often sounded as though he wanted to go back to the nineteenth century. Speaking to the farmers and small business people who constituted most of the party's supporters, Wilson pledged to work for the small capitalist and to restore the free marketplace.

The first major piece of legislation passed in Wilson's administration was the Underwood-Simmons Tariff, which lowered tariffs for the first time since the Civil War. For farmers, small business people, and consumers' groups, Wilson's New Freedom seemed to be a reality. Congress also passed income tax legislation after the Sixteenth Amendment to the Constitution was ratified in 1913. Congressional acceptance of the Clayton Anti-Trust Act (1914) seemed further evidence that the large corporations had lost control. So did the Seventeenth Amendment, which allowed the people to elect senators (1913).

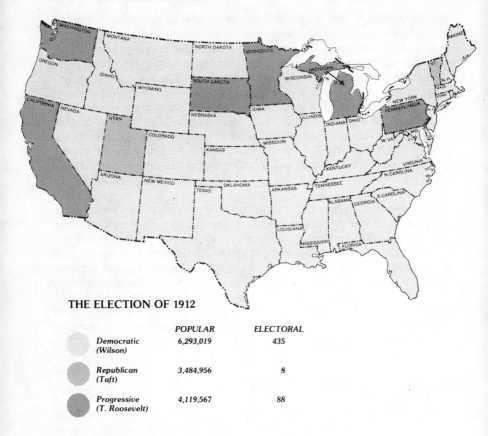

THE ELECTION OF 1912

		POPULAR	ELECTORAL
Democratic (Wilson)		6,293,019	435
Republican (Taft)		3,484,956	8
Progressive (T. Roosevelt)		4,119,567	88

Wilson, the New Nationalism, and the South

By the 1912 campaign, Wilson had come to share a large part of Roosevelt's belief that the growth of large corporations was inevitable. Although his New Freedom speeches during the campaign implied a return to the small-scale capitalism of the mid-nineteenth century, Wilson took the presidency in 1913 certain that the large corporations had to be regulated, not destroyed. He supported legislation to create a Federal Trade Commission (FTC). This commission, which Roosevelt had called for in 1912, was to have the power to regulate coporate activities. Wilson appointed business leaders to be the commissioners of the FTC. They immediately helped large corporations in areas such as steel and rubber to form trade associations. The trade associations made it possible for pricing agreements to be worked out by the three or four major companies that dominated production in many economic areas. These companies could thereby escape the instability of price competition. The great burst of progressive legislation in Wilson's administration, compared to the small amount while Roosevelt was president, was made possible by Wilson's ability to bring the Democratic party, especially in the South, to support the kinds of laws that the Republican Roosevelt had wanted.

The Federal Reserve System was the greatest achievement of this fusion of northern Republican progressives and southern Democratic progressives under Wilson's leadership. From the end of the Civil War on, southern and western farmers and small business people had been critical of the way in which New York banks controlled the nation's currency and interest rates. They wanted the national government to assume this power. The legislation that established the Federal Reserve System (1913) also created a Federal Reserve Board, to be appointed by the president, that could control the amount of currency in circulation and regulate interest rates. The Federal Reserve Board accomplished these tasks through twelve Federal Reserve Banks located throughout the country.

Once again, however, while farmers and small business people were pleased, so were the large banks. The privately owned national banks in each region owned the Federal Reserve Bank located there. And the president appointed men from the capitalist banking community to the Federal Reserve Board. Indeed, the large banks wanted such a system to provide stability. There had been a great deal of instability in banking between 1900 and 1914, and the smaller state banks were prospering more than the larger national banks. After 1914, the state banks lost their competitive edge, and the national banks began to gain more control.

Although Wilson, like Roosevelt, accepted large corporations in 1913, he did not agree at that time with Roosevelt that the specific economic interests of agriculture and labor should be given government support in order to make them healthy parts of a corporate economy. After many Democratic congressmen were defeated by Republicans in the 1914 elections, however, Wilson changed his mind and was ready to support legislation specifically helpful to labor and agriculture.

The Adamson Act (1916), which established an eight-hour workday for railroad workers, was seen as a model for private employers to imitate. The situation with farmers paralleled that of workers. After the collapse of populism, many farmers had accepted the corporate system and formed organizations that worked for narrow economic gains, much as the AFL did for labor. The Wilson administration responded to these pressure groups by creating a system of Federal Farm Loan Banks that made credit easier. A Federal Highway Act (1916), which committed the national government to the funding of roads throughout the country, was passed. Farm groups felt that the roads would help them get their crops to market as the rapid development of trucks began to provide an alternative to shipping by railroads. Congress also passed the Smith-Lever Act (1914), which sent federal funds to the states to help support agricultural education. By 1916, the national government had become a significant force in the economic marketplace because of pressures from a variety of capitalist groups, ranging from small farmers to large corporations.

Wilson, Blacks, and Northern Segregation

When Wilson became president, he had toilets segregated in federal office buildings so that white women would not have to use the same facilities as black women. Lunchrooms were also segregated, so whites would not have to eat with blacks. This segregation was not the result solely of Wilson's southern background, the many southerners in his cabinet, or the fact that southern Democrats had become the leaders of Congress. White northerners not only had accepted the crusade against blacks when it developed during the 1890s, they had participated in it. Many restaurants, bars, hotels, and theaters in northern cities had excluded blacks after 1900. Black grocers, caterers, carpenters, barbers, and other small business people, who had had white customers during the 1890s, found that whites refused to patronize them after the turn of the century.

By 1900, the expanding black population in the South could no longer find agricultural opportunities in that region. The slowly growing number of industrial jobs were monopolized by whites, and there were too few cities in the South to absorb the increased population. A small but steady stream of southern blacks, therefore, had begun to move north by 1900. The black population increased by 50 percent between 1900 and 1910 in New York City and by 30 percent in Philadelphia and Chicago.

The Urban Ghetto

Blacks, mostly poor, had lived scattered among the white poor of northern and southern cities before the end of the century. Then, between 1900 and 1916, there were social and legal efforts to separate black neighborhoods from white. As southern blacks came into northern cities, they found that they had to live within the existing limits of the black neighborhoods. The black ghettos contained denser populations than other areas of the cities. This pressure forced rents to go higher. With no choice as to where they could shop, blacks also paid more for other commodities.

The white ethnic minorities whose low incomes kept them from moving out of the central cities into the WASP suburbs desperately tried to keep blacks out of their neighborhoods. Largely limited to blue-collar jobs since the WASPs kept the white-collar jobs, the ethnic minorities also tried to exclude blacks from their trades and unions. Most AFL unions refused black apprentices. Irish-Catholic bosses accepted the fact that they would have to share city jobs and patronage with leaders from Italian and Polish and Jewish neighborhoods, but they refused to share power with black neighborhoods. While many of the white ethnic groups had only slow economic mobility from 1900 to 1940, rural blacks in the South and urban blacks in the North had almost no economic mobility during those decades.

Black Leaders and Accommodation in the South

Most black leaders during the progressive era pointed to the exceptional blacks who had been economically successful to argue that there was a frontier of opportunity open to all blacks. By 1910, there were 220,000 black land-owning farmers in the South. A major magazine of the black middle class in the South, the *Southern Workman,* pointed to these figures as evidence of a hopeful future. But this was the high point of black ownership. By the end of the 1920s, the number of farms owned by blacks had declined to 180,000. (It has continued to decline to the present.) The emphasis on the success of the landowners obscured the fact that 80 percent of blacks were sharecroppers in 1910. Many of the sharecroppers were held in peonage and were denied their legal right of geographic mobility. Labor contracts, enforced by local sheriffs, pledged blacks to work for whites for a set period of time. Often going in debt during the year, they were forced to renew the contracts.

Black Leaders and Accommodation in the North

In the northern cities, the mass of the poor blacks, male and female, left the ghettos in the morning to work as servants or unskilled laborers for whites and returned at night to black leaders whose economic existence depended on the workers' small earnings. The small black middle class, including doctors, lawyers, real estate brokers, and business people, accepted the status quo because the ghettos protected them from competition from powerful whites. This attitude also was typical of black insurance brokers, bankers, morticians, and managers of cemeteries.

The black leaders and the many fraternal organizations, such as the Odd Fellows, that developed in the black communities, gave blacks a sense of pride. But they did nothing to challenge the white system that excluded and exploited the blacks. In this way, the black communities were like those of the white ethnic minorities. The same kinds of organizations gave meaning to the ethnic neighborhoods. And much of the black life focused on Baptist and Methodist churches, as ethnic life focused on the Catholic church and the Jewish temple. Most black preachers, like most Catholic priests and Jewish rabbis, preached acceptance and accommodation to the dominant WASPs.

Black Radicals

Between 1900 and 1906, ordinary black people had engaged in boycotts in twenty-five southern cities to protest the segregation of streetcars. But, without militant black leadership and without the support of the

Born into slavery in Virginia, Booker T. Washington (1856-1915) took advantage of the freedom of blacks to gain an education after emancipation in 1865. Working his way through college, he provided the leadership to establish Tuskegee Institute in Alabama. He emerged as a national leader of the black community in the 1890s as he struggled to save the Negro educational system in the South during the years when blacks were losing the right to vote and the system of Jim Crow segregation was being solidified. (Courtesy of Library of Congress.)

national government, they had no hope of success. President Roosevelt had appointed a few blacks to minor federal government positions in the South, and he had invited Booker T. Washington to dinner at the White House, but he did not take a strong stand in opposition to violence against blacks in the southern states. Instead, he reacted with blind rage in upholding the caste system, which denied blacks the right to use violence against whites. He dismissed without honor three entire companies of a black regiment in Brownsville, Texas — including six winners of the Medal of Honor — without a hearing because a few of their number had purportedly shot up the town and killed one white citizen. After 1909, Taft wanted to drive the few remaining blacks out of the Republican parties in the southern states and to make those parties "lily-white."

Dissatisfaction with Booker T. Washington's philosophy of accommodation appeared in 1905 when a group of young black militants met at Niagara Falls, Canada, to begin a new abolitionist movement. The Niagara Movement, which met again in 1906 and 1907 in Boston under the leadership of men such as Monroe Trotter (editor of the black newspaper, the *Boston Guardian*), called upon black and white liberals to work together to abolish Jim Crow segregation as they had worked together to abolish slavery. A few white Socialists and progressives were interested in beginning such a reform movement. In 1909, William English Walling, Lillian Wald, Mary White Ovington, and Oswald Garrison Villard were leaders in establishing the National Association for the Advancement of Colored People (NAACP) to provide the institutional structure for this reform. They invited a militant black, W. E. B. DuBois, to become the editor of *The Crisis*, the voice of the NAACP published in New York. DuBois was born in Massachusetts and had a Harvard Ph.D. as well as a period of study at German universities. After several years of teaching at black colleges in the South, he returned north to become a major leader of those blacks who would not accept a permanent policy of patience and second-class citizenship. In contrast to Washington's emphasis on vocational education for survival, DuBois called for the very best college education for young black leaders who would make a better future.

Black radicals such as DuBois shared with white liberals the belief that political and legal change was the crucial issue for blacks, as it was for women. The NAACP was very active in the courts, arguing that the Fourteenth and Fifteenth Amendments were being violated. Their policy met with limited success when the Supreme Court struck down the Grandfather Clauses in the voting laws of several southern states, clauses which had excluded from voting persons whose grandparents had been slaves. City ordinances enforcing residential segregation also were found unconstitutional (1917).

W. E. B. DuBois (1868-1963) became Washington's strongest critic. Born in Massachusetts and educated at Harvard, DuBois taught at a Negro college in Atlanta. He was outraged by the way in which blacks were denied their constitutional rights. He felt that Washington should speak out more against segregation and disfranchisement. In 1909, DuBois came North to become a leader of the new organization, the National Association for the Advancement of Colored People (NAACP). The NAACP worked through the courts to restore the rights of blacks under the Fourteenth and Fifteenth Amendments to the Constitution. (The Granger Collection.)

But white racism dominated the nation. This fact is explained by the segregationist policies of Woodrow Wilson. The commitment of whites to preserve the caste system also had been demonstrated in the case of the boxer Jack Johnson. Johnson had violated the caste code, which said blacks must accept violence from whites but must not retaliate, when he became the heavyweight champion of the world. Johnson infuriated whites by demanding the right of first-class citizenship. He further violated the caste system by openly establishing a sexual relationship with a white woman. A crusade was begun to put Johnson in jail, or drive him into exile, and to find a "Great White Hope" who would reclaim the championship for the white race. The crusade was successful in driving Johnson out of the country and in taking the championship from him.

Supplementary Reading

The continuation of the crusade against blacks during the twentieth century is the subject of I. Newby, *Jim Crow's Defense: Anti-Negro Thought in America* (1965). Black response to the crisis is outlined in A. Meier's *Negro Thought in America, 1880-1915* (1963). Black life in the North is described by G. Osofsky, *Harlem: The Making of a Ghetto, 1890-1920* (1966), and A. Spear, *Black Chicago: The Making of a Negro Ghetto, 1890-1920* (1967).

Attitudes toward efficiency are the subject of S. Hays, *Conservation and the Gospel of Efficiency* (1958); S. Haber, *Efficiency and Uplift: Scientific Management in the Progressive Era* (1964); D. W. Noble, *The Progressive Mind* (1970); and D. F. Noble, *America by Design* (1977). G. White, *The Eastern Establishment and the Western Experience* (1968), stresses the concern of the elite for vitality and militancy, as does J. Gillis, *Youth and History* (1974).

The use of education to Americanize the immigrants is described in D. Tyack, *The One Best System* (1974); J. Spring, *Education and the Rise of the Corporate State* (1972); and W. Bullough, *Cities and Schools in the Gilded Age* (1974).

S. Fine, *Laissez-faire and the General Welfare State* (1957), J. Weinstein, *The Corporate Ideal in the Liberal State, 1900-1918* (1968), and G. Kolko, *The Triumph of Conservatism* (1963), provide perspectives on corporate progressivism. The role of middle-class women during the Progressive era is discussed by D. Pivar, *Purity Crusade: Sexual Morality and Social Control* (1973); D. Kennedy, *Birth Control in America: The Career of Margaret Sanger* (1970); and R. Lubove, *The Progressives and the Slums* (1962). Lubove also discusses the limits of progressive reforms in *The Struggle for Social Security* (1968). J. Blum, *The Republican Roosevelt* (1954), G. Mowry, *The Era of Theodore Roosevelt* (1958), and W. Harbough, *Power and Responsibility: The Life and Times of Theodore Roosevelt* (1961), relate Roosevelt to the progressive movement. D. Chalmers, *The Social and Political Ideas of the Muckrakers* (1964), describes the important role of newspapers and magazines in fostering a national progressive movement. Wilson's place in that movement is discussed by A. Link, *Woodrow Wilson and the Progressive Era* (1954).

R. Ginger, *The Bending Cross: A Biography of Eugene Debs* (1949), D. Shannon, *The Socialist Party in America* (1955), and J. Diggins, *The American Left in the Twentieth Century* (1973), provide good analyses of radicalism during the early twentieth century.

Studies of Roosevelt's foreign policy are H. Beale, *Theodore Roosevelt and the Rise of America to World Power* (1956), and D. Burton, *Theodore Roosevelt, Confident Imperialist* (1968). W. and M. Scholes, *The Foreign Policies of the Taft Administration* (1970), show the continuity from the Roosevelt administration. P. Varg, *The Making of a Myth: The United States and China, 1879-1912* (1968), provides perspective on national policy in the Far East.

Chapter

23

World War I and the Climax of Progressivism

The magazines of the new middle class had called for a dynamic hero during the 1890s, and Theodore Roosevelt, as a soldier, seemed to be that hero. From 1900 until 1912, these magazines (for example, *McClure's*) had stressed muckraking articles. Their reporters investigated corruption in the United States Senate, in city and state governments, and in large corporations. They investigated crime and poverty in the slums and described the poor working conditions of children and women. During that time, the magazines presented heroes who purged the evils revealed by the muckrakers and restored virtue to the nation. Roosevelt as president seemed to be that kind of hero. By 1912, however, the editors of the magazines had gradually dropped their emphasis on muckraking. They believed that the country had been purified and stabilized. Then, their stories presented heroes without dynamic, forceful personalities. The new heroes were calm administrators, whose task it was to preserve the order achieved by the earlier, more forceful heroes. Woodrow Wilson, with his background as a college professor and a college president, seemed to be that kind of hero.

When a major war broke out in Europe in 1914, Theodore Roosevelt urged immediate and decisive action to fight on the side of Britain and France against Germany. President Wilson, however, called for calm and stressed the need for neutrality. Most of the new middle class supported Wilson, rather than Roosevelt.

Roosevelt, Wilson, and a European Policy

The new middle class supported Wilson because the United States had no clear foreign policy toward Europe. Until the 1890s, American leaders had assumed that the United States would limit its activities to the Western Hemisphere and develop its trade with Latin America. Then, at the end of the 1890s, WASP leaders developed an Asian foreign policy that tried to treat China in the same open-door fashion as the South American nations.

When Theodore Roosevelt became president, he believed that the United States should act as a great power, equal in strength to the strongest European nations (Britain, Germany, and France) in developing policies toward Latin America and Asia. The population and the industrial production of the United States had surpassed that of Britain, which had been a major world empire for centuries. America, therefore, was potentially the most powerful country in the world. With that power, the United States had replaced Britain as the enforcer of the Monroe Doctrine in the Western Hemisphere. With the withdrawal of British power from the Western Hemisphere, the chief threat to American control came from Germany.

During the second half of the nineteenth century, the German population had doubled and Germany had surpassed France as the most populous country in western Europe. By 1900, German coal and steel production also had surpassed that of England, making Germany second only to the United States as an industrial power. German leaders, like those of the United States, believed in the importance of selling surplus factory products abroad while securing raw materials from overseas. By the 1890s, the Germans had expanded their commercial activity in South American and Asia. Unlike the Americans, the Germans were not content with an Open Door empire. They wanted to seize colonies, especially in Africa, and they sought a colonial empire as had Britain and France.

Representing the two most dynamic nations, German and American leaders saw each other as major rivals in the future. Naval leaders in both countries recognized the possibility of a future war that would pit the navies of the United States and Germany against each other. In 1905, tension between Germany and France over control of Morocco nearly led to war. Roosevelt, acting on the principle that the United States as a great power had a responsibility to intervene even in a European crisis, took leadership of a conference at Algeciras, Spain, at which American and British diplomats backed France against Germany and forced a German retreat.

Balance of Power and an Open Door

Roosevelt was not able to develop a European policy that was compatible with the progressive outlook of the new middle class. The only possible European policy in 1905 seemed to be American participation in the European balance of power. Until 1890, European overseas expansion had cost predominantly white nations little in the way of casualities or armaments. Modern political, economic, and military organization had easily overpowered premodern Asian and African peoples, as it had been easy for American WASPs to overpower the American Indians during the western expansion. After 1890, however, European nations faced increased competition with one another in their continued overseas expansion. The British faced the Germans in Africa and Asia, and the weapons and the organizational skills of the two modern nations were essentially equal. The policy of WASP leaders during the 1890s of replacing the closed western frontier with an overseas frontier, of course, brought the United States into competition with the strong navies and armies of European nations, as well as with Japan, whose leaders had chosen during the 1870s and 1880s to develop a modern growth economy and build modern military forces.

After 1890, as military and naval armaments accumulated in Europe and tensions grew, the European nations formed two major power blocs. Britain and France set aside their competition over colonies to unite against Germany, and they allied themselves with Russia, which faced German expansion in eastern Europe. Germany, in turn, allied itself with the Austro-Hungarian Empire of central Europe.

Middle-class Americans disapproved of the British and French empires as much as they did of German expansionism. Empires stopped the free flow of trade, which American progressives wanted to become worldwide. Even though most progressives were becoming more friendly toward Britain and more hostile toward Germany, they feared that entangling alliances with Britain and France might force America into a war to defend the European empires. By 1914, tensions among the militarized nations of Europe had reached a breaking point, and a small incident in central Europe brought the English-French-Russian Allies into total war with the German-Austro-Hungarian Central Powers. Wilson and most other progressives hoped that the war would result in a stalemate. Then, they believed the United States could play a peacemaking role and persuade the European nations to give up their empires. Under such new circumstances, the American position of economic competition in a world open to free trade might usher in a peaceful world order.

The American Peace Movement

In spite of the outbreak of war in 1914, most American leaders believed that permanent world peace was close at hand. By 1900, American progressives had begun to think of an international world in which there might be peaceful, restrained, and rational competition among the modern nations in the same way that there might be peaceful, restrained, and rational competition among the large corporations within the United States.

More than 100 peace organizations had been formed in Europe and the United States by 1914. Edward Ginn, a publisher, gave much of his fortune to the World Peace Foundation, and Andrew Carnegie gave millions to the Carnegie Endowment for International Peace. The major Protestant denominations, following their social gospel, came together in the Federation of the Churches of Christ in America and put much energy into their department of peace. Protestants, Catholics, and Jews shared in the Church Peace Union. The United States sent delegates to international conferences that met in the Netherlands in 1899 and 1907 and established international courts for the arbitration of disputes between nations. Presidents Roosevelt, Taft, and Wilson encouraged their secretaries of state to negotiate conciliation treaties with other nations that pledged that neither nation agreeing to the treaty would go to war before there was an attempt at peaceful negotiation. Former president Taft became a leader in the League to Enforce Peace, an organization that was to institute many of the principles upon which President Wilson's League of Nations was based in 1919.

Women and the Peace Movement

Many middle-class American women, who hoped to make public life less competitive and more cooperative (as life in the home was), formed the Woman's Peace party (1915). The party's major leaders were the settlement house workers Jane Addams and Crystal Eastman. The Woman's Peace party called on the neutral countries, including the United States, to mediate the conflict in Europe. It also opposed any increase in American armaments. Crystal Eastman was especially active in New York, where she tried to block legislation that would put all high school boys in uniforms and give them military training.

By 1916, there was a significant division between the men and women in the peace movement. Many of the men had begun to say that the only way to achieve lasting peace was to destroy German militarism. Increasingly, they identified modern, industrial Germany as a medieval country where an evil and corrupt feudal aristocracy was keeping the German people in bondage. War against these wicked leaders would liberate the people, and then a democratic Germany could participate in a world of free trade and open-door competition.

Woodrow Wilson and Preparedness

By 1915, Wilson disappointed the people in the peace movement when he turned away from his previous opposition to a big army and navy and accepted the position of Theodore Roosevelt on the need for American military preparedness. Under Wilson's leadership, Congress passed the National Defense Act and the Naval Appropriations Act in the summer of 1916, which greatly strengthened the army and the navy.

As armaments increased rapidly in nations in Europe as well as the United States from the 1880s to 1914, many organizations dedicated to peace also developed. While men from the upper-middle class dominated preparedness groups, women from that class provided much of the leadership for the peace groups. This was especially true after 1915 when President Wilson converted to the preparedness position. Until war was declared in 1917, many women, including Jane Addams, tried to win the public to the side of peace by organizing marches in the big cities. (The Bettman Archive, Inc.)

A significant part of the WASP elite had insisted that the United States must model its navy and army after the new military developments taking place in Europe. The agitation of this group had been successful during Roosevelt's administration in establishing the Army War College. Just as the Navy War College had been established in 1890 to plan overseas strategy, the Army War College planned overseas activity for the army. The army also borrowed directly from the Germans the idea of a general staff. Under General Leonard Wood, the staff was to make overall strategy and planning more efficient.

During the Roosevelt administration, the leaders of the WASP elite had brought about the replacement of the autonomous state militias with the National Guard. This change made the state militias a direct reserve for the national army. By 1916, many college presidents were enthusiastic about the establishment of Reserve Officers Training Corps (ROTC) programs at their institutions, which would greatly supplement the number of officers turned out by the military academies at West Point and Annapolis.

Woodrow Wilson and Good Leaders

Wilson, like Taft, accepted the Roosevelt corollary to the Monroe Doctrine. Taft had encouraged business people to invest in Central America and had been willing to send troops there to stabilize governments so American investments could be protected. Wilson continued this dollar diplomacy and established American military governments in Haiti (1915) and Santo Domingo (1916). Wilson, however, placed dollar diplomacy within a missionary context. American capitalism helped backward people become hardworking, honest, and efficient; American presidents were teaching them how to practice representative government. When a revolution in Mexico overthrew President Francisco Madero and General Victoriano Huerta took power (1913), Wilson decided not to recognize Huerta's government. Wilson intended to force Huerta out of power and to teach the Mexican people how to choose what he called good leaders. Wilson was willing to sacrifice the short-run economic stability of Huerta's reactionary government in order to establish a more constitutional form of government, comparable to that of the United States, for the Mexican people. Wilson, unlike most American presidents after World War II, believed that long-run economic stability depended upon the triumph of constitutional government throughout the world. The stability of Mexico was particularly important to Wilson, because American investment in Mexico had expanded rapidly and, by 1913, Americans owned half of Mexico's mineral and oil resources, as well as most of its railroads. On April 21, 1914, Wilson ordered the attack and occupation of the Mexican port of Vera Cruz in order to block military supplies arriving on a German ship for Huerta's forces. Huerta fled the country and was replaced by President Venustiano Carranza. One of Carranza's generals, Pancho Villa, rebelled against him and planned to create chaos by drawing American troops into Mexico. Villa attacked the town of Columbus, New Mexico (March 1916), and Wilson ordered General John Pershing to pursue Villa into Mexico. After penetrating 300 miles into Mexico, Pershing withdrew. The American relationship with Mexico was stabilized by March of 1917.

As Wilson had faced the question of war with Germany during this spring month of 1917, he established a policy involving the use of military force to create constitutional governments committed to the open-door policy principle of free world trade. An important way to achieve such an ideal situation, for Wilson, was to drive bad leaders out of political power.

Wilson, Germany, and the Freedom of the Seas

As a representative of American progressives, Wilson was committed to the free flow of American trade throughout the world. But, in 1914, Britain and Germany declared blockades against each other, which, according to the American government, violated existing international law. Wilson disliked Britain's actions, since they interfered with American shipping, but he never considered going to war against Britain in order to defend American rights. Wilson had shared the friendship for Britain that had grown among WASP cultural leaders between 1900 and 1914. He also shared their growing dislike for Germany during that period. Given his dislike for Germany, he was prepared to enforce international law against the Germans. The difference between the two blockades also made it easier for newspapers to dramatize German actions. The British blockade slowly starved people, but German submarines struck suddenly and killed people on ships. No match for British naval superiority with surface ships, which kept merchant vessels from reaching Germany, the Germans concentrated on building submarines to sink freighters sailing for England.

In May 1915, a German submarine sank an English passenger ship, the *Lusitania,* killing 1,198 people, including 128 Americans. The *Lusitania* was carrying munitions, as well as people. Still, Wilson sent an angry warning to Germany to stop attacking passenger ships. Wilson's warnings to Germany continued until May 1916, when the sinking of the *Sussex* led him to send an ultimatum to Germany. The Germans then agreed that they would search ships rather than sink them on sight. Wilson, however, had placed American honor on the line. If Germany resumed unrestricted submarine warfare, Wilson threatened to ask for war to enforce his position of May 1916. The crisis came in February 1917.

William Jennings Bryan had resigned as secretary of state in 1915 to protest Wilson's policy of overlooking the illegal British blockade while putting extreme pressure on Germany. His successor Robert Lansing wanted immediate war against Germany and persuaded Wilson to allow unrestricted loans to the Allies. By 1917, these loans totaled more than $2 billion, and trade had grown from $800 million in 1914 to $3 billion. Loans to Germany were $27 million, and trade had dropped from $170 million to $1 million by 1917.

Wilson sent Colonel Edward House, a close friend, to Europe in 1916 to try to achieve an armistice and begin negotiations that would lead to peace. House told British leaders that the United States would probably go to war against Germany if that country refused a peace conference. Another of Wilson's friends, Walter Hines Page, the ambassador to Britain, also promised American participation.

Wilson and the Election of 1916

When Wilson stood for reelection in November 1916, he still hoped for a negotiated peace, so he could pressure the Allies as well as the Central Powers to move away from imperial economies to free trade. He was afraid that, if the United States became a wartime ally of Britain and France, he would no longer be able to pressure them into surrendering their empires or to keep them from punishing Germany. Wilson wanted the German leaders removed, but he believed that a peaceful world of modern nations must include an economically healthy Germany.

Although he did not call for war, Charles Evan Hughes, the Republican candidate, was identified by many voters with that part of the WASP upper-middle class that wanted immediate war against Germany. People such as Theodore Roosevelt and Charles Eliot, the president of Harvard, denounced Wilson for continuing neutrality and hoped for a Republican victory, which would take the United States into the war. But Wilson, who had won the presidency in 1912 because the national Republican majority divided its votes between Taft and Roosevelt, was reelected in 1916 because a number of Republicans, especially in the Midwest, voted for him in the hope of preserving neutrality. They were persuaded by the Democrats' slogan: "He kept us out of war." Then, on February 1, 1917, Germany announced the resumption of unrestricted submarine warfare against all Allied and neutral ships traveling to English, French, and Italian ports.

The willingness of President Wilson and many congressmen to defend Wilson's commitment of American honor against this kind of warfare was intensified on February 24 by the interception of a secret telegram from Germany to the Mexican government that discussed war against the

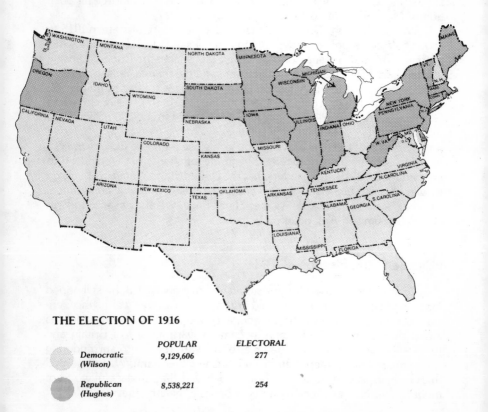

THE ELECTION OF 1916

		POPULAR	ELECTORAL
	Democratic (Wilson)	9,129,606	277
	Republican (Hughes)	8,538,221	254

United States. German leaders assumed that the United States would come into the war after their February announcement. They were taking a calculated risk that their submarines would sink so many ships before America could mobilize that Britain, dependent on overseas supplies, would collapse and make peace. The German foreign secretary, Arthur Zimmerman, therefore, contacted Mexican leaders to offer a wartime alliance. Mexico, if it fought against the United States, could recover the areas of the Southwest it had lost to the United States in the war of 1846.

Then, on February 26, Wilson asked Congress for the authority to arm American merchant ships traveling to England. This request was blocked by congressmen who believed that the majority of the people wanted to stay out of the war. Republicans from the Midwest, such as Senator George Norris from Nebraska and Senator Robert LaFollette from Wisconsin, argued that it was the large eastern corporations, bankers, and munitions makers who would benefit from the war. They argued that British imperialism was as evil as German. Wilson then bypassed Congress and used his executive power early in March to order the arming of the merchant ships. German submarines sank several of the armed ships at the end of March, and Wilson called Congress into special session on April 2, 1917, to face a shooting war that the president had begun. Wilson asked Congress for a declaration of war and got it on April 6, with votes of 82 to 6 in the Senate and 373 to 50 in the House.

Progressivism and the War Economy

Farmers, small business people, laborers, and consumers all had wanted government commissions to regulate large corporations in an effort to protect the marketplace from control by a few large companies. These groups made up part of the coalition that is known as the progressive movement. A number of corporate leaders, however, also joined the progressive coalition to call for regulatory commissions. These corporate progressives disliked the instability of a marketplace of many small competitors. They especially disliked price competition, which made it difficult for the large corporations to plan ahead and predict their expenses and income. Corporate progressives thought that regulatory commissions would help provide that kind of stability. Lawyers who worked for corporations and university professors who believed in a rational, efficient, and controlled marketplace shared in this corporate progressivism.

In 1917, President Wilson called in men from elite groups of Americans to mobilize the American economy. Extensive mobilization would be necessary if a huge army of more than 4 million men was to be assembled and uniforms, guns, trucks, and tanks produced for them. A huge fleet of warships and merchant vessels would have to be built to take the American forces to Europe. And the domestic economy, especially the segment that supplied food, would have to be sustained and, if possible, strengthened.

To accomplish these ends, a Council of National Defense, including members of the cabinet and corporate leaders, was organized. Under its leadership, a War Industries Board was created to control production. It decided which goods were essential and which were not. It decided which materials must be sent into war production and which could go to the civilian economy. The Emergency Fleet Corporation began to build the ships needed for the expedition to Europe. Herbert Hoover directed the Food Administration, which suggested food prices, advised meatless days, and directed the flow of food from the farms to the military and civilians. The Railroad Administration created a national system out of the many private lines. The War Trade Board controlled imports and exports. The Fuel Administration regulated the use of the most important fuel, coal.

The corporate progressives who had encouraged a conservative labor movement through the National Civic Federations then were able to overcome the long period from 1904 to 1917 when union membership had grown very little. Through the National War Labor Board and the War Labor Policies Board, pressure was put on companies with war contracts to permit unionization, to raise pay, and to move toward the eight-hour workday. In this way, Wilson won the full support of Gompers and most AFL leaders, and union membership doubled from 2.5 to 5 million. The same government agencies worked against the radical Industrial Workers of the World (IWW).

The Mobilization of Public Opinion

Congress passed the Selective Service Act (1917) to draft men into the armed forces. But the whole society had to be conscripted to support a mobilized economy. President Wilson had been very critical of those he called "hyphenated Americans," those who had opposed his preparedness programs in 1916. Large numbers of Irish-Americans refused to support England, since it still kept Ireland under imperialistic exploitation. But German-Americans created special problems. Only WASPs were more numerous than German-Americans, and the German-Americans had resisted the pressures to acknowledge WASP leadership more than any other ethnic group. German-Americans knew that Germany had provided the leadership in music, literature, history, social sciences, and physical sciences for all of Western civilization during the nineteenth century, and they knew that young WASPs had gone to study in the German universities. In cities such as Cincinnati, St. Louis, and Milwaukee, German-Americans still used the German language and perpetuated the German culture. In these cities, many newspapers were printed in German, and, because of the international importance of German science and music, even WASPs were encouraged to study German in high schools. In 1917, many in the German-American community were reluctant to support what they saw as British imperialism.

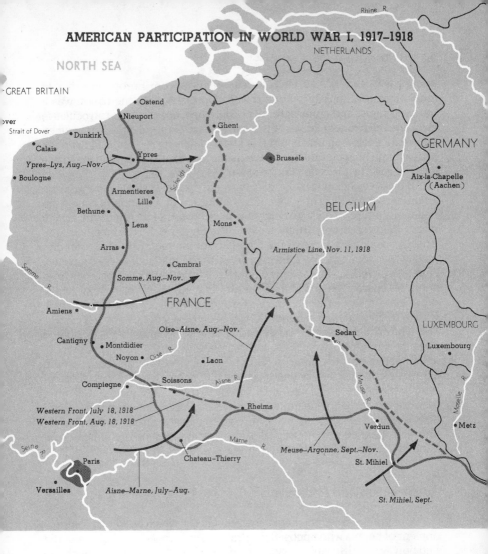

AMERICAN PARTICIPATION IN WORLD WAR I, 1917–1918

NORTH SEA

GREAT BRITAIN

Strait of Dover

NETHERLANDS

GERMANY

BELGIUM

LUXEMBOURG

FRANCE

Ostend
Nieuport
Ghent
Dunkirk
Calais
Ypres
Boulogne
Ypres–Lys, Aug.–Nov.
Brussels
Aix-la-Chapelle (Aachen)
Armentieres
Lille
Bethune
Lens
Mons
Armistice Line, Nov. 11, 1918
Arras
Cambrai
Somme, Aug.–Nov.
Amiens
Oise–Aisne, Aug.–Nov.
Sedan
Luxembourg
Cantigny
Montdidier
Noyon
Laon
Compiegne
Soissons
Western Front, July 18, 1918
Western Front, Aug. 18, 1918
Rheims
Verdun
Metz
Meuse–Argonne, Sept.–Nov.
Chateau-Thierry
St. Mihiel
Paris
Versailles
Aisne–Marne, July–Aug.
St. Mihiel, Sept.

Rhine R.
Scheldt R.
Somme R.
Oise R.
Aisne R.
Marne R.
Seine R.
Meuse R.
Moselle R.

But, in 1917, Congress created the Committee on Public Information (CPI) under the leadership of a muckraking journalist, George Creel. Most of the public that had voted for peace in 1916 did not seem to understand the extent to which WASP leaders had decided to end American isolation during the 1890s and pursue the policy of becoming a great power in international affairs. They did not seem to be aware of the ability of Roosevelt, Taft, and Wilson to shape foreign policy without involving Congress or the public. They were not informed that Wilson and the corporate progressives hoped to see a worldwide Open Door policy emerge after the European war.

The propaganda strategy of the CPI, therefore, was to present the war as the defense of America against German aggression. Transatlantic communications had been controlled by England between 1914 and 1917, and British leaders had filtered news reports from Europe in order to emphasize the English attitude toward Germany (that the nation was a barbaric rapist and a murderer of children because of alleged atrocities in Belgium and France). Major American newspapers and magazines owned by WASPs also had presented this image of Germany. The CPI used the propaganda image of the Germans as the new Huns and urged all Americans to rally to the defense of the United States.

The overwhelming majority of university professors were enthusiastic volunteers for CPI. They were committed to the creation of a uniform national culture. Their participation in a crusade for American loyalty would help force conformity to WASP standards. Irish-Americans, the English-speaking leaders of the Catholic community, would be forced to pledge their loyalty to WASPs in order to prove that they were completely American. German-Americans would have to give up their attempt to preserve a separate language and culture. Indeed, the efforts of all ethnic groups to preserve their languages through newspapers printed in Italian, Polish, Yiddish, Swedish, and Finnish became suspect.

The CPI organized thousands of patriotic speakers and distributed millions of patriotic pamphlets. It also mobilized artists for a very powerful and effective poster campaign that put visual images of the German Hun on every street corner. Beyond this, the CPI encouraged every local community to engage in vigilante activities and to report un-American activities and use extralegal means to suppress them. Local communities burned books printed in German, forced Lutheran ministers to stop preaching in German, painted the houses of some German-Americans yellow, and banned the teaching of German in the schools.

Americanism and Radicalism

Congress passed the Espionage Act (1917), which allowed the imprisonment of people who opposed the draft or encouraged disloyalty, and the Sedition Act (1918), which made it a crime to criticize the government, the Constitution, the armed forces, and the flag during wartime. These laws enabled the government to ban Socialist newspapers from the mails and to jail Socialist leaders. The Socialist party argued that the war was capitalist and that it would refuse to kill other members of the international proletariat. Many important Socialists deserted the party and supported Wilson, and some even joined the CPI. But many top leaders of the Socialist party, including Eugene Debs and Rose Pastor Stokes, chose to go to jail. Pacifists and anarchists (Emma Goldman, for example) also opposed the war and went to jail. Just as the war gave the WASP elite the opportunity to define officially every other ethnic culture as un-American, it gave them the opportunity to define all anticapitalists as un-American. The violence of lynch mobs was directed especially against the WASP leaders of the IWW.

The War and Blacks

Since the CPI stressed that the United States was fighting to defend democracy against German tyranny, W. E. B. DuBois and other black leaders believed that the government would soften its segregationist policies. They urged blacks, therefore, to support the war effort. Government leaders did plan to draft blacks, but they planned to use the blacks as enlisted men under white officers.

In the earlier crusade against blacks, whites had emphasized their belief that all blacks were cowards. The Sambo image that whites were trying to reestablish characterized blacks as childish and lacking courage. This attitude was so strong among whites by 1917 that generals believed that blacks could only serve as supply personnel and not as combat soldiers. White leaders had forgotten that black regiments had been the major assault troops against the Apaches and that they had been the first to land in Cuba. Writers such as Owen Wister, who were presenting cowboys as manly, fighting heroes for adolescents to imitate, also ignored the important role of black cowboys in the West.

In 1917, blacks were barred from the Marine Corps, which was considered to include the toughest fighters in the armed forces. In the Navy, blacks could only serve as messboys. Black leaders protested so strongly, however, that a small number of black army troops were trained for combat and an officer's training camp for blacks was created. General Pershing, the American commander in France, wanted his white troops to fight as an American army and not be absorbed by the British or French armies. But he sent the black regiments to serve with French units. The French did not have a strong caste attitude toward blacks, and American generals warned French soldiers not to socialize with blacks or to allow French civilians, especially women, to associate with them.

The war effectively checked European immigration, which had been averaging a million people a year since 1900. The increase of production and the taking of millions of men into the army combined with the restricted immigration to cause a labor shortage. Northern capitalists sent agents into the South to recruit blacks to come North to work in the mining, meatpacking, and steel-producing industries. Newspapers published by blacks in northern cities also encouraged southern blacks to come north to escape Jim Crow segregation. During the war, a half-million blacks moved to the North. Black leaders established branches of the National Urban League in every major northern city and tried to find jobs and housing for the migrants. But the Urban League failed to get the AFL to accept black members. Lower-income whites resented the increase in the number of black workers in basic industries and the expansion of black ghettos into their neighborhoods. Bloody race riots broke out in cities such as Philadelphia and East St. Louis (1917) and continued across the country until fifteen whites and twenty-three blacks were killed in a riot in

Like the European nations in World War I, the United States conscripted its civilians into a mass army. (Signal Corps photo.)

Chicago (1919). White soldiers returning from the war fought the blacks who had taken their jobs. And the blacks no longer passively tolerated white violence but fought back against the white police.

The War and Women

Most women leaders of the National American Women's Suffrage Association (NAWSA) pledged support for the war. Jane Addams and many other leaders of the Women's Peace party decided not to defy the government openly. Many middle-class women became active in the Red Cross or joined the new United States Army Corps of Nurses and went overseas. Lower-income women went to work in munitions factories and in other basic industries; however, most lost their jobs when the war was over and they were replaced by men. The middle-class women who had been leaders of the Purity Crusade saw the increased social discipline of a total war effort as an opportunity to complete their efforts by protecting the millions of men in army camps from liquor and prostitutes. During the war years, the Women's Christian Temperance Union (WCTU) won wider support for national prohibition, and Congress moved to accept the Eighteenth Amendment, which would ban the sale of alcoholic beverages. Some members of the WCTU favored sex education that would warn against the dangers of promiscuity and venereal disease. They were successful in persuading the army to include sex education as part of basic training for soldiers.

Alice Paul and other young women who wanted the vote broke from NAWSA to form the National Woman's party, which maintained that there could be no war for democracy as long as women were not participants in that democracy. They borrowed the tactic of direct confrontation from English suffragists and marched on the White House. When jailed, they went on hunger strikes and were force-fed by the authorities. Again, the logic of a total war, which needed the cooperation of women, helped push Congress toward acceptance of the Nineteenth Amendment (1920), which gave the vote to women.

Confrontations by middle-class women with authorities intended to force legislative reform had been pioneered in 1915 and 1916 by Margaret Sanger, when she defied the law by establishing birth-control clinics in the poor districts of New York City. Sanger's group had been willing to go to jail and endure police harassment. By 1920, she had won the open support of many middle-class women.

Throughout the nineteenth century respectable American women were supposed to be sexless. In the language of the culture, they had limbs and not legs. Dresses before World War I preserved this illusion. But by 1912, when these fashions were designed, middle-class women already were leaving the privacy of their homes, where their innocence was to be preserved, and nineteenth-century patterns of middle-class sexual behavior were breaking down. (From Ladies' Home Journal, *September 1912.)*

By 1924, when these fashions were designed, the sexuality of the middle-class woman was beginning to be publicly accepted, and the changes in sexual behavior that had begun before World War I and which challenged the double standard of the nineteenth century were being discussed by the younger middle-class people. It had become permissible, therefore, for fashions to reveal that women had legs. (From Vogue, September 1, 1924.)

Wilson and Wartime Politics

Wilson was able to get a majority of people to support a war meant to defeat German aggression. Those who supported the war obeyed the corporate progressives who managed the economy and supplied the armed forces. The men drafted into the military obeyed their officers. The mobi-

lized economy and the military effort it supported were successful in bringing the defeat of the Central Powers. The navy was the deciding factor in
the battle against German submarines as it helped convoy supplies to England and later the American Expeditionary Force (AEF) to France. The
American troops gave the Allies numerical superiority; and, by the fall of
1918, the British, French, and American soldiers had broken the German
lines in France and Belgium. German leaders, facing inevitable military
defeat, forced the kaiser to go into exile, created a republic, and surrendered their still-powerful armies in November 1918. German leaders were
willing to surrender because they believed what Wilson had said about
American war aims. Wilson insisted that the United States did not want to
punish the German people. He believed that the people had been forced
into the war because Germany did not have representative government. It
was ruled, he said, by a medieval emperor and a feudal aristocracy. Once
these remnants from the Dark Ages were destroyed, according to Wilson,
the German nation under republican institutions could play a responsible
role in the family of modern nations.

But, in November 1918, Wilson was in no position to control peace at
home. Most German-Americans and Irish-Americans had supported the
war effort, but they and many Scandinavian-Americans deeply resented
the ability of the WASPs to wage a war that they and the majority of other
Americans had voted against in 1916. Many working-class Americans resented the upper-class monopoly of economic authority at home and military authority abroad. Most of the new officers had come from the small
percentage of young men in college in 1917. Southern and western farmers
were critical of the eastern leadership that dominated American diplomacy.

Upper-class Republicans, who had wanted war in 1916, resented the
Democratic president who belatedly had become the war's leader. Many
Republican big business people, who had supported Taft in 1912, had not
accepted the idea of corporate progressivism and resented the regulations
imposed on them during the war. Wartime inflation hurt many people, and
most citizens had been pressured into buying Liberty Bonds to pay for the
war. Although income taxes had been raised, it was obvious that a small
group had profited immensely from war production. Wilson begged the
voters to elect a Democratic Congress to help him make the peace, but
because of all these resentments, the Republicans won landslide victories
in November 1918 and took firm control of the House and the Senate.

Wilson and the Peace Conference

When Wilson sailed to Paris in early 1919, he ignored the Republican
majority and took Democrats as his major advisers. Wilson had made
most of the crucial decisions between 1914 and 1917 that had led to war. In
1919, he acted as though he could make most of the major decisions leading to peace. At Paris, however, he was forced to compromise with the

Allied nations of Britain, France, Italy, and Japan. After the United States had entered the war, Wilson, as he had feared, failed to persuade the Allies to agree to a peace in which they dismantled their empires or that would not demand the punishment of Germany. The German empire in Africa and Asia was divided among the Allies; parts of Germany were given to France and Poland; the Austro-Hungarian Empire was divided into a number of independent nations; and Germany was forced to pay billions in reparations to Britain and France to defray the cost of their war efforts. Wilson persuaded the Allies to establish a League of Nations, in which all nations could resolve international problems before they led to war. He also hoped that the league's assembly, meeting as a world parliament, would help move the world toward free trade. As American regulatory commissions established before 1914 had been designed to keep corporations from engaging in unfair competition, the league, for Wilson, was

President Woodrow Wilson (1856-1924) believed strongly in Anglo-American tradition, which went back to the seventeenth-century Puritans, that the United States was chosen by God to be a "redeemer nation" and had the responsibility of leading the nations of the Old World out of darkness into the divinely inspired patterns of America. He believed that World War I provided the United States with the opportunity to fulfill this destiny. When he landed in Europe in 1919, he expected a dramatically purified world to emerge from the peace negotiations. (UPI.)

designed to keep nations from engaging in unfair competition. This was especially true of Article X of the league's constitution, which said that members of the League of Nations would protect the territorial integrity of all members of the league.

Wilson and the Senate

Most Democrats and Republicans in the Senate were prepared to accept the terms of the Treaty of Versailles (1919), including American entry in the League of Nations, but Henry Cabot Lodge, the leader of the Republican majority in the Senate, insisted that Article X be dropped before Republicans would accept the treaty. Article X, he argued, ended freedom of action for the United States because the League of Nations, not American leaders, could decide on the issues of war and peace. Wilson rejected Lodge's demand, and he refused to allow the Democratic minority to compromise on Article X. This pushed Republican moderates into an alliance with Republican "irreconcilables," a group of western and midwestern Republican isolationists who opposed any cooperation with European nations. Wilson began a speaking tour of the nation in the hope of mobilizing public opinion to force the Senate Republicans to accept the treaty without reservations. Overtired, Wilson suffered a stroke and spent the last year of his administration as an invalid isolated in the White House. The impasse in the Senate continued, and the treaty had not been signed by the time of the presidential election of 1920.

Wilson and the Collapse of Progressivism

Both Roosevelt and Wilson, as progressive leaders, had been able to forge successful political coalitions of different, even conflicting groups. Many persons had believed that the establishment of government commissions would restore the small-scale capitalism of the nineteenth century. Others had seen the commissions as leading to a new order of corporate capitalism. Many had seen the emphasis on renewed democracy as restoring the Jacksonian democracy of the common man. Others had seen this democratic emphasis ending boss rule and establishing leadership by highly trained experts. Wilson's personal collapse marked the collapse of this coalition. Already, in 1917, foreign policy had produced a division between many midwestern progressives like LaFollette and Norris who opposed the war and eastern progressives who supported it.

Many of the university professors who admired Theodore Roosevelt's progressivism in 1912 had shifted to Wilson in 1916. As the professional associations of historians, political scientists, economists, and sociologists developed during the 1880s and 1890s, the members of the new professions had defined the shift from small-town agricultural America to an urban-industrial society as progress. Progress, they argued, was evolutionary change upward, from dark-age cultures like those in medieval Europe, from contemporary societies in India and China, and from the tribal cultures of Africa and the Americas. Such backward societies, according to the professors, were based on superstition and tradition. Modern, progressive society, they believed, was based increasingly on science and reason.

Rural and small-town Americans who were mostly evangelical Protestants, the professors continued, still lived with superstition and tradition. Proof of this was their rejection of Darwin's theory of evolution. Black Americans, American Indians, and Catholic and Jewish immigrants also lived with superstition and tradition. But the professors were certain that the discipline of industrial life would liberate all people from their superstitions and traditions. The economist Thorstein Veblen and the historian Charles Beard wrote many articles and books that tried to demonstrate that both the workers and the managers of factories had to live in a world of rationality and science. They shared some of the views of efficiency expert Frederick W. Taylor, who held that the logic of factories was maximum and efficient production and that this kind of production could be measured by the impersonal standards of speed and weight. John Dewey, an educational philosopher, argued that compulsory education in the public schools could speed up the process by which children were liberated from the irrational customs of their parents so that they could live by the rational standards of the factory. The sociologist Robert Park also argued that the logic of city life was impersonal and would help break down the personal qualities of rural peasant and tribal life. People like Veblen, Beard, Dewey, and Park felt that the United States had become more progressive than any other nation. But they believed that patterns of industrialism and urbanism would spread everywhere in the world and that all humans would be freed eventually from traditional culture.

Before 1917, Veblen and Dewey had suggested that most Germans lived by the rational logic of industrialism and urbanism and that only a small ruling aristocracy lived by the traditions of the medieval past. The theorists were sure, therefore, that it would be easy to liberate the Germans so that they, too, could become progressives. These progressive intellectuals believed that political and military power was personal and irrational and that a completely industrialized and urbanized world would be run by experts whose authority was impersonal because it was based on rational and scientific principles. According to them, American military might was destroying the personal and irrational military power of Germany. They believed that Britain and France had moved in the direction of the American commitment to a progressive urban-industrial society. They were sure, too, that the forced cooperation of American corporations under the guidance of the experts who ran the wartime agencies had purged the remaining business leaders who thought in terms of personal profits rather than about how productive and efficient their factories were.

Expecting World War I to be a major turning point in world history, many of these professors were deeply disillusioned when British and French leaders insisted on playing power politics at the Paris peace conference. They were bitterly disappointed when Wilson brought back the Treaty of Versailles, which incorporated so much of the selfish interests of Britain, France, Italy, and Japan.

Many of the internationalistic professors who had enthusiastically supported the war and who had joined the Democratic party joined with isolationist Republicans like LaFollette and Norris to oppose the treaty and the League of Nations. Such leading historians as Charles Beard accepted the arguments that LaFollette had made in 1917 about the nature of British and French imperialism and the way in which the war would strengthen selfish corporate power at home.

The disillusionment was shared by the liberal Protestants who had moved away from fundamentalism during the 1890s and had accepted the social gospel and the idea of evolution. They also identified evolution with progress and were sure that the changes taking place between 1900 and 1918 were leading to the establishment of the kingdom of God on earth. They saw the values of rationality and science as the values of liberal Protestantism. The liberal Protestant churches were getting ready for a worldwide missionary effort when the war ended, and they were sure masses of people were ready to be converted from their traditional religions. But, by 1919, social gospel theologians like Walter Rauschenbusch were as confused and as unsure about the future as historian Charles Beard and economist Thorstein Veblen.

The Russian Revolution and the Red Scare

Until 1919, most American leaders were certain that the United States represented the future of the entire world. Evolution and progress were to lead all other nations to follow the American example. But, by 1919, many of these leaders were afraid that progressivism had failed at home, and they knew that Wilson had failed to end the imperialism of the western European nations and establish a worldwide Open Door policy. The dramatic shift from extreme optimism in 1917 to extreme pessimism in 1919 caused the progressives to be especially fearful of the triumph of communism in Russia. In March 1917, a revolution had overthrown the Russian czar and the feudal aristocracy and had established a republic. At first, American leaders rejoiced, because it had been embarrassing to fight a war for democracy with an undemocratic ally. But the revolution soon fell into the hands of Bolsheviks, who rejected Western capitalism and Western forms of government. The Bolshevik leader Nicolai Lenin said that he was establishing a communist society based on the principles of Karl Marx.

Between 1850 and 1870, the writings of Marx had made a slight impact in Europe and the United States. Marx had pointed to the alienation of workers under industrial capitalism as they lost control of the means of production and lost any meaningful relation to the products they made. Marx warned of growing alienation for the whole society when production was for profit and not for use. He promised, moreover, that industrial capitalism would cause a growing division between the few capitalist owners and the many unpropertied workers (the proletariat). Eventually, the proletariat would engage in a revolution to destroy the capitalist elite and create an economy based on production for use and not for profit.

Lenin, working from the Marxist idea that there were no limits to the capitalists' desire for profits, predicted that the capitalist nations would go to war against each other in order to command ever-expanding markets and to get increasing supplies of raw materials. In 1917, Lenin argued that Wilson was mistaken in his hope that the capitalist nations could end colonial imperialism and enter into a worldwide open-door economy. For Lenin, the only way to end imperialism was to end capitalism, and he promised that the Russian Revolution was only the beginning and that the logic of industrialism would sweep the world. But industrialism would liberate people to become communists, not capitalists. Soviet Russia, not the United States, would be the model for the industrial future.

Lenin had taken Russia out of the war in 1917, allowing Germany to concentrate on the western front. Britain, France, and Japan had sent troops into Russia to help anti-Bolshevik groups try to overthrow communism. Wilson had also sent American troops, but they did not engage in active fighting. This Allied effort failed to destroy the Bolshevik government, and, in 1919, there were threats of communist revolutions in the new nations formed out of the Austro-Hungarian Empire and even in Germany itself.

The Red Scare of 1919

In 1912, the Socialist party accepted Foreign Language Federations of new immigrants. These federations, like the IWW, tried to push the party toward direct confrontations with the establishment. In 1919, the Socialist party expelled the federations because of their radicalism, thus losing 50 percent of its membership. Many of the federationists then helped form the Communist party, while others joined the Communist Labor party. During May and June of 1919, bombs were sent through the mails to members of the corporate elite, such as John D. Rockefeller and Attorney General A. Mitchell Palmer. Bombs exploded in cities across the country. Major strikes also occurred: 35,000 shipyard workers in Seattle; the Boston police; 350,000 steelworkers in Chicago, Gary, and Pittsburgh.

Attorney General Palmer told the nation that a major effort at communist revolution was beginning and that drastic measures were needed to smash it. He appointed J. Edgar Hoover to head an antiradical division in the Department of Justice. In a series of raids, Palmer jailed more than 4,000 people who, he claimed, were leaders of the coming revolution. They were arrested without warrants and held without bail or access to lawyers, and they often were beaten. Throughout the country, vigilante groups executed suspected radicals.

Elbert Gary and other leaders of the steel industry used the red scare to smash the largest strike in American history. AFL chiefs had decided that the gains they had made during the war would be consolidated if they could unionize the nation's largest industry. Twenty-four AFL unions planned to work together to win membership among the steelworkers. They did not plan to create one large industrial union but to divide the workers into twenty-four specialties that fit into the existing union structures.

New immigrant workers who had been able to act with great solidarity during the coal strike of 1902 and the Lawrence strike of 1912 enthusiastically joined the strike for union recognition. Half of them were working twelve hours a day, seven days a week. Wages were so low that several families often shared a house and boarders sometimes took turns using a single bed.

But many skilled workers refused to go on strike, and some AFL unions failed to fulfill their pledge to send money. Mayors refused to grant the strikers the right to assemble, and police broke up their meetings. Newspapers persuaded their readers that the strikers were part of the international communist conspiracy. They stressed that most of the strikers were new immigrants and that these "foreigners" were dangerous radicals who had to be stopped. Attorney General Palmer sent agents to investigate the "radical" leaders of the strike. Fragmented and isolated, the strikers surrendered.

1920: The End of Progressivism and the Return to Normalcy

The failure of the war to achieve American world leadership had weakened the position of corporate progressives, university professors, and liberal Protestants in both the Republican and the Democratic parties. The demand for conformity during the war and the red scare had discredited Socialists. Superpatriotism during the war had hurt the antitrust progressives such as William Jennings Bryan in the Democratic party and Robert LaFollette in the Republican party. The dominant groups in the conventions of both the Democratic and the Republican parties in the summer of 1920, therefore, were the big and small business people who had opposed progressivism since the 1890s. They were opposed to government commissions, to aid to farmers, and to paternalism toward labor. They wanted a return to "normalcy." The Democrats nominated Governor James Cox of Ohio and the Republicans, Warren Harding, a senator from Ohio. Harding smashed Cox, with 16 million votes to Cox's 9 million votes. Participation by eligible voters dropped to 50 percent or less,

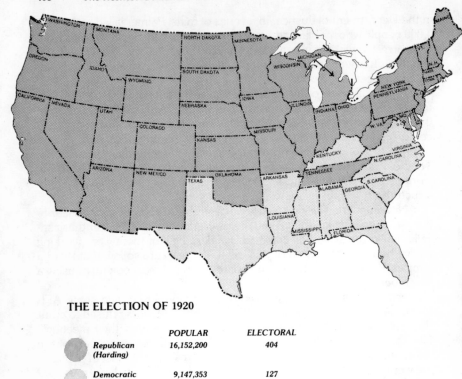

THE ELECTION OF 1920

		POPULAR	ELECTORAL
	Republican (Harding)	16,152,200	404
	Democratic (Cox)	9,147,353	127

down from 90 percent during the 1880s. Obviously, many voters were disillusioned with the leadership of the parties, especially that of the Democrats, who had disappointed so many Americans by going to war after promising peace in 1916 and by failing to achieve a satisfactory peace settlement in 1919.

Supplementary Reading

The changing character of middle-class heroes is described in S. Diamond, *The Reputation of the American Businessman* (1955), and T. Greene, *America's Heroes* (1970). B. Tompkins, *Anti-Imperialism in the United States: 1890-1920* (1970), provides a general outline of the peace movement, and A. Davis, *American Heroine: The Life and Legend of Jane Addams* (1973), discusses the particular role of women in that movement. W. Kuehl, *Seeking World Order: The United States and World Organization to 1920* (1969), describes the background of the League of Nations.

The growing role of the military in American life is the subject of R. Challener, *Admirals, Generals, and American Foreign Policy, 1898-1914* (1973), and J. Clifford, *The Citizen Soldiers* (1972). Wilson's attitudes toward Central America are analyzed in R. Quirk, *An Affair of Honor: Woodrow Wilson and the Occupation of Vera Cruz* (1962). R. Gregory, *The Origins of American Intervention in the First World War* (1971), and J. Cooper, Jr., *The Vanity of Power: American Isolation and the First World War, 1914-1917* (1969), deal with the conflicts and contradictions in the outlook of Americans toward the war in Europe. Wilson's hope that America could drastically change Europe is clarified in E. Tuveson, *Redeemer Nation* (1968). The mobilization of the economy is described in R. Cuff, *The War Industries Board: Business-Government Relations during World War I* (1973), and in several essays in *A New History of Leviathan* (1972), edited by R. Radosh and M. Rothbard. The enforcement of unity is described by W. Preston, *Aliens and Dissenters: Federal Suppression of Radicals* (1963), and J. Jensen, *The Price of Vigilance* (1968). The role of professors in mobilizing public opinion is dealt with by G. Blakey, *Historians on the Home Front* (1970), and C. Gruber, *Mars and Minerva: World War I and the Uses of Higher Learning in America* (1975).

W. O'Neill, *Everyone Was Brave: The Rise and Fall of Feminism in America* (1969), and P. Filene, *HimHerself* (1974), describe the role of women in the war. J. Foner, *Blacks and the Military in American History* (1974), describes the segregated army of 1917.

Wilson's relationship to the peace settlement is analyzed in N. Levin, Jr., *Woodrow Wilson and World Politics* (1968), and A. Meyer, *Politics and Diplomacy of Peacemaking: Containment and Counter-Revolution at Versailles* (1967). R. Stone, *The Irreconcilables: The Fight against the League of Nations* (1970), looks at the political forces that defeated Wilson at home.

Some of the major tensions in American society in 1919 are described by W. Tuttle, *Race Riot: Chicago in the Red Summer of 1919* (1970); D. Brody, *Labor in Crisis: The Steel Strike of 1919* (1965); and R. Murray, *The Red Scare* (1955).

Chapter 24

Progressivism
for Business Only
1920-1932

Many voters in 1914 were not aware of the decision by government and business leaders in the 1890s to develop systematically overseas markets and sources of raw materials. Then, in 1920, most voters believed that the United States was returning to a traditional policy of isolation after momentarily engaging in a foreign adventure during World War I. They did not recognize that members of the Harding administration, especially Secretary of State Charles Evans Hughes and Secretary of Commerce Herbert Hoover, were deeply concerned with questions of foreign policy.

Harding, Hoover, and Hughes and the Open Door Frontier

Both Hughes and Hoover wanted to continue the Open Door policies in Latin America and Asia. Both wanted the policy to be applied to Europe, as had Woodrow Wilson. Less committed than Wilson to the League of Nations, they were confident that the American economy was so strong that it could provide stability for the world without the use of the political and military power that was part of the league's covenant. In other words, Hughes and Hoover knew that the United States was already a great world power. During the 1920s, 50 percent of all industrial production in the world was located in the United States. The economy of Germany, the second-strongest industrial power in 1914, was in shambles, and Britain, the third-strongest industrial power, had been badly weakened.

In 1914, the United States owed Europe $4 billion that it had borrowed to pay for its earlier industrial growth. By 1920, America had become a creditor nation for the first time; it was owed $12 billion by Europeans. The government had loaned $4 billion to Britain and $3 billion to France. The rest had been loaned to private bankers. Private bankers and investors loaned another billion dollars abroad during each year of the 1920s.

At the peace conference, Britain and France had forced Germany to agree to pay them $33 billion in reparations. The battered German economy could not meet those debts, so Hughes and Hoover moved to get American bankers to loan large sums to Germany. That country then used the borrowed money to pay Britain and France. Britain and France, in turn, made payments on their debts to the United States. The American leaders believed that a stable Germany, which was not in conflict with Britain and France, was necessary for a healthy European economy. A prosperous Europe could serve as a market for agricultural and industrial products from the United States. The unity of the western European nations was also necessary if communism was to be contained in Russia.

The United States and Japan

With the collapse of German and British power, there was no danger to the American Open Door policy in Latin America. Although government officials from the United States were in control of the financial affairs of ten Central American and Caribbean countries during the 1920s, diplomatic leaders were beginning to consider an end to the use of military intervention in Latin America. But the American Open Door policy in Asia was not so secure.

Japan had begun to modernize during the 1880s. With very limited resources for industrial growth, the Japanese were dependent upon foreign sources of raw materials, and they were prepared to enter into competition with European nations for those resources. The Japanese navy had defeated Russia in 1905. American leaders believed at that time that Japan was the greatest threat to the Open-Door policy in China. But Theodore Roosevelt felt that America did not have enough naval power to stop the Japanese conquest of Korea, a peninsula jutting out from the Chinese mainland toward the Japanese islands. He also made concessions to Japan by recognizing a special Japanese interest in the northern Chinese province of Manchuria. Japan then joined the Allies in the war against Germany and seized the German-held Mariana, Caroline, and Marshall islands. During the war, Japanese leaders pressured Wilson to recognize that Japan, as the closest modern nation to China, had special interests there that were different from those of any of the other industrial countries.

The greatest problem for Secretary of State Hughes, therefore, was to try to preserve the Open Door policy in China against Japanese expansion. Acting as the representative of the greatest world power, he called on the most powerful nations of Europe and Asia to meet in Washington, D.C. (1921). At this Washington conference, Hughes persuaded Japan to reaffirm the Open Door policy for China. In one of the treaties signed at the conference, the United States, Britain, Japan, France, and Italy pledged to stop building battleships and to accept a ratio of five ships for the United States, five for Britain, three for Japan, and one and two-thirds each for France and Italy.

It appeared to American leaders that their diplomatic intervention had made American investments secure without the price of political and military entanglements. Indeed, it seemed that the United States did not have to increase its own navy or army to provide stability in Europe and Asia. As secretary of commerce, Hoover felt free to encourage business people to invest overseas. Under the Webb-Pomerene Act (1918), Hoover could promise that there would be no antitrust action against business combinations formed to engage in overseas investment.

Business, Progress, and the New Era

Hoover considered himself a progressive, but he disagreed with other corporate progressives about the need for government regulatory commissions to provide order and discipline to the marketplace. In Hoover's opinion, the large corporations would be able to overcome destructive competition by voluntarily joining trade associations. As secretary of commerce under Harding and Coolidge and then as president in 1928, Hoover encouraged the corporations to reach agreement on prices and a fair share of the market.

With the 200 largest industrial corporations controlling as much wealth as the other 200,000, many corporate leaders shared Hoover's hope that business could achieve a high level of efficiency and rationality. Business schools had been part of the new universities of the 1890s, but there was an extensive expansion of the existing schools at Harvard and Pennsylvania during the 1920s, and many other universities established business schools at that time, also. Increasingly, business executives were college trained and had been taught to run businesses by "scientific" methods. Business leaders believed that time and motion studies of each worker's performance would provide maximum efficiency throughout the economy. Henry Ford's experiments with assembly-line production between 1912 and 1914 had cut the time of assembly for his Model T from twelve hours to one. Such efficiency had enabled Ford to raise wages, cut the cost of his cars, and still make a personal profit of $80 million a year after taxes. The number of autos in use had more than tripled, from 2.5 million in 1915 to 9 million in 1920.

The triumph of the assembly line assured business leaders that they could control the productive part of the economy. The development of research laboratories further assured them of their ability to control the flow of new technologies. Borrowing from Germany, which had pioneered the use of research laboratories, American business people gathered scientists, engineers, and technicians together to work systematically at the invention of new machines and new chemicals. The research laboratories achieved spectacular advances in steel and aluminum technology and in new drugs and chemicals, including synthetic fiber for clothing.

New business magazines, such as *System,* promised that systematic approaches to production and invention guaranteed ever-increasing prosperity. Leaders, like Hoover and Ford, agreed that a "new era" had been reached and that old-fashioned business cycles would disappear.

Business, Labor, and the New Era

Business leaders argued that there should be no competition between management and labor if there was to be a completely rational and controlled economy. Strikes would interrupt the productive process, and even collective bargaining would upset a planned economy. Management claimed that labor's demands for higher wages would threaten long-range planning. The business leaders of the 1920s created company unions in which workers could express grievances but had no power to influence wages, working hours, or working conditions. In return for the workers' acceptance of management's leadership, managers offered to provide health care for the workers and recreational facilities for their leisure activities.

Supported by the Supreme Court and many state courts, many business leaders worked to keep unions out of industry. They also tried to destroy the whole idea of independent unions. Taking advantage of the red scare, they advocated an American Plan for labor that they claimed would save the independence of workers. Reverting to pre-World War I policies, they argued that a worker who was forced to join a union was in a closed shop and had lost his or her right as an American to make a choice. Management offered to protect that right by creating open shops. But management further restricted workers' choices by having new employees sign yellow-dog contracts, in which workers promised not to join unions. During the 1920s, American management also spent as much as $65 million a year on private detectives to infiltrate and disrupt unions.

The 1920s, therefore, were the first prosperous years in which unions did not gain recruits. Union membership dropped from 5 million in 1920 to 3 million in 1930. Only the unions of skilled construction craftsmen, printers, and railroad workers kept their strength during the decade. From 20 percent of the nonagricultural work force in 1920, union membership dropped to 10 percent in 1930.

Business and Farmers

After the hard times of the 1880s and 1890s, farmers had recovered some prosperity from 1900 to 1914 as agricultural prices rose. World War I had created a huge demand for food. Farm prices had leapt still higher, and marginal land had been brought into cultivation. Then, suddenly, farm income dropped from $14 billion in 1919 to $8 billion in 1922 and remained at $8 billion a year until a further drastic reduction after 1930. Competing with each other for survival, the wealthier farmers bought more machinery and fertilizer. Their investments increased farm production on fewer acres. Less successful farmers were driven from the land, and 4 million people moved from the country into the city during the 1920s.

The farmers who remained on the land suffered severe economic pressure. The Republican Congress had passed the Fordney-McCumber Tariff (1922), which reversed the Underwood-Simmons Tariff and increased protection of manufactured goods. During the 1920s, farmers bought machinery and other products on a protected national market but had to sell most of their crops on an unprotected international market. Under the leadership of Secretary of the Treasury Andrew Mellon, Congress also cut taxes for the wealthy in 1921 and 1926. Such programs set a pattern for the 1920s in which taxes rested more heavily on farmers and workers than on urban business people.

Working as a pressure group through the American Farm Bureau Federation, the Grange, and the Farmer's Union, farmers created a farm bloc of southern and western congressmen. In 1927 and 1928, Congress passed the McNary-Haugen bill, which gave the government the responsibility of buying crop surpluses at American prices and selling them abroad at the existing world prices. President Coolidge successfully vetoed the bill. He argued that it violated the American spirit of free enterprise.

LaFollette and the Progressive Party of 1924

A number of labor leaders, especially those from the railroad unions, refused to accept the antiunion crusade passively. Frustrated by the fact that both the Democrats and the Republicans accepted antilabor leadership, labor leaders called a Conference for Progressive Political Action (1922). There they planned a third-party movement for 1924 that was to be headed by Senator Robert LaFollette. The AFL endorsed the new Progressive party, as did what remained of the Socialist party. The party platform proposed (1) the nationalization of the railroads and the natural resources necessary for industrial production; (2) a reversal of the current tax situation, so the rich would pay more and the poor less; (3) a constitutional amendment to allow Congress to override the Supreme Court; (4) the end of court injunctions against union activity; and (5) economic relief for the farmers.

The leaders of the Progressive party hoped that the major scandals during the Harding administration would discredit the Republican policy of normalcy. Corruption had surrounded Attorney General Harry Daugherty and the Veterans' Bureau, and two government officials had committed suicide. Secretary of the Interior Albert Fall was convicted of taking bribes for transferring government oil reserves to oil-corporation executives. Harding had shown signs of great stress as his friends brought disgrace to his administration, and he died suddenly in 1923. Calvin Coolidge, Harding's vice-president, persuaded many Republicans that he was free of corruption and won the Republican nomination in 1924. He defeated both the Democratic candidate John W. Davis and LaFollette; the vote was 15 million for Coolidge, 8 million for Davis, and 5 million for LaFollette. While the vote for the Progressives was impressive for a third party, labor leaders were discouraged and accepted the advice of the new president of the AFL, William Green, to withdraw from politics and save the remaining craft unions.

The Ku Klux Klan and Cultural Politics

A major reason that the lower-income worker-farmer majority was unable to form a political alliance against the upper-income business minority was the continuing cultural hostility of southern and western farmers and small business people (overwhelmingly Anglo-Saxon evangelical Protestant) toward the Catholics and Jews in the northern and midwestern cities. By 1914, white southerners felt that their crusade against blacks had been successful. Blacks were excluded from southern politics, and Jim Crow laws forced segregation in public places. During the 1920s, white southerners believed that they had the responsibility of saving the rest of the nation from the corrupt Old World cultures of Catholic and Jewish immigrants. In the view of white southerners, WASP biological superiority would be destroyed if Nordic blood were mixed with the inferior blood of southern and eastern Europeans.

A new Ku Klux Klan was founded in Georgia (1915). Like the original KKK, it was concerned with keeping blacks in their place. But its major responsibility was seen as keeping Catholics and Jews in their places as second-class citizens. The new KKK quickly became a national organization, with its greatest strength in Ohio and Indiana and especially in smaller midwestern cities, such as Indianapolis and Columbus, that had not received many new immigrants. It was also strong in fast-growing cities of the Southwest, such as Tulsa, Oklahoma, and Houston, Texas. Newly emerging WASP business elites were expressing their insecurities about the urban environment by searching for Catholic and Jewish scapegoats.

At the same time, the children of Catholic and Jewish immigrants were beginning to come of age and to become involved in politics. No longer content to control the Democratic parties in the cities, they sought power in the states where they formed a numerical majority. Alfred E.

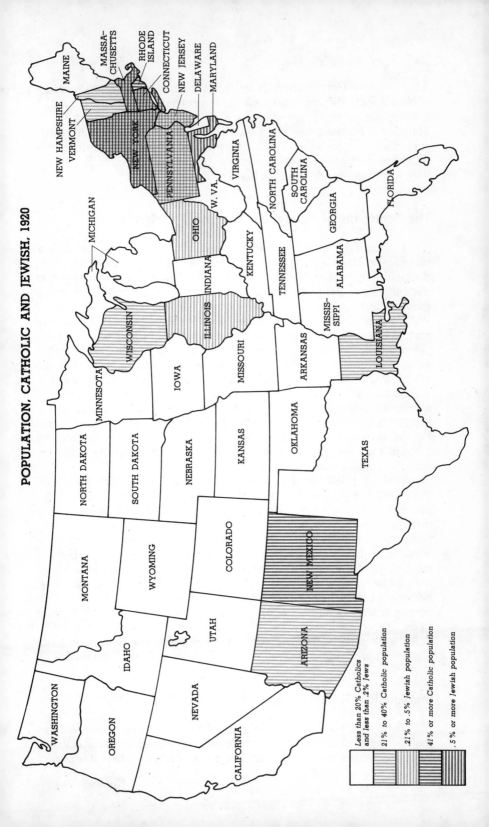

POPULATION, CATHOLIC AND JEWISH, 1920

Less than 20% Catholics
and less than .2% Jews

21% to 40% Catholic population

.21% to .5% Jewish population

41% or more Catholic population

.5% or more Jewish population

Smith, an Irish-Catholic from New York City, had been elected governor of New York (1919), the most powerful state in the union in terms of wealth and population. In 1924, just as the KKK reached its peak in the South, Southwest, Midwest, and Far West, big-city Democrats from the Northeast made a major effort to win the presidential nomination for Smith. Southern delegates at the convention hysterically opposed Smith, but they were barely able to block his nomination.

The South, the West, and the East and Prohibition

Prohibition helped evangelical Protestants to emphasize their monopoly of first-class citizenship. The failure of Prohibition, therefore, served to discredit that monopoly. The everyday use of beer and wine was part of the cultures of the Catholic and Jewish immigrants. Prohibition forced these groups to surrender their culture according to the dictates of WASPs. Until 1920, southern and western WASPs thought that they were part of a national movement to save the purity of the nation. By 1900, upper-middle-class WASPs from the Northeast had come to support the drive for prohibition of the Anti-Saloon League. But saloons served the ethnic neighborhoods as cultural and political centers where workers discussed their jobs and planned union activities. Saloons preserved a sense of community solidarity that made it easier to pressure each individual to support a strike effort. Ethnics kept their language alive in the saloons. But, while it was in the class interest of WASP leaders to destroy the saloons, they, too, were developing a life-style that included the daily consumption of alcoholic cocktails.

When the WASP elites helped to establish Prohibition, therefore, they were not prepared to enforce it against themselves. If neither the upper-class WASPs nor the lower-class Catholics of the cities wanted to prohibit the use of alcoholic beverages, there was no way to stop drinking. Speakeasies (underground saloons) sprang up in every city and were supplied by illegal stills or by smuggling from Canada. The problem of supplying illegal alcohol to much of the nation was one that could be solved only by large-scale economic organization. Organized crime, therefore, became a national institution during the 1920s. Many of the underworld corporate leaders, like Al Capone, came from Italian backgrounds. Unable to use their organizational talents in the national economy dominated by WASPs or in the Catholic church or urban politics dominated by Irish-Catholics, people like Capone used their talents where they could.

Immigration, WASP Decadence, and the Scopes Trial

From the Civil War until World War I, a major economic problem was the development of machinery that could produce rapidly and efficiently. With production as a major concern, there was a constant shortage of labor. But, by 1920, the problem of production seemed to be solved. Although industrial production increased more rapidly during the 1920s than in any previous decade, there was no significant increase in the indus- trial work force. A million workers who lost their jobs to new machines never found other jobs, and unemployment stayed around 6 percent dur- ing those prosperous years. WASP corporate leaders, therefore, responded to the pleas of labor and farmers to restrict immigration. Con- gressional legislation in 1921 and 1924 made it impossible for large-scale immigration to resume. The major restrictions were on southern and east- ern Europeans and were based openly on the assumption that Latins and Slavs were biologically and culturally inferior. Finally, in 1929, immigration was restricted to 150,000 per year. The quota for each nation was related to its proportion of the American white population in 1920. In terms of the Anglo-Saxon bias of this legislation, more than one-third of the 150,000 immigrants, 65,000, could come from England each year, while only 6,000 could come from Italy.

The restriction of immigration by Catholics and Jews, however, did not serve to reunite southern and western WASPs with those of the North- east. Rural and small-town Protestants were horrified by what they saw as the corruption of the urban WASP elites. Besides the vices of drinking and smoking, the WASP elite seemed to accept the sinfulness of dancing to sensual African rhythms. Starting in the 1890s, ragtime and then blues and jazz had become major influences in urban popular music and dancing styles. Fundamentalist Protestants were correct in seeing a different atti- tude toward the body and sexuality in this music, which incorporated Afri- can traditions that had survived in black American culture.

It was during this same period that the WASP urban middle class stopped requiring the chaperoning of unmarried young women. Premari- tal sexual experiences for the WASP women became much more common between 1900 and 1920. The lengths of women's skirts had become short- er before World War I, and, in the 1920s, they reached the knee and some- times went above it.

These trends convinced conservatives in the South and the West that, when many northern Protestants had converted to liberalism during the 1890s and accepted the idea of evolution, they had ushered in a climate of permissiveness and sinfulness. As members of the Anti-Evolution League or as Bible Crusaders, they urged state legislatures to pass laws barring the teaching of evolution in the public schools. They won such laws in Oklahoma, Tennessee, North Carolina, Florida, and Texas and came close to victory in many other southern and midwestern states.

This clash of cultures was vividly expressed in Tennessee in 1925, when a young high school teacher named John Scopes, supported by the American Civil Liberties Union, challenged the state law. The defense was led by Clarence Darrow, a nationally famous trial lawyer and an outspoken agnostic. The prosecution was assisted by William Jennings Bryan. Scopes lost, but the national elite believed that the provincial culture represented by Bryan was shown to be shallow and foolish.

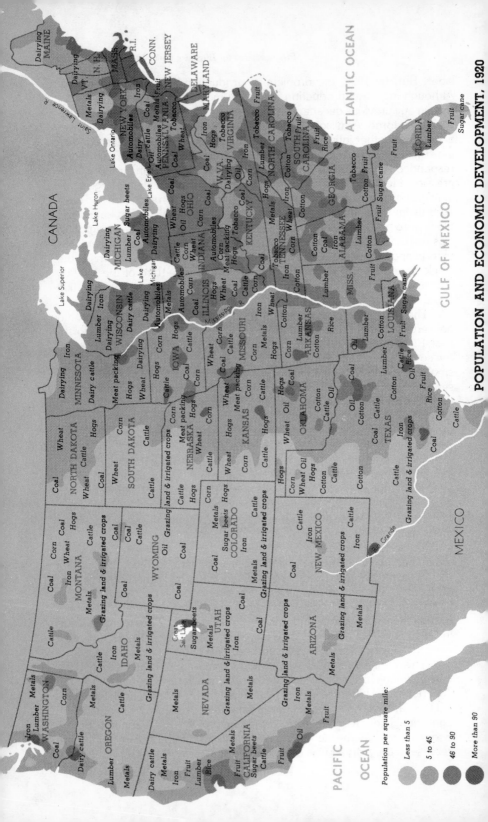

POPULATION AND ECONOMIC DEVELOPMENT, 1920

Population per square mile:

Less than 5
5 to 45
46 to 90
More than 90

This picture of the Ku Klux Klan marching in Washington, D.C. in 1926 illustrates the frustrations of lower-middle-class Protestantism with the social trends of the 1920s. Unlike the upper-middle-class WASPs who believed that Catholics and Jews could be Americanized, the lower-middle-class WASPs believed that the new immigrants must be controlled and regulated. Afraid of the corruption of American life by Catholics and Jews, the lower middle class also doubted, by the 1920s, the willingness of the upper-middle-class WASPs to preserve national virtue. As a result, many of the lower-middle-class WASPs mobilized themselves in the KKK. (Underwood & Underwood Photo, Courtesy of Library of Congress.)

The Novelists of the Lost Generation

Ironically, the most sophisticated and talented poets and novelists of the WASP elite shared the belief of the provincial culture that the establishment was corrupt and decadent. A generation of young writers born between 1890 and 1900 was bitterly disillusioned that a better society had not emerged after World War I. Lost Generation writers such as Ernest Hemingway had witnessed the meaningless slaughter of the war. Hemingway and other writers felt that their elders had lied to them by preaching virtue but practicing corruption. In America, Hemingway felt trapped by hypocrisy, and so he returned to Europe. Many expatriate American artists in Berlin, Rome, London, and, above all, Paris believed that the Old World was better than the New. Hemingway's early collection of short stories, *In Our Time*, dealt with his disillusionment with the promise of America.

The Lost Generation writers refused to believe in the rationality of the corporation preached by the leaders of big business. John Dos Passos and Sinclair Lewis wrote novels about the irrational selfishness of American business. F. Scott Fitzgerald in his novel *The Great Gatsby* described a young man fleeing from the agricultural frontier to find a career in the urban-industrial frontier of New York. Gatsby encounters only decadent and immoral people in this eastern society. In a world without ideals or hope, many of the young people presented in the novels and poems of the period drowned their sorrows in drink or tried to forget in fleeting sexual encounters.

The Movies: National Culture versus Regional Culture

By 1900, a new form of entertainment — vaudeville — had become popular in American cities. Besides singing, dancing, acrobatics, and magic acts, there were also comedy acts. A high proportion of the comedians were Irish-Catholic or Jewish. The new urban culture added to the fears of rural and small-town evangelical Protestants. Vaudeville continued to be popular into the 1920s, but movies had begun to replace vaudeville as the major form of mass entertainment as early as World War I. For instance, D. W. Griffith's movie *Birth of a Nation* (1915) grossed $18 million. By 1930, the average weekly attendance at movie theaters was 90 million and the annual income of the movie industry reached $1 billion.

The entrance of young Jews into the eastern preparatory schools and Ivy League colleges continued to be severely restricted during the 1920s. Since many leaders of major corporations and banks were recruited from these institutions, the possibility of Jewish leadership in these corporations and banks was greatly limited. The possibility of Jewish leadership was further limited by the continued restrictions on Jewish membership in major business clubs and country clubs, where important business deals were worked out. Without these outlets for their skills and capital, Jewish business people invested in the new entertainment industry and dominated the major Hollywood studios. During the pre-World War I Purity Crusade, there had been an anti-Semitic attitude that linked Jews to white slavery. The anti-Semitism of the provincial culture then was strengthened by the heavy emphasis on sex in the movies. Movies attracted audiences with titles such as *Rouged Lips, The Joy Girl, Pleasure Mad,* and *A Woman of Affairs*. Theda Bara and Mae West became stars as vamps, vampires who destroyed men. In contrast to these bad women, there were good women stars, such as Mary Pickford, who saved men from the temptations of vamps by offering them virtuous sex within marriage.

Women during the 1920s

In 1880, a good married woman was defined as free from sexual passion. In 1920, a good married woman was defined as having sexual feelings. This revolutionary acceptance of the sexuality of middle-class women had the ironic effect of helping to stop their movement out of the home. Middle-class women had argued from 1880 to 1920 that they could bring their pure sexlessness out of the home and apply it to public life. But, if good women as well as bad women had sexual feelings, then those feelings must be kept under control in the home, where a wife could be a virtuous lover to her husband. Movies and magazines encouraged women to be feminine and to express their feminity in marriage. No longer were women like Jane Addams, who had chosen public life and celibacy, models for young women. Although more middle-class women were going to college during the 1920s, fewer chose to become doctors, lawyers, professors, ministers, and social workers. College led to marriage, not to a career. It is not surprising that the two women who were successful business people, Elizabeth Arden and Helena Rubenstein, and became millionaires during the 1920s sold cosmetics that encouraged women to see themselves as feminine in an unbusinesslike way.

Having won the vote in 1920, some of the women of NAWSA formed the League of Women Voters, which was designed as a nonpartisan group that studied political issues and made recommendations. Opposed to this position of neutrality was the National Woman's party. This small group of radicals began to lobby Congress for the passage of an equal rights amendment for women. The General Federation of Business and Professional Women opposed such an amendment, as did the old progressives in the National Women's Trade Union League (NWTUL). The leaders of the NWTUL had attempted, since 1900, to get state and national governments to limit the hours of work and to establish a minimum wage for women. They feared that an equal rights amendment would result in greater exploitation of working women.

One of the major technological breakthroughs to take place at the end of the nineteenth century had been the development of electric motors. Increasingly, factories had turned to electric power because of its flexibility. The use of electric horsepower had jumped from 0.5 million in 1900 to 9 million in 1914 and to 30 million in 1930. There also was a tremendous increase in the use of electricity in middle-class homes. During the 1920s, the number of white-collar workers increased more rapidly than the number of workers in any other employment group, and advertising focused on the young wives of this growing middle class as the model consumers for all other Americans to imitate.

These women were revolutionary leaders, according to advertising, who were bringing the latest advances of technology to homemaking. Every woman needed an electric stove, refrigerator, vacuum cleaner, iron, toaster, and washing machine. Between 1920 and 1930, advertising expenditures jumped from $1 billion to $3 billion a year and installment buying increased from $1 billion to $7 billion a year.

The housing industry also influenced the middle-class consumers. Until World War I, city limits had expanded to incorporate the new housing built out along the trolley lines. Most of urban growth during the 1920s, however, was outside the city limits in independent suburbs. Chicago, for example, grew by 25 percent during the 1920s, but its suburbs grew by 700 percent. Detroit grew by 50 percent, while its suburbs also grew by 700 percent.

The white-collar workers of the suburbs drove in to the inner city in their cars and demonstrated their superior social status to the lower middle-class and blue-collar workers who had to commute within the city on trolley cars. It was prestigious for the wives in these suburbs to buy expensive furniture and household appliances for their new houses, and installment buying increased greatly. Only the middle class was defined as responsible enough to have charge accounts in the large department stores.

By emphasizing women as consumers, many Americans were able to ignore the shift in national values from a producing people to a consuming one. The great economic problem of the 1920s was finding ways to get people to buy the products made on the assembly lines. Until that time, WASP capitalist tradition had emphasized the importance of thrift so that savings could be invested in production. From the 1920s on, the capitalist middle class was urged to spend and even to go into debt.

The Heroes of the 1920s

The great heroes at the end of the nineteenth century were men who, like Carnegie and Rockefeller, increased production. In the 1920s, Henry Ford and Herbert Hoover were still heroes of production related to the old value of hard work. Their personalities were sober, careful, and restrained. But, if Americans were to become consumers, they needed different kinds of heroes. Movie stars became models for young men and women. They were heroes who played for a living and who produced nothing substantial. Such heroes lived in a personal world of conspicuous consumption. Other national heroes of the 1920s who did no productive work included the heavyweight champion Jack Dempsey, who drew the first million-dollar gate, and Babe Ruth, a baseball hero whose drinking and sexual exploits were as great as his home-run hitting. College football also had a national hero in Red Grange, the Illinois running back.

Blacks, like women, had never been associated with the Protestant work ethic or its emphasis on competition, saving, and investment. But sentiment against blacks was so strong during the 1920s that blacks could not become heroes in entertainment and sports. Until after World War II, the only acceptable role for them in movies was that of servants. Blacks were also barred from major league baseball until 1947. Between 1920 and 1930, radio became a major form of entertainment. Sales of 100,000 sets a year at the beginning of the decade had risen to 5 million a year by 1930.

The most popular radio comedy was "Amos 'n' Andy." White actors, pos-
ing as blacks, got laughs by using the Sambo stereotype of blacks as childlike, inept, and irresponsible in business. The heroes also were easily
cheated by the petty thieves who were presented as being accepted
members of the black community. But the heroes, in the Sambo tradition,
were always happy and carefree in spite of all their troubles.

Many whites were not aware that, since the 1890s, they had been listening and dancing to music influenced by black rhythms. But, during the
1920s, WASP elites in major cities did identify jazz with black musicians. A
large number of whites began to appreciate that aspect of black culture. As
long as the Protestant work ethic had been dominant, Afro-American
music, with its strong emphasis on rhythm, was seen as evil because it celebrated free-moving bodies. But the increased acceptance of sexuality and
the human body during the 1920s reversed the situation. Listening to black
musicians play jazz in speakeasies, upper-class whites created a group of
underground heroes that included Louis Armstrong, Cab Calloway, and
Duke Ellington. Blues and jazz performed by black musicians also became
available through increasingly popular phonograph records. Radio stations, however, played jazz by white musicians, such as Paul Whiteman,
which had more restrained rhythm and less obviously sexual lyrics.

The Harlem Renaissance

The great urban growth between 1890 and 1914 had resulted largely
from the almost 20 million Catholic and Jewish emigrants from southern
and eastern Europe. The migration of blacks from the South into northern
cities had seemed insignificant compared to European immigration. But,
during the 1920s, black migration continued to increase while emigration
from Europe declined. During the 1920s, 400,000 southern blacks moved
into Illinois, Pennsylvania, and New York, mostly into urban centers such
as New York City, where the Harlem ghetto population doubled from
73,000 to 165,000 during the 1920s.

Young black people who hoped to be poets, novelists, and playwrights came from all over the country to Harlem. They were excited by
the knowledge that there were white cultural leaders in New York City
who believed that blacks were capable of artistic achievement and were
willing to provide some financial support. Several of the novelists and
poets expressed a sense of personal crisis comparable to that of the white
writers of the Lost Generation. Jean Toomer's *Cane,* Wallace Thurman's
Infants of the Spring, and Nella Larson's *Quicksand* expressed the agony
of living in a world without meaning. Claude McKay and Countee Cullen
wrote excellent poetry; but more powerful was the work of Langston
Hughes and Sterling Brown, who linked their poetry with the blues tradition. Older black leaders, including W. E. B. DuBois, were upset that black
artists found strength in the sexual and musical traditions of the black
masses. The black pride of Hughes and Brown differed from that of

Louis Armstrong (1900-1971) was the most important black jazz musician of the 1920s and 1930s. It was not until after World War II, however, that he was accepted by white America as one of the great jazz musicians. Although jazz was developed by Negro musicians in New Orleans in the early twentieth century and carried by them up the Mississippi River to St. Louis, Kansas City, and Chicago, prejudice against blacks was so strong that they could not become major recording or radio stars before 1945. Most whites did not go to the small clubs where blacks like Armstrong played in the 1920s. But they learned about jazz from records and the radio where they listened to all-white bands. The most popular of these bands was that of Paul Whiteman. (Courtesy of Library of Congress.)

The majority of southern blacks for whom Booker T. Washington was a spokesman were rural before World War II. W. E. B. DuBois represented a small elite of educated blacks in the North. By 1920, however, large numbers of southern blacks had moved into northern cities and Marcus Garvey (1887-1940) became the major spokesman of the urban poor. Born in the West Indies, Garvey preached black pride and voluntary segregation to develop a self-sufficient economic community. Convicted of fraud, he was deported by the United States government. (The Granger Collection.)

Booker T. Washington and DuBois, who stressed the achievement of specific individuals. The poets were proud of what the black people were and proud of their Afro-American cultural traditions.

Marcus Garvey, a black emigrant from the West Indies, appealed to the black masses in the northern cities to turn their backs on the whites, who imprisoned them in ghettos and kept them in menial jobs. He preached black pride to the black children of the black God and His son, the black Christ. Suggesting that Africa was the chosen land for blacks, Garvey urged blacks to separate from white society and prepare to return to Africa. Strengthened through the African Orthodox church, blacks were to build a separate economy through the Universal Negro Improvement Association. Garvey's followers marched through Harlem in the uniforms of the African Legion and the Black Cross Nurses.

The Great Crash of 1929

The overwhelming majority of rural blacks in the South and urban blacks in the North lived in poverty in 1929. But their poverty was shared by many whites. Sixty percent of all families in that year had incomes of $2,000 or less. More efficient machines had made it possible for the productivity of industrial workers to increase by 32 percent during the 1920s, but their wages had increased by only 10 percent. Profits from the industrial corporations grew 62 percent and went largely to the wealthiest 5 percent of the people.

Until 1925, the increase in installment buying by the expanding number of white-collar workers had made it possible for the nation to consume most of the goods pouring off the assembly lines. But the use of automobiles, which had doubled from 9 to 20 million between 1920 and 1925, only increased to 27 million by 1930. The saturation of the market had led Alfred Sloan of General Motors to reject Henry Ford's practice of turning out a Model T that did not change from year to year and was always painted black. Using advertising techniques, Sloan tried to persuade the public that car styling should change every year and that cars should be painted in attractive colors. Sloan won much of the automobile market from Ford, but he could not increase car sales.

By 1929, cars had become crucial to the consumer economy. Twenty percent of the steel, 75 percent of the glass, and 80 percent of the rubber produced was absorbed by the automobile industry. The oil industry and the many filling stations, garages, roadside restaurants, and motels depended upon the car. Much of cement production went into road building.

The slump in car sales was paralleled by a decline in the construction of new housing, which caused unemployment in the building trades. Fewer suburban houses also meant fewer markets for refrigerators and the many other electric appliances. While the consumer economy was slowing and agriculture was in a depression, the wealthy were pouring their profits into the stock market. Corporate profits had been high during the early 1920s, and elite investors had accepted President Hoover's promise that the "new era" had brought permanent prosperity and endless growth. The stock market went higher and higher until October 1929. Suddenly, confidence in the earning power of the overpriced stocks collapsed, and the stock market fell. As it fell, the business slowdown continued, making confidence in corporate stocks still more unsteady. American investments abroad stopped. The German economy collapsed without the inflow of American money. The loss of payments from Germany shattered the already weak British and French economies. They, in turn, could not pay the American government or American private investors.

Hoover and the Great Depression

In 1928, urban Democrats won control of their nominating convention from southern Democrats and chose Al Smith. In the election that followed, all of the border southern states and many western states that usually voted Democratic voted instead for the Republican candidate Her-

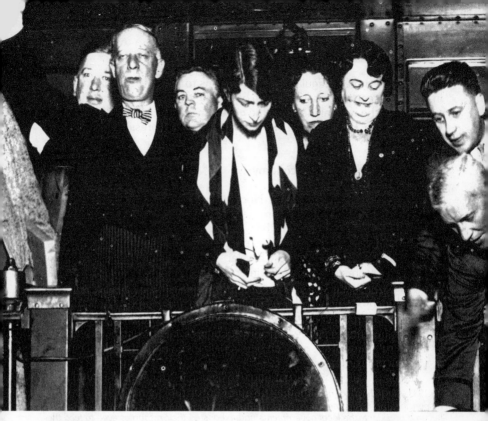

Alfred E. Smith (1873-1944) was the first Catholic to be nominated as the presidential candidate of one of the major parties. By the 1920s, the Catholic immigrants from Europe, who had flooded into northern cities until 1914, had become familiar enough with America to develop political power within the Democratic party. But the other major bloc of voters in the Democratic party were white Protestants in the South who were very hostile to Catholicism. Many of those southern Democrats, especially in the border states, voted for the Republicans in 1928 because of their anti-Catholicism. (The Granger Collection.)

bert Hoover. Rural and small-town Protestants would not accept a Catholic as president. Anti-Catholic prejudice was just as strong in the Deep South. But belief in the necessity of white loyalty to a single party to keep blacks out of politics was stronger than anti-Catholicism in South Carolina, Georgia, Alabama, Mississippi, Louisiana, and Arkansas, and all of these states voted for Smith. The Catholic issue was so intense that many more voters participated in the election than in 1920 or 1924. Hoover, with southern support, won, with 21 million votes to 15 million for Smith. Smith, however, inspired many Catholics to vote for the first time and was the first Democrat to carry the northern cities.

Throughout the 1920s, Hoover had been certain that there was no need for government interference in the economy beyond the enactment of tariffs to encourage trade agreements among large corporations. Then, six months after he took office, he was faced with the most dramatic economic collapse in American history. Populists and progressives had wanted government regulatory commissions to regulate the marketplace in order to keep corporations from becoming too powerful. They had not considered the radical idea that the government should try to control the business cycle. But, because of the severity of the depression, Hoover felt pressure to do just that.

The Collapse of the Economy

As a corporate executive, Hoover knew how interdependent the parts of the economy had become, and he feared that the collapse of the large corporations would bring the whole capitalist system to an end. One percent of the 25,000 banks held 50 percent of all assets. Three companies — Ford, General Motors, and Chrysler — produced 85 percent of all the cars. Chain stores, such as A&P in groceries and Rexall in drugs, had as many as 15,000 stores across the country. Insurance companies had invested in the stocks of the industrial corporations. As the stock market lost $74 billion from 1929 to 1933, the stock of major corporations fell; General Motors fell from 73 to 8 points, and United States Steel fell from 262 to 21 points.

By 1933, more than a quarter of the work force was unemployed. Welfare in 1932 was the responsibility of local and state governments. But by 1933, when Franklin D. Roosevelt became president, the local governments had exhausted their resources even to feed the unemployed. The desperation of the situation forced the national government in 1933 into the unprecedented step of providing relief to the unemployed. Here are unemployed in New York City in 1930 waiting in a breadline. (UPI.)

Hoover had already been worried about the depression in agriculture when he took office. He persuaded Congress to pass the Agricultural Marketing Act. It established a Farm Board that was authorized to loan money to help farmers establish cooperatives. Hoover hoped that these cooperatives would serve farmers in the same way that trade associations served corporations to stop cutthroat competition. But the millions of farmers could not reach agreement on prices and production as easily as the three large automobile producers or the three large steel companies. Each independent farmer struggled to raise more crops as prices fell, and the increased production caused prices to fall more. Farm income dropped from $8 billion in 1929 to $3 billion in 1933, and thousands of farms were lost as banks foreclosed on mortgages.

The large companies refused to allow their prices to fall and, instead, cut production and fired many workers and cut the wages of others. Unemployment leaped from 1.5 million in 1929 to 13 million — 25 percent of the work force — in 1933, and industrial wages fell from $25 to $17 a week. Hoover's answer to this disaster was to get almost a billion dollars from Congress for public works projects that would boost employment. He also asked the states and cities to start similar projects. He got a tax cut from Congress and signed the Norris-LaGuardia Act (1932), which outlawed yellow-dog contracts.

But Hoover refused to give direct federal relief to the unemployed and the starving. When thousands of veterans marched to Washington, D.C., to beg Congress to give them the bonuses that they were not supposed to receive until 1945, Hoover asked Army Chief of Staff Douglas MacArthur to conduct a military operation to drive what he believed to be potential revolutionaries out of the capital. And Hoover persuaded Congress to establish a Reconstruction Finance Corporation (RFC) based on the model of the World War I War Finance Corporation. The RFC loaned $1.5 billion to large banks, insurance companies, railroads, and industrial corporations. Hoover felt that aid to the poor would cause them to lose their commitment to competitive capitalism. He had much more faith that the corporations, if saved by government aid, would preserve their commitment to capitalism.

Hoover and Foreign Policy

Hoover was the first president to try actively to control the business cycle. The onset of the Great Depression also forced him to reconsider his views on foreign policy. Hoover believed that the depression was caused by the weakness of the European economy. He believed that the health of the American economy was interrelated with the world economy, and he called for a year's moratorium on the payment of international debts (1931). Hoover hoped that this interval would stabilize Europe by curtailing the debt payments that dated from World War I. Hoover contradicted these actions, however, by signing the Hawley-Smoot bill (1930), which raised tariffs still higher and made it more difficult for Europeans to get money to pay their debts by exporting goods to America. The angry Europeans raised tariffs against American goods, and American exports to Europe fell 50 percent between 1930 and 1932.

Hoover and Japan

Japan reluctantly had accepted the American Open-Door policy in China because it could not compete with American, British, and French naval power in Asia. With the disintegration of the economies of the Western nations, however, Japan felt free to act and so marched armies into all of Manchuria (1931).

In 1920, Hoover had believed that the American economy was so strong that it could bring order to the world without the use of military force. With a shattered economy, however, Hoover faced the probability that the only way to stop Japan's defiance of the Open-Door policy was through war. Hoover refused to commit the nation to another war. He remembered that, while capitalist nations had fought each other in World War I, communism had managed to establish itself in Russia. Hoover greatly feared that another capitalist war would allow communism to spread from Russia and threaten capitalism everywhere. He refused, therefore, to take the advice of Secretary of State Henry Stimson to be tough with Japan.

In March 1933, when he turned over the presidency to Franklin D. Roosevelt, Hoover's hopes for a "new era" at home and abroad were as shattered as the economy.

Supplementary Reading

W. A. Williams, *The Tragedy of American Diplomacy* (1962), was the first major book to stress the activist foreign policy of the 1920s. J. Wilson, *American Business and Foreign Policy* (1971), and E. Lieuwen, *U.S. Policy in Latin America* (1965), present aspects of that policy in greater detail. *The American Economy between the World Wars* (1974) by J. Potter and *Main Currents in Modern American History* (1976) by G. Kolko examine the major patterns of the business economy during the 1920s. J. Wilson, *Herbert Hoover: Forgotten Progressive* (1975), and M. Heald, *The Social Responsibilities of Business* (1970), describe the continuation of corporate progressivism.

The difficulties of the labor movement are explored in I. Bernstein's *The Lean Years: A History of the American Worker, 1920-1933* (1960). Problems of farmers are the subject of G. Fite, "The Farmer's Dilemma, 1919-1929, in *Change and Continuity in Twentieth-Century America: The 1920s* (1968), edited by J. Braemen, R. Bremner, and D. Brady. The problems of farmers are also discussed in T. Saloutos and J. Hicks, *Twentieth-Century Populism: Agricultural Discontent in the Middle West, 1900-1939* (1951).

The political patterns of the 1920s are discussed in R. Murray, *The Politics of Normalcy* (1973); B. Noggle, *Teapot Dome: Oil and Politics in the 1920s* (1962); G. Tindall, *The Emergence of the New South* (1967); E. Moore, *A Catholic Runs for President* (1956); R. Krickus, *Pursuing the American Dream: White Ethnics and the New Populism* (1976); and D. Burner, *The Politics of Provincialism: The Democratic Party in Transition, 1918-1932* (1976).

J. Higham, *Strangers in the Land: Patterns of American Nativism* (1955), analyzes the legislation designed to stop immigration; and N. Clark, *Deliver Us from Evil: An Interpreta-*

tion of American Prohibition (1976), places that movement within the larger cultural context. K. Jackson, *The Ku Klux Klan in the City, 1915-1930* (1967), relates the KKK to national patterns.

The standard book on the novelists is F. Hoffman, *The Twenties* (1949). P. Fass, *The Damned and the Beautiful: American Youth in the 1920s* (1977), is an excellent anaylsis of youth culture.

W. Chafe, *The American Woman: Her Changing Social, Economic, and Political Role* (1972), and S. Lemans, *The Woman Citizen: Social Feminism in the 1920s* (1973), describe the changing role of women.

R. Sklar, *Movie-made America* (1976), and J. Fink, *The Car Culture* (1975), indicate the dramatic changes in urban culture.

The continued frustrations of blacks are analyzed in J. Sochen, *The Unbridgeable Gap: Blacks and Their Quest for the American Dream* (1972).

J. Galbraith, *The Great Crash* (1961), and R. Himmelberg, *The Origins of the National Recovery Administration: Business, Government, and the Trade Association Issue, 1921-1933* (1976), provide evidence of the unprecedented role of the Hoover administration in fighting the economic collapse.

Chapter
25

Depression and War
1932-1945

Franklin D. Roosevelt, unlike Herbert Hoover, was not a self-made millionaire; he had been born into a wealthy New York family that traced its heritage to colonial America. Raised on a country estate, Roosevelt was tutored at home and then educated at private schools and Harvard University. He had been attracted to the progressivism of Woodrow Wilson and had served as an undersecretary of the navy in Wilson's administration. He had been the vice-presidential candidate of the Democrats in their disastrous defeat of 1920. After his legs had been crippled by polio, he returned to politics to become the governor of New York in 1928. Democratic party leaders were impressed by his ability to win votes at the same time Hoover and the Republicans were gaining a smashing victory. They were especially impressed by the ability of the aristocratic Protestant to win the votes of working-class and lower-middle-class Catholics, as well as the votes of New York's large Jewish population. Governor Roosevelt was reelected in 1930; in 1932, he won the Democratic presidential nomination, because it seemed that he would be able to unite southern Protestants and northern Catholics.

During the presidential campaign, Roosevelt disagreed with Hoover about the nature of the depression. Whereas Hoover said the depression was caused by international problems, Roosevelt said the depression was a national problem. Immediately after he became president, Roosevelt sent Secretary of State Cordell Hull to the London Economic Conference (1933). However, Roosevelt then instructed Hull not to cooperate with the other nations in their effort to stabilize the currencies used for international trade.

Roosevelt also disagreed with Hoover about the role of the government in the economy. Like Theodore Roosevelt and Woodrow Wilson, Roosevelt believed that political leaders and government experts could be constructive leaders of the capitalist economy and that government regulatory commissions could stabilize economic patterns. As governor of New York, he had been particularly concerned with the conservation of forest lands and water resources and the preservation of family-owned farms. He also had been willing to provide relief for the urban poor and unemployed. His progressive heritage from Theodore Roosevelt and Woodrow Wilson, however, included a commitment to a balanced budget. During the 1932 campaign, he criticized Hoover for allowing the national budget to have deficits. There was nothing in his progressive heritage to provide guidelines for controlling the business cycle.

Roosevelt's Election and the Triumph of Corporate Progressivism

Roosevelt won 22 million votes; Hoover, 15 million. The Democrats won majorities of 311 to 119 in the House of Representatives and 60 to 35 in the Senate. These statistics reversed those of 1928 and marked the end of the Republicans as the majority party. The Republicans had become the majority party in 1896, because they had become identified with the urban-industrial society that was becoming more important than rural and small-town American society with which the Democrats traditionally were identified. By 1932, however, the Democrats were more strongly linked with the cities because of the strong support they received from Catholics and Jews, who formed the majority in many northeastern and midwestern cities.

The nomination of the Catholic Al Smith as the presidential candidate of the Democratic party in 1928 had dramatically changed the image of the party established in 1896, when William Jennings Bryan had stood for the preservation of an evangelical Protestant America. Many more Catholics and Jews were eligible to vote by 1928, in contrast to the 1890s, because the growing stability of urban neighborhoods by 1914 allowed them to meet residency requirements. By the end of the 1920s, many also had overcome the language barrier and had gained a greater understanding of the political process.

Smith, therefore, had been able to win many of the northern cities in 1928, the first time a Democratic presidential candidate had been successful there since the election of 1892. But many white southerners, traditionally Democratic, had voted against him and his Catholicism. In 1932, however, Roosevelt was able to combine the Jewish and Catholic voters in the northern cities and the white Protestants of the rural and small-town South into a national majority that has persisted up to the present. The return of the Democratic majority was marked by a reversal of the trend of fewer people participating in politics. Coming into the 1890s, more than 80 percent of eligible voters participated in presidential elections. During the years of the Republican majority, 1896-1928, the rate of participation dropped below 50 percent. Between 1928 and 1936, the rate of participation began to rise, going over 60 percent in 1936 and adding further strength to the Democratic majority.

Between his election in November 1932 and his inauguration in March 1933, Roosevelt established contact with the corporate leaders (such as Gerard Swope of General Electric) who had been in favor of the establishment of government regulatory commissions that would limit price competition. The corporate progressives had been frustrated by the Republican administrations between 1920 and 1932, but, with the election of FDR, they became optimistic that they could return to the kind of policies represented by the FTC and the Federal Reserve System in the Wilson administration and by the large numbers of governmental agencies that had regulated the economy during World War I.

The major proposal of the corporate progressives in response to the economic crisis of the depression was the National Recovery Administration (NRA), which was established in 1933. Roosevelt considered the creation of the NRA his most important legislative accomplishment. Under the NRA, members of the trade associations reached agreements on prices, wages, and production quotas. Unlike earlier agreements, these codes ceased to be voluntary; after 1933, they could be enforced by the Justice Department. All the companies in one industry, such as steel or rubber or auto, were encouraged to participate in creating a code for their part of the economy. The government did not use laws to force them to join, but great pressure was put on companies to participate and to show their participation by marking their products with the emblem (a blue eagle) of the NRA.

Roosevelt's concern, like Hoover's, was to save the corporate structure of the economy. Unlike Hoover, however, Roosevelt was not afraid to use the power of the government to influence the economy, and he did not feel the need to support only voluntary activities. These attitudes were expressed further by his acceptance of the plans for stabilizing agriculture that were put forward by the large farm organizations. Under these plans, farmers growing crops such as wheat, cotton, and corn were to come together to decide how many acres of the crops would be planted in a given year. In 1933, the Agricultural Adjustment Administration (AAA) encouraged the farmers to cut back production by paying the participating farmers for not growing crops or raising animals.

Both the NRA and the AAA were designed to reduce production at the same time there was great poverty and hunger throughout the country. Both worked in favor of big businesses and farmers over small businesses and farmers, especially tenant farmers, as well as laborers.

*For the National Recovery Act,
one of Roosevelt's attempted
remedies for the depression,
General Hugh Johnson
designed a blue eagle as a
symbol of cooperation between
business and government.*

Roosevelt and the War against the Depression

Roosevelt sent the bills establishing the NRA and the AAA to Congress, where leaders of the Democratic party asked congressmen to vote for them without studying or even reading them. During his 1932 speeches, Roosevelt had asked people to see the depression as an enemy similar to Germany during World War I, and he insisted that unquestioning loyalty was necessary to defeat the new enemy. Many Democratic and Republican leaders agreed with the president that Congress should give him uncritical support in the spring of 1933, just as Congress had supported Wilson in 1917 by passing emergency measures to mobilize the nation in the face of danger. Between November 1932 and March 1933, the economy continued to fall apart. So many banks were failing that governors closed the remaining state banks in order to save them from having all their funds withdrawn by panic-striken customers. As soon as he became president, Roosevelt used an emergency law passed during World War I to establish a bank holiday that closed all the national banks (March 4, 1933). He promised that the government would back solvent banks and would permit those that were sound to reopen. This policy proved effective; the panic passed, and the larger banks survived. Congressional leaders then, in 1933, created the Federal Deposit Insurance Corporation (FDIC), which guaranteed the savings people placed in the banks against loss by the failure of the banks. Swift and powerful government action had saved the private banking system, especially the wealthier banks. The Security Act created a commission to regulate the Wall Street Stock Exchange and restore confidence in that major capitalist institution. Many middle-class homeowners were saved from losing their property by the Home Owners Loan Corporation (HOLC, 1933), which gave them new mortgages at lower interest rates.

Roosevelt, Relief, and Reform

These New Deal programs, like Hoover's RFC, were helpful to property owners. But Roosevelt, unlike Hoover, was also willing to provide federal money for the relief of the many poor and starving people. The Federal Emergency Relief Administration (FERA, 1933) was established to grant money to states, which provided matching funds. The Public Works Administration (PWA, 1933) began large-scale building projects and the Civil Works Administration (CWA, 1933) engaged in small-scale projects to give work to the unemployed. Never before had the national government taken responsibility for the poor and the unemployed. The Roosevelt administration continued to break precedent through the establishment of the Civilian Conservation Corps (CCC, 1933). Young, unemployed males were recruited and put in workcamps, where they were given uniforms and were commanded by army officers. They received a small amount of money in addition to their clothes, food, and housing to carry out such tasks as replanting the national forests.

In addition to these relief measures, Roosevelt supported the creation of the Tennessee Valley Authority (TVA, 1933). This was a project that Republican progressives from the Midwest, such as George Norris of Nebraska, had long supported. The TVA built a series of dams and electric and fertilizer plants throughout the Tennessee River Valley. Besides stimulating the economy of this very poor region, it was hoped that the cost of running the government plants would provide a yardstick to judge the prices charged by private utilities throughout the country.

The New Deal, Professors, and Social Workers

The trend that put professors from the universities into the administrations of Theodore Roosevelt and Woodrow Wilson, which had been checked between 1920 and 1932, was renewed and accelerated under Franklin Roosevelt. Raymond Moley from Columbia University played a major role in drawing up the NRA. Rexford Tugwell, also from Columbia, and Milburn Wilson, a professor from Montana, did much of the planning for the AAA. Many law professors also took positions in the numerous government agencies. This group of intellectuals came to be known as the Brain Trust.

Social workers who had become so important during the progressive era had limited influence during the 1920s. After 1933, however, they were given many government offices, especially in the FERA, which was headed by Harry Hopkins. FERA offered government jobs to an unprecedented

The South did not participate greatly in the increase in industrial wealth from the Civil War to World War II. As its population increased, therefore, more of its white population as well as its black population was forced into sharecropping. By the 1930s, the Roosevelt administration recognized that there was a special problem of rural poverty in the South. The problem had been solved ironically, however; since World War II the mechanization of southern agriculture has driven both white and black sharecroppers into the ghettos of northern and southern cities. (USDA Photo.)

number of women, many of them in positions of leadership. Frances B. Perkins, Roosevelt's secretary of labor, was the first woman cabinet member.

Many fewer social workers, professors, and Protestant ministers were attracted to socialism during the years of the New Deal than during the first dozen years of the century. Norman Thomas, the presidential candidate of the Socialist party in 1932, got only 800,000 votes, and the Socialist party became still weaker in 1936 and 1940. William Z. Foster, the candidate of the Communist party, received only 100,000 votes in 1932, and the Communists could not expand their support in 1936 and 1940 even though economic recovery had not been achieved. Seeing the weakness of the Socialist and Communist parties and hoping that Roosevelt would begin new economic and social experiments, most radical intellectuals tried to work within the Democratic party and push it to the left. Many farmers and city workers who were not satisfied with Roosevelt's legislative record in 1933 also wanted more radical legislation.

Huey Long, the South, and the New Deal

In 1934, Huey Long, a senator from Louisiana, became the most powerful critic of the New Deal. Since the 1880s, southern farmers had been bitterly critical of the large corporations centered in the Northeast. They had called for state and national government commissions to regulate the corporations and for government financial policies to help farmers. Many had become Populists in 1892, and others had helped William Jennings Bryan get the nomination of the Democratic party in 1896. They had also voted for Woodrow Wilson in 1912, when he promised to fight the large corporations. In the 1920s, they were very critical of the support given the large corporations by the Republicans, but they could not accept Al Smith, a Catholic, as a leader against the Republicans. Again, they had hoped that Franklin Roosevelt would strike out against the corporations, but, instead, NRA gave the corporations protection from antitrust action. Long, whose father had been a Populist, strongly attacked Roosevelt for protecting the corporations and the wealthiest people in the country.

After developing a ruthless personal dictatorship in Louisiana that gave him a secure base of operations, Long reached out from the South to build a national organization. His ambition was to become the first southerner to be elected president since before the Civil War. (Although Woodrow Wilson was from the south, he was elected president as the governor of New Jersey, a northern state. In this sense, Jimmy Carter, the former governor of Georgia, in 1976 became the first southerner to be elected president since the mid-nineteenth century.) Long built his national organization around Share Our Wealth clubs that claimed 5 million members. Long proposed to tax much of the wealth of the very rich and redistribute the money to provide a house and an income of $5,000 for every family. He also proposed that the government pay the college expenses of every interested and qualified young person. He planned to challenge Roosevelt for the Democratic nomination in 1936 and then win the nomination in 1940 after Roosevelt had failed to take the country out of the depression. But Long was assassinated in 1935, and the major protests against the conservatism of the New Deal began to come more from the workers of the North than from the farmers of the South.

Workers and the NRA

New Deal leaders, who were trying to reestablish the corporate progressivism of World War I, moved to include labor in the war against the depression. Under the leadership of corporate progressives, union membership had doubled during the war before it declined rapidly during the 1920s, when antiunion corporate leaders had gained control of national politics. The antiunion business leaders had been discredited by the collapse of the economy, and corporate progressives were in a position to encourage the safe, nonradical unionism of the AFL. Section 7-A of the NRA legislation stated that the codes worked out by business leaders must include provisions for minimum wages, maximum hours, and the right of collective bargaining for unions. Business leaders, however, tried to take advantage of the large number of unemployed workers to set the minimum wage at a very low level and moved to bring workers into company unions. At first, they were successful, and a million workers joined company unions. But many workers then refused to accept the leadership of business people who had not been able to sustain prosperity after 1929. The workers engaged in strikes in order to force the recognition of independent unions. Other workers in industries where unions did not exist, such as trucking, began to engage in strikes to force employers to accept unionization.

The elections of 1928 and 1932 had demonstrated that the 20 million immigrants who had come to America from southern and eastern Europe between 1890 and 1914 were learning to use the political process. These same people also were beginning to understand the world of industrial work. By 1934 and 1935, they no longer could be as easily divided and conquered by their employers as they had been before World War I. Something like a common working-class experience existed by 1933, and solidarity among workers was much more possible. When truck drivers went on strike in Minneapolis in 1934, employers called on the police to use force against the strikers and also armed themselves in an attempt to intimidate the workers. During the 1890s, this kind of force had been successful in stopping unionization and in destroying already existing unions. But in 1934, workers in many kinds of jobs were able to identify with the truck drivers, and thousands of men and women went into the streets to give them support. The workers were ready to use violence if they were attacked by the police or their employers. Faced with a mass uprising, the officials from the trucking companies made concessions that led to the recognition of the union.

The New Deal, Progressivism, and Labor

The wave of strikes in 1934 and the growing strength of Huey Long's Share Our Wealth program indicated a grass-roots rebellion against corporate leadership. This rebellion expressed itself in the congressional elections of November 1934, when, for the first time since 1902, a party in power (the Democrats) increased its congressional majority. Franklin Roosevelt, like Theodore Roosevelt and Woodrow Wilson, expected that corporate progressives would give labor fair pay and fair working conditions. These progressive presidents expected, however, that the middle class would provide leadership and that labor would follow that leadership.

But in 1935, Democratic congressmen and senators from northern cities began to express the discontent of workers with Roosevelt's politics, which had stressed recovery by stabilizing big business and big agriculture and had provided only relief for the unemployed. The workers wanted reform as well as relief and recovery.

Catholics, Jews, Reform, and the New Deal

Most Jews had never accepted the dominant philosophy of nineteenth-century American Protestants, that it was wrong to help the poor. In the minds of nineteenth-century Protestants, the poor had chosen to be poor and therefore had sinned against God. They believed it was God's will that everyone work as hard as possible, and they believed there was work for everyone who wanted it. Anyone who helped a poor person shared in the sin of rebellion against God.

However, the Jewish culture stressed giving charity to the poor, as did the Catholic culture. Both the Jewish and the Catholic cultures had a much stronger commitment to social solidarity and responsibility than the Protestant culture did. Wealthier Jews provided a great deal of help to the millions of poor Jews who came from Russia between 1890 and 1914. And, since the 1890s, popes had been issuing encyclicals that were critical of competitive capitalism when it ignored the issues of social justice. They also spoke in favor of labor unions. During the election of 1932, most leaders of the American Catholic church had used the social justice position to criticize Hoover for ignoring the suffering of the poor and the unemployed. Most cardinals, archbishops, and bishops openly supported Roosevelt. Since 1919, the Catholic Bishops' Program for Social Reconstruction had called for minimum-wage laws and unemployment, health, and old-age insurance. Roosevelt, in contrast to the Republican presidents of the 1920s, appointed large numbers of Catholics, as well as Jews, to federal offices. James Farley and Thomas Walsh were Catholics appointed to the cabinet. But Roosevelt had little interest in the issues of unemployment and old-age insurance. Senator Robert Wagner, a Catholic from New York, led the drive in Congress during 1935 to create a Social Security Act and to force Roosevelt to accept it.

The Social Security Act (1935) was to begin paying pensions to people over sixty-five in 1940. Not all workers were covered under the act, however, and the pensions of those who were came from taxes on their salaries. It was assumed that there was such a strong tradition against Social Security in the country that it could be accepted only if workers paid for it themselves. The Social Security legislation also provided for unemployment compensation. The money for the unemployment programs was to come from taxes on payrolls and was to be administered by the states so that the amount of money an unemployed worker received varied from state to state. A program of assistance for blind and disabled people and for dependent children was begun with the federal government granting money to states, which provided matching funds.

Most states used sales taxes to provide their matching funds, although sales taxes, like the Social Security payroll tax, were regressive and fell more heavily on lower-income families, rather than higher-income families. Some states provided more matching funds and made their welfare programs more attractive than others. Northern states tended to have more generous welfare programs; this encouraged the poor to move from the South into the northern cities. Since the southern states taxed themselves less, they, in turn, attracted industry from northern states because of their more favorable tax rates.

Senator Wagner, the NLRB, and the CIO

Congress passed the Wagner Act (1935), which established a National Labor Relations Board (NLRB). The board was given the power to conduct elections in which workers could choose whether or not they wanted to be represented by a union. If two unions wanted to represent the workers, an election would determine which union the workers preferred. The NLRB also had the responsibility of keeping management from firing workers for union activity and from trying to force them into company unions.

Encouraged by the wave of strikes in 1934, union leaders, including John L. Lewis of the United Mine Workers, Sidney Hillman of the Amalgamated Clothing Workers, and David Dubinsky of the International Ladies' Garment Workers, had begun a rebellion within the AFL. Then, they argued, was the time to unionize the unskilled industrial workers. Top leadership in the AFL, however, refused to take advantage of the weakness of the business community and break from their cautious tradition of preserving the skilled craft unions. But, in 1935, further encouraged by the creation of the NLRB, the rebellious leaders broke from the AFL to form the Congress of Industrial Organizations (CIO). Helped by the NLRB, the CIO began to win some elections and provide unions to large numbers of industrial workers for the first time since the collapse of the Knights of Labor at the end of the 1880s. Business leaders, unable to count on federal troops or even local police to repress union activity as they had in previous decades, redoubled their spending for labor spies and armies of private police to fight union organizers.

Taking advantage of the sense of worker solidarity that had been expressed in the strikes of 1934, union organizers encouraged the workers to take over their factories until management recognized their right to unionize. Workers, for example, struggling to unionize in Toledo and Minneapolis in 1934, had been able to withstand police violence against them because thousands of people went into the streets to support them. In 1937, 400,000 workers engaged in sit-down strikes in steel, auto, and rubber plants. Owners were limited in their ability to use force to get the workers out because their factories might have been destroyed in the struggle. Small armies of private police were used by Henry Ford, however, in bloody clashes with union organizers, and Ford was able to delay unionization until World War II. By 1938, United States Steel and General

Motors had accepted collective bargaining with the CIO, and union membership reached 9 million in 1939, three times the 3 million union members in 1930.

The Election of 1936

When Roosevelt was forced to accept the reforms of 1935, he lost much of the support he had had from big business. Business and political leaders from both the Republican and the Democratic parties accused him of undermining the capitalist system. These men, including Al Smith, formed the Liberty League and tried unsuccessfully to keep Roosevelt from being renominated in 1936.

Reflecting the way in which it had lost its hold on urban-industrial society, the Republican party nominated Governor Alfred Landon of Kansas, one of the most rural states, as its presidential candidate. More than 80 percent of the nation's newspapers backed Landon, but Roosevelt still won an even greater victory than he had in 1932, with his 27 million votes to Landon's 16 million. Roosevelt got the votes of 5 million people who had not voted in 1932. Increasing numbers of women, blacks, and workers participated in the election, because they were excited by Roosevelt's promise to shift the attention of the nation from the very rich to the poor, the bottom third of the population. Much more than in 1932, Roosevelt's speeches spoke of shifting power from corporations to average Americans.

Roosevelt and Blacks

In 1932, Roosevelt had won the support of only 20 percent of the black voters. With blacks disfranchised in the South, the northern black voters had remained loyal to the Republicans as the party of Lincoln and emancipation. By 1936, Roosevelt had reversed Woodrow Wilson's policies against blacks and had appointed more blacks to positions of importance in the federal government than had been appointed by any previous president. Robert Weaver and William Hastie were appointed to the Department of Interior. Mary Bethune was named to the National Youth Administration, as was Ira DeA. Reid to the Social Security Administration. Lawrence Oxley was appointed to the Department of Labor, and R. K. Jones, to the Department of Interior.

At the same time, however, blacks experienced discrimination in receiving relief and in getting jobs on TVA projects. They were limited to quotas in the CCC and the WPA. But blacks, who were traditionally last hired and first fired, suffered even more from the depression than whites did, and many were grateful that they were included in New Deal relief projects that kept them from starving. Because of the importance of white southerners in the Democratic party and in Congress, Roosevelt was afraid to alter patterns of discrimination and segregation. He resisted efforts by the black leaders Walter White of the NAACP and A. Philip Randolph of the Brotherhood of Sleeping Car Porters to get him to support antilynching legislation in Congress.

But, by 1936, many white southerners were already angry with Roosevelt because he had included blacks in relief programs and had named blacks to leadership positions in his administration. And these whites were frightened by the participation of blacks in the victory of the Democratic party in 1936, when 75 percent of northern blacks voted as Democrats. Having kept southern blacks out of politics since 1900, white southern Democrats had to face sharing power in the national Democratic party with northern blacks.

Racist Democracy and Sambo

In 1933, Adolf Hitler had established what he called a racist democracy in Aryan Germany. He had called on all Aryan Germans to unite in the Nazi party in order to drive the Jews who lived in Germany out of politics. In the way that blacks were legally segregated socially in the South, Hitler wanted Jews to be segregated in Germany. By 1936, the American tradition of racist democracy, especially the extreme form that it took in the South, was becoming embarrassing to American leaders because it could so easily be compared to the philosophy of Nazi Germany. The need of American WASP leaders to show that the United States was different from Germany made it possible for them to tolerate a major break in the caste system by 1936.

The caste system had demanded that black men appear to be Sambos, adult children. These grown children, called boys even when they were very old, were no threat to the caste system, which denied white women to black men and kept black men from being violent toward white men. Black men could not compete with white men. The typical figure of a black in the movies in the 1930s was the very slow and lazy Step 'n' Fetchit. Always portrayed as a servant, he never threatened the leadership roles of whites. On the very popular Jack Benny radio show, Benny had a black servant named Rochester. The low status of blacks was emphasized by the fact that Rochester always addressed his employer as Mr. Benny, while he, like a boy, was called by his surname Rochester.

But, in 1936, a black man — Joe Louis — became the heavyweight boxing champion of the world after defeating a German, Max Schmeling. And Louis, unlike Jack Johnson, was not driven out of the country. Jesse Owens was the American hero at the Olympic Games held in Berlin in 1936. Louis and Owens broke the caste system by competing against whites and defeating them. It was much easier for American whites to accept this challenge to the caste system, since Louis and Owens were defeating white representatives of German racist democracy.

Women and the Great Depression

Pearl Buck, one of the major women novelists of the 1930s, used Nazi Germany also as a way to criticize the traditional American definition of the role of women. In *Of Men and Women* (1941), she pointed out how strongly Hitler had tried to confine women to the home, insisting that the only role for a woman was as a wife and mother. How, she asked, was this different from public policy toward women in the United States?

The Economy Act (1933) had stated that wives should be fired before husbands when federal jobs were cut. Most states had laws ending the employment of women teachers when they married. At the end of the 1930s, a public opinion poll indicated that three-fourths of men and women were opposed to wives working outside the home. Fewer women went to college than in the 1920s, and the number of women professionals (doctors, lawyers, and college teachers) had also declined.

But, as in the case of blacks, the 1930s demonstrated contradictory and conflicting patterns. In contrast to Hitler's policies, Roosevelt had appointed Jews, blacks, and women to high offices in his administration. Even if male WASPs remained in control of the most important economic and social institutions throughout the New Deal, they had to share political power with groups who had been outsiders. Eleanor Roosevelt was more active and influential than any previous president's wife. She had helped her husband campaign when he was crippled by polio, and she continued her political activity after 1933. She insisted that a woman's first duty was to her family, but, herself the mother of five, she also advocated roles outside the home. She was much more committed to social justice than was her husband, and she was enthusiastic about the new coalition of labor, women, blacks, and ethnic minorities that became such an important part of the Democratic party in 1936. An illustration of the contradictory pattern of the New Deal was Rose Schneiderman, who served on the NRA Labor Advisory Board but could not keep the pay scale for women doing equal work from being lower than that of men.

The most popular programs on radio were soap operas such as "Ma Perkins," in which the major figure was a woman. These strong women provided the wisdom and the strength to help their families and neighbors, males and females, with their troubles. The decline of male prestige after the great crash of 1929 was shown even more dramatically in the movies. Women stars who expressed their sexuality, such as Mae West, Greta Garbo, and Marlene Dietrich, were much more independent than the heroines of the 1920s, and they displayed more initiative in choosing their lovers. Another group of women stars with powerful personalities — Joan Crawford, Bette Davis, Katharine Hepburn, and Rosalind Russell — played roles of lawyers, businesswomen, and athletes. Often, the scripts had them surrender their independence to men at the conclusion of the movies, but they displayed great competence and skill in their professions before the traditional ending.

The movies were the most popular of the arts in the 1930s, and few movies were concerned with criticism of the status quo. Rather, most offered an escape from the serious economic and social problems. Many were comedies that focused on the lives of wealthy people. Others, such as the one pictured here, were lavish musicals. The escapism of the movies of the 1930s represented, therefore, the refusal of the average voter of that decade to seriously consider a radical political solution to his economic and social problems. (From Paramount Pictures, Inc.)

Martha Gellhorn reporting on the Spanish civil war, Anne O'Hare McCormick writing for the *New York Times*, Dorothy Thompson writing for the *New York Herald Tribune*, and Freda Kirchway as editor of the *Nation* provided leadership in journalism. Until their breakthrough in the 1930s, it had been assumed that only males were tough enough to work in the competitive world of journalism. Discriminated against in established academic areas, women such as Ruth Benedict and Margaret Mead excelled in the new field of anthropology.

American Indians and the Great Depression

By World War I, American Indians were beginning to recover from the shock of the rapid conquest of the West by whites. Their populations had stopped declining, and there were new signs of cultural vitality. One of these signs was the development of the Native American Church. It began in Oklahoma as a blend of Indian and Christian doctrines and rituals. The drug peyote was used in the religious ceremony. At first, the government tried to suppress the ceremonies, as it had suppressed the Ghost Dance of 1890; but, by 1920, it had given up these efforts. By that time, the church had won converts in tribes throughout the entire country, but it was especially strong in the tribes of the Great Plains.

The Native American Church indicated that the tribes were not going to accept white culture passively but would use aspects of it creatively. This was what blacks had done in developing Afro-American churches and Afro-American music. Some whites had begun to appreciate black creativity during the 1920s, and some whites also began to appreciate the creativity of the Indians. When the Great Depression called the white man's ways into question, some whites suggested that Congress reverse the policy of the 1880s that had proposed the destruction of tribal cultures. Already in 1924, Congress had voted to accept Indians as citizens even when they had not left communal life. Then, in 1934, Congress passed the Indian Reorganization Act (IRA), which stopped the further breakdown of tribal land into individual allotments and recommended that the dictatorial control of Indian life by superintendents appointed by the Bureau of Indian Affairs (BIA) be limited. Instead, the tribes were to obtain the right of self-government through the development of tribal councils. Encouraged by the resurgence of tribal independence and the survival of the Native American Church, young American Indians began to develop a sense of pan-Indianism, or Indian nationalism, which found political expression in the formation of the National Congress of American Indians (NCAI) in 1944.

Radical Literature and Conservative Culture

Small groups of writers and painters reacted to the Great Depression by rejecting capitalism completely. Unlike the artists who became socialists between 1900 and 1914 and believed in peaceful and gradual political change, many of these intellectuals were committed to violent revolution. They accepted the guidance of Lincoln Steffens, who had been a leading muckraking journalist in 1914. Writing in 1930, Steffens said that he and others of his generation had been mistaken in hoping for the evolutionary reform of capitalism. Only a revolution by the proletariat, Steffens argued, could bring a new order. Younger writers, like Michael Gold, asked that novelists, poets, playwrights, and painters produce revolutionary art. This art, labeled social realism, was to educate its audience to the need for revolution. Only a few of the plays and novels of social realism were artistic successes. Clifford Odets wrote effective plays (*Let Freedom Ring, Awake and Sing,* and *Waiting for Lefty*), which were first produced in 1935. Effective too were John Steinbeck's novels *In Dubious Battle* and *The Grapes of Wrath* (1939).

Studies by sociologists Helen and Robert Lynd provided an explanation of the fact that so few Americans were converted to revolution against the system. According to the Lynds, many Americans blamed themselves, not the system, for their economic distress. Radio programs for children, such as "Jack Armstrong: The All-American Boy," reinforced the cultural values of capitalism, as did comic strips such as "Little Orphan Annie" and "Terry and the Pirates." Few movies offered criticism of the economic system. Movies with cowboy heroes that reaffirmed the value of individual self-sufficiency were immensely popular. Many movies of the 1930s celebrated the winning of the West from villainous Indians and kept alive the importance of conquering frontiers.

1937 and the Collapse of the New Deal

Roosevelt's own point of view represented the cultural confusion of the period. In some of his speeches, he said that the frontier experience of America was over and that an America with limits must take its place. But, in other speeches, he praised traditions of frontier individualism and expansion. And these attitudes affected his fiscal policies. His national budgets averaged a deficit of $3 billion a year between 1933 and 1940. Roosevelt always hoped to end this deficit spending. He had not accepted the ideas of the English economist John Keynes, who advocated deficit spending to encourage economic growth. In 1937, after his reelection, Roosevelt reduced government spending. The economy had been slowly recovering in 1935 and 1936, and Roosevelt believed that he could safely stop a number of government programs and cut back the WPA.

The Works Progress Administration (WPA) had been created by Congress in 1935 to provide government jobs for many of the unemployed. Between 1935 and 1941, $11 billion was spent to employ about 2 million people at an average monthly wage of $52. Artists and writers, as well as unskilled workers, received help under the WPA. The Federal Theater Project, for instance, employed more than 12,000 theater people. Support from the government helped keep many artists from losing faith in the system and becoming revolutionaries.

When Roosevelt cut back government spending in 1937, including WPA funds, the economy collapsed again, and 4 million people lost their jobs. Once more, there were 12 million unemployed. Roosevelt reluctantly resumed deficit spending, but many people who had praised him for ending the depression in 1933 then blamed him for the new setback. The Republicans made major gains in the congressional elections of 1938.

Roosevelt had also lost the confidence of many people in 1937 because of his plan to add judges to the Supreme Court. Under Roosevelt's plan, when a justice reached the age of seventy and did not choose to retire, another justice would be added to the Court. Roosevelt wanted to create a new majority on the Court because it had ruled the NRA and the AAA unconstitutional. Many who had welcomed Roosevelt's almost dictatorial power in 1933 had begun to fear his power and opposed this attempt at presidential manipulation of the Court. Congress rejected his plan. Members of the Court, however, had begun to change their minds about government regulation of the economy and were willing to accept a second AAA and new legislation regulating hours and wages (the Fair Employment Act, 1938). Older justices did retire and were replaced by Roosevelt's appointees, and the Court accepted the Social Security Act (1935) and the Wagner Act (1935).

But northern congressmen could no longer push through reform legislation like that of 1935. Southern Democrats, who had supported the power of the New Deal to engage in national economic planning from 1933 to 1936, began to worry that this national power might be used to overthrow the Jim Crow segregation laws of the southern states. Some major southern political leaders, such as Governor Eugene Talmadge of Georgia, asked white southerners to return to their old tradition of upholding states' rights. A coalition of southern Democrats and northern Republicans kept northern liberal Democrats from establishing an effective public housing program, extending Social Security coverage, raising the minimum wage, and taxing the rich.

The Coming of World War II, 1937-1939

Fearful that another major war was about to begin, WASP political, economic, and cultural leaders began to focus their attention on Europe in 1937. In 1939, Germany invaded Poland, leading Britain and France, allies of Poland, to declare war on Germany. Hitler had decided that the key to German economic recovery was the expansion of German power and trade throughout Europe and the world. His plan was to create a unified Europe under German leadership and to increase German trade with Latin America and Africa.

Roosevelt also had reversed his isolationistic position of 1933 and had concluded by 1935 that the expansion of American overseas trade was crucial to recovery from the depression. Secretary of State Cordell Hull made reciprocal trade treaties with twelve countries and inaugurated a Good Neighbor policy with Latin America. To discourage German and Japanese influence in South America, Roosevelt withdrew the marines from Central American and Caribbean nations and promised at the Inter-American Conference in Buenos Aires, Argentina (1936), that the United States would never again send troops into another American country. The increasing aggressiveness of Germany was matched by Japan. In 1937, Japan rejected the Open Door policy completely and attacked and captured all the major coastal cities in China.

In his famous "Quarantine" speech delivered in Chicago in 1937, Roosevelt warned against German and Japanese aggression and indicated that he wanted to defend American interests in Asia and Europe. But public opinion in 1937 was overwhelmingly opposed to the use of force to protect those interests. Most Protestant ministers who had been enthusiastic supporters of World War I in 1937 declared themselves opposed to American participation in another war. Many Americans declared themselves to be pacifists. More than 100,000 college students participated in demonstrations against war in 1934 and 1935.

Neutrality Legislation, 1934-1939

In 1934, a special Senate committee, chaired by Senator Gerald Nye of North Dakota, began to study the role of munitions makers in World War I and concluded that these business people had played a major role in getting the United States into the war. The committee's findings agreed with the position taken in Walter Millis's best-selling book *Road to War* (1934). Charles Beard and other revisionist historians of the 1920s called for government policies that would keep the nation from being tricked into another war. Beard's book *Open Door at Home* (1934), which called for a noninterventionistic policy, was well received by college teachers. And, in 1936, Robert Sherwood won a Pulitzer Prize for his play *Idiot's Delight*, which attacked war profiteers.

Congress responded to this strong public demand for nonintervention by passing neutrality legislation. In 1935, sales of arms and ammunition to warring nations were banned. In 1936, loans to warring nations also were banned. And, in 1937, Congress forbade American ships to enter war zones.

But, in 1937, Hitler absorbed Austria into Germany and, in 1938, took control of Czechoslovakia. When war in Europe seemed inevitable, Roosevelt asked Congress for large appropriations to build up the American armed forces. Congress agreed and also repealed the embargo on arms sales (1939). When Germany successfully defeated France (1940) and took control of all of western Europe, except the British Isles, Roosevelt named a Republican, Henry Stimson, as secretary of war. Stimson represented the wing of the Republican party that wanted to go to war to support Great Britain. He helped Roosevelt create a coalition of Republicans and Democrats in Congress that voted to begin the first peacetime conscription of young men into the armed forces. And, in September 1940, Roosevelt gave fifty destroyers to Britain in return for leases on British bases in North America. After his reelection to an unprecedented third term in November 1940, Roosevelt moved further to repeal the neutrality legislation by asking Congress to create the Lend-Lease Act, which gave the president the power to lend supplies to Britain, which was too poor to pay for them.

Even before Congress passed the lend-lease legislation in the spring of 1941, Roosevelt and his military advisers had begun talks with British military leaders in anticipation of America's entry into the war. Roosevelt was determined to save Britain and defeat Germany. He ordered the navy to escort British merchant ships across the Atlantic to Iceland, which the

United States then occupied. Fighting between German submarines and American destroyers began in the fall of 1941. On October 16, the destroyer the U.S.S. *Kearney* was damaged by a torpedo, and, on October 20, the U.S.S. *Reuben James* was sunk. The undeclared war became official in December 1941, when Japan attacked the American fleet at Pearl Harbor in Hawaii. When the United States declared war against Japan after the attack, Germany and Italy, which had mutual defense treaties with Japan, declared war on the United States.

Roosevelt and the Coming of the War

In his campaign speeches of 1940, Roosevelt had promised that, if re-elected, he would see that no young Americans were sent overseas to fight. Unlike Wilson in 1916, however, Roosevelt anticipated America's entry into the war. He was not as concerned as Wilson had been that the war result in a new and better world. Roosevelt was part of the eastern, upper-class culture that identified very closely with England. Like many other Ivy Leaguers, Roosevelt admired England and despised Germany. He wanted to save the existing democratic nations and those with constitutions upholding individual liberties from being overwhelmed by the totalitarianism represented by Nazi Germany. He wanted, therefore, to keep England, which he saw as the mother of constitutional tradition throughout the world, from being defeated by Hitler's dictatorship. Beyond his desire to fight to defend an old cultural friend, Roosevelt also was motivated by the German threat to American trade with Europe and Latin America. In 1940, he also anticipated war with Japan. Again, he was prepared to resist the Japanese effort to dominate China and to force American economic interests out of the Far East.

Public opinion polls indicated that the majority of Americans did not want to go to war in 1940. This was especially true of Americans of German, Italian, Scandinavian, and Irish descent. But cultural leadership in 1940 tended to be in the hands of upper-class Anglo-Americans from the east coast, and they were able to direct American opinion toward support of England. Midwestern WASPs tended to be more isolationistic than those in the East, but again the easterners were able to control national identity and define the midwesterners as people who were limited by their regional outlook and unable to provide national leadership. In moving from the neutrality legislation of 1939 to active fighting in the fall of 1941, Roosevelt used the opinion polls that showed that many people wanted to help England but not to the extent of actual fighting. He had defined each step in 1939, 1940, and 1941 as help for England, not as war against Germany.

Roosevelt also used the threat of war as the reason for breaking the two-term tradition. As a strong leader, he argued, he could guide the nation through the troubled times ahead, as he had guided the nation through the troubled years of the Great Depression. In 1940, the more internationalistic Republicans from the eastern cities were able to win the nomination for Wendell Willkie, a Wall Street lawyer originally from Indiana. Willkie was ready to accept much of the New Deal legislation, and he shared Roosevelt's foreign policy views. However, he criticized Roosevelt for his ambition to become the first third-term president. Willkie reduced Roosevelt's huge margin of victory in 1936 and attracted 5 million more votes than Landon had. But the Democratic majority still gave Roosevelt an easy victory.

Roosevelt had ordered trade restrictions against Japan in an effort to force the Japanese to withdraw from China. Limits on sales of oil and iron were imposed in 1940, and, in the spring of 1941, a total embargo of American goods to Japan was announced. A conflict had developed in Japan between moderates, who believed that they could expand Japanese economic control throughout Asia without war with the United States, and militants, who insisted that American leaders would make no concessions to Japan without war. In the fall of 1941, the moderates were given a last chance to win concessions from the United States, while war plans were put into motion in case they failed. American intelligence had broken Japanese secret codes, and Roosevelt and Secretary of State Hull knew that war would come if they refused to negotiate. When they refused the Japanese offers, they knew that the Japanese would wage attacks throughout the Far East, including the Philippines. But American leaders were unprepared for the devastating attack on Pearl Harbor, which destroyed much of the Pacific Fleet on December 7, 1941.

Organizing the Economy for War

While the New Deal of 1933 had been dominated by corporate progressives concerned with stability, farmers and workers had pushed the New Deal toward reform in 1935 and 1936. But these reformers lost strength by 1938, and corporate progressives were able to regain control by 1940.

Concerned about American participation in the war by 1939, Roosevelt wanted to gain the support of the large corporations that controlled most of the nation's production. Therefore, he appointed a top executive of United States Steel, Edward Stettinius, as head of the War Resources Board. In Roosevelt's opinion, there was a chain of continuity that linked the government boards that planned the economy during World War I to the NRA in 1933 and then to the War Resources Board in 1939. In every situation, the corporations were to be exempt from price competition and would be able to work together to determine their share of the market. Once the United States had entered the war in 1941, the War Production Board took the place of the War Resources Board and other agencies similar to those of World War I were established: the War Manpower Commission, the Office of Price Administration, and the Food Administration. As in World War I, this "military-industrial complex" was

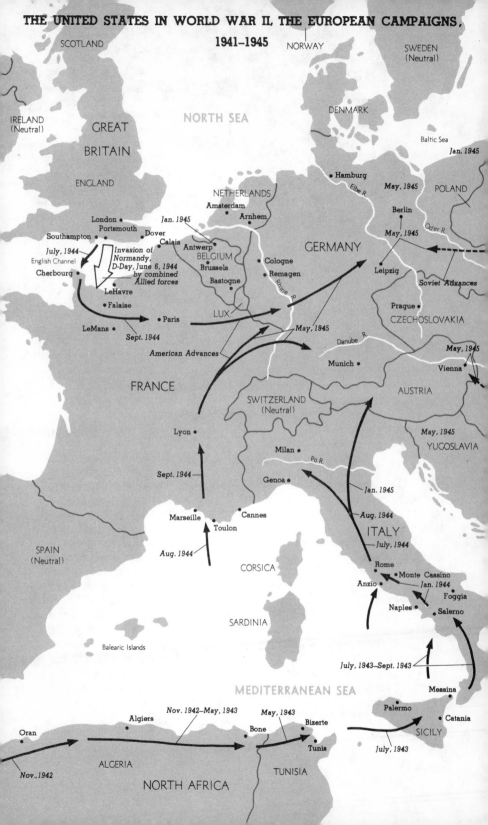

THE UNITED STATES IN WORLD WAR II. THE EUROPEAN CAMPAIGNS, 1941–1945

SCOTLAND

NORWAY

SWEDEN (Neutral)

IRELAND (Neutral)

GREAT BRITAIN

ENGLAND

NORTH SEA

DENMARK

Baltic Sea

Jan. 1945

Hamburg

Elbe R.

May, 1945

POLAND

Berlin

Oder R.

NETHERLANDS

Amsterdam

Arnhem

May, 1945

London

Portsmouth

Jan. 1945

Southampton

Dover

Calais

Antwerp

BELGIUM

Brussels

Cologne

GERMANY

Leipzig

Soviet Advances

July, 1944

English Channel

Invasion of Normandy, D-Day, June 6, 1944 by combined Allied forces

Remagen

Prague

Cherbourg

Bastogne

Rhine R.

May, 1945

CZECHOSLOVAKIA

LeHavre

Falaise

LUX.

May, 1945

May, 1945

LeMans

Paris

American Advances

Danube R.

Vienna

Sept. 1944

Munich

FRANCE

SWITZERLAND (Neutral)

AUSTRIA

May, 1945

Lyon

Sept. 1944

Milan

Po R.

YUGOSLAVIA

Genoa

Jan. 1945

Marseille

Cannes

Aug. 1944

Toulon

ITALY

July, 1944

SPAIN (Neutral)

Aug. 1944

CORSICA

Rome

Monte Cassino

Anzio

Jan. 1944

Foggia

Naples

Salerno

SARDINIA

July, 1943–Sept. 1943

Balearic Islands

Messina

MEDITERRANEAN SEA

Palermo

Catania

Algiers

Nov. 1942–May, 1943

May, 1943

Bone

Bizerte

SICILY

Oran

Tunis

July, 1943

Nov., 1942

ALGERIA

TUNISIA

NORTH AFRICA

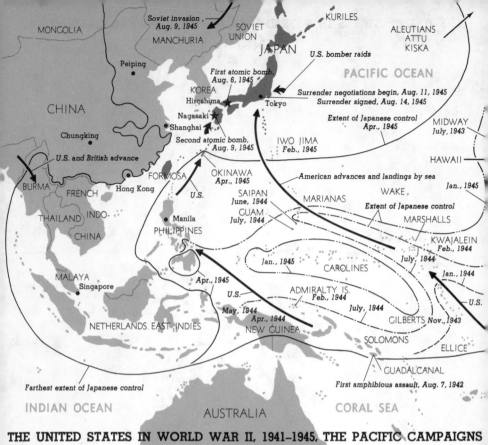

THE UNITED STATES IN WORLD WAR II, 1941–1945, THE PACIFIC CAMPAIGNS

headed by major corporation leaders. More of the nation's manpower and resources had to be mobilized than in World War I, and the government, for the first time, engaged in the rationing of food and other scarce resources.

The 200 largest corporations received most of the government contracts to turn out the guns, tanks, airplanes, and other supplies needed for the war, and their share of national production increased to more than two-thirds. The government provided the money for the companies to build new plants and install new machinery and to retool old plants. There was no bidding on the contracts received from the government, and the contracts were open-ended on costs. Whatever the cost of fulfilling the contracts, the businesses were guaranteed their profits. The business leaders who had objected to the $24-billion deficit that was added to the national debt between 1933 and 1940 to pay for relief for the poor and the unemployed had little objection to the almost $200 billion of deficit spending from 1940 to 1945 because much of this money went directly to the business community.

Industrial production doubled during the war, while 14 million men and women were taken out of the job market and put into the armed services. The unemployment of 11 million workers in 1940 was replaced by a shortage of workers in 1943. While corporation profits doubled, wages increased about 50 percent during the war, in spite of wage and price controls. As during World War I, unions were supported by the government as a reward for their loyalty to the war effort. Union membership increased rapidly, from 9 million in 1940 to 15 million in 1945.

Ideals and Power in World War II

A major effort had been made to pay for World War I through taxes. Although there was some deficit spending that needed to be financed through the selling of bonds for World War I, that was a tiny amount compared to deficit spending necessary for World War II, for which taxes payed no significant part of the expenses. Roosevelt's willingness not to worry about the means to be used to reach his ends in 1933 became even more obvious during the war. During World War I, the American government expected its allies to repay wartime loans that came from the United States, but Roosevelt gave $50 billion to Britain and Russia under the Lend-Lease Act with no real expectation that the money would be repaid.

Hitler had invaded Russia in June 1941. Although American policy since 1917 had been very hostile toward the existence of a communist government there, Roosevelt and British prime minister Winston Churchill were willing to send money and supplies to Soviet Russia to keep German troops tied down on the eastern front, while the United States and Britain prepared to invade western Europe.

Most male college students during World War II were members of army or navy programs. (Courtesy of University of Minnesota Archives.)

Unlike American generals who accepted the strategy developed by British and French generals in World War I, American military leaders in, World War II assumed leadership in Europe and the Pacific. General Dwight Eisenhower made the final decisions for troops from England and the British Empire, as well as for American troops, in Europe, and General Douglas MacArthur commanded Australian and New Zealand soldiers, as well as Americans, in the Pacific. In the spring of 1941, before the official American entry into the war, Roosevelt, Churchill, and their military advisers had decided to concentrate on defeating Germany first and then turn to the defeat of Japan. While much of the Germany army was fighting in Russia, the American-British allies planned to drive the Germans and their Italian allies out of North Africa and then invade Italy. Finally, when the German armies and air force had been weakened in these battles, a major invasion from England into France would take place.

Although Roosevelt and Churchill were willing to support Soviet Russia as a means of defeating Germany and Japan, they were concerned with containing the spread of communism from Russia once victory had been gained. Already in 1942, the United States had cooperated with the French right-wing political leader Admiral Jean Darlan and other conservative leaders in the Balkans, although most of the underground groups fighting against the Germans throughout Europe were associated with the left wing.

When the United States and Britain invaded France in June of 1944, the Allied political and military leaders, therefore, had conflicting attitudes because the invasion would help the Russians crush the Germans. Fearful of their Russian allies, it was necessary to rush Allied troops to western Germany to keep the Russians from overrunning the entire continent to the North Sea.

In February 1945, Roosevelt and Winston Churchill met with Stalin at the Russian resort city of Yalta to discuss the peace settlement in Europe that would come after the Germans were defeated. They also discussed the continued conduct of the war against Japan. Agreement was reached to divide Germany into four zones, separately occupied by Russia, the United States, Britain, and France. It was assumed that a permanently divided, disarmed, and deindustrialized Germany could never again wage aggressive war.

Stalin also agreed to allow anticommunist Polish leaders in London to become part of the communist government the Russians had established in that country when they liberated it from the Germans. Roosevelt hoped that the Russians would not choose to keep complete control of the areas of eastern Europe, such as Poland, that had been overrun by Soviet armies.

Roosevelt also won agreement from Stalin on disputed details about the shape of the United Nations. Roosevelt's experience of the 1930s was that Hoover's concept of the Open Door empire had failed and that the economic objections to political participation in the League of Nations had been proved false. For Roosevelt, American participation in World War II proved that ongoing political and military power was necessary to supplement economic power and that a vigorous international agency was essential to providing the stable and peaceful environment needed for economic growth.

Roosevelt and his advisers were influenced by the current attack of intellectuals and Protestant theologians on the American tradition of innocence that had insisted that the United States must never engage in the sinful use of political power. Dismissing the idealism of Wilson, Roosevelt wanted a United Nations divided between those nations that had great power and those that had little power. Although only the United States, Russia, and Britain had significant power, Roosevelt was willing to include France and China as permanent members of a United Nations Security Council, which would have six other members elected for two-year terms by less powerful nations. The council would have the power to apply economic and military sanctions against aggressive nations who challenged the world status quo. Each of the five permanent members, however, would have an absolute veto over any decision the council made. Thus, the United States could retain its national freedom of action while becoming a member of an international organization. All the little nations were to be members of a General Assembly, in which world issues could be discussed but where no policy decisions could be made.

When President Roosevelt died in April 1945 and was succeeded by Vice-President Harry S. Truman, the traditional American fear of communist Russia began to become the dominant attitude among American foreign policy leaders.

In 1945, Stalin was not supporting any communist groups he could not control directly. He refused to aid communist forces in Greece, Italy, and France because they insisted on their independence. He refused to aid the communists in China or Ho Chi Minh in Vietnam for the same reason. But American leaders could not escape the tradition of dividing the world into two geographic parts, one evil and contaminated by wicked conspirators, the other pure and virtuous and characterized by liberty and goodness. This tradition, by which the founding fathers had defined the meaning of the American Revolution and which justified the Monroe Doctrine of 1823, became dominant again in the American political imagination of 1945. Instead of the forces of enlightenment of 1917 fighting to liberate the entire world from the conspiracy of medieval darkness, the free world forces of 1945 were fighting to preserve half of the world from the threat of communist conspiracy.

American strategy, therefore, shifted from persuading Russia to play a major role in the war against Japan to planning ways to have the United States monopolize victory in the Far East. The development of the atomic bomb made this strategy possible. This development had been a top-

As Americans tried to retreat to isolation in the 1920s and 1930s, they returned to symbols of the nineteenth century. Even art critics in New York City applauded artists like John Steuart Curry for refusing to abandon a realistic style of painting and refusing, therefore, to be corrupted by the increasing use of abstract symbolism by European painters. Eastern intellectuals committed to isolation in the 1930s could celebrate this painting by Curry, "Baptism in Kansas," for keeping America free from European style. (Collection of Whitney Museum of American Art, New York.)

priority program from the beginning of the war, when scientists had warned President Roosevelt that the Germans were working on a nuclear weapon. The completion of the bomb followed the surrender of Germany in May 1945, and in August atomic bombs were dropped on the Japanese cities of Hiroshima and Nagasaki, with almost complete destruction of buildings and population. Fearing heavy American casualties in an invasion of Japan, Truman and his advisers seemed to feel little anguish in making the decision to obliterate these cities. Although American policy had called for the unconditional surrender of Japan, American leaders allowed the Japanese to surrender with the understanding that the United States would not depose the emperor.

The abruptness of the Japanese defeat under the threat of more atomic bombing allowed the United States to monopolize the control of Japanese reconstruction without sharing power with Russia, and General

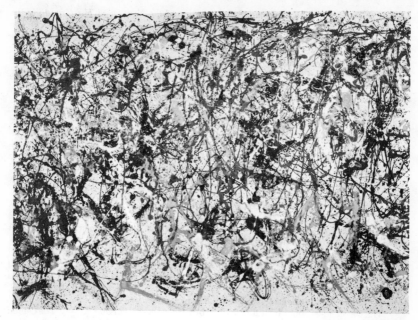

Nowhere is the dramatic revolution of American intellectuals from isolation to internationalism in the 1940s more clearly demonstrated than in the movement of the art critics to reject their loyalty to realism in the 1930s to embrace the abstract expressionism of painters like Jackson Pollock (here in "Autumn Rhythm") in the 1940s. For the first time American painters like Pollock were accepted by Europeans in the 1940s and 1950s as the leaders of international painting. (The Metropolitan Museum of Art, George A. Hearn Fund, 1957.)

Douglas MacArthur was given absolute authority to remake Japan into a political democracy and a friend of the United States.

In the fall of 1945, the United States returned to peace. President Roosevelt had been successful in defeating Germany and Japan and in protecting American overseas interests in Europe and Asia. Massive deficit spending and the mobilization of production for war had restored prosperity. The new president, Harry Truman, had to find ways of preserving this wartime prosperity and of defending America's overseas economic frontiers from competition with communist Russia.

Supplementary Reading

W. Leuchtenburg's *Franklin D. Roosevelt and the New Deal* (1963) is an excellent overview. The differences in the economic philosophies of Hoover and Roosevelt are discussed in G. Smith, *The Shattered Dream: Herbert Hoover and the Great Depression* (1970), and E. Hawley, *The New Deal and the Problem of Monopoly: A Study in Economic Ambivalence*

(1966). J. Patterson, *Congressional Conservation and the New Deal: The Growth of the Conservative Coalition in Congress, 1933-1939* (1967), and L. Baker, *Back to Back: The Duel between FDR and the Supreme Court* (1967), describe conservative resistance to the New Deal. T. H. Williams, *Huey Long* (1969), and J. Huthmacher, *Senator Robert F. Wagner and the Rise of Urban Liberalism* (1968), describe two major critics of Roosevelt who found him too conservative. The New Deal is linked to World War I by W. Leuchtenburg, "The New Deal and the Analogue of War" in *Change and Continuity in Twentieth Century America* (1964), edited by J. Braeman, R. Bremner, and E. Walters.

L. Fishel, Jr., "The Negro and the New Deal" in R. Resh, editor, *Black Americans: Accommodation and Confrontation in Twentieth-Century America* (1969), describes Roosevelt's limited concern for blacks. J. Boskin, *The Life and Death of Sambo* (1970), however, describes the weakening of the Sambo image. H. Hertzberg, *The Search for an American Indian Identity* (1974), discusses the growing strength of Indian culture. The economic difficulties of women during the depression are the subject of the chapters on the 1930s in W. Chafe, *The American Woman: Her Changing Social, Economic, and Political Role, 1920-1970* (1972).

The issues of radicalism and conservatism in literature and the movies are outlined by D. Aaron, *Writers on the Left* (1961); R. Pells, *Radical Visions and American Dreams: Culture and Social Thought in the Depression Years* (1973); and R. Sklar, *Movie-made America: A Cultural History of the American Movies* (1976).

The issues leading to World War II are discussed by L. Gardner, *Economic Aspects of New Deal Diplomacy* (1964), and D. Borg, *The United States and Far Eastern Crises of 1933-1938* (1964). The movement away from isolation is the subject of R. Divine, *Second Chance: The Triumph of Internationalism in America during World War II* (1967), and D. Meyer, *The Protestant Search for Political Realism, 1919-1941* (1960).

The war years at home are well described by R. Polenberg, *War and Society: The United States, 1941-1945* (1972), and J. Blum, *V Was for Victory; Politics and American Culture during World War II* (1976). M. Sherwin, *A World Destroyed: The Atomic Bomb and the Grand Alliance* (1975), discusses the revolutionary implications of the atomic weapon.

Chapter
26

Cold War, Prosperity, and an Uncertain Future
1945-1960

Woodrow Wilson had hoped that World War I would hasten the creation of an international marketplace in which all nations could trade freely. He saw the American Open Door policy for China as the model for a world of free trade. During the 1920s, Herbert Hoover believed that the Open Door policy was being established because of the great strength of the American economy. But, by 1938 and after the collapse of the economy, Franklin Roosevelt felt the need to substitute military power for economic power in order to defend American overseas frontiers against Germany and Japan.

Then, in 1945, President Truman's advisers told him that continued prosperity depended upon the expansion of American overseas trade. They urged him to put pressure on Soviet Russia to allow the free penetration of American economic interests into Russia and its satellites in eastern Europe. Stalin and other communist leaders, however, did not believe in the capitalist marketplace. Committed to government control of economic policies, they refused to accept the American idea of free trade and they refused to withdraw from eastern Europe, including the part of Germany occupied by their armies.

Truman and the Cold War

Although Truman and his advisers showed great hostility toward the Russians at the Potsdam Conference (August 1945) after the Russians refused to accept a new American proposal for the unification of Germany, the president did not issue a formal challenge to Russian expansion. American policy, nevertheless, presumed that there was a worldwide conflict with Soviet Russia, and, in April 1947, Truman articulated the concept of containment of Russian communism that had been worked out by men such as George Kennan and Dean Acheson, trained in Ivy League universities.

The policy of containment by economic and military pressure without actual fighting was called the Cold War. Truman had the support of former isolationists as well as the Democratic and Republican leaders who had supported Roosevelt in 1940 and 1941 in his policies for containing Germany and Japan. A number of American leaders in 1940 and 1941 had taken seriously Herbert Hoover's warning that another civil war among the capitalist nations would permit the spread of communism from Russia. These conservatives were called isolationists because they had argued against American entry into World War II. After the war, however, most of the isolationists felt that they could not object to Truman's policy of containing communism. Communism, for them, was much more dangerous to capitalism than German fascism and Japanese imperialism had been in the 1930s.

Arthur Vandenberg, the Republican chairman of the Senate Foreign Relations Committee, declared in February 1947 that he had abandoned his prewar isolationism. He said that the American economic and political system could survive only if it were spread throughout the entire world. Vandenberg led a number of Republican senators and congressmen into open bipartisan support of the Truman administration's foreign policy, particularly its willingness to use political and military force throughout the world in order to contain Russian communism. Senator Robert Taft of Ohio, a leading isolationist in 1941 and another leader of the Senate Republicans, was left in a minority position when he remained critical of a policy of military internationalism. He warned that the use of military power to spread capitalism abroad would undermine it at home because it would cause the growth of huge government bureaucracies. These bureaucracies, Taft said, would end free enterprise within the United States. Nearly all political figures felt the need, however, to declare their willingness to support the nation's forceful involvements around the world or be branded isolationists, a term that in postwar America implied a failure to adapt to the realities of the world as it was. Consensus in this bipartisan policy became so strong that foreign policy issues were no longer debated in Congress or during presidential election campaigns.

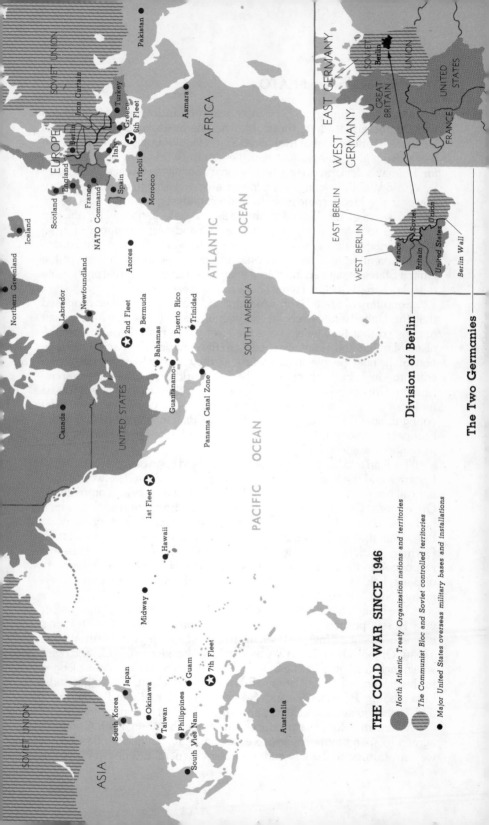

THE COLD WAR SINCE 1946

- ○ North Atlantic Treaty Organization nations and territories
- ▨ The Communist Bloc and Soviet controlled territories
- ● Major United States overseas military bases and installations

Division of Berlin

The Two Germanies

The Marshall Plan and NATO

President Truman had congressional support from most Republican and Democratic leaders, therefore, when he proclaimed in the Truman Doctrine (April 1947) that the United States would supply aid to any nation that was fighting communism anywhere in the world. The specific cause for Truman's declaration was revolutionary activity in Greece. Weakened by World War II, Britain was no longer able or willing to exercise military power in the Mediterranean. If the anticommunist government of Greece was to survive, the United States was the only nation with sufficient resources to give it the necessary financial and military support. Large-scale economic aid and military supplies were sent to Greece. The American intervention in Greece marked the first time in the history of the United States that it had interfered in another nation's internal political life outside of the Western Hemisphere during peacetime.

Secretary of State George Marshall, a former general, then proposed that the United States rebuild the economies of the western European nations so that they would have the strength to resist Russian communism. Marshall and Truman appealed to the American humanitarian tradition of helping people in distress and they warned of the danger to constitutional liberty throughout the free world from Soviet totalitarianism. But Congress showed little enthusiasm for the idea until Soviet Russia took control of Czechoslovakia (February 1948). Congress reacted by voting to spend $13 billion for the Marshall Plan for the rebuilding of the European economy (March 1948). The aid accelerated economic recovery throughout western Europe.

Truman and his advisers, however, wanted to go beyond the Truman Doctrine and the Marshall Plan to work out a coordinated network of military alliances to carry on the Cold War against Russian communism. Once more, Congress was reluctant to break from the tradition, which had existed since 1789, of avoiding European political or military alliances. But, when the United States, Britain, and France decided to merge their German districts into a single nation — West Germany — the Russians responded to the decision with a blockade of land routes into those parts of Berlin held by the Allies. Berlin was well within the eastern part of Germany controlled by Russia.

The United States broke the blockade with an airlift, but the conflict with Russia pushed Congress to support the Truman administration's desire for alliances. In April 1949, the treaty establishing the North Atlantic Treaty Organization (NATO) was signed in Washington, D.C., and overwhelmingly accepted by the Senate. The United States then was pledged to the military support of Britain, France, Italy, Belgium, the Netherlands, Luxembourg, Portugal, Iceland, Norway, and Denmark. In 1952, Greece and Turkey joined the alliance, and, in 1954, West Germany joined.

When the Russians produced an atomic bomb in 1949, Congress agreed to spend more billions to establish American military bases from western Europe to Turkey and to appoint General Eisenhower as commander of NATO forces in the Cold War against Russia. By 1949, American military strategy was completely different from what it had been in 1939. In 1939, it was assumed that the Atlantic and Pacific oceans made it possible for the United States to have military security without alliances and without large military and naval forces. It was further assumed in 1939 that the oceans would provide time for the United States to mobilize if a threat to its security developed. In 1949, however, American leaders assumed that the United States needed extensive military alliances throughout the world to contain the permanent threat of Russian aggression and that the United States must always have massive military power to deter the Russians from attacking anywhere in the world.

This revolutionary new policy meant that large military expenditures would be a permanent part of the peacetime national budget and that generals and admirals would play a major role in making peacetime governmental decisions. A Department of Defense (DOD) was created in 1947 to consolidate the Departments of the Army and the Navy. Congress also established the Joint Chiefs of Staff, which coordinated military leadership and linked the military to the presidency through a National Security Council (NSC). Congress approved the formation of the Central Intelligence Agency (CIA), which was to carry out undercover intelligence operations throughout the world.

Communism in Asia

The American fear of communism that had been building up between 1945 and 1949 because of events in Europe was greatly increased by events in Asia. American military strategists during World War II had assumed that, while the United States had the economic and human resources to place armies in Europe, the country did not have the resources to operate armies on the Asian mainland. Military strategy, therefore, had been to fight the Japanese only on the islands lying off the coast of Asia. With the defeat and occupation of Japan in 1945, American leaders felt very secure about the American position in Asia. Russia did not seem to have the power to compete with the United States in that area. Japan was then an American satellite, and China was a friend.

After 1945, however, the Truman administration increasingly became worried about the political situation in China, where native communists, who had developed sufficient strength during the 1930s to fight the Japanese, were rapidly expanding their power with little help from Russia. Chiang Kai-shek's government, supported by the United States, was weakened by corruption and its refusal to provide land reform for the peasants. But the United States sent money and supplies to Chiang Kai-shek's nationalist armies to battle against the communists headed by Mao Tsetung. As the communists won support from the peasants, they captured supplies from the nationalists for their own armies and, in 1949, took complete control of mainland China. Chiang fled to the island of Formosa (Taiwan), where he established a government in exile that could be protected by the American navy.

The War in Korea

Since 1900, American foreign policy had assumed that China would become a vast market for American goods. American leaders also assumed that the United States was the friend and protector of China and that American influence would Christianize and modernize the Chinese. These half-century-old attitudes were shattered by the communist victory, and Truman received tremendous criticism for having "lost" China. Reacting to that criticism, he was ready to ignore military advice against committing American troops on the Asian mainland when war broke out between North and South Korea in 1950. Exercising the same extensive presidential control over foreign policy and war that Wilson and Roosevelt had used in 1917 and 1941, Truman ordered American troops stationed in Japan into combat in Korea to stop the advances of the North Koreans. In making this decision, Truman (like Kennedy and Johnson after him) did not ask Congress for a formal declaration of war. But Congress, in these cases, felt the need to back the president in crusades against communism.

The Korean peninsula, which extends from northern China toward Japan, had been ruled by the Japanese for fifty years. At the end of World War II, it had been divided, with Russians occupying the northern half and Americans, the southern. The tensions of the Cold War made it impossible for the nations to reach an agreement on unifying the country. But, when American armies under the command of General Douglas MacArthur had pushed the North Koreans out of South Korea, Truman permitted the forces to carry the war into North Korea despite warnings from the Chinese communists that they would not allow Americans to conquer that country.

In ignoring that threat, the Truman administration revealed some of the less explicit factors that influenced foreign policy during the Cold War. Just as white racism had led Americans to underestimate the fighting ability of the Japanese during World War II, it led them to underestimate in 1951 the fighting ability of the Chinese. (The same outlook affected American foreign policy toward the Viet Cong during the 1960s.) When MacArthur approached the Chinese border, Chinese troops rapidly drove him back to the original border between North and South Korea, where a stalemate developed. Truman and his advisers reluctantly accepted their inability to defeat communist China without the use of the atomic bomb. They did not use the bomb because they feared atomic retaliation from Russia. MacArthur publicly criticized Truman's decision to wage a limited war, and he appealed to the traditions of World War I and World War II in which Wilson and Roosevelt had demanded total victory and the unconditional surrender of the enemy. Truman removed MacArthur from his military command in 1951 when he refused to obey the president's order to stop his public criticism of Truman's military policy. And, when MacArthur returned home, he failed to rally Congressional and popular support for his policy of total victory.

MacArthur had not obtained popular support because the majority of American voters, between 1940 and 1952, were not enthusiastic about the Roosevelt-Truman policy of using military force to protect American overseas interests. Only the pressure of the Cold War and the belief in the need to contain communist Russia had persuaded Congress to support Truman's policies. Part of his administration's strategy for sustaining the Cold War was establishing peacetime conscription as a regular and permanent part of American life. Congress responded to the emotionalism of the Korean War by establishing Selective Service for young men, by expanding American military bases in North Africa, by the rearmament of Germany, and by a peace treaty with Japan that established American military bases there and allowed Japanese industrialization.

When Dwight Eisenhower became president in 1952, he was willing to carry on the Truman administration's Cold War policy of the containment of communism. But, like Truman, he was afraid to enter into a total war in Korea that might mean total war with China and perhaps Russia. Reluctantly, Eisenhower and Secretary of State John Foster Dulles reached an armistice with North Korea that left the peninsula divided (1953).

The Cold War and Civil Liberties

The psychology of the Cold War was like that of World War I and World War II; it was one of conformity. The demand for national unity was so great that there was little concern for civil liberties. At the beginning of World War II, the government had created the Office of Censorship and the Office of War Information. Unlike the situation in 1917, when one-third of the population was made up of immigrants and the children of immigrants, there was little fear of those who had German, Italian, and Central European ancestors. The Roosevelt administration had used the Espionage Act of 1917 to arrest people who had been identified with fascist or Nazi movements during the 1930s.

Congress also had passed in 1939, the Hatch Act, which excluded from federal employment persons who belonged to organizations that advocated the overthrow of the American government. In 1943, the Interdepartmental Committee on Employee Investigations was scrutinizing all government employees. Six thousand conscientious objectors, mostly Jehovah's Witnesses, had been jailed for refusing to register for the draft. Because of the strong peace movement active during the 1930s, during World War II there were three times as many conscientious objectors who registered for limited government service than in World War I and four times as many went to jail as in 1917.

Although Roosevelt felt confident in dealing with Italian- and German-Americans (many of whom supported the Democratic party in the northeastern states), he shared the racist prejudice toward the Japanese that grew on the west coast after the attack on Pearl Harbor. Roosevelt responded to anti-Japanese hysteria in the Pacific coast states by ordering most Japanese-Americans into concentration camps. The majority of the 112,000 people put into the camps were born in America and were American citizens. The Supreme Court declared, however, that all civil liberties of individuals could be suspended during wartime and that the government had the legal right to imprison the Japanese-American citizens even though they were guilty of no crimes. During Truman's administration, Congress passed the McCarran Internal Security Act (1950), which drew up plans for a number of secret prison camps that were to hold subversive Americans if the president decided that there was a crisis.

During the war years, 1941-1945, the government had emphasized friendship with the Soviet Union as a necessary military ally. Major magazines such as *Life* were encouraged to carry pro-Russian stories, and Hollywood was encouraged to produce pro-Russian movies. Then, there was a deliberate reversal of this policy by the Truman administration, which instituted an Internal Securities program and ordered the Federal Bureau of Investigation (FBI) to use wiretaps to uncover communist conspiracies in the country. The House Un-American Activities Committee (HUAC) carried out hearings on the communist influence in Hollywood. A number of movie actors and writers, as well as people in radio, were blacklisted and could no longer find jobs because they were accused of having communist connections. Some were imprisoned for refusing to testify before the committee. The post office banned communist materials from the mails, and most states passed laws demanding loyalty oaths from all state employees, including teachers.

Democrats, Republicans, and Anticommunist Hysteria

Upper-middle-class WASPs, especially those who had been educated in the eastern universities, had been Roosevelt's major supporters as he led an unwilling majority of Americans into World War II. The same group had provided advisers to Truman when he led the nation into the Cold War with Soviet Russia. But there was not as much resentment toward the Democratic party as the party of World War II and the Cold War as there had been toward the Democrats in 1918. The decreased amount of resentment resulted from the fact that there was a sense of greater participation in the Roosevelt administration of labor and lower-income and ethnic groups than there had been in the Wilson administration.

These groups had demanded much of the major New Deal legislation (such as Social Security and the Wagner Act) when the majority of college-educated Democrats had opposed it in 1935. But the college-educated Democrats still controlled foreign policy between 1939 and 1948, and there was resentment against that control by lower-income Democrats. While lower-income Protestants and Catholics could not show their resentment of this upper-class leadership by opposing a strong stand against communism, they could show it by supporting leaders who criticized eastern Democrats for not being anticommunist enough. Richard Nixon, a young Republican congressman from California, and Joseph McCarthy, a Republican senator from Wisconsin, were the most important figures mobilizing this resentment toward upper-class, eastern Democrats.

In a series of extravagant speeches during the early 1950s, McCarthy claimed that the State Department (in which most of the employees were graduates of the eastern universities) had been infiltrated by communist sympathizers. Alger Hiss, a former State Department official with an Ivy League background, was accused of espionage and was convicted of perjury. Midwestern Republicans in the Senate allowed McCarthy to make wild and sweeping accusations against men like Dean Acheson and George Marshall who were founders of the Cold War policies against communism. Democrats in Congress also were afraid to criticize McCarthy's unfounded statements because they feared that they would be branded as communist sympathizers. Radio and newspaper reporters helped McCarthy become a national figure by reporting his accusations without asking him for evidence to support his claims. Even liberal eastern Republicans with the same Ivy League background as Dean Acheson hoped that McCarthy would help destroy the Democratic majority and make possible a Republican victory in 1952.

1948: The End of the New Deal Coalition

Resentment against Democratic politics during World War II had led to Republican victories in the congressional elections of 1946. In control of Congress, Republicans had looked forward to winning the presidency in 1948. In 1946, polls indicated that Truman had the support of only 32 percent of the people, and the Republicans were sure that Thomas Dewey of New York could defeat the president. Dewey had run well as the Republican candidate in 1944, when Roosevelt narrowly won reelection to a fourth term. In 1947, the Republican Congress sent to the states for ratification the Twenty-second Amendment to the Constitution, which officially limited a president to two terms in office. They also struck at the power gained by organized labor during the Democratic administrations by passing the Taft-Hartley Act (1947). The act outlawed the closed shop (the requirement that workers in a particular plant belong to a union). It also made illegal the use of union dues for political activities and gave the president the legal power to order strikers back to work.

Most workers, therefore, felt that they could not vote their resentment against Democratic foreign policy in 1948 but that they had to vote for Truman to protect their economic interests. Truman campaigned on the platform of a Fair Deal, which asked for higher minimum wages for labor, the repeal of the Taft-Hartley Act, high price supports for farmers, public housing, medical insurance, federal aid to education, and moderate civil rights legislation. Truman won a narrow victory in 1948, holding much of the labor vote among Catholics in the North as well as the vote of many midwestern farmers who feared that Dewey would end agricultural price supports. Jews and blacks who had converted to the Democratic party during the 1930s also remained loyal. And Truman won in 1948 despite the defection of many white southern voters.

White southerners had provided the most loyal group of voters for Roosevelt in 1936. They also were the strongest group in the country in favor of reforms such as Social Security. From 1936 to 1944, however, they had begun to fear that the power of the federal government might be used to help blacks break out of the subordinate political and social positions in which southern whites kept them. Their fears had been fulfilled in the Democratic party's 1948 platform, which called for the recognition of the civil rights of blacks. The result was the appearance of a third party, the States Rights party, headed by J. Strom Thurmond of South Carolina. These "Dixiecrats" argued that the national government did not have the constitutional right to interfere with racial patterns in the states. Thurmond won the votes of many white southerners, especially in the Deep South from South Carolina to Louisiana.

When these white southerners were willing to vote for a Republican candidate in 1952, they helped make possible the Republicans' recapture of the presidency from the Democrats. (Still, although Republicans, with the support of white southern votes, have won the presidency in 1952, 1956, 1968, and 1972, they have not recaptured their position as the majority party in the country. Many southern whites have continued to call themselves Democrats or to call themselves independents, and they have continued to vote for Democrats at the state and local levels. This pattern also has been true for many northern voters since 1952. They have voted for Republican presidential candidates but not for state and local Republicans.)

World War II, Blacks, and Civil Rights

In 1941, the caste system was still intact in the armed services. The white belief that adult black males were boys who could not or should not engage in violence kept blacks out of the marines, considered the toughest fighting units, and out of the air force. Blacks served only as messboys in the navy and were service, not combat, troops in the army.

Blacks leaders from the NAACP, the National Urban League, and the Congress of Racial Equality (CORE) put continual pressure on the Roosevelt administration to modify these caste patterns. Gradually, blacks were permitted into the air force, into the marines, into the navy as regular sailors, and into combat units in the army. Always, however, blacks were placed in segregated units, and generals and admirals saw to it that no black officers commanded white men. The most dramatic breakdown of the caste system during the war came when the army began to train whites and blacks together in officers' training schools.

Although a black (Dr. Charles Drew) had developed the techniques for utilizing blood plasma, the Red Cross kept blood from white and blacks separated in its blood banks. Army camps also were totally segregated, with separate theaters, post exchanges, chapels, and buses for white and black soldiers. In 1944, protests from black leaders finally forced President Roosevelt to order an end to these practices in the army camps. Military units, however, continued to be divided by race. One of Roosevelt's considerations was his need for the blacks' votes when he tried for a fourth term in that year, since he knew that the Republicans were gaining strength because of the resentment toward the war.

At the beginning of the war, pressure from an organization of blacks called the March on Washington Movement had caused Roosevelt to issue an executive order that prescribed that industries with defense contracts stop discriminating against blacks and begin to hire black workers. Later, the Fair Employment Practices Commission was established to enforce this policy.

The shortage of labor for industry during World War II, as during World War I, pulled many blacks out of the South and into northern cities. The pressure alarmed northern whites and led to major race riots. In Detroit, for example, a riot in 1943 killed twenty-five blacks and nine whites. The renewed migration of blacks into the North increased the importance of black voters within the Democratic party. President Truman ordered the desegregation of the armed forces before the 1948 election, and black votes in key northern states provided the margin for his victory. In Korea, black and white soldiers served in the same platoons for the first time (1950), and it was possible for black commissioned and noncommissioned officers to give orders to white men.

The official desegregation of the nation's armed services and the symbolic rejection of the caste system had been speeded by the need of the Roosevelt administration to separate itself from the racist democracy of Nazi Germany and then by the need of the Truman administration to avoid the criticism of Soviet Russia that the United States subjugated black people in a caste system. The communists' criticism was especially important to American leaders because of the new foreign policy that committed the United States to the role of a world power. If the United States was going to check communist influence among the people of Asia and Africa, it had to prove to those people that American policy was not racist.

This kind of pressure led the white community to accept a black man as a participant in the national sport — baseball. In 1947, Jackie Robinson became a member of the Brooklyn Dodgers. Again, the transition was eased by Robinson's college education, his good manners, his high intelligence, and, of course, his outstanding skill as a baseball player. He was ordered by management to turn the other cheek when he was insulted by white players. But once again the caste system had been shattered. A black man was accepted as someone who could be physically aggressive toward white men on the playing field and who would not be punished for that aggressiveness. After Robinson, the number of black players in professional baseball, football, and basketball increased steadily. However, caste attitudes remained, making it difficult for many whites to accept black leadership. (In 1976, there still are no black head coaches in professional football and it has been difficult for a black quarterback to establish himself. Frank Robinson was the only black manager in baseball, and his appointment did not come until the 1970s. Black players have become so dominant in professional basketball, however, that there are a number of black head basketball coaches; the first was Bill Russell, appointed as coach of the Boston Celtics in the 1960s.)

The Supreme Court, which had upheld the patterns of racist democracy in its decisions during the 1890s, also responded to the changing definition of full citizenship. Reversing earlier decisions, the Court ruled in 1944 that it was unconstitutional for the Democratic parties in the southern states to deny blacks the right to vote in the party primaries because of their race. In 1944, less than 5 percent of southern blacks were registered to vote. Those who were registered had to be registered as Republicans. Slowly between 1944 and 1948 and then more rapidly by 1952, the number of southern blacks registering to vote increased, and they registered as Democrats. This change intensified the crisis of southern whites within the national Democratic party and caused many of them to vote for the Dixiecrats (the States' Rights party) in 1948 and the Republicans in 1952.

World War II and Women

In 1940, the percentage of women in the work force was the same as it had been in 1910. The labor shortage of the war years, however, caused the number of women workers to increase by 50 percent while the number of working wives doubled. Between 1941 and 1945, women's membership in unions increased by 400 percent. And the divorce rate almost doubled during the war years. Women also entered the armed services for the first time in special units such as the Women's Army Corps (WAC).

Cultural leaders, however, assumed that this dramatic increase in the number of women working outside the home was temporary and that the pattern of 1940 would be reestablished when returning veterans took back their jobs from women workers. Women, it was believed, would resume their roles as housewives. Anthropologists and psychologists, many of them women, insisted that women were happy and fulfilled only in the home. The best women's colleges taught their students to prepare for marriage, not for careers after graduation, and polls indicated that almost 90 percent of women graduates hoped for marriage and a family.

Magazines and advertisers renewed the messages of the 1920s that women should be skilled wives, mothers, and consumers. After the long period between 1929 and 1945 when marriages had been delayed, the birthrate had dropped, and few houses had been built, the return of prosperity in 1945 produced an explosive increase in the number of marriages as men and women married at an earlier age. There was a 50

There was still large-scale unemployment in the country in 1940. But the massive deficit spending of the war years financed a huge increase of industrial production, and the mobilization of 14 million men in the armed forces forced many women to take over the responsibility of producing the planes and tanks for the war effort. The war, therefore, accelerated the trend of taking women out of the privacy of the home and into public life.(Wide World Photos.)

percent increase in the birthrate between 1945 and 1955. And so many new houses were built that, by 1960, 25 percent of all houses in the United States had been built after 1945.

It seemed as though a successful conservative movement had restored traditional roles for women. In the movies, the strong women stars of the 1930s were replaced by weaker women (such as Debbie Reynolds and Doris Day) during the 1950s. A symbol of sexuality like Marilyn Monroe had none of the ability to control her own life or choose her lovers as Mae West, Greta Garbo, and Marlene Dietrich had during the 1930s.

Indeed, during the late 1940s and 1950s, a series of movies had taken strong women like Joan Crawford and Bette Davis and presented them as monsters who tried to destroy the independence and masculinity of men. The fear and hatred of women was a central theme in the best-selling detective novels of Mickey Spillane during the 1950s.

As television became the most important form of home entertainment during the 1950s, children watched a whole group of cowboy programs, such as "The Lone Ranger," that presented women as kinds of Sambos. Women were usually depicted as being silly and helpless. Often, because they could not think or act constructively, they got the cowboy hero into trouble. The male hero, however, usually had a horse or a dog who was not frightened into helplessness by danger and, unlike the women, was capable of intelligent and decisive actions that helped, rather than hindered, the hero. The message, like those in the books used to teach children reading in the schools, was clear: helpless women needed the protection of the home, and only men had the courage and the intelligence to deal with the frontiers outside the home.

The years between 1945 and 1960 did not see a return to the 1920s. A slow trend toward women becoming a larger part of the work force continued, as did a slow upward trend in the divorce rate. And, by the end of the 1950s, the birthrate had begun to decline.

The new prosperity increased the number of jobs that women traditionally held. More schools and hospitals were built, and there were more jobs for teachers and nurses. There was more paperwork in the growing corporations and in the growing government bureaucracies and, therefore, more clerical jobs for women. Here, too, women were defined as Sambos. A typist or secretary was a girl until she retired. She was always dependent upon her boss, who called her by her first name but whom she called mister.

On the surface, therefore, the period between 1945 and 1960 seemed to be one of contentment for middle-class women in their renewed roles as suburban housewives and successful consumers. Beneath the surface, however, the increasing number of working women and the increasing number of divorces called into question the housewife's role and foreshadowed the explosive questioning of women's roles that began during the 1960s.

1952, Eisenhower, and the Return to Normalcy

In 1952, the Republican party nominated General Eisenhower as its presidential candidate. He easily defeated the Democratic candidate, Governor Adlai Stevenson of Illinois. The Republican victory, however, did not mean that the renewed progressivism of the New Deal had ended as the Republican victory in 1920 had ended the progressive movement. Republicans who leaned toward corporate progressivism at home and intervention abroad, with their greatest strength in the East, had nominated

Wendell Willkie in 1940, Thomas Dewey in 1944 and 1948, and Eisenhower in 1952. These liberal Republicans accepted the progressive position of both Theodore Roosevelt and Franklin Roosevelt that political leadership was necessary to direct the economy and the society. They also accepted the position that military and political power were necessary for the defense of American interests overseas.

Eisenhower, who had commanded the military campaigns in Europe and then had served as commander of NATO, clearly was committed to the use of political and military power abroad. He also pledged his loyalty to modern Republicanism. He accepted the idea of the Full Employment bill passed by Congress at the end of World War II, which committed the government to use its policies to avoid economic depressions. During the campaign, he said that he would use the Council of Economic Advisers created by Congress (1946) to keep the country prosperous. He argued, however, that since the economy was going well, there was no need for more governmental activity. He was especially opposed to the idea of national health insurance. Since 1945, the American Medical Association (AMA) had been mounting a major campaign to persuade the people that such insurance would constitute socialized medicine and therefore was un-American.

This social conservatism was made possible, in part, by the fact that, by 1952, the two groups — farmers (especially in the South) and northern workers — that had provided the driving force for Social Security in 1935 were no longer actively pushing for social and economic reform. By 1952, much of the energy of white southerners was directed at preserving the caste system in their region, and most blue-collar workers had been unionized and had won a higher standard of living than unskilled and unorganized workers. In a sense, the unions had become part of the establishment. Their major concern was to save what they had gained between 1935 and 1950. The increasing automation of the economy also had stopped the expansion of the industrial work force. During the 1950s, the number of industrial workers and union members decreased as the number of white-collar workers increased.

Eisenhower pledged to operate the government within a balanced budget and end deficit spending. He vetoed legislation for public housing, which would have gone to the poor who were not part of the union establishment. He did accept legislation that raised Social Security payments and minimum wages, legislation wanted by union leaders.

One-quarter of the rural population, mostly the rural poor, had been driven off the land during the 1940s as prosperity made possible the rapid mechanization of agriculture. The remaining farmers also felt themselves part of the establishment and worked to save or increase the price supports they had gained under Roosevelt and Truman. Even though Eisenhower's secretary of agriculture (Ezra Taft Benson, a conservative) wanted to end farm price supports, they were raised from $1 billion to $5 billion between 1952 and 1960. This made up most of the increase of $8 billion in federal spending during Eisenhower's eight years as president.

But the economy did not continue the rapid growth of the 1940s during Eisenhower's administrations, and it lagged behind the growth rates of Russia, Germany, Japan, France, Italy, and Britain. By 1957, a serious recession had set in and unemployment had increased from 4 percent to almost 8 percent. Eisenhower and his advisers tried to stimulate the economy with legislation to build a national system of highways, at the cost of $26 billion. Congress also passed the National Defense Education Act (1958), which sent federal funds to private and state universities to pay for the expansion of their science and language programs. This money helped union construction workers and college teachers but not the poor and the unemployed. Eisenhower rejected advice to cut taxes in order to stimulate economic recovery. The recession continued until the end of his administration in 1960 and caused reduced tax revenues that resulted in major budget deficits.

Eisenhower and the Cold War

When he left the presidency in 1960, Eisenhower warned the country against the danger of a "military-industrial complex" gaining power over the lives of Americans. During World War II, much of the national budget had gone to finance the war, and then, under Truman, much of the national budget had gone to finance the Cold War. This pattern continued

The South had remained a rural region from the Civil War to World War I, while the Northeast, Midwest, and Far West were becoming more and more urban. The economy of the South, however, benefited more from the prosperity brought by government spending during World War II and continued to benefit from the defense spending of the Cold War. Southern cities such as Atlanta, pictured here, have grown very rapidly, therefore, since World War II, and southern population structure now resembles that of the nation. (Courtesy of Atlanta Chamber of Commerce.)

THE SOUTHEAST ASIA TREATY ORGANIZATION
(SEATO) SINCE 1954

Pakistan and New Zealand membership presently withdrawn (1972).
★ Nations which have bilateral treaties with U.S.

European members: UNITED KINGDOM, FRANCE

during Eisenhower's presidency, with many large companies making most of their profits from building missiles, airplanes, and other armaments.

Eisenhower hoped to conduct the Cold War without involving the government still further in the economy through increased defense spending. He wanted to reduce the armaments race with Soviet Russia, and he wanted to depend upon allies to supply troops to contain communism in China, as well as in Russia. Secretary of State Dulles persuaded many nations in the Pacific to join the Southeast Asia Treaty Organization (SEATO), which surrounded China (1954). Dulles then negotiated the Central Treaty Organization (CENTO) with Turkey, Iraq, Iran, and Pakistan (1959); CENTO linked SEATO to NATO. The United States then was allied with the nations that encircled both Russia and China.

To cut back the expenses of a large army, navy, and air force to be stationed at bases in all these allied countries, Eisenhower preferred to concentrate on developing more powerful atomic weapons and the missiles and planes to deliver them. He hoped that this threat of massive nuclear destruction would deter communist Russia and China from aggressive acts.

Eisenhower and his advisers continued the outlook held by Franklin Roosevelt in 1944 and thought it was realistic to see a few major powers policing the world. Truman and then Eisenhower had seen the world divided between two power centers, the United States and the Soviet Russia (allied with communist China). This perspective did not take into account the collapse of European imperialism in Asia and Africa and the development of revolutionary nationalism throughout a Third World that included Latin America.

One of the Third-World areas included the French colonies of Laos, Cambodia, and Vietnam in Southeast Asia. France had tried to suppress revolutions for independence there between 1945 and 1954. After military defeat, France entered into peace talks in Geneva, Switzerland, that resulted in independence for the three colonies. The major revolutionary group in Vietnam was headed by Ho Chi Minh, who used Marxist ideology as part of his struggle for national independence from France. Ho Chi Minh's forces had taken the northern part of the country from the French, who still held power in the south when the peace agreement was signed in Geneva. According to the agreement of 1954, there would be national elections by 1956 to elect a government that included representatives from both the northern and southern parts of the country. Dulles and Eisenhower refused to accept the Geneva agreement because they were sure that the majority in South Vietnam would vote for Ho Chi Minh. Instead, they sent arms and money to the anticommunist military and political leaders in South Vietnam, who were headed by Ngo Dinh Diem, to help them establish a separate country, South Vietnam. Momentarily, Eisenhower had restrained revolutionary nationalism in Vietnam. This was not the case, however, in Cuba.

Cuba and the Near East

Revolutionary leaders in China and Vietnam had used Marxist ideology in their efforts to overthrow unjust systems that exploited the majority of the people. These leaders did not intend, however, to take orders from Soviet Russia; there was great friction between communist China and communist Russia. American foreign policy leaders, however, believed that all Marxists were part of a single international conspiracy centered in Moscow. This attitude caused American leaders to be very hostile toward Fidel Castro when he overthrew a right-wing dictatorship in Cuba in 1959. Knowing that Castro called himself a Marxist, American leaders tried to drive him from power by refusing to buy Cuban sugar and by cutting off other forms of trade. This policy forced Castro to ask Russia for economic aid and made Cuba much more dependent on Soviet communism.

In Egypt, General Gamal Abdel Nassar had taken the Suez Canal out of British colonial rule in 1956. Secretary of State Dulles tried to force Nasser into an anti-Russian position. When Dulles failed and Nasser barred Israeli ships from the Suez Canal, Israel (backed by Britain and France) invaded Egypt and occupied the Egyptian territory up to the canal. Eisenhower forced Britain and France out of Egypt because he feared war with Russia and the lasting hostility of all the Arab states against the United States. Since the Arabs controlled so much of the world's oil reserves, it was especially important not to drive them into the arms of Russia.

American Jews and Israel

When Russian Jews came to America in large numbers after 1890, they brought with them the idea of Zionism. It was the belief of orthodox Jews that some day God would return them to their ancient home in Israel. Besides this religious Zionism, many Jews from eastern Europe brought a commitment to political Zionism. By the 1890s, some Jews in Europe had lost hope that anti-Semitism would disappear in the European countries. In order for Jews to escape persecution, leaders of political Zionism argued that Jews must establish a political nation for themselves in Israel.

Most of the eastern European Jews coming to the United States believed that they could escape anti-Semitic persecution here. America could be their new Israel. But they believed that a nation of Israel was necessary as a refuge for their relatives in Europe. At first, the German Jews who had come to America before 1880 resisted the idea of Zionism. But, by World War I, led by Louis Brandeis, many had accepted the belief that a nation of Israel must be created. A number of European Jews had settled in Palestine by World War I. Then, after Hitler had ordered death for all European Jews during World War II, the survivors believed that a political state for Jews must be created in Palestine. The horror of the holocaust in Nazi Germany, where 6 million Jews were killed in concentration camps, convinced American Jews to raise as much money as possible to support Jews living in Israel and to put pressure on Britain and the United States to allow a Jewish state to be built among the Palestinian Arabs. When Jews in 1948 declared their separation from the Palestinian Arabs and declared the existence of the nation of Israel, President Truman granted the new country instant recognition.

Jews and Intellectual Life

From the 1880s up to World War II, the WASP establishment had systematically kept Jews outside its major economic, social, and educational institutions. President Franklin Roosevelt believed that the tradition of anti-Semitism was so strong in the country at the beginning of World War II that public opinion would not permit him to admit large numbers of Jewish refugees from Nazi Germany. During the war, however, as the WASP establishment disassociated itself from Hitler's racist democracy in its extreme form (killing Jews), a dramatic change took place in American policies of segregating Jews. Barriers that had kept Jews from teaching American history and American literature at major universities were broken. Quotas that had limited Jewish enrollment at many eastern universities also were abandoned in many cases, as were quotas in the private schools that prepared students for those universities.

There has been a significant split within the WASP establishment, therefore, since the 1940s. While education and government have been largely open to Jews, large banks and corporations, and the business and social clubs to which business executives belong, have largely continued to discriminate against Jews.

The Ecumenical Movement

First in the New Deal and then during World War II, national leaders had made an attempt to show that Catholics and Jews were first-class citizens who were fully a part of American life. At patriotic events, a Jewish rabbi and a Catholic priest were present along with a Protestant minister. These changes during the 1930s and 1940s expressed a trend that had begun as early as 1910, when most of the major Protestant groups, with the exception of the Baptists and the Lutherans, talked in terms of institutional cooperation. This led to a broadening of the Federal Council of Churches under its new name, the National Council of Churches (1950). The United Presbyterian Church, the United Church of Christ, and the Methodist and Episcopal churches also began to discuss the possibility of merger into a single church. Lutherans consolidated from a large number of divisions into three or four major groups. Another indication that the major Protestant denominations were no longer committed to isolation was the establishment of the National Conference of Christians and Jews (1928).

Catholics, however, largely avoided Protestant overtures for a discussion of ecumenical concerns until Pope John XXIII, in the second Vatican Council (1962), ended the traditional barriers to communication between Catholics and Protestants. The desire of the major American Protestant denominations to end their nineteenth-century identity of isolated purity also led them to enter into ecumenical discussion at the world level. This brought about the establishment of the World Council of Churches (1948). By the late 1960s, theologians of the major Protestant groups followed European and Latin American Catholics into a dialogue with Marxists that was based on their common concern for social justice. This dialogue marked a lessening of the great hostility toward Marxism that had been characteristic of American Protestant, Catholic, and Jewish theologians, as well as university intellectuals, during the 1940s and 1950s.

Reinhold Niebuhr and the New Realism

The changes in American Protestantism since World War I found their most powerful expression in the Protestant theologian Reinhold Niebuhr during the 1940s. Many people believed Niebuhr was the most important American theologian since Jonathan Edwards during the eighteenth century. Niebuhr, a young man in 1917, had hoped that World War I would convert the whole world to American democracy and Protestantism. Disillusioned in the 1920s, he had become an isolationist. Then, at the end of the 1930s, he began to persuade the many Protestant ministers who had become isolationists and pacifists during the 1930s that they should support Roosevelt in his war against the evil leaders of Germany and Japan. Niebuhr argued that American Protestants had been prisoners of a false theology of innocence in 1917, when they hoped that the world could be made perfect. And, for Niebuhr, who had been a Marxist during the early 1930s, they were still prisoners of innocence when they wanted to isolate American perfection from the imperfections of the rest of the world. Developing a theology of neo-orthodoxy, Niebuhr emphasized that Americans shared the sinfulness of all other people and that, because of original sin, the world could never be made perfect. People must choose to support positions that were partially good. For Niebuhr, it was important to defend and conserve the imperfect virtues of democracy and capitalism against the attempt of Nazi Germany to purify the world through the bloody purge of war.

Liberalism, Marxism, and Consensus, 1940-1960

Niebuhr believed that the middle classes of western Europe and America had committed the greatest sin, that of pride, in believing in endless progress toward perfection. But he found that this pridefulness was qualified by their Jewish-Christian heritage that did stress human weakness and by their commitment to political and economic traditions that stressed checks and balances. It was easier, in his analysis, for them to turn from innocence to realism than it was for Marxists. Marxists not only believed in progress and perfection, but they had totally rejected religious traditions of sinfulness and they had rejected decentralized politics and economics in favor of centralization.

The social scientists, literary critics, and Protestant theologians who shared Niebuhr's rejection of the traditional American view of history as progress translated this rejection into support for a foreign policy of containment of communist aggressiveness. As America had the responsibility to preserve the qualified virtues of democracy and capitalism against Nazi Germany, so it had the responsibility to restrain the revolutionary attempts of communist Russia to force the world into ideological perfection.

Many of the secular intellectuals in the universities during the 1940s and 1950s shared Niebuhr's belief that the progressive tradition was naive. Such literary criticism as Leslie Fiedler's *The End of Innocence* (1948) and Lionel Trilling's *The Liberal Imagination* (1950) pointed to the weakness of the American utopian tradition. Other literary critics — Henry Nash Smith in *Virgin Land* (1950), R. W. B. Lewis in *The American Adam* (1955), and Charles Sanford in *The Quest for Paradise* (1960) — analyzed and criticized the way in which this vision of American purity, in contrast to European corruption, had dominated the perspective of American writers from the seventeenth through the twentieth centuries.

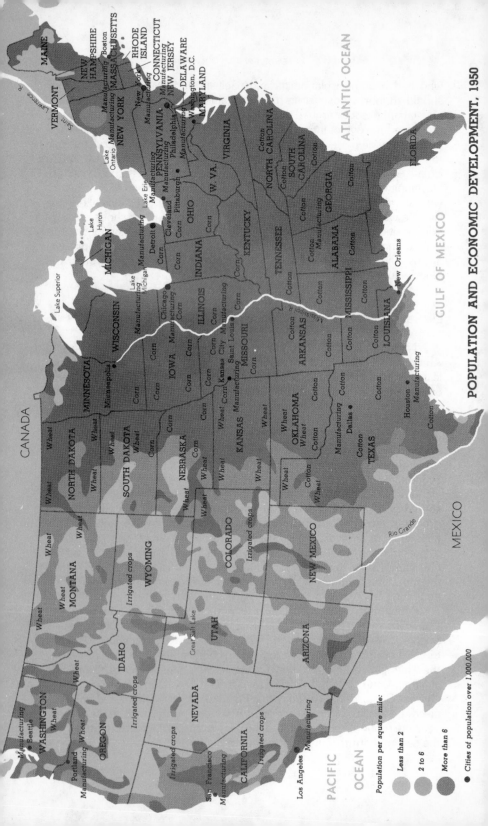

POPULATION AND ECONOMIC DEVELOPMENT, 1950

Population per square mile:

Less than 2

2 to 6

More than 6

• Cities of population over 1,000,000

Historians, political scientists, and sociologists began, during the 1950s, to argue that the American political tradition defined change as gradual and pragmatic. This view was expressed in Daniel Boorstin's *The Genius of American Politics* (1953), Clinton Rossiter's *American Conservatism* (1955), and Daniel Bell's *The End of Ideology* (1960). These scholars stressed the realism of the founding fathers in fearing the sinfulness of human nature and of establishing a government of checks and balances that ensured that no one could exercise great power over anyone else. Because the heritage of the founding fathers was pragmatic, according to these scholars, there was no tradition of ideological conflict in American politics. All Americans shared a consensus on the values of democracy and capitalism. They claimed that this consensus persisted into the 1950s, when there were no significant differences between the Republicans and the Democrats on foreign policy or domestic issues. It was the responsibility of the many institutions — governments, schools, and churches — to preserve this consensus and not allow un-American right-wing or left-wing ideas to divide the American people and lead them into conflict.

Civil Religion and the Churches

With the new definition of America as a country of Protestants, Catholics, and Jews, there was new emphasis on the president as the major symbol of American religious life. America, leaders claimed, was a religious country, in contrast to the official atheism of Soviet Russia. But only the president could represent the different religious traditions of Protestants, Catholics, and Jews. Eisenhower said that all Americans should believe in God but that it did not matter what the particular belief was. He opened cabinet meetings with nondenominational prayers and held prayer breakfasts at the White House. Sociologists have called this association of religion with politics *civil religion*. More Americans than at any time in history, 95 percent, identified themselves as religious. The phrase "under God" was added to the Pledge of Allegiance and a new postage stamp declared that "in God We Trust."

As during the 1920s, all of the religious groups spent a great deal of money on building churches and temples. The new prosperity made it possible for the Catholics to enlarge their parochial school system, and, by 1960, there were 11,000 elementary schools, 2,500 high schools, 295 colleges and universities, and 112 seminaries supported by the Catholic community.

The Youth Culture during the 1950s

Adults seemed to cling to security during the 1950s, and they found the right kind of leader in Eisenhower, the oldest American president. But there was a contradiction between this view of an elderly, cautious generation and the population patterns of the Eisenhower era. The 50 percent rise in the birthrate caused the population to jump from 150 million to 180 million between 1950 and 1960, the largest ten-year increase in American history. This huge increase in the number of children was related to the restoration of prosperity, which made it possible for young couples starting large families to move out of the cities and into the suburbs. While the people on farms and in small towns and central cities grew older on the average, national attention focused on the suburbs with their young couples and children.

Part of the new prosperity reflected the federal government's support of higher education. Under the G.I. Bill of Rights (1944), the federal government provided economic assistance to veterans for education. The number of college students immediately doubled. Veterans graduating from college found white-collar jobs in expanding corporations and government agencies. This trend paralleled another significant pattern: the number of self-employed persons declined from 9 to 8 million, while the number of persons employed in professional and managerial occupations doubled, from 7 to 14 million between 1945 and 1960.

The children of these successful middle-class fathers living in the suburbs were aware of the dramatic changes in their families. Many of their grandparents were blue-collar workers and belonged to the lower-middle class. The children's sense of separation from the past was increased by the fact that the grandparents did not live in the suburbs but in cities or in small towns or on farms. The sense of separation was made greater by the fact that their parents often had moved out of the state or region where the grandparents lived. When industrialization became significant at the end of the nineteenth century, white-collar workers tended to be rooted in a city, while unskilled workers tended to move from city to city and state to state. Then, after World War II, this pattern was reversed. While blue-collar or unskilled workers tended to be rooted, white-collar workers tended to move from city to city and state to state.

The children of the dramatically enlarged suburban middle class were aware that they were a part of a new wealthy life-style. During the 1950s, suburban Americans spent twice as much on entertainment as on rent. Leisure activities became a major part of the economy. Children shared in the affluent, leisurely life-style of their parents. The sale of records to young people became a billion-dollar enterprise, and advertisers took advantage of the large number of well-to-do children by identifying special clothing styles for them as well as special foods and soft drinks.

Young People and Music

A particular style of music developed during the 1950s for young people. Elvis Presley, a white entertainer, became famous for his use of black rhythm and blues. As in the 1920s, young whites emphasized the sexuality expressed in black music. Presley projected this sexuality in his

During the depression of the 1930s little new housing was built. The prosperity brought by World War II made possible an explosion of new housing, most of which went into suburbs that formed an urban sprawl around the central cities. Most of the people moving into these suburban developments were white Protestants, Catholics, and Jews. Blacks, driven off the land in the South by mechanization, then filled the ghettos of the central cities in the 1950s and 1960s. (Courtesy of HUD.)

performances, as did black performers such as Chuck Berry and Little Richard who were popular with white audiences.

The stress on the need to use all of one's energy in the competition of the marketplace had led WASP cultural leaders during the nineteenth century to warn young men not to waste their energy on sexuality or music. But such sociological studies as David Riesman's *The Lonely Crowd* (1950) and William Whyte's *The Organization Man* (1955) argued that middle-class men who worked in the corporations and government agencies no longer valued extreme competition. Teamwork, cooperation, and getting along with one's fellow workers were important values in the large organizations. Children during the 1950s saw their fathers come home with extra energy, which they put into entertainment or hobbies. Their parents urged the schools to teach their children about life adjustment, about getting along with other people. Promotions in the large organizations depended at least as much on sociability and not making enemies as they did on beating out your opponent in tough competition.

Suburban parents were not only teaching their children to be less competitive, their own life-styles undermined the loyalty of their children to the major institutions of American society. The suburban middle class taught their children that they must respect the institutions of government, business, education, and church. But children observed the way in which their parents' life-styles emphasized private life rather than public life. Fathers came home from the city to the suburban home, showing that their major concern was not with the public problems of the city but with the life of the family. Most of the family's money and energy was spent on its own entertainment, its own hobbies, and its own vacations.

The young people of 1960, therefore, had learned contradictory values from their parents. They were told to respect authority, social institutions, and their elders, but they also were told to do their own thing. They were told to respect the capitalist system but not the competitive spirit that was essential to capitalism. They were told to accept the morals and manners of the older generation, but they were taught to accept their bodies, too. Their parents wanted them to be taught about sexuality in schools and churches but to live with the antisexual morality of nineteenth-century America.

Affluent, suburban, middle-class youth, therefore, passed from the 1950s into the 1960s confused and rebellious. Eisenhower's economic and foreign policies were in crisis by 1960. The social life of the suburban middle class, his strongest supporters, was also in crisis.

Supplementary Reading

W. LaFeber, *America, Russia, and the Cold War* (1976), provides an excellent overview of the subject. Specific issues are explored more deeply in D. Yergin, *Shattered Peace: The Origins of the Cold War and the National Security State* (1977), and F. Block, *The Origins of International Economic Disorder* (1977). See also R. Caridi, *The Korean War and American Politics* (1968). The impact of the Cold War on civil liberties is the subject of A. Theoharis, *Seeds of Repression: Harry S. Truman and the Origins of McCarthyism* (1971); R. Freeland, *The Truman Doctrine and the Origins of McCarthyism* (1972); and M. Rogin, *The Intellectuals and McCarthy* (1967). The major patterns of postwar politics are discussed by A. Hamby, *Beyond the New Deal: Harry S. Truman and American Liberalism* (1973), and J. Boss and W. DeVries, *The Transformation of Southern Politics: Social Change and Political Consequence Since 1945* (1976).

The revolution in race relations is described by R. Kluger, *Simple Justice: The History of Brown v. Board of Education and Black America's Struggle for Equality* (1976), and R. Ruetten, *Quest and Response: Minority Rights and the Truman Administration* (1973). W. Chafe, *The American Woman* (1972), charts the economic changes in the status of women brought by World War II; and M. Haskell, *From Reverence to Rape* (1974), analyzes the growing hostility toward women expressed in the movies.

The political and diplomatic issues of the Eisenhower administration are discussed in H. Parmet, *Eisenhower and the American Crusades* (1972), and P. Lyon, *Eisenhower* (1974). T. Hoopes, *The Devil and John Foster Dulles* (1973), and V. Marchetti and J. Marks, *The CIA and the Cult of Intelligence* (1974), are especially good on foreign policy.

J. Goulden, *The Best Years: 1945-1950* (1976), and D. Miller and M. Nowak, *The Fifties: The Way We Really Were* (1977), provide perspective on the social and cultural history of those years. Specific aspects of American culture are explored in E. Barnouw, *The Image Empire* (1970), a look at television, and G. Gow, *Hollywood in the Fifties* (1971).

A. Gordon, *Jews in Suburbia* (1959), and A. Guttman, *The Jewish Writer in America: Assimilation and the Crisis of Identity* (1971), discuss the impact of World War II on Jewish-American culture. A good starting point in the study of civil religion is W. Herberg, *Protestant-Catholic-Jew* (1958).

Chapter 27

The New Frontier at Home and Abroad

1960-1968

In 1960, the Democrats regained the presidency from the Republicans. Their candidate, John F. Kennedy, was the first Roman Catholic to be elected president of the United States. Although the majority of white Protestants voted against him, the religious issue was not as intensely divisive as it had been when Al Smith was the Democratic candidate in 1928. Most leaders of major northern Protestant denominations in 1960, unlike the large majority in 1928, declared that leadership by a Catholic was acceptable. Unlike 1928, only a few leaders of southern Baptists and Methodists declared a Catholic president unacceptable. The New Deal and World War II had enabled Catholics to achieve status as first-class citizens capable of leadership.

Political Loyalties in 1960

Kennedy could be accepted more easily, as Jackie Robinson had been more easily accepted in baseball, because he was exceptional. He was more handsome, more intelligent, and had more charm than the average politician. Kennedy's father was a millionaire, and the candidate had been educated at Harvard. White Protestants also were less prejudiced against Irish Catholics than they were against Italian, Polish, and Chicano

John F. Kennedy (1917-1963) was the first Catholic to be elected president of the United States. By 1960, prejudice against Catholics was considerably less than it had been in 1928 when it helped defeat Al Smith. Although a Democrat, Kennedy played much the same role that Theodore Roosevelt had in 1901. Once again, upper-middle-class leaders believed that urban problems were being ignored in the 1950s and that Kennedy would provide more vigorous leadership than President Eisenhower had. The assassination of Kennedy in 1963 did much to break the mood of enthusiasm and optimism that Kennedy had been able to inspire. (UPI.)

Catholics. By the 1960s, Irish-Catholics on the average were reaching levels of education and income equal to those of the most elite Protestant groups (such as the Presbyterians and Episcopalians). This was not true of Italian and Polish Catholics, who, on the average, remained in blue-collar occupations, or the Chicanos (Spanish-speaking Americans), who were mostly unskilled and very poor.

Although Kennedy won the votes of 77 percent of the Catholics, 76 percent of the blacks, and 85 percent of the Jews, he defeated the Republican candidate, Richard Nixon, by only 118,000 votes out of the 69 million cast. His victory surprised many political experts, who had believed that Eisenhower's victories in 1952 and 1956 were evidence that the Republicans had replaced the Democrats as the majority party. These experts had expected the growing middle class, which resulted from the new prosperity after World War II, to vote Republican. During the 1930s, most upper-income and college-educated people had been Republicans. But Jews and Catholics, as they became more prosperous, tended to remain Democrats. The many Jews who had come from Russia and eastern Europe around 1900, unlike the earlier Jewish immigrants from Germany, were very poor. But, by 1960, their educational level and salaries, on the average, were surpassing those of the Episcopalians and the Presbyterians. The Protestant elites, however, remained richer because much of their wealth came from stocks and property, rather than from salaries. The Protestant elites also remained more powerful than the Jews and the Irish-Catholics because they continued to monopolize the leadership of the largest corporations and banks.

Increasing numbers of the Protestant middle class were moving away from the Republican party. In 1940, only 30 percent of white Protestant business and professional people in the North said that they would support a Democrat, but, by 1960, this proportion had risen to 50 percent. Many professionals in colleges, government agencies, and corporations identified the growth of their institutions with policies begun by the Democratic party during the 1930s and 1940s. They believed that, if growth was to continue so that there would be more opportunities for promotion within these institutions, the policies of the Democratic party must continue.

This change was most dramatic in the Northeast, with its concentration of universities, corporations, and government agencies. The following chart shows the growing strength of the Democrats at the congressional level during the Eisenhower years.

Percentages of Democrats in the House of Representatives

	Northeast	Midwest	South	West
1952	38%	26%	92%	33%
1956	41	36	92	45
1960	53	40	93	56

During the 1950s, polls indicated that people saw the Republicans as the group best able to handle foreign policy and preserve peace and that they saw the Democrats as the group best able to handle the economy and preserve prosperity. Voters during the 1950s chose a Republican president to keep peace and a Democratic Congress to keep prosperity. In 1960, many more people voted for Democratic congressmen than voted for Kennedy, the Democratic candidate.

The extent of ticket splitting and independence from party loyalty during the 1950s (which has continued up to the present) is something new in American history. The ability of presidential candidates to present themselves to the public on television has made them more independent of political parties. Before television, national candidates depended on local political organizations to carry their message to the public. But Eisenhower during the 1950s and Nixon in 1960 could hope to reach and win independent and even Democratic voters even though Republican parties at the state and local levels were growing weaker. This is one reason that Nixon was ready to engage in television debates with Kennedy during the 1960 campaign.

Kennedy and the New Frontier

During the campaign, Kennedy blamed the Eisenhower administration for slow economic growth and high unemployment. He also attacked Eisenhower's vice-president, Richard Nixon, then the Republican presidential candidate, for administration policies that had allowed communist Russia to get ahead of the United States in the arms race, especially in long-distance missiles. Kennedy promised that he would speed up economic growth and change America's defensive position on communism to an aggressive one. Kennedy called his policy of expansion at home and abroad the New Frontier.

The youngest president since Theodore Roosevelt, Kennedy believed his academic advisers who thought that governmental activity could easily make the American economy work well. Economists such as Walt Whitman Rostow also argued that the entire world was developing along the lines of American capitalism. According to this view, communism was abnormal. Progress, or modernization, followed capitalistic patterns. Countries in Africa, Asia, and Latin America would move from primitive and backward peasant societies into ones something like the United States unless they developed a disease while they were changing. In Rostow's opinion, communism was a disease that could strike countries while they were modernizing. But the United States, like a doctor, could stop the disease from spreading or could cure a diseased country.

For the first time since World War I, young Americans were encouraged to be missionaries who would help Americanize the whole world. Congress established the Peace Corps (1961) for young volunteers who wanted to teach people in backward countries how to achieve progress.

Certain that the Cuban people did not support Fidel Castro and that the disease of communism could easily be cut out of Cuba, Kennedy supported a CIA plan to invade Cuba with an army of anti-Castro Cubans who had been trained and armed in America. Castro's troops crushed the invasion at the Bay of Pigs (April 1961). But in October of 1962, Kennedy was ready to threaten the Russian leader Nikita Khrushchev with atomic warfare when he learned that Russian missiles were being installed in Cuba. Russia agreed to withdraw the missiles if Kennedy would agree to end United States military activity against Cuba. The Soviet Union also signed a treaty with the United States that banned the testing of atomic weapons except underground, where there would be no danger of fallout (1963).

Kennedy persuaded Congress to appropriate money to increase the numbers of marines and soldiers and airplanes and naval ships to wage conventional wars. It was the argument of Kennedy's advisers that Eisenhower's reliance on massive deterrence made it impossible for the United States to fight small wars to stop the disease of communism when it was just beginning in the modernizing nations of Asia, Africa, and Latin America. Applying this logic to Vietnam, Kennedy increased the number of troops there from 600 to 16,000. It is probable that he permitted the assassination of Ngo Dinh Diem, the leader of South Vietnam, by South

Vietnamese army officers who promised to fight the Viet Cong (the South Vietnamese Marxists) more vigorously. It is also probable that the CIA, which had successfully intervened against leftists in Guatemala and Iran during the 1950s, then tried a number of unsuccessful plots to assassinate Castro.

The New Frontier at Home

When Kennedy was assassinated in November 1963, his efforts to take the offensive against communism had not succeeded. Castro was stronger in Cuba, and the Viet Cong were stronger in South Vietnam. But the increase of government spending for the armed forces and for the space program did stimulate the rate of economic growth and decrease the number of unemployed. Corporate progressives were reassured that political leadership was able to control the business cycle. The number of business people who were in favor of the political control of the economy was larger than during the 1930s, because at least 10 percent of industrial production was financed by the Department of Defense. More of the economy and the universities obtained funds from the Atomic Energy Commission (AEC). And the Apollo project to put a man on the moon by the end of the 1960s sent $30 billion into industry and the universities. Kennedy's advisers included cabinet members from the business community (for example, the banker Douglas Dillon and Robert McNamara, who had been the head of the Ford Motor Company). They agreed with Kennedy's economists that the economy would be further stimulated by a tax cut. After Kennedy's death, Congress passed a tax program that reduced the rates for corporations and the wealthy more than it did for middle- and low-income families. Until 1969, the Kennedy-Johnson economic policies seemed to work well. The economy grew so rapidly that there was more corporate and personal income to tax. These increased revenues paid for the larger government expenditures for defense, so there was little deficit spending and little change in the national debt.

Johnson, Goldwater, and the Landslide of 1964

Lyndon Johnson from Texas, the majority leader in the Senate during the 1950s, was chosen as the vice-presidential candidate in 1960 to give Kennedy additional strength in the South. Running as the Democratic presidential candidate in 1964, Johnson won a landslide victory, with 43 million votes in contrast to 27 million for Republican candidate Barry Goldwater.

Johnson had little of Kennedy's charm. People voted against Goldwater rather than for Johnson. Goldwater lost the votes of most independents as well as liberal Republicans because he represented the right wing of the Republican party. Polls indicated that the largest number of Republicans wanted Governor William Scranton of Pennsylvania, a moderate, as

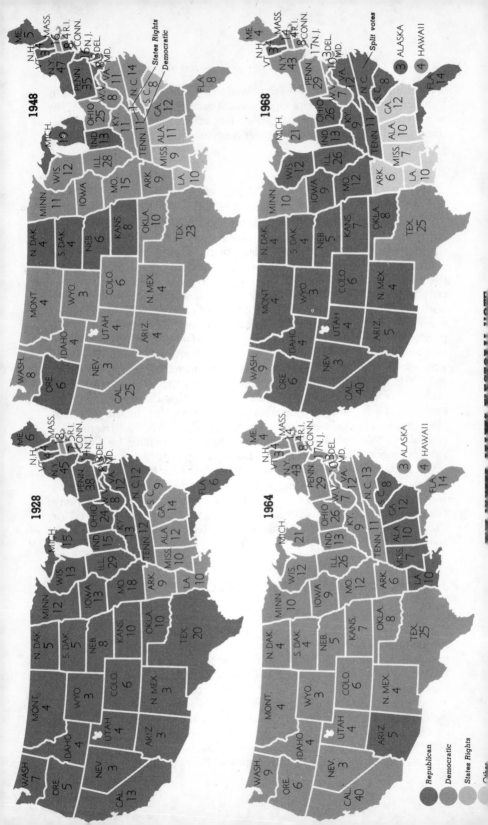

their presidential candidate. But conservative Republicans with intense ideological commitments succeeded in capturing control of the Republican national convention, and they nominated Goldwater. These were Republicans who had refused to go along with the qualified acceptance of the New Deal represented by Thomas Dewey during the 1940s and by Eisenhower during the 1950s.

As college presidents and professors; newspaper, radio, and television journalists; church leaders; and business leaders in the Northeast tended to move from the Republican to the Democratic party between 1940 and 1960, the number of liberal Republicans tended to decline. This trend in the Northeast was accompanied by the rise of conservative Republicanism in the South and Southwest. The rapid industrialization and urbanization of those regions had produced large numbers of new business people. Unlike many of the older business class in the Northeast who had moved to corporate progressivism with Theodore Roosevelt in 1901, many of this new business class in the 1960s believed in the competitive marketplace of the nineteenth century. They talked about destroying labor unions and Social Security. Their conservative values led them to support Goldwater in 1964, while liberal Republicans crossed party lines and voted for Johnson.

College students during the 1950s and 1960s, unlike students in the 1930s, also showed a strong preference for the Democratic party. Those college students who remained Republicans became more intensely conservative. They liked the ideological novels of Ayn Rand, including *Atlas Shrugged* and *The Fountainhead,* which called for destruction of welfare capitalism and a return to nineteenth-century individualism. A small group of well-educated young Republicans even joined the extremely conservative John Birch Society. The founder of the society, businessman Robert Welch, accused President Eisenhower of being part of the communist conspiracy because Eisenhower accepted welfare legislation at home and refused to fight a total war against communism abroad.

Although Goldwater won support from conservative Republicans, most voters saw him as an extremist who might use atomic weapons in Vietnam and who might try to end Social Security at home. Goldwater won only his home state of Arizona and states in the Deep South (South Carolina, Georgia, Alabama, Mississippi, and Louisiana).

The South and Massive Resistance

White southerners had become increasingly hostile toward northern Democrats and liberal Republicans after 1948, because the national government had become more active in attacking Jim Crow patterns throughout the South. The blacks who could meet literacy tests and pay poll taxes continued their revolutionary return to political participation after a Supreme Court decision outlawed the white primary (1944). The pattern of increased black voting centered in the southern cities and in the most recently developed agricultural areas. An example was the increased voting in Florida cities and the citrus-growing counties in the center of the state. The slowest increase in black voting in Florida was in the old, established cotton-planting counties along the Georgia border. Another example was Mississippi, the most rural of all southern states, where the increase of black voting lagged far behind the other southern states. In the rural counties, whites owned the land and threatened to fire black workers if they registered to vote. Stable population patterns made it possible for white leaders to know when anyone did register. In the cities and the rapidly changing agricultural counties, such control was impossible. The following chart shows the growing percentages of voting-age blacks who were registered in the southern states.

Percentages of Voting-Age Blacks Registered in the South

	1940	1952	1960	1966
Mississippi	0%	4%	6%	14%
Alabama	0	5	14	31
South Carolina	0	20	27	38
Louisiana	0	25	32	39
Georgia	2	23	27	46
Arkansas	3	27	38	54
Virginia	5	16	23	49
Texas	9	31	39	59
North Carolina	10	18	38	49
Tennessee	16	27	48	72

Another series of decisions by the Supreme Court dealing with education also drove white southerners to develop a position of massive resistance to racial desegregation. Under legal pressure from the NAACP, the Supreme Court during the 1930s had begun to warn white politicians in the southern states that they were not providing separate educational facilities for blacks that were equal in quality to those for whites. This strategy of the NAACP, however, changed during the 1940s to the argument that any segregated facilitiy was a violation of the rights of equal citizenship under the Fourteenth Amendment because segregation was based on the assumption of white superiority and black inferiority. Equal education for black children could not be provided when black children were taught that they were segregated because they were not equal to whites.

In 1954, the Supreme Court accepted this argument (presented by Thurgood Marshall, the lawyer for the NAACP) in a unanimous decision in the case Brown v. Board of Education of Topeka and ruled that all laws establishing segregated education were unconstitutional. This reversed the Court's decision of 1896 in Plessy v. Ferguson, which had upheld separate-but-equal facilities.

President Eisenhower criticized this decision, which was presented by his appointee, Chief Justice Earl Warren, because Eisenhower believed that integration could not be forced by governmental action. However, he also believed that he had no choice but to uphold the federal courts, and, in 1957, he used troops at Central High School in Little Rock, Arkansas, when Governor Orval Faubus mobilized state troops to block integration. Faubus represented a new group of southern governors who called on states' rights to prevent national intervention in racial patterns. Unlike northern conservatives for whom states' rights meant a complete laissez-faire attitude, however, they continued to stress the need for their state governments to provide social services and welfare. Faubus won six terms as governor of Arkansas by presenting himself as a martyred representative of the white people who defied national power.

Most southern governors and most members of Congress from the South signed statements denying the constitutional right of the national government to interfere with social patterns in the states. But the momentum in national politics to dismantle the Jim Crow structure continued. Congress established the Civil Rights Commission and the Civil Rights Division in the Department of Justice (1957). The attorney general was given the power to restrain southern registrars who kept blacks from registering to vote. In 1961, the Twenty-third Amendment to the Constitution permitted the residents of Washington, D.C., mostly blacks, to vote in presidential elections. In 1962, the Twenty-fourth Amendment barred the use of state poll taxes in federal elections. In 1964, the Civil Rights Act called for the end to discrimination in all public places, made it illegal for employers and unions to discriminate, affirmed that federal funds would be withheld from state-administered programs that discriminated, and gave the power to the national government to help people register to vote.

White southerners had organized themselves in white citizens' councils during the 1950s in the hope that they could intimidate southern blacks so that they would not work for change. They also hoped to be a successful pressure group in national politics. By 1964, the white citizens' councils had failed to preserve the status quo in the South or change the policies of the national Democratic party. But they had helped take the Republican party from the control of liberal Republicans.

Martin Luther King, Jr., and the Fight against Jim Crow

Between 1920 and 1950, blacks had replaced whites as the leaders of the NAACP and, by the 1950s, were beginning to take over leadership from white liberals in the more recently formed Congress of Racial Equality (CORE). The strategy of this group emphasized passive but uncompromising resistance to the Jim Crow system. Their ideas for passive resistance derived, in part, from Mahatma Gandhi's peaceful protests against the English in India and from labor's use of the sit-down strike during the 1930s. In 1955-1956, a spontaneous black protest against segregated buses in Montgomery, Alabama, began the use of these tactics. The most important leader who emerged from the Montgomery bus boycott was Martin Luther King, Jr., a Baptist minister.

The existence of a whole group of black leaders like King in the southern cities demonstrated the failure of the crusade against blacks in the
South that was to have forced blacks back into the dependent condition of
slavery. Jim Crow had established a pattern in which blacks in public situa-
tions had to act like dependent children. But the denial of dignity to adult
blacks, which was the essence of the caste system, operated only when
whites and blacks met in public. Unlike the situation in the Union of South
Africa, white southerners did not go into the black ghettos of the cities to
stop the development of black leaders as ministers, business people, lawyers, doctors, and teachers. By 1955, therefore, large numbers of skilled
black leaders lived in the ghettos of southern cities. At that time, they
began visible challenges of the Jim Crow system. King, for example, had
gone to a black high school and a black college in Atlanta before he went
North to receive a divinity degree and a doctorate at integrated
universities.

King became the most important leader of the many protest movements throughout the South in part because his philosophy of nonviolence
and love for his enemies made him more acceptable to whites as the first
major southern black leader to challenge patterns of white racism. By
1960, black college students, with the aid of some white students, were
using the technique of nonviolent direct action for sit-ins at lunch counters
and stores to break the patterns of discrimination that existed throughout
the South.

King had established the Southern Christian Leadership Committee
(SCLC) as his organization to bring about change. But, by 1961, many of
the black students thought he was too cautious in challenging the status
quo and turned to the Student Nonviolent Coordinating Committee
(SNCC) for direction. And CORE responded to the enthusiasm of young
blacks for achieving an immediate breakthrough in civil rights by organizing a freedom ride (1961) to desegregate bus lines in Alabama and Mississippi. This action focused national attention on the continued
discrimination in public transportation in those states. The more moderate
NAACP and the National Urban League also supported these successful
efforts at direct action.

White liberals accepted and supported the commitment of black
organizations to nonviolent and direct action. A conference on race and
religion called by Protestant, Catholic, and Jewish leaders in 1963
endorsed this new strategy for civil rights reform. And they joined black
leaders who planned a march on Washington, D.C., that would focus on
the poverty and unemployment of blacks.

Black Power

By 1965, black protest groups had succeeded in destroying patterns
of public discrimination and winning strong civil rights legislation from the
national government. But none of these gains helped the desperate economic and social conditions of the millions of blacks living in the urban

In the 1960s, for the first time in American history, a black rather than a white Protestant was the most powerful spiritual leader in the nation. Raised in Georgia, King, a Baptist minister, became a spokesman of the bus boycott in Montgomery, Alabama, in 1958. From that date until his assassination in Memphis, Tennessee, in 1968, King was successful in appealing to the consciences of many whites for their help in breaking down Jim Crow segregation and regaining the vote for blacks in the southern states. At the end of his life, he had shifted his attention to the problem of poverty in the black ghettos of northern cities and to criticizing the war in Vietnam. (Wide World Photos.)

slums. These people experienced low incomes and high unemployment, terrible overcrowding in decaying housing, a lack of personal safety in areas of high crime and drug use, and few job prospects for their children.

Once more, therefore, during the 1960s as during the 1920s, there was a major movement for black nationalism among the lower-income people. Black Muslims, under the leadership of Elijah Muhammad, preached the need for black people to separate themselves from whites because the whites were devils who were attempting to destroy blacks by creating the hellish conditions of the ghettos. The Muslims preached the need for the greater religious commitment and self-discipline necessary for the blacks in order to gain the strength to overcome the temptations of the slums and to build a self-sufficient economy separate from the white world. However, Malcolm X, who was assassinated in 1965, broke away from Elijah Muhammad and started a movement that stressed the common struggle of oppressed blacks and whites against the establishment. Later, the Black Panthers expressed a somewhat similar outlook.

The hopelessness and frustration of the black masses exploded in riots in New York and Los Angeles in 1964 and 1965. In the Watts ghetto of

Los Angeles, thirty-five people were killed and property worth $30 million was burned. The police and the national guard used violence to stop the spread of the riots throughout the country. In 1967, the dead numbered forty-three in Detroit and twenty-six in Newark. The 164 riots in 1967 destroyed property valued at more than $100 million. Young middle-class blacks began to question the logic of focusing their reforms on destroying segregation to facilitate black assimilation into a white society that caused so much misery.

Stokely Carmichael, the young leader of SNCC, began to doubt that blacks could teach whites to be more loving and charitable as King had hoped. Perhaps, he argued in 1966, blacks must save themselves with a philosophy of black power. Blacks in 1967 and 1968 were divided as to whether black power meant the development of a totally separate black society (as the black Muslims advocated) or whether it meant forging an alliance with other groups in America who wanted to gain control of the economy in order to redirect it toward economic justice for lower-income people (this second view was held by the Black Panthers and their leader Eldridge Cleaver).

The strong sense of black pride that had developed among young blacks during the 1960s, expressed in the slogan "black is beautiful," meant that when they attended the major universities, which until the 1950s had been almost totally white, they wanted a symbol of continuing black identity in the creation of Afro-American studies departments. No longer forced to go to segregated black colleges as they had been before World War II, blacks wanted to be accepted as first-class citizens. But they did not want their equality with whites defined in white terms. To have an African heritage was no longer seen as a mark of humiliation but as a reason for pride.

The South and the Black Migration to the Cities

The riots in the northern cities during the 1960s were the result, in large part, of the migration of blacks out of the South after 1940. The massive spending for World War II had an even greater impact on the South's economy than on the rest of the nation. At the end of the 1930s, the South's per-capita income was half that of the national average. By 1950, it had increased to two-thirds of the national average. A rapid mechanization of agriculture and an even more rapid growth of industry were the reasons for this prosperity. The proportion of agricultural workers declined from 43 percent to 21 percent of the region's work force during the years 1940-1960, while the percentage of service workers increased from 38 to 62 percent, thereby reaching the national average. Income from manufacturing increased 400 percent, and 500,000 industrial jobs were created.

But the mechanization of agriculture that allowed one machine to do the work of twenty-four people in picking cotton drove millions of blacks off the land in the South. Most of the blacks in southern agriculture were

Blacks did not share equally in the prosperity of the postwar years. Indeed, moving from rural poverty in the South into urban poverty both North and South was a cultural shock with the new experience of overcrowding and urban crime. By the 1960s frustration with the urban slums and frustration with the failure to be included in the national economic growth caused blacks to riot in the cities of the Southwest and North. Without organization, the rioters were suppressed by local police and national troops. (UPI.)

sharecroppers or day laborers, not landowners, and they had no choice but to go to the cities for work. In 1910, almost 90 percent of the black population lived in the South, most of it on the land. In 1970, less than 50 percent lived in the South, and most of the blacks still in the South lived in southern cities. This migration and the impact of mechanization can be seen in the following table.

Black Migration from the South

1910-1920	450,000
1920-1930	750,000
1930-1940	350,000
1940-1950	1,600,000
1950-1960	1,500,000
1960-1966	600,000

Most of the migrants to the North flowed into the largest cities. The increase in the percentages of blacks in the total populations of some of these cities for the period 1950-1970 is shown in this table.

Percentages of Blacks in Populations of Northern Cities

	1950	1960	1970
New York	10%	14%	31%
Chicago	14	23	33
Los Angeles	9	14	18
Detroit	16	29	45
Cleveland	16	29	40
Washington, D.C.	35	54	70
Newark	17	34	60

The growth of white prosperity allowed many whites to leave the slums of the central city for the suburbs. Between 1950 and 1966, 11 million whites left the central cities. It was into these urban centers that southern rural blacks moved.

Unlike the peasant immigrants who came from southern and eastern Europe to prospering American cities between 1890 and 1914, blacks came to cities that were in economic decline. Moreover, the modern cities had a fundamentally different economy. Cars facilitated the expansion of housing throughout a larger metropolitan area around the central city. In 1900, central cities had 70 percent of the population in their metropolitan areas; by 1960, this figure had dropped to 50 percent. Trucks made it possible for jobs to follow the population into the suburbs. The railroads, which had made the central city the key to economic distribution, no longer held a monopoly on freight distribution. The central cities' share of jobs in retail businesses in comparison to the suburbs' dropped from 80

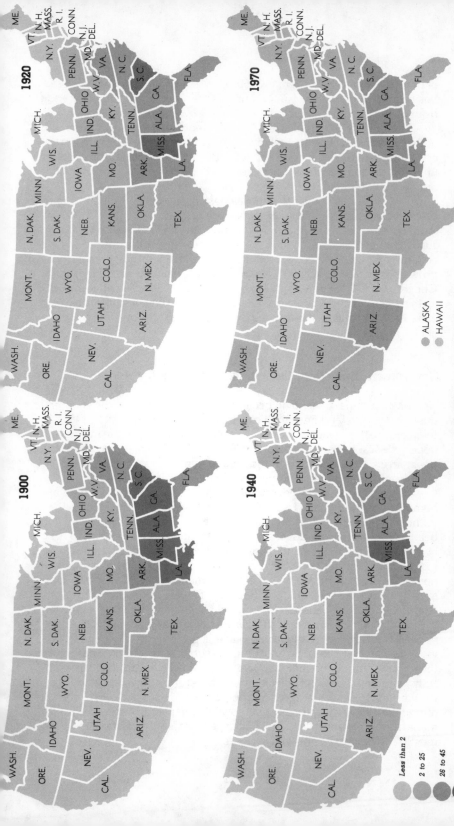

AMERICAN BLACK POPULATION DISTRIBUTION   *Percentage of total population, by States*

1900

1920

1940

1970

● ALASKA
● HAWAII

Less than 2

2 to 25

26 to 45

More than 45

percent in 1930 to 60 percent in 1960. Their share of the jobs in wholesale businesses dropped from 93 percent to 80 percent, and in manufacturing from 67 percent to 57 percent.

The unskilled rural blacks who migrated to the city were frustrated not only by this decline of urban economic activity but by the change in the economy from unskilled to skilled jobs. Because there was little need for unskilled laborers, teenage unemployment among blacks was 25 percent during the 1960s.

The social and political explosiveness of the concentration of poor blacks in the central cities caused welfare to become a major economic issue by the end of the 1960s. The nation spent $15 billion on welfare in 1969. Half of this sum came from the states and half from the federal government. In 1950, money from the state and federal governments was providing welfare to 635,000 families. Aid to Families with Dependent Children (AFDC) increased to 745,000 families in 1960. But, after the riots in the black ghettos began in 1964, state governments began a rapid expansion of welfare assistance. By 1969, 800,000 more families were added to welfare rolls.

Government Spending, the Middle Class, and the Poor

As government spending became an important part of the economy during the 1930s and an even more important part during World War II, the major pattern was for most of the spending to benefit the middle and upper classes. It was expected that money would trickle down from the upper levels of the economy to the bottom. Only enough relief to keep the poor from starving would come directly to lower-income people.

During the 1930s, the government also gave more help to middle-class homeowners through the Home Owners Loan Corporation (HOLC) than to the poor through public housing. The pattern of housing in the cities had been that of a trickling down since the late nineteenth century. Housing was built for the middle and upper classes. As they grew wealthier and moved out of the central cities, poor people moved into their abandoned housing. After World War II, the government, through specially guaranteed mortgages for veterans (G.I. mortgages) and other mortgages guaranteed by the Federal Housing Administration (FHA), encouraged the building of new houses in the suburbs by the expanding middle class. Federal subsidies to roadbuilding made it possible for the middle-class workers living in these new houses in the suburbs to commute easily into the central cities. The federal government, however, allowed the mass transit systems of the central city, used by lower-income people too poor to own cars, to deteriorate. When Congress voted funds for urban renewal during the 1950s, much housing for low-income people was torn down to make room for the new office buildings, theaters, and stadiums used mostly by the middle and upper classes.

Defense Spending and Corporations

Government spending for defense was a major part of the economy between 1945 and 1968. Most of the contracts, as in World War II, went to the larger corporations. By the end of the 1960s, there were 300,000 legally incorporated companies in the United States. The largest 100 of these controlled one-third of all manufacturing. Three or four companies controlled 80 to 100 percent of production in aluminum and automobiles, synthetic fibers and glass, electric equipment and copper, cereal and cigarettes, tires and rubber, soap and steel. Furthermore, the 1960s were a period of mergers in which the large companies began a new pattern of merging with companies outside their original area of production. For example, R. J. Reynolds, one of the giant cigarette companies, merged with poultry, canned soup, egg noodles, pie mix, soft drink, and freight-shipping companies. Between 1948 and 1968, the 200 largest companies absorbed 600 other companies with assets of more than $30 billion. By 1968, these 200 largest companies were engaged in 2,200 different business enterprises. Most Americans, therefore, were employed by large corporations (for example, American Telephone and Telegraph with 745,000 employees and General Motors with 625,000 employees).

The increasingly corporate nature of the economy was also reflected in the stock market, where the number of individual investors became static during the 1960s as more and more investment was done by groups. Individual investors often put their money in mutual funds, whose managers then invested in the market. Such investment increased by $50 billion between 1948 and 1968. Pension funds that had grown from $2.5 billion in 1940 to $80 billion in 1968 also became a major part of the market investment. Insurance companies and banks were other large corporate investors during the 1960s. The continued growth of the corporate economy meant that in 1968 only one-third of the work force was engaged in the production of goods while two-thirds was engaged in distribution and service. This was a reversal of the 1930 figures.

Government Subsidies

The late-nineteenth-century trend for corporate growth to be paralleled by government growth continued during the twentieth century and became more dramatic than ever. In 1929, state, local, and national governments purchased 11 percent of the goods and services of the economy. By 1968, they purchased 20 percent.

More important, the government was providing much of the money for the research that helped the economy continue to expand. During the 1930s, 0.5 percent of the GNP was spent for research and development. During the 1960s, this figure reached 3 percent. Much of this money came from the Department of Defense (DOD), the National Aeronautics and

Space Administration (NASA), and the Atomic Energy Commission (AEC). In 1968, there were 570,000 professional scientists and engineers in the country. Eighty-two percent of them were receiving federal financial support through government contracts to the private companies and universities where they worked.

This meant a dramatic shift in the way in which universities have been financed since World War II. The best private and state universities had become large-scale business enterprises competing for research contracts from the national government. The Massachusetts Institute of Technology (MIT) received 80 percent of its budget from the federal government in 1968. The University of Chicago was receiving two-thirds of its annual budget from federal funds and only one-tenth from tuition. The University of Michigan received 50 percent of its budget from federal funds.

The businesslike nature of the major universities gave rise to satellite businesses. The small city of Ann Arbor, the location of the University of Michigan, had only one private research firm before World War II. In 1965, it had more than fifty. These private research firms either were headed by university professors or made extensive use of their skills. One such company, Tracor, Inc., was making $40 million a year by the 1960s. The vast influx of federal funds that financed the expansion of the major universities as research centers is reflected in the 400 percent growth of the University of Michigan's budget between 1951 and 1966.

Government's support of university research was largely the result of the new military strategy of the worldwide deterrence of communism. Between 1945 and 1968, the United States spent almost $1 trillion for defense. This was about 60 percent of the national budget. In contrast, $96 billion, or 6 percent of the budget, was spent for health, education, and welfare during these years.

This expenditure meant that the national government subsidized the growth of a number of private companies, as well as universities. Government funds from 1945 to 1968 supplied 60 percent of the income of aircraft companies, 33 percent of radio and television manufacturers, and 26 percent for machine shop companies. It is estimated that 10 percent of the total national work force was supported by defense spending in 1968, while 42 percent of the workers in Seattle and 43 percent of those in Los Angeles were dependent on national contracts. The Department of Defense itself had become the single most important element in the American economy in 1968, with its ownership of 29 million acres and weapons and buildings worth $400 billion.

Much of this expenditure for defense was spent abroad to finance the ring of American bases around the Soviet Union and China and to provide arms to those countries that would support the United States' foreign policy. Between 1949 and 1966, the Pentagon sold $16 billion in arms and gave away $30 billion in arms to allies of the United States.

The flow of much of this wealth abroad and the fact that so much of the economy produced weapons, rather than civilian goods, in factories that were increasingly automated discouraged the growth of an industrial work force.

Private Investment Abroad

Corporate profits grew twice as fast as wages during the 1960s. Corporation leaders and other wealthy people, however, tended to invest this money abroad, where they could make larger profits than in the United States. This overseas investment again discouraged the expansion of the American work force. Between 1955 and 1965, private investment abroad grew from $19 billion to $65 billion, and, by 1968, many large companies (such as Standard Oil of New Jersey, National Cash Register, and Colgate-Palmolive) were getting more than half their income from their foreign investments; others (such as Eastman Kodak, International Harvester, and Minnesota Mining and Manufacturing) were getting more than one-third.

Most of this investment in Canada and Western Europe went into the establishment of manufacturing plants. While American industry increased its domestic production 72 percent in the decade between 1958 and 1968, overseas production increased 471 percent. Forty percent of Ford's, 30 percent of Chrysler's, and 25 percent of General Motors' automobile production came from their foreign factories. This meant that American foreign sales began to shift from exports from the United States to sales from American-owned factories abroad. In 1950, one-third of the American foreign sales of $37 billion were exports. In 1968, only one-sixth of the $200 billion in foreign sales were exports. An example of this foreign expansion was the American ownership in 1968 of 1,600 companies in Britain, which produced 10 percent of the industrial output and 20 percent of the exports of that nation.

Continuing Poverty at Home

The prosperity that came with World War II and continued with the Cold War did not eliminate poverty in America. Economists assumed that a family during the 1960s with an income of $4,000 or less was living in poverty. The growth of national wealth, however, did decrease the number of the poor, as can be seen in this table.

Income	1935	1960
$4,000 or less	68%	23%
$4,000 to $6,000	17	23
$6,000 to $7,500	7	31
$15,000 or above	2	7

A second table that gives the changing percentages of national income controlled by each of these groups demonstrates the economic power of a well-to-do middle class and helps to explain why government policies expressed the interests of that class.

Income	1935	1960
$4,000 or less	35%	7%
$4,000 to $6,000	21	15
$6,000 to $7,500	10	14
$7,500 to $15,000	16	40
Over $15,000	18	24

By 1968, the percentage of the population living in poverty stopped decreasing and the number of middle-income people stopped increasing. While one-fourth of the nation's population lived in poverty during the 1960s, more than one-half of the black population did. During the 1930s, the average wage of a black was 50 percent of the average wage of a white. During the years between 1940 and 1960, this percentage rose to 60 percent but had begun to slip back toward 50 percent by 1968.

Johnson and the War on Poverty

With the Johnson landslide in 1964, the Democrats strengthened their majority in Congress. Democrats outnumbered Republicans 68 to 32 in the Senate and 295 to 140 in the House. The assassination of Kennedy and the riots in the cities had forced political leaders to face the major social and economic problems of urban America. The ability of the Democratic president to work with a Democratic Congress made possible the passage of the first major welfare legislation since 1935. By using increased Social Security taxes, Medicare extended health care to the elderly. Medicaid established clinics in the cities to provide free medical care to the poor. Educational aid sent money from the national government into elementary and high schools throughout the country. Nearly $1 billion was appropriated to encourage economic growth in the Appalachian Mountain area of the upper south, where there was much poverty among rural whites. A housing act for the urban poor gave them rent supplements. New departments for housing and urban development and transportation were added to the president's cabinet.

As part of his War on Poverty, Johnson persuaded Congress to establish the Office of Economic Opportunity (OEO, 1965), which was to provide aid to farmers and migrant agricultural workers, as well as to the urban poor. The urban poor were to be taught job skills by VISTA (Volunteers in Service to America — a program in which young, middle-class people were to go into the slums), by the Job Corps, and by the Neighborhood Youth Corps. The Community Action Program (CAP) was to help people in poor neighborhoods organize themselves. CAP programs included legal services for the poor and Head Start programs for the preschool children of lower-income families.

By 1968, serious doubts had developed about many of these programs, especially those that dealt with housing and jobs for the poor. These programs provided jobs for middle-class college graduates who gave services to the poor. But increasing mechanization in agriculture and automation in the factories continued to reduce the number of jobs available to the poor, while teenage unemployment, especially among blacks, grew larger. Capital continued to be invested abroad by corporations; this increased overseas jobs but did not add domestic jobs. Within the United States, economic growth focused in the suburbs, not the central cities, and companies tended to move more of their operations from the northeastern and midwestern cities, where many of the poor were concentrated, to the South and the West. Another problem was that many of the poor, especially the blacks, were being trained for skilled construction jobs. But, by 1968, the construction industry had ceased to expand, and unemployment was growing among skilled construction workers.

In 1968, there was no question that Medicare and Medicaid would be continued, but the Office of Economic Opportunity and the Community Action Program were being challenged. City political leaders were especially hostile toward CAP, because they believed it established a rival political system. Congressional legislation also had not created a major effort to improve mass transit or public housing, both of which were of crucial importance to the poor.

Johnson's War on Poverty, therefore, had failed to solve the economic and social problems of the cities. His administration had extended Social Security through Medicare and welfare through Medicaid. The Twenty-fourth Amendment (1964), which banned the poll tax in national elections, and the Civil Rights Act of 1965, which barred literacy tests, however, did break resistance in the rural South to the registration of blacks. In states such as Mississippi and Alabama where black registration had been held below 20 percent as late as 1966, registration jumped to 60 percent by 1968. Blacks also began to win political power in the North. Edward Brooke, elected in Massachusetts in 1966, was the first black from the North to sit in the United States Senate. Carl Stokes in Cleveland, Ohio, and Richard Hatcher in Gary, Indiana, were the first blacks elected as mayors of major northern cities.

Johnson and the War in Vietnam

By 1968, the major political concern of the nation was the war in Vietnam. The failures of Johnson's domestic policies were not nearly as important as the failures of his foreign policy. When he became president in November 1963, Johnson was warned that the Viet Cong were succeeding in their efforts to overthrow the pro-American generals in South Vietnam.

Only increased American aid, including troops, could keep the Marxist rebels from victory. Johnson decided that he would provide that aid. But, until his victory over Goldwater in November 1964, he promised the American people that he would not send large numbers of American troops to Vietnam. During the presidential campaign, Johnson defined himself as a peacemaker and Goldwater as a warmaker.

Despite these public statements, Johnson sent Congress a report of an attack on American ships in the Tonkin Gulf near the North Vietnam shoreline by North Vietnamese torpedo boats (August 1964). The American ships had not been damaged. And Johnson did not report that they had been helping an attack by South Vietnamese soldiers. Johnson ordered heavy bombing of North Vietnam and asked Congress to give him the power to protect American military forces in Vietnam. Congress passed the Tonkin Gulf Resolution, giving the president such power with no negative votes in the House and only two in the Senate.

Throughout 1965 and 1966, Johnson used this power to order the increased bombing of North Vietnam, and he sent 200,000 soldiers to South Vietnam. As the United States increased its forces in South Vietnam, the Marxist government in North Vietnam stepped up its flow of supplies and troops to help the Viet Cong. Since so many of the peasants in the countryside helped the Viet Cong rebels, American military strategy was to move the peasants into the cities and destroy the crops and even the jungles with chemicals so that the Viet Cong would lose the food and hiding places they needed to carry out guerrilla warfare against the American forces. Johnson was confident, as Kennedy had been, that social scientists had learned how to engage in the social engineering that would result in the successful modernization of peasant societies.

Robert McNamara, as secretary of defense, promised that with enough troops, enough firepower, and enough bombing by the air force victory would be inevitable. But victory did not come, even though 500,000 soldiers were committed by 1967 and more bombs were dropped than in World War II. (As American troops grew more frustrated, they sometimes engaged in massacres, such as the one at My Lai in 1968, when 347 children, women, and old men were killed.) Even though there were assurances from the American generals that United States forces were winning, the Viet Cong with help from North Vietnam started battles everywhere throughout South Vietnam in February 1968, including important areas that were supposed to have been pacified by American troops. This Tet Offensive caused many of Johnson's advisers to break from him. They no longer believed the generals' claims that another 100,000 soldiers and more bombing would bring victory. Only the use of atomic weapons to destroy all of North Vietnam might bring victory and that would bring the threat of atomic retaliation from Russia and China.

Johnson had announced that he would run for reelection and that he would continue the war. But he was challenged in the 1968 primaries of the Democratic party by Senator Eugene McCarthy from Minnesota who called for an end to the war. When McCarthy had demonstrated the popu-

The major American military problem in Vietnam was that of controlling the countryside, which supported the guerrilla warfare of the enemy. Many American soldiers came to doubt whether they could tell the difference between an enemy soldier and a friendly civilian. Here are American soldiers leading a group of suspected guerrillas. (UPI.)

larity of the cause, Senator Robert Kennedy, President Kennedy's brother, also challenged Johnson on the war issue. Johnson finally recognized how widespread antiwar feeling was and how fast it was growing. He announced that he would not accept renomination and that he would stop escalating the war.

The Election of 1968

The decreasing strength of liberal Republicans forced them to support Richard Nixon as the presidential candidate of the Republican party in 1968. In 1952, Nixon had been chosen as the vice-presidential candidate because, as a conservative, he balanced the liberalism of Eisenhower. Although he had been defeated in an effort to be elected governor of California in 1962, he was one of the few leaders who could gain support from both liberal and conservative Republicans in 1968.

Nixon's strategy was to appeal to the voters to trust that he had a plan to end the war in Vietnam and to remember that the war, like all other wars in the twentieth century, had started during a Democratic administration. Nixon planned a "southern strategy" to hold the South by promising to end the trend toward more civil rights legislation and more welfare legislation. He hoped that these issues would also appeal to the white working class in the northern cities. Their ethnic neighborhoods often had been disrupted by the massive migration of blacks into the cities, and they resented paying taxes to pay for the welfare that often went to black families.

Blue-collar and lower-middle-class whites in the cities, as well as in the small towns and rural areas, were upset by the rising divorce and crime rates and by the increased use of alcohol and drugs. They believed that upper-middle-class cultural leaders were taking a permissive view toward these social patterns, and they also blamed upper-middle-class leaders for the civil rights and welfare legislation that they believed was disrupting their neighborhoods. Nixon focused this resentment on the Supreme Court. Led by Chief Justice Earl Warren, a liberal Republican appointed by Eisenhower, the court had upheld the constitutionality of the sit-ins of the early 1960s, while it ruled against compulsory prayers and Bible reading in the public schools. The liberal Court also forced the states to reapportion their legislatures to reflect changing population trends from the country to the cities. The Warren Court also made a series of rulings that protected the civil rights of those accused of crimes and ordered that lawyers be available to the accused who were too poor to hire them. Other rulings by the Supreme Court that declared that censorship of pornography was unconstitutional and that denied restrictions on the distribution of birth-control devices also enraged those who believed that permissiveness was responsible for crime and for the changing sexual patterns of the society.

Nixon used these social issues to discredit Democratic leadership and so did Governor George Wallace of Alabama, who headed a third-party movement, the American party. Wallace argued that the permissive upper-middle class controlled both the Republican and the Democratic parties and that both parties protected the economic interests of the rich rather than those of middle-income people. In 1967, 43 percent of the whites in the country said that they had a favorable attitude toward Wallace, but he won only 13 percent of the vote in the 1968 election. In the South, the vote was divided 34 percent for Wallace, 34 percent for Nixon, and 32 percent for Humphrey.

In the national election, the Democratic candidate, Hubert Humphrey, lost Johnson's huge majority of 61.3 percent and won only 43 percent of the votes. Humphrey was hurt by his refusal to reject Johnson's Vietnam policy until the last few weeks of the campaign, as well as by Nixon's and Wallace's successful efforts to link Humphrey with the social issues of civil rights, welfare for the poor, and permissiveness. Humphrey also lost some liberal support for failing to criticize Chicago's Mayor Richard Daley when the Chicago police attacked McCarthy supporters at the Democratic National Convention in 1968. Nixon's narrow victory, with

43.4 percent of the votes, was made possible by major shifts of white voters. In 1964, 59 percent of whites voted for Johnson, but only 38 percent voted for Humphrey in 1968. Republican support among whites increased from 41 percent in 1964 to 47 percent in 1968, while 15 percent of whites voted for Wallace. Nonwhite voters shifted only slightly from their overwhelming 94 percent support for the Democrats and only 6 percent for the Republicans in 1964 to 85 percent support for the Democrats, 12 percent for the Republicans, and 3 percent for Wallace in 1968.

Among white Protestants, the change was from 55 percent for the Democrats and 45 percent for the Republicans in 1964 to 35 percent for the Democrats, 49 percent for the Republicans, and 16 percent for Wallace in 1968. Catholics changed from their strong 76 percent support for the Democrats and only 24 percent for the Republicans in 1964 to a reduced majority of 59 percent for the Democrats, 33 percent for the Republicans, and 8 percent for Wallace in 1968.

The changes in voting patterns for occupational groups were more dramatic among farmers, who voted 53 percent Democratic and 47 percent Republican in 1964 but only 29 percent Democratic, 51 percent Republican, and 20 percent for Wallace in 1968. Blue-collar workers also shifted their support significantly, from 71 percent Democratic and 29 percent Republican in 1964 to 50 percent Democratic, 35 percent Republican, and 15 percent for Wallace in 1968. Professional and business people changed from a slight Democratic majority of 54 percent and a slight Republican minority of 46 percent in 1964 to a definite Democratic minority of 34 percent, a Republican majority of 56 percent, with 10 percent for Wallace, in 1968.

The 1968 election also marked the beginning of a trend for young people to stay out of politics. Large numbers of babies born as part of the baby boom that began in 1954 were coming of age during the 1960s. Many joined the antiwar movement, which was more powerful than in any previous war. Many also were attracted by counterculture values that were critical of the traditional Protestant work ethic and most of the major American institutions, including corporations, schools, and family. Others became involved in the ecology movement, which led them to be critical of national patterns of economic growth as well as the environmental destruction caused by the war in Vietnam.

Believing that there was no hope of changing the conservative attitudes of the Republican party, large numbers of young people went to Chicago in 1968 with the hope that they could influence the Democratic party. By mass marches and protests, they believed they could get major Democratic leaders such as Humphrey to reconsider the war and orthodox economic and social policies. The Chicago police, however, under orders from Mayor Richard Daley (one of the last city bosses), used extreme violence to break up the protest marches. But the young people who were not completely disillusioned by politics began to make plans to gain control of the convention of the Democratic party in 1972 and nominate a presidential candidate who, unlike Hubert Humphrey, would reject politics as usual.

Supplementary Reading

J. Heath has two useful books on the 1960s, *John F. Kennedy and the Business Community* (1969) and *Decade of Disillusionment: The Kennedy-Johnson Years* (1975). T. White, *The Making of the President, 1960* (1961), describes the presidential election of 1960. B. Miroff, *Pragmatic Illusions: The Presidential Politics of John F. Kennedy* (1976), provides a critical analysis of both domestic and foreign policy. R. Walton, *Cold War and Counter-Revolution* (1972), concentrates on foreign policy. N. Nie, *The Changing American Voter* (1976), explores in detail voting patterns during the 1960s.

Assassination: Dallas and Beyond (1976), edited by P. Scott, P. Hock, and R. Stetler, and C. Oglesby, *The Yankee and Cowboy War: Conspiracies from Dallas to Watergate and Beyond* (1976), offer theories about the assassinations of the decade between 1963 and 1973.

E. Goldman, *The Tragedy of Lyndon Johnson* (1969), interprets the Johnson administration. The problems of the cities are the subject of *American Urban History* (1969), edited by A. Callow, Jr., and *The Liberal Tradition in Crisis* (1974), edited by J. Mileur. Johnson's problems with foreign policy are described by D. Halberstam, *The Best and the Brightest* (1972), and T. Hoopes, *The Limits of Intervention* (1972).

Economic patterns are the subject of J. Galbraith, *The New Industrial State* (1967); R. Barber, *The American Corporation* (1970); and S. Melman, *Pentagon Capitalism* (1970). The problem of poverty is discussed by G. Kolko, *Wealth and Power in America* (1972); H. Miller, *Rich Man, Poor Man* (1964); and M. Harrington, *The Other America* (1962). An excellent critical analysis of welfare is provided by F. Pivan and R. Cloward, *Regulating the Poor: The Function of Public Welfare* (1971).

D. Lewis, *King: A Critical Biography* (1970), A. Meier, *The Transformation of Activism: Black Power* (1970), C. Hamilton and S. Carmichael, *Black Power* (1967), and R. Fogelson, *Violence as Protest: A Study of Riots and Ghettos* (1971), provide perspective on the civil rights movement in general and problems of blacks in the cities in particular. The changing patterns of politics resulting from black migration and the civil rights movement are discussed by D. Mathews and J. Prothro, *Negroes and the New Southern Politics* (1966), and H. Holloway, *The Politics of the Southern Negro* (1969). White backlash in the North and South is the subject of S. Lipset and E. Raab, *The Politics of Unreason* (1970); K. Phillips, *The Emerging Republican Majority* (1970); and L. Howe, editor, *The White Majority* (1970).

The best study of the 1968 presidential election is G. Wills, *Nixon Agonistes: The Crisis of the Self-made Man* (1971).

Chapter 28

Nixon and a Revolutionary World
1968-1976

Nixon, after his election in 1968, did not reveal the secret peace plan he had talked about during the campaign. But he did begin a slow withdrawal of American ground troops from Vietnam and promised in the Nixon Doctrine that pro-American Asians would provide all the infantry forces in any future wars to contain communism in Southeast Asia. The United States, he said, would continue to supply only air power in Vietnam or in any new war. Antiwar sentiments in the United States continued to grow, and Congress began to consider legislation that would cut off funds for the war in 1970. In November 1969, more than a million people marched in Washington, D.C., to protest the continuation of the war.

Nixon and the Cold War, 1968-1973

Nixon, like Lyndon Johnson, did not want to be known as the first president to lose a war. He escalated bombings and in May of 1970 sent American troops into Cambodia to attack North Vietnamese troops who used bases in that country to raid across the border into Vietnam. Nixon hoped that such surprise actions would deflect attention from the continued withdrawal of American troops from Vietnam. But the immediate result of the invasion was to strengthen Marxist rebels in Cambodia in their effort to overthrow the right-wing government that had allowed the American invasion. New waves of protest rolled over hundreds of college campuses in the United States. Many people were outraged when unarmed white students were killed by the National Guard at Kent State University in Ohio and black students were killed by police at Jackson State College in Mississippi.

Nixon, like Johnson, used the FBI, the CIA, and army intelligence to harass protesters and suspected radicals. Although the FBI engaged in a major COINTELPRO program of illegal break-ins and burglaries against protesters and radicals and tried to persuade organized crime, including the Mafia, to fight against the radicals, Nixon did not get as much cooperation from J. Edgar Hoover, the head of the FBI, as he wanted. Nixon, therefore, began to organize an intelligence organization to work directly from the White House. The White House organization was to tap phones and burglarize the offices of those suspected of giving secret government plans about the war to the press. The Nixon administration also indicted eight leaders of the protests at the Democratic convention in Chicago in 1968. The Nixon administration's attempt to suppress radicalism by prosecution of dissidents in the federal courts, however, built on precedents from the Johnson administration, which had brought to trial a number of antiwar spokespeople such as Dr. Benjamin Spock and the Rev. William Sloane Coffin, Jr., for conspiring to disrupt the draft.

Nixon failed, however, to silence the opposition with this kind of pressure. He also failed in his attempt to persuade Americans to elect a Republican Congress in 1970. President Nixon and Vice-President Spiro Agnew blamed the campus protests on a philosophy of permissiveness encouraged by the Democratic party and asked for the election of Republicans to restore law and order. Instead, Democrats strengthened their control of Congress and defeated many Republican governors.

After November 1970, Nixon abandoned his hope of creating a Republican majority and began to plan his reelection as a spokesman for all the American people and not as the head of the Republican party. By 1972, Nixon had withdrawn almost all ground troops from Vietnam, had promised to end the draft, and had supported a constitutional amendment to give the vote to eighteen-year-olds. He hoped these policies would end antiwar protests, especially by the young.

Nixon had decided that he could gain reelection and win an important place in American history by dramatically reducing the tensions of the Cold War. Reversing the criticism he had made of communist China between 1949 and 1969, Nixon asked for a new policy of detente with both communist China and Soviet Russia. In February 1972, Nixon traveled to China; three months later, he flew to Russia. It was much easier for a Republican than for a Democrat to seek better relations with communist countries because Republicans had been successful since 1945 in defining the Democrats as the party that was permissive about communism. It was also much more difficult for the Democrats to criticize the Republicans for being soft on the communist challenge.

By the time of the election of 1972, therefore, Nixon had led a major retreat of American power from the Kennedy-Johnson policies of rolling back communism. Nixon obscured this retreat by ordering the heavy bombing of North Vietnam and the mining of North Vietnamese ports in May 1972, and he forced North Vietnamese leaders to negotiate for peace by smashing North Vietnam's cities with the heaviest bombing of the war in December 1972. The peace agreement signed in Paris in January 1973 was, nevertheless, another retreat of American power, and Secretary of State Henry Kissinger agreed to withdraw all American troops from South Vietnam while allowing troops from North Vietnam to remain in the South even though the pro-American government of Nguyen van Thieu continued in office.

Nixon and the Economy, 1968-1972

One reason that Nixon felt the need to get along with Russia and China was the weakness of the American economy during his first administration. He believed that increased trade with the communist nations would stop the growing American trade deficit that threatened the stability of the American dollar. By 1968, the Kennedy-Johnson economic policy of increased government spending and decreased taxes, especially for corporations, was beginning to cause higher rates of inflation (which went from 2 percent in 1965 to 4.5 percent in 1968) and budget deficits. There was a deficit of $25 billion in Johnson's last budget in 1968, the largest since World War II.

Nixon's advisers told him that he could halt inflation by allowing the economy to slow its growth. This policy, however, resulted in increased unemployment, which jumped from 3.5 percent in 1969 to 6 percent in 1971. And inflation continued, while the slower rate of economic growth resulted in smaller tax revenues. After balancing the budget in 1970, the Nixon administration created large budget deficits of $23 billion in both 1971 and 1972.

Nixon also faced a crisis in foreign trade. In 1971, the United States bought more than it sold abroad for the first time since 1890. Inflation was making American goods too expensive to sell abroad. To stabilize the economy before the election of 1972, Nixon declared that he accepted the Democrats' commitment to the theories of the English economist John Keynes and that increased government management of the economy could restore prosperity.

One of the major actions taken by Nixon in 1971 was to devalue the dollar by 9 percent. This made American goods more competitive on the world market. Again, in 1973, Nixon devalued the dollar by 10 percent. Nixon also declared that dollars no longer could be exchanged for gold because government gold reserves had shrunk from $23 billion in 1956 to $13 billion in 1966. As American dollars lost value as a world currency, gold rose in value from $35 an ounce in 1971 to $120 an ounce in 1973.

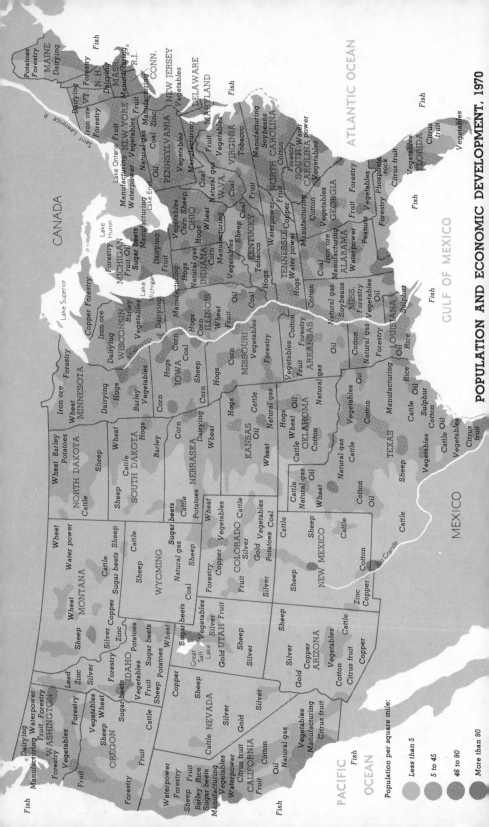

POPULATION AND ECONOMIC DEVELOPMENT, 1970

Population per square mile:

Less than 5

5 to 45

46 to 90

More than 90

Nixon's actions were an admission that the American domination of the free-world's economy had ended and that free-world currencies would no longer depend on the dollar. In addition to devaluing the dollar in 1971, Nixon placed a 10 percent tariff on imports to improve the balance of trade. To check inflation, he placed a ninety-day freeze on all prices, rents, wages, and salaries in the United States and asked Congress for a tax cut. These actions helped persuade voters in 1972 that Nixon was in control of the economy and helped him win the election. But inflation became more of a problem after his reelection, reaching 10 percent in 1973 and 12 percent in 1974. Economists could not understand what was happening to the economy, because this inflation was accompanied by the most serious collapse of the economy since 1929. In all earlier depressions, the cost of living had gone down. But, in the early 1970s, there was both recession and inflation. Between 1973 and 1975, the GNP dropped by 8 percent, industrial output declined by 14 percent, and unemployment jumped to 9 percent.

The sharp increase in the national debt after 1969 was paralleled in the rest of the economy. Americans borrowed more and more money to try to stay even with inflation. Commercial bank loans increased from $279 billion in 1969 to $445 billion in 1973; consumer installment credit increased from $9 billion in 1969 to $21 billion in 1973; and new mortgage debt jumped from $35 billion in 1969 to $63 billion in 1973. The weakening of the economy caused the budget deficits of the national government to jump to the enormous figures of $40 billion in 1974 and 1975 and $65 billion in 1976, with an expected deficit of $50 billion in 1977. The recession and inflation doubled medical costs between 1968 and 1976, causing a crisis in health care. The price of the average house also doubled in this period to $46,000. This meant that, for the first time in American history, the average family could not afford to buy a house.

The slowing of economic expansion was paralleled by a continued decline of the birthrate. Again, for the first time in American history, the average new family was having fewer than two children. Economists talked of a permanent end to the expansion of professional and managerial jobs and estimated that perhaps 30 percent of college students were overqualified for the jobs that were available to them. This shortage of skilled jobs resulted in the decline of salaries for college graduates. In 1969, a college graduate could expect a starting salary 24 percent higher than a job-seeker without a degree. But, by 1976, this margin had dropped to 6 percent. The 1970s, therefore, saw the end of the trend from 1945 to 1969 for more and more high school students to go on to college. In 1969, 44 percent of middle-class males went on to college, but, by 1976, this proportion had dropped to 33 percent.

Between 1970 and 1973, middle-class white people also continued to flee from the cities of the Northeast and Midwest to the South and the Southwest to escape the recession, high taxes, and crime and to obtain jobs in industrial and corporate headquarters that had moved to those regions. Cities such as Minneapolis, St. Louis, Cleveland, Detroit, Buffalo, and Pittsburgh lost between 8 percent and 12 percent of their populations in these three years. The number of jobs available declined by 18 percent in Detroit and St. Louis during the same three years, while Baltimore and Philadelphia lost 12 percent of their jobs. Meanwhile, the number of crimes increased by 71 percent in Boston, 38 percent in Buffalo, 90 percent in Chicago, and 67 percent in Milwaukee between 1970 and 1974. The increase in the national rate of crime for these four years was 27 percent.

The nation's largest city, New York, faced bankruptcy in 1975 because of these trends. With a million people out of a total population of 8 million on welfare, and two-thirds of them children, New York was spending $2 billion a year to support the poor and the unemployed. The number of public jobs increased by 50 percent between 1963 and 1973, and the city paid $7 billion a year for city salaries, as well as $1 billion a year for retirees. From 1964 on, New York officials began to borrow to balance the city budget, although city taxes increased from 7 to 10 percent of an average person's income. Many corporations moved their headquarters out of the city, and 500,000 jobs were lost between 1969 and 1975. Three hundred thousand middle- and high-income people left the city during these years, further cutting back the tax base that had already declined with the loss of the corporations. Interest on the city's debt reached $1.8 billion in 1974, more than the entire city budget in 1960. Reluctantly, the Ford administration loaned money to New York in 1975 to pay interest on the debt. He criticized city officials for living beyond the tax revenues available to them. Still, the national budget itself had increased from $45 billion in 1951 to $250 billion in 1973 to $400 billion in 1977, and the nation was paying $45 billion in interest on the national debt in 1977, with a national deficit of at least $50 billion in that year after the deficit of $65 billion in 1976.

The Election of 1972 and the New Politics

The election of 1972 was similar to the election of 1964 in that a highly motivated minority with strong ideological commitments was able to capture control of the convention of one of the major parties and nominate a presidential candidate disliked by the majority of that party. In 1964, this happened in the Republican party; in 1972, it happened in the Democratic party. In 1972, polls indicated that Senator Edmund Muskie of Maine was preferred by most Democrats as their presidential candidate and that he had a very good chance of defeating President Nixon in the election. The Nixon administration engaged in dirty tricks to discredit Muskie, which made it easier for Senator George McGovern of South Dakota to gain the nomination. Nixon and his advisers believed that they could more easily defeat McGovern than Muskie. But it was the enthusiasm of a minority within the Democratic party, which wanted a "new politics," that won control of the convention and nominated McGovern. Organizing at the local level to elect their delegates, new politics Democrats radically changed the makeup of the convention from what it had been in 1968. In 1968, 10 percent of the delegates had been women; in 1972, 40 percent were women. In

Shirley Chisholm, in 1968, was the first black woman to be elected to the United States Congress. Representing the Democratic party in Brooklyn, New York, she was an active feminist and concerned with increasing the role of women in politics. In 1971, she joined with Bella Abzug, Gloria Steinem, and Betty Freidan to help form the National Women's Political Caucus, which was designed to increase the proportion of delegates in the Democratic and Republican parties who were women. The organization was successful in enlarging the proportion in the Democratic party from 13 percent in 1968 to 39 percent in 1972 and in the Republican party from 17 percent in 1968 to 29 percent in 1972. (UPI.)

1968, 5 percent of the delegates had been black; in 1972, 15 percent were black. In 1968, 4 percent were under thirty years old; in 1972, 22 percent were under thirty.

New politics Democrats were opposed to the law-and-order policies of the Nixon administration, which they believed repressed civil liberties. They refused to make heroes of military leaders, J. Edgar Hoover, or other law-enforcement leaders. They supported the development of new life-styles associated with the counterculture. They were critical of the major economic and social institutions, because they believed that these institutions blocked the development of black power, women's liberation, and justice for the poor. New politics Democrats also wanted immediate withdrawal from Vietnam and amnesty for the many young men who had fled to Canada or Sweden or who had gone underground to avoid conscription, as well as for those who had deserted from the armed forces after being drafted.

In 1970, political scientists found that 14 percent of the voters identified with the new politics Democrats, while 17 percent of the voters were extreme conservatives who were strongly opposed to the kinds of public protests used by the civil rights, antiwar, and women's liberation movements. The extreme conservatives were violently opposed to the new life-styles of the counterculture and expressed complete trust in the military leaders, the FBI, and the local police. And they wanted the military and the police to defend the major economic, political, and social institutions by using force to suppress protest and the development of new life-styles. The political scientists found 69 percent of the voters to be in the center between the extreme conservatives and the new politics Democrats. The people of the center were divided on issues such as the war, with 40 percent favoring immediate withdrawal and 36 percent wanting to push on to victory, and on civil rights, with 31 percent wanting the government to help minorities while 44 percent were opposed to such help.

When eighteen-, nineteen-, and twenty-year-olds were added to the electorate by the Twenty-sixth Amendment to the Constitution (1971), the number of new politics Democrats almost doubled to 25 percent of the voters. Fifty-four percent of these new voters identified themselves with the new politics, and 46 percent with the political center, while none of them identified with the extreme conservatives, who made up only 7 percent of the voters by 1972.

McGovern, however, was unable to persuade many Democrats and independents from the center to join the new politics minority. President Nixon, who was popular for winding down the war, for attempting to establish good relations with Russia and China, and trying to stabilize the economy, won the votes of 42 percent of the Democrats and 60 percent of the independents. Labeled by Nixon as the candidate of "amnesty, acid, and abortion," McGovern was unable to win the trust of the voters in the center; even some of the new politics Democrats distrusted him. Almost exactly reversing the figures of 1964, Nixon won 47 million votes, to 29 million for McGovern. But 86 percent of Democrats voted for Democratic congressional candidates and reelected a Congress with a strong Democratic majority. Nixon's narrow victory in 1968 and his overwhelming victory in 1972, therefore, did not end the decline of the number of people who identified themselves as Republicans. In 1974, 46 percent of the voters identified themselves as Democrats, 32 percent as independents, and 22 percent as Republicans. But, when Richard Nixon began his second term in January 1973, he had the approval of 68 percent of the American people.

Ecology and the End of the American Frontier

The dramatic fluctuations in the elections of 1964 and 1972, the dwindling number of Americans who voted in elections, and the increasing number of political independents all indicated increasing confusion about political issues. Most Americans had assumed that there would be continual economic growth and that political action could help keep the economy growing. But the new science of ecology, which had developed since World War II, insisted that there were limits to growth. This scientific position provided justification for a counterculture that rejected the Protestant work ethic.

The Protestant realism, expressed by Reinhold Niebuhr in the 1940s, had argued against the possibility of constant progress. During World War II, WASP leaders had insisted that the American people accept the necessity of political and military power. These leaders, however, did not apply the ideas of spiritual limits to economic limits or of military power to the physical power or of energy needed to run the economy. But scientists, by the end of the 1940s, did begin to make these connections.

According to ecological thinking, all plants and animals, including human beings, exist as links in biological chains. The sun's energy, interacting with the earth's unique atmosphere of oxygen and water, supports simple plant life. These plants become food for the more complex plants and animals that are eaten by humans. The survival of humans as a biological species depends upon the continued existence of a balanced amount of oxygen, water, and productive soil.

Ecological scientists agreed that there are natural cycles of renewal and regeneration that replenish the supply of oxygen, purify the water, and renew the fertility of the land. These scientists, as exemplified by Barry Commoner and his book *The Closing Circle* (1971), then argued that the economic policies of American corporations and the political policies of the American government were based on a philosophy of constant growth that upset the balance of the cycles of regeneration necessary to the preservation of the supplies of oxygen, water, and fertile land on which all forms of life depend.

As early as the middle of the nineteenth century, there had been men, like George Perkins Marsh, who were developing ecological concepts in their writings. But it was not until the end of the 1940s that men like Fairfield Osborn (*Our Plundered Planet*, 1948) and William Vogt (*Road to Survival*, 1948) began to persuade a small group of people that the ecological perspective was true. The first reaction of many cultural, political, and economic leaders was to deny the accuracy of the arguments of Osborn and Vogt. In the late eighteenth century, Thomas Malthus, an Englishman, had warned that population would grow faster than resources. For a century and a half, his prophecy had seemed false, and so the prophecies of Osborn and Vogt were linked to that of Malthus and ridiculed. By the 1960s, however, many community leaders had begun to believe these warnings, and books like *The Population Bomb* (1968) by the biologist Paul Ehrlich had become best-sellers. Apparently, many people sensed the limits of growth, and the birthrate fell rapidly during the 1960s and early 1970s. By 1976, it had reached the point advocated by the group known as Zero Population Growth (ZPG).

Large numbers of scientists had also begun to take these warnings seriously during the 1950s, when the dramatic impact of the atomic bomb testing began to convince them of the interrelatedness of all things. During the 1950s, the fallout from the atomic tests began to enter the food chain and went into the milk drunk by children. In 1956, it was clear that radioactive fallout from across the Pacific Ocean in the form of strontium 90 was harming babies in the United States. Adlai Stevenson, the Democratic presidential candidate, put the issue of fallout into American politics for the first time that year.

As more scientists began to accept the ecological concept, many average citizens were converted to the concept by the furor over Rachel Carson's book *Silent Spring* (1961). She had written the book to warn the public that the insecticide DDT, which was successful in the control of insects for commercial farming, was entering food chains and poisoning many fish and birds and that DDT would rise through the food chain to poison human beings. At first, most public officials and agricultural specialists derided her arguments, but, by the end of the 1960s, it was clear that the poisoning of birds was occurring. The most dramatic impact on a species was the death of many eagles, who fed on fish in which DDT had become concentrated.

The first major conference of scholars that focused on the way human populations changed the landscape was held in 1955, and the scholarly papers were published in 1956 with the title of *Man's Role in Changing the Face of the Earth*. The rapidly growing acceptance of the ecological perspective led to a calling of an Earth Day celebration on May 1, 1970, by young people across the country. The impact of ecological thinking throughout the entire world led to another Conference on the Human Environment, sponsored by the United Nations in Stockholm, Sweden (in June 1972). Also in 1972, a group of international scientists published a study called *The Limits of Growth,* which predicted from data fed into computers that continued rates of economic, technological, and population growth would lead to the collapse of world society by the end of the twentieth century.

As more and more people were persuaded that the ecologists were correct about the weblike character of nature and the need to protect the environment from overpopulation, pollution, and overuse of resources, they put pressure on the states to create environmental protection agencies. These agencies worked to control the use of pesticides like DDT, they established standards for industry to follow in reducing their pollution of air and water, and they demanded environmental impact studies before they permitted the construction of large-scale industry, power plants, and major highways. The Johnson administration also responded to ecological issues by getting congressional passage in 1965 of the Water Quality Act, the Clean Water Restoration Act, and the Solid Waste Disposal Act.

The first Nixon administration continued this momentum by backing the Clean Air Act of 1970, which called for the automobile industry to design engines by 1975 that would have a low level of polluting emissions. The growing oil shortage of the 1970s, however, forced Congress to give the automakers more time to change the engines. But the government imposed a national fifty-five-mile-an-hour speed limit to reduce the use of gasoline. The Environmental Protection Agency (EPA) also was added to the structure of the national government. The 1970s, therefore, have been marked by sharp political debate on whether to give priority to economic growth or to air and water quality.

The prosperity of the 1950s and 1960s was accompanied by a number of social and economic problems. But the ability of more Americans to buy houses in the suburbs and to buy cars to commute to their jobs also caused a major ecological problem — smog. Air pollution created by the exhaust fumes from cars first became a crisis situation in Los Angeles, pictured here. The greater decentralization of Los Angeles and the necessary greater use of cars, accompanied by peculiar air currents, forced Americans in every city to think about their future as the use of cars for transportation continued to accelerate. (Courtesy of County of Los Angeles Air Pollution Control District.)

The warnings of scientists and ecological experts about the need to limit population growth that were rejected as irrelevant by President Eisenhower during the 1950s were accepted by many government leaders during the 1960s. Former presidents Eisenhower and Truman agreed in 1965 to serve as cochairmen for Planned Parenthood/World Population. In that same year, President Johnson sent a message to Congress warning of the disastrous consequences of the world population explosion. Congress responded in 1966 by granting money to the Department of Health, Education, and Welfare (HEW) and to the Office of Economic Opportunity (OEO) to support birth-control programs at home and abroad. The Nixon and Ford administrations continued this government commitment to encourage birth control. The development of birth-control pills made it much easier for American women to practice birth control and lower the birthrate. In 1971, the Supreme Court ruled that state laws barring abortions during the first twenty weeks of pregnancy were unconstitutional. This ruling made legal abortions possible and hospitals receiving public funds could not refuse abortions to women who wanted them.

The Emergence of a Counterculture

Biologists, such as Garrett Hardin in his book *Exploring New Ethics for Survival* (1972), argued that the modern commitment to technological growth and the Protestant work ethic were the major causes of the ecological crisis. He and other ecologists believed that poets who saw humans as part of nature, living in harmony with the rhythms of natural cycles, could help teach young people to stop trying to dominate and manipulate nature through technology and a work ethic that kept people from enjoying the beauty of nature. Scholars of the 1960s such as Theodore Roszak (*The Making of a Counter-Culture*), Charles Reich (*The Greening of America*), Philip Slater (*The Pursuit of Loneliness* and *Earthwalk*), and William Irwin Thompson (*At the Edge of History* and *Passages around the Earth*) saw young people breaking away from the values of their parents. This generation gap pointed in the direction of poets of the 1950s like Allen Ginsberg and Gary Snyder, who had turned to Asia to find philosophies and religions that gave humans a sense of living in harmony with the universe. According to the sociologist Philip Slater, the young people of the counterculture were rejecting the values of the older generation, which they saw as giving "preference to property rights over personal rights, technological requirements over human needs, competition over cooperation, violence over sexuality, concentration over distribution, the producer over the consumer, means over ends, secrecy over openness, social forms over personal expression, striving over gratification, Oedipal love over communal love" (Philip Slater, *The Pursuit of Loneliness: American Culture at the Breaking Point* [Boston: Beacon Press, 1970], p. 100). The rejection of materialism and rationalism also took the form of searching for spiritual insight through the use of drugs, especially LSD. For a time in the 1960s, a former professor of psychology, Timothy Leary, led a psychedelic drug cult.

Music, the Arts, and the Counterculture

One of the most important ways in which the counterculture expressed its opposition to the establishment was through its music, which built on that of the 1950s. At the beginning of the 1960s, there was a renewal of the use of folk songs to protest social and economic injustices. Going back to the songs of the 1930s and earlier, this music (as sung by people like Joan Baez and Bob Dylan) focused on the problems of civil rights, poverty, and war. However, there was a revolution (led by the Beatles) in the patterns of musical composition itself, as young people created new and complex musical forms. Many lyrics of this music also dealt with the problems of social injustice and the war in Vietnam, but, by the end of the 1960s, the trend was to express concern with the private world of drug and sexual experience and personal freedom.

At the end of the 1960s, there was still much critical analysis of the establishment in the lyrics of groups such as Jefferson Airplane, Iron Butterfly, and the Mothers of Invention and in the songs of Paul Simon and Art Garfunkel. All stressed the artificiality of the adult world, its lack of real feeling and commitment, and its repressiveness and destructive violence. There were also descriptions of the disintegration of the institutions of the establishment. In this revolutionary situation, however, most of the lyrics did not emphasize the possibility of a political solution; they emphasized a personal one. Unity was to be found in the rhythms of the masses, in the intensity of the sound, and in the psychedelic light shows that sometimes accompanied musical performances.

The novel use of popular music to criticize the establishment during the 1960s was paralleled by a radical change in the movies of that decade. The existing restrictions on sex that could be shown in films collapsed, and the explicit sex mentioned in popular song lyrics was also shown on the screen. Equally revolutionary was the way in which movies, which largely had supported traditional values since 1920, began to mock and challenge those values. Directors like Sam Peckinpah and Robert Altman in films such as *The Wild Bunch* and *McCabe and Mrs. Miller* debunked the romantic myths about the cowboy as hero. Movies such as *Dr. Strangelove, Catch-22,* and *M*A*S*H* satirized the nation's political and military leadership. Others such as *The Graduate* and *Easy Rider* attacked the way in which the establishment repressed and destroyed the young people who wanted to live their own lives. Still others such as *Little Big Man* criticized the white culture that had conquered the Indians. Novelists of the 1960s, including Kurt Vonnegut, Jr. (*Cat's Cradle*) and Ken Kesey (*One Flew over the Cuckoo's Nest*), who were popular with the youth culture, used their novels to describe an America where the individual was trapped in senseless institutions.

The traditional western hero had also vanished from television by the end of the 1960s, as television westerns changed from a celebration of the self-reliant individual in the 1950s to programs like "Bonanza" in the 1960s that emphasized group activity in defending property.

A student of public opinion, Daniel Yankelovich, reported the strong development of counterculture values on college campuses during the 1960s in *Changing Values on Campus* (1972). In his next book *The New Morality* (1974), he reported his surprise at the rapid spread of these values to lower-income young people who were not attending college. In 1969, only 22 percent of young people not in college said that they would welcome more sexual freedom, in contrast to 43 percent of college students who were so inclined. But, by 1973, 47 percent of young people not attending college wanted sexual freedom.

Another area of dramatic change was in attitudes toward homosexuality; 42 percent of college students and 72 percent of young people not attending college were opposed to homosexual relations between consenting adults in 1969, but only 43 percent of the second group opposed homosexual relations in 1973. There was another major shift in attitudes toward religion; only 38 percent of college students thought it was a very important value in 1969, in contrast to the 64 percent of young people not attending college who thought so. But, in 1973, only 42 percent of young people who were not college students continued to think it was a very important value. In 1969, 60 percent of young people not in college thought patriotism was important, in contrast to 35 percent of college students. However, in 1973, the percentage of young people outside college who admired patriotism had dropped to 40 percent. But perhaps most significant was the changing attitude toward work; 79 percent of the young people not in college in 1969 believed that hard work pays off, in contrast to the 56 percent of college students. But, by 1973, only 56 percent of the first group continued to believe in hard work. One of the signs of the changing attitudes of young blue-collar workers toward work was their increasing reluctance to accept the discipline of the assembly line.

American Indians

Like blacks, young American Indians during the 1960s were aware of the confusion in the WASP establishment that was leading to the creation of a counterculture and an ecological perspective. This awareness inspired a red power movement comparable to the black power movement. But the red power movement of the 1960s, like the black power movement, had its roots in the past. A Native American Church, which combined tribal rituals with Christian rituals, had spread from Oklahoma to many other regions of the country after World War I, giving Indian people a sense of solidarity. Congress, in 1924, had voted to accept Indians as citizens even when they had not left communal life. Then, in 1934, Congress passed the Indian Reorganization Act (IRA), which stopped the division of tribal lands into individual allotments and recommended that the absolute dictatorship of the superintendents of the Bureau of Indian Affairs (BIA) be limited by establishing the principle that the tribes had the right of self-government.

The development of tribal governmental councils after 1934 strengthened the Indians' will to preserve their identity and pan-Indianism, the sense of an Indian identity beyond that of particular tribes, found expression in the formation of the National Congress of American Indians (NCAI) in 1944.

During the 1940s, however, Congress decided to reverse the policy of 1934 that had accepted the separate cultural identity of American Indians. Congress established the Indian Claims Commission that permitted Indians to file suit against the government when they believed that the government had violated legal agreements it had made with Indians in the past. Apparently generous to the Indians, the logic of the legislation, however, was to integrate the Indians into the legal and property systems of the white society. This logic was spelled out by Congress in 1953, when it declared that government's policy should be the termination of the Indians' tribal status. Termination was forced on the Klamath tribe in Oregon and the Menominee of Wisconsin with disastrous social and economic results for the Indians. Most individuals in the tribes became economically dependent on subsidies from the federal government.

Under this congressional philosophy, the powers of the BIA were reduced by turning over governmental medical services for the Indians to the United States Public Health Service, and, during the 1960s, the Office of Economic Opportunity began to work through Indian communities to try to help Indians improve their economic condition. In the 1960s, an Indian's average yearly income was $1,500; the average length of life was forty-four years, compared to the national average of sixty-eight; infant mortality was three times higher than the national average; and 70 percent of Indian housing was substandard.

The overwhelming majority of American Indians rejected the new policy of termination and asked instead for Indian control of the BIA. Recognizing the confusion of the WASP establishment, Indians responded by emphasizing pride in their cultural traditions, including its ecological logic, and insisted that they would not be assimilated into white society.

Despite their poor health statistics since World War II, Indians were healthier than they had been earlier in the century, and, because of a very high birthrate, Indian population was increasing more rapidly than the white population. The higher population meant that many Indians were coming into cities from the reservations, where there was no longer room for them. During the 1960s, half of the American Indians in the country were living in cities such as Los Angeles, San Francisco, Chicago, and Minneapolis.

In the cities, younger Indians organized themselves as the National Indian Youth Council and used militant tactics to force colleges to create Indian studies programs in which Indian languages and history were taught. To call attention to the economic and social problems of urban and reservation Indians, the American Indian Movement (AIM) was formed by Dennis Banks and Russell Means. Borrowing the confrontation techniques used earlier by blacks, the Indians seized the Bureau of Indian Affairs Building in Washington, D.C., in 1972 and, in 1973, seized Wounded Knee, South Dakota, where the AIM warriors held off local police and the FBI for several months before surrendering.

Chicano Power

The Spanish-speaking Americans of the Southwest, who had been overrun by Anglo-Americans during the 1830s and 1840s, also began to

Clyde Bellecourt (center) and Russell Means (right) were two of the leaders of the American Indian Movement (AIM) when this radical organization seized the town of Wounded Knee, South Dakota, in February 1973 and resisted the FBI for two months before surrendering. They represent the development of a sense of red power, which paralleled the appearance of black power in the 1960s. They wanted young Indians to develop a sense of pride in themselves and to confront the white establishment. This confrontation was to call attention to the refusal of white America to honor treaties made with Indian tribes. (UPI.)

rebel against a long tradition of discrimination. A high birthrate and the recruitment of farm labor from Mexico after World War II led to a population explosion that brought millions of Chicanos into the cities of Texas, New Mexico, Arizona, California, and Colorado, as well as into such midwestern cities as Chicago and St. Paul, where they met another people with a Spanish-American culture, the Puerto Ricans. A similar population explosion in Puerto Rico had forced hundreds of thousands of Puerto Ricans off their small island into New York City, where they formed a large ghetto and began to spread out to other eastern and midwestern cities. Cesar Chavez organized the economic power of Chicano farm workers in the West, while political leaders such as Jose Angel Gutierrez started Chicano political parties in Texas and other southwestern states. Pride in a Spanish-American culture that existed before the English reached America led the Chicanos to insist on the teaching of Chicano culture in colleges and the right of their children to be educated in Spanish as well as in English. The WASP establishment that had been able to insist that English was the only language for American citizens then had to compromise about the use of the Spanish language. Numbering about 20 million, the Chicanos and Puerto Ricans also were rebelling against the domination of the Catholic church by the smaller number of Irish-Americans and the Irish-American demand that Catholic schools use English as the standard language.

Women's Liberation

During the 1960s, young women were aware that women had been a growing part of the labor force since World War II. They also were aware that the number of women professionals had been dropping since the 1920s. Even though more and more women went to college, they could expect only low-paying and relatively unskilled jobs after they graduated. As some of these young women participated in the civil rights movement and the antiwar movement or became members of the organizations of the new left, they began to question the system that exploited them. Their anger grew even more intense when they realized that the men in the protest movements also expected them to play passive and supportive roles rather than participate as equals who could provide leadership. While middle-class women such as Betty Friedan worked with organizations such as the National Organization of Women (NOW) or the Women's Equity Action League (WEAL) and Federally Employed Women (FEW) to force men to accept women as equals in the professions, younger, more radical women such as Jo Freeman and Shulamith Firestone questioned whether women should try to win acceptance in the male-dominated establishment. Some of these women radicals, for example Jane Johnson, advocated that women live apart from men and build a separate female-dominated society. Other radicals, like Caroline Heilbrun, advocated a revolution in male and female roles so that there could be a new society in which women and men were equal to each other.

At the beginning of the 1970s, women increasingly used the Civil Rights Act of 1964, which guaranteed equal pay for equal jobs to women as well as blacks, to try to force companies to change pay scales that discriminated against women. Universities were pressured by the federal government to hire women as professors and to provide equal athletic facilities for female students. If the colleges failed to comply, they were threatened with losing their federal funding.

During the 1970s, increasing numbers of young women were choosing either not to marry or to postpone marriage so that they could enter the work force. More middle-aged women, after their children were grown, also entered the work force. But the economy, which had not been growing rapidly since the late 1960s, did not provide many job opportunities, except at lower levels of skill and pay. As a result, the average woman worker in 1974 earned $6,772, compared to the $11,835 earned by the average male worker. Only 5 percent of the people paid more than $15,000 a year in 1974 were women.

Women, however, were working not only to be independent but also to help their husbands provide an income that would make possible a middle-class standard of life. Economists believed that only 40 percent of the jobs in 1974 paid enough by themselves to allow an employed person to support a family above the poverty level.

During the 1970s, economists talked about the great revolutionary entry of women into the work force. Sociologists talked about the great revolution taking place in the way in which women defined their sexuality, their role in the home, and their role as mothers and the number of children they planned. Perhaps these revolutions in the expectations of women, as well as those of blacks, American Indians, and Chicanos, contributed to the insecurities that President Nixon felt in the White House. Troubled by changes he disliked or failed to understand, Nixon developed a kind of secret police in the White House that could spy on his enemies and harass them.

The Resignation of Richard Nixon

In June 1972, James McCord, a former CIA agent and director of security for the Committee to Reelect the President (CREEP), and four other men were arrested for breaking into the offices of the Democratic National Committee located in the Watergate Apartment Complex in Washington, D.C. They were sent to jail in September without having implicated any leaders of the Republican party. But, in March 1973, McCord notified the judge that his illegal mission had been planned in the White House. In April 1973, John Dean and Jeb Magruder, two minor officials in the White House, gave testimony to the Watergate grand jury and the Senate Watergate Committee, headed by North Carolina Senator Sam Ervin, which implicated White House officials in the planning of the break-in. President Nixon then asked his two chief White House advisers, Robert Haldeman and John Erhlichman, to resign. Nixon also appointed a special Watergate prosecutor, Archibald Cox, and promised that he would help in every way to find out who planned the Watergate break-in.

In July 1973, the Senate committee discovered that all conversations in the president's White House office were recorded on tape, and they requested that the president turn over his tapes to the committee. The president refused and, in October, caused a national crisis by firing the Watergate prosecutor as well as Attorney General Elliot Richardson. The crisis over President Nixon's credibility worsened with the resignation of Vice-President Spiro Agnew. There was evidence that Agnew had systematically accepted bribes from Maryland building contractors while he was a Maryland state official and while he was vice-president. Agnew threatened a national crisis unless he was allowed to resign with the promise that he would not be prosecuted. Under the recently passed Twenty-fifth Amendment, Gerald Ford, the leader of the Republicans in the House of Representatives, became the new vice-president.

Under continued pressure from public opinion, the Senate Watergate Committee, and the Watergate grand jury, Nixon finally released edited transcripts of his taped conversation with his aides about the Watergate break-in. Although there was no direct evidence to show that the president shared in the cover-up of the involvement of Erlichman, Haldeman, and Attorney General John Mitchell in the plan carried out by McCord and the others, the transcripts did suggest that the president was involved.

The Judiciary Committee of the House of Representatives then began to consider the impeachment of the president. And the Supreme court ordered Nixon to release all tapes that might relate to the Watergate affair. On August 5, 1974, Nixon released tapes that showed that he had participated in the cover-up in the summer of 1972. His remaining White House advisers and the Republican leaders of the House and Senate told him that he must resign. On August 8, 1974, Richard Nixon became the first American president to resign. He admitted mistakes in judgment but denied any wrongdoing. The new president, Gerald Ford, however, pardoned him for any illegal acts he might have committed while in office.

Kissinger and Détente

Nixon had depended on Henry Kissinger, a Jewish refugee from Nazi Germany, for many of the negotiations in Vietnam and for establishing a policy of détente with communist Russia and China. Previously a professor of political science at Harvard University, Kissinger seemed the only strong figure in the Nixon administration during 1973 and 1974. Appointed secretary of state in February 1973, Kissinger believed in power and compromise, rather than in idealism and total victory. Overshadowing the president as Nixon lost the confidence of many Americans in 1973, Kissinger seemed the only person in control of foreign policy as the pro-American governments in Cambodia and Vietnam showed signs of collapsing. Finally, on May 1, 1975, the Viet Cong and the North Vietnamese captured Saigon, the capital of South Vietnam. As they abandoned Vietnam, American forces took with them 100,000 South Vietnamese who eventually settled in the United States.

Accepting American defeat in Southeast Asia, Kissinger spent most of his energy after 1973 trying to avert total war in the Near East. In the fall of 1973 on the Day of Atonement (Yom Kippur), Egypt and Syria had attacked Israel. While Israel won a military victory, as it had done so often since 1948, the victory was more costly than the previous wars against the Arab countries. The Arab countries placed an embargo on oil sent to the United States, western Europe, and Japan, which deepened the economic depression troubling all the industrial nations. During the 1960s, oil boycotts by the Arabs had not hurt the United States because America was exporting oil at that time. But American oil production had begun to drop while the use of oil increased, and Americans depended on the Arab countries for 30 percent of their oil supply by 1973.

Kissinger, therefore, put pressure on Israel to return some of the territories it had taken from Egypt and to work toward a policy of détente with

Egypt and Syria as the United States had worked toward a policy of détente with Russia and China. The weakening of American power was also evident when the United States had to acknowledge a successful socialist revolution in Portugal in 1975 that undermined the American attempt to keep Marxist influence out of western Europe.

Southern Africa was another area where Kissinger was desperately active in an attempt to avoid the outbreak of war. After Portugal surrendered its African colonies, Rhodesia and the Union of South Africa were the last African countries dominated by whites. Throughout 1975 and 1976, Kissinger worked to get the white minority in Rhodesia to agree to a peaceful transition to rule by the black majority. Kissinger and other American leaders were afraid that bloody revolution would allow communist influence to spread throughout Africa. American policy also was directed toward forcing white South African leaders to modify their policy of apartheid (segregation), which denied citizenship to the black majority in that country.

Ford, the Economy, and the Election of 1976

Throughout 1973, Nixon had tried to control the rapidly rising inflation by vetoing nine major bills that would have spent money in such areas as education and pollution, by refusing to spend money that Congress had appropriated, and by cutting back government funds for welfare. In 1974, President Ford announced that his administration also would work to "Whip Inflation Now." The WIN program, however, had to be abandoned when industrial production dropped and unemployment increased. Ford reluctantly accepted the advice of the Democrats in Congress to cut taxes in order to stimulate consumer buying. By cutting taxes and retaining the same level of domestic and military spending, Ford accepted the huge budget deficits of 1975 and 1976.

The Democrats, helped by the Nixon scandals and the unsolved economic problems, won a smashing victory in the congressional elections of 1974, although only 45 percent of those eligible to vote did so, including only 21 percent of the young people eighteen to twenty years old. Generally, a small turnout of voters helps the Republicans because older and wealthier people, who tend to be Republicans, are more apt to vote than the young and the poor, who tend to be Democrats.

Outnumbering Republicans in the House of Representatives by a margin of 290 to 145 and in the Senate by 62 to 38, the Democrats refused to accept the Ford administration's plan to solve the oil crisis by removing all controls from oil prices. After the Arab oil embargo of 1973, the major oil-producing countries of Asia, Africa, and South America had joined together in OPEC (Organization of Petroleum Exporting Countries) to force world oil prices much higher. To keep billions of American dollars from being paid for foreign oil, and thus hurting the American balance of trade, the Ford administration wanted to force Americans to use less gasoline by having the price of oil produced in the United States go up drastically and by putting a high tax on each gallon of gasoline sold. Congressional Democrats, on the other hand, wanted to reduce gasoline use by rationing. They argued that sharply higher oil prices would deepen the depression. As a result of the impasse between Congress and President Ford, the country had no energy policy when the new president, Jimmy Carter, prepared to take office in January 1977.

Although it is almost impossible to keep an incumbent president from winning renomination by his party, Ronald Reagan, a former governor of California, came very close to defeating President Ford at the Republican convention in Kansas City during the summer of 1976. Representing the most extreme Republican conservatives, Reagan criticized Ford for his compromise with the welfare state and for accepting detente with communist nations. To keep the support of the right wing, Ford dropped his vice-president, the moderate Republican Nelson Rockefeller, and accepted the more conservative Robert Dole, a Kansas senator, as his running mate.

Ford asked the voters to elect him in 1976 because he had restored integrity to the White House and the people's trust in the national government. Democratic candidate Jimmy Carter won more primaries than any other Democratic leader by arguing that he, too, could restore integrity and trust. A former governor of Georgia, Carter was the first person from the Deep South to be elected president since before the Civil War. Carter stressed that his conversion experience as a southern Baptist gave him a special strength that would help the American people regain faith in the future of the country.

In the election of 1976, however, voters found Ford a stronger symbol of integrity and trust than Carter. Carter's narrow majority of 51 percent in the popular vote came from the fact that the southern states, with the exception of Virginia, voted solidly for the Democratic presidential candidate for the first time since 1944. Unlike 1944, however, when blacks were disfranchised throughout the South, the large numbers of black voters made it possible for Carter to win such southern states as Texas, Florida, Louisiana, and Mississippi, where the majority of whites voted for Ford.

More than 90 percent of the blacks who voted supported Carter in the North as well as in the South and made the difference in his carrying New York, Pennsylvania, and Ohio. The majority of white Protestants in the North and the West, as in the past, voted Republican, and Ford carried almost every state in the West, where very few Jewish, Catholic, or black voters lived. Many Catholics and Jews expressed an uneasiness with Carter because of his southern and Baptist roots. But a majority of Catholics voted for him because they believed he would do more to solve the problems of unemployment and inflation than Ford would.

Although Ford won 49 percent of the popular vote, the Republicans regained none of the House and Senate seats they had lost in 1974. Furthermore, Republicans continued to lose strength in state legislatures, as they had since 1966, and the number of Republican governors dropped from thirty-two in 1970 to only twelve in 1976.

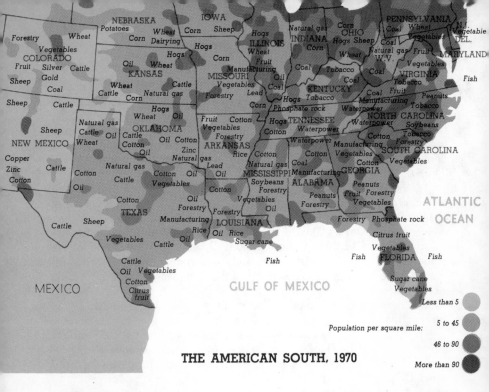

THE AMERICAN SOUTH, 1970

As Americans celebrated their bicentennial in 1976, many political scientists feared that the two-party system was in danger because of the possible collapse of the Republican party. They were also concerned with the failure of increasing numbers of citizens to vote. Sixty-three percent of the eligible voters had gone to the polls in 1960, but only 53 percent had in 1976.

The instability of domestic politics was accompanied by the instability of foreign affairs. And the possibility that 1976 marked a new revolutionary era for the United States was increased by the instability of family life, of male and female roles, and of experiments in new life-styles. The issues of ecology and energy had no precedents in the past and seemed to demand totally new ways of looking at the world. It seemed certain that the history Americans experienced after 1977 would be as surprising and dramatic as that which they had experienced since the assassination of John Kennedy in 1963.

Supplementary Reading

The concerns of the average white worker are the subject of M. Novak, *The Rise of the Unmeltable Ethnics* (1972); S. Aronowitz, *False Promises: The Shaping of American Working Class Consciousness* (1974); and R. Krickus, *Pursuing the American Dream: White Ethnics and the New Populism* (1976). Excellent analyses of the changing political patterns are provided by E. Ladd, Jr., and C. Hadley, *Transformations of the American Party System* (1975), and W. Miller and T. Levitan, *Leadership and Change: Presidential Elections from 1952 to 1976* (1976).

A fascinating study of the Nixon administrations is J. Schell, *The Time of Illusion* (1975). The major scandals of the Nixon administrations are described by J. Witcover, *A Heartbeat Away: The Investigation and Resignation of Vice President Spiro T. Agnew* (1974), and C. Bernstein and B. Woodward, *All the President's Men* (1974).

Diplomatic patterns are the subject of H. Brandon, *The Retreat of American Power* (1972), and W. Brown, *The Last Chopper: The Denouement of the American Role in Vietnam, 1963-1975* (1976).

K. Sale, *Power Shift: The Rise of the Southern Rim and Its Challenge to the Eastern Establishment* (1975), helps explain the capture of the presidency by Jimmy Carter, a southerner. I. Unger, *The Movement: A History of the American New Left, 1959-1972* (1974), provides perspective on the failure of political radicalism after 1970.

The importance of the ecological point of view is the subject of W. Anderson, *A Place of Power: The American Episode in Human Evolution* (1976), and J. Petulla, *American Environmental History* (1977). P. Slater, *The Pursuit of Loneliness* (1970), T. Roszak, *The Making of a Counter-Culture* (1969), R. Braden, *The Age of Aquarius* (1970), R. Wuthnow, *The Consciousness Reformation* (1976) and C. Glock and R. Bellah, editors, *The New Religious Consciousness* (1977), provide descriptions of the new cultural and religious values. M. Dickstein's *Gates of Eden* (1977) is the most recent book on the youth culture. The weakness of traditional heros is described by R. Brauer, *The Horse, the Gun, and the Piece of Property: Changing Images of the TV Western* (1975).

S. Steiner, *The New Indians* (1968), provides a perspective on the changes taking place among American Indians, as do M. Meier and F. Rivera, *The Chicanos* (1972) for Americans of Spanish heritage. B. Deckard, *The Woman's Movement* (1975), and G. Yates, *What Women Want: The Ideas of the Movement* (1975), are excellent studies of the revolutionary changes in the outlooks of women.

Appendix A
The Declaration of Independence

When in the Course of human Events, it becomes necessary for one People to dissolve the Political Bands which have connected them with another, and to assume among the Powers of the Earth, the separate and equal Station to which the Laws of Nature and of Nature's God entitle them, a decent Respect to the Opinions of Mankind requires that they should declare the causes which impel them to the Separation.

We hold these Truths to be self-evident, that all Men are created equal, that they are endowed by their Creator with certain unalienable Rights, that among these are Life, Liberty, and the Pursuit of Happiness — That to secure these Rights, Governments are instituted among Men, deriving their just Powers from the Consent of the Governed, that whenever any Form of Government becomes destructive of these Ends, it is the Right of the People to alter or to abolish it, and to institute new Government, laying its Foundation on such Principles, and organizing its Powers in such Form, as to them shall seem most likely to effect their Safety and Happiness. Prudence, indeed, will dictate that Governments long estabished should not be changed for light and transient Causes; and accordingly all Experience hath shewn, that Mankind are more disposed to suffer, while Evils are sufferable, than to right themselves by abolishing the Forms to which they are accustomed. But when a long Train of Abuses and Usurpations, pursuing invariably the same Object, evinces a Design to reduce them under absolute Despotism, it is their Right, it is their Duty, to throw off such Government, and to provide new Guards for their future Security. Such has been the patient Sufferance of these Colonies; and such is now the Necessity which constrains them to alter their former Systems of Government. The History of the present King of Great-Britain is a History of repeated Injuries and Usurpations, all having in direct Object the

Establishment of an absolute Tyranny over these States. To prove this, let Facts be submitted to a candid World.

He has refused his Assent to Laws, the most wholesome and necessary for the public Good.

He has forbidden his Governors to pass Laws of immediate and pressing Importance, unless suspended in their Operation till his Assent should be obtained; and when so suspended, he has utterly neglected to attend to them.

He has refused to pass other Laws for the Accommodation of large Districts of People, unless those People would relinquish the Right of Representation in the Legislature, a Right inestimable to them, and formidable to Tyrants only.

He has called together Legislative Bodies at Places unusual, uncomfortable, and distant from the Depository of their public Records, for the sole Purpose of fatiguing them into Compliance with his Measures.

He has dissolved Representative Houses repeatedly, for opposing with manly Firmness his Invasions on the Rights of the People.

He has refused for a long Time, after such Dissolutions, to cause others to be elected; whereby the Legislative Powers, incapable of Annihilation, have returned to the People at large for their exercise; the State remaining in the mean time exposed to all the Dangers of Invasion from without, and Convulsions within.

He has endeavoured to prevent the Population of these States; for that Purpose obstructing the Laws for Naturalization of Foreigners; refusing to pass others to encourage their Migrations hither, and raising the Conditions of new Appropriations of Lands.

He has obstructed the Administrations of Justice, by refusing his Assent to Laws for establishing Judiciary Powers.

He has made Judges dependent on his Will alone, for the Tenure of their Offices, and the Amount and Payment of their Salaries.

He has erected a Multitude of new Offices, and sent hither Swarms of Officers to harrass our People, and eat out their Substance.

He has kept among us, in Times of Peace, Standing Armies, without the consent of our Legislatures.

He has affected to render the Military independent of and superior to the Civil Power.

He has combined with others to subject us to a Jurisdiction foreign to our Constitution, and unacknowledged by our Laws; giving his Assent to their Acts of pretended Legislation:

For quartering large Bodies of Armed Troops among us:

For protecting them, by a mock Trial, from Punishment for any Murders which they should commit on the Inhabitants of these States:

For cutting off our Trade with all Parts of the World:

For imposing Taxes on us without our Consent:

For depriving us, in many Cases, of the Benefits of Trial by Jury:

For transporting us beyond Seas to be tried for pretended Offences:

For abolishing the free System of English Laws in a neighbouring Province, establishing therein an arbitrary Government, and enlarging its Boundaries, so as to render it at once an Example and fit Instrument for introducing the same absolute Rule into these Colonies:

For taking away our Charters, abolishing our most valuable Laws, and altering fundamentally the Forms of our Governments:

For suspending our own Legislatures, and declaring themselves invested with Power to legislate for us in all Cases whatsoever.

He has abdicated Government here, by declaring us out of his Protection and waging War against us.

He has plundered our Seas, ravaged our Coasts, burnt our Towns, and destroyed the Lives of our People.

He is, at this Time, transporting large Armies of foreign Mercenaries to compleat the Works of Death, Desolation, and Tyranny, already begun with circumstances of Cruelty and Perfidy, scarcely paralleled in the most barbarous Ages, and totally unworthy the Head of a civilized Nation.

He has constrained our fellow Citizens taken Captive on the high Seas to bear Arms against their Country, to become the Executioners of their Friends and Brethren, or to fall themselves by their Hands.

He has excited domestic Insurrections amongst us, and has endeavoured to bring on the Inhabitants of our Frontiers, the merciless Indian Savages, whose known Rule of Warfare, is an undistinguished Destruction, of all Ages, Sexes, and Conditions.

In every stage of these Oppressions we have Petitioned for Redress in the most humble Terms: Our repeated Petitions have been answered only by repeated Injury. A Prince, whose Character is thus marked by every act which may define a Tyrant, is unfit to be the Ruler of a free People.

Nor have we been wanting in Attentions to our British Brethren. We have warned them from Time to Time of Attempts by their Legislature to extend an unwarrantable Jurisdiction over us. We have reminded them of the Circumstances of our Emigration and Settlement here. We have appealed to their native Justice and Magnanimity, and we have conjured them by the Ties of our common Kindred to disavow these Usurpations, which, would inevitably interrupt our Connections and Correspondence. They too have been deaf to the Voice of Justice and of Consanguinity. We must, therefore, acquiesce in the Necessity, which denounces our Separation, and hold them, as we hold the rest of Mankind, Enemies in War, in Peace, Friends.

We, therefore, the Representatives of the United States of America, in General Congress, Assembled, appealing to the Supreme Judge of the World for the Rectitude of our Intentions, do, in the Name, and by Authority of the good People of these Colonies, solemnly Publish and Declare, That these United Colonies are, and of Right ought to be, Free and Independent States; that they are absolved from all Allegiance to the British Crown, and that all political Connection between them and the State of Great-Britain, is and ought to be totally dissolved; and that as Free and Independent States, they have full Power to levy War, conclude Peace, contract Alliances, establish Commerce, and to do all other Acts and Things which Independent States may of right do. And for the support of this Declaration, with a firm Reliance on the Protection of divine Providence, we mutually pledge to each other our Lives, our Fortunes, and our sacred Honor.

Signed by Order *and in* Behalf *of the* Congress,
John Hancock, President.

Attest:
Charles Thomson, Secretary.

Appendix B
The Constitution

We, the People of the United States, in order to form a more perfect union, establish justice, insure domestice tranquility, provide for the common defence, promote the general welfare, and secure the blessings of liberty to ourselves and our posterity, do ordain and establish this Constitution for the United States of America.

ARTICLE I.

Section 1. All legislative powers herein granted shall be vested in a Congress of the United States, which shall consist of a Senate and House of Representatives.

Sect. 2. The House of Representatives shall be composed of members chosen every second year by the people of the several states, and the electors in each state shall have the qualifications requisite for electors of the most numerous branch of the state legislature.

No person shall be a representative who shall not have attained to the age of twenty-five years, and been seven years a citizen of the United States, and who shall not, when elected, be an inhabitant of that state in which he shall be chosen.

Representatives and direct taxes shall be apportioned among the several states which may be included within this Union, according to their respective numbers, which shall be determined by adding to the whole number of free persons, including those bound to service for a term of years, and excluding Indians not taxed, three-fifths of all other persons. The actual enumeration shall be made within three years after the first meeting of the Congress of the United States, and within every subsequent term of ten years, in such manner as they shall by law direct. The number of representatives shall not exceed one for every thirty thousand, but each state shall have at least one representative; and until such enumeration shall be made, the state of New-Hampshire shall be entitled to chuse three, Massachusetts eight, Rhode-Island and Providence Plantations one, Connecticut five, New-York six, New-Jersey four, Pennsylvania eight, Delaware one, Maryland six, Virginia ten, North-Carolina five, South-Carolina five, and Georgia three.

When vacancies happen in the representation from any state, the Executive authority thereof shall issue writs of election to fill such vacancies.

The House of Representatives shall chuse their Speaker and other officers; and shall have the sole power of impeachment.

Sect. 3. The Senate of the United States shall be composed of two senators from each state, chosen by the legislature thereof, for six years; and each senator shall have one vote.

Immediately after they shall be assembled in consequence of the first election, they shall be divided as equally as may be into three classes. The seats of the senators of the first class shall be vacated at the expiration of the second year, of the second class at the expiration of the fourth year, and of the third class at the expiration of the sixth year, so that one-third may be chosen every second year; and if vacancies happen by resignation, or otherwise, during the recess of the Legislature of any state, the Executive thereof may make temporary appointments until the next meeting of the Legislature, which shall then fill such vacancies.

No person shall be a senator who shall not have attained to the age of thirty years, and been nine years a citizen of the United States, and who shall not, when elected, be an inhabitant of that state for which he shall be chosen.

The Vice-President of the United States shall be President of the senate, but shall have no vote, unless they be equally divided.

The Senate shall chuse their other officers, and also a President pro tempore, in the absence of the Vice-President, or when he shall exercise the office of President of the United States.

The Senate shall have the sole power to try all impeachments. When sitting for that purpose, they shall be on oath or affirmation. When the President of the United States is tried, the Chief Justice shall preside: And no person shall be convicted without the concurrence of two-thirds of the members present.

Judgment in cases of impeachment shall not extend further than to removal from office, and disqualification to hold and enjoy any office of honor, trust or profit under the United States; but the party convicted shall nevertheless be liable and subject to indictment, trial, judgment and punishment, according to law.

Sect. 4. The times, places and manner of holding elections for senators and representatives, shall be prescribed in each state by the legislature thereof; but the Congress may at any time by law make or alter such regulations, except as to the places of chusing Senators.

The Congress shall assemble at least once in every year, and such meeting shall be on the first Monday in December, unless they shall by law appoint a different day.

Sect. 5. Each house shall be the judge of the elections, returns and qualifications of its own members, and a majority of each shall constitute a quorum to do business; but a smaller number may adjourn from day to day, and may be authorized to compel the attendance of absent members, in such manner, and under such penalties as each house may provide.

Each house may determine the rules of its proceedings, punish its members for disorderly behaviour, and, with the concurrence of two-thirds, expel a member.

Each house shall keep a journal of its proceedings, and from time to time publish the same, excepting such parts as may in their judgment require secrecy;

and the yeas and nays of the members of either house on any question shall, at the desire of one-fifth of those present, be entered on the journal.

Neither house, during the session of Congress, shall, without the consent of the other, adjourn for more than three days, nor to any other place than that in which the two houses shall be sitting.

Sect. 6. The senators and representatives shall receive a compensation for their services, to be ascertained by law, and paid out of the treasury of the United States. They shall in all cases, except treason, felony and breach of the peace, be privileged from arrest during their attendance at the session of their respective houses, and in going to and returning from the same; and for any speech or debate in either house, they shall not be questioned in any other place.

No senator or representative shall, during the time for which he was elected, be appointed to any civil office under the authority of the United States, which shall have been created, or the emoluments whereof shall have been encreased during such time; and no person holding any office under the United States, shall be a member of either house during his continuance in office.

Sect. 7. All bills for raising revenue shall originate in the house of representatives; but the senate may propose or concur with amendments as on other bills.

Every bill which shall have passed the house of representatives and the senate, shall, before it become a law, be presented to the president of the United States; if he approve he shall sign it, but if not he shall return it, with his objections to that house in which it shall have originated, who shall enter the objections at large on their journal, and proceed to reconsider it. If after such reconsideration two-thirds of that house shall agree to pass the bill, it shall be sent, together with the objections, to the other house, by which it shall likewise be reconsidered, and if approved by two-thirds of that house, it shall become a law. But in all such cases the votes of both houses shall be determined by yeas and nays, and the names of the persons voting for and against the bill shall be entered on the journal of each house respectively. If any bill shall not be returned by the President within ten days (Sundays excepted) after it shall have been presented to him, the same shall be a law, in like manner as if he had signed it, unless the Congress by their adjournment prevent its return, in which case it shall not be a law.

Every order, resolution, or vote to which the concurrence of the Senate and House of Representatives may be necessary (except on a question of adjournment) shall be presented to the President of the United States; and before the same shall take effect, shall be approved by him, or, being disapproved by him, shall be repassed by two-thirds of the Senate and House of Representatives, according to the rules and limitations prescribed in the case of a bill.

Sect. 8. The Congress shall have power

To lay and collect taxes, duties, imposts and excises, to pay the debts and provide for the common defence and general welfare of the United States; but all duties, imposts and excises shall be uniform throughout the United States;

To borrow money on the credit of the United States;

To regulate commerce with foreign nations, and among the several states, and with the Indian tribes;

To establish an uniform rule of naturalization, and uniform laws on the subject of bankruptcies throughout the United States;

To coin money, regulate the value thereof, and of foreign coin, and fix the standard of weights and measures;

To provide for the punishment of counterfeiting the securities and current coin of the United States;

To establish post offices and post roads;

To promote the progress of science and useful arts, by securing for limited times to authors and inventors the exclusive right to their respective writings and discoveries;

To constitute tribunals inferior to the supreme court;

To define and punish piracies and felonies committed on the high seas, and offences against the law of nations;

To declare war, grant letters of marque and reprisal, and make rules concerning captures on land and water;

To raise and support armies, but no appropriation of money to that use shall be for a longer term than two years;

To provide and maintain a navy;

To make rules for the government and regulation of the land and naval forces;

To provide for calling forth the militia to execute the laws of the union, suppress insurrections and repel invasions;

To provide for organizing, arming, and disciplining, the militia, and for governing such part of them as may be employed in the service of the United States, reserving to the States respectively, the appointment of the officers, and the authority of training the militia according to the discipline prescribed by Congress;

To exercise exclusive legislation in all cases whatsoever, over such district (not exceeding ten miles square) as may, by cession of particular States, and the acceptance of Congress, become the seat of the government of the United States, and to exercise like authority over all places purchased by the consent of the legislature of the state in which the same shall be, for the erection of forts, magazines, arsenals, dock-yards, and other needful buildings; — And

To make all laws which shall be necessary and proper for carrying into execution the foregoing powers, and all other powers vested by this constitution in the government of the United States, or in any department or officer thereof.

Sect. 9. The migration or importation of such persons as any of the states now existing shall think proper to admit, shall not be prohibited by the Congress prior to the year one thousand eight hundred and eight, but a tax or duty may be imposed on such importation, not exceeding ten dollars for each person.

The privilege of the writ of habeas corpus shall not be suspended, unless when in cases of rebellion or invasion the public safety may require it.

No bill of attainder or ex post facto law shall be passed.

No capitation, or other direct, tax shall be laid, unless in proportion to the census or enumeration herein before directed to be taken.

No tax or duty shall be laid on articles exported from any state. No preference shall be given by any regulation of commerce or revenue to the ports of one state over those of another: nor shall vessels bound to, or from, one state, be obliged to enter, clear, or pay duties in another.

No money shall be drawn from the treasury, but in consequence of appropriations made by law; and a regular statement and account of the receipts and expenditures of all public money shall be published from time to time.

No title of nobility shall be granted by the United States: — And no person holding any office of profit or trust under them, shall, without the consent of the Congress, accept of any present, emolument, office, or title, of any kind whatever, from any king, prince, or foreign state.

Sect. 10. No state shall enter into any treaty, alliance, or confederation; grant letters of marque and reprisal; coin money; emit bills of credit; make any thing but gold and silver coin a tender in payment of debts; pass any bill of attainder, ex post facto law, or law impairing the obligation of contracts, or grant any title of nobility.

No state shall, without the consent of Congress, lay any imposts or duties on imports or exports, except what may be absolutely necessary for executing its inspection laws; and the net produce of all duties and imposts, laid by any state on imports or exports, shall be for the use of the Treasury of the United States; and all such laws shall be subject to the revision and controul of the Congress. No state shall, without the consent of Congress, lay any duty of tonnage, keep troops, or ships of war in time of peace, enter into any agreement or compact with another state, or with a foreign power, or engage in war, unless actually invaded, or in such imminent-danger as will not admit of delay.

II.

Section 1. The executive power shall be vested in a president of the United States of America. He shall hold his office during the term of four years, and, together with the vice-president, chosen for the same term, be elected as follows.

Each state shall appoint, in such manner as the legislature thereof may direct, a number of electors, equal to the whole number of senators and representatives to which the state may be entitled in the Congress: but no senator or representative, or person holding an office of trust or profit under the United States, shall be appointed an elector.

The electors shall meet in their respective states, and vote by ballot for two persons, of whom one at least shall not be an inhabitant of the same state with themselves. And they shall make a list of all the persons voted for, and of the number of votes for each; which list they shall sign and certify, and transmit sealed to the seat of the government of the United States, directed to the president of the senate. The president of the senate shall, in the presence of the senate and house of representatives, open all the certificates, and the votes shall then be counted. The person having the greatest number of votes shall be the president, if such number be a majority of the whole number of electors appointed; and if there be more than one who have such majority, and have an equal number of votes, then the house of representatives shall immediately chuse by ballot one of them for president; and if no person have a majority, then from the five highest on the list the said house shall in like manner chuse the president. But in chusing the president, the votes shall be taken by states, the representation from each state having one vote; a quorum for this purpose shall consist of a member or members from two-thirds of the states, and a majority of all the states shall be necessary to a choice. In every case, after the choice of the president, the person having the greatest number of votes of the electors shall be the vice-president. But if there should remain two or more who have equal votes, the senate shall chuse from them by ballot the vice-president.

The Congress may determine the time of chusing the electors, and the day on which they shall give their votes; which day shall be the same throughout the United States.

No person except a natural born citizen, or a citizen of the United States, at the time of the adoption of this constitution, shall be eligible to the office of president; neither shall any person be eligible to that office who shall not have attained to the age of thirty-five years, and been fourteen years a resident within the United States.

In the case of the removal of the president from office, or of his death, resignation, or inability to discharge the powers and duties of the said office, the same shall devolve on the vice-president, and the Congress may by law provide for the case of removal, death, resignation or inability, both of the president and vice-president, declaring what officer shall then act as president, and such officer shall act accordingly, until the disability be removed, or a president shall be elected.

The president shall, at stated times, receive for his services, a compensation, which shall neither be encreased nor diminished during the period for which he shall have been elected, and he shall not receive within that period any other emolument from the United States, or any of them.

Before he enter on the execution of his office, he shall take the following oath or affirmation:

"I do solemnly swear (or affirm) that I will faithfully execute the office of president of the United States, and will to the best of my ability, preserve, protect and defend the constitution of the United States."

Sect. 2. The president shall be commander in chief of the army and navy of the United States, and of the militia of the several States, when called into the actual service of the United States; he may require the opinion, in writing, of the principal officer in each of the executive departments, upon any subject relating to the duties of their respective offices, and he shall have power to grant reprieves and pardons for offenses against the United States, except in cases of impeachment.

He shall have power, by and with the advice and consent of the senate, to make treaties, provided two-thirds of the senators present concur; and he shall nominate, and by and with the advice and consent of the senate, shall appoint ambassadors, other public ministers and consuls, judges of the supreme court, and all other officers of the United States, whose appointments are not herein otherwise provided for, and which shall be established by law. But the Congress may by law vest the appointment of such inferior offices, as they think proper, in the president alone, in the courts of law, or in the heads of departments.

The president shall have power to fill up all vacancies that may happen during the recess of the senate, by granting commissions which shall expire at the end of their next session.

Sect. 3. He shall from time to time give to the Congress information of the state of the union, and recommend to their consideration such measures as he shall judge necessary and expedient; he may, on extraordinary occasions, convene both houses, or either of them, and in case of disagreement between them, with respect to the time of adjournment, he may adjourn them to such time as he shall think proper; he shall receive ambassadors and other public ministers; he shall take care that the laws be faithfully executed, and shall commission all the officers of the United States.

Sect. 4. The president, vice-president and all civil officers of the United States, shall be removed from office on impeachment for, and conviction of, treason, bribery, or other high crimes and misdemeanors.

III.

Section 1. The judicial power of the United States, shall be vested in one supreme court, and in such inferior courts as the Congress may from time to time ordain and establish. The judges, both of the supreme and inferior courts, shall hold their offices during good behaviour, and shall, at stated times, receive for their services, a compensation, which shall not be diminished during their continuance in office.

Sect. 2. The judicial power shall extend to all cases, in law and equity, arising under this constitution, the laws of the United States, and treaties made, or which shall be made, under their authority; to all cases affecting ambassadors, other public ministers and consuls; to all cases of admiralty and maritime jurisdiction; to controversies to which the United States shall be a party; to controversies between two or more States, between a state and citizens of another state, between citizens of different States, between citizens of the same state claiming lands under grants of different States, and between a state, or the citizens thereof, and foreign States, citizens or subjects.

In all cases affecting ambassadors, other public ministers and consuls, and those in which a state shall be a party, the supreme courts shall have original jurisdiction. In all the other cases before mentioned, the supreme court shall have appelate jurisdiction, both as to law and fact, with such exceptions, and under such regulations as the Congress shall make.

The trial of all crimes, except in cases of impeachment, shall be by jury; and such trial shall be held in the state where the said crimes shall have been committed; but when not committed within any state, the trial shall be at such place as the Congress may by law have directed.

Sect. 3. Treason against the United States, shall consist only in levying war against them, or in adhering to their enemies, giving them aid and comfort. No person shall be convicted of treason unless on the testimony of two witnesses to the same overt act, or on confession in open court.

The Congress shall have power to declare the punishment of treason, but no attainder of treason shall work corruption of blood, or forfeiture except during the life of the person attained.

IV.

Section 1. Full faith and credit shall be given in each state to the public acts, records, and judicial proceedings of every other state. And the Congress may by general laws prescribe the manner in which such acts, records and proceedings shall be proved, and the effect thereof.

Sect. 2. The citizens of each state shall be entitled to all privileges and immunities of citizens in the several states.

A person charged in any state with treason, felony, or other crime, who shall flee from justice, and be found in another state, shall, on demand of the executive authority of the state from which he fled, be delivered up, to be removed to the state having jurisdiction of the crime.

No person held to service or labour in one state, under the laws thereof, escaping into another, shall, in consequence of any law or regulation therein, be discharged from such service or labour, but shall be delivered up on claim of the party to whom such service or labour may be due.

Sect. 3. New states may be admitted by the Congress into this union; but no new state shall be formed or erected within the jurisdiction of any other state; nor any state be formed by the junction of two or more states, or parts of states, without the consent of the legislatures of the states concerned as well as of the Congress.

The Congress shall have power to dispose of and make all needful rules and regulations respecting the territory or other property belonging to the United States; and nothing in this Constitution shall be so construed as to prejudice any claims of the United States, or of any particular state.

Sect. 4. The United States shall guarantee to every state in this union a Republican form of government, and shall protect each of them against invasion; and on application of the legislature, or of the executive (when the legislature cannot be convened) against domestic violence.

V.

The Congress, whenever two-thirds of both houses shall deem it necessary, shall propose amendments to this constitution, or, on the application of the legislatures of two-thirds of the several states, shall call a convention for proposing amendments, which, in either case, shall be valid to all intents and purposes, as part of this constitution, when ratified by the legislatures of three-fourths of the several states, or by conventions in three-fourths thereof, as the one or the other mode of ratification may be proposed by the Congress; Provided, that no amendment which may be made prior to the year one thousand eight hundred and eight shall in any manner affect the first and fourth clauses in the ninth section of the first article; and that no state, without its consent, shall be deprived of its equal suffrage in the senate.

VI.

All debts contracted and engagements entered into, before the adoption of this Constitution, shall be as valid against the United States under this Constitution, as under the confederation.

This constitution, and the laws of the United States which shall be made in pursuance thereof; and all treaties made, or which shall be made, under the authority of the United States, shall be the supreme law of the land; and the judges in every state shall be bound thereby, any thing in the constitution or laws of any state to the contrary notwithstanding.

The senators and representatives beforementioned, and the members of the several state legislatures, and all executive and judicial officers, both of the United States and of the several States, shall be bound by oath or affirmation, to support this constitution; but no religious test shall ever be required as a qualification to any office or public trust under the United States.

VII.

The ratification of the conventions of nine States, shall be sufficient for the establishment of this constitution between the States so ratifying the same.

Articles in addition to, and Amendment of the Constitution of the United States of America, proposed by Congress, and ratified by the Legislatures of the several States, pursuant to the fifth Article of the original Constitution.

ARTICLE I

Congress shall make no law respecting an establishment of religion, or prohibiting the free exercise thereof; or abridging the freedom of speech, or of the press; or the right of the people peaceably to assemble, and to petition the Government for a redress of grievances.

ARTICLE II

A well regulated Militia, being necessary to the security of a free State, the right of the people to keep and bear Arms, shall not be infringed.

ARTICLE III

No Soldier shall, in time of peace be quartered in any house, without the consent of the Owner, nor in time of war, but in a manner to be prescribed by law.

ARTICLE IV

The right of the people to be secure in their persons, houses, papers, and effects, against unreasonable searches and seizures, shall not be violated, and no Warrants shall issue, but upon probable cause, supported by Oath or affirmation, and particularly describing the place to be searched, and the persons or things to be seized.

ARTICLE V

No person shall be held to answer for a capital, or otherwise infamous crime, unless on a presentment or indictment of a Grand Jury, except in cases arising in the land or naval forces, or in the Militia, when in actual service in time of War or public danger; nor shall any person be subject for the same offence to be twice put in jeopardy of life or limb; nor shall be compelled in any criminal case to be a witness against himself, nor be deprived of life, liberty, or property, without due process of law; nor shall private property be taken for public use, without just compensation.

ARTICLE VI

In all criminal prosecutions, the accused shall enjoy the right to a speedy and public trial, by an impartial jury of the State and district wherein the crime shall have been committed, which district shall have been previously ascertained by law, and to be informed on the nature and cause of the accusation; to be confronted with the witnesses against him; to have compulsory process for obtaining witnesses in his favor, and to have the Assistance of Counsel for his defence.

ARTICLE VII

In Suits at common law, where the value in controversy shall exceed twenty dollars, the right of trial by jury shall be preserved, and no fact tried by a jury, shall be otherwise re-examined in any Court of the United States, than according to the rules of the common law.

ARTICLE VIII

Excessive bail shall not be required, nor excessive fines imposed, nor cruel and unusual punishments inflicted.

ARTICLE IX

The enumeration in the Constitution, of certain rights, shall not be construed to deny or disparage others retained by the people.

ARTICLE X

The powers not delegated to the United States by the Constitution, nor prohibited by it to the States, are reserved to the States respectively, or to the people.

ARTICLE XI

The Judicial power of the United States shall not be construed to extend to any suit in law or equity, commenced or prosecuted against one of the United States by Citizens of another State, or by Citizens or Subjects of any Foreign State.

ARTICLE XII

The Electors shall meet in their respective states, and vote by ballot for President and Vice-President, one of whom, at least, shall not be an inhabitant of the same state with themselves; they shall name in their ballots the person voted for as President, and in distinct ballots the person voted for as Vice-President, and they shall make distinct lists of all persons voted for as President, and of all persons voted for as Vice-President, and of the number of votes for each, which lists they shall sign and certify, and transmit sealed to the seat of the government of the United States, directed to the President of the Senate; — The President of the Senate shall, in the presence of the Senate and House of Representatives, open all the certificates and the votes shall then be counted; — The person having the greatest number of votes for President, shall be the President, if such number be a majority of the whole number of Electors appointed; and if no person have such majority, then from the persons having the highest numbers not exceeding three on the list of those voted for as President, the House of Representatives shall choose immediately, by ballot, the President. But in choosing the President, the votes shall be taken by states, the representation from each state having one vote; a quorum for this purpose shall consist of a member or members from two-thirds of the states, and a majority of all the states shall be necessary to a choice. And if the House of Representatives shall not choose a President whenever the right of choice shall devolve upon them, before the fourth day of March next following, then the Vice-President shall act as President, as in the case of the death or other constitutional disability of the President. — The person having the greatest number of votes as Vice-President, shall be the Vice-President, if such number be a majority of the whole number of Electors appointed, and if no person have a majority, then from the two highest numbers on the list, the Senate shall choose the Vice-President; a quorum for the purpose shall consist of two-thirds of the whole number of Senators, and a majority of the whole number shall be necessary to a choice. But no person constitutionally ineligible to the office of President shall be eligible to that of Vice-President of the United States.

ARTICLE XIII

Section 1. Neither slavery nor involuntary servitude, except as punishment for crime whereof the party shall have been duly convicted, shall exist within the United States, or any place subject to their jurisdiction.

Sect. 2. Congress shall have power to enforce this article by appropriate legislation.

ARTICLE XIV

Section 1. All persons born or naturalized in the United States, and subject to the jurisdiction thereof, are citizens of the United States and of the State wherein they reside. No State shall make or enforce any law which shall abridge the privileges or immunities of citizens of the United States; nor shall any State deprive any person of life, liberty, or property, without due process of law; nor deny to any person within its jurisdiction the equal protection of the laws.

Sect. 2. Representatives shall be apportioned among the several States according to their respective numbers, counting the whole number of persons in each State, excluding Indians not taxed. But when the right to vote at any election for the choice of electors for President and Vice President of the United States, Representatives in Congress, the Executive and Judicial officers of a State, or the members of the Legislature thereof, is denied to any of the male inhabitants of such State, being twenty-one years of age, and citizens of the United States, or in any way abridged, except for participation in rebellion, or other crime, the basis of representation therein shall be reduced in the proportion which the number of such male citizens shall bear to the whole number of male citizens twenty-one years of age in such State.

Sect. 3. No person shall be a Senator or Representative in Congress, or elector of President and Vice President, or hold any office, civil or military, under the United States, or under any State, who, having previously taken an oath, as a member of Congress, or as an officer of the United States, or as a member of any State legislature, or as an executive or judicial officer of any State, to support the Constitution of the United States, shall have engaged in insurrection or rebellion against the same, or given aid or comfort to the enemies thereof. But Congress may by a vote of two-thirds of each House, remove such disability.

Sect. 4. The validity of the public debt of the United States, authorized by law, including debts incurred for payment of pensions and bounties for services in suppressing insurrection or rebellion, shall not be questioned. But neither the United States nor any State shall assume or pay any debt or obligation incurred in aid of insurrection or rebellion against the United States, or any claim for the loss or emancipation of any slave; but all such debts, obligations and claims shall be held illegal and void.

Section 5. The Congress shall have power to enforce, by appropriate legislation, the provisions of this article.

ARTICLE XV

Section 1. The right of citizens of the United States to vote shall not be denied or abridged by the United States or by any State on account of race, color, or previous condition of servitude.

Sect. 2. The Congress shall have power to enforce this article by appropriate legislation.

ARTICLE XVI

The Congress shall have power to lay and collect taxes on incomes, from whatever source derived, without apportionment among the several States, and without regard to any census or enumeration.

ARTICLE XVII

The Senate of the United States shall be composed of two Senators from each State, elected by the people thereof, for six years; and each Senator shall have one vote. The electors in each State shall have the qualifications requisite for electors of the most numerous branch of the State legislatures.

When vacancies happen in the representation of any State in the Senate, the executive authority of such State shall issue writs of election to fill such vacancies: *Provided,* That the legislature of any State may empower the executive thereof to make temporary appointments until the people fill the vacancies by election as the legislature may direct.

This amendment shall not be so construed as to affect the election or term of any Senator chosen before it becomes valid as part of the Constitution.

ARTICLE XVIII

Section 1. After one year from the ratification of this article the manufacture, sale, or transportation of intoxicating liquors within, the importation thereof into, or the exportation thereof from the United States and all territory subject to the jurisdiction thereof for beverage purposes is hereby prohibited.

Sect. 2. The Congress and the several States shall have concurrent power to enforce this article by appropriate legislation.

Sect. 3. This article shall be inoperative unless it shall have been ratified as an amendment to the Constitution by the legislatures of the several States, as provided in the Constitution, within seven years from the date of the submission hereof to the States by the Congress.

ARTICLE XIX

The right of citizens of the United States to vote shall not be denied or abridged by the United States or by any State on account of sex.

Congress shall have power to enforce this article by appropriate legislation.

ARTICLE XX

Section 1. The terms of the President and Vice President shall end at noon on the 20th day of January, and the terms of Senators and Representatives at noon on the 3rd day of January, of the years in which such terms would have ended if this article had not been ratified; and the terms of their successors shall then begin.

Sect. 2. The Congress shall assemble at least once in every year, and such meeting shall begin at noon on the 3rd day of January, unless they shall by law appoint a different day.

Sect. 3. If, at any time fixed for the beginning of the term of the President, the President shall have died, the Vice President elect shall become President. If a President shall not have been chosen before the time fixed for the beginning of his term, or if the President elect shall have failed to qualify, then the Vice President elect shall act as President until a President shall have qualified; and the Congress may by law provide for the case wherein neither a President elect nor a Vice President elect shall have qualified, declaring who shall then act as President, or the manner in which one who is to act shall be elected, and such person shall act accordingly until a President or Vice President shall have qualified.

Sect. 4. The Congress may by law provide for the case of the death of any of the persons from whom the House of Representatives may choose a President whenever the right of choice shall have devolved upon them, and for the case of the death of any of the persons from whom the Senate may choose a Vice President whenever the right of choice shall have devolved upon them.

Sect. 5. Sections 1 and 2 shall take effect on the 15th day of October following the ratification of this article.

Sect. 6. This article shall be inoperative unless it shall have been ratified as an amendment to the Constitution by the legislatures of three-fourths of the several States within seven years from the date of its submission.

ARTICLE XXI

Section 1. The eighteenth article of amendment to the Constitution of the United States is hereby repealed.

Sect. 2. The transportation or importation into any State, Territory, or possession of the United States for delivery or use therein of intoxicating liquors, in violation of the laws thereof, is hereby prohibited.

Sect. 3. This article shall be inoperative unless it shall have been ratified as an amendment to the Constitution by conventions in the several States, as provided in the Constitution, within seven years from the date of the submission hereof to the States by the Congress.

ARTICLE XXII

Section 1. No person shall be elected to the office of the President more than twice, and no person who has held the office of President, or acted as President, for more than two years of a term to which some other person was elected President shall be elected to the office of the President more than once. But this Article shall not apply to any person holding the office of President when this Article was proposed by the Congress, and shall not prevent any person who may be holding the office of President, or acting as President, during the term within which this Article becomes operative from holding the office of President or acting as President during the remainder of such term.

Sect. 2. This article shall be inoperative unless it shall have been ratified as an amendment to the Constitution by the legislatures of three-fourths of the several States within seven years from the date of its submission to the States by the Congress.

ARTICLE XXIII

Section 1. The District constituting the seat of Government of the United States shall appoint in such manner as the Congress may direct:

A number of electors of President and Vice President equal to the whole number of Senators and Representatives in Congress to which the District would be entitled if it were a State, but in no event more than the least populous State; they shall be in addition to those appointed by the States, but they shall be considered, for the purposes of the election of President and Vice President, to be electors appointed by a State; and they shall meet in the District and perform such duties as provided by the twelfth article of amendment.

Sect. 2. The Congress shall have power to enforce this article by appropriate legislation.

ARTICLE XXIV

Section 1. The right of citizens of the United States to vote in any primary or other election for President or Vice President, for electors for President or Vice

President, or for Senator or Representative in Congress, shall not be denied or abridged by the United States or any State by reason of failure to pay any poll tax or other tax.

Sect. 2. The Congress shall have power to enforce this article by appropriate legislation.

ARTICLE XXV

Section 1. In case of the removal of the President from office or of his death or resignation, the Vice President shall become President.

Sect. 2. Whenever there is a vacancy in the office of the Vice President, the President shall nominate a Vice President who shall take office upon confirmation by a majority vote of both Houses of Congress.

Sect. 3. Whenever the President transmits to the President pro tempore of the Senate and the Speaker of the House of Representatives his written declaration that he is unable to discharge the powers and duties of his office, and until he transmits to them a written declaration to the contrary, such powers and duties shall be discharged by the Vice President as Acting President.

Sect. 4. Whenever the Vice President and a majority of either the principal officers of the executive departments or of such other body as Congress may by law provide, transmit to the President pro tempore of the Senate and the Speaker of the House of Representatives their written declaration that the President is unable to discharge the powers and duties of his office, the Vice President shall immediately assume the powers and duties of the office as Acting President.

Thereafter, when the President transmits to the President pro tempore of the Senate and the Speaker of the House of Representatives his written declaration that no inability exists, he shall resume the powers and duties of his office unless the Vice President and a majority of either the principal officers of the executive department or of such other body as Congress may by law provide, transmit within four days to the President pro tempore of the Senate and the Speaker of the House of Representatives their written declaration that the President is unable to discharge the powers and duties of his office. Thereupon Congress shall decide the issue, assembling within forty-eight hours for that purpose if not in session. If the Congress, within twenty-one days after receipt of the latter written declaration, or, if Congress is not in session, within twenty-one days after Congress is required to assemble, determines by two-thirds vote of both Houses that the President is unable to discharge the powers and duties of his office, the Vice President shall continue to discharge the same as Acting President; otherwise, the President shall resume the powers and duties of his office.

ARTICLE XXVI

Section 1. The right of citizens of the United States, who are eighteen years of age or older, to vote shall not be denied or abridged by the United States or by any State on account of age.

Sect. 2. The Congress shall have power to enforce this article by appropriate legislation.

Appendix C
Presidential Elections

Year	Candidates	Parties	Popular Vote	Electoral Vote
1789	GEORGE WASHINGTON	No party designations		69
	John Adams			34
	Minor Candidates			35
1792	GEORGE WASHINGTON	Federalist		132
	John Adams	Federalist		77
	George Clinton	Democratic-Republican		50
	Minor Candidates			5
1796	JOHN ADAMS	Federalist		71
	Thomas Jefferson	Democratic-Republican		68
	Thomas Pinckney	Federalist		59
	Aaron Burr	Democratic-Republican		30
	Minor Candidates			48
1800	THOMAS JEFFERSON	Democratic-Republican		73
	Aaron Burr	Democratic-Republican		73
	John Adams	Federalist		65
	Charles C. Pinckney	Federalist		64
	John Jay	Federalist		1
1804	THOMAS JEFFERSON	Democratic-Republican		162
	Charles C. Pinckney	Federalist		14
1808	JAMES MADISON	Democratic-Republican		122
	Charles C. Pinckney	Federalist		47
	George Clinton	Independent-Republican		6

Presidential Elections (continued)

Year	Candidates	Parties	Popular Vote	Electoral Vote
1812	JAMES MADISON	Democratic-Republican		128
	DeWitt Clinton	Fusion		89
1816	JAMES MONROE	Republican		183
	Rufus King	Federalist	?	34
1820	JAMES MONROE	Republican		231
	John Quincy Adams	Independent Republican		1
1824	JOHN QUINCY ADAMS	Democratic-Republican	108,740	84
	Andrew Jackson	Democratic-Republican	153,544	99
	Henry Clay	Democratic-Republican	47,136	37
	William H. Crawford	Democratic-Republican	46,618	41
1828	ANDREW JACKSON	Democratic	647,286	178
	John Quincy Adams	National Republican	508,064	83
1832	ANDREW JACKSON	Democratic	687,502	219
	Henry Clay	National Republican	530,189	49
	William Wirt	Anti-Masonic }		7
	John Floyd	Nullifiers }	33,108	11
1836	MARTIN VAN BUREN	Democratic	765,483	170
	William H. Harrison	Whig		73
	Hugh L. White	Whig		26
	Daniel Webster	Whig	739,795	14
	W. P. Mangum	Anti-Jackson		11
1840	WILLIAM H. HARRISON	Whig	1,274,624	234
	Martin Van Buren	Democratic	1,127,781	60
	James G. Birney	Liberty	7,069	
1844	JAMES K. POLK	Democratic	1,338,464	170
	Henry Clay	Whig	1,300,097	105
	James G. Birney	Liberty	62,300	
1848	ZACHARY TAYLOR	Whig	1,360,967	163
	Lewis Cass	Democratic	1,222,342	127
	Martin Van Buren	Free Soil	291,263	
1852	FRANKLIN PIERCE	Democratic	1,601,117	254
	Winfield Scott	Whig	1,385,453	42
	John P. Hale	Free Soil	155,825	
1856	JAMES BUCHANAN	Democratic	1,832,955	174
	John C. Frémont	Republican	1,339,932	114
	Millard Fillmore	American	871,731	8
1860	ABRAHAM LINCOLN	Republican	1,865,593	180
	Stephen A. Douglas	Democratic	1,382,713	12
	John C. Breckinridge	Democratic	848,356	72
	John Bell	Constitutional Union	592,906	39
1864	ABRAHAM LINCOLN	Republican	2,206,938	212
	George B. McClellan	Democratic	1,803,787	21
1868	ULYSSES S. GRANT	Republican	3,013,421	214
	Horatio Seymour	Democratic	2,706,829	80
1872	ULYSSES S. GRANT	Republican	3,596,745	286
	Horace Greeley	Democratic	2,843,446	66

Presidential Elections (continued)

Year	Candidates	Parties	Popular Vote	Electoral Vote
1876	RUTHERFORD B. HAYES	Republican	4,036,572	185
	Samuel J. Tilden	Democratic	4,284,020	184
1880	JAMES A. GARFIELD	Republican	4,453,295	214
	Winfield S. Hancock	Democratic	4,414,082	155
	James B. Weaver	Greenback-Labor	308,578	
	Neal Dow	Prohibition	10,305	
1884	GROVER CLEVELAND	Democratic	4,879,507	219
	James G. Blaine	Republican	4,850,293	182
	Benjamin F. Butler	Greenback-Labor	175,370	
	John P. St. John	Prohibiton	150,369	
1888	BENJAMIN HARRISON	Republican	5,477,129	233
	Grover Cleveland	Democratic	5,537,857	168
	Clinton B. Fisk	Prohibition	249,506	
	Anson J. Streeter	Union Labor	146,935	
1892	GROVER CLEVELAND	Democratic	5,555,426	277
	Benjamin Harrison	Republican	5,182,690	145
	James B. Weaver	People's	1,029,846	22
	John Bidwell	Prohibition	264,133	
	Simon Wing	Socialist Labor	21,164	
1896	WILLIAM McKINLEY	Republican	7,102,246	271
	William J. Bryan	Democratic	6,492,559	176
1900	WILLIAM McKINLEY	Republican	7,218,491	292
	William J. Bryan	Democratic; Populist	6,356,734	155
	John C. Wooley	Prohibition	208,914	
1904	THEODORE ROOSEVELT	Republican	7,628,461	336
	Alton B. Parker	Democratic	5,084,223	140
	Eugene V. Debs	Socialist	402,283	
	Silas C. Swallow	Prohibition	258,536	
1908	WILLIAM H. TAFT	Republican	7,675,320	321
	William J. Bryan	Democratic	6,412,294	162
	Eugene V. Debs	Socialist	420,793	
	Eugene W. Chafin	Prohibition	253,840	
1912	WOODROW WILSON	Democratic	6,296,547	435
	Theodore Roosevelt	Progressive	4,118,571	88
	William H. Taft	Republican	3,486,720	8
	Eugene V. Debs	Socialist	900,672	
	Eugene W. Chafin	Prohibition	206,275	
1916	WOODROW WILSON	Democratic	9,127,695	277
	Charles E. Hughes	Republican	8,533,507	254
	A. L. Benson	Socialist	585,113	
	J. Frank Hanly	Prohibition	220,506	
1920	WARREN G. HARDING	Republican	16,143,407	404
	James M. Cox	Democratic	9,130,328	127
	Eugene V. Debs	Socialist	919,799	
	P. P. Christensen	Farmer-Labor	265,411	

Presidential Elections (continued)

Year	Candidates	Parties	Popular Vote	Electoral Vote
1924	CALVIN COOLIDGE	Republican	15,718,211	382
	John W. Davis	Democratic	8,385,283	136
	Robert M. LaFollette	Progressive	4,831,289	13
1928	HERBERT C. HOOVER	Republican	21,391,993	444
	Alfred E. Smith	Democratic	15,016,169	87
1932	FRANKLIN D. ROOSEVELT	Democratic	22,809,638	472
	Herbert C. Hoover	Republican	15,758,901	59
	Norman Thomas	Socialist	881,951	
1936	FRANKLIN D. ROOSEVELT	Democratic	27,752,869	523
	Alfred M. Landon	Republican	16,674,665	8
	William Lemke	Union	882,479	
1940	FRANKLIN D. ROOSEVELT	Democratic	27,307,819	449
	Wendell L. Willkie	Republican	22,321,018	82
1944	FRANKLIN D. ROOSEVELT	Democratic	25,606,585	432
	Thomas E. Dewey	Republican	22,014,745	99
1948	HARRY S. TRUMAN	Democratic	24,105,812	303
	Thomas E. Dewey	Republican	21,991,291	189
	J. Strom Thurmond	States' Rights	1,176,125	39
	Henry A. Wallace	Progressive	1,157,326	
1952	DWIGHT D. EISENHOWER	Republican	33,936,234	442
	Adlai E. Stevenson	Democratic	27,314,992	89
1956	DWIGHT D. EISENHOWER	Republican	35,590,472	457
	Adlai E. Stevenson	Democratic	26,022,752	73
1960	JOHN F. KENNEDY	Democratic	34,226,731	303
	Richard M. Nixon	Republican	34,108,157	219
1964	LYNDON B. JOHNSON	Democratic	43,126,566	486
	Barry M. Goldwater	Republican	27,176,799	52
1968	RICHARD M. NIXON	Republican	31,785,480	301
	Hubert H. Humphrey	Democratic	31,275,166	191
	George C. Wallace	American Independent	9,906,473	46
1972	RICHARD M. NIXON	Republican	47,169,911	520
	George S. McGovern	Democratic	29,170,383	17
	John G. Schmitz	American Independent	1,099,482	
1976	JIMMY CARTER	Democratic	40,830,763	297
	Gerald Ford	Republican	39,147,793	241
	Eugene McCarthy	Independent	756,691	
	Roger L. MacBride	Libertarian	173,011	
	Lester G. Maddox	American Independent	170,531	

Source: *Historical Statistics of the United States, Colonial Times to 1968* (1975), pp. 1073-1074.

Appendix D

Political Party Affiliations in Congress 1789-1979

(Letter symbols for political parties: Ad — Administration; AM — Anti-Masonic; C — Coalition; D — Democratic; DR — Democratic-Republican; F — Federalist; J — Jacksonian; NR — National Republican; OP — Opposition; R - Republican; U — Unionist; W — Whig. Figures are for the beginning of the first session of each Congress.)

Year	HOUSE Majority Party	HOUSE Principal Minority Party	HOUSE Other	SENATE Majority Party	SENATE Principal Minority Party	SENATE Other	President
1789-1791	Ad-38	OP-26	—	Ad-17	OP-9	—	F (Washington)
1791-1793	F-37	DR-33	—	F-16	DR-13	—	F (Washington)
1793-1795	DR-57	F-48	—	F-17	DR-13	—	F (Washington)
1795-1797	F-54	DR-52	—	F-19	DR-13	—	F (Washington)
1797-1799	F-58	DR-48	—	F-20	DR-12	—	F (John Adams)
1799-1801	F-64	DR-42	—	F-19	DR-13	—	F (John Adams)
1801-1803	DR-69	F-36	—	DR-18	F-13	—	DR (Jefferson)
1803-1805	DR-102	F-39	—	DR-25	F-9	—	DR (Jefferson)
1805-1807	DR-116	F-25	—	DR-27	F-7	—	DR (Jefferson)
1807-1809	DR-118	F-24	—	DR-28	F-6	—	DR (Jefferson)

Political Party Affiliations in Congress: 1789 to 1979 (continued)

Year	HOUSE Majority Party	Principal Minority Party	Other	SENATE Majority Party	Principal Minority Party	Other	President
1809-1811	DR-94	F-48	—	DR-28	F-6	—	DR (Madison)
1811-1813	DR-108	F-36	—	DR-30	F-6	—	DR (Madison)
1813-1815	DR-112	F-68	—	DR-27	F-9	—	DR (Madison)
1815-1817	DR-117	F-65	—	DR-25	F-11	—	DR (Madison)
1817-1819	DR-141	F-42	—	DR-34	F-10	—	DR (Monroe)
1819-1821	DR-156	F-27	—	DR-35	F-7	—	DR (Monroe)
1821-1823	DR-158	F-25	—	DR-44	F-4	—	DR (Monroe)
1823-1825	DR-187	F-26	—	DR-44	F-4	—	DR (Monroe)
1825-1827	Ad-105	J-97	—	Ad-26	J-20	—	C (John Q. Adams)
1827-1829	J-119	Ad-94	—	J-28	Ad-20	—	C (John Q. Adams)
1829-1831	D-139	NR-74	—	D-26	NR-22	2	D (Jackson)
1831-1833	D-141	NR-58	14	D-25	NR-21	8	D (Jackson)
1833-1835	D-147	AM-53	60	D-20	NR-20	—	D (Jackson)
1835-1837	D-145	W-98	—	D-27	W-25	4	D (Jackson)
1837-1839	D-108	W-107	24	D-30	W-18	—	D (Van Buren)
1839-1841	D-124	W-118	—	D-28	W-22	—	D (Van Buren)
							W (W. Harrison)
1841-1843	W-133	D-102	6	W-28	D-22	2	W (Tyler)
1843-1845	D-142	W-79	1	W-28	D-25	1	W (Tyler)
1845-1847	D-143	W-77	6	D-31	W-25	—	D (Polk)
1847-1849	W-115	D-108	4	D-36	W-21	1	D (Polk)
							W (Taylor)
1849-1851	D-112	W-109	9	D-35	W-25	2	W (Fillmore)

Political Party Affiliations in Congress: 1789 to 1979 (continued)

Year	HOUSE Majority Party	HOUSE Principal Minority Party	HOUSE Other	SENATE Majority Party	SENATE Principal Minority Party	SENATE Other	President
1851-1853	D-140	W-88	5	D-35	W-24	3	W (Fillmore)
1853-1855	D-159	W-71	4	D-38	W-22	2	D (Pierce)
1855-1857	R-108	D-83	43	D-40	R-15	5	D (Pierce)
1857-1859	D-118	R-92	26	D-36	R-20	8	D (Buchanan)
1859-1861	R-114	D-92	31	D-36	R-26	4	D (Buchanan)
1861-1863	R-105	D-43	30	R-31	D-10	8	R (Lincoln)
1863-1865	R-102	D-75	9	R-36	D-9	5	R (Lincoln)
1865-1867	U-149	D-42	—	U-42	D-10	—	R (Lincoln) / R (A. Johnson)
1867-1869	R-143	D-49	—	R-42	D-11	—	R (A. Johnson)
1869-1871	R-149	D-63	—	R-56	D-11	—	R (Grant)
1871-1873	R-134	D-104	5	R-52	D-17	5	R (Grant)
1873-1875	R-194	D-92	14	R-49	D-19	5	R (Grant)
1875-1877	D-169	R-109	14	R-45	D-29	2	R (Grant)
1877-1879	D-153	R-140	—	R-39	D-36	1	R (Hayes)
1879-1881	D-149	R-130	14	D-42	R-33	1	R (Hayes)
1881-1883	R-147	D-135	11	R-37	D-37	1	R (Garfield) / R (Arthur)
1883-1885	D-197	R-118	10	R-38	D-36	2	R (Arthur)
1885-1887	D-183	R-140	2	R-43	D-34	—	D (Cleveland)
1887-1889	D-169	R-152	4	R-39	D-37	—	D (Cleveland)
1889-1891	R-166	D-159	—	R-39	D-37	—	R (B. Harrison)
1891-1893	D-235	R-88	9	R-47	D-39	2	R (B. Harrison)

Political Party Affiliations in Congress: 1789 to 1979 (continued)

Year	HOUSE Majority Party	Principal Minority Party	Other	SENATE Majority Party	Principal Minority Party	Other	President
1893-1895	D-218	R-127	11	D-44	R-38	3	D (Cleveland)
1895-1897	R-244	D-105	7	R-43	D-39	6	D (Cleveland)
1897-1899	R-204	D-113	40	R-47	D-34	7	R (McKinley)
1899-1901	R-185	D-163	9	R-53	D-26	8	R (McKinley)
1901-1903	R-197	D-151	9	R-55	D-31	4	R (T. Roosevelt)
1903-1905	R-208	D-178	—	R-57	D-33	—	R (T. Roosevelt)
1905-1907	R-250	D-136	—	R-57	D-33	—	R (T. Roosevelt)
1907-1909	R-222	D-164	—	R-61	D-31	—	R (T. Roosevelt)
1909-1911	R-219	D-172	—	R-61	D-32	—	R (Taft)
1911-1913	D-228	R-161	1	R-51	D-41	—	R (Taft)
1913-1915	D-291	R-127	17	D-51	R-44	1	D (Wilson)
1915-1917	D-230	R-196	9	D-56	R-40	—	D (Wilson)
1917-1919	D-216	R-210	6	D-53	R-42	—	D (Wilson)
1919-1921	R-240	D-190	3	R-49	D-47	—	D (Wilson)
1921-1923	R-301	D-131	1	R-59	D-37	—	R (Harding)
1923-1925	R-225	D-205	5	R-51	D-43	2	R (Coolidge)
1925-1927	R-247	D-183	4	R-56	D-39	1	R (Coolidge)
1927-1929	R-237	D-195	3	R-49	D-46	1	R (Coolidge)
1929-1931	R-267	D-167	1	R-56	D-39	1	R (Hoover)
1931-1933	D-220	R-214	1	R-48	D-47	1	R (Hoover)
1933-1935	D-310	R-117	5	D-60	R-35	1	D (F. Roosevelt)
1935-1937	D-319	R-103	10	D-69	R-25	2	D (F. Roosevelt)
1937-1939	D-331	R-89	13	D-76	R-16	4	D (F. Roosevelt)
1939-1941	D-261	R-164	4	D-69	R-23	4	D (F. Roosevelt)

Political Party Affiliations in Congress: 1789 to 1979 (continued)

Year	HOUSE Majority Party	HOUSE Principal Minority Party	HOUSE Other	SENATE Majority Party	SENATE Principal Minority Party	SENATE Other	President
1941-1943	D-268	R-162	5	D-66	R-28	2	D (F. Roosevelt)
1943-1945	D-218	R-208	4	D-58	R-37	1	D (F. Roosevelt)
1945-1947	D-242	R-190	2	D-56	R-38	1	D (Truman)
1947-1949	R-245	D-188	1	R-51	D-45	—	D (Truman)
1949-1951	D-263	R-171	1	D-54	R-42	—	D (Truman)
1951-1953	D-234	R-199	1	D-49	R-47	—	D (Truman)
1953-1955	R-221	D-211	1	R-48	D-47	1	R (Eisenhower)
1955-1957	D-232	R-203	—	D-48	R-47	1	R (Eisenhower)
1957-1959	D-233	R-200	—	D-49	R-47	—	R (Eisenhower)
1959-1961	D-283	R-153	—	D-64	R-34	—	R (Eisenhower)
1961-1963	D-263	R-174	—	D-65	R-35	—	D (Kennedy)
							D (Kennedy)
1963-1965	D-258	R-177	—	D-67	R-33	—	D (L. Johnson)
1965-1967	D-295	R-140	—	D-68	R-32	—	D (L. Johnson)
1967-1969	D-247	R-187	—	D-64	R-36	—	D (L. Johnson)
1969-1971	D-243	R-192	—	D-57	R-43	—	R (Nixon)
1971-1973	D-254	R-180	—	D-54	R-44	2	R (Nixon)
1973-1975	D-239	R-192	1	D-56	R-42	2	R (Nixon)
1975-1977	D-290	R-145	—	D-61	R-39	—	R (Ford)
							R (Ford)
1977-1979	D-285	R-146	—	D-61	R-38	1	D (Carter)
							D (Carter)

Source: Congressional Quarterly's *Guide to U.S. Elections*, 1975

Index